# Contents

| | | |
|---|---|---|
| *Editor's foreword* | | v |
| *Preface* | | vii |

**INTRODUCTION** — 1

| | | |
|---|---|---|
| 1 | A Management Accounting Framework | 3 |
| | 1.1 What is meant by the term 'management accounting'? | 4 |
| | 1.2 Management accounting topics | 4 |
| | 1.3 Related disciplines | 7 |
| | 1.4 The framework for management accounting | 7 |
| | 1.5 The emphasis of management accounting | 11 |
| | 1.6 Organisation structure and the management accountant | 12 |
| | 1.7 Reporting to management | 12 |
| | 1.8 The control period | 19 |
| | 1.9 Summary | 19 |

**FINANCIAL STATEMENT CLASSIFICATION** — 23

| | | |
|---|---|---|
| 2 | Financial Data Classification and Terminology | 25 |
| | 2.1 The effectiveness of the system of classification | 26 |
| | 2.2 Limitations on financial data division | 26 |
| | 2.3 Characteristics for data division | 26 |
| | 2.4 Responsibility centres | 27 |
| | 2.5 Cash and accrual accounting | 29 |
| | 2.6 Normal divisions of business transactions | 30 |
| | 2.7 Business activity and cost classification | 32 |
| | 2.8 Accounting terminology | 35 |
| | 2.9 A concluding comment | 36 |
| 3 | Financial Data Division | 41 |
| | 3.1 Capital acquisition | 42 |
| | 3.2 Capital investment | 42 |
| | 3.3 Resources use | 43 |
| | 3.4 Investment results | 44 |
| | 3.5 Profit disposal | 44 |
| | 3.6 Marketing information | 44 |
| | 3.7 Production cost information | 47 |
| | 3.8 Capital expenditure and research and development cost information | 50 |
| | 3.9 Working capital information | 50 |
| | 3.10 Administration cost information | 53 |
| | 3.11 A concluding comment | 53 |

**FINANCIAL STATEMENT INTERPRETATION** — 59

| | | |
|---|---|---|
| 4 | Accounting Information Relationships | 61 |
| | 4.1 Manufacturing statement relations | 62 |
| | 4.2 Trading statement relationships | 64 |

|       |                                                                                      |     |
|-------|--------------------------------------------------------------------------------------|-----|
| 4.3   | Profit and loss statement relationships                                              | 65  |
| 4.4   | Balance sheet relationships                                                          | 69  |
| 4.5   | Accounts charts                                                                      | 70  |
| 4.6   | A concluding comment                                                                 | 71  |
| 5     | Ratio Analysis and Interfirm Comparison                                              | 78  |
| 5.1   | Forms of ratio analysis                                                              | 79  |
| 5.2   | Limitations of ratio analysis                                                        | 79  |
| 5.3   | The return on investment concept                                                     | 80  |
| 5.4   | The interpretation of capital employed                                               | 82  |
| 5.5   | The interpretation of profit                                                         | 84  |
| 5.6   | Divisional and product assessment of capital employed                                | 84  |
| 5.7   | Primary ratio interpretation factors                                                 | 85  |
| 5.8   | Subsidiary ratio interpretation factors                                              | 85  |
| 5.9   | An illustrative example of representative key ratios                                 | 86  |
| 5.10  | Inter-statement ratios                                                               | 88  |
| 5.11  | Balance sheet ratios                                                                 | 89  |
| 5.12  | Profit statement ratios                                                              | 89  |
| 5.13  | Monetary and non-monetary relationships                                              | 90  |
| 5.14  | Non-monetary relationships                                                           | 90  |
| 5.15  | Interfirm comparison                                                                 | 91  |
| 5.16  | Summary                                                                              | 93  |
| 6     | Cost − Volume − Profit Analysis                                                      | 101 |
| 6.1   | The profit graph                                                                     | 102 |
| 6.2   | Profit graph assumptions                                                             | 102 |
| 6.3   | The division of costs into their fixed and variable elements                         | 103 |
| 6.4   | The planned range of activity                                                        | 105 |
| 6.5   | The profit graph and the economist                                                   | 106 |
| 6.6   | Marginal cost and contribution                                                       | 107 |
| 6.7   | The break-even point and the margin of safety                                        | 107 |
| 6.8   | The conventional break-even chart                                                    | 109 |
| 6.9   | Break-even charts for particular purposes                                            | 110 |
| 6.10  | Cost−volume−profit analysis formulae                                                 | 113 |
| 6.11  | Summary                                                                              | 116 |
| 7     | Funds Analysis                                                                       | 123 |
| 7.1   | The profit or loss for the period                                                    | 124 |
| 7.2   | Increases or reductions in long, medium and short-term liabilities                   | 125 |
| 7.3   | New capital introduced into the business                                             | 125 |
| 7.4   | Increases or reductions in long, medium- and short-term assets                       | 125 |
| 7.5   | Cash flow and working capital terminology                                            | 125 |
| 7.6   | An example of funds and cash flow                                                    | 126 |
| 7.7   | The working capital cycle                                                            | 130 |
| 7.8   | Estimating working capital requirements                                              | 130 |
| 7.9   | The control of cash                                                                  | 131 |
| 7.10  | The uses of the funds statements                                                     | 132 |
| 7.11  | Summary                                                                              | 132 |
|       | **ACCOUNTING AND FORWARD PLANNING**                                                  | 143 |
| 8     | The Managerial Control Process                                                       | 145 |
| 8.1   | Establishing business objectives                                                     | 146 |
| 8.2   | Planning                                                                             | 146 |
| 8.3   | Integration of long and short term plans                                             | 147 |

657·4

Mr Wylie
(loan)

THE HEINEMANN
ACCOUNTANCY AND ADMINISTRATION SERIES

*General Editor:*
J. BATTY, D Com (S A), M Com (Dunelm), A C M A,
M Inst A M, M I P M

# MANAGEMENT ACCOUNTING

# MANAGEMENT ACCOUNTING

## NORMAN THORNTON

MA, MSc, FCMA, AMBIM

*Principal Lecturer in Accountancy*
*Manchester Polytechnic*

HEINEMANN : LONDON

William Heinemann Ltd
15 Queen St, Mayfair, London W1X 8BE

LONDON   MELBOURNE   TORONTO
JOHANNESBURG   AUCKLAND

First published 1978

434 91960 8

Text set in 10/12 pt IBM Press Roman, printed by photolithography, and bound
in Great Britain at The Pitman Press, Bath

# Editor's Foreword

The *Heinemann Accountancy and Administration Series* is intended to fill a gap in the literature that caters for accountants, company secretaries, and similar professional people who are engaged in giving a vital information service to management. As far as possible, due recognition is given to the fact that there are two distinct bodies of readers: those who aspire to professional status — the students — and others who are already managing or serving management.

Around fifteen years have elapsed since any major British textbook for undergraduate and professional students on management accountancy has been published. During that time many changes have taken place and, therefore, it is desirable to take a fresh look at the theory and practice of this tremendously important subject.

With rising costs and shrinking profit margins the need to plan and control is of vital importance. Without information managers have difficulty in making rational decisions. Yet unless properly organised, the management information system does not give the facts required at the appropriate time.

If accountants are to understand how best they can serve managers they must be prepared to learn about managing. There must be a departure from the traditional approach to accounting and an adaptation to the needs of planners, decision-makers and controllers.

In this book Norman Thornton shows how the main techniques may be employed in industry and commerce. More important for the student, a real attempt is made to show how examination questions may be tackled in an effective manner.

This new book should find a prominent place in the studies of those preparing for accountancy, banking and administrative examinations.

J. BATTY

# Preface

This textbook provides students with the basic material for an understanding of the management accounting process. The majority of students studying the subject of management accounting will have taken a general accounting course and this is assumed, although the text is written in a form suitable for students whose main subject of study is not accountancy based. The text is primarily directed to students in polytechnics, colleges and other establishments of higher education whose studies are undertaken for professional qualifications and diplomas in management accounting.

The subject is logically presented in a classified framework developed in the following sections:

Introduction
Financial statement classification
Financial statement interpretation
Accounting and forward planning
Accounting and business control
Accounting and business decision-making
Associated topics for study
Conclusion.

A feature of the book is the clear statement of the objective and outline of each chapter to guide the student's attention to principal aspects of the topics covered in the text. For further study, supplementary reading has been recommended and a variety of discussion questions, exercises and case studies provided. It is difficult to distinguish types of problem material and they are merged under the general title of 'questions'. The questions are of varying difficulty and, where possible, given in the order of the topic coverage in the appropriate chapter.

I am indebted to the authors of the works listed in each chapter, including the chapter footnotes, and their recommendation is my thanks. I also record my thanks to the Institute of Cost and Management Accountants and Association of Certified Accountants for permission given to quote examples from their examination papers. Where appropriate, they have been altered to show metric units of measurement.

My thanks are due to Mr M. L. Houlton, ACMA, of William Heinemann, who made many valuable suggestions on the original manuscript and these have been incorporated in the text.

I am deeply indebted to my wife who has given me the support, understanding and constant encouragement that has enabled me to carry through my intention to write this textbook.

NORMAN THORNTON

| | | |
|---|---|---|
| 8.4 | Fixing standards | 148 |
| 8.5 | Fixing the responsibility | 148 |
| 8.6 | The appraisal of performance | 149 |
| 8.7 | Executive action | 150 |
| 8.8 | Guidance to management and the communications problem | 150 |
| 8.9 | The control of costs in different types of business activity | 151 |
| 8.10 | Types of control systems | 151 |
| 8.11 | Behavioural aspects of management | 151 |
| 8.12 | Co-ordination of business activities | 152 |
| 8.13 | The provision of information | 152 |
| 8.14 | The place of the accountant in the control process | 153 |
| 8.15 | Summary | 153 |
| **9** | **Business Objectives** | **159** |
| 9.1 | The meaning of policies and objectives | 160 |
| 9.2 | Aims and considerations guiding policy formation | 160 |
| 9.3 | Principles applicable to objectives | 161 |
| 9.4 | The nature of objectives | 162 |
| 9.5 | Setting the objectives of the company | 163 |
| 9.6 | Communication of company objectives | 169 |
| 9.7 | The corporate model and business objectives | 169 |
| 9.8 | Management by objectives | 169 |
| 9.9 | Summary | 169 |
| **10** | **Budgetary Control (1) — A Management Control Techniques** | **173** |
| 10.1 | Representations of the Budget | 174 |
| 10.2 | The approach to budgeting | 174 |
| 10.3 | Budgeting co-ordination | 176 |
| 10.4 | Essentials of a budgetary control system | 177 |
| 10.5 | Installation of a budgetary system | 177 |
| 10.6 | Top management support for budgeting | 178 |
| 10.7 | The use of associated techniques in budgeting | 178 |
| 10.8 | The budget period | 178 |
| 10.9 | The budgeted level of attainment | 179 |
| 10.10 | The budget time-table | 179 |
| 10.11 | Budget responsibility | 180 |
| 10.12 | The benefits and limitations of budgetary control | 180 |
| 10.13 | Summary | 182 |
| **11** | **Budgetary Control (2) — Budget Type Aspects** | **186** |
| 11.1 | Budget revisions | 187 |
| 11.2 | Flexible budgeting | 187 |
| 11.3 | Sectional budgets | 191 |
| 11.4 | Preparation of sectional budgets | 198 |
| 11.5 | Period reporting | 200 |
| 11.6 | The budget committee | 200 |
| 11.7 | The budget manual | 201 |
| 11.8 | Summary | 201 |
| | | |
| **ACCOUNTING AND BUSINESS CONTROL** | | **213** |
| **12** | **The Acquisition of Long-term Resources** | **215** |
| 12.1 | Essentials of a capital expenditure control system | 216 |
| 12.2 | The cost of capital | 217 |
| 12.3 | Capital investment commitment | 218 |
| 12.4 | Risk and uncertainty in capital expenditure forecasting | 218 |

|  |  |  |
|---|---|---|
| 12.5 | Priorities and the evaluation of capital expenditure projects | 219 |
| 12.6 | Cost escalation including the effects of inflation | 219 |
| 12.7 | Levels of responsibility for project approval | 220 |
| 12.8 | Case presentation | 220 |
| 12.9 | Types of asset acquisition | 220 |
| 12.10 | The buy or lease decision | 221 |
| 12.11 | Project evaluation methods | 221 |
| 12.12 | Other factors affecting project evaluation | 224 |
| 12.13 | Comparison of the evaluation methods | 227 |
| 12.14 | Capital expense accumulation and classification | 228 |
| 12.15 | Progress reporting | 228 |
| 12.16 | Summary | 229 |
| 13 | Use of Resources (1) − Material Control | 235 |
| 13.1 | Material control requirements | 236 |
| 13.2 | Stores accounting procedure | 237 |
| 13.3 | Purchase cost of materials and supplies | 237 |
| 13.4 | Costing material issues | 239 |
| 13.5 | Issue cost as a residual calculating | 242 |
| 13.6 | The use of material | 242 |
| 13.7 | Stock checking | 243 |
| 13.8 | Stock limits | 244 |
| 13.9 | Stores cost control | 245 |
| 13.10 | Summary | 245 |
| 14 | Use of Resources (2) − Labour Control | 251 |
| 14.1 | Labour control requirements | 252 |
| 14.2 | Labour recruitment and selection | 253 |
| 14.3 | Training | 253 |
| 14.4 | Wage and salary payment | 254 |
| 14.5 | Financial incentives and productivity | 255 |
| 14.6 | Work study | 255 |
| 14.7 | Financial incentive schemes | 256 |
| 14.8 | Employee expense factors | 259 |
| 14.9 | Labour utilisation | 259 |
| 14.10 | Labour turnover | 262 |
| 14.11 | Summary | 263 |
| 15 | Use of Resources (3) − Expense Control and Depreciation Methods | 269 |
| 15.1 | Factors concerned with facility availability and use | 270 |
| 15.2 | Research and development | 281 |
| 15.3 | Advertising | 282 |
| 15.4 | Other expenses | 282 |
| 15.5 | Reconciliation of profit per the management and financial accounts | 285 |
| 15.6 | A concluding comment | 285 |
| 16 | Investment Results | 290 |
| 16.1 | Work-in-progress and finished goods stock valuation | 290 |
| 16.2 | The stock valuations compared | 292 |
| 16.3 | Possibilities for improving business efficiency | 294 |
| 16.4 | Profit improvement emphasis | 295 |
| 16.5 | Cost reduction factors | 298 |
| 16.6 | The cost reduction approach | 301 |
| 16.7 | Value engineering and value analysis | 302 |
| 16.8 | Variety reduction | 303 |
| 16.9 | Summary | 303 |

17 Standard Costing (1) – Basic Procedure and Primary Variance
   Analysis 307
   17.1 The advantages of standard costing 308
   17.2 Limitations of standard costing 308
   17.3 The essentials of a standard costing system 309
   17.4 The standard hour 309
   17.5 The revision of standards 310
   17.6 The standard of attainment 310
   17.7 The level of activity 310
   17.8 The standard cost sheet 311
   17.9 Control at source 312
   17.10 Accounting system integration 312
   17.11 Standard costing and the reporting system 313
   17.12 Variance analysis 313
   17.13 Summary 322
18 Standard Costing (2) – Further Variance Analysis 330
   18.1 Direct materials – additional variances 330
   18.2 Direct labour – additional variances 333
   18.3 Factory overhead – additional variances 335
   18.4 Sales – additional variances 340
   18.5 The revision variance 343
   18.6 The causes of variance 343
   18.7 Limitations of variance calculation 343
   18.8 Treatment of standard cost variances 344
   18.9 The relationship of efficiency and activity ratios to variance
        analysis 345
   18.10 Summary 345

ACCOUNTING AND BUSINESS DECISION-MAKING 353

19 Marginal Costing 355
   19.1 Marginal cost and absorption cost 356
   19.2 Marginal costing difficulties 358
   19.3 The value of marginal costing to management 359
   19.4 The acceptance of special orders 360
   19.5 The possible elimination of a product 361
   19.6 The make or buy decision 362
   19.7 Selling of a product in a limited market 362
   19.8 Short-term pricing 363
   19.9 Product emphasis using the key factor 363
   19.10 Standard marginal costing 365
   19.11 Summary 366
20 Decision-Making Techniques 374
   20.1 Defining the context in which a decision must be made 375
   20.2 Relevant information as a basis for decision-making 376
   20.3 Examples of relevant costs in decision-making 377
   20.4 The possibilities available to the decision-maker 378
   20.5 Making the decision 378
   20.6 Implementing the decision 379
   20.7 Follow-up action on the implemented decision 379
   20.8 The operational research approach to decision making 379
   20.9 The operational research model 380
   20.10 Operational research techniques 381
   20.11 Probability theory and the decision-maker 382

20.12 Behavioural factors in decision-making 383
20.13 The management accountant's contribution to decision-making 383
20.14 A concluding comment 383
21 Decision-Making Problems 388
  21.1 Considerations for various types of decisions 389
  21.2 Possible solutions to business problems 392
  21.3 Summary 407

ASSOCIATED TOPICS FOR STUDY 417

22 Source Documentation and Data Processing 419
  22.1 Aspects of source documentation and data processing 420
  22.2 Source preparation of data 420
  22.3 Accuracy of documentation 421
  22.4 Data sorting 422
  22.5 Data summarisation and tabulation 422
  22.6 Documentation costs 422
  22.7 Form design 423
  22.8 Document data retention and disposal 423
  22.9 Basic documentation flow 425
  22.10 Data processing control 431
  22.11 Double entry book-keeping 431
  22.12 Profit reconciliation 440
  22.13 Impact of methods of data processing 440
  22.14 A concluding comment 441
23 Cost Accounting Methods 450
  23.1 Costing the cost centres 451
  23.2 Assigning the manufacturing service cost 452
  23.3 An example of cost allotment to producing cost centres 453
  23.4 Assigning the producing cost centre costs to products produced 455
  23.5 Over- and /under-absorption of overhead cost 456
  23.6 Assigning other cost centre costs to products 456
  23.7 Job costing 457
  23.8 An example of contract costing 458
  23.9 Process costing 460
  23.10 The treatment of losses and gains in process costing 462
  23.11 Equivalent units of production 464
  23.12 Joint products and byproducts 467
  23.13 Inter-process profits 468
  23.14 Uniform costing 468
  23.15 A concluding comment 469
24 Accounting for Changing Price Levels 479
  24.1 The effect of changing price levels 480
  24.2 Methods used to reflect changing price levels in the accounts of the business 483
  24.3 Appropriation for excess depreciation 483
  24.4 A charge in the accounts for excess depreciation 484
  24.5 The issue of supplementary statements 484
  24.6 Bases for adjustments to the accounts caused by changing price levels 484
  24.7 Professional valuation of assets 485
  24.8 Use of replacement costs 485

|        |                                                      |     |
|--------|------------------------------------------------------|-----|
| 24.9   | Use of index numbers                                 | 486 |
| 24.10  | Value variation and inflation                        | 487 |
| 24.11  | Recognising changing price levels in stock           | 488 |
| 24.12  | An example of accounts conversion using a general price index | 488 |
| 24.13  | The Effect of Introducing Current Cost Accounting    | 494 |
| 24.14  | A concluding comment                                 | 495 |

25  Performance Assessment                                       501
| 25.1   | The effectiveness of company objectives and policies | 502 |
| 25.2   | Satisfactory standards of comparison                 | 502 |
| 25.3   | Financial control system effectiveness               | 503 |
| 25.4   | Decentralised control and performance assessment     | 505 |
| 25.5   | Transfer pricing                                     | 507 |
| 25.6   | Motivation of Management for better performance      | 509 |
| 25.7   | Management audit                                     | 510 |
| 25.8   | Summary                                              | 510 |

CONCLUSION                                                       515

26  The Future of Management Accounting                          517
| 26.1   | Likely developments to affect the management accountant | 518 |
| 26.2   | Keeping in touch with management accounting developments | 521 |
| 26.3   | Management accounting developments and the common body of knowledge | 522 |
| 26.4   | A concluding comment                                 | 522 |

APPENDICES                                                       525

A  The Use of Compound Interest Formulae and Tables             527
Formulae and definition of terms                                 527
Compound interest tables — forms of presentation                 529
Application of formulae to business problems                     531

B  Compound Interest Tables                                      536

Table 1. Present value of £1                                     536
Table 2. Present value of £1 per period                          537
Table 3. Future value of £1 per period                           539
Table 4. Periodic amount of an annuity — present value of £1     540

C  Aspects of Taxation and Management Accounting                 542

The principal taxes concerned                                    542
Income Tax on incomes of unincorporated businesses               542
Corporation tax on incomes of companies                          543
Expansion area incentives                                        544
Stock increase relief                                            545
Value added tax (VAT)                                            545

D  Management Accounting in Retail Organisations                 547

A retail classification                                          547
Retail selling and buying control                                548
Estimating gross profit                                          550

INDEX                                                            553

# INTRODUCTION

# 1 A Management Accounting Framework

## OBJECTIVE OF THE CHAPTER

To provide a conceptual framework for management accounting indicating its coverage and emphasis in the provision of information for management.

## OUTLINE OF THE CHAPTER

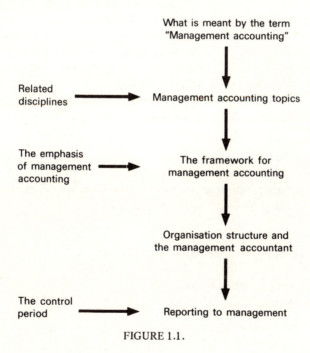

FIGURE 1.1.

What is management accounting and its contribution to the achievement of company objectives? What are the duties of the management accountant and his place in the organisation structure of the business? The purpose of this book is to answer these questions in reasonable detail. This chapter provides the framework for the logical development of the subject and integrates topics that are often isolated from the main theme of management accounting.

3

## 1.1 WHAT IS MEANT BY THE TERM 'MANAGEMENT ACCOUNTING'?

To answer this question an obvious approach is to define separately the terms 'management' and 'accounting' and merge the definitions to give the meaning required. Standard definitions are as follows:

> *Management:* 'Seeing that the job gets done efficiently. Its tasks all centre on decisions for planning and guiding the operations that are going on in the enterprise.'*
> *Accounting:* 'Accounting is a system for collecting, summarising, analysing and reporting, in monetary terms, information about an organisation.'†

A typical merged definition describes management accounting as 'the application of professional knowledge and skill in the preparation and presentation of accounting information in such a way as to assist management in the formulation of policies and in the planning and control of the operations of the undertaking.'‡

In an attempt to be more explicit it is not uncommon to expand the above definitions and an example defines management accounting as 'the application of accounting and statistical techniques to the specific purpose of producing and interpreting information designed to assist management in its functions of promoting maximum efficiency and in envisaging, formulating and co-ordinating future plans and subsequently in measuring their execution.'§

From these definitions it is clear that a book on management accounting should recognise the decision-making responsibilities of internal management in the following areas:

1. Fixing the objectives and policies to be adopted to plan the acquisition, use and disposition of the resources of the business
2. Assuring the effectiveness and efficiency with which the objectives of the business are accomplished.

## 1.2 MANAGEMENT ACCOUNTING TOPICS

The management accounting system should:
1. Facilitate the preparation of reports for management to assess:

    (*a*) Company profitability
    (*b*) The financial status of the business
    (*c*) The anticipated future progress of the business

---

\* E. F. L. Brech, ed., *Principles and Practice of Management* (Longmans, 1963), p. 9.
  † Robert N. Anthony, *Management Accounting – Text and Cases* (Richard D. Irwin, Homewood, Illinois, 1970), p. 1.
  ‡ *Terminology of Management and Financial Accountancy* (Institute of Cost and Management Accountants, 1974), p. 9.
  § *Management Accounting – a Concise Appraisal* (Association of Certified and Corporate Accountants, 1954), p. 3.

(*d*) The stability and security of the investment in the business
(*e*) Company liquidity and the ability to pay debts

2. Ensure that, within reason, those financial factors which should influence a business decision are readily available
3. Make possible the provision of consistent information for the preparation of management reports in a uniform manner.

This list suggests a structure of topics in the following classification which is used in this book:

Introduction
Financial statement classification
Financial statement interpretation
Accounting and forward planning
Accounting and business control
Accounting and business decision-making
Associated topics for study
Conclusion.

The content for each of these classifications is briefly described below.

## 1.21 INTRODUCTION

The objective of this section is stated at the beginning of the chapter. The emphasis is on information for use within the organisation. In common with other general texts this book concentrates on management accounting for manufacturing companies but the principles are equally applicable to other types of business. Aspects of retailing applications are explained in Appendix D.

## 1.22 FINANCIAL STATEMENT CLASSIFICATION

In management accounting, classification is the central feature which governs the whole process. The recording and sorting aspects facilitate the classification of data in a form of value to management. At an early stage in the study of management accounting, financial data classification should be considered and the characteristics for data division to produce an assembly in logical order of grades of information for management.

## 1.23 FINANCIAL STATEMENT INTERPRETATION

The classified financial data emphasises financial relationships which can be studied by the technique of ratio analysis. The financial relationships are considered in profit planning and the technique for their interpretation in this area is cost—volume—profit analysis. To strengthen areas of potential weakness in an organisation or to capitalize on more attractive opportunities for the business, asset flows must be interpreted and the technique of funds analysis requires study for this purpose.

## 1.24 ACCOUNTING AND FORWARD PLANNING

The management accounting system of control is built around the specific plans formulated to achieve the objectives of the business. The sequence of operations to produce a co-ordinated integrated system is described in the management control process and the accounting technique that uses this process is budgetary control.

## 1.25 ACCOUNTING AND BUSINESS CONTROL

Financial control is possible at each operational stage of the business:

- (*a*)  Capital acquisition
- (*b*)  Capital investment
- (*c*)  Resources use
- (*d*)  Investment results
- (*e*)  Profit disposal.

Management accounting is a tool of management to assist in ensuring that the specific business plans are carried out at each operational stage. A technique of particular value in detail control is standard costing.

## 1.26 ACCOUNTING AND BUSINESS DECISION-MAKING

Managers are concerned in decision-making and this usually involves weighing up alternative opportunities in the light of relevant information. The relevant information includes financial data and many decision-making techniques have evolved to assist managers in this important area of their work. The marginal costing technique is particularly useful in providing relevant information for decision-making and is considered in this section.

## 1.27 ASSOCIATED TOPICS FOR STUDY

The increasing attention being given to management control systems has influenced management to recognise the need for an integrated system of data provision; the establishment of a system of data flow between departments; and data processing for departments. The expansion of recording systems to give management the information they want includes cost accounting data, not only in the form of predetermined costs mentioned in an earlier section but historical costs too.

In a period of inflation the unstable monetary unit renders the measurement of profit difficult. Traditionally, accounting measurement has used historical costs but the marked upward trend of prices in recent years demands a recognition of the price level problem in accounting practice.

The emphasis of management accounting in the earlier sections provides valuable information for performance assessment but special problems must be considered in this area, particularly in large organisations, where decentralisation of the decision-making power is practised.

1.28 CONCLUSION

The objective of this section is to recognise that the practice of management accounting is not static. It can only be valuable where there is a dynamic response to the changes taking place in business today and the relevance of the reported information is maintained for the decision-making situations faced by management.

## 1.3 RELATED DISCIPLINES

The topics above indicate the close relationship of management accounting to other disciplines such as:

1. Finance, financial accounting and economics
2. Mathematics and the quantitative techniques
3. Behavioural and social sciences
4. Management information systems and computer science.

In this book, the view is taken that little value can be gained from discussion aimed at claiming specific topics for one discipline or claiming special merit for the emphasis that one discipline places on aspects of the subject. It appears sensible to use the valuable results of research in other disciplines to develop and apply to maximum advantage the techniques of management accounting. The relevant features of related disciplines are incorporated in the appropriate sections.

## 1.4 THE FRAMEWORK FOR MANAGEMENT ACCOUNTING

The existing framework for management accounting is not consistent and integrated to the extent that one might expect an organised discipline of study to be. This section is an attempt to provide a reasonable framework for management accounting capable of further development.

### A BASIC CLASSIFICATION OF DATA

Financial information for business management may be considered from two points of view:

1. An analysis of data on the basis of manager(s) actions in the business. This approach is illustrated in Figure 1.2.
2. An analysis of data on the basis of the economic cycle of the activities of the business. This approach is illustrated in Figure 1.3.

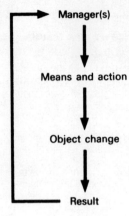

FIGURE 1.2. Data analysis on the basis of manager(s) actions

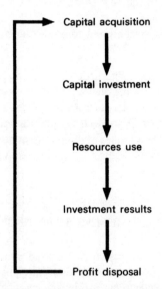

FIGURE 1.3. Data analysis on the basis of the economic cycle of the business

The terms used in Figures 1.2 and 1.3 are defined as follows:

| Term | Definition |
| --- | --- |
| Manager(s) | The person(s) responsible for taking managerial action (the control of the work of others in the business) |
| Means | The methods, skills, techniques and knowledge enabling the manager to take the action required |

| Action | That which is done or performed |
|---|---|
| Object change | That which is the subject of the action |
| Result | The product of the action |
| Capital acquisition | The acquisition of the means of making investment |
| Capital investment | The investment of capital in the resources of the business |
| Resources use | The measurement of the use made of the resources of the business |
| Investment results | The revenue/cost relationships arising from the use of the resources of the business |
| Profit disposal | The use made of the investment results |

Applying the first approach to management functions, the additional analysis provided is illustrated in Figure 1.4.

The acts of management have received wide coverage in management literature* and from an analysis of research in this area the following definitions for the framework given have emerged:

Strategic planning — is the process of deciding on objectives of the organisation, on changes in these objectives, on the resources used to attain these objectives, and on the policies that are to govern the acquisition, use, and disposition of these resources.

Management control — is the process by which managers assure that resources are obtained and used effectively and efficiently in the accomplishment of the organisation's objectives.

Operational control — is the process of assuring that specific tasks are carried out effectively and efficiently.†

The comprehensive nature of the economic cycle approach is illustrated in Figure 1.5.

In this illustration the time cycle of one year begins with a capital of £70,000, £50,000 provided by proprietors and investors and £20,000 retained in the business

---

* A good summary appears in Appendix A of Robert N. Anthony, *Planning and Control Systems — a Framework for Analysis* (Graduate School of Business Administration, Harvard University, Boston, Mass., 1965), pp. 117–47.
† Ibid, pp. 16, 17, 18.

to finance future operations. The £70,000 is invested in fixed and working capital and throughout the year resources of £200,000 are acquired and are available for use. Resources amounting to £80,000 are not used in the current year and are carried forward to the following year represented by the original capital from proprietors and investors of £50,000 and the retained profits increased to £30,000 as

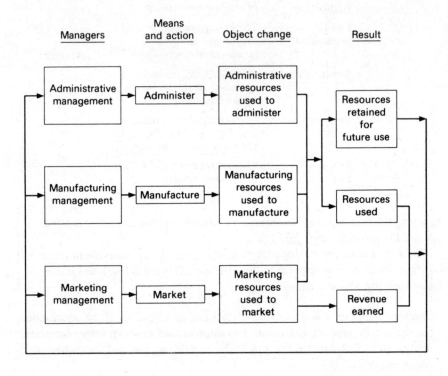

FIGURE 1.4. An illustration of data analysis — manager(s) actions basis

a result of the profit disposal decision to limit the distribution to proprietors and investors to £10,000. The resources used of £120,000 represents the expenses of running the business and the cost of manufacturing the products which have been sold for £140,000. When the resulting profit of £20,000 is distributed, the economic cycle is complete.

Data analysis on the bases illustrated are clearly related since the actions of managers produce the economic cycle. There is no logical reason why the two approaches should not be merged because the formula represented by Figures 1.4 and 1.5 permits independent classifications, if desired, based on the properties or characteristics inherent in the data to be classified. This proposition is the one adopted in this book.

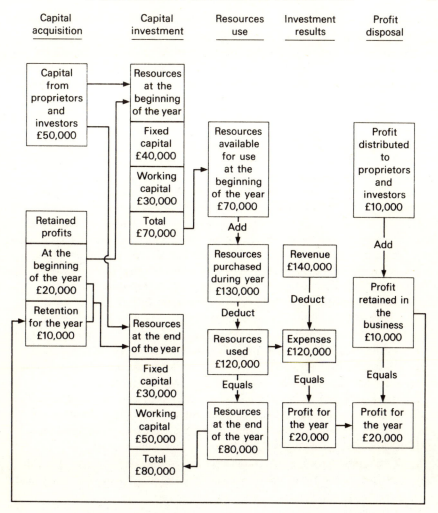

FIGURE 1.5. An illustration of data analysis — economic cycle basis

## 1.5  THE EMPHASIS OF MANAGEMENT ACCOUNTING

In the provision of information for management, the essential qualities which underlie a management accounting system are as follows:

1.  Relevance — the system should assist in the provision of useful information to achieve a desired result
2.  Comprehensiveness — the system should cover the basic features of business activity
3.  Flexibility — the system should be adaptable to the needs of a variety of users

4. Realism — the system should recognise the practical limitations in the business situation regarding the provision of financial data and its potential use
5. Accuracy — the system should recognise the degree of accuracy required of source data to provide output within the prescribed limits of accuracy to meet the objectives laid down by management.

## 1.6 ORGANISATION STRUCTURE AND THE MANAGEMENT ACCOUNTANT

There is little uniformity among companies regarding their organisation for financial control; the duties and extent of influence of accounting staff; and titles used. The American title of controller for the chief accounting officer of the company is often replaced in Britain by the title 'chief accountant' and the management accountant may be one member of the chief accountant's staff. From the meaning of management accounting given earlier it is clear that the function is advisory providing a control service to management. A breakdown of this advisory service could provide a statement of the responsibilities of a controller. This confusion is only resolved in each company by the clear definition of the responsibilities of each individual in the organisation, whatever the title chosen for a given task. The title is unimportant; what is important is what the individual does and whether the company recognises the vital service that management accounting can provide, and allows the company officials to realise that potential. In this book, the official practising management accounting is described as the management accountant.

The responsibilities and accountability of managers in an organisation are provided by an organisation chart and a typical structure for a manufacturing business is illustrated in Figure 1.6. This is a simple diagram and the interrelationships recognised by functional responsibilities have not been incorporated.

In large organisations, the central management of the company may take over central services for the group and expenses may be incurred in the following areas:

1. Accounting
2. Personnel
3. Research and development
4. Marketing
5. General administration.

## 1.7 REPORTING TO MANAGEMENT

The responsibilities of specific managers in the business will dictate the type of financial information reported to each manager and reports may be identified by description or code linked to the organisation pattern of the business in the form of an information chart. Such a chart for a divisionalised company is illustrated in Figure 1.7. This chart is useful because it shows in a clear manner the relation-

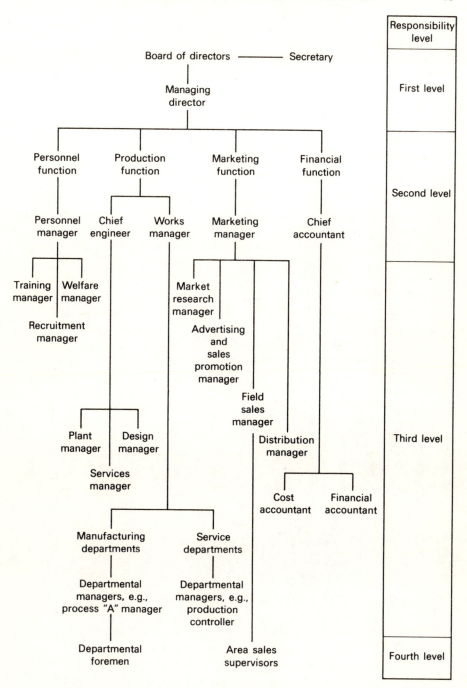

FIGURE 1.6. A typical manufacturing organisation structure

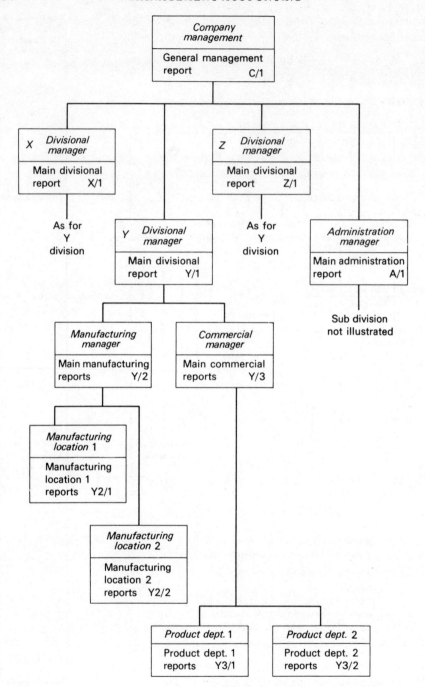

FIGURE 1.7. An information chart

ship between different forms in the reporting procedure and the appropriate level of management responsibility.

## 1.71 INTEGRATION OF REPORTING

Integration of reporting procedures may be considered as:

1. Providing schedules which explain in greater detail sections of an overall report for management (*see* Figure 1.8)
2. Providing reports for different levels of management which progressively break down the overall report for management (*see* Figure 1.9).

The reports produced from financial and cost accounting procedures should be reconciled and this point is considered in greater detail in Chapter 22.

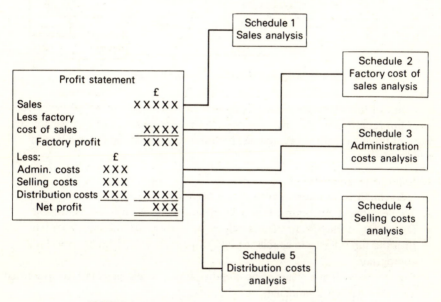

FIGURE 1.8. Integrated reporting – classification analysis

## 1.72 REPORTING TERMINOLOGY

Accounting terms are capable of misinterpretation, and to the manager receiving the accounting reports, meaningful interpretation can only follow if he understands the accounting terminology used. Acceptable terminology within the business should be consistently applied in report presentation.

## 1.73 MANAGEMENT RELATIONSHIPS

Reporting to management places the accountant in a difficult position with his colleagues because the information issued must reflect upon individual performance

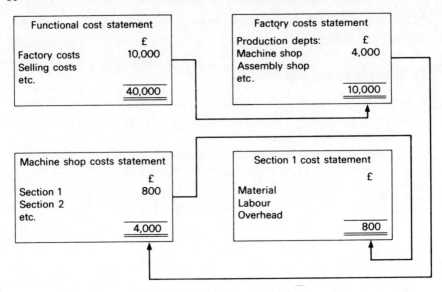

FIGURE 1.9. Integrated reporting – levels of management analysis

and most of the information must be reported to the individual's supervisor. To meet this requirement, yet maintain the effective co-operation of managers in the work of the management accountant, the following points should be borne in mind:

1. Report the facts
2. Use standards for assessment that have been independently compiled
3. To the extent that comments may be necessary, be as objective as possible
4. Depending on the circumstances, release information to the supervisor later than the subordinate to enable the latter to conduct inquiries he may think appropriate
5. Where information appears to be unduly critical, check the detail to ensure that a mistake has not been made.

### 1.74 INTERPRETATION OF INFORMATION

Reports are prepared to encourage action by those responsible for any unsatisfactory tendencies disclosed in the reports to improve performance. This function assumes that those receiving the reports understand the information given and can interpret the detail provided. Any time spent in educating managers in the meaning of the reports supplied and the conclusions that may be reached as a basis for action is worth while.

To ascertain the true cause of an unfavourable result can sometimes be a time-consuming job since the apparent cause may hide more fundamental problems. If more rigorous analysis and investigation are not followed, subsequent reporting may continue to show unfavourable results until the basic cause has been established and rectified. It follows that in the interpretation of information it is unwise to apply a superficial diagnosis.

## 1.75 FLEXIBILITY AND THE REPORTING SYSTEM

Business conditions change rapidly and if the information service is to be efficient it must be sufficiently flexible to provide the information required under the new conditions, whether the new situation is a result of external influence or internal action. A change of internal method as, for example, the installation of a computer, may make possible the provision of information which was earlier thought desirable but uneconomic.

## 1.76 ROUTINE/SPECIAL REPORTING

Financial matters that are significant to managers and repetitive are the subject of routine reports. Matters of singular or infrequent occurrence do not warrent continuous reporting and are made the subject of special reports. Both types of reporting may be made orally in individual conversation or through the medium of committee meetings but most companies find it necessary to supplement this form of exchange of information by the use of:

1. Tabular reports and charts mainly for routine reporting
2. Narrative reports mainly for special reporting.

An outline tabular report is illustrated in Figure 1.10 and a narrative report in Figure 1.11.

| Title | | | | | | |
|---|---|---|---|---|---|---|
| Period _____ | | | | | | |
| | | This period | | | To date | | |
| | | Actual | Comparable data | Variation | Actual | Comparable data | Variation |
| | | £ | £ | £ | £ | £ | £ |
| Analysis headings | | | | | | | |
| | Sub total | | | | | | |
| | | | | | | | |
| | Sub total | | | | | | |
| | Total | | | | | | |

FIGURE 1.10. An outline tabular report

To: . . . . . . . . . . . . . . . . . . . . . . . . . . .                    Date . . . . . . . . . . . .

     Copies to: . . . . . . . . . . . . . . . . . . . .

     . . . . . . . . . . . . . . . . . . . .

     . . . . . . . . . . . . . . . . . . . .

From: . . . . . . . . . . . . . . . . . . . . . . . .

Subject of the report

1. Introduction
2. Main section of the report – including reference to appendices (if applicable)
3. Conclusions
4. Recommendations.

Signature . . . . . . . . . . . . . . . . . . . . .

FIGURE 1.11. An outline of a narrative report

    Graphs are a common form of chart as shown, for example, in the illustrations in the chapter on cost–volume–profit analysis.

    The tabular reports for routine reporting may be pre-printed to show:

1. The title
2. The period covered by the report
3. The classified information headings with a clear indication of the key figures by sub-totals and totals (the comparable data title in Figure 1.10 is usually specifically identified by type, e.g., 'budget' or 'last year actual')
4. Columns for figures to be recorded.

In addition, the following may be shown:

(*a*) Distribution details
(*b*) Panels for comments and possibly recommendations
(*c*) The signature of the person responsible for the preparation of the report
(*d*) The date of preparation.

    The personal contact between managers and the management accounting department is the most effective way of achieving meaningful communication and the smaller the company the greater the ease with which the accounting service can be applied through individual conversation to assist management in running the business. As companies increase in size, this direct contact is not always possible although as reporting procedures develop it should not be forgotten that any opportunity to obtain personal contact is valuable and should be used to maximum advantage in improving reporting links with the 'man on the job'.

## 1.77 REPORT REVIEW

To ensure that routine reports are continuing to give the information required by managers as efficiently as possible, a regular review of internal reporting should be made regarding:

1. The cost of reports in relation to the benefits expected
2. The frequency of reports — frequency may be reduced
3. The promptness of producing the report — can the speed of production be increased?
4. Report accuracy — can the accuracy limits be altered without loss in value of the report?
5. Use of the report — is all the report used for managerial control?
6. Content of the report — may the contents be improved?

## 1.8 THE CONTROL PERIOD

The frequency with which reports for management are produced depends on the extent effective action can be taken as a result of interpreting the information contained in the statements. The control period selected should reflect significant variations in performance and make reasonable allowance for the random effect of short-period fluctuations which can average out when larger periods are taken.

Some statements for management may be produced weekly; others, four-weekly, or monthly. Some organisations split the quarter year into two four-weekly periods followed by a five-weekly period or other combinations of dates to take account of specific conditions affecting the company — for example, a fixed holiday period. Management requirements for some information may be adequately met by quarterly or half-yearly reports. The general aim is to produce statements for control periods of equal working duration so that comparable data may aid the interpretative process.

## 1.9 SUMMARY

The output from a management accounting system is information for management which should be relevant, comprehensive and accurate. The system to deal with the data input should be flexible to ensure a realistic response to the needs of management and the changing business environment.

The framework for management accounting is provided by the basic classification of data in the economic cycle of capital acquisition, capital investment, resources use, investment results and profit disposal.

# FOR FURTHER STUDY

## QUESTIONS

1. *Interpretation of definition of accounting*
   'Accounting is a system for collecting, summarising, analysing and reporting in monetary terms information about an organisation.'
   (R. N. Anthony, *Management Accounting — Text and Cases,* Richard D. Irwin, Homewood, Illinois, 1964, page 1)
   *Required:*
   What do you understand by this statement?

2. *The role of the management accountant and the function of management accountancy*
   Discuss the role of the management accountant and the function of management accountancy in a manufacturing company.

3. *Classification of business operations*
   As a basis for management accounting, describe the business operations of a manufacturing company, classifying these operations to give a logical presentation of the economic cycle affecting the business.

4. *Duties of the management accountant*
   What are the duties of a management accountant in a medium-sized manufacturing company?

5. *Behavioural implications of the management accountant's task.*
   'Reporting to management places the accountant in a difficult position with his colleagues because the information issued must reflect upon individual performance and most of the information must be reported to that individual's supervisor.'
   *Required:*
   What action may be taken to meet this requirement yet maintain the effective co-operation of managers in the work of the accountant.

6. *The role of the management accountant and the extent of the authority of the works manager over the works accounting and management accountant*
   The top management of the Motor Engineering Co. Ltd held differing views regarding the role of the management accountant, especially regarding the extent to which such an official of the company should participate in the running of the functional departments concerned with manufacturing and marketing. It was generally agreed that the management accountant should occupy an advisory position relative to these departments but the problem concerned the power of the management accountant when views were expressed contrary to the opinions of the heads of the functional departments. The company had recently employed a management accountant with a forceful personality with undoubted ability, and the soundness of his views had received the managing director's support to such an extent that the factory and sales managers had recently resigned. They maintained that the management accountant was

exceeding his authority and the top management action left them no alternative but to resign. At this time the management accountant secured a lucrative position in another company and top management felt that this was an ideal opportunity to review the role of the management accountant.

Another problem was relevant. When the company was a smaller organisation, most of the management accounting concerned with the manufacturing operations was controlled by a works accountant responsible to the works manager. Now this work was controlled by the chief accountant and carried out by the management accountant's department. Some members of the company considered that this work should be under the direct control of the works manager and the management accountant should report direct to him. In support of this view they maintained that the interpretation of information demanded a closeness to the job not possible where the accounting was segregated.

*Required:*

(*a*) Comment on the role of the management accountant in the situation described in this case. What advice would you give to top management?

(*b*) Do you agree with the view that the management accountant should carry out the management accounting within the works administration and report direct to the works manager?

7. *Factors affecting the structure of the reporting system*
What factors affect the structure of the reporting system for financial information for the internal management of a manufacturing company?

8. *Points to consider when preparing a special report*
What are the preliminary questions to consider when preparing a special report? How should such a report be presented?

9. *The nature of an investigation and its results in preparation for report submission*
To complete a special report, investigation, recording and analysis of the subject of the report are necessary. What steps should be taken at the investigation stage? In reaching the conclusions and making the recommendations from the results of the investigation, what faults should be avoided?

10. *Features of a financial report*
What do you consider to be the essential features of an effective financial report for management? (ACA — Modified)

11. *The choice of the accounting period for control reports for management*
What factors affect the frequency with which financial reports for management are produced? Indicate three common accounting periods adopted and comment on their use.

12. *Sufficiency of the reports received and the possible modification of the reports supplied*
As part of the reorganisation of Medical Chemicals Ltd, a medium-sized manufacturing company, it was the intention of the management to alter the report-

ing system for internal control of the business. Reports currently supplied to management consisted of:

(a) An annual financial report based on the final accounts of the business (balance sheet and profit and loss account) as at the end of the year together with detailed schedules of operating expenses

(b) Monthly statistics as to the value of orders received

(c) Statistics as to the value of deliveries to customers daily, weekly and monthly

(d) Weekly reports for the works manager showing the output of various departments in product units

(e) As requested, labour costs and some of the direct manufacturing expense, expressed as average costs per unit or as a percentage to the sales value of output.

Certain members of the management team believed that these reports did not furnish sufficient information to management to control the business adequately. On the other hand, they were aware that in the provision of reports the cost of gathering the data could exceed the value received from the additional information. In addition, there was the possibility that so many figures might be provided that management would be unable to identify the key information for control.

*Required:*

(a) Do you agree with the members of the management team who believed that the reports supplied were insufficient for adequate control of the business? Why?

(b) If your answer to (a) is 'yes', what reports would you expect to find as a result of a modification of the reporting system? Give the likely frequency of your reports with reasons.

FURTHER READING

Anthony, Robert N. *Planning and Control Systems − a Framework for Analysis.* Division of Research, Graduate School of Business Administration, Harvard University, Boston, Mass., 1965.

Bostock, Christopher. *Management, Accounting and Profitability.* Pitman, 1960. Chs 1, 2, 8, 9 and 10, and Appendices A and C.

*The Presentation of Information to Management.* Institute of Cost and Works Accountants, 1950.

# FINANCIAL STATEMENT CLASSIFICATION

# 2 Financial Data Classification and Terminology

OBJECTIVE OF THE CHAPTER

To study the grouping of units of financial data into classes and the characteristics for data division to produce meaningful information for management.

OUTLINE OF THE CHAPTER

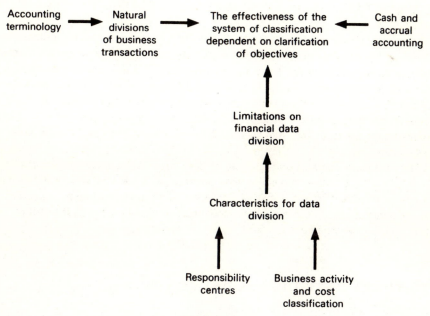

FIGURE 2.1.

A central factor in the success or failure of the provision of relevant financial information for management is the effectiveness of the system of classification upon which the management accounting system is based. Constituent elements of the classification are the classes and to identify a class, or classes, from a number of things is to classify. The process of dividing the total data for classification into classes requires the interpretation of data by characteristics. In this chapter, the principal characteristics applicable in the management accounting classification process are examined and the basic features emerging from this sorting of data.

## 2.1 THE EFFECTIVENESS OF THE SYSTEM OF CLASSIFICATION

To ensure the management accounting system of classification will be effective, answers are required to the following questions:

1. Which system objectives are essential and which may be rejected as non-essential within the resources available?
2. Given the decision on the objectives to be adopted, what is the best form of classification for their realisation?

As financial data grows in bulk and variety of subject matter, the need for an adequate classification increases.

## 2.2 LIMITATIONS ON FINANCIAL DATA DIVISION

The possible characteristics for financial data division are numerous but the view is taken in this text that there are limitations on the number of characteristics that may be chosen and applied. There are few essential characteristics for data division because unlimited analysis would provide so much detail that it could seriously be questioned as to whether the volume of information that would be available could be assimilated by management. Not only must the additional data be relevant to the user's needs, but its incremental value should be in excess of its incremental provision cost.

In some cases, the data unit may not be divisible; in other cases, the unit itself may be a total. It is to be expected that aggregated data will be regularly supplied as input for classification and it may be unproductive to sub-classify this data, either at the point of origin or intermediate accounting entity where the classification process is being carried out.

## 2.3 CHARACTERISTICS FOR DATA DIVISION

The minimum classification, as a basis for sub-division, is the identification of the nature of resources available and used in terms of the function or activity performed for a particular period of time. The nature of the resources available and used are related to the time scale as shown in Figure 2.2.*

---

* An application of the 'flow of input' chart in E. O. Edwards and P. W. Bell, *The Theory and Measurement of Business Income* (University of California Press, Berkeley, 1967), p. 72.

The significant properties* or qualities which enable the units of data of financial information to be classified are:

| Property | Relationship of the property to the type of analysis provided | Example(s) |
|---|---|---|
| 1. Source | The origin of what is acquired | Funds may be analysed as to their source, e.g., investors and creditors |
| 2. Accountability | The nature of the responsibility of a member of the business | Factory costs may be assignable to the factory manager and marketing costs to the marketing manager |
| 3. Controllability | The degree of influence exercised by a member of the business | The commitment to pay rent for a building to be used for the production of a product may be made by a factory manager. The rental cost assignable to the manager of a department in the factory is not controllable by the departmental manager |
| 4. Liquidity | The ease with which assets may be converted into cash | Short-term investment may be converted into cash quicker than investments made for a long term |
| 5. Importance | The magnitude and significance of the activities of the business | Data may be identified with the major, minor and ancillary activities of the business |
| 6. Regularity | Similarities produced as a result of normal or ordinary conditions being attained | The isolation of an abnormal cost which may arise owing to an abnormal loss in a process or extraordinary profit earned as a result of an activity not in the ordinary course of business |
| 7. Variability | The relative effect of fluctuations in activity level | Costs may vary directly with variations in the volume of production, i.e., a variable cost. |

## 2.4 RESPONSIBILITY CENTRES

Management is delegated to responsible members of the organisation, and their sections of activity are termed responsibility centres. These sections may be engaged in a separate production process or group of processes; in the provision of a service;

* A modified version of the properties considered by A. A. Fitzgerald and L. A. Shumer in *Classification in Accounting* (Butterworth & Co. (Australia) Ltd, 1952), pp. 78–88.

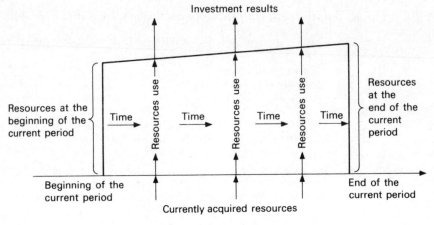

FIGURE 2.2. The basis for data division

or in the execution of an administrative or managerial function. Typical definitions may be:

| Term | Description |
|---|---|
| Production department | A section of the works under separate managerial control which is concerned with the manufacture of a particular product or group of products |
| Process | A complete and independent production operation carried out within a department or part of a department |
| Sub-process | A sub-division of a process |
| Service department | A section of a works under separate managerial control which provides a service for the operation of one or more departments or processes |
| General department | Sections outside the works activities concerned with selling, distribution, and the execution of administrative functions. |

Examples of responsibility centres used in management accounting classifications are as follows:

| Data for classification | Classification |
|---|---|
| Expenses of a business in a period | Manufacturing, marketing and administration expense responsibility centres |
| Sales revenue for a period | On the basis of product division responsibility; on the basis of geographical area responsibility |
| Assets of a business as at a certain date | On the basis of functional controllability; on the basis of geographical controllability. |

In these examples, it is evident that the responsibility centre may be limited to expenses; include revenue in addition to expenses; or relate the revenue and expenses to the responsibility for assets assigned to that centre. These centres may be termed expense, profit (the difference between the revenue and expenses for the period) and investment centres, respectively. The responsibility centre classification is illustrated in Figure 2.3.

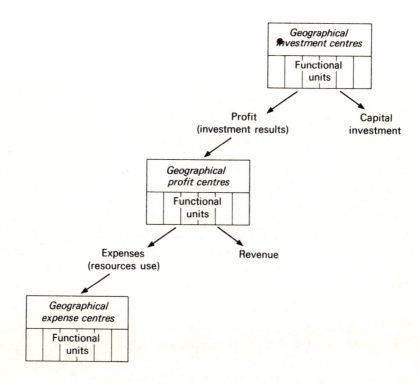

FIGURE 2.3. Responsibility centre classification

## 2.5 CASH AND ACCRUAL ACCOUNTING

Fundamental business transactions are recorded in cash either received or paid in a control period. Financial information limited to cash flows does not show the financial effects of the business events taking place in the period. The attempt to match revenue earned with expenses incurred in earning that revenue in a period is termed accrual accounting. This involves the recognition of the rights to receive and obligations to pay cash at the time when the right or obligation is created. Financial information applicable to a current control period on the accrual accounting basis is illustrated below:

<table>
<tr><td>Current control period</td><td>Future control period</td></tr>
<tr><td>Allocation of expected future receipts and payments for goods and services (accruals) for the current period)</td><td></td></tr>
<tr><td align="center">+</td><td></td></tr>
<tr><td>Allocation of past receipts and payments for goods and services (deferred revenue or expense for the current period)</td><td>Allocation of past receipts and payments for goods and services (deferrals for the future period)</td></tr>
<tr><td align="center">+</td><td></td></tr>
<tr><td>Present receipts and payments for goods and services for the current period</td><td></td></tr>
<tr><td align="center">=</td><td></td></tr>
<tr><td>Revenue earned and expenses incurred</td><td></td></tr>
</table>

Costs which represent a sacrifice of values may extend beyond any one control period. Costs applicable to a particular period are known as expenses.

Where allocations are involved, as shown above, the measurement process is important. Precise allocations of costs between periods are not always possible and estimates based on judgment are necessary. The inaccuracy introduced into the system is only permissible if the resulting information given to management is of a standard sufficient to meet the purpose demanded by the user when using the information.

## 2.6 NORMAL DIVISIONS OF BUSINESS TRANSACTIONS

The names of the transactions carried out by the business is the simplest form of classification and is known as natural or normal classification. A typical series of normal divisions of business transactions is shown below:

1. Capital acquisition
   (a)  Company equity — capital issued; capital and revenue reserves
   (b)  Other long-term liabilities — debentures and loans

2. Capital investment
   (a)  Fixed assets and depreciation
   (b)  Other long-term assets — goodwill; patents and trade marks; investments in associated and subsidiary companies; trade investments
   (c)  Cash — deposit and current accounts; petty cash; bills receivable; marketable securities
   (d)  Trade debts — trade debtors; bad debts provision
   (e)  Stock — raw materials; supplies; work-in-progress; finished goods

(*f*)  Other current assets – debts from employees; short-term deposits; prepaid expenses and accrued income

(*g*)  Short-term borrowings – bank overdraft facilities; bills payable

(*h*)  Other current liabilities – accounts payable to suppliers; accrued current taxation; current accounts with associated companies; accrued expenses and deferred income; suspense and clearing accounts

3. Resources use

(*a*)  Materials – direct and indirect

(*b*)  Manpower – direct and indirect labour; labour allowances; overtime and night shift premiums

(*c*)  Supplies – consumable materials; maintenance and tool materials

(*d*)  Services – rent and insurances

(*e*)  Utilities – electricity; gas; water; fuel oil; solid fuel; petrol and diesel oil

(*f*)  Contractors' charges – hiring plant and equipment; repairs and maintenance; plant overhaul; tool design and maintenance

(*g*)  Travelling and representation – domestic and foreign travelling and entertaining

(*h*)  Advertising

(*i*)  Communications – telephone and teleprinters; postage and telegrams

(*j*)  Information and knowledge – books, journals and literature; subscriptions to trade and professional associations

(*k*)  Employment expense – pension fund; national insurance; and state graduated pension fund

(*l*)  Professional fees – legal; market research; accounting, auditing and taxation

(*m*)  Donations

(*n*)  Depreciation

(*o*)  Imputed interest

(*p*)  Miscellaneous expense – not classified elsewhere

(*q*)  Taxation and government fees – rates; training levy; motor vehicle tax; stamp duty; registration fees

(*r*)  Expense credits and allocations – canteen revenue; training grants receivable; service charges from associated companies; variable and fixed expenses allocated

4. Investment results

(*a*)  Revenue – net sales

(*b*)  Other income – rents receivable; receipts from sales of scrap and waste; cash discount receivable; interest receivable; dividends receivable

5. Profit disposal

(*a*)  Dividend payment

(*b*)  Other expenditure – interest on debentures; other interest payable

(*c*)  Taxation – income and corporation tax.

These divisions of financial data when assembled in logical order provide hierarchies of information for management – the subject of Chapter 4.

## 2.7  BUSINESS ACTIVITY AND COST CLASSIFICATION

Two features of business activity are production output and sales, and manufacturing companies seek to balance the output and sales levels in relation to minimum planned stock levels to deal with seasonal and cyclical fluctuations. These activity levels have an important effect on cost behaviour and produce cost classifications that are useful to the management accountant. Some costs fluctuate with changes in activity levels while other costs do not alter with such changes. The former are known as variable costs and the latter, fixed costs. The volume measure used should be the one that reasonably reflects the conditions that cause the costs to change: factory costs may be expected to have a correlation with production output and selling costs with sales. Costs do not fit easily into the fixed and variable categories named above and it is necessary to be more precise in the definitions given and to extend this classification to include the following:

1. Variable costs — costs which vary in direct proportion to changes in the level of activity, i.e., constant per unit of volume. Material directly identifiable as a constant per unit produced is used as an example in Figure 2.4.

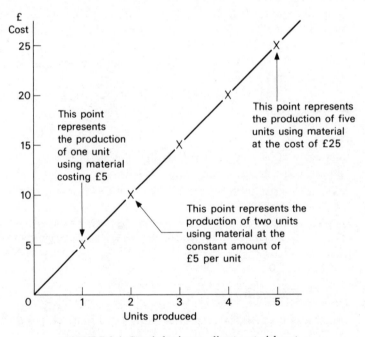

FIGURE 2.4. Cost behaviour — direct material cost

2. Fixed costs — costs unaffected by a change in the level of activity and which tend to vary with time or when there is a substantial change in financial policy. If a long enough period is taken, the cost may change as, for example, in the case of rent illustrated in Figure 2.5.

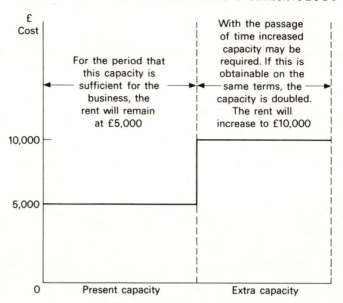

FIGURE 2.5. Cost behaviour – rent cost

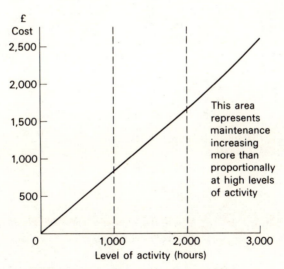

FIGURE 2.6. Cost behaviour – maintenance cost

In this illustration, the decision to rent additional capacity has varied the 'fixed cost'. This cost is fixed for a particular range of output and then increases to a new level for another range of output. Once the commitment is made to rent the additional capacity the charge is fixed at £10,000. Diagramatically represented as in Figure 2.5 the cost is sometimes known as a stepped cost.

3. Semi-variable costs – maintenance is a variable cost but showing its behaviour graphically it may appear as in Figure 2.6.

Costs which although capable of variation as production facilities are utilised over or below normal levels and not automatically changing with the production rate are known as semi-variable costs. If the planned range of output of such a cost includes the portion of the graph where almost a linear relationship is evident (almost a constant cost per unit—say between 1,000 and 2,000 hours in Figure 2.6) the portions of the graph where the costs vary indirectly with the level of activity (e.g., 2,000 to 3,000 hours in Figure 2.6) may be ignored and the expenditure treated as a variable cost. In Figure 2.6 it has been assumed that a minimum cost has not been incurred. Sometimes such a charge must be incurred as, for example, in the case of a telephone charge — shown in Figure 2.7.

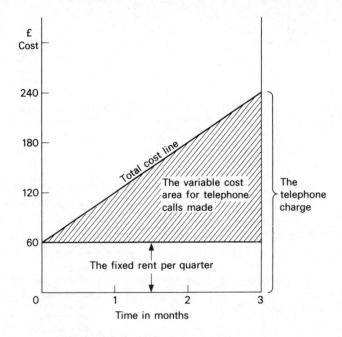

FIGURE 2.7. Cost behaviour — telephone cost

This is a semi-variable cost. Where the fixed and variable elements are clearly identifiable, as in Figure 2.7, the expenditure is sometimes known as a mixed cost.

The decisions taken by management affect the divisions of cost into their fixed and variable elements and where the cost is not directly related to the manufacturing operations of the business this discretionary factor may have important consequences because the costs can be whatever management wants them to be. Professor Anthony* calls these costs, for example, research and development cost and advertising cost, managed costs. The decision on how much to spend for a managed

* Robert N. Anthony, *Management Accounting — Text and Cases* (Richard D. Irwin, Homewood, Illinois, 1970), pp. 474—6.

cost item may take several forms as shown in Figure 2.8 and diagrammatically the graphs appear to show a fixed, variable and semi-variable cost subject to the inevitable pattern of manufacturing operation. Professor Anthony points out that these relationships are not inevitable — the level of cost can be changed simply by changing the management decision.

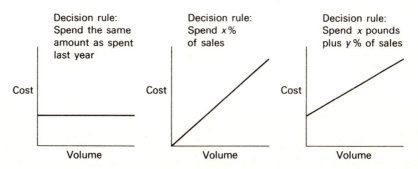

FIGURE 2.8. Cost behaviour — managed costs

## 2.8  ACCOUNTING TERMINOLOGY

Many terms used in accountancy are capable of misinterpretation and even accountants sometimes disagree as to the precise meaning to be given to a particular term. The important thing to establish is that those responsible for using information in a particular business are clear as to the meaning of the financial terms used on the statements provided. Once agreed, the same terms should be used on all statements giving financial information and consistently applied.

In a financial classification, terms in common use are often given a technical meaning and this is to be preferred because such terminology is likely to be more precise than popular terms. This text uses conventional accounting terminology but technical terminology particular to a business may be preferred if more easily understood by the managers in the company.

There are two principal aims* to be kept in mind when deciding on the terms to be used in financial information supplied to management. They are:

1.  Clarity — this involves attention to the following points:
    (a)  Simplicity. Concise expressions and simple words should be used.
    (b)  Presentation of detail. Where it is necessary or desirable to amplify items by means of notes or in statements annexed to accounting information, the items and the relevant details should be identifiable by appropriate reference numbers or letters and the wording used in the notes or statements should correspond with the descriptions used in the items to which they relate.

* A slightly modified version of the points made in the introduction to *Terms Used in Published Accounts of Limited Companies* (Institute of Chartered Accountants in England and Wales, 1962), pp. 3—4.

2. Significance — information should be so presented as to enable significant descriptions to be applied to the figures. This involves attention to the following
points:

(*a*) Composite items. The inclusion of dissimilar components in one narrative
should be avoided. It is preferable to state them as separate items.

(*b*) Immaterial items. Where a single amount comprises several components no
useful object is attained by referring in the narrative to any component
which is not material in amount.

(*c*) Sub-totals. Appropriate descriptions are desirable for all significant sub-
totals; and it is desirable to avoid sub-totals having no significance.

## 2.9  A CONCLUDING COMMENT

The simplicity of the basic structure of the natural classification described in this
chapter in the context of characteristics to be identified to produce meaningful
information for management enables its use in the smallest organisations. The
possible sub-analysis makes its application valid in the largest organisations and this
extended analysis is examined in subsequent chapters.

## FOR FURTHER STUDY

### QUESTIONS

1. *Classification systems*
'Expenses and losses may be classified according to the function performed, the
person responsible for the disposition, the form in which the services were
contained, or any other satisfactory classification system.'
(Norton M. Dedford, *Income Determination Theory. an Accounting Framework* Addison-Wesley, Reading, Mass., 1965), p. 170)
*Required:*
Explain and comment on this statement indicating 'other satisfactory classification systems' in your answer.

2. *Analysis of controllable and uncontrollable costs*
To the extent that managers of departments may be held accountable for the
results of their departments, i.e., division on the basis of accountability, is
division on the basis of the controllability characteristic a duplication? Give the
analysis of expenses into their controllable and uncontrollable categories for a
company with which you are familiar.

3. *Exceptional, normal and abnormal costs*
Give examples of:
(*a*) Income or expenditure that may not be directly connected with the main
object of a company
(*b*) Exceptional costs that require separate classification

(c) Types of cost that may be normal and those abnormal where the stoppage of plant and machinery is involved.

**4.** *Departmental company organisation*
Describe the departmental organisation of a company with which you are familiar.

**5.** *Cost limits of classification*
To assist the classification of departmental costs, limits of classification may be identified for each department. The cost manual may give such cost limits in the following format:

| Name of department | Departmental description | Limits of classification | |
|---|---|---|---|
| | | Cost from | Cost to |
| — | — | — | — |

*Required:*
Give examples of such cost limits for the departments in a section of the organisation with which you are familiar. If no cost manual is in existence, find out the information by examination of the accounting system.

**6.** *Costs applicable to subsequent trading periods*
Costs currently incurred may extend beyond any one control period.
*Required:*
Itemise costs that may be placed in this category and the reason for carrying forward the expenditure into a subsequent trading period.

**7.** *Analysis of fixed and variable costs*
List the overheads of a company with which you are familiar classified into their fixed and variable elements.

**8.** *Analysis of fixed, variable and semi-variable costs*
A company runs a fleet of motor vehicles. Itemise the type of transport costs you would expect incurred by the company, grouping these costs into fixed, variable and semi-variable categories. State for each cost the reason why you have classified the item as fixed, variable or semi-variable.

**9.** *The activity measure used for the graphical presentation of the behaviour of costs*
In the graphical presentation of the behaviour of costs different activity measures may be used on the $X$ axis.
*Required:*
Give four examples of the activity measure that may be used, expressing an opinion as to the volume factor that you prefer.

**10.** *The assumptions made when costs are classified into their fixed and variable elements*
The production management of Steel Products Ltd are discussing the behaviour of production costs with the accountant and are concerned about estimating

cost levels and interpreting cost reports produced. In an attempt to explain cost behaviour patterns the accountant has produced the following graph:

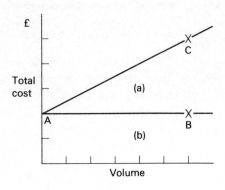

FIGURE 2.9.

and explains that *AC* is the total cost line; *AB* the fixed cost line; area (*a*), the variable cost; and area (*b*), the fixed cost.

After examining the graph, the machine-shop manager says that he imagines area (*a*) to include costs directly involved with the manufacture of the product and therefore graphically presented as a fixed cost per unit. He further imagines that area (*b*) includes costs such as the rent of the factory that will not vary whether the production activity is nil or at the maximum capacity use of the factory. What puzzles him is the apparent simplicity of the graph in the context of estimating and report interpretation because not all his costs behave in this way.

The factory manager states that the graph is obviously based on certain assumptions and asks the accountant to qualify his graph accordingly.
*Required:*
(*a*) Reply to the factory manager's request for a statement of the assumptions on which the graph is based.
(*b*) Do you agree with the views expressed by the machine-shop manager? Explain the apparent absence of the other costs that this manager suggests do not behave as simply as the accountant has suggested.

11. *Characteristics of managed costs*
What characteristics signify a managed cost in the context of management's financial control responsibility?

12. *Requirements of a system of classification and developments expected in the system*
The classification of accounts used by Ventures Ltd is based on a two-part system reflecting the financial accounts as follows:

*Part 1 – Balance Sheet*

| *Main classification* | *Sub-classification* |
|---|---|
| Fixed assets | Leasehold land and buildings |
| | Plant and machinery |
| | Fixtures and fittings |
| | Commercial vehicles |
| | Motor cars |
| | Other assets |
| Depreciation provisions | As for fixed assets |
| Current assets | Stocks |
| |    Raw materials |
| |    Work-in-progress |
| |    Finished goods |
| |    Other stocks |
| | Trade debtors control |
| | Prepaid expenses |
| | Other debtors |
| | Cash at bank |
| | Cash in hand |
| Current liabilities | Trade creditors control |
| | Accrued expenses |
| | Other creditors |
| Share capital | Ordinary shares |
| | Preference shares |
| Capital reserves | Capital reserve |
| Revenue reserves | Profit and loss account |
| Deferred liabilities | Future tax |

*Part 2 – Profit and Loss Account*

| | |
|---|---|
| Sales | Sales by product group |
| Factory cost of sales | Factory cost of sales by product groups |
| Material purchases | Raw materials |
| | Components |
| Expenses | Direct wages |
| | Indirect wages |
| | Salaries |
| | National insurance |
| | Pension fund |
| | Rent |
| | Rates |
| | Light, heat and power |
| | Carriage inwards |
| | Carriage outwards |
| | Car expenses |
| | Insurance |
| | Printing and stationery |

|  | Postage and telephones |
|  | Travelling and entertaining |
|  | Bad debts |
|  | Discounts allowed |
|  | Bank charges |
|  | Legal and professional fees |
|  | Depreciation |
|  | Directors remuneration |
|  | Other expenses |
| Other income | Discounts received |
|  | Rent receivable |
| Other expenditure | Loss on sale of fixed assets |
| Taxation | Corporation tax |
|  | Income tax |
| Appropriations | Dividends – ordinary shares |
|  | Dividends – preference shares |

*Required:*

(*a*) In this case, the classification has formed a general ledger pattern divided into two main sections. It has been designed to meet certain requirements of a system of classification. What are these requirements and how have they been met in this case?

(*b*) What developments could be expected in this classification to meet the needs of a management accounting system?

**FURTHER READING**

Anthony, R. N., Deardon, J. and Vancie, Richard F. *Management Control Systems.* Richard D. Irwin, Homewood, Illinois, 1965. Ch. 5, readings 5–1 and 5–2.
Fitzgerald, A. A. and Schumer, L. A. *Classification in Accounting.* Butterworth & Co (Australia) Ltd, 1962. Chs 1, 3 and 5; Appendices A, B and C.
Kohler, Eric L. *A Dictionary for Accountants.* Prentice Hall, New Jersey, 1963. (For reference: the meaning of terms.)

# 3 Financial Data Division

OBJECTIVE OF THE CHAPTER

To indicate the type of financial information for management that may be produced as a result of the application of characteristics for division. These characteristics applied to the financial data used as input into the management accounting system.

OUTLINE OF THE CHAPTER

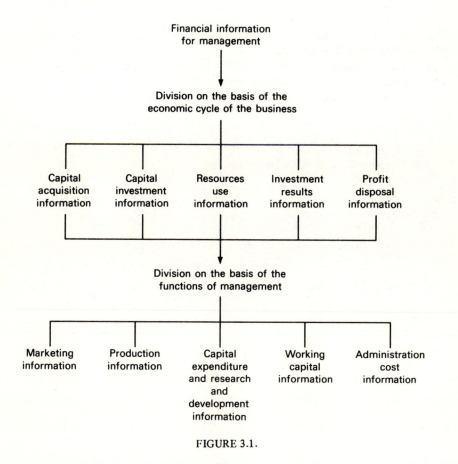

FIGURE 3.1.

41

Within the economic cycle classification, the application of the characteristics mentioned in the previous chapter to financial data may produce financial information for management as detailed below.

## 3.1  CAPITAL ACQUISITION

| *Capital acquisition changes in the period* | £ | £ |
|---|---|---|
| Increases in financial obligations resulting from: | | |
| New capital contributions | – | |
| Increases in long-term liabilities | – | |
| Increases in medium-term liabilities | – | – |
| Deduct reductions in financial obligations resulting from: | | |
| Repayment of capital | – | |
| Reductions in long-term liabilities | – | |
| Reductions in medium-term liabilities | – | – |
| Net result of capital acquisition changes | | – |

## 3.2  CAPITAL INVESTMENT

| *Commitments as at a certain date* | £ | £ | £ |
|---|---|---|---|
| Short-term commitments | | | |
| Taxation | – | | |
| Trade creditors – major classifications of accounts | – | | |
| | – | – | |
| Sundry creditors | | – | – |
| Long-term commitments | | | |
| Capital expenditure – major classifications | – | | |
| | | – | – |
| Total commitments | | | – |

| *Capacity changes in the period* | | | |
|---|---|---|---|
| Purchase of fixed assets – major classifications of facilities | – | | |
| | | – | – |
| Deduct sale of fixed assets – major classifications of facilities | – | | |
| | | – | – |
| Net result of capacity changes | | | – |

|  | £ | £ | £ |
|---|---|---|---|
| *Resources available as at a certain date†* | | | |
| Operating resources – major classifications of facilities | – | | |
| | – | – | |
| – major classifications of stock | – | | |
| | – | – | – |
| | – | | |
| Patents and research and development | | | |
| Patents and trademarks | – | | |
| Research and development – major classifications of research programmes | – | | |
| | – | – | – |
| Monetary resources | | | |
| Cash – at bank | – | | |
| – in hand | – | | |
| | – | – | |
| Short-term investments – major classifications | – | | |
| | – | – | |
| Trade debtors – major classifications of accounts | – | | |
| | – | | |
| Sundry debtors | | – | – |
| Non-operating resources – major classifications of outside investments | | – | |
| | | – | – |
| Total resources available | | | – |

## 3.3 RESOURCES USE*

|  | £ | £ | £ |
|---|---|---|---|
| *Operating expenses incurred in the period* | | | |
| Variable costs | | | |
| Responsive to production volume – major classifications of cost | – | | |
| | – | – | |
| Responsive to sales volume – major classifications of cost | – | | |
| | – | – | – |
| Period costs – major classifications of costs incurred in the use of company facilities | | – | – |
| Programmed costs – major classifications of managed costs | | – | |
| | | – | – |
| Total operating expenses incurred | | | – |

|  | £ | £ |
|---|---|---|
| *Non-operating expenses incurred in the period* | | |
| Abnormal costs – major classifications of costs abnormal in size and incidence derived from events in the ordinary course of business | – | |
| | – | – |
| Extraordinary expenses – major classifications of expenses derived from events outside the ordinary course of business | – | |
| | – | – |
| Other non-operating expenditure – major classifications | – | |
| | – | – |
| Total non-operating expenses incurred | | – |

* Classified controllable/uncontrollable and by product divisions, if possible.
† Classified by product divisions, if possible.

## 3.4  INVESTMENT RESULTS

| *Revenue receivable in the period* | £ | £ | £ |
|---|---|---|---|
| Operating revenue – major classifications of revenue receivable from operations as defined by the company's principal business | | – | – |
| Non-operating revenue | | | |
|     Abnormal revenue – major classifications of revenue abnormal in size and incidence derived from events in the ordinary course of business | – | – | |
| Extraordinary revenue – major classifications of revenue derived from events outside the ordinary course of business | – | – | |
| Other non-operating revenue – major classifications | – | | |
| | – | – | – |
| Total revenue receivable | | | – |

| *Earnings available for retention or disposal in the period* | £ | £ |
|---|---|---|
| Operating revenue receivable | | – |
| Deduct operating expenses incurred | | – |
| Operating profit | | – |
| Non-operating revenue receivable | – | |
| Deduct non-operating expenses incurred | – | – |
| Disposable profit for the period | | – |

## 3.5  PROFIT DISPOSAL

| *Financial obligation reductions in the period* | £ | £ |
|---|---|---|
| Taxation | | – |
| Dividends payable – major classifications according to priority of payment | – | – |
| Interest payable – major classifications | – | |
| | – | – |
| Total reduction in financial obligations | | – |

Withing these classifications, sub-division may be related to the functions of managment. The type of information that may be provided is given in the remaining sections of this chapter.

## 3.6  MARKETING INFORMATION

Funds are generated by sales, and managements recognising this fact give a fair amount of their time to the study of matters relating to sales. Generally, the same attention is not given to selling costs which arise as a result of the effort necessary to obtain sales. Sales and selling costs should be considered together and the term 'marketing' integrates these factors with the distribution function. Significant marketing information may cover the following sectors of the marketing organisation.

1. Market research
2. Product development
3. Sales promotion
4. Field sales
5. Sales service
6. Warehousing
7. Distribution
8. Sales office services.

The significant information that may be provided to management is considered in the sections that follow.

### 3.61 MARKET RESEARCH INFORMATION

This information may take the form of:

(a) Salesmen's reports
(b) The results of investigations into competitors' products and methods of marketing
(c) The results of consumer studies
(d) Trade and government statistics and journal reports
(e) University economic services
(f) New product tests.

### 3.62 PRODUCT DEVELOPMENT INFORMATION

Product information may be divided into the following three categories.*

(a) The strong and established items of the line. These products provide the main sales volume and the company depends on these products for its main source of profits in relation to capital employed.
(b) Products that are new and as yet unproved. These products are expected to provide good future profits and management is prepared to subsidise them during their development period.
(c) Products that have passed their peak in growth and profitability. Since these products can offer little in the way of future profits it may be expected that management effort may be diverted to the other categories.

* This classification is taken from *Management: a Book of Readings,* ed. H. Koontz and C. O'Donnell (McGraw-Hill, New York, 1964), p. 527, from the contribution by T. C. Mackenson in the article, 'Return on invested capital', reprinted from *How H. J. Heinz Manages its Financial Planning and Controls* (American Management Association, 1953).

This diversion to more profitable products may demand the following information:

(i) The timing of new product introduction
(ii) The analysis of the profit impact of the new products
(iii) The impact of the new products on:

    (*a*) product line strategy
    (*b*) product elimination
    (*c*) competitors' reaction
    (*d*) stock levels.

### 3.63 SALES PROMOTION INFORMATION

The sales promotion effort may be judged by information analysed as follows:

(*a*) The costs of each type of sales effort and the per cent distribution of each sales promotion medium
(*b*) The sales promotion costs expressed as a per cent of sales
(*c*) Where possible, the information in (*a*) and (*b*) compared with similar detail applicable to competitors.

### 3.64 FIELD SALES INFORMATION

The following information in respect of field sales staff is significant:

(*a*) The action of salesmen in the form of the number of calls made to customers and potential customers
(*b*) The results of their action in the form of the number and value of orders received analysed by salesmen, sales areas, order size, and sales outlet. Product profitability of sales secured is particularly relevant.
(*c*) The field sales costs, e.g., travelling expenses, subsistence allowances, entertaining, telephone charges, and other expenses.

The aim is not to obtain the maximum volume of sales but to recognise the relative profitability of products and credit-worthiness of customers. There is no point in obtaining a large volume of sales with little or no profit, or sales to customers who may not pay for the goods received. Information for management should emphasise these points.

### 3.65 SALES SERVICE INFORMATION

Sales services in the form of installation, inspection and repair activities also include dealing with warranty claims, allowances and rectification. Important information covers costs of these activities and the number of warranty claims received, possibly analysed by sales outlet and product.

## 3.66 WAREHOUSING INFORMATION

Stock level information should be provided showing stock in relation to planned quantities for each product or product group. Information required for efficient warehousing stock control includes in respect of each product: provision times, demand patterns and stock costs. Warehousing expenses may be related to sales.

## 3.67 DISTRIBUTION INFORMATION

Distribution costs consist of packaging costs, carriage outwards and vehicle costs. Standards should be available for packaging costs per product and the comparison of own vehicle costs with other forms of transport or transport contractor costs will give an indication of whether the company is operating efficiently in terms of distribution costs.

Vehicle cost information may be provided per vehicle or per vehicle group, the groups being fixed according to the make and type of each vehicle. Operational statistics such as mileage run (loaded and empty), fuel consumption and miles per gallon are usually combined with costs to enable an assessment to be made of the operating efficiency of each vehicle.

## 3.68 SALES OFFICE SERVICE INFORMATION

In many companies, sales office costs may be considered as general administration. If separated, the following costs may be identified: salaries and national insurance, printing and stationery, postages and telephones and accommodation costs.

## 3.7 PRODUCTION COST INFORMATION

In a manufacturing organisation, the area of major cost is usually in the factory and the accountant has an important part to play in assisting the works manager to control this important sector of the business. The works manager's training is concentrated on the technical aspects of business operation but as part of senior management he should have a broader appreciation of company problems. The type of information provided should recognise this general need as well as the sectional requirements of the works organisation. Significant production cost information may cover the following sectors of the works organisation:

1. Production departments
2. Maintenance
3. Tool room
4. Drawing and works office
5. Estimating
6. Planning and progress
7. Stores
8. Inspection
9. Purchasing
10. Design.

The significant information that may be provided to management is considered in the sections to follow.

## 3.71 PRODUCTION DEPARTMENT INFORMATION

The information may take the form of:

(a) An idle time report – an analysis of idle time by causes and location. Costs of idle time may be given.
(b) Output levels – activity ratios may be indicated by expressing the standard hours for the work produced as a percentage of the planned standard hours for the planned production.
(c) Efficiency measurements – for example, the expression of the standard hours for the work produced as a percentage of the actual hours for the production achieved.
(d) Materials usage analysis – waste may be analysed by cause.
(e) Labour costs – labour directly identified with the manufacture of the product. The effect of overtime or the use of inexperienced labour may also be indicated.
(f) Material costs – material directly identified with the manufacture of the product. Price variations and the financial effects of changes in material mix and yield may be given.
(g) Factory overhead – specific costs to the direct producing departments, e.g., wages and salaries of indirect labour: supervisors and foremen.

Productive capacity may be expressed in numbers of units or in standard hours and should reflect the best production-line speeds that can be maintained on a continuous basis under usual production conditions. This may be different from 'peak' line speeds for the short period or from 'theoretical' line speeds which are never achieved.

## 3.72 MAINTENANCE DEPARTMENT INFORMATION

The following information is significant:

(a) Preventative maintenance costs – equipment type analysis may be given
(b) Breakdowns – may be analysed by location, equipment and cause. The cost of the breakdowns may be provided.

## 3.73 TOOL-ROOM INFORMATION

Although this is usually a small department, costs are normally high owing to the employment of high-grade personnel and high quality machinery. Management information may take the form of tool-room costs and tool availability.

## 3.74 DRAWING OFFICE AND WORKS OFFICE INFORMATION

Management information may consist of the administration costs of these departments.

## 3.75 ESTIMATING DEPARTMENT INFORMATION

In addition to the administration costs of the estimating department, the supply of information to management may consist of:

(*a*) The value of estimates given against the orders received
(*b*) Variations between actual and estimated costs.

## 3.76 PLANNING AND PROGRESS DEPARTMENT INFORMATION

Management information in connexion with the planning and progress departments may be provided as follows:

(*a*) Jobs in arrear – the arrear detail may be analysed by cause
(*b*) Production control department costs.

Relevant information for the planning and progress department reflects the close liaison between these sections and the stores and production departments. Stock information mentioned in the working capital section is an example of associated detail of considerable importance to the planning and progress department.

## 3.77 INSPECTION DEPARTMENT INFORMATION

The inspection department is responsible for checking actual performance against the standards set for the production departments. The comparisons are against physical standards but the cost of rejected units may be given to management and scrap cost may be analysed according to:

(*a*) Operator faults
(*b*) Material faults:
    (i) Defective outside guarantee period
    (ii) Defective material content recoverable
(*c*) Faulty tools
(*d*) Other causes.

## 3.78 PURCHASING DEPARTMENT INFORMATION

Purchasing department information may include the following:

(*a*) The number and value of purchase orders placed
(*b*) The percentage of low-value orders to total orders
(*c*) The percentage of rush orders to total orders
(*d*) The value of overdue orders
(*e*) The cost of operating the purchasing department
(*f*) Price differences between planned and actual purchase prices.

### 3.79 DESIGN DEPARTMENT INFORMATION

The cost of the design department is not the main information provided to design staff. Estimated product costs may be prepared from the best information available as a guide to profitable product development. The work of the design department is closely connected with research and development and the information for management for this sector of the business unit is considered in greater detail in the next section.

## 3.8 CAPITAL EXPENDITURE AND RESEARCH AND DEVELOP-MENT COST INFORMATION

Capital expenditure is expenditure incurred which is expected to benefit the business in the long term, that is costs beneficial to the company in future accounting periods such as the cost of a new asset or its improvement. Management information in this area usually begins with the completion of a capital project form and an example is given in Figure 3.2.

This form is completed by the departmental executive requiring the authority to incur the expenditure and the accountant is usually called upon to assist in the evaluation of the project before authority is given to invest in the project. The approval of a project does not necessarily release the funds for purchase and a separate form may be completed to obtain the funds necessary.

Subsequent financial control of projects may be obtained by the provision of the following information for management:

(a) Project sanction number and brief details of the capital project
(b) The cost for the current control period
(c) Cost to date
(d) An estimate of the cost to complete the project
(e) The total cost (c) plus (d)
(f) The amount authorised
(g) The amount of over/under spending.

The request to incur expenditure on research for new products or improvements in products or methods may also be subject to project sanction and such sanctions form the basis for cost control.

## 3.9 WORKING CAPITAL INFORMATION

In accounting, working capital is the excess of current assets over current liabilities. In this context, the word 'current' usually means possession of the asset or obligations for a period less than a year.

Working capital may be a significant proportion of the funds invested in a manufacturing business and to secure an adequate return on investment management

| Capital expenditure proposal | Reference no. |
|---|---|
| **Location/function** | |

| Description of project | Asset classification |
|---|---|
| | Land ☐ <br> Buildings ☐ <br> Leasehold improvement ☐ <br> Machinery and equipment ☐ <br> Other (named) ☐ |

| Justification and purpose | Purpose of expenditure |
|---|---|
| | New product ☐ <br> Cost saving ☐ <br> Replacement ☐ <br> Expansion ☐ |
| | Total of this proposal £_____ <br> To be capitalised £_____ <br> To be expensed £_____ |
| | Total cost of project £_____ <br> Amount of this proposal £_____ <br> Amount previously proposed £_____ |
| **Estimated completion date** | Amount to be proposed in the future £_____ |

Profit and investment summary

| Submitted by | Date | Approved by | Date |
|---|---|---|---|
| _____ | _____ | _____ | _____ |

FIGURE 3.2. Capital expenditure proposal form

should be provided with relevant information on the current assets and current liabilities of the business. It is particularly important to keep a check on the movement of funds because of the dangers of overtrading and undertrading.

### 3.91 FACTORS AFFECTING THE SIZE OF THE WORKING CAPITAL

The nature of the business undertaken affects the amount of working capital required. The production policy for a seasonal business may be to equalise the production rate throughout the year and in the application of this policy stock balances may significantly increase in the slack trade periods.

As companies expand, an increase in working capital is necessary and information presented to management should emphasise the liquidity of the business. An expanding business is particularly vulnerable to cash shortage and a balanced relationship between fixed investment and working capital is vital. A shortage of working capital may restrict the growth of a company and this position may be worsened by the competitive situation. Where competition is increasing, the demand for new products or more generous credit terms increases the working capital required.

The length of the cash cycle, which may be defined as the period commencing with the cash payment for the raw material to be used in manufacture and ending with the date when cash is received from the customer for the finished goods, governs working capital requirements. The quality of management can significantly alter the need for working capital. Good management will tend to shorten the cash cycle by effective stock control and credit control. Efficient production planning and control can reduce the length of time goods are in progress in the factory.

During a period of inflation holders of monetary assets, such as cash and debtors, lose general purchasing power. These items should, therefore, be carefully controlled.

## 3.92 FUNDS AND CASH-FLOW INFORMATION

In this section funds and cash-flow information have been brought together because of their relationship but a distinction is usually made in accounting literature. This distinction is described in greater detail in a later chapter but for the purpose of this section it should be noted that the term 'funds' is synonymous with the term 'working capital'. Where the working capital changes are analysed on the statement for management the term 'cash flow' is appropriate. The importance of a change in liquid resources may be emphasised by providing information on the change in net quick assets. Quick assets include cash, temporary investment and trade debtors.

## 3.93 STOCK CONTROL INFORMATION

Without efficient stock control over-investment of working capital in stock is likely, with the result that the return on investment may be much lower than it should be. Stock may be analysed as follows:

(a) Product material or stores type
(b) Raw materials, general stores, semi-manufactured stocks and finished goods
(c) Factory produced, sub-contracted and imported stock
(d) Fast, slow and non-current parts inventory.

## 3.94 DEBTORS AND CREDITORS CONTROL INFORMATION

Analysis of debtors and creditors for control is usually by age of debt. Trade creditor detail normally presents little difficulty since payment by the company is either early to secure cash discounts or in the normal credit period. Outside the normal credit period, special arrangements may be made with suppliers. In the case of trade debtors, close control is essential to ensure that customers are not extending the credit period to the detriment of the company's cash flow.

## 3.10 ADMINISTRATION COST INFORMATION

In smaller companies, administrative costs are not significant and detailed statements may not be considered necessary but in larger companies administrative costs are significant. In the case of the larger companies administration costs may be analysed by type of expense for each administrative department. The expenses that may be itemised include office staff salaries, management salaries, national insurance, rent and rates, printing and stationery, car expenses, postage and telephone charges, professional charges and sundry office expenses.

## 3.11 A CONCLUDING COMMENT

This chapter has surveyed the type of information that may be provided by the accounting function for management and this may be related to the profit and loss statement and balance sheet of standard format as illustrated in Figure 3.3. The increased detail relative to production cost is illustrated in Figure 3.4.

## FOR FURTHER STUDY

QUESTIONS

1. *Classifications of sales costs for planning*
   The sales manager of a company manufacturing a range of household electrical appliances is responsible for all sales in the UK market and his sales force is organised in territorial divisions. He prepares his own sales plans and his office keeps records of sales for comparison with the planned sales levels. No cost plans are prepared for the department and the only information on costs incurred is obtained from the following account headings in the general ledger:

   Sales salaries and commissions
   Travelling and car expenses
   Advertising
   Sales Office expenses.

   *Required:*
   What further analysis of the department's costs do you suggest to enable adequate cost plans to be prepared in relation to the sales plans?

2. *Product development and product strategy information requirements*
   Modern Machines Ltd manufactures electrical motors for use in the domestic appliance industry and over the years has managed to establish a dominant position in the market with a stable product supported by a range of equipment where progress and change are always taking place in the models which the company handle. To hold the market in this sector it is necessary for the company to frequently redesign old types or bring out entirely new machines. Because of the dominant position of the main product the detailed examination

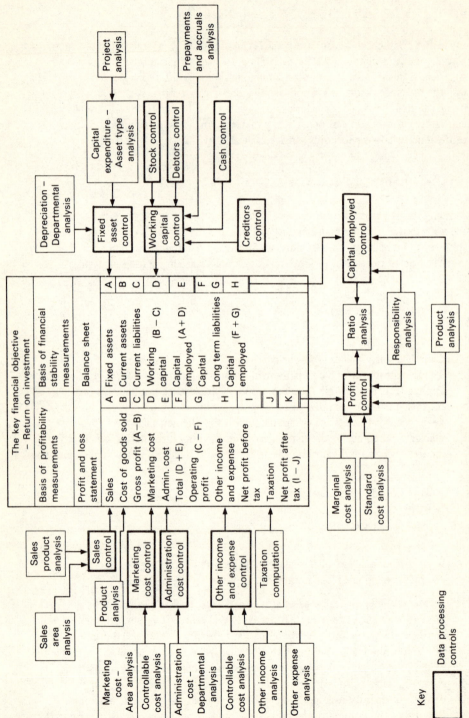

FIGURE 3.3. Accounting information for control – summary

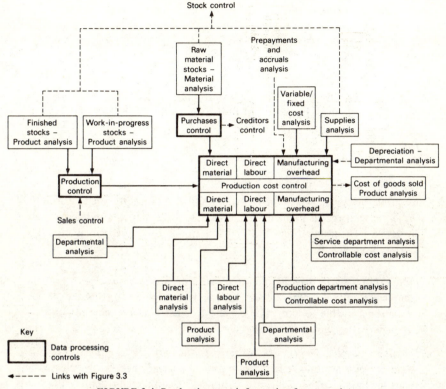

FIGURE 3.4. Production cost information for control

of the market relative to product development is not given the attention that some executives consider the subject deserves. Currently, the sales trend of the main product is declining and these executives feel that their view is of increasing importance to the company.

*Required:*

(*a*)  What information may be supplied that will assist the executives in deciding on future product strategy?

(*b*)  What analysis of this product information will identify the key areas for management attention? Suggest the emphasis that management should give to the categories identified.

(*c*)  What information may be demanded if the executives decide to divert their attention to new products?

3.  *Distribution cost classifications and their value*

Distribution costs may be classified by (*a*) form of transport; (*b*) delivery routes; and (*c*) product.

*Required:*

Indicate the anticipated value of these classifications to management mentioning related information, where appropriate.

(ICMA — Modified)

4. *Sales, purchases and overhead analysis in a department store*
Itemise the analyses you would prepare for management of a retail departmental store regarding (*a*) sales; (*b*) purchases; and (*c*) overheads. Explain why you have chosen the items in your answer.

(ICMA)

5. *The possible restriction of managerial information to controllable costs*
'In the provision of information for management it is only necessary to give a specific manager details of costs that he can control.'
*Required:*
Comment on this statement giving your view of the practice.

6. *Classified information provided to different levels of management*
Describe the type of classified information that may be provided regarding factory operations to the managing director, works manager and departmental supervisor. The integration of this information in the three reports should be given in your answer.

7. *Production meeting agenda to consider control information*
Many companies hold production management meetings to consider the information available for control. Give the agenda for such a meeting for a company with which you are familiar.

8. *Details required to sanction the release of funds for capital expenditure*
The approval of a capital expenditure project does not necessarily release the funds for purchase and a separate form may be completed to obtain the funds necessary.
*Required:*
Itemise the detail that may be needed from managers requiring funds to be released for a capital expenditure project already approved on the basis of the submission of a capital expenditure proposal form.

9. *Research and development proposal information required*
Itemise the detail that may be required from research and development personnel when completing a proposal form requesting funds for a research and development project.

10. *The meaning of the terms 'current assets' and 'current liabilities'*
A company balance sheet includes the classifications current assets and current liabilities.
*Required:*
Explain and comment on each of these classifications giving examples to illustrate your answer.

11. *Stores classifications and standardisation*
A large number of products provided a stock problem for the Engineering Equipment Co. Ltd, and its difficulties were increased by the new products constantly being developed. The company aimed to keep the investment of

funds in stock at the minimum to conserve funds, avoid losses on realisation, and reduce the expenses of holding and handling the stock. Recently the stock value had increased considerably and an examination of the stock had revealed duplicated items stored under different names; numerous types of stock which could be used interchangeably for products but individual designs dictate different material to be used; and slow-moving stock items.

A new stock controller has been appointed who recommends an improved classification system for stores items and a programme of standardisation to be applied with the help of the design and production departments.

*Required:*

(*a*)  What classifications are normally used for stock that may assist the company with their problem?

(*b*)  How may the classification system make a contribution to the standardisation of material and component use?

12.  *The type of information supplied to top management*
Outline the type of financial information supplied to the top management of a company with which you are familiar. An indication of the nature of the business and its size should support the details of the reports supplied to management.

FURTHER READING

Burney, A. G. B. *Illustrations of Management Accounts in Practice.* Gee, 1959. Chs 2 and 3.

Dobson, R. Warwick. *Management Information and Accounting.* Gee, 1964. Chs 6, 8 and 12–20.

*An Evaluation of External Reporting Practices – A Report of the 1966/8 Committee on External Reporting.* Accounting Review Supplement. American Accounting Association, 1969, pp. 79–122. (This report is the result of research into the form of accounting information for external users but includes the consideration of divisions of financial data of considerable value to management for internal use in the business.)

# FINANCIAL STATEMENT
# INTERPRETATION

# 4 Accounting Information Relationships

## OBJECTIVE OF THE CHAPTER

To show the grouping of classified financial information in ordered sequence as a basis for the identification of important accounting information relationships. These relationships are expanded in the framework of conventional accounting summary statements.

## OUTLINE OF THE CHAPTER

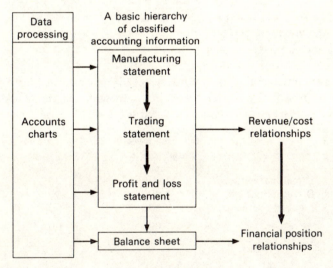

FIGURE 4.1.

The divisions of financial data mentioned in the previous two chapters, when assembled in a logical order, provide hierarchies of information for management. Accounting information is based on the manufacturing, trading, profit and loss statement and balance sheet and it is normal to use these summary statements, with possibly a flow of funds statement, as a basic hierarchy of classified information. The flow of funds statement will be described in detail in Chapter 7 and the remaining statements introduced in the previous chapter are used as the basis for the description of important accounting information relationships in the sections to follow.

61

## 4.1 MANUFACTURING STATEMENT RELATIONSHIPS

Manufacturing statement relationships may be identified as follows:

|  | £ | £ | £ |
|---|---|---|---|
| Direct material cost |  |  |  |
|   Direct materials purchases cost |  | 5,000 |  |
|   Direct materials stock at the beginning of the period | 1,000 |  |  |
|   Direct materials stock at the close of the period | 800 |  |  |
|   Add direct materials stock variation |  | 200 | 5,200 |
| Direct labour cost |  |  | 2,700 |
| Direct expense |  |  | 100 |
| Prime cost |  |  | 8,000 |
| Factory overhead |  |  |  |
|   Variable factory overhead |  | 2,000 |  |
|   Fixed factory overhead |  | 3,000 |  |
|   Total factory overhead |  |  | 5,000 |
| Total factory cost |  |  | 13,000 |
| Work-in-progress stock at the beginning of the period |  | 7,000 |  |
| Work-in-progress stock at the close of the period |  | 6,000 |  |
| Add work-in-progress stock variation |  |  | 1,000 |
| Factory cost of goods completed |  |  | 14,000 |

On the assumption that work-in-progress stock is valued at total factory cost, an alternative presentation is given below. In this presentation, the values of work-in-progress stocks are assumed to be calculated as follows:

|  | Opening work-in-progress Stock | Closing work-in-progress stock |
|---|---|---|
|  | £ | £ |
| Direct material cost | 3,000 | 2,500 |
| Direct labour cost | 2,000 | 1,900 |
| Factory overhead | 2,000 | 1,600 |
|  | 7,000 | 6,000 |

|  | £ | £ | £ |
|---|---|---|---|
| Direct materials purchases cost |  | 5,000 |  |
| Direct materials stock at the beginning of the period | 1,000 |  |  |
| Direct materials stock at the close of the period | 800 |  |  |
|   Add direct materials stock variation |  | 200 |  |
| Direct materials cost |  | 5,200 |  |
| Direct materials in work-in-progress stock at the beginning of the period | 3,000 |  |  |
| Direct materials in work-in-progress stock at the close of the period | 2,500 |  |  |
|   Add direct materials work-in-progress stock variation |  | 500 |  |

|  | £ | £ | £ |
|---|---|---|---|
| Direct materials cost of finished goods manufactured |  |  | 5,700 |
| Direct labour cost |  | 2,700 |  |
| Direct labour cost in work-in-progress stock at the beginning of the period | 2,000 |  |  |
| Direct labour cost in work-in-progress stock at the close of the period | 1,900 |  |  |
| Add direct labour cost work-in-progress stock variation |  | 100 |  |
| Direct labour cost of finished goods manufactured |  |  | 2,800 |
| Direct expense |  |  | 100 |
| Factory overhead |  | 5,000 |  |
| Factory overhead in work-in-progress stock at the beginning of the period | 2,000 |  |  |
| Factory overhead in work-in-progress stock at the close of the period | 1,600 |  |  |
| Add factory overhead work-in-progress stock variation |  | 400 |  |
| Factory overhead of finished goods manufactured |  |  | 5,400 |
| Factory cost of goods completed |  |  | 14,000 |

If costs can be directly identified with the manufacture of a product they are known as direct costs. Although costs may be directly identified with the manufacture of a product they may not be allotted to that product as direct costs if, for example, the cost is insignificant or the cost of accumulation is not warranted. In this situation the unallotted costs are included with those not directly identified with the manufacture of the product (indirect costs) to provide factory overhead. Factory overhead shown above may be analysed as follows:

|  | £ | £ |
|---|---|---|
| Materials and supplies |  |  |
| Indirect materials | — |  |
| Consumable materials | — |  |
| Maintenance and tool materials | — | — |
| Factory manpower |  |  |
| Indirect labour | — |  |
| Overtime and night shift premiums | — |  |
| Contribution to pension fund and National insurance | — |  |
| Sick and accident pay | — |  |
| Holiday pay | — | — |
| Factory utilities |  |  |
| Electricity | — |  |
| Gas | — |  |
| Water | — |  |
| Fuel Oil | — | — |
| Factory contractors' charges |  |  |
| Hire of plant and equipment | — |  |
| Repairs and maintenance | — | — |

|                                              | £ | £ |
|----------------------------------------------|---|---|
| Factory occupancy                            |   |   |
| Rent                                         | – |   |
| Rates                                        | – |   |
| Cleaning                                     | – |   |
| Buildings depreciation                       | – |   |
| Buildings repairs and maintenance            | – | – |
| Factory services                             |   |   |
| Storekeeping expenses including stock losses | – |   |
| Production control expenses                  | – |   |
| Plant and machinery depreciation             | – |   |
| Plant and machinery repairs and maintenance  | – | – |
| Other factory overhead                       | – |   |
| Factory overhead                             |   | 5,000 |

The conversion cost of converting the material in the factory to the finished product may be identified as follows:

|                      | £     |
|----------------------|-------|
| Direct labour cost   | 2,700 |
| Direct expense       | 100   |
| Factory overhead     | 5,000 |
| Conversion cost      | 7,800 |

## 4.2  TRADING STATEMENT RELATIONSHIPS

Trading statement relationships may be identified as follows:

|                                                 | £      | £      | £      |
|-------------------------------------------------|--------|--------|--------|
| Gross sales                                     |        | 32,000 |        |
| Less sales returns and trade discounts          |        | 2,000  |        |
| Net sales                                       |        |        | 30,000 |
| Less cost of sales                              |        |        |        |
| Factory cost of goods completed                 |        | 14,000 |        |
| Finished goods at the beginning of the period   | 10,000 |        |        |
| Finished goods stock at the close of the period | 9,000  |        |        |
| Add finished goods stock variation              |        | 1,000  | 15,000 |
| Gross profit                                    |        |        | 15,000 |

Where product costs are calculated on a pre-determined cost basis (e.g., estimated factory overhead allotted to products), the cost of sales shown above should include an adjustment for the difference between actual factory overhead and estimated factory overhead charged to products. The effect of this adjustment, known as over- or under-absorbed overhead, is to restore the cost of sales to actual cost from the predetermined figures used. This point is developed in Chapter 23.

In the judgement of operating cost levels, profits may be related to net sales. If the opening and closing stocks of work-in-progress are significantly different the cost relationships may be interpreted by taking account of this factor using the value of output in place of net sales. Judgement of the efficiency of the factory may involve the use of value added information. Value of output and value added are calculated as follows:

|  | £ | £ | £ |
|---|---|---|---|
| Net sales |  | 30,000 |  |
| Work-in-progress stock at the beginning of the period | 7,000 |  |  |
| Work-in-progress stock at the close of the period | 6,000 |  |  |
| Deduct the work-in-progress stock variation |  | 1,000 |  |
| Value of output |  |  | 29,000 |
| Deduct: materials consumed |  | 5,200 |  |
| bought out services |  | 800 | 6,000 |
| Value added |  |  | 23,000 |

## 4.3 PROFIT AND LOSS STATEMENT RELATIONSHIPS

Profit and loss statement relationships may be identified as follows:

|  | £ | £ |
|---|---|---|
| Operating revenue — net sales |  | 30,000 |
| Less operating cost of sales (absorption costing basis) |  | 15,000 |
| Gross profit |  | 15,000 |
| Less operating expenses |  | 9,000 |
| Operating profit |  | 6,000 |
| Add non-operating revenue | 500 |  |
| Less non-operating expenses | 300 |  |
| Non operating profit |  | 200 |
| Net profit before taxation |  | 6,200 |
| Taxation |  | 3,000 |
| Net profit after taxation (disposable profit for the period) |  | 3,200 |
| Less: dividends payable | 1,000 |  |
| interest payable | 500 | 1,500 |
| Disposable profit retained in the business |  | 1,700 |
| Less appropriations (e.g., reserves) |  | 1,000 |
| Unappropriated profit for the period |  | 700 |
| Add disposable profit brought forward from the previous period |  | 5,000 |
| Total profit carried forward to the next period |  | 5,700 |

The above statement is related to the trading statement of the preceding section on the basis that absorption costing is used. Absorption costing is the procedure adopted where product costs are ascertained on the basis that fixed and variable costs are allotted to products as manufactured.

An alternative costing procedure known as marginal costing may be used. In this procedure, product costs are restricted to variable costs, a product contribution emerging towards fixed costs. When these fixed costs are covered by the total contribution of products sold, the residual figure is profit. The presentation described is illustrated below and the implications of this procedure are described in Chapter 19.

|                                              | £ |
|----------------------------------------------|---|
| Operating revenue – net sales                | – |
| Less variable cost of sales (marginal cost basis) | – |
| Contribution                                 | – |
| Less period and managed costs                | – |
| Operating profit                             | – |

The word 'operating' used in the illustrations in this section is used to define the boundaries of the revenue and expenses to give a figure of operating profit. In this instance, the meaning covers the business events forming the principal activities undertaken by the company in the ordinary course of business. This classification identifies other income and expense as non-operating revenue and non-operating expense, that is revenue and expense for business events not forming the principal activities undertaken by the company in the ordinary course of business – for example, for a manufacturing company, rents receivable and investment income.

Where opening and closing stocks of work-in-progress are significantly different, the interpretation of results may be assisted by the alternative form of operating profit calculation shown below:

|                          | £      | £      |
|--------------------------|--------|--------|
| Value of output          |        | 29,000 |
| Less output cost         |        |        |
| Factory cost             | 13,000 |        |
| Other operating expenses | 9,000  | 22,000 |
| Operating profit         |        | 7,000  |

The difference in the two operating profits of £1,000 is the finished goods stock variation.

The identification of the financial effects of events in the ordinary course of business mentioned above implies the segregation of items that are extraordinary in the period in which the profits are being calculated. These items such as the discontinuance of a significant part of a business should be an adjustment to the profit after tax – the extraordinary items recorded less taxation attributed to them.

To isolate the effect of abnormal events on the profits of the business, the operating profit may be calculated prior to the adjustment for costs abnormal in size and incidence derived from events in the ordinary course of business, for example, abnormal charges for bad debts and write-offs of stocks and work-in-progress.

Operating expenses as a title shown in the first illustration in this section may be analysed as follows:

| | £ | £ | £ |
|---|---|---|---|
| *Administration costs* | | | |
| Administtation manpower | | | |
|     Office staff salaries | — | | |
|     Management salaries | — | | |
|     Contribution to pension fund and | | | |
|     National insurance | — | | |
|     Sick pay | — | | |
|     Holiday pay | — | — | |
| Administration office utilities | —— | | |
|     Electricity | — | | |
|     Gas | — | | |
|     Water | — | — | |
| Administration office occupancy | | | |
|     Rent | — | | |
|     Rates | — | | |
|     Cleaning | — | | |
|     Building depreciation | — | | |
|     Building repairs and maintenance | — | — | |
| Administration travelling | | | |
|     Car expenses | — | | |
|     Subsistence allowances | — | — | |
| Administration office supplies and services | | | |
|     Printing and stationery | — | | |
|     Office furniture depreciation | — | | |
|     Office machinery depreciation | — | | |
|     Hire of office machinery | — | | |
|     Insurance | — | — | |
| Administration communications | | | |
|     Telephones and teleprinters | — | | |
|     Postage and telegrams | — | — | |
| Information and knowledge | | | |
|     Books and journals | — | | |
|     Subscriptions to professional | | | |
|     associations | — | — | |
| Professional fees | | | |
|     Legal | — | | |
|     Accounting | — | | |
|     Auditing and taxation | — | — | |
| Other administration expenses | — | — | — |

|  | £ | £ | £ |
|---|---|---|---|
| *Selling and distribution costs* | | | — |
| Marketing manpower | | | |
|    Marketing staff salaries | — | | |
|    Drivers' wages | — | | |
|    Contribution to pension fund and | | | |
|    National insurance | — | | |
|    Sick pay | — | | |
|    Holiday pay | — | — | |
| Marketing office utilities | | | |
|    Electricity | — | | |
|    Gas | — | | |
|    Water | — | — | |
| Marketing office occupancy | | | |
|    Rent | — | | |
|    Rates | — | | |
|    Cleaning | — | | |
|    Building depreciation | — | | |
|    Building repair and maintenance | — | — | |
| Marketing office supplies and services | | | |
|    Printing and stationery | — | | |
|    Office furniture — depreciation | — | — | |
| Travelling representation | | | |
|    Car expenses | — | | |
|    Entertaining | — | | |
|    Subsistence allowances | — | — | |
| Marketing communications | | | |
|    Telephones and teleprinters | — | | |
|    Postage and telegrams | — | — | |
| Professional fees — market research | — | | |
| Advertising and sales promotion | — | | |
| Collection charges including bad debts | — | | |
| Vehicle costs | | | |
|    Running expenses | — | | |
|    Van depreciation | — | — | |
| Packing and other delivery expenses | — | | |
| Other selling expenses | — | — | |
| Operating expenses | | | 9,000 |

In large organisations where the central management of the company may have taken over central services for the group, their expenses may be charged to operational units. If this procedure is adopted, profit statements produced for the operating units will show within the classification for administration expenses a separate heading titled: 'Head office expenses' or 'Central services'.

In the statements above no indication is given of the attitude of management towards changing price levels. If, for example, depreciation is calculated on the basis of historical cost or opening stock values at price levels of an earlier period, a recognition of changing price levels may be recorded in the profit and loss statement, assuming prices have increased, as follows:

|  | £ | £ |
|---|---|---|
| Profit before tax unadjusted for changing price levels |  | — |
| Deduct the price adjustment for |  |  |
| Stock | — |  |
| Depreciation | — | — |
| Adjusted profit before tax |  | — |

Other adjustments may be made for changing price levels and these are considered in Chapter 24.

In control period reporting the 'total to date' may be recorded on statements for management and it may be anticipated that, for example, the total of profits previously reported to management for control periods 1, 2 and 3 should equal the 'to date' figure reported as at the end of period 3. It may be that significant errors have been made in earlier statements and to preserve this arithmetical link the adjustments made may be to the current period figures (period 3). Unfortunately, this has the effect of distorting the current period financial results. An alternative approach is to adjust the operating profit for period 3 for prior period adjustments. This procedure permits the correct financial results to be reported for period 3 and allows the 'to date' total profit as at the end of period 3 to be reconciled with earlier reports issued.

## 4.4 BALANCE SHEET RELATIONSHIPS

Balance sheet relationships may be identified as follows:

|  | £ |
|---|---|
| *Capital acquisition* |  |
| Issued share capital | 4,000 |
| Capital reserves | 1,000 |
| Revenue reserves | 7,500 |
| Loan capital | 3,000 |
| Long-term deferred liabilities | 3,500 |
|  | 19,000 |

| *Capital investment* | £ | £ |
|---|---|---|
| Fixed assets |  | 11,000 |
| Deferred assets |  | 3,000 |
| Working capital |  |  |
| Current assets | 13,000 |  |
| Current liabilities | 8,000 | 5,000 |
|  |  | 19,000 |

The capital acquisition category can be sub-classified to identify the net worth of the business:

|  | £ |
|---|---|
| Issued share capital | 4,000 |
| Capital reserves | 1,000 |
| Revenue reserves | 7,500 |
| Deferred liabilities | 3,500 |
|  | 16,000 |

16,000 (£19,000 minus loan capital: £3,000)

Capital reserves are amounts not regarded as free for distribution through the profit and loss account and revenue reserves, those reserves other than capital reserves. Revenue reserves include amounts set aside for the financial strengthening of the business and the profit carried forward into subsequent trading periods. The intentions of the directors are pertinent to the classification of reserves.

The capital investment figure of £19,000 is also known as net assets. An alternative classification for capital investment may be used to identify total assets:

|  | £ |
|---|---|
| Fixed assets | 11,000 |
| Deferred assets | 3,000 |
| Current assets | 13,000 |
|  | 27,000 |

The total assets may be sub-divided to identify:

1. Operating assets – total assets less non-operating assets. This category identifies assets available for use in the principal activities undertaken by the company in the ordinary course of business
2. Employed assets – available assets less idle facilities
3. Tangible assets – total assets less intangible assets. Intangible assets are assets that have no physical existence but their possession confers a right to the business, e.g., goodwill.

An alternative term for the capital amounts described above is 'capital employed' and this general term needs qualification. The many interpretations of capital employed reflect the varying responsibilities of members of management and this point will be examined in greater detail in the next chapter.

Also examined in greater detail in the next chapter will be the possible changes in the valuations given. In this section, the figures given are based on the assumption that the valuations are not changed when, in fact, there may be good reasons for recording different valuations.

## 4.5 ACCOUNTS CHARTS

In the processing of data to provide the various classifications described in this and earlier chapters, transactions should be arranged in ordered sequence to allow management to obtain the accounting information required. The ordered sequence adopted* is known as an accounts chart and to assist the data processing function the transactions may be coded for the following reasons:

1. It is a means by which the classification terminology is applied to the source documentation
2. It is often the means of expressing the terms of the classification in a convenient manner
3. It is the key to the organisation and structure of the classification.

Coding is subordinate to classification and it should not be allowed to restrict classification either in the accommodation of the items of the classification or the structure which is considered to be the required framework for analysis.

## 4.6 A CONCLUDING COMMENT

In the provision of accounting information to management a choice is made regarding the relative importance of data and its emphasis. The choice provides arrangements of financial data to match the objectives laid down by the users of that information. The flexibility of the classifications provided by the conventional accounting summary statements, as shown in this chapter, provide key information relationships explored in the next chapter.

## FOR FURTHER STUDY

QUESTIONS

1. *Problems associated with the analysis of product costs into their direct and indirect elements*
   Define direct and indirect costs of production indicating the problems that may arise in respect of this analysis of product costs.

2. *Preparation of trading statement*
   The following information is obtained from the accounting records of the company for the three months ended 31st March 19. .:

|                                  | £     |
|----------------------------------|-------|
| Direct materials purchased       | 6,000 |
| Direct labour cost               | 3,000 |
| Direct expense                   | 200   |
| Maintenance materials consumed   | 100   |
| Indirect labour                  | 1,000 |
| Electricity, gas and water       | 700   |
| Rent and rates                   | 1,100 |

* Examples of ordered sequence from Chapter 2 include: (*a*) the normal divisions of business transactions; (*b*) question 12.

| Plant and machinery | |
|---|---|
| depreciation | 800 |
| Sundry factory expenses | 1,200 |
| Net sales | 25,000 |

*Stocks:*

|  | *Opening* £ | *Closing* £ |
|---|---|---|
| Raw materials | 1,500 | 1,700 |
| Work-in-progress | 9,000 | 8,000 |
| Finished goods | 12,000 | 14,000 |

*Required:*

Using the information given above, prepare a trading statement for the three months ended 31st March 19. . indicating:

(a) Prime cost
(b) Total factory cost
(c) Factory cost of goods completed
(d) Cost of sales
(e) Gross profit.

3. *Preparation of a profit statement*

The following information is obtained from the accounting records of the company for the three months ended 31st March 19 . .:

|  | £ |
|---|---|
| Net sales | 35,000 |
| Investment income | 2,000 |
| Cost of sales | 17,000 |
| Office staff salaries | 3,000 |
| Office rent and rates | 1,000 |
| Printing and stationery | 500 |
| Telephones and postage | 600 |
| Audit fee | 200 |
| Sundry office expenses | 1,000 |
| Salesmen's salaries and commission | 3,000 |
| Salesmen's entertaining expenses | 100 |
| Salesmen's car expenses | 700 |
| Carriage outwards | 1,000 |
| Taxation | 2,000 |

*Required:*

Using the information given above prepare a profit statement for the three months ended 31st March 19 . . indicating:

(a) Operating profit
(b) Net profit before tax
(c) Net profit after tax
(d) Administration expenses total
(e) Selling and distribution expenses total.

**4.** *Preparation of a trading and profit statement*

The following information is obtained from the accounting records of the company for the three months ended 31st March 19 . .:

|  | £ |
|---|---|
| Lubricants | 500 |
| Factory supervision salaries | 3,000 |
| Administration salaries | 2,000 |
| Salesmen's commissions | 900 |
| Van expenses | 1,000 |
| Closing stocks – work-in-progress | 2,900 |
| – finished goods | 4,800 |
| Labour cost incurred on defective work | 1,000 |
| Factory insurance | 500 |
| General office rent | 1,000 |
| Inspection labour cost | 700 |
| Plant and machinery repairs | 500 |
| Audit fee | 1,000 |
| Sales salaries | 2,000 |
| Cariage outwards | 1,500 |
| Factory clerk's wages | 1,100 |
| Direct material cost | 5,000 |
| Telephone and telegrams | 500 |
| Advertising | 2,000 |
| Opening stocks – work-in-progress | 3,000 |
| – finished goods | 5,000 |
| Factory rent | 1,000 |
| Direct labour cost | 4,000 |
| Postage and stationery | 700 |
| Travelling and entertaining – salesmen | 600 |
| Plant and machinery depreciation | 800 |
| Factory power | 900 |
| Sales office rent | 900 |
| Net sales | 40,000 |

*Required:*

Using the information given above prepare for the three months ended 31 March 19 . .:

(*a*) A trading statement showing:

(i) Prime cost
(ii) Total factory cost
(iii) Factory cost of goods completed
(iv) Cost of sales
(v) Gross profit.

Support this statement with a schedule of fixed and variable factory overhead costs.

(b) A profit statement showing:

    (i) Administration expenses total
    (ii) Selling expenses total
    (iii) Distribution expenses total
    (iv) Operating profit.

5. *The profit calculation*
'The profit calculation is made by combining in the trading and profit statements fact and opinion.'
*Required:*
Comment on this statement.

6. *Preparation of a balance sheet*
The following information is obtained from the accounting records of the company for the three months ended 31st March 19 . .:

| | £ |
|---|---|
| Issued share capital | 5,000 |
| Profit and loss account balance at the end of the period | 9,000 |
| Trade creditors | 5,000 |
| Current taxation | 2,000 |
| Freehold land and buildings | 6,000 |
| Plant and machinery | 4,000 |
| Office furniture and fixtures | 1,000 |
| Trade debtors | 6,000 |
| Stocks | 7,000 |
| Cash at bank and in hand | 2,000 |

*Required:*
Using the information given above prepare a balance sheet as at 31 March 19 . . indicating:

(a) Current liabilities
(b) Current assets
(c) Fixed assets
(d) Working capital
(e) Capital employed.

7. *Intangible asset definition and presentation*
Because of the controversy regarding the nature of intangible assets their treatment in financial statements is a difficult accounting problem.
*Required:*
(a) What do you understand by an intangible asset?
(b) How may these items be shown in the balance sheet?

8. *Causes and effect of idle plant capacity*
Losses due to idle facilities may occur in the most carefully managed plants.

*Required:*

(*a*) Define idle factory plant capacity

(*b*) List the possible causes of idle plant capacity

(*c*) Comment upon the fixed costs associated with idle facilities.

9. *Working capital assumptions*

What do you understand by the term 'working capital'? What assumptions are made in the provision of this figure in the accounts of the business?

**10.** *Modification of company accounts for inter-firm comparison*

Engineering Products Ltd is a company producing the following accounts for the year ended 31 December 19 . .:

### Trading Statement

| | £ | £ | | £ | £ |
|---|---|---|---|---|---|
| Opening stocks | | | Sales | | 400,000 |
| Materials and goods | 10,000 | | Closing stocks | | |
| Work-in-progress | 20,000 | 30,000 | Materials and | | |
| Purchases | | 140,000 | goods | 9,000 | |
| Factory wages | | 150,000 | Work-in-progress | 25,000 | 34,000 |
| | | 320,000 | | | |
| Gross profit carried | | | | | |
| down | | 114,000 | | | |
| | | 434,000 | | | 434,000 |

### Profit Statement

| | £ | | £ |
|---|---|---|---|
| Salaries | 20,000 | Gross profit brought | |
| Rates | 7,000 | down | 114,000 |
| Miscellaneous expenses | 20,000 | | |
| Other administration | | | |
| expenses | 10,000 | | |
| Other selling and | | | |
| distribution expenses | 29,000 | | |
| | 86,000 | | |
| Net profit carried down | 28,000 | | |
| | 114,000 | | 114,000 |

| | £ | | £ |
|---|---|---|---|
| Taxation | 10,000 | Net profit brought down | 28,000 |
| Proposed dividend | 20,000 | Balance brought forward | |
| Balance carried forward | 6,000 | from previous year | 8,000 |
| | 36,000 | | 36,000 |

*Balance Sheet as at 31st December 19 . .*

| | £ | £ | | £ | £ |
|---|---|---|---|---|---|
| Share capital | | 400,000 | Fixed assets at cost | 300,000 | |
| Revenue reserves — | | | Less depreciation | 50,000 | 250,000 |
| Profit and loss | | | Current assets | | |
| account balance | | 6,000 | Stocks: | | |
| Future taxation | | 10,000 | Materials and | | |
| Current liabilities | | | goods | 9,000 | |
| Trade and sundry | | | Work-in-progress | 25,000 | |
| creditors | 5,000 | | | 34,000 | |
| Current taxation | 4,000 | | Trade and sundry | | |
| | | | debtors | 141,000 | |
| Proposed dividend | 20,000 | 29,000 | Cash | 20,000 | 195,000 |
| | | 445,000 | | | 445,000 |

The company subscribes to a Trade Federation Scheme for company financial information to be shared so that the detail provided may be used to increase their efficiency and profitability. To accomplish this objective more information is required and the company provides the following notes to its accounts:

(*a*) Factory wages analysis:

| | £ |
|---|---|
| Production employees | 144,000 |
| Van drivers | 6,000 |
| | 150,000 |

(*b*) Salaries analysis:

| | |
|---|---|
| Works manager | 4,000 |
| Sales manager | 5,000 |
| Management and clerical employees | 11,000 |
| | 20,000 |

(*c*) Miscellaneous expenses include factory expenses of £15,000
(*d*) Other selling and distribution expenses include distribution expenses of £9,000.

*Required:*
From the information given above:

(*a*) Calculate the following:

    (i) Operating assets
    (ii) Value of output
    (iii) Operating profit
    (iv) Value added
    (v) Factory cost
    (vi) Administration cost
    (vii) Selling cost
    (viii) Distribution cost.

(*b*) What other adjustments may be necessary to ensure that the company information is comparable with information of other organisations participating in the Trade Federation Scheme?

11. *Purpose and construction of an accounts chart*
What is the purpose of an accounts chart and how may such a chart be constructed?

12. *Coding of a chart of accounts*
Refer to Question 12 in Chapter 2 and code the classification of accounts used or possibly developed by Ventures Ltd. The symbolisation adopted should reflect the principal and subclassifications envisaged in such an accounting system.

FURTHER READING

*Extraordinary Items and Prior Year Adjustments.* Statement of Standard Accounting Practice No. 6. Accounting Standards Committee, 1974.
Fitzgerald, A. *Analysis and Interpretation of Financial Statements.* Butterworth & Co (Australia) Ltd, 1963. Chapters 4–8.
Risk, J. M. S. *The Classification and Coding of Accounts.* Institute of Cost and Works Accountants, 1956. Chapters 3–14.

# 5  Ratio Analysis and Interfirm Comparison

## OBJECTIVE OF THE CHAPTER

To examine the technique of ratio analysis and indicate its value to management in the identification of key relationships regarding the financial stability and profitability of the business.

## OUTLINE OF THE CHAPTER

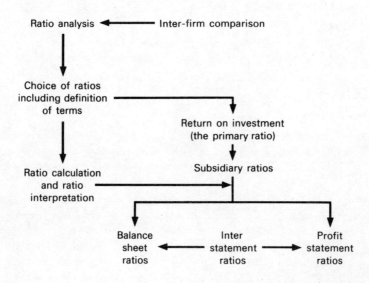

FIGURE 5.1.

The classified information provided in the summary financial statements when further analysed as shown in the last chapter provides management with the basic data to assess key relationships. The significant relationships may be examined by the use of the technique known as ratio analysis and preferably presented in sequence to stimulate inquiry and develop understanding of the business.

## 5.1 FORMS OF RATIO ANALYSIS

*Data*

Profit: £8,000 (for Year 1)
Sales: £80,000 (for Year 1); £100,000 (for Year 2)
Capital employed: £20,000 (as at the end of Year 1)
Costs: £70,000 (for Year 1); £80,000 (for Year 2)

Using the above data, accounting ratios may be expressed in the following forms:

1. A percentage, e.g., $\dfrac{\text{Profit}}{\text{Sales}} \times 100 = \dfrac{£8,000}{£80,000} \times 100 = 10\%$

2. A quotient, e.g., $\dfrac{\text{Sales}}{\text{Capital employed}} = \dfrac{£80,000}{£20,000} = 4$ times or $4:1$

3. A rate, e.g., The difference in costs: £80,000 − £70,000 = £10,000
   The difference in sales: £100,000 − £80,000 = £20,000
   i.e., a variation of £1 cost for every £2 sales.

The form adopted will be that chosen to convey to the user the information wanted for checking the performance of the business.

## 5.2 LIMITATIONS OF RATIO ANALYSIS

Ratios are not a standard formula for judging the performance of a business. Many ratios are in common use and express standard relationships but are only a guide since management cannot be reduced to a formula. What the standard relationships do convey is a logical and important operational sequence of related key control figures. The absolute figures by themselves are of limited value to management.

Ratios are not a substitute for judgement. Management is not provided with answers to its problems by ratios. Not only must judgement be used in the selection of key ratios to suit the business but also judgement in their evaluation. In this connexion, a meaningful figure for comparison may be crucial. Unfortunately, in some areas absolute standards have been adopted. It is possible to read, for example, of the desirability of current assets to current liabilities as a ratio of 2 : 1. There is generally no such absolute standard ratios common to all businesses. Ratios calculated on an industrial basis where there is a common basis of calculation are likely to be of greater value. In this area, information may be gained regarding the optimum level for specific ratios or acceptable range variations.

Unless the make-up of ratios is chosen with care the relationships may be misleading. A simple presentation of the ratio profit to capital employed disguises the complexity of the choice of what constitutes profit and what constitutes capital employed. It would appear to be reasonable that the profit figure given should arise from the use of the resources represented by the capital employed figure. This apparent logicality is not necessarily applied to the calculation of this ratio.

When ratios are compared on an historical basis the time periods may be of equivalent duration but price level changes between the periods may give distorted results if no allowance is made for this factor. It should not be forgotten that where historical ratio information is used this detail is not, necessarily, a guide to the future.

A sense of proportion should be exercised in the choice and calculation of ratios. Some advocates of ratio analysis have developed elaborate systems and it is questionable whether so much detail is worth the effort. In this chapter, key ratios for control of the business are examined.


## 5.3  THE RETURN ON INVESTMENT CONCEPT

In Chapter 3 a key financial objective was identified as earning the required return on the funds invested in the business, consistent with maintaining the sound financial position of the business. The prominence given to this measure of performance in the accounting literature confirms its importance and this section gives a brief examination of the concept as a basis for subsequent ratio analysis.

Using the return on investment ratio $\left(\dfrac{\text{Profit}}{\text{Capital employed}}\right)$ an informative measurement can be supplied to management. Consider the following figures:

Data for an accounting period

|  | Product 'Y' £ | Product 'Z' £ |
|---|---|---|
| Sales | 1,000 | 2,000 |
| Profit | 80 | 160 |
| Capital employed | 800 | 800 |

Calculated information for management from the data:

|  | Product 'Y' % | Product 'Z' % |
|---|---|---|
| Profit to sales | 8 | 8 |
| Profit to capital employed | 10 | 20 |

Both products appear equally profitable under the profit to sales assessment whereas product 'Z', in fact, gives the better return because of the increased turnover of capital employed in the case of this product.

Many take-over bids have been prompted by the realisation that better profits could be made through the better use of capital employed. A company might consider its profit to be at a reasonable level without realising that the value of assets employed in earning that profit is out of proportion to the return achieved.

## 5.31 LIMITATIONS OF THE RETURN ON INVESTMENT CONCEPT

It is often very difficult to assess with reasonable accuracy the amount of capital employed. What items to be included in the amount and their valuation are matters of dispute and further reference will be made to this point later in this chapter.

Where the units of a business form a vertically integrated company, each making a contribution to overall performance and these separate units cannot be considered in isolation, the return on investment measure of performance is not appropriate to the unit.

The return on investment ratio, as an assessment of efficiency, creates a tendency to rent or lease rather than purchase property. In the long run, ownership of property may be more advantageous to the company. While matters of this kind could be controlled by, for example, a check on hiring of assets as well as a check on capital expenditure, the return on investment concept like all tools of management should be applied with care, the method of calculation being clearly defined.


## 5.32 SHOULD THE RETURN BE CALCULATED ON OWNERS' EQUITY?

The view that the return should be judged on the basis of owners' equity is based on the principle that the cost of equity capital may be considered as the minimum return that equity investors can expect from their investment. It follows from this that the management is only operating efficiently if it earns at least this minimum rate of return. On this basis, any project that gives more than the minimum rate of return should be accepted using finance from any sources available providing that its cost is less than the equity capital. The effect of this action would be an increase in the earnings per equity share but it may encourage the use of too high a proportion of borrowed funds giving a low return. In the normal business situation, investment projects of varying profitability are available to management and for reasons such as administrative limits it is necessary to ration projects and concentrate one's efforts on those giving at least as good a return as that currently experienced from existing assets.

Through ratio analysis a relationship can be established between the return on capital employed and return on owners' equity. The ratio that indicates the extent to which the capital employed of the company has been derived from shareholders as distinct from other investors is expressed as:

$$\frac{\text{Capital employed}}{\text{Owners' equity}}$$

If this is shown related as follows:

$$\frac{\text{Profit}}{\text{Capital employed}} \times \frac{\text{Capital employed}}{\text{Owners' equity}}$$

this equals:

$$\frac{\text{Profit}}{\text{Owners' equity}}$$

## 5.4  THE INTERPRETATION OF CAPITAL EMPLOYED

If the measure of efficiency is considered to be the return on capital employed it should be established whether the reference is to total assets or fixed assets plus working capital. Within this broad classification what items to exclude should also be established. The valuation of assets is a controversial matter for decision.

### 5.41  TOTAL ASSETS OR FIXED ASSETS PLUS WORKING CAPITAL?

There seems to be a weight of evidence in favour of the fixed assets plus working capital approach* but the key to this problem is the responsibility factor. If operating management is responsible for creditors they should be deducted from the assets because this may encourage the management to obtain the best possible terms. There is the need to view each item in the balance sheet according to its function and relevance to management responsibility in order to decide what items should be included in capital employed. For example, a bank overdraft used as a continuing source of funds, although recorded as a current liability in the balance sheet, should be considered as part of the capital employed.

### 5.42  ITEMS TO BE EXCLUDED FROM CAPITAL EMPLOYED

An indication of the application of principles to the choice of items to be excluded from capital employed may be gained from the comments recorded below:

*Idle assets.* The basic feature here is the one already mentioned of responsibility. If operating management is not responsible for the non-employment of assets, as might arise when trade is slack and there is a temporary surplus of capacity, the usual view is to exclude such assets from the asset base. By excluding such assets the profit to capital employed ratio is improved but if these assets are unemployed it represents an inefficient use of funds, and for an overall assessment such assets should be included in capital employed.

*Surplus cash.* The same arguments can be put forward as those above for non-operating assets. Again, the purpose of the ratio should be the deciding factor.

*Outside investments.* Outside investments in, for example, the form of shares in other companies, should be segregated from the capital employed calculation since they are not the responsibility of operating management.

*Intangible assets.* As these items, represented by goodwill, patents and trademarks,

---

* Many interfirm comparison schemes are based on the fixed assets plus working capital approach. See, for example, H. Ingham and L. Taylor Harrington, *Interfirm Comparison for Management.* (British Institute of Management, 1958), page 49, Appendix 2. This view of capital employed was the considered view of the British Institute of Management Study Group which included representatives of companies of considerable standing. They were: Courtaulds Ltd, Distillers Ltd, Metal Box Ltd, Imperial Chemical Industries Ltd, Bowater Paper Corporation Ltd, T.I. (Group Services) Ltd, Shell Petroleum Co. Ltd (*Efficiency Comparisons Within Large Organisations*, B.I.M. and the Centre for Interfirm Comparison, 1962).

are included in balance sheets only when they have been the subject of purchase and sale, and are then usually written off as soon as possible, any figure remaining is likely to be unrepresentative of their true value. Companies may have a large goodwill element but not show this in the balance sheet. On the grounds of practicality it appears necessary to exclude intangible assets from the capital employed calculation. The point at issue here is the valuation given to the assets — a point to be considered in the next section — but, for example, patents and trademarks may have a definite market value and they should be included in the capital employed at that figure.

## 5.43  THE VALUATION OF ASSETS

This heading covers three points:

1.  Should the original cost of assets be used or their book value?
2.  Should assets be valued at their current value?
3.  Should the average value of assets in the control period be taken?

In the overall appraisal of company performance, to value assets at their original cost is to duplicate the effect of the depreciation amount since this may accumulate in the form of working capital. In the appraisal of a section of the business where the manager is not responsible for the reinvestment of the funds represented by the depreciation charge, the original cost of assets may be the better method of valuation. The purpose of the figures calculated, whether as an overall or sectional company appraisal, governs whether assets should be valued at original cost or shown at their book value.

Although common practice, it seems absurd to calculate the profit to capital employed ratio where the profit is overstated, owing to depreciation on original cost in inflationary conditions, and capital employed is understated, owing to book values on the same original cost. Both errors serve to give a higher rate of return on capital employed and the result can be very misleading. It is sometimes suggested that to allow for this factor a higher return on capital employed can be required, say, 25% where the calculations are in conventional form, so that this would give an effective 15% return on capital employed, based on current values. Unless an assessment of this type is based on current values it is difficult to avoid the conclusion that the results may be very unreliable.

The conversion of historical costs to current values may be on the basis of replacement costs less depreciation on the replacement costs. Alternatively, published indices, own company indices or valuations by company personnel with professional assistance may be used. This point is explored in greater detail in Chapter 24.

The remaining point to cover in this section is whether the capital employed should be an average value of assets employed in the control period. Capital employed as calculated at the beginning or end of the control period is often used although there may be large movements in the capital employed figure throughout the accounting period. An average capital employed figure is the answer although to take the opening and closing figures of a lengthy accounting period could be misleading. Monthly figures of capital employed taken as an average would help to remove any distortion in the ratio but figures on such a frequent basis may not be available. In this situation, quarterly or yearly figures may have to be used and the following general formula applied:

$$\frac{\text{the sum of the balances at the end of the accounting periods available in the year to date}}{\text{the number of accounting periods in the year to date.}}$$

## 5.5 THE INTERPRETATION OF PROFIT

The profit figure calculation depends on the interpretation of capital employed. For example, if outside investments are excluded from capital employed, the profit figure should be after deduction of the income from those investments. If a bank overdraft is considered as capital employed the bank interest on the overdraft should be added back in the profit calculation. The profit calculated should be the profit earned by the assets included in the asset base.

Where assets have been calculated on a replacement cost basis the old depreciation charges will be added back to profit and the depreciation on the replacement costs deducted from the resulting profit figure.

Taxation presents a problem in the return on capital employed calculation because the taxation figure as a period assessment may be a distorted amount. For this reason, profit before tax is often used. The view may be taken that it is important for management to be aware of the level of taxation affecting their final profit figures and a company calculation of tax may be made restricting the factors to those under the direct control of the unit management.

## 5.6 DIVISIONAL AND PRODUCT ASSESSMENT OF CAPITAL EMPLOYED

The application of the concept of return on capital employed to product lines is theoretically attractive but it involves serious apportionment problems not only in respect of costs but also in respect of investment. For this reason, as a regular routine, capital employed is not often analysed to products unless products are divisionalised and the automatic identification of divisional facilities removes many of the apportionment problems.

A lot of attention has been given to the apportionment of common costs through the development of costing theory but the same attention has not been given to investment apportionment. For special excerises, where it is necessary to examine individual product investment, the principles of apportionment may be illustrated by the following examples:

| Asset(s) | Basis of apportionment |
|---|---|
| Plant and equipment | As used to manufacture products |
| Service facilities | An estimation of service received |
| Stocks | Finished goods and work-in-progress as identified to specific products; raw material consumption data may be used as the basis for raw materials |
| Trade debtors | As a per cent of product sales |
| Cash | As a per cent of cost of sales |

The apportionment base chosen should reflect the incidence of the items to be apportioned to the products. Where other assets are relatively insignificant a general base such as cost of sales or sales may be chosen. If other assets are significant and an equitable base for apportionment cannot be found, it is better practice to exclude such items from the assessment procedure.

## 5.7 PRIMARY RATIO INTERPRETATION FACTORS

The return on capital employed ratio is often termed the primary ratio and its two constituent elements: the profit margin and turnover of capital rate are the basis of the ratio analysis technique. The profit margin may be expressed in one of its forms as:

$$\frac{\text{Profit}}{\text{Sales}}$$

The turnover of capital rate may be expressed in one of its forms as:

$$\frac{\text{Sales}}{\text{Capital employed}}$$

These ratios are related and, in fact:

$$\frac{\text{Profit}}{\text{Sales}} \times \frac{\text{Sales}}{\text{Capital employed}} = \frac{\text{the return on}}{\text{capital employed}}$$

Further analysis is possible through the application of subsidiary ratios.

## 5.8 SUBSIDIARY RATIO INTERPRETATION FACTORS

Further analysis of the profit to sales ratio can follow the elements of cost and the sales to capital employed ratio, the asset classification, as indicated in Figure 5.2.

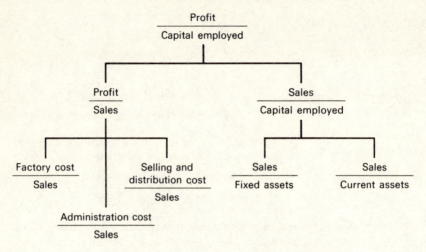

FIGURE 5.2. Subsidiary ratio analysis

Subsidiary analysis can be extended considerably given the basic data related to the above overall information. Numerators and denominators may be changed for more informative measurement of efficiency but this does not nullify the relationships shown. The changes generally accepted to give the ratio information management require are given in the sections to follow analysed to preserve the relationships developed in Chapter 4: inter-statement ratios; balance sheet ratios; profit statement ratios. The ratios may be calculated on the basis of current values.

## 5.9 AN ILLUSTRATIVE EXAMPLE OF REPRESENTATIVE KEY RATIOS

In this illustration, the figures have been reduced to the simplest terms to illustrate principles.

*Data for an accounting period*

*Profit Statement for the period . . .*
(£000)

|  | £ | £ |
|---|---|---|
| Net sales | | |
| Credit | 60 | |
| Cash | 20 | 80 |
| Less cost of sales | | |
| Opening stock | 14 | |
| Add factor cost | 62 | |
|  | 76 | |
| Less closing stock | 16 | 60 |
| Gross profit | | 20 |

| | | | |
|---|---|---|---|
| Less administration cost | | 3 | |
| selling and distribution cost | | 7 | 10 |
| Net profit | | | 10 |

Balance Sheet as at . . .<br>(£000)

| | £ | | | £ | £ |
|---|---|---|---|---|---|
| Capital and | | Fixed assets | | | 24 |
| reserves | 40 | Current assets | | | |
| Current liabilities | 16 | Stock | | 16 | |
| | | Debtors | | 10 | |
| | | Cash | | 6 | 32 |
| | 56 | | | | 56 |

## Calculated ratios from the data

Return on capital employed ratio:

$$\frac{\text{Profit before tax}}{\text{Capital employed}} = \frac{10}{40} \times 100 = 25\%$$

Net profit ratio:

$$\frac{\text{Profit before tax}}{\text{Net sales}} = \frac{10}{80} \times 100 = 12\tfrac{1}{2}\%$$

Capital turnover ratio:

$$\frac{\text{Net sales}}{\text{Capital employed}} = \frac{80}{40} = \text{twice (the number of times the capital turned over)}$$

Gross profit ratio:

$$\frac{\text{Gross profit}}{\text{Net sales}} = \frac{20}{80} \times 100 = 25\%$$

Factory cost ratio:

$$\frac{\text{Factory cost}}{\text{Net sales}} = \frac{62}{80} \times 100 = 77\tfrac{1}{2}\%$$

Administration cost ratio:

$$\frac{\text{Administration cost}}{\text{Net sales}} = \frac{3}{80} \times 100 = 3\tfrac{3}{4}\%$$

Selling and distribution cost ratio:

$$\frac{\text{Selling and distribution cost}}{\text{Sales}} = \frac{7}{80} \times 100 = 9\%$$

Liquid ratio:

Liquid assets : Current liabilities = 16 : 16 i.e. 1 : 1

| | |
|---|---|
| (Cash, | (Creditors |
| readily | and accruals, |
| realisable | i.e., short- |
| securities | term liabilities) |
| and good | |
| debtors) | |

Current ratio:
Current assets : Current liabilities = 32 : 16 i.e., 2 : 1
(Stock and          (short-term
liquid assets,      liabilities)
i.e., short-
term assets)

Fixed to total assets ratio:

$$\frac{\text{Fixed assets}\ \text{(Land and buildings, plant and machinery, fixtures and fittings and other physical long-term assets held for profit earning)}}{\text{Fixed assets plus current assets}} = \frac{24}{56} \times 100 = 43\%$$

Stock turnover ratio:

$$\frac{\text{Cost of sales}}{\text{Average stock}} = \frac{60}{(14 + 16) \div 2} = 4 \text{ times}$$ (the number of times the stock turned over)

Sales to debtors ratio:

Net credit sales: Debtors = 60 : 10 i.e., 6 : 1

or

$$\frac{\text{Debtors}}{\text{Average sales per day}}$$

Assuming given data for a twelve-months period $= \frac{10}{60 \div 12}$

$$= 2 \text{ months}$$

(average collection period)

## 5.10 INTER-STATEMENT RATIOS

In the above example, the following are inter-statement ratios:

1. Return on capital employed ratio ⎫ already described
2. Capital turnover ratio            ⎬
3. Sales to debtors ratio.           ⎭

If the required credit period is less than the average period calculated this indicates that customers are taking extended credit from the company by not paying their accounts as promptly as desired.

Other inter-statement ratios generally calculated are as follows:

(a) Creditors to purchases ratio — this ratio will check the credit period being taken by the company in the settlement of its trade debts
(b) Sales to fixed assets ratio   ⎫ A more detailed check on the
(c) Sales to current assets ratio ⎬ turnover of capital rate

(*d*) Net profit to ordinary shareholders' equity ratio — this ratio indicates the profit performance in relation to ordinary share capital, general reserves and retained profits

(*e*) Value added to plant and machinery ratio — this ratio gives an indication of how effectively the plant and machinery has been used.

## 5.11 BALANCE SHEET RATIOS

In the illustrative example, the following are balance sheet ratios:

1. Liquid ratio — this ratio indicates the availability of liquid assets to meet short-term liabilities.
2. Current ratio — this ratio is also an indication of a company's liquidity, expressing the working capital relationship in terms of short-term assets to short-term liabilities.
3. Fixed to total assets ratio — this ratio indicates the proportion of capital invested in long-term assets.

The capital gearing ratio may be calculated. This is the ratio of shareholders' equity to outside liabilities in the form of borrowed funds. A satisfactory relationship between these two sources of funds is necessary to give a balanced financial structure to the business.

## 5.12 PROFIT STATEMENT RATIOS

In the illustrative example, the following are profit statement ratios:

1. Net profit ratio
2. Gross profit ratio
3. Factory cost ratio
4. Administration cost ratio
5. Selling and distribution cost ratio

6. Stock turnover ratio.

} Ratios indicating the extent of operating efficiency with possibly the areas worthy of further investigation for improved performance

If the required turnover rate is greater than the average turnover rate calculated, this indicates that stock is being held for periods longer than considered necessary. The ratio may be analysed to show turnover rates for types of stock. e.g.

$$\frac{\text{Raw materials consumed}}{\text{Raw materials stock}}$$

Other profit statement ratios generally calculated are as follows:

(*a*) Value of output to net sales ratio — the objective of this ratio is to qualify the profit to sales ratio where there is a marked variation in opening and closing stocks of work-in-progress (*b*) Cost element ratios – each element of cost may be related to factory cost.

## 5.13 MONETARY AND NON-MONETARY RELATIONSHIPS

Financial analysis may be assisted by the inclusion of non-monetary data into ratios. Typical ratios in this category include:

1. Employee data giving rates per employee, e.g.
   Value added per factory employee
   Factory wages per factory employee.

2. Responsibility centre data giving rates per responsibility factor, e.g.
   Occupancy costs per 100 sq.ft occupied
   Sales per sq.ft of selling area.

3. Cost unit data giving rates per cost unit, e.g.
   Factory cost per job
   Value of output per job.

4. Share data giving rates per share, e.g.

   Earnings per share $\left(\dfrac{\text{Profit after tax}}{\text{Number of shares}}\right)$

   (If preference shares are issued, the profit after tax will be reduced by the preference share dividend and this figure as the numerator will be divided by the number of ordinary shares to give the earnings per ordinary share)

   Price earnings ratio $\left(\dfrac{\text{Market price per share}}{\text{Earnings per share}}\right)$

   Dividend yield $\left(\dfrac{\text{Dividend per share}}{\text{Market price per share}} \times 100\right)$

## 5.14 NON-MONETARY RELATIONSHIPS

Non-monetary data in the numerator and denominator of the ratio gives information that is often incorporated in financial statements to assist management to interpret the financial information given. Common ratios in this category include the following:

1. Labour performance:

   Efficiency ratio $= \dfrac{\text{Standard labour hours for actual output*}}{\text{Actual labour hours worked}} \times 100$

   \* Example of the calculation of standard labour hours for actual output:
   Each unit produced should take 2 hours labour time
   100 units produced
   Standard labour hours for actual output: 100 x 2 = 200 hours.

$$\text{Activity ratio} \quad = \frac{\text{Standard labour hours for actual output}}{\text{Planned production in terms of standard labour hours}} \times 100$$

2. Machine performance:

$$\text{Efficiency ratio} \quad = \frac{\text{Standard machine hours for actual output}}{\text{Actual machine hours in operation}} \times 100$$

$$\text{Utilisation ratio} \quad = \frac{\text{Actual machine hours in operation}}{\text{Machine time available in machine hours}} \times 100$$

$$\text{Availability ratio} = \frac{\text{Machine time available in machine hours}}{\text{Total machine capacity in hours}} \times 100$$

$$\text{Capacity ratio} \quad = \frac{\text{Actual machine hours in operation}}{\text{Planned machine hours in operation}} \times 100$$

## 5.15  INTERFIRM COMPARISON

Interfirm comparison schemes using ratios may be organised by a trade association or the Centre for Interfirm Comparison* and their objective is to provide information regarding the competitive position of participating companies to improve the profitability and productivity of those companies. This objective is achieved in the manner illustrated in Figures 5.3 and 5.4.

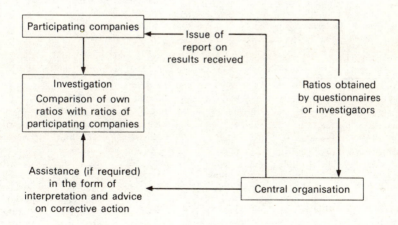

FIGURE 5.3. Interfirm ratio comparison schemes — basis of operation

* The Centre for Interfirm Comparison (CIFC) is a non-profit-making organisation established by the British Institute of Management.

The data selected for ratio comparison is chosen by the trade association or the Centre for Interfirm Comparison for a particular industry after considering:

1. The practical issues involved in introducing an interfirm comparison scheme for the industry
2. The best ratios to express the information required
3. The relationships that can be established in the ratios chosen to assist interpretation and corrective action where necessary
4. The adjustments necessary to accounting information to ensure comparability in the ratios produced.

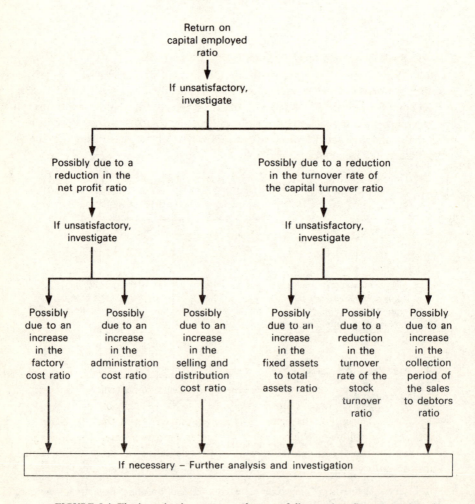

FIGURE 5.4. The investigation sequence that may follow an interfirm comparison

## 5.16 SUMMARY

Ratio analysis is a useful financial technique to assist management in the control of the business providing its limitations are understood.

The primary ratio in the form of the return on capital employed serves as the basis for subsidiary analysis in the two constituent elements of that ratio: the profit margin and the turnover of capital rate. Detailed analysis and investigation may continue as necessary in these key financial areas.

Internal comparisons may be extended with advantage to participating companies who share ratio information in interfirm comparison schemes.

## FOR FURTHER STUDY

QUESTIONS

1. *The dangers of using ratios*
   'Ratios are indicators, sometimes pointers, but not in themselves powerful tools of management. In the wrong hands ratios can be very dangerous, as it is easy to draw incorrect conclusions from them, particularly when based on insufficiently detailed data.' (A. W. Howitt, 'Higher financial control', *The Cost Accountant* (April, 1961), page 112).
   *Required:*
   Explain and comment on this statement.

2. *Capital employed as a basis for expressing profit*
   Profit is very often expressed for comparative purposes as a percentage of sales or of the cost of goods sold.
   *Required:*
   As management accountant of a long-established manufacturing company, enumerate the advantages and disadvantages of using capital employed for this purpose instead of sales or cost. (ICMA)

3. *The calculation of the capital employed figure*
   On the assumption that an organisation has decided that its profit target should be expressed in terms of return on capital employed what problems are likely to arise in determining the figure of capital employed? Using the figures disclosed in the following balance sheet, and notes, prepare a statement showing the capital employed figure you would use in calculating the profit target. You may make any assumption which you consider reasonable about any figure disclosed in the balance sheet and adjust it accordingly, but your adjustment should be accompanied by a brief note explaining why this has been done.

*Balance Sheet as at 31st December 19 . .*                    (£000)

| | £ | £ | | Cost £ | Depn. £ | £ |
|---|---|---|---|---|---|---|
| Issued share capital | | 810 | Fixed Assets | | | |
| Reserves – profit and loss account | | 217 | Freehold land/ buildings | 350 | 10 | 340 |
| | | | Plant and machinery | 150 | 60 | 90 |
| | | 1,027 | Fixtures/fittings | 80 | 25 | 55 |
| | | | Motor vehicles | 70 | 30 | 40 |
| Future taxation | | 95 | | 650 | 125 | 525 |
| Loan stock | | 300 | | | | |
| Current liabilities | | | Research/development | | | 225 |
| Sundry creditors and accruals | 550 | | Loose tools at valuation | | | 20 |
| Current taxation | 85 | | Goodwill at cost | | | 25 |
| Bank overdraft | 750 | | Investments | | | |
| Proposed dividend | 38 | 1,423 | Trade | | 150 | |
| | | | Quoted (market value) | | 30 | 180 |
| | | | Current assets | | | |
| | | | Stocks | | 1,050 | |
| | | | Sundry debtors and prepayments | | 750 | |
| | | | Cash and bank balances | | 70 | 1,870 |
| | | 2,845 | | | | 2,845 |

*Notes to balance sheet*

(a) The freehold property was valued by experts three years ago at £400,000. Since then the valuers have supplied the company with an index of valuation which at present is 102 on the basis of three years ago = 100.

(b) The plant engineer has estimated that to replace the present plant and equipment would cost £200,000 but that if the company were to try and dispose of it it would only realise £125,000.

(c) The company spends considerable sums on research and development, the benefits of which are always reaped some time in the future. The amount under this heading in the balance sheet represents that part of this type of expenditure which has been capitalised and which will gradually be written off.

(d) Stocks consist of the following:
Raw materials: £342,000; valued on a FIFO basis
Work-in-progress, £200,000; valued at prime cost
Finished goods: £508,000; valued at factory cost or net realisable value, whichever is lower.

(e) The bank has agreed it will not call upon the company for repayment of the bank overdraft within the next three years without first giving the company nine months notice of its intention to do so.  (ACA – Modified)

**4.** *The apportionment of capital employed to products*

A large-scale manufacturing company makes three types of product, X, Y and Z, and occupies two factories. Factory 1 is rented and is used for the manufacture of product X. Factory 2 is owned by the company, and comprises: machine and assembly shops for products Y and Z; a central machine shop which provides services for products Y and Z at cost; and an administration block including a central sales ledger section. The central machine shop attempts to achieve capacity working by undertaking sub-contract machining for outside customers.

There is a separate general manager for each product and for the central machine shop, each controlling his own buying, selling, invoicing and cost accounting functions.

The company calculates its overall return on capital employed (at cost) and now wishes to analyse this calculation by product types to provide a yardstick for the control of management performance and a guide to future product policy.

*Required:*

Recommend appropriate bases for the analysis of capital employed in the above company.                                             (ICMA)

**5.** *The constituent elements of the primary ratio*

Your managing director has recently attended a conference at which a speaker made the statement that return on capital is the product of the profit margin and asset turnover, and it is to these that management's attention should be directed.

*Required:*

He has asked you to send him a memorandum explaining and elaborating on what the speaker meant and stating the extent to which you agree with him.

(ACA)

**6.** *The significance of a specific ratio*

The managing director of a manufacturing concern claims that the only information he requires to measure the progress of the company is a weekly calculation of the selling value of the goods produced minus the cost of direct materials used in that production, divided by the number of workers employed, which he compares with a pre-determined standard.

*Required:*

What criticism would you make of the director's assertion?          (ICMA)

**7.** *Balance sheet ratios*

From the information given below, illustrate the calculation of six ratios which might be of use to the management of the company concerned. Explain the object of each ratio, and indicate, where appropriate, how it might be refined by the use of more detailed information than is here available. By what standards of comparison would the significance of each ratio be judged?

### Balance Sheet of XYZ Ltd at 31st July 19 . .

|  | £000 |  | £000 |
|---|---:|---|---:|
| Ordinary share capital issued and fully paid | 1,395 | Fixed assets at cost | 4,923 |
| Reserves | 963 | Less depreciation | 2,599 |
| Profit and loss account |  |  | 2,324 |
|   Opening balance less dividend | 695 |  |  |
|   Profit for year | 1,750 | Stocks |  |
|  | 2,445 |   Finished goods | 1,407 |
|   Less taxation | 900 |   Raw materials and work-in- |  |
|  | 1,545 |     progress | 840 |
|  |  | Trade debtors | 1,277 |
| Bank loan secured on assets | 690 | Cash | 41 |
| Provision for future taxation | 750 |  |  |
| Trade creditors and current taxation | 546 |  | 5,889 |
|  | 5,889 |  |  |

Sales less returns for the year ended 31st July 19 . .: £7,000,000.  (ICMA)

## 8. Significant features for profit improvement

You are required to comment on the significant features of the information given below, highlighting the relationships between the turnover ratio and the return on capital employed, and identifying areas which you feel would be worthy of further investigation if the profit position is to be improved within the second half of the year and thereafter.

The management of the A.B. Co. Ltd is concerned at the relatively low net profit margin which they make on sales. Over the last few years this margin has fallen to as low as 2% and has never been higher than 5%. The company does not manufacture, but sells to retailers a wide variety of products which it purchases from overseas manufacturers. Although there is a wide variety of products the selling prices of these do not vary significantly.

### Summary Profit and Loss Account for six months ended last month

|  | £ | £ |
|---|---:|---:|
| Sales revenue |  | 142,500 |
|  |  | 114,000 |
|  |  | 28,500 |
| Selling expenses | 4,900 |  |
| Warehouse expenses | 6,750 |  |
| Handling and clerical expenses | 10,250 |  |
| Administration expenses | 3,750 | 25,650 |
|  |  | 2,850 |

Capital employed: £95,000.
Target return on capital: $12\frac{1}{2}$%.

| Order size | Number of orders | Sales income £ |
|---|---|---|
| Under £5 | 4,000 | 8,000 |
| £5 to £29·9 | 1,750 | 17,500 |
| £30 to £54·9 | 1,200 | 48,000 |
| £55 to £79·9 | 400 | 24,000 |
| £80 to £104·9 | 300 | 27,000 |
| £105 plus | 120 | 18,000 | (ACA)

9. *Key ratio calculation and their interpretation*

The following information relates to an engineering company making consumer durables:

*Profit and loss account for the year*

| | £000 Actual Year 1 | Year 2 | Plan Year 3 |
|---|---|---|---|
| Sales | 200 | 220 | 280 |
| Materials | 80 | 81 | 101 |
| Direct labour | 30 | 31 | 36 |
| Indirect labour | 30 | 32 | 37 |
| Other costs | 22 | 24 | 29 |
| Factory cost | 162 | 168 | 203 |
| Administration | 21 | 26 | 47 |
| Selling | 5 | 7 | 8 |
| Distribution | 2 | 3 | 4 |
| Total cost | 190 | 204 | 262 |
| Net profit before tax | 10 | 16 | 18 |
| | 200 | 220 | 280 |

*Balance sheets at the end of the year*

| | | | |
|---|---|---|---|
| Fixed assets at cost | 120 | 169 | 187 |
| Less depreciation | 67 | 67 | 80 |
| | 53 | 102 | 107 |
| Stock and work-in-progress | 54 | 60 | 70 |
| Debtors | 32 | 27 | 31 |
| Other current assets | 4 | 3 | 5 |
| | 143 | 192 | 213 |
| Less current liabilities | 18 | 12 | 15 |
| Total capital employed | 125 | 180 | 198 |

*Required:*

Give your interpretation of the management of the company over the period shown, illustrating your answer with a tabulation of selected key ratios.

(ICMA)

**10.** *Interfirm comparison ratio choice*

'Looking back over the past three years of operation one of the most striking points to emerge is the wide range of results as between one firm and another in the same industry. Operating profit on assets employed ranges in many industries from 35% to minus 5%. The number of days required by firms to collect outstanding debts ranges from 29 to 107. Examples of this kind show what scope there is for most firms in industry to improve their performance.' (H. Ingham, Information circular on interfirm comparison from the CIFC, October 1962.)

*Required:*

Are the results of such studies comparable and how would you choose the key ratios in an IFC scheme to indicate the potential for improved business performance?

**11.** *The value of interfirm comparisons to trade association members*

(*a*) You are the secretary of a trade association which looks after the general interests of its member firms. Some of these firms feel that it would be useful if a scheme of interfirm comparison could be introduced within the association.

*Required:*

Draft a circular pointing out the advantages and limitations of such a scheme and the type of information which could be produced.

(*b*) After such a scheme has been introduced it is found that in a given year certain of company A's costs compare with the average costs provided by the association as follows:

*Costs per unit of product (£)*

|  | Average for all firms | Company A |
|---|---|---|
| Direct labour | 15 | 10 |
| Direct material | 32 | 30 |
| Overhead | 16 | 26 |

*Required:*

Give possible explanations of these differences and indicate what investigations it might pay company A to make.          (ACA)

**12.** *Interfirm comparison*

Mr Brown, the managing director of Electric Parts Ltd, had recently joined the Centre of Interfirm Comparison for his industry and forty firms of similar size and making similar products were taking part. The decision to join the CIFC arose out of a wish to be able to compare the company's performance with an external assessment of efficiency.

Initially, the board of Electric Parts Ltd were concerned about two aspects of the management ratios scheme conducted by the CIFC. They were:

(*a*) Whether the company's figures would be disclosed to others, particularly competitors, whom they did not wish to have access to them

(*b*) Whether the firms taking part, and their figures, would be really comparable.

A representative from the CIFC satisfied the Board of Electric Parts Ltd on these points and as a result of this conversation the company submitted their own figures to the Centre, analysed as requested. Later, Electric Parts Ltd received the following information:*

*Management Ratios, Year . . .*

| Ratio | Measurement | | Figures for forty companies | Figures for Electric Parts Ltd |
|---|---|---|---|---|
| 1. Operating profit / Capital employed | % | 1st Quartile<br>Median<br>3rd Quartile | 6<br>9<br>13 | 5 |
| 2. Operating profit / Sales | % | 1st Quartile<br>Median<br>3rd Quartile | 3<br>6<br>11 | 4 |
| 3. Cost of production / Sales | % | 1st Quartile<br>Median<br>3rd Quartile | 80<br>84<br>88 | 88 |
| 4. Cost of administration / Sales | % | 1st Quartile<br>Median<br>3rd Quartile | 5<br>6<br>7 | 5 |
| 5. Cost of selling and distribution / Sales | % | 1st Quartile<br>Median<br>3rd Quartile | 3<br>4<br>6 | 3 |
| 6. Sales / Capital employed | % | 1st Quartile<br>Median<br>3rd Quartile | 120<br>145<br>166 | 125 |
| 7. Fixed assets / Capital employed | % | 1st Quartile<br>Median<br>3rd Quartile | 60<br>63<br>70 | 65 |
| 8. Materials consumed / Stock | Times | 1st Quartile<br>Median<br>3rd Quartile | 2<br>3<br>4 | 2 |
| 9. Average trade debts / Average sales per day | Days | 1st Quartile<br>Median<br>3rd Quartile | 52<br>62<br>67 | 70 |

* These figures are based on the article: 'Interfirm comparisons' by H. W. G. Kendall, *Cost Accountant* (October 1962), page 362.

The company was informed that for each ratio the figures are listed in order of size from the lowest to the highest. The median is the figure that comes half way down the list. The first and third quartiles are the figures one quarter and three-quarters down the list. The median and quartiles are, therefore, figures of actual firms but for each ratio it is very probable that they will be of different firms. The three figures are given to provide an indication of the range of results.

*Required:*

(*a*) If you were the representative from the CIFC how would you satisfy the company on the points that concerned the board?

(*b*) What meanings would you give to the terms quoted in the ratios?

(*c*) What comments would you make on the performance of Electric Parts Ltd, as compared with the other firms in the scheme? Do you consider the membership of Electric Parts Ltd in the management ratios scheme worth while?

## FURTHER READING

*Efficiency Comparisons within Large Organisations.* British Institute of Management and Centre for Interfirm Comparison, 1962.

Ingham, H. and Harrington, L. Taylor. *Interfirm Comparison for Management.* British Institute of Management, 1958.

*The Planning and Measurement of Profit – a Technique of Management Accounting.* Association of Certified Accountants, n.d.

# 6 Cost–Volume–Profit Analysis

## OBJECTIVE OF THE CHAPTER

To explain the technique of cost–volume–profit analysis which charts the significant financial relationships as a basis for profit planning.

## OUTLINE OF THE CHAPTER

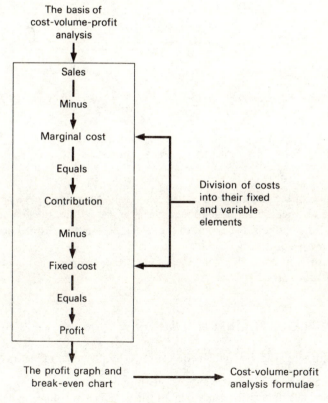

FIGURE 6.1.

The financial relationships considered in earlier chapters may be conveniently expressed in chart form and the techniques of cost–volume–profit analysis enables the data to be used for profit planning and decision-making.

## 6.1  THE PROFIT GRAPH

Planning concerns the future of the business and the decisive factor is usually sales. This activity level governs costs and profit and if plans have been made in advance on a particular volume the manager requires an answer to the question: 'What will happen to profit if the sales level changes?' This is a significant question and a graph may be useful in giving the answer. Figure 6.2 shows a chart known as a profit graph which may be used as an aid to interpreting the cost—volume—profit relationships.

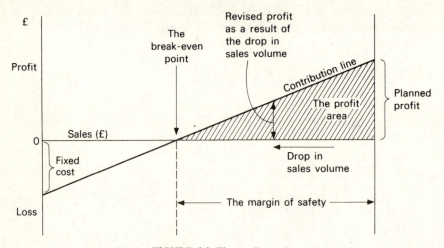

FIGURE 6.2. The profit graph

The *X* axis of the graph gives the sales volume and the plan shows a profit at a given volume of sales. If this volume is reduced, on the basis of the planned cost structure of the business, the extent of the reduction can be measured on the *X* axis and a revised profit calculated.

This illustration shows that a number of important assumptions have been made regarding the business.


## 6.2  PROFIT GRAPH ASSUMPTIONS

The assumptions particular to the period covered by the graph in Figure 6.2 are:

1. That variable costs are a constant cost per unit of volume
2. That fixed costs are at the same amount for the range of volume indicated in the graph
3. That the efficiency of operations is unchanged over the range of volume illustrated
4. That mixed costs can be separated into their fixed and variable elements

5. That the sales price per unit of sale is a constant
6. That in the case of a multi-product business the sales mix will be constant
7. That the volume measure adopted in the graph measures the variability of the variable costs presented
8. That stock levels will not significantly vary in the period.

The point arises as to whether these assumptions are valid. A study of cost behaviour is relevant to this problem and in Chapter 2 business activity in cost classification was examined in some detail. This study is the clue to the division of costs into their fixed and variable elements.

## 6.3  THE DIVISION OF COSTS INTO THEIR FIXED AND VARIABLE ELEMENTS

With mixed costs, the fixed cost component may be allocated to fixed costs and the variable cost component to the variable cost classification. Costs varying not in direct proportion to changes in the level of activity but predominently variable or fixed may be regarded as such. This view may be taken if the error introduced is considered to be insignificant and unlikely to mislead management. Stepped costs may be regarded as fixed for the planned range of output.

Scattergraphs or the application of the statistical technique of least squares may assist in the division of costs into their fixed and variable elements.

### 6.31  THE SCATTERGRAPH

This graphical method discloses visually the regression line on the basis of plotted data and the fixed and variable elements of cost may then be obtained by inspection. This procedure is applied as follows:

*Data for an accounting period*

| Control period | Volume measure units | Period cost |
|---|---|---|
|  |  | £ |
| 1 | 200 | 240 |
| 2 | 300 | 340 |
| 3 | 250 | 280 |
| 4 | 400 | 380 |
|  |  | 1,240 |

This information plotted on a graph is illustrated in Figure 6.3. The regression line is drawn by inspection of the plotted points and it is evident that the fixed cost is £105. The variable cost per unit is calculated as follows:

Select a volume — say, 150 units
Read off the graph the cost: £210
Deduct the fixed cost: £210 − £105 = £105
Variable cost per unit = $\frac{£105}{150}$ = £0·70.

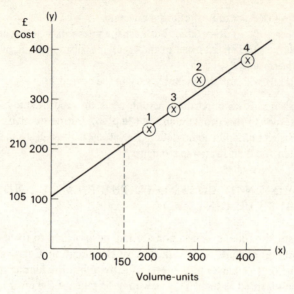

FIGURE 6.3. The scattergraph

## 6.32 THE LEAST SQUARES TECHNIQUE

The graph illustrated in Figure 6.3 may be described by the general formula:

$$y = a + bx$$

where

$y$ = the dependent variable (period cost)
$x$ = the independent variable (volume units)
$a$ = the fixed costs
$b$ = the slope of the regression line (variable cost per unit).

The data given in the previous section may be extended as follows:

| Control period | Volume measure | Period cost | | |
|---|---|---|---|---|
| | $x$ units | $y$ £ | $xy$ £ | $x^2$ units |
| 1 | 200 | 240 | 48,000 | 40,000 |
| 2 | 300 | 340 | 102,000 | 90,000 |
| 3 | 250 | 280 | 70,000 | 62,500 |
| 4 | 400 | 380 | 152,000 | 160,000 |
| N = 4 (number of control periods) | Σ 1,150 | 1,240 | 372,000 | 352,500 |

Using this information, the equations to give the values of $a$ and $b$ are as follows:

$$a = \frac{\Sigma x^2 \, \Sigma y - \Sigma x \, \Sigma xy}{N \, \Sigma x^2 - (\Sigma x)^2}$$

$$b = \frac{N \, \Sigma xy - \Sigma x \, \Sigma y}{N \, \Sigma x^2 - (\Sigma x)^2}$$

The calculations are as follows:

$$\text{The fixed cost} = \frac{(352,500)(1,240) - (1,150)(372,000)}{(4)(352,500) - (1,150)^2}$$

$$= £106$$

$$\text{The variable cost per unit} = \frac{(4)(372,000) - (1,150)(1,240)}{(4)(352,500) - (1,150)^2}$$

$$= £0\cdot70$$

## 6.4  THE PLANNED RANGE OF ACTIVITY

The reference in the previous section to the 'planned range of output' is a key factor in cost–volume–profit analysis. Figure 6.4 illustrates the importance of this point.

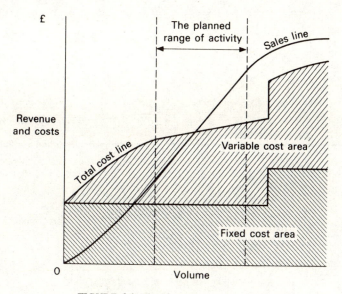

FIGURE 6.4. The planned range of activity

The 'straight line' relationships shown within the planned range of activity change outside these limits; therefore, linear assumptions in cost–volume–profit analysis should be re-examined if data is used outside these limits. For planning purposes, the planned range of activity makes possible the use of conventional cost—volume—profit formulae as being not significantly in error within the limits given.

## 6.5 THE PROFIT GRAPH AND THE ECONOMIST

If the following fixed and variable costs are plotted as costs per unit the presentation is as illustrated in Figure 6.5.

*Data*

| Volume | Variable costs | Fixed costs | Average Variable cost | Cost per unit Fixed Costs | Total cost |
|---|---|---|---|---|---|
| units | £ | £ | £ | £ | £ |
| 1 | 80 | 100 | 80 | 100 | 180 |
| 2 | 160 | 100 | 80 | 50 | 130 |
| 3 | 240 | 100 | 80 | 33·3 | 113·3 |
| 4 | 320 | 100 | 80 | 25 | 105 |
| 5 | 400 | 100 | 80 | 20 | 100 |

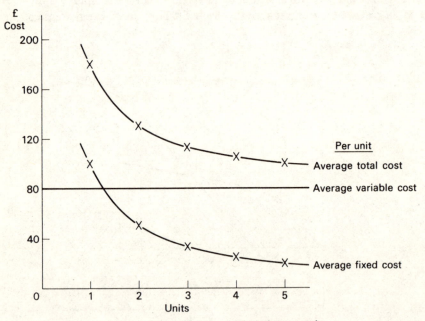

FIGURE 6.5. Costs per unit plotted on a graph

The economist views variable unit costs as shown in figure 6.6.

The economist's variable unit costs are not constant for a change in output because of changes in the efficiency of the business. Also shown in Figure 6.6 is the economist's marginal cost which is the extra cost of producing one more unit. Again, this marginal cost varies with a change in output. Providing the additional

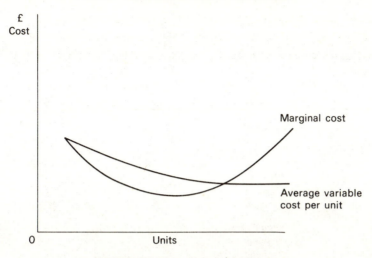

FIGURE 6.6. The economist's unit costs

revenue from selling an additional unit exceeds this additional cost, the additional business will be profitable.

The planned range of activity helps the accountant and economist to come together for cost–volume–profit analysis and some eminent economists (for example, Professor Joel Dean) have conducted research which suggests that the views of both sides are not so far apart as might be imagined. It may be noted that cost–volume–profit analysis does not recognise the increase in capital employed (working capital) that may be necessary to cover the increased volume of business.

The conclusion to draw from this section is that data should be used with great care and its interpretation governed by the validity of the assumptions made in the processing of the data.

## 6.6 MARGINAL COST AND CONTRIBUTION

Given the ability to segregate fixed and variable cost, it is possible to calculate the marginal cost and contribution per unit of product. Marginal cost may be defined as the total variable cost per unit of product. Contribution equals the selling price minus the marginal cost per unit and is the amount available to contribute to fixed costs and profit.

The contribution per unit makes possible the plotting of the contribution line as illustrated in Figure 6.2 and it will be noted that up to the point where this line crosses the sales volume axis the contribution has been used to cover the fixed costs. From this point on the chart, contribution gives profit.

## 6.7 THE BREAK-EVEN POINT AND THE MARGIN OF SAFETY

Where the contribution line crosses the activity line is known as the break-even point. The break-even point may, therefore, be defined as the level of activity where total costs equal total revenue. If the level of activity increases beyond the break-even point, a profit is obtained; if the level of activity drops below the break-even point, a loss is incurred. The profit graph, therefore, in disclosing the estimated profit or loss at different levels of activity also gives the extent to which a planned activity level can fall before a loss is experienced. This is known as the margin of safety and is the difference between planned sales and the break-even point.

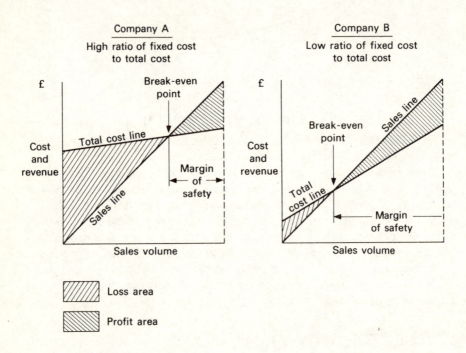

FIGURE 6.7. The effect of company cost structure on the break-even point and the margin of safety

If reference is made to Figure 6.7, where the cost–volume–profit structures of two companies are illustrated, it will be noted that two companies with the same total costs and sales amounts may have differing break-even points and, therefore, different margins of safety. In the case of Company A, once the break-even point is reached, large profits will be quickly made as volume increases. With Company B, once the break-even point is reached, profits will be achieved but at a slower rate than in Company A. Where trading conditions are difficult, the activity level in the case of Company B can drop much further than in Company A before a loss is sustained. In other words, the margin of safety of Company B is greater than in Company A.

## 6.8 THE CONVENTIONAL BREAK-EVEN CHART

The features of the profit graph illustrated in Figure 6.2 have now been described and in the process a different form of graphical presentation has emerged. This is illustrated in Figure 6.8 and is usually called a break-even chart.

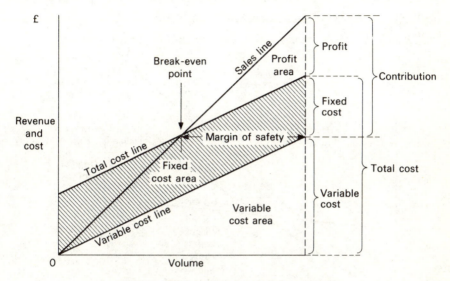

FIGURE 6.8. The conventional break-even chart

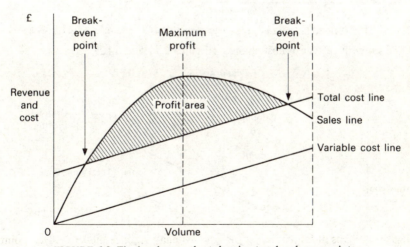

FIGURE 6.9. The break-even chart showing two break-even points

Two break-even points may be indicated when company profit planning data are plotted on such a chart and an example is given in Figure 6.9. In this example, sales revenue may have declined as a result of lowering selling prices to sell the increased volume of goods and the point is reached where the company again moves into a loss-making situation. The graph shows the level of activity where profit is at the maximum.

## 6.9 BREAK-EVEN CHARTS FOR PARTICULAR PURPOSES

The break-even chart may be used to illustrate the effect of many planning alternatives and a number of examples are given below:

1. To show the effect of sales price changes on profit (Figure 6.10).

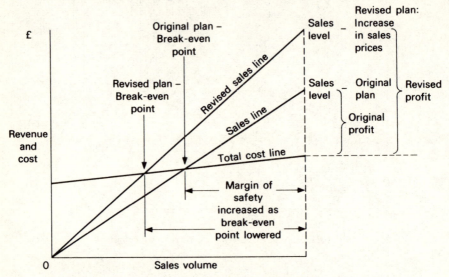

FIGURE 6.10. Break-even chart to show the effect of a sales price increase

2. To show the effect of cost changes (Figures 6.11 and 6.12).

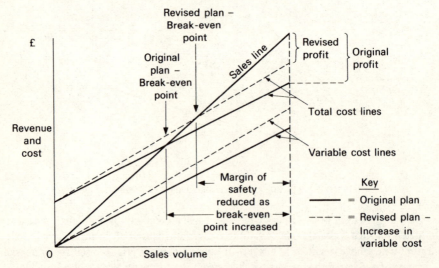

FIGURE 6.11. Break-even chart to show the effect of an increase in variable cost

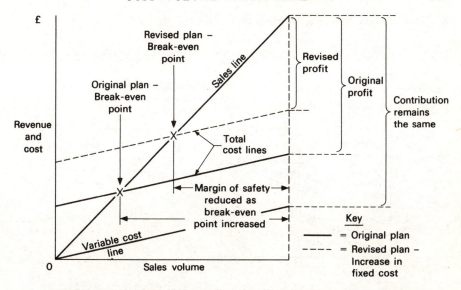

FIGURE 6.12. Break-even chart to show the effect of an increase in fixed cost

3. To show the effect of planned increases in capacity (Figure 6.13).

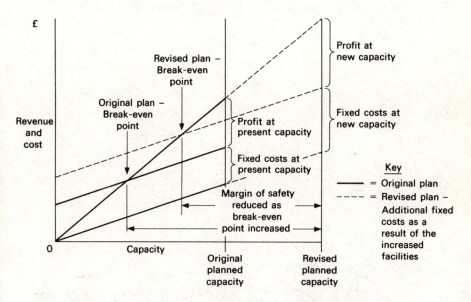

FIGURE 6.13. Break-even chart to show the effect of an increase in capacity

4. To show the effect of appropriations of profit (Figure 6.14).

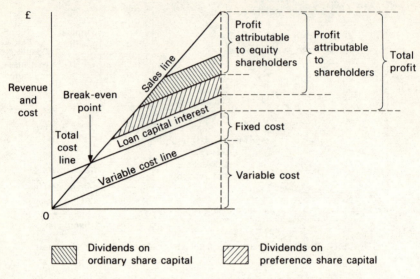

FIGURE 6.14. Break-even chart to show the effect of appropriations of profit

5. To show the effect of contribution by products to overall profitability (Figure 6.15).

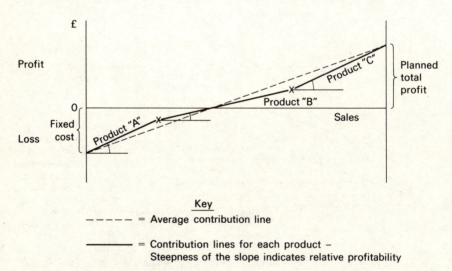

FIGURE 6.15. Profit graph to show the contribution effect of three products to overall profitability

## 6.10 COST–VOLUME–PROFIT ANALYSIS FORMULAE

On the assumptions described for the conventional break-even chart it is now possible to represent the graphs given in this chapter by formulae. Symbols used in the formulae are as follows:

Fixed cost: $FC$
Contribution: $C$
Profit: $P$
Sales: $S$
Profit/volume ratio: $P/V$ ratio
Break-even point: $B/E$ point
Margin of safety: $MS$

May also be calculated by using the formulae:

$$FC = C - P$$

$$(P/V \text{ ratio} \times S) - P$$

$$C = FC + P$$

$$P/V \text{ ratio} \times S$$

$B/E$ point:
in sales: £s

$$= \frac{FC}{C} \times S$$

$$\frac{FC}{P/V \text{ ratio}}$$

in sales: units

$$= \frac{FC}{C \text{ per unit of product}}$$

$$MS = S - B/E \text{ point}$$

$$P = C - FC$$

$$P/V \text{ ratio} \times MS$$

The term '$P/V$ ratio' has been introduced into the above formulae. It is calculated as a percentage as follows:

$$P/V \text{ ratio} = \frac{C}{S} \times 100$$

The $P/V$ ratio determines the angle of the profit graph.

The interrelationships of these formulae may be illustrated by the following example:

*Data for an accounting period*

|  | £ |
|---|---|
| Sales | 8,000 |
| Variable cost | 4,000 |
| Contribution | 4,000 |
| Fixed cost | 3,000 |
| Profit | 1,000 |

$$P/V \text{ ratio} = \frac{£4,000}{£8,000} \times 100 = 50\%$$

Units manufactured and sold: 4,000.

Inter-relationships of the data are shown in figure 6.16.

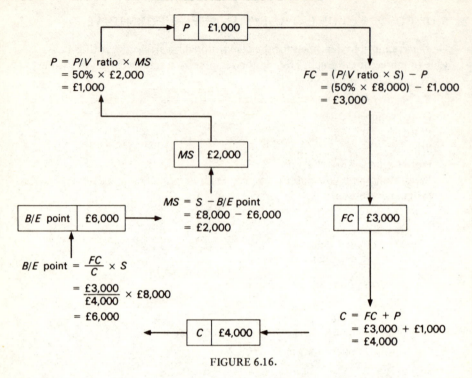

FIGURE 6.16.

It is possible to develop the formulae to give the results of varying the cost–volume–profit data as follows:

*Possible independent changes to the above data*

(*a*) Fixed expenses increased to £3,500
(*b*) £1,000 minimum additional profit required for extra fixed costs of £500
(*c*) Extra £600 profit required
(*d*) Selling price per unit reduced to £1·50.

(the new $P/V$ ratio, therefore: $\dfrac{£0·50}{£1.50} \times 100 = 33\tfrac{1}{3}\%$.

*Required: the level of sales in £s*

1. To achieve a given profit

|  *Given* | *Formula* |
|---|---|
| Fixed cost $P/V$ ratio | $\dfrac{\text{Given profit} + \text{fixed cost}}{P/V \text{ ratio }\%}$ |

Example: $\dfrac{£1,000 + £3,000}{50\%} = £8,000$

2. To maintain the current profit after an increase in fixed expenses.

*Given*        *Formula*

New fixed    $\dfrac{\text{Current profit} + \text{New fixed cost}}{P/V \text{ ratio \%}}$

cost

$P/V$ ratio.

Example using change $(a)$: $\dfrac{£1,000 + £3,500}{50\%} = £9,000$

£

Proof: Contribution = 50% × £9,000 = 4,500

Less fixed cost            3,500

Profit                    1,000

3. To earn a minimum return on a new investment in plant and machinery as well as the current profit.

*Given*             *Formula*

New fixed cost   $\dfrac{\text{Current Profit} + \text{Minimum return in additional profit} + \text{New fixed cost}}{P/V \text{ ratio \%}}$

$P/V$ ratio

Example using change $(b)$: $\dfrac{£1,000 + £1,000 + £3,500}{50\%} = £11,000$

£

Proof: Contribution = 50% × £11,000 = 5,500

Less fixed cost            3,500

Profit                  2,000

4. To achieve an increased profit.

*Formula*

*Given*

Current sales   Current     $+ \left( \dfrac{\text{Increased profit required}}{P/V \text{ ratio \%}} \right)$

level            sales

$P/V$ ratio      level

No change in

fixed costs

Example using change $(c)$: $£8,000 + \left( \dfrac{£600}{50\%} \right) = £9,200$

Proof:                           £

Contribution = 50% × £9,200 = 4,600

Less fixed cost           3,000

Profit                1,600

*Required: the sales volume in units*

5. To maintain the current profit when a reduction in selling prices is contemplated.

*Given*             *Formula*

Current contribution      $\dfrac{\text{Total contribution prior to price reduction}}{\text{New } P/V \text{ ratio \% as a result of the price reduction}} \div \text{New selling price per unit}$

New $P/V$ ratio

New selling price

per unit

Example using change ($d$): $\dfrac{£4,000}{33\frac{1}{3}\%} \div £1\cdot 50 = 8,000$ units

|  |  | £ |
|---|---|---|
| Proof: | Sales 8,000 x £1·50 = | 12,000 |
|  | Variable cost 8,000 |  |
|  | x £1 = | 8,000 |
|  | Contribution | 4,000 |
|  | Fixed cost | 3,000 |
|  | Profit | 1,000 |

6. To maintain the current profit after an increase in fixed costs.

| Given | Formula |
|---|---|
| New fixed cost | New    Profit prior to |
| Contribution | fixed + the increase in |
| per unit | cost        fixed costs |
| No change in |  |
| the $P/V$ ratio. | Contribution per unit |

Example using change ($a$): $\dfrac{£3,500 + £1,000}{£1} = 4,500$ units

|  |  | £ |
|---|---|---|
| Proof: | Contribution = 4,500 x £1 = | 4,500 |
|  | Less fixed cost | 3,500 |
|  | Profit | 1,000 |

## 6.11  SUMMARY

It is now possible to draw a number of conclusions from the break-even chart and profit-graph presentations. These are:

1. A high proportion of fixed cost to total cost represents a company with a high break-even point. Such a company can rapidly make substantial profits once the break-even point is passed.
2. A low proportion of fixed cost to total cost represents a company with a low break-even point. Such a company has greater flexibility in terms of profitable operation than the company described in (1).
3. When sales prices are increased the break-even point is lowered which increases the margin of safety of the company.
4. An increase in costs increases the break-even point and reduces the margin of safety of the company.

The conventional break-even chart is based on a number of assumptions which should be clearly stated and understood by management. Amongst these assumptions is a fixed set of conditions and to change these conditions demands revised charting. The profit graph is useful for the purpose of representing the cost—volume—profit relationships of the business in simple form to aid profit planning. This simplicity is a danger particularly in conveying the impression that the company only needs to increase sales to increase profit.

## FOR FURTHER STUDY

### QUESTIONS

1. *Difficulties in break-even analysis*
   You wish to employ break-even analysis to indicate likely profits and losses at different levels of sales activity but you are aware of several factors which could invalidate your findings. What might these factors be, and how could they be suitably allowed for in the use of break-even analysis? (ICMA)

2. *The value of the break-even chart*
   (*a*) Comment briefly on the information provided by a break-even chart
   (*b*) Discuss the usefulness of the break-even chart as aid to profit planning
   (*c*) How useful is a break-even chart in a multi-product company?

   (ACA – Part)

3. *An interpretation of cost–volume–profit relationships*
   John Smith, the sales manager of Brown & Green Ltd, had returned from a management meeting where profitability in the following year had been discussed in relation to the poor profit record of the current year. John Smith had emphasised his belief that greater volume in terms of sales was the answer to the company problem. An increase in volume in the previous year had not materialised. In fact, the sales value was the same as the year before with no major volume change yet the profit had dropped. John Smith mentioned that product 123 had not sold in the current year as well as in the previous year.

   Bill Green, the factory manager, mentioned that he hoped that John Smith would achieve a higher sales level next year because he had taken delivery of a costly new piece of plant and machinery and this should mean an increased production rate.

   Tom Brown, the managing director, in planning for the future had presented the following chart prepared by his accountant, Jim Grey:

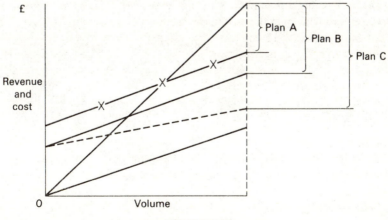

FIGURE 6.17.

Jim Grey had explained the chart and then the meeting was adjourned for lunch.

*Required:*

(*a*) Describe the cost–volume–profit relationships implied in the statements made by John Smith and Bill Green.

(*b*) Give the possible explanation of the chart supplied by Jim Grey.

4. *Interpretation of the break-even chart*

The imports for the year of a firm of shippers were as follows:

| Product | Quantity (litres) | Cost per litre £ |
|---------|-------------------|------------------|
| A | 30,000 | 2 |
| B | 20,000 | 3 |
| C | 40,000 | 10 |

The sales value of these imports is £825,000. Distribution and bottling costs average £4 for every twelve litres. Management, clerical, and selling costs tend to remain fixed in the short term at £100,000 per annum. Rates, depreciation, and other fixed costs amount to £50,000. Additional sales of 20% all round are proposed and these are likely to add £50,000 per annum in respect of advertising, selling, and other fixed costs.

*Required:*

Prepare a break-even chart to reflect operations on the existing and proposed scales. Read from the chart:

(*a*) break-even point before and after sales expansion;

(*b*) margin of safety before and after sales expansion.      (ICMA – Modified)

5. *Alternative product profitability charting*

The following information relates to three products A, B and C, each of which has the same selling price and the same potential level of sales but only one of which can be included in the next period's budget

| | Products | | |
|---|---|---|---|
| | A | B | C |
| Selling price | £1 | £1 | £1 |
| Profit/volume ratio | 20% | 15% | 10% |
| Fixed costs | £9,500 | £6,000 | £3,750 |
| Estimated sales | 60,000 units | 60,000 units | 60,000 units |

*Required:*

Present this information in a suitable graphical form and comment on it in respect of the particular problem under consideration.      (ACA)

6. *Preparation of a scattergraph*

The following figures are extracted from the books of a manufacturing company using actual cost methods:

| Year | Sales totals | Profit before tax |
|------|--------------|-------------------|
|      | £            | £                 |
| 1    | 64,400       | 12,600            |
| 2    | 56,000       | 7,700             |
| 3    | 75,600       | 19,600            |
| 4    | 70,000       | 16,800            |
| 5    | 67,200       | 15.400            |

From information supplied about results for the nine months ended 30th September, year 6, it seems probable that sales for the year will amount to £78,400, and profit before tax to £16,800. Price levels for costs and sales have been practically constant throughout.

*Required:*

Plot suitable 'scatter' dots and complete a graph to enable you to ascertain if the cost–volume–profit relationship is being maintained for the current year. What conclusions can you draw with the help of the graph?

(ICMA – Slightly modified)

7. *Preparation of a profit graph by products*

The following figures apply to a manufacturing company producing a wide range of products which may be classified into three main groups:

| Product group | Annual sales | Variable costs |
|---------------|--------------|----------------|
|               | £            | £              |
| A             | 3,000,000    | 1,000,000      |
| B             | 3,000,000    | 2,000,000      |
| C             | 3,500,000    | 3,000,000      |

The fixed costs total £2,500,000.

*Required:*

Plot on a graph the contribution lines for the three product groups in alphabetical order to enable you to plot the average contribution line for the total output.

(ICMA – Part)

8. *The application of break-even formulae*

The budgeted sales of three companies are as follows:

|                                   | Company 1 | Company 2 | Company 3 |
|-----------------------------------|-----------|-----------|-----------|
| Budgeted sales in units           | 10,000    | 10,000    | 10,000    |
| Budgeted selling price per unit   | £2        | £2        | £2        |
| Budgeted variable costs per unit  | £1·50     | £1·25     | £1        |
| Budgeted fixed expenses total     | £3,000    | £5,500    | £8,000    |
| Budgeted capacity                 | 80%       | 80%       | 80%       |

*Required:*

From the above information you are required to compute the following for each company:

(*a*) The budgeted profit
(*b*) The budgeted break-even point in unit sales
(*c*) The budgeted margin between break-even point and budgeted sales in units expressed as a percentage of total capacity
(*d*) The impact on profits of a ± 10% deviation in budgeted sales.

     Comment briefly on the effect of this in relation to the distribution between the companies' fixed and variable expenses.      (ACA)

**9.** *The relationship of break-even formulae*
The following figures related to a company manufacturing a varied range of products:

| Year | Total sales | Total costs |
|------|-------------|-------------|
|      | £           | £           |
| 1    | 39,000      | 34,800      |
| 2    | 43,000      | 37,600      |

*Required:*

Assuming stability in prices, with variable costs carefully controlled to reflect pre-determined relationships, and an unvarying figure for fixed costs, calculate:

(*a*) The fixed cost
(*b*) The profit/volume ratio
(*c*) The break-even point
(*d*) The margin of safety for years 1 and 2.

     How may the profit/volume ratio be improved, apart from increasing selling prices or reducing costs.      (ICMA – Modified)

**10.** *Modifying the break-even chart to indicate specific information*
An engineering company manufactures in batches to customers' instructions and an order is regarded as profitable only if the contribution to general fixed overheads is equal to the labour cost.

     An inquiry is received for the manufacture of certain components which would necessitate the purchase of special jigs and tools at a cost of £240. Costs per component are estimated at:

|                    | £ |
|--------------------|---|
| Direct material    | 4 |
| Direct labour      | 2 |
| Variable overheads | 5 |

A selling price of £16 per component is quoted.

*Required:*

From the above data, prepare a chart showing at what sales level contribution towards general fixed overheads will commence, and also the sales level at which the order will be considered profitable.                    (ICMA — Modified)

11. *The use of break-even analysis for the consideration of profit planning possibilities*

The accountant at Electric Tools Ltd has produced the following break-even chart for the company:

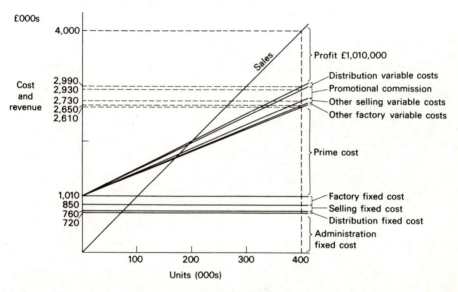

FIGURE 6.18.

The tools produced sell at £10 each and a meeting has been convened to consider the following sales proposals:

A  If unit selling price is reduced by 5% the present sales volume will be increased by $12\frac{1}{2}\%$

B  If unit selling price is reduced by 10% the present sales volume will be increased by 25%.

*Required:*

(*a*) The accountant has not indicated the break-even point on his chart. What is the break-even point?

(*b*) Calculate the profit under each of the sales proposals.

(*c*) Calculate the quantity to be sold under the price arrangement referred to in proposal B in order for the profit to be the same as in proposal A.

(*d*) Is this use of cost–volume–profit analysis of value to the company?

(ACA — Modified)

**12.** *Break-even data assumptions and formulae*

   (*a*) Discuss the underlying assumptions in the use of cost–volume–profit data for profit planning and cost control.

   (*b*) With the normal assumptions made, give formulae for each of the following:

      (i) The level of sales in £s to obtain a given profit.

      (ii) Sales volume in units needed to maintain the current profit given a reduction in selling price.

      (iii) Sales volume in units required to maintain the current profit after an increase in fixed costs (assuming no change in the *P/V* ratio).

FURTHER READING

Holmes, Geoffrey. 'Break-even and P/V analysis'. *Accountancy*, October 1970, pp. 737–40; November 1970, pp. 807–10; February 1971, pp. 80–2.

Kelvie, William E. and Sinclair, John M. 'New technique for break-even charts'. *Management Accounting*, December 1968, pp. 519–28.

Tse, John Y. D. *Profit Planning through Volume Cost Analysis*. Macmillan, New York, 1960.

# 7 Funds Analysis

OBJECTIVE OF THE CHAPTER

To explain the sources and applications of funds and changes in the cash balance of a business as a basis for cash and funds management.

OUTLINE OF THE CHAPTER

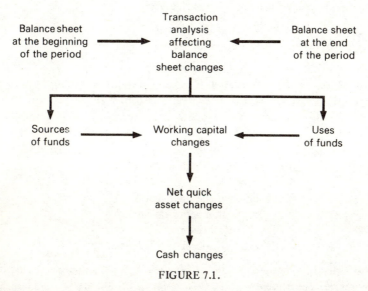

FIGURE 7.1.

Funds analysis is concerned with the funds flow of the business: the changes in its financial structure in terms of the sources of funds that have become available and the way the funds have been used in the accounting period.

The sources of the funds include:

1. Profits earned by the business
2. Increases in long-, medium- and short-term liabilities
3. New capital introduced into the business
4. Reductions in long-, medium- and short-term assets
5. Receipts from the disposal of fixed assets and long-term investments.

The uses of funds include:

1. Losses sustained by the business

2. Reductions in long-, medium- and short-term liabilities
3. Capital withdrawn from the business
4. Dividend payments
5. Increases in medium- and short-term assets
6. Fixed asset and long-term investment purchases.

The sources of funds equal the uses of funds but the interpretation of the movements in the above items governs the form of statement produced. In this chapter, the changes in particular accounts are examined as a preliminary to the preparation of the statements possible from such analysis.

## 7.1 THE PROFIT OR LOSS FOR THE PERIOD

The profit after tax in the profit and loss statement for the period (profit prior to appropriations) needs adjustment for the following:

1. Depreciation and amortisation of fixed assets
2. Profit or loss on the disposal of fixed assets and long-term investments.

Depreciation does not represent a flow of funds and the period change for this item should be cancelled by a reversal of the period transaction. This involves an addition to profit and a reduction of accumulated depreciation.

The profit or loss on disposal of fixed assets is a net figure on the disposal transaction as follows:

| Item | | £ | £ |
|---|---|---|---|
| 1 | Amount received from the disposal of fixed assets | | – |
| 2 | Original cost of the fixed assets | – | |
| 3 | Less accumulated depreciation | – | |
| 4 | Book value of the assets sold | | – |
| 5 | Profit/loss on disposal of fixed assets | | – |

Only the first item represents a flow of funds and the remaining items are cancelled by reversal adjustments:

| Item | Adjustment |
|---|---|
| 2 | Fixed asset values increased by this item |
| 3 | Accumulated depreciation increased by this item |
| 5 | If a profit on disposal, the profit after tax is reduced by this item; if a loss on disposal, the profit after tax is increased by this item. |

If the effect of taxation is to be shown in the funds statement, taxation will be added back to the profit after tax to give the profit before tax figure.

Other adjustments to assets that do not represent a flow of funds such as a bad debts provision or book adjustments for changing price levels should be eliminated from the funds analysis.

## 7.2 INCREASES OR REDUCTIONS IN LONG-, MEDIUM- AND SHORT-TERM LIABILITIES

The profits earned by the business are an important source of funds but it is necessary on occasions to increase the funds available by short- and medium-term loans including the bank overdraft. These funds usually finance needed working capital but the loans concerned may be reduced or eliminated when possible or desired and funds analysis must identify these changes.

This section includes the movement in liabilities other than loans such as, for example, deferred taxation and current liabilities in the form of trade creditors and current tax.

## 7.3 NEW CAPITAL INTRODUCED INTO THE BUSINESS

With a shortage of cash, many companies require an injection of capital not only to finance permanent investment and expansion programmes but also to support the increasing sales in an expanding business which may be under continual pressure for cash to finance the additional working capital required.

## 7.4 INCREASES OR REDUCTIONS IN LONG-, MEDIUM- AND SHORT-TERM ASSETS

The analysis of the profit or loss on the disposal of assets in an earlier section discloses changes in fixed assets which are recorded separately in funds analysis in terms of cash flow. Fixed asset purchases represent significant movements of funds and separate classificaiton of this item is desirable.

If current assets other than cash are increased or decreased these will be shown on a cash flow statement. The significance of this point is that where the source and use of funds is extended beyond the working capital stage the analysis must go further to show the effect of changes in current assets on cash.

## 7.5 CASH FLOW AND WORKING CAPITAL TERMINOLOGY

The type of funds analysis given to management is governed by the stage chosen to show the net result of funds movement. The net result may be shown in terms of:

1. Working capital
2. Net quick assets (another term for liquid items, e.g., the exclusion of stock from current assets)
3. Cash.

There is a considerable body of opinion that identifies 'funds' with working capital. Statements for management may be given the titles:

(a) Working capital changes – the funds flow statement or sources and applications of funds statement

(b) Cash changes – the cash flow statement

(c) Net quick asset changes – the net quick asset flow statement.

## 7.6 AN EXAMPLE OF FUNDS AND CASH FLOW

The analysis of the given data below shows the relationship of the information in the three types of statement that may be produced.

*Data for an accounting period*

| As at 1st January 19.. | | Balance Sheets in £000 | As at 31st December 19.. | |
|---|---|---|---|---|
| £ | £ | | £ | £ |
| | 52 | Ordinary share capital | | 60 |
| | | Revenue reserves | | |
| 2 | | General reserve | 5 | |
| 6 | 8 | Profit and loss account balance | 6 | 11 |
| | 60 | | | 71 |
| | | Current liabilities | | |
| 14 | | Creditors | 15 | |
| 4 | | Taxation | 5 | |
| 2 | 20 | Proposed dividend | 3 | 23 |
| | 80 | | | 94 |
| | 44 | Fixed assets | | 50 |
| | | Current assets | | |
| 15 | | Stock | 20 | |
| 11 | | Debtors | 13 | |
| 10 | 36 | Cash | 11 | 44 |
| | 80 | | | 94 |

*Profit and Loss Statement in £000*
*Year ended 31st December 19..*

| | £ |
|---|---|
| Sales | 34 |
| Less cost of sales | 18 |
| Gross profit | 16 |
| Less expenses | 8 |
| Operating profit | 8 |
| Add profit on sale of fixed assets | 1 |
| Net profit before tax | 9 |
| Less taxation | 3 |
| Net profit after tax | 6 |
| Less proposed dividend | 3 |
| Profit for the year retained | 3 |

*Movement on Fixed Asset Accounts in £000*
*Year ended 31st December 19 . .*

|                                        | £   |
|----------------------------------------|-----|
| Opening balance                        | 44  |
| Add additions at cost                  | 17  |
|                                        | 61  |
| Less disposals (net book value)        | 6   |
|                                        | 55  |
| Less depreciation for the year         | 5   |
| Closing balance                        | 50  |

*Movement in Revenue Accounts in*
*Year ended 31st December 19 . .*

|                                            | General reserve £ | Profit and loss account £ |
|--------------------------------------------|-------------------|---------------------------|
| Opening balances                           | 2                 | 6                         |
| Add profit for the year retained           |                   | 3                         |
| Add/(Deduct) general reserve transfer      | 3                 | (3)                       |
|                                            | 5                 | 6                         |

From the given data the following statements may be prepared:

(*a*)

*Sources and Applications of Funds Statement*
*for the year ended 31st December 19 . . (£000)*

|                                                   | £  | £  |         |
|---------------------------------------------------|----|----|---------|
| *Sources of funds*                                |    |    |         |
| Profit for the year (see note 1 below)            | 2  |    |         |
| Depreciation added back                           | 5  | 7  |         |
| Proceeds from the sale of fixed assets (see note 2) |    | 7  |         |
| Proceeds from issue of ordinary share capital     |    | 8  |         |
|                                                   |    | 22 | (A)     |
| *Application of funds*                            |    |    |         |
| Cost of additional fixed assets                   |    | 17 | (B)     |
| *Increase in working capital* (see note 3)        |    | 5  | (A − B) |

| *Notes:*                                          | £  |
|---------------------------------------------------|----|
| 1.  Profit for the year retained                  | 3  |
|     Less profit on sale of fixed assets           | 1  |
|     Profit for the year used above                | 2  |
|                                                   |    |
| 2.  Disposal of assets (net book value)           | 6  |
|     Add profit on sale of fixed assets            | 1  |
|     Proceeds from sale of fixed assets            | 7  |

|  | £ | £ |
|---|---|---|
| 3. Closing working capital |  |  |
| Current assets | 44 |  |
| Current liabilities | 23 | 21 |
| Opening working capital |  |  |
| Current assets | 36 |  |
| Current liabilities | 20 | 16 |
| Increase in working capital |  | 5 |

(b) (i)

*Cash Flow Statement*
*for the year ended 31st December 19 . . (£000)*

|  | £ | £ |  |
|---|---|---|---|
| *Increase in cash available* |  |  |  |
| Operating profit | 8 |  |  |
| Depreciation for the year added back | 5 | 13 |  |
| Increase in creditors |  | 1 |  |
| Proceeds from issue of ordinary shares |  | 8 |  |
| Proceeds from sale of fixed assets |  | 7 |  |
|  |  | 29 | (A) |
| *Reduction in cash available* |  |  |  |
| Increase in stock |  | 5 |  |
| Increase in debtors |  | 2 |  |
| Cost of additional fixed assets |  | 17 |  |
| Payment of tax (see note below) |  | 2 |  |
| Payment of dividend |  | 2 |  |
|  |  | 28 | (B) |
| *Net increase in cash* |  | 1 | (A − B) |

| *Note:* | £ |
|---|---|
| Opening tax liability | 4 |
| Add taxation provision | 3 |
|  | 7 |
| Less closing tax liability | 5 |
| Tax payment | 2 |

The above statement may be presented as follows:

(ii)                *Cash Flow Statement*
*for the year ended 31st December 19 . . (£000)*

|  | £ |  |
|---|---|---|
| *Opening cash balance* | 10 |  |
| *Receipts* |  |  |
| From customers (see note 1 below) | 32 |  |
| From shareholders | 8 |  |
| From sales of fixed assets | 7 |  |
|  | 57 | (A) |

| *Payments* | £ | |
|---|---|---|
| To suppliers and for expenses (see note 2) | 25 | |
| For additional fixed assets | 17 | |
| For taxation | 2 | |
| Of dividend | 2 | |
| | 46 | (B) |
| *Closing Cash Balance* | 11 | (A − B) |

| *Notes:* | £ |
|---|---|
| 1. Opening debtors balance | 11 |
| Add sales | 34 |
| | 45 |
| Less closing debtors balance | 13 |
| Cash received from customers | 32 |

| 2. Opening creditors balance | | 14 |
|---|---|---|
| Add stock increase | | 5 |
| cost of sales | | 18 |
| expenses | | 8 |
| | £ | 45 |
| Less depreciation | 5 | |
| closing creditors balance | 15 | 20 |
| Payment to suppliers and for expenses | | 25 |

(c)             *Net Quick Asset Flow Statement*
*For the year ended 31st December 19 . . (£000)*

| | £ | £ | |
|---|---|---|---|
| *Sources of funds* | | | |
| Profit for the year retained less profit on the sale of fixed assets | 2 | | |
| Depreciation added back | 5 | 7 | |
| Proceeds from sale of fixed assets | | 7 | |
| Proceeds from issue of ordinary share capital | | 8 | |
| | | 22 | (A) |
| *Application of funds* | | | |
| Cost of additional fixed assets | | 17 | |
| Increase in stock | | 5 | |
| | | 22 | (B) |
| Increase in net quick assets (see note below) | | Nil | (A − B) |

| | £ | £ |
|---|---|---|
| *Note:* | | |
| Closing net quick assets | | |
| Liquid nassets (£13 plus £11) | 24 | |
| Less current liabilities | 23 | 1 |
| Opening net quick assets | | |
| Liquid assets (£11 plus £10) | 21 | |
| Less current liabilities | 20 | 1 |
| | | Nil |

## 7.7  THE WORKING CAPITAL CYCLE

Working capital is the portion of total funds of the company used in current operations of the business and this gives a cycle that starts with the purchase of raw materials increasing creditors. Operating expenses representing the use of resources to convert the material to finished goods creates stock for sale. When the sales are made the debtors increase. Settlement of customers' accounts creates an inflow of cash.

Funds statements provide information as to whether a company is solvent, that is, able to settle its debts and obligations when due. The indication of the extent of the working capital generated in the cycle described above and how it is used can assist management in planning for the future. It is not easy to estimate working capital requirements. Stocks may vary significantly owing to seasonal factors not operating as expected; when the company is expanding, a greater volume of purchases will increase creditors; production delays may affect work-in-progress stocks and customers may be slow in settling their accounts. Sometimes it is difficult for a company to remain solvent and only control of working capital can prevent a serious shortage of funds.

## 7.8  ESTIMATING WORKING CAPITAL REQUIREMENTS

Given estimated data for a year where sales and production are equal and carried on evenly throughout the year of 50 weeks (5-day week).

| *Item* | |
|---|---|
| Sales | 150,000 units at £1 per unit sold on credit |
| | Customers allowed 60 days credit |
| Production cost | |
|    Raw  material | £0·50 per unit. The production cycle is 20 days and all material will be issued at the commencement of each production cycle. Fifty days credit will be taken from suppliers. |
|    Labour | £0·20 per unit |
|    Expenses | £0·25 per unit |
| Cash | One quarter of the average remaining current assets required |
| Stock levels | |
|    Raw materials | 40 days supply |
|    Finished goods | 20 days supply. |

From the data the estimated working capital requirements would be as follows:

|  | £ | £ | *Basis of calculation* |
|---|---|---|---|

Stock

| Raw materials | 12,000 | | $\dfrac{150{,}000 \text{ units}}{250 \text{ days}} \times \dfrac{40}{\text{days}} \times £0\cdot50$ |

Work-in-progress

Work-in-progress in units:

$$\dfrac{150{,}000 \text{ units}}{250 \text{ days}} \times \dfrac{20}{\text{days}}$$

$$= 12{,}000 \text{ units}$$

£

Material:

$$12{,}000 \times £0\cdot50 = 6{,}000$$

Labour: on average
50% complete:

$$6{,}000 \times £0\cdot20 = 1{,}200$$

Expenses: on average
50% complete:

$$6{,}000 \times £0\cdot25 = \underline{1{,}500}$$

|  | 8,700 | | $\underline{8{,}700}$ |
| Finished goods | $\underline{7{,}600}$ | 28,300 | $8{,}000 \times (£0\cdot50 + £0\cdot20 + £0\cdot25)$ |
| Trade debtors | | 36,000 | $\dfrac{150{,}000 \text{ units}}{250 \text{ days}} \times \dfrac{60}{\text{days}} \times £1$ |
| Cash | | 16,075 | $\dfrac{£36{,}000 + £28{,}300}{4}$ |
|  | | 80,375 | |
| Less trade creditors | | 15,000 | $\dfrac{150{,}000 \text{ units}}{250 \text{ days}} \times \dfrac{50}{\text{days}} \times £0\cdot50$ |
| Estimated working capital | | 65,375 | |

## 7.9 THE CONTROL OF CASH

The aim of cash control is to have sufficient funds available to meet all day-to-day operations of the business with the smallest balance of unused cash to allow for contingencies. If too much cash is available, this represents funds lying idle and can reduce the return on capital employed. To obtain a return the surplus cash may be invested in short-term securities so that these funds can be made available when needed. If surplus cash is not likely to be needed in the near future, longer-term securities may be purchased.

When trade is slackening, the cash balance is likely to improve because cash will be received from debtors although purchases and other expenses will be reduced. If trade is improving, the opposite situation will arise and management may be puzzled that rising profits may be accompanied by a reducing cash balance. An effective way of explaining this position to management is to produce a cash flow statement of the type adjusting the profit to give an increase or decrease in cash available (illustration (*b*) (i) in the earlier section).

The control of cash is a difficult task, particularly in large companies, and the free movement of surpluses to centralised bank accounts and the supply of cash to subsidiary companies when needed is usually arranged through the medium of appropriate bank facilities. To prevent a shortage of cash and the danger of being caught by an emergency, careful cash budgeting is a necessity.

## 7.10 THE USES OF THE FUNDS STATEMENTS

The funds and cash flow statements are useful to interpret the quality of the company's financial management. This is accomplished by emphasis on the significant financial changes in the period. This emphasis also enables the management to plan for the future: long-term planning with the help of the sources and applications of funds statement, and short-term planning with the help of the cash flow statement.

The planned sources and application of funds statement gives the relationship between profits and working capital — information of value in debt control and plans for business development. The planned cash flow statement gives management an indication as to whether the expected cash inflow will be sufficient to meet expected short-term cash requirements.

## 7.11 SUMMARY

Funds flows in an accounting period in terms of their sources and applications may be calculated by analysis of the transactions involved in the changes between opening and closing company balance sheets for that period. The statement produced may be limited to working capital changes or the analysis developed further to explain cash movements and plan the funds and cash flow for the future.

## FOR FURTHER STUDY

### QUESTIONS

1. *Comparison of profit statement with funds analysis*
   Why is funds analysis important to management? Compare the funds flow statement and the cash flow statement with the company profit statement.

2. *Alternatives to the cash budget*
   'Cash budget — this budget is the plan of the receipts and payments of cash for

the budget period and for shorter terms, drawn up so that the balance can be forecast at regular intervals.'

(*An Introduction to Budgetary Control*, ICWA)

*Required:*
Some accountants operating systems of budgetary control claim that it is not necessary to draw up a cash budget. Explain what takes its place and indicate how the probable cash position at any time is made available to management.

(ICMA)

3. *The need to check liquidity*
'Many a good business with a full order book and producing goods at a reasonable profit has come to grief through neglecting to keep a close watch on its liquid position; this is a key requirement in all circumstances.'

(L. W. Robson, 'Management accounting from a director's point of view', *The Cost Accountant*, June 1957, p. 15)

*Required:*
Explain and comment on this statement.

4. *Working capital management*
The average daily sales of a wholesale trading company increased from £5,000 per day in period 1 to £6,000 per day in period 2, while the average working capital employed changed as shown in the table.

|  | Period 1 £ | Period 2 £ |
|---|---|---|
| Average daily sales | 5,000 | 6,000 |
| Average working capital employed: |  |  |
| Cash | 41,000 | 2,000 |
| Receivables | 235,000 | 330,000 |
| Inventory | 134,500 | 144,000 |
| Prepaid expenses | 6,500 | 7,000 |
| Total current assets | 417,000 | 483,000 |
| Current liabilities | 156,500 | 244,000 |
|  | 260,500 | 239,000 |

The managing director claims that due to good financial management the rate of working capital turnover has increased.
*Required:*
(a) Check the managing director's calculations.
(b) Add any relevant calculations of your own.
(c) Give your own comments on the financial direction of the company.

(ICMA)

5. *Cash budget on a receipts and payments basis*
A. B. Stores Ltd, a retail business, has provided its planned accounts for the

three months ending 31st August 19 .. as follows:

### AB Stores Ltd
### Budgeted Balance Sheet as at 31st August 19 ..

| 31st May 19.. £000 | £000 | | £000 | £000 |
|---|---|---|---|---|
| 21,250 | | Fixed assets at cost | 22,750 | |
| 4,950 | 16,300 | Less depreciation | 5,150 | 17,600 |
| | | Current assets | | |
| 4,130 | | Stock | 4,330 | |
| 2,070 | | Debtors | 3,820 | |
| 175 | | Loan to associated company | 25 | |
| 80 | | Prepayments | 75 | |
| 1,100 | | Cash | 450 | |
| 7,555 | | | 8,700 | |
| | | Current liabilities | | |
| 2,220 | | Trade creditors | 2,570 | |
| 385 | | Other creditors (wages and expenses) | 630 | |
| 1,775 | | Taxation | 1,875 | |
| 75 | | Debenture interest | 75 | |
| 4,455 | | | 5,150 | |
| | 3,100 | Net current assets | | 3,550 |
| | 19,400 | Total | | 21,150 |
| | | Financed by | | |
| | 12,500 | Ordinary share capital | | 12,500 |
| | 5,400 | Reserves | | 5,650 |
| | 1,500 | 10% debentures | | 3,000 |
| | 19,400 | | | 21,150 |

*Notes on the budgeted balance sheet:*

1. New fixed assets to be purchased during the quarter amount to £2,000,000
2. New debentures to be issued on 1st June 19 ... Interest payable half-yearly, 1st June and 1st December.

### Budgeted Profit Statement
### Quarter ended 31st August 19 ..

| | £000 | £000 |
|---|---|---|
| Sales: Credit | 7,000 | |
| Cash | 5,500 | 12,500 |
| Cost of sales | | 8,050 |
| Gross profit | | 4,450 |

|  |  |  |
|---|---|---|
| Less wages and expenses | 2,350 |  |
| depreciation | 600 | 2,950 |
|  |  | 1,500 |
| Less debenture interest |  | 75 |
| Trading profit prior to tax |  | 1,425 |
| Tax |  | 600 |
|  |  | 825 |
| Proposed 5% interim dividend payable on 31st August 19 .. |  | 625 |
|  |  | 200 |
| Profit on sale of surplus fixed assets |  | 50 |
| Profit retained |  | 250 |

*Required:*

From the above information prepare for A. B. Stores Ltd a cash budget on a receipts and payments basis for the three months ending 31st August 19 . ..

(ICMA)

6. *The working capital flow statement and its relationship to other statements compiled in funds analysis*

The accounts of a company for the last completed year ended 30th April (described as the current year) are summarised below:

*Balance Sheets as at 30th April (£000)*

|  | Current year £ | Previous year £ |  | £ | Current year £ | £ | Previous year £ | £ |
|---|---|---|---|---|---|---|---|---|
| Ordinary share capital | 80 | 80 | Fixed assets |  |  |  |  |  |
|  |  |  | At cost at the beginning of the current year | 200 |  |  |  |  |
| Profit and loss account: £ |  |  | Additions at cost | 30 |  |  |  |  |
| Balance at the beginning of the |  |  |  | 230 |  |  |  |  |
| current |  |  | Less sales | 10 | 220 |  | 200 |  |
| year 65 |  |  | Depreciation provision at the beginning of |  |  |  |  |  |
| Less dividends |  |  | the current |  |  |  |  |  |
| paid 10 |  |  | year | 100 |  |  |  |  |
| 55 |  |  | Additional |  |  |  |  |  |
| Add profit for the |  |  | provision | 8 |  |  |  |  |
|  |  |  |  | 108 |  |  |  |  |
| year 23 | 78 | 65 | Less |  |  |  |  |  |
| Future tax | 10 | 10 | withdrawals | 3 | 105 | 115 | 100 | 100 |
| Mortgage |  |  | Current assets |  |  |  |  |  |
| debentures | 65 | — | Stock and work-in-progress |  | 123 |  | 74 |  |
| Sundry creditors including current taxation | 66 | 66 | Sundry debtors |  | 56 |  | 41 |  |
|  |  |  | Cash at bank and in hand |  | 5 | 184 | 6 | 121 |
|  | 299 | 221 |  |  |  | 299 |  | 221 |

*Profit and Loss Account for the current year (£000)*

|  | Debits £ | Credits £ |
|---|---|---|
| Sales |  | 597 |
| Profit on disposal of fixed assets |  | 3 |
| Works cost of sales | 350 |  |
| Administration expenses | 212 |  |
| Depreciation of fixed assets | 5 |  |
| Provision for taxation | 10 |  |
| Net profit after tax | 23 |  |
|  | 600 | 600 |

*Required:*

Using the above information you are required to:

(*a*) Prepare a working capital flow statement for the current year showing the sources and disposal fo working capital funds.

(*b*) Explain how such a statement differs from a liquid asset flow statement and a cash flow statement.

(*c*) Explain the purpose of these various statements.    (ICMA – Modified)

## 7. *Preparation of monthly cash budget*

X Y Trading Co. Ltd sells on both cash and credit terms. Customers who pay their accounts within 15 days are given a cash discount of 5% and likewise the X Y Co. always pays cash on receipt of purchases in order to obtain a 4% discount. Forecast sales for the next three months are as follows:

|  | June £ | July £ | August £ |
|---|---|---|---|
| Credit sales | 80,000 | 80,000 | 90,000 |
| Cash sales | 20,000 | 25,000 | 27,000 |
| Total sales | 100,000 | 105,000 | 117,000 |

The profit mark-up on sales gives a gross profit margin of 50% on gross cost. It is estimated that the above sales will require a stock of goods of £90,000 in sales value to be maintained.

An analysis of customer accounts discloses that on average only 75% of each month's credit sale customers settle their accounts within the month. Eighty per cent of credit customers pay in time to take advantage of the cash discount, 10% pay at the end of 30 days and the remainder at the end of 60 days. There are virtually no bad debts in this business. Of the 25% who settle their accounts in the month following the month of sale the proportions on average taking the discount and deferring payment are the same as given.

The estimated other expenses payable monthly are as follows:

| Fixed | £14,000 per month |
|---|---|
| Variable | 10% of gross sales. |

Included in the fixed expense is a depreciation charge of £3,000.

A capital payment of £20,000 is required to be made during July. The balances at the beginning of June are as follows:

| | |
|---|---|
| Cash | £16,000 |
| Stock | £50,000 |
| Debtors | £18,000. |

Credit sales for May — a low sales month — were £35,000 of which £14,000 were still outstanding at the end of the month. The remainder of the debtors represent April sales. On average, each month's debtors show the same relationship.

*Required:*

The directors of X Y Trading Co. Ltd have been concerned about the problems of cash shortages and ask you to prepare a cash budget for each of the next three months.                                                (ACA)

8. *Cash flow statement with interpretation*

The summary balance sheets of D. J. W. Co. Ltd as at the beginning and end of the trading year along with the profit and loss account for the year are as follows:

### D. J. W. Co. Ltd
*Summary Balance Sheet as at the end of the current year*

| Last year £ | Share Capital | £ | Last year £ | Fixed Assets | £ |
|---|---|---|---|---|---|
| 195,500 | Ordinary shares | 195,500 | 100,330 | Land/Buildings | 92,830 |
| 40,000 | Redeemable preference shares | 38,000 | 475,000 | Plant/Machinery cost | 569,950 |
| | Reserves | | 104,500 | depreciation | 140,250 |
| | Capital redemption | | 370,500 | | 429,700 |
| — | reserve | 2,000 | 1,230 | Loose tools (at valuation) | 1,870 |
| 26,000 | General | 32,000 | 15,000 | Goodwill | 18,000 |
| 276,000 | Unappropriated profits | 290,970 | 487,060 | | 542,400 |
| 32,000 | *Taxation* | 30,500 | 35,550 | *Trade Investments* | 15,750 |
| 180,000 | *Loans* | 160,000 | | *Current Assets* | |
| | Current Liabilities | | 175,150 | Stock | 160,750 |
| | | | 8,050 | Investments | 4,500 |
| 41,000 | Taxation | 41,313 | 252,090 | Debtors | 280,000 |
| 10,560 | Dividends | 14,717 | 5,750 | Bills receivable | 2,500 |
| 152,500 | Creditors | 160,375 | 500 | Cash | 425 |
| 10,500 | Bank overdraft | 40,950 | | | |
| 964,150 | | 1,006,325 | 964,150 | | 1,006,325 |

*Summary Profit and Loss Account for the current year*

|  | £ | £ | £ |
|---|---:|---:|---:|
| Sales turnover |  |  | 1,100,000 |
| Trading profit (prior to deducting the undernoted items) |  |  | 183,600 |
| Depreciation |  |  |  |
|   Plant and machinery | 46,500 |  |  |
|   Loose tools | 2,500 | 49,000 |  |
| Audit fee |  | 500 |  |
| Directors' remuneration |  |  |  |
|   Fees | 7,500 |  |  |
|   Other remuneration | 37,500 | 45,000 | 94,500 |
|  |  |  | 89,100 |
| Loan interest paid |  |  | 13,600 |
|  |  |  | 75,500 |
| Income from investment |  |  | 2,000 |
| Profit before taxation |  |  | 77,500 |
| Corporation tax based on profit for the year |  |  | 30,500 |
| Net profit for year after Corporation tax |  |  | 47,000 |
| Appropriations |  |  |  |
|   Transfer to General reserve |  | 6,000 |  |
|   Transfer to Capital redemption reserve fund |  | 2,000 |  |
|   Dividends |  | 24,030 | 32,030 |
|  |  |  | 14,970 |
| Unappropriated profits brought forward |  |  | 276,000 |
| Unappropriated profits carried forward |  |  | 290,970 |

*Notes:*

1. During the period, plant and machinery with an original cost of £15,800 and book value of £5,050 was sold for £2,500. The loss on the sale is included in the trading profit of £183,600. There was no gain or loss on the sale of any other assets.
2. Loose tools are valued at the end of each year and depreciation calculated accordingly.

The general manager is disappointed with the results for the year. A pre-tax profit of £77,500 has been achieved which as a percentage of total net assets at 10·3% (based on values as at the end of the year) is no better than the average for the industry. The cash position has deteriorated during the year in that there has been a substantial increase in the bank overdraft. This is particularly disappointing, because during the year the company, through its cost reduction programme and new marketing policy, managed to achieve a net profit margin higher than most other companies in the industry. In addition, the general manager had hoped that in the ensuing period it would have been possible to have built up cash resources in the light of the extension programme he has been contemplating, but now he is doubtful if this can be achieved.

*Required:*

(*a*) Prepare a statement for the general manager highlighting the reasons for the increase in bank overdraft.

(*b*) Comment on the information revealed by the statement you have prepared in (*a*) above, and suggest an area where further investigation might disclose opportunities for improving the company's profitability.                    (ACA)

9. *The relationship between the cash balance and profits*

A business is expanding rapidly, and although the four-weekly accounts presented to management show that a profit is being made, the bank overdraft is increasing. Management is concerned at this increase, and suggests:

(*a*) That your accounts may be overstating the profit

(*b*) That arrangements must be made for an increase in the overdraft facilities.

*Required:*

Draft a report to management, pointing out:

(*a*) That the figures shown in your accounts are to be expected

(*b*) That finance can be provided from within the business by certain improvements in efficiency, which you describe.                    (ICMA)

10. *The control of working capital*

As management accountant you are required to prepare a report for your board of directors on measures which could be used to assist in controlling the level of stocks and total working capital on a regular monthly basis.

To illustrate the measures you propose and their purpose all the following information from the latest available accounts should be used in your report.

|  | *£000* |
|---|---|
| Annual cost of sales | 1,000 |
| Annual purchases of raw materials | 330 |
| Current liabilities (creditors, tax and dividends) | 200 |
| Current assets |  |
| Debtors | 125 |
| Stock of raw materials | 55 |
| Stock of finished goods | 60 |
| Cash | 10 |

(ICMA)

11. *The working capital cycle*

Jim Spencer, the managing director of Nuts & Bolts Ltd, had been reading a financial journal and passed to his accountant the following extract from an article on working capital control:

'Companies pay considerable attention to sales and profits. They increase the sales in an attempt to improve profits. This may be an attractive policy for the business but if followed without a check on the working capital cycle it may encourage over-trading.'

'Working capital requirements vary according to the nature of the business.

A company concentrating on cash trade yet purchasing on credit is in a different position from the company that operates on the opposite basis and needs cash to pay for purchases and finance sales on credit. The cash cycle time represented by the difference between the time when payments must be made before cash is received from customers is vital. In this cycle the stock turnover rate is significant as also the manufacturing time span in its effect on capital held in work-in-progress.'

Jim Spencer wants to know what is meant by 'overtrading' and how they may reduce the working capital cycle for their business.

*Required:*

As the company accountant, reply to Jim Spencer.

12. *Funds analysis as an aid to cash management*

The accountant of Tar Products Ltd has examined the company cash budget for the following year and noted the uneven cash balance between periods. In general, the months in the early period of the year show a steady drain on cash matched by substantial surpluses in the closing three months of the year. This is owing to the maintenance of a constant production rate with materials ordered in the month of production, trade creditors paid by the end of the month and trade debtors allowed two months' credit.

The accountant believes that this uneven cash flow may be altered with advantage if production is co-ordinated with sales needs. He recognises the possible need for lead time both in the ordering of materials and producing the products for sale, and believes that reasonable allowances are to produce one month in advance the expected sales and purchase materials one month in advance of production. Assuming purchases and sales terms as originally planned he modifies the cash budget and finds the early periods of the planned year showing improved balances of cash but closing periods still substantial. This has the effect of considerable deficits of cash in the middle of the year.

The accountant attempts to improve the cash plans further by varying the financing policies to reduce sales terms to one month's credit and negotiate extended credit with raw materials suppliers to two months. In conjunction with these changes he assumes that he can avoid the lead time on production and produce products in the month of sale. His calculations on these assumptions produces an even cash flow between accounting periods and he feels that he has a good basis for discussion with the sales and factory managers.

*Required:*

(a) What changes do you anticipate in the planned period profit statements and balance sheets as a result of the possible changes in the cash budget?

(b) What advantage is the above procedure to the company?

(c) What are the likely reactions of the sales and factory managers to the accountant's proposals?

FURTHER READING

Jaedicke, Robert K. and Sprouse, Robert T. *Accounting Flows: Income, Funds, and Cash.* Prentice-Hall, Englewood Cliffs, New Jersey, 1965. Chapters 5 and 6.

*Statements of Source and Application of Funds.* Statement of Standard Accounting
  Practice No. 10. Accounting Standards Committee, 1975.
Staubus, George J. 'Cash flow analyses and projections'. *Management Accounting*,
  February 1967, pp. 48—57.

# Accounting and Forward Planning

# 8 The Managerial Control Process

## OBJECTIVE OF THE CHAPTER

To outline the nature of the managerial control process to enable the reader to understand the use of accounting techniques in forward planning aspects of the management control system.

## OUTLINE OF THE CHAPTER

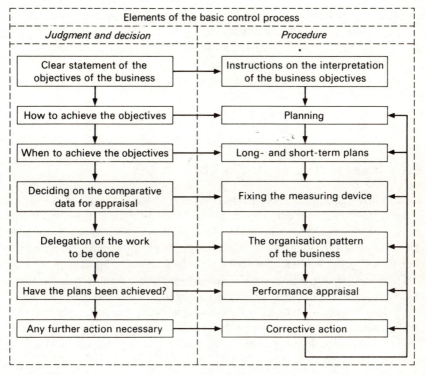

FIGURE 8.1.

A technical process is concerned with the monitoring of performance against technical standards with the feedback of instructions to adjust for variations in the process. It is tempting to compare the control of a business with the control of an automatic technical process but business is not an automatic process. Business is conducted by people with individual skills, experience and attitudes which significantly affect the managerial control process. It is, however, possible to use the technical process analogy to define the elements of the basic control process which are:

1. Establish the business objectives
2. Decide how to achieve the objectives of the business — planning
3. Consider when to achieve the objectives — this involves the integration of long- and short-term planning
4. Ascertain what constitutes good performance — the fixing of standards
5. Decide on who will carry out the plans — fix the responsibility
6. Check that the plans have been achieved — appraisal of performance
7. Decide whether executive action is necessary — corrective action may be necessary starting with the planning phrase and proceeding through the various stages of the control process.

For the effective operation of the basic control process, the following must be operative:

(a) Advice, particularly of a financial nature. The accountant's professional expertise is valuable to the business.
(b) A recognition of the behavioural aspects of management — an individual's motivation, aspirations and aptitudes.
(c) Integration of related areas of management.
(d) The provision of relevant control information.
(e) Communication up and down the traditional lines of management and between the various service departments.

## 8.1 ESTABLISHING BUSINESS OBJECTIVES

For effective management, it is necessary to have a clear statement of the objectives of the business and secondary objectives should be identified as subordinate to the primary objectives of the undertaking. For objectives to be achieved they should be clearly expressed and accepted by managers to the extent that employees may be guided by effective leadership to accomplish the aims of the business.

The nature and establishment of business objectives is developed in greater detail in the next chapter but essentially the company should be looking for profitable opportunities, possibly expanding the business with existing customers or finding new customers either for existing products or for new products to be developed. Objectives may include the aim to achieve cost reduction or the use of additional resources for increased profitability.

## 8.2 PLANNING

To achieve the objectives of the business, it is necessary to determine the action required in a period in the selection and use of resources, techniques and procedures.

This is the planning phase and the concern is with the future rather than the past, although past information may be useful in indicating trends. The latest techniques of forecasting in, for example, the use of market research, may be necessary but managers should watch for signs of any pending change in business activities to be in the position of anticipating the future and alter plans accordingly. Without a plan, changes that are taking place may be unrecognised or, if recognised, their profit impact may be difficult to assess. The following changes are relevant to this assessment:

1. The effect of research and development by competitors on the type of competing products offered to customers
2. Changes in demand owing to population movements or buying habits
3. Changes in the balance between production and sales for the company
4. Fiscal policy changes as a result of the national and international economic climate to the extent that they affect company operation.

The types of information that form the plans for the business may be expressed in different terms but there is only one practical common denominator and that is money. Plans should be expressed in monetary terms to obtain the co-ordination of the planning process. The plans expressed in money terms form an essential tool for the accountant to help managers to control the business.

## 8.3 INTEGRATION OF LONG- AND SHORT-TERM PLANS

Short-term plans are plans that are likely to mature within one year. Long-term plans are likely to extend over a much longer period which may be up to ten or more years from the date of inception. Short-term plans should be integrated with long-term objectives and the following matters are particularly important in this integration:

1. Significant market changes
2. Facility changes — in particular, major policies of contraction or expansion
3. Important product changes
4. Changes in key personnel
5. Fundamental alterations to the structure of the business organisation
6. Finance with particular reference to capital investment
7. Predicted rate of inflation.

Long-term plans are subject to a greater probability of error than short-term plans but they should be conceived to give direction and purpose to current activities. Without the long-term planning, the powerful external factors such as economic, technical and political forces can quickly drive a company off its course of survival or growth.

In the short term, it may not be too difficult to estimate expenditure for the coming year. If management is faced with the problem of estimating the costs associated with an expansion of manufacturing facilities in three years time, existing cost classifications may be of limited use. Much of the existing information which has been collected in the past may also be of limited use since this information will relate to operating conditions different from those under consideration. Inflationary effects are particularly significant in long-term planning. In an attempt to optimise the use of the company's resources and test long-term plans as realistically as possible the company may develop its own company model and use computers to simulate alternative strategies under consideration.

Long-range planning is the responsibility of top management but in a large company, strategic planning advice may come from executives whose task is to try to ascertain where the business should be in the industry in, say, five years time and attempt to judge the risks concerned with the potential growth of segments of the business.

## 8.4 FIXING STANDARDS

Standards are fundamental to the control process. They are established to serve as an incentive to action and as a measuring device in judging the efficiency with which the business is conducted. Finding an adequate standard for comparison with actual results may be difficult. To assist the interpretation of information presented to management some kind of comparable information is usually given. As management information is provided for each control period (week, month or quarter), the previous control period's result in the current year or the same period in the previous year can be used as the comparable information. To establish trends, cumulative information in the current and previous years or moving annual totals may be calculated. If the company is a large group operating comparable businesses, their results may be compared for control purposes, or advantage taken of membership of the Centre for Interfirm Comparison or Trade Association where management ratios or uniform costs may be calculated for comparison. If budgetary control and standard costing are in use, the budget or standard cost may be the comparable information given.

Standards fixed should take account of the progressive increase in operating skill that comes with experience.

## 8.5 FIXING THE RESPONSIBILITY

For managerial control, responsibilities should be defined and accepted. Top management carries a burden which cannot easily be delegated and, in general, it is difficult to decentralise the following responsibilities:

1. The formulation of the general policies of the business
2. The determination of overall company objectives
3. The possible changes in overall company policies and objectives
4. The appraisal of long- and short-term plans for the business

5. The general control of finance with particular reference to major capital expenditure projects.

To delegate responsibility yet maintain control is a difficult aspect of management, particularly bearing in mind that responsibility involves an acceptance of risk by the manager given the authority to discharge a particular function of the business. If the element of risk is an accepted part of the manager's job, the control system should recognise the consequences of this delegated risk-taking. The delegation process should be based on the recognised organisation structure of the business. The distinctive segments of the business will vary with different organisations. In large companies, products or product class divisions may be appropriate; in other companies, functional classifications may be more relevant.

The management of a company is delegated to many managers at various levels of management in the business. Where the accounting system prepares and reports information applicable to a segment of the organisation controlled by a manager the term 'responsibility accounting' may be used.

Managers given responsibility should have the authority to discharge their responsibilities and the choice of men able to manage effectively is of particular importance to the business. Systems of control may be developed until they are applied in their most sophisticated form but, without personnel of the required calibre, efficient operation of the business will not be achieved. Considerable progress has been made in technological factors affecting business operation but the ability to motivate key personnel to achieve the best results possible from the resources available have not been so successful.

## 8.6 THE APPRAISAL OF PERFORMANCE

Appraisal of performance in modern systems of control takes the form of comparing the actual results with the standard that represents good performance. This procedure takes advantage of the management principle of control by exception. This means the direction of management effort to matters requiring their attention such as operations seriously below expected performance. Without the application of this principle, effort may be diffused over all operations showing good and bad performance. In the limited time available for control purposes executives need their attention concentrated on the exceptions rather than on the normal. The techniques of budgetary control and standard costing make use of this principle.

It is not sufficient to measure the difference between the actual results and the standard; the difference should be interpreted and the technique of variance analysis assists in meeting this requirement.

The application of the principle of exception depends on the ability to identify what is significant as compared with what is insignificant. This is a normal feature of accounting practice and is usually a matter of judgement but statistical techniques are being used to an increasing extent in business problems of this type. The danger of relying too much on the exception principle is the implied assumption that conformation to the standard is always desirable whereas departure from the standard is always undesirable. This does not necessarily follow and in the appraisal of performance a broader view is necessary. Performance might be improved by concentrating attention on why a unit has improved on an accepted standard so that the lessons learned may be applied with advantage to other units, rather than directing the effort to eliminate deviations from the plan. Managers should be encouraged at all times to compare their performance with what they could achieve given the will to be really successful at their jobs.

## 8.7  EXECUTIVE ACTION

The reporting of the performance against the plan may indicate action that should be taken to maintain the required standard of business efficiency. Management should respond to opportunities as they arise and changes in events which demand managerial attention. It follows that however efficient the data processing and the reporting service may be this does not alter the need for management decisions to be made and action taken as a result of these decisions.

The standard of management may be poor and the reluctance to take decisions may take the form of using every opportunity to postpone action, particularly if as a result of making a decision the manager will be unpopular with his associates or staff.

It is unfortunately true that many business decisions have to be made without an adequate background of facts, owing to the information not being available or the cost of providing the information being prohibitive. To refrain from taking action when the information provided indicates that this is necessary is to neglect the responsibility of the management function.

## 8.8  GUIDANCE TO MANAGEMENT AND THE COMMUNICATIONS PROBLEM

For the control system of the business to be effective it should be understood at all levels of management. All too often, members of an organisation can feel isolated and management difficulties be traced to poor communication. The manager should be able to communicate effectively so that his staff can work as a team. Departmental productivity is dependent on the communication of relevant information for each employee to perform his job in a satisfactory manner. This information includes a statement of departmental objectives and how these objectives are to be achieved by personal endeavour.

Good communication is more important as companies increase in size, decentralise work programmes, attempt greater specialisation, and when technical progress accelerates.

## 8.9 THE CONTROL OF COSTS IN DIFFERENT TYPES OF BUSINESS ACTIVITY

In the manufacturing sections of the business a significant proportion of cost is particular to the products manufactured. The product specification determines the qualities and costs of the elements incurred in manufacture, and control of actual expenditure is, therefore, facilitated. In the non-manufacturing sections of the business the costs are principally non-variable and it is difficult to select a unit against which such costs can be measured. The control of non-manufacturing costs is possible by greater reliance on the experience and personal judgement of the manager responsible for authorising expenditure.

## 8.10 TYPES OF CONTROL SYSTEMS

The procedures designed to achieve the objectives of the business efficiently and effectively are collectively known as the system. In systems terminology, there are three types of control system:

1. The deterministic system – there is no intervention by the manager until a breakdown of the process occurs. This implies the incorporation in the system of a control mechanism to maintain automatically the process operating efficiently and effectively.
2. The probabilistic system – there is periodic intervention by the manager for the purpose of adjusting or otherwise influencing the process. The states in the system may have varying probabilities of achievement.
3. The adaptive system – there is intervention based on the information obtained from the process. The information and possible intervention is continuous as, for example, when actual results are compared with plans to ensure the business is on course.

## 8.11 BEHAVIOURAL ASPECTS OF MANAGEMENT

Effective performance depends on individual employees being motivated to do a good job and, in general, staff will respond if they are made to feel an important part of the company. Managers are responsible for creating the right atmosphere for business success; an apathetic management breeds apathy on the part of staff. By comparison, a go-ahead enthusiastic manager can encourage others to adopt the same attitude to their work.

Accounting criteria for evaluating performance is often criticised* but the

---

* Professors Backer and Jacobsen give three criticisms:
'(a) Accounting criteria are regarded by supervisory personnel as pressure instruments.
(b) Accounting performance standards arouse inter-departmental conflicts.
(c) Accounting performance standards lack flexibility.'
*Cost Accounting – a Managerial Approach* (McGraw-Hill, New York, 1964), p. 409.

financial form of motivation is particularly relevant to business control, providing it is supported by praise and criticism and rewards and penalties as necessary.

The manager should attempt to understand the objectives and ambitions of his subordinates so that it is possible to identify the aims of the individual with company objectives.

## 8.12  CO-ORDINATION OF BUSINESS ACTIVITIES

The efforts of different sections of management should be co-ordinated to achieve maximum efficiency but this is more easily said than done. A technique such as budgetary control can be of help with this problem. Any effort in this direction will be rewarded since it is not uncommon to find that co-ordinated business activity has a combined total effect of greater value to the business than the sum of individual actions taken in isolation.

In the practical situation, co-ordination involves making the most of the resources available by attempting to remove conflicts between functional managers. These managers may be working, probably to the best of their ability, in their own sections without realising the full effect of the interrelationship of their work with other departments. Integrated systems analysis can help with this problem and the control process can attempt to recognise the strengths and weaknesses in the company. In this way the maximum advantage can be taken of the strong points in the company and effort directed to improve the weak areas at the earliest opportunity.

A company system is made up of a number of sub-systems that perform basic functions. The review of sub-systems within the main system is essential to optimise the integrated total system. The aim should be to secure the effective working of system segments that interact properly in the company system.

## 8.13  THE PROVISION OF INFORMATION

Control can only be effective where the information service is tailored to the specific management needs of every key executive. The required information should be available when it is wanted and adequate for the purpose intended, provided the cost of supplying that information is reasonable. High levels of accuracy increase the cost of supplying that information and the level of accuracy adopted should be relative to the control problem. Control information should not be unduly delayed because a delay in the provision of information may prompt executive action that is too late to correct an unsatisfactory tendency in the business. It may also induce an instability referred to in systems terminology as oscillation: this is corrective action exceeding the limits of desirable activity. If the corrective action could have been taken in time it is expected that activity changes would not exceed the desirable limits.

Information is required at every stage of the management control process and the information flow is continuous. The information flow related to the management control process is illustrated in Figure 8.2.

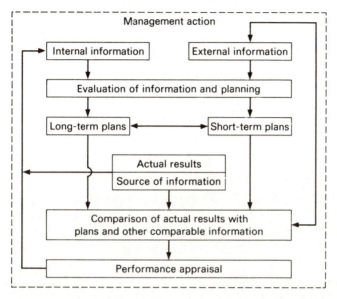

FIGURE 8.2. Information flow and the management control process

## 8.14 THE PLACE OF THE ACCOUNTANT IN THE CONTROL PROCESS

The line authority of the management accountant is limited to his own department but in the choice of relevant information for management, with the interpretation where necessary, the accountant performs a control task far outside the limits of his own department. Many accountants fall short of this standard of service to management but the new generation of managers are no longer mystified by the accountant's terminology. If managers do not receive this standard of performance from the accountant they will go to other specialists willing and able to take a dynamic role in the top management team controlling the business.

## 8.15 SUMMARY

Managerial control begins when there is a clear statement of the objectives of the business and policies are agreed at top management level to achieve the objectives. The objectives are given detailed expression in the plans for the business and the achievement of the objectives is made possible by managers being held accountable for any deviations from the plans. The control mechanism is developed to a high level when an integrated system is operational in the business with the accountant satisfying management needs for information using modern procedures and business methods.

## FOR FURTHER STUDY

QUESTIONS

1. *Meaning and principles of cost control*
Write an essay on cost control dealing with its meaning, principles and techniques, and describe briefly the part which cost control plays in business management.                                                           (ACA)

2. *Essential aspects of cost control*
An existing business sytem lacks the essential aspects of cost control.
*Required:*
List the main matters to be introduced to make good the system's deficiencies.
                                                                        (ICMA)

3. *Nature and scope of the managerial control process*
Discuss the nature and scope of the managerial control process making appropriate references in your answer to
(*a*)  Organisation structure
(*b*)  The planning and control functions of management
(*c*)  The principle of management by exception.                        (ACA)

4. *Responsibility accounting*
It has been decided to introduce a system of responsibility accounting in your company.
*Required:*
What do you understand by the term 'responsibility accounting' and what matters have to be decided before such a system is introduced.

5. *Accounting techniques and the managerial control process*
'By control is meant the guiding of the company towards a pre-determined objective by means of pre-determined policies and decisions.'
*Required:*
Comment on this statement in relation to the accounting techniques which it presupposes are in use.                                          (ACA)

6. *Integration of control techniques*
One of the criticisms frequently levelled at industrial management is that although control systems are introduced into manufacturing units, these controls are rarely integrated with one another.
*Required:*
If one accepts that the main controls required are of output, its quality and

cost, what contribution would you, as management accountant, make towards integration of cost control techniques with production control and quality control.                                                                (ICMA)

7. *Financial control in the non-manufacturing sections of the business*
Discuss the special problems which arise in establishing financial control in the non-manufacturing sections of the business.

8. *Types of control systems*
The control system is a plan formulated by management to indicate when intervention should take place. Three types of control systems are generally possible. The first involves no intervention by the manager until a breakdown of the process occurs. The second type of control system consists of periodic intervention by the manager for the purposes of adjusting or otherwise influencing the process. The third approach bases the intervention decision on the information obtained from the process.
*Required:*
Discuss the features involved in selecting a particular type of control system and the information necessary to operate it.                                (ICMA)

9. *The relevance of the accounting process to cost control*
'Cost control is not exclusively or even primarily an accounting process, although accounting methods do have an important part to play in cost control. In general, control of operations must precede control of cost.'
*Required:*
Explain and comment on this statement.

10. *The planning and control of material costs*
One of the most important functions of the management accounting department is to assist in the planning and control of material costs.
*Required:*
Name three other departments whose assistance would be required. Indicate why this is so and specify an accounting function in relation to material control for which this co-operation is essential.                                (ACA)

11. *The application of management control*
Three interviews with three company executives are recorded below.

*Company 1*

*Interviewer:* When you started your career as an executive in research and development with the company, what management problems did you find?
*Executive:* The problem was to get the basic information I wanted. It was also difficult to get the money needed and understand the costs involved to substantiate my case for needed finance. It was also a problem to control the spending of the money. If one overspends and doesn't attain the objective one can be in real trouble.

*Interviewer:* Did you find the accountant a help with the problems?

*Executive:* Yes. Unfortunately, the accountant's job tends to put him in opposition to everybody else. He tends to be the pessimist in the company. When one is enthusiastic about a project he seems to find the weak spots and dampen the enthusiasm.

*Interviewer:* When you went into general management what did you regard as your key problem?

*Executive:* I think supply is the key problem — the supply of raw materials inwards and the supply of manufactured goods outwards. The efficient control of total supply seems to be the key to considerable savings in cost and increases in efficiency. Such control must occupy a central point in many manufacturing businesses.

*Interviewer:* Referring to the information requirement mentioned earlier. How do you ensure that the things that are going wrong are communicated to you?

*Executive:* This is a case of using management control techniques if you are in a large organisation. In the small company there is no communication problem: such a manager can see for himself what is going wrong. A large organisation can go badly wrong and managers not be aware of the situation unless you have the system to feed back the information. In a large organisation, this means mass data handling. Tight control is important with the rapid response to changing situations.

*Interviewer:* In your experience, has the control system supplied you with the information needed to solve the problem of the business off course?

*Executive:* Not always. Further research has often been needed to get the facts behind evidence of something going wrong.

*Interviewer:* Have the facts usually surprised you?

*Executive:* Often, but part of the solution is finding the specific problem to be solved which is not necessarily the apparent problem.

## Company 2

*Interviewer:* Are the principles of business management the same when applied to the big company as to the small company?

*Executive:* I think the principles of business management are the same for a company, large or small. It's carrying out the principles that must be different.

*Interviewer:* In a large organisation there must be considerable delegation. Is delegation easy?

*Executive:* No. A manager usually thinks he can do a job better than his subordinate and having delegated the task there is a temptation to interfere. This should be resisted. Unless management are prepared to delegate and let people use their initiative they will certainly not reap the potential from the individual.

*Interviewer:* Do the junior management levels have an opportunity to state their views to top management?

*Executive:* Yes. I try to discuss policies with junior managers whenever possible.

*Interviewer:* Is there a danger that you will short-circuit the chain of command?

*Executive:* Not on the broad issues. Top management is concerned with the broad issues — other people are employed to deal with the detail.

*Interviewer:* As a member of top management do you need to have an extensive knowledge of accountancy, statistics, technical manufacturing and marketing?

*Executive:* A person with such extensive knowledge would be a remarkable person. What top management needs is the capacity to ask the right questions and make a judgement on the expert advice given.

### Company 3

*Interviewer:* What special management problem have you faced in your industry?

*Executive:* Finding the best managers.

*Interviewer:* You have tended to let the managers appointed exercise considerable personal initiative. Did this approach provide you with a big problem of co-ordination and control?

*Executive:* Not in the early stages of the growth of the company. As the company has grown we have met the problem of co-ordination by centralizing a number of activities.

*Interviewer:* How much influence does the managing director have in a company like yours?

*Executive:* Enormous. Management is a team effort but the managing director's personality must pervade the organisation. Other members of top management must also significantly influence others in the business.

*Interviewer:* What modern management technique or techniques have you employed successfully?

*Executive:* The most fundamental technique is planning ahead for about five years and then setting detailed targets for each section of the business to make sure that the plans are achieved.

*Interviewer:* Do you have a very long chain of command in your business?

*Executive:* No — we have it as short as possible. The shorter the chain of command the quicker things get done.

*Interviewer:* Your background is in financial management. How have you managed to develop your company to its present position?

*Executive:* I didn't do it. We did it as a team. I was able to add to the team elements that were missing such as financial management and forward planning.

*Required:*

Discuss the implications of the statements made by the executives in the three companies in the context of the management control process.

**12.** *Managerial style and the management control process*

Joe Sprocket is an ambitious executive of Chain Supplies Ltd, and has attended a business management course and studied the nature of management, its elements, foundation and structure. One seminar impressed him considerably. The course members were asked to clarify their own ideas of what constituted good management. They attempted to rate their own performance and management style. After discussion of a number of work situations, each team member assessed the performance of the individual manager. The managers then compared their own rating with the later assessments given by team members. Joe found that management style was concerned with two key elements: the practical side in terms of the use of resources, and the personal side in terms of personal relationships.

*Required:*

How may the key elements of managerial style be integrated in the context of the managerial control process?

## FURTHER READING

Brech, E. F. L., *Organisation – the Framework of Management.* Longmans, Green, 1957. Chapters 1 to 5.

Bruns, Jr., William J. and DeCoster, Don T. *Accounting and its Behavioural Implications.* McGraw-Hill, New York, 1969. Section IV.

Donald, A. G. 'Explaining system concepts'. *Management Accounting,* March 1970, pp. 103–105.

# 9 Business Objectives

OBJECTIVE OF THE CHAPTER

To show the importance of defining the long- and short-term objectives of the business, the nature of these objectives, and the involvement of managers in this process.

OUTLINE OF THE CHAPTER

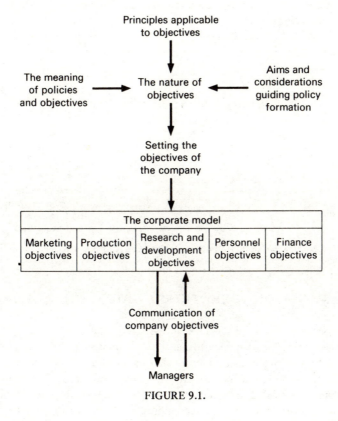

FIGURE 9.1.

A business control system begins with the recognition of objectives by every manager whose performance affects the future of the business. It is fundamental, therefore, to the management control process.

159

## 9.1 THE MEANING OF POLICIES AND OBJECTIVES

A policy is a company's decision to be continually applied to repetitive problems, providing the conditions that formed the basis of the decision have not changed. An objective is a company goal to be used to guide the company managers in managing the business. Both terms are linked in the management control process where managers implement policies to accomplish objectives. A policy is a general statement and an objective a specific statement of intent. For example:

A policy statement: to distribute the products of the company nationally
An objective: to establish distribution facilities in a regional network so that company products will be distributed throughout Great Britain by the end of 19. . .

Policies have a curious relationship in company operations because they appear to have a primary role in moving from the general to the specific yet arise out of and reflect company objectives. To be significant, policies should affect company results by clarifying objectives for the business and personnel ordered to apply the policies in day-to-day management.

The relationship between policies and objectives and the control process is illustrated in Figure 9.2.

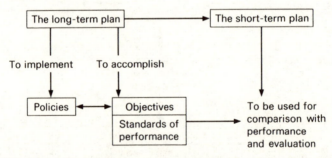

FIGURE 9.2. The relationship of policies and objectives to the management control process

## 9.2 AIMS AND CONSIDERATIONS GUIDING POLICY FORMATION

Before proceeding from the general to the specific a company should establish its aims and considerations in policy formation. It is unusual in Great Britain for companies to publish this information believing that their operating activities imply a general attitude to the factors affecting the survival and prosperity of the business. To a certain extent this is true, but the apparent vagueness of general beliefs in this area requires deeper inquiry and direct expression to emphasise company ethics and the philosophy of management.

Typical aims and considerations cover the following:

1. The type of business to be operated at a profit, e.g., a diversified manufacturing

business. This heading may also include the general types of products manufactured and the type and extent of their projected markets.

2. The product quality characteristics, e.g., good products supplied at fair prices
relative to consumer needs.

3. The approach to company growth, e.g., attitudes to research and development
and company acquisitions with, possibly, a statement of considerations affecting
take-over ethics.

4. Management calibre, e.g., the expected quality of management personnel and
their personal commitment and integrity.

5. Staff terms and conditions of employment, e.g., a statement of the framework to
produce a loyalty, satisfaction and identity with the company only possible by
sustained good industrial relations.

6. The continuity and long-term future for the business. This point might include
statements on brand identity.

7. Public relations, e.g., the recognition of the implications of company actions on
wide groups of people and responsibilities towards local, national and international
society.

8. To foster the confidence and co-operation of all groups in association with the
company to achieve its objectives.


## 9.3 PRINCIPLES APPLICABLE TO OBJECTIVES

In emphasising the segments of the company where it is vital to be effective, certain
principles are applicable to objectives. Professor Strong gives five principles:*

1. The principle of acceptability
2. The principle of attainability
3. The motivational principle
4. The principle of simplicity
5. The principle of communication.

Managers should understand that they are expected to attain the objectives
applicable to their responsibility in the organisation. The best results are likely to
be achieved where the objectives are framed in such a way as to be acceptable to
all personnel responsible for implementing them.

Objectives should be realistic. They should be possible of attainment under
efficient operation of existing or proposed facilities, and they should be attainable
within a reasonable period. The balancing of long- and short-term objectives is
particularly important in this context.

Co-operative effort is so necessary to efficient management that any attempt
made to secure the required result at all levels will be a valuable contribution to the
production of significant results. The motivation should be at the highest level

*Earl P. Strong. *The Management of Business—An Introduction.* (Harper & Row, New York,
and John Weatherhill, New York, 1965), pp. 491–2.

incorporating social and other ideals not capable of measurement in monetary terms.

A multiplicity of objectives for any one manager will clearly work against their attainment and the more simply the objectives can be stated the better.

Objectives should be linked with responsibility levels and secondary objectives may be developed from the primary objectives for levels of responsibility below top management. For example, the primary objective may be to increase the return on capital invested from 19% to 20% by the end of the year. One of the secondary objectives to secure this attainment may be to increase the stock turnover rate by 10% and reduce stock levels accordingly in the same period. The primary objective may be linked with the managing director while the secondary objective may be linked with the materials controller. The relationship of the primary and secondary objectives to the levels of management is illustrated in Figure 9.3.

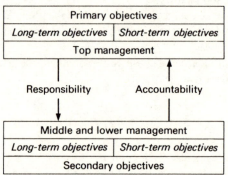

FIGURE 9.3. The relationship of primary and secondary objectives to levels of management

## 9.4 THE NATURE OF OBJECTIVES

Management literature emphasises the multiple responsibilities of management but most companies are profit orientated and it may be expected that key objectives reflect this factor for business success. The nature of objectives for a specific business will reflect the key features of the industry which include:

1. *The profit pattern for the industry.* Profit stability is a characteristic of some types of business but in others wide fluctuations in profitability are almost inevitable owing to the nature of the trade undertaken.
2. *The cost structure of the industry.* Proportions of total costs applicable to elements of cost are likely to be dictated by the type of goods manufactured. For example, 70% of total cost may be the cost of the material used in producing the product.
3. *Industry production control difficulties.* In some industries it can be difficult to balance work programmes to use machinery to maximum advantage.
4. *Development opportunities in the industry.* These opportunities may be restricted in a declining industry.

Attempts may be made by companies to overcome profit instability or the other difficulties of an industry by extending company activities to other areas where greater opportunities for profitable development are possible. This may be difficult and some companies may be forced to recognise as their primary objective the ability to remain in business.

The number and variety of business objectives is almost limitless and selection is necessary. The objectives that may be considered are suggested in the next section.

## 9.5  SETTING THE OBJECTIVES OF THE COMPANY

The fixing of objectives is closely linked to the company's organisation structure typically illustrated in Figure 1.6. At the first level of responsibility, the overall objective is usually earning the required return on the funds invested in the business, consistent with maintaining the sound financial position of the business. At the second level of responsibility, typical functional objectives that may be fixed are related to the following functions:

1. Marketing
2. Production
3. Research and development
4. Personnel
5. Finance.

At the third level of responsibility, sectional objectives may be developed to secure the functional objectives. These may be analysed further at the fourth level where 'front-line' activity takes place to achieve overall objectives.

### 9.51  MARKETING OBJECTIVES

To establish marketing objectives, answers are required to the following questions:

1. What is the overall strategy of the company relative to the marketing function?
   In what direction is the company moving?
   Where could or where should the company be moving?
2. What is the present market share?
   What could or should the market share be?
   How can the market share be improved?
   What are the strategies of competitors?
   What are the profit implications of variations in the market share?
3. What is the company success rate in achieving sales targets?
   What effect have various selling methods on sales achievement?
   What are the acceptable levels of sales expenditure for specific sales levels?
4. What is the effect of price changes on product demand?
   What is the effect of order size on pricing and demand?
   What price changes are required in order to secure the required profit return on investment?

5.  What distribution methods are applicable to company products?
    How may the distribution methods be improved for company products?
    What are the acceptable levels of distribution costs?

From answers to the above questions, typical marketing objectives include the following:

(a)  To produce products to satisfy customers in terms of quality and value for money
(b)  To improve market penetration with existing products
(c)  To replace declining sales on products that have passed their peak with new products
(d)  To effect price changes to secure a more balanced price structure, including a review of discount policy
(e)  To increase the effectiveness of sales staff in terms not only of sales level but also of sales costs and profitability of products sold
(f)  To improve distribution methods including support facilities such as dealer services
(g)  To review advertising effectiveness and redirect resources into better publicity media
(h)  To introduce revised sales incentive plans to secure improved sales performance
(i)  To change sales territory coverage to maximise market potential
(j)  To improve delivery service to customers by improved finished goods stock control
(k)  To develop market intelligence services to secure relevant information to improve the quality of marketing decisions.

Marketing operates in an area in which many factors affecting the business are uncontrollable by individual companies, government regulations significantly affecting businesses to an increasing extent. The company should aim to control as many as possible of its activities, for example, in the areas of product mix and advertising. It should also seek to exert an influence favourable to the company in respect of customer reaction to its products. The business should aim to take advantage of weaknesses in competitor strategy and capitalise on company strength.

## 9.52 PRODUCTION OBJECTIVES

To establish production objectives answers are required to the following questions:

1.  What are the products required to meet marketing requirements?
    What changes could or should be made to existing products?
    What new products are expected to be introduced?
2.  Are product controls satisfactory in the area of value analysis, design and quality standards?
    Are product designs all they should be?
    Are quality specifications reviewed and accurate?
    Is scrap and rectification adequately controlled?

3. What are the production resources available to the company?
   How could or should production resources be extended?
   How can existing production resources be improved?
   What time-scale is involved in securing needed plant improvements?
4. Are support facilities such as plant maintenance adequate and effective?
5. Is purchasing of raw materials controlled satisfactorily?
   Are purchasing procedures effective?
   Are purchasing objectives being achieved compatible with the requirements of
   the production departments?
6. Is raw material and work-in-progress effectively controlled?
   Are obsolete stocks retained?
   Is raw material used as effectively as possible?
   Are raw material stocks minimised consistent with ensuring supplies are available
   when required?
7. Are production control procedures effective?
   Are balanced work programmes in relation to sales requirements usually achieved?
   When work requirements change, is the system sufficiently flexible to deal with
   the situation without undue dislocation?
   Are related activities effectively co-ordinated to secure maximum plant utilisa-
   tion?
8. Is labour effectively controlled?
   Is indirect labour effectively controlled?
   Are employee relationships conducive to achieving reasonable standards of
   productivity?

From answers to the above questions typical production objectives include the
following:

(a) To produce an even flow of production according to the production schedule
    which in turn depends on marketing needs
(b) To ensure that the products produced are to the required quality standards
(c) To control raw materials, purchased parts and sub-assemblies, consumable
    stores and work-in-progress at acceptable levels consistent with supply require-
    ments
(d) To reduce wastage in product manufacture and improve yield percentages
(e) To improve the design of products causing manufacturing difficulties and
    alter methods as necessary
(f) To negotiate new sources of supply of materials where existing contracts are
    not satisfactory to the company
(g) To review product specifications regarding labour use and improve manpower
    utilisation
(h) To secure improvements in machine efficiency including set-up times, work or
    tool change-over periods and breakdown experience
(i) To facilitate the rearrangement, replacement or expansion of plant and
    machinery to secure the most effective use of the production resources
(j) To develop improved production methods

(*k*) To remove production bottlenecks experienced in sections of the plant at stated periods.

The type of manufacture carried out and whether products are manufactured to customer specifications or for stock affects many of the issues described in this section. Objectives should recognise the type of organisation.


## 9.53 RESEARCH AND DEVELOPMENT OBJECTIVES

To establish research and development objectives answers are required to the following questions:

1. What major changes are required in the company in the future?
   New or improved products?
   New applications of materials?
   New or improved methods?
2. What means are or should be employed to secure the changes needed?
   What proportions of effort and cost should be devoted to pure and applied research?
3. To what questions or problems are specific projects directed to provide the answers?
   What are the priorities?
   What is the value of the research result to be obtained?
   How is the research result to be applied?
4. How many research and development projects be evaluated?
   What is the impact of new products on product line strategy, product elimination, future years performance and competitors' reaction?
5. What exploratory work has been done which may indicate lines along which further investigation may proceed?
   What references are available to relevant reports or other literature?

From answers to the above questions, typical research and development objectives include the following:

(*a*) To provide research facilities adequate for the programmes of pure and applied research considered desirable for the business and to finance such activities in a systematic manner
(*b*) To improve the evaluation of research and development work
(*c*) To carry out research to provide new products, methods and procedures for the company
(*d*) To convert the results of research into commercially viable products and procedures
(*e*) To secure the growth of the business by the introduction of new products that are timed to meet marketing requirements, production requirements and maintain the company in a significant position relative to competitors
(*f*) To control research projects in an attempt to obtain the results anticipated

when the proposal for research and development was accepted as a project for the business

(g) To secure results in accordance with the strategic decisions of the business.

Research and development requires long-range planning and the company must be able to capitalise on the results of this research by appropriate changes in the business. There is always resistance to change and the planning should include a determination to overcome such resistance so that expenditure on research and development can be justified.

## 9.54 PERSONNEL OBJECTIVES

To establish personnel objectives answers are required to the following questions:

1. Is the organisation structure of the business satisfactory?
   Does the structure of the business facilitate the work of the company?
   Does the structure of the business facilitate the integration of related activities and promote staff co-operation?
2. Is management development planned and related to promotion, training and selection procedures?
   What opportunities will be granted to managers and potential managers to give their best performance in their present jobs and advance with the company?
   How will the company ensure that the skills of managers are developed to meet the needs of the future?
   How may a management development programme be operated to provide the number and type of managers that will be needed in the future?
3. Is the personnel function operating within the framework of sound personnel policies?
4. How might personal relationships in the business be improved?

From answers to the above questions, typical personnel objectives include the following:

(a) To engage in manpower planning to anticipate staff requirements at all levels and provide the organisation to satisfy the needs identified
(b) To fill appointments, whenever possible, through promotion and transfer
(c) To train staff of the required potential to fill anticipated vacancies
(d) To relate jobs by job analysis and description to identify the characteristics required by a good employee
(e) To improve selection procedures to enable the company to secure the best employees possible
(f) To improve placement procedures to ensure that staff are placed in jobs best suited to their qualifications and experience
(g) To improve personnel records so that sound personnel action may be taken on the basis of reliable staff information
(h) To establish reasonable terms and conditions of employment
(i) To reduce labour turnover to a reasonable level for the type of business undertaken.

The overall requirement of personnel objectives is to secure the right quality of staff when and where they are required to carry out the efficient operations of the business. Adequate terms and conditions of employment are necessary to satisfy and motivate personnel in the interests of the business, bearing in mind government legislation affecting these factors such as restrictions on wage and salary levels.

## 9.55 FINANCE OBJECTIVES

To establish finance objectives answers are required to the following questions:

1. What financial resources are available to the company?
2. What could or should the financial resources be in order to meet current and future requirements of the business?
3. How can the company resources be improved and what are the important timing considerations to obtain this improvement?
4. Are the key factors affecting business performance clearly identified and controlled?
5. What is the company's return on investment and how may it be improved to the return considered desirable?
6. Does the accounting system make an effective contribution to the management of the company?

From answers to the above questions, typical finance objectives include the following:

(a) To provide the finance to enable the business to carry out its planned operations
(b) To secure the best mix of sources of finance and allocation to the activities of the business to optimise the use of finance in the company
(c) To use the resources of the business effectively to achieve overall objectives
(d) To secure adequate cash flows within control periods to balance short-term needs with long-term demands
(e) To obtain a balanced financial structure for the business between equity and loan capital and between fixed and working capital
(f) To incorporate in the financial planning growth requirements realistically fixed for the business within a reasonable time-scale
(g) To provide a return to shareholders indicative of the stability and strength of the enterprise related to funds to be retained in the business to finance the future growth of the business
(h) To invest short-term funds surplus to current requirements in temporary investments to obtain some return on idle cash.

Long-term financial planning is essential to ensure the survival of the business and satisfy the needs of investors and other claimants on the company. The use of techniques such as budgetary control can identify the financial implications of management plans and materially assist in the achievement of the planned objectives in all areas of the business.

## 9.6 COMMUNICATION OF COMPANY OBJECTIVES

All managers should be deeply involved in the achievement of company objectives and this implies that appropriate objectives are effectively communicated to all concerned. This aim is assisted if objectives are in written form to specific managers, and meetings held to remove any misunderstanding. The quality of staff affects the understanding of objectives. It is an educative task to get lower management to understand what is being done and why.

## 9.7 THE CORPORATE MODEL AND BUSINESS OBJECTIVES

The different assumptions made in fixing objectives should be evaluated and their consequences individually determined. A useful technique for this purpose is corporate modelling where the quantifiable aspects of company plans are expressed in mathematical terms identifying rules and relationships which can be used to simulate business problems in an attempt to reduce the areas of uncertainty. Models can be manipulated and analysed and where they are complex, as in the corporate planning area, computers are frequently used. Development of the model needs management involvement, considerable financial knowledge and a volume of relevant input data. The accountant can make an effective contribution to corporate planning in providing the financial input data to be used for selecting specific objectives.

## 9.8 MANAGEMENT BY OBJECTIVES

The need to define objectives for individuals and the company when linked with management development and appraisal may be termed management by objectives. This systematic approach to management involves the control and review of assigned objectives to specific managers. The manager participates in setting the objectives to the extent of stating his own objectives for the resources he controls. If these are agreed, in relation to company objectives, they become a commitment that the manager seeks to accomplish through the medium of personal development, concentration on the key result areas of his job, use of facilities made available and the use of control information on the progress being made.

## 9.9 SUMMARY

The successful company emphasises areas of the business where it is vital to be effective by considering where the business must be in one, three, five or more years time; how it is going to get there from the position it is in now; and defining the part to be played by each key executive to overcome problems that could prevent the company achieving its overall objectives. The quality of management is vital in this process and if the development of staff can be incorporated in the task greater success is likely.

## FOR FURTHER STUDY

### QUESTIONS

1. *Policy formation and its relationship to business objectives*
   What is a business policy and what is its relationship to the business objective? How should a new policy be established or an existing policy altered?

2. *Principles applicable to objectives*
   What are the principles applicable to the formation and use of company objectives as an essential feature of the management control process?

3. *Communicating objectives*
   Describe the methods that may be used by a company to communicate its objectives to managers.

4. *Nature of objectives for business success*
   What are the requirements for company success that should be incorporated in business objectives?

5. *Fixing the overall objectives of the business*
   What questions should be asked in trying to define the overall objectives of the business?

6. *Objectives reflecting the key features of an industry*
   The nature of objectives for a specific business will reflect the key features of the industry.
   *Required:*
   Give the key features of an industry with which you are familiar, explaining the implication of each feature on setting company objectives.

7. *Company response to changes in the business environment*
   In fixing objectives, consideration must be given to the business environment which is changing continually.
   *Required:*
   Classify the changes in a company's business environment that may be expected and comment on how these changes may be used to profit the company.

8. *Importance of defining objectives*
   'A cost control system cannot be made operational in an organisation until objectives have been defined and a planning system based on these objectives implemented.'
   *Required:*
   Comment on this statement.                                      (ACA)

**9.** *Policy considerations in connexion with automation*

Your board is about to make a policy decision on the subject of the installation of an expensive piece of automated equipment which will result in the redundancy of a considerable amount of semi-skilled labour.

*Required:*

The board requires you to brief them on policy considerations which require to be taken into account. Do so.                                    (ACA – part)

**10.** *Role of the management accountant in selling price policies*

What do you consider to be the role of the management accountant in the pricing of an organisation's products or services? Make reference in your answer to:

(*a*) The determination of price strategies in general

(*b*) The cost information which should be made available to the marketing management function.                                    (ICMA)

**11.** *Multiple objectives of a company*

*The company.* Control Instruments Ltd is a large company operating through subsidiary companies. The group headquarters is in London and control is decentralised to each subsidiary of the company which is divisionalised according to the principal product range. For example: Process Meters Ltd, located in Manchester; Engineering Gauges Ltd, located in Glasgow; Automation Ltd, located in Birmingham.

*The control of performance.* Subsidiaries are expected to meet a profit objective related to sales and investment in the company in the planning period. This requirement is fixed by H.Q. recognising long-term goals and interrelated factors demanding policy decision.

*Views regarding future performance objectives.* A number of executives in the group have expressed views regarding the significance of multiple objectives and the points made can be summarised as connected with the key result areas identified by Professor Drucker:

Profitability
Market standing
Innovation
Productivity
Worker performance and attitude
Financial and physical resources
Manager performance and development
Public responsibility.

Top management decided to review its assessment of performance in terms of organisational objectives.

*Required:*

The major objectives of business are usually profit orientated. Give your opinion regarding the nature of company objectives and their emphasis in a company of the type described in this question.

**12.** *Management development and management by objectives*
A company become alarmed at their shortage of trained managers able to succeed their senior executives who were nearing retiring age. A programme of management development was considered necessary, and a small committee was established to look into the matter. Their report stipulated the following practical steps that should be taken as a basis for further action:

(*a*) An identification of specific responsibilities of individual managers and the qualifications and experience required to discharge those responsibilities

(*b*) An interpretation of expected company developments and anticipated retirements in terms of specific needs for general managers, functional executives and supervisors

(*c*) An appraisal scheme for managers to indicate training needs to remedy experience deficiencies

(*d*) An encouragement to selected personnel to assume greater responsibilities in the areas where such effort will not only benefit the company in the context of their own jobs, but will also prepare the managers to assume positions anticipated in stage (*b*) of this process.

It was suggested that the requirements of stages (*c*) and (*d*) could be met by adopting a management-by-objectives scheme and the company accountant was asked to:

(i) Define the background conditions that must be provided for such a scheme to be a success

(ii) Indicate the initial action that would be taken by managers if this scheme was adopted

(iii) State the subsequent action that should be taken by managers.

*Required:*
As the accountant in this case, prepare notes as the basis of your submission to the top management of the company on the proposed adoption of a management-by-objectives scheme.

FURTHER READING

Broom, H. N. *Business Policy and Strategic Action.* Prentice-Hall, Englewood Cliffs, New Jersey, 1969. Chapters 14—20.
Hague, D. C. *Managerial Economics.* Longmans, 1969. Chapter 2.
Humble, J. W. *Improving Business Results.* McGraw-Hill, New York, 1968.

# 10 Budgetary Control (1)—A Management Control Technique

OBJECTIVE OF THE CHAPTER

To show how the budgetary control technique may be used as a management tool for controlling the business.

OUTLINE OF THE CHAPTER

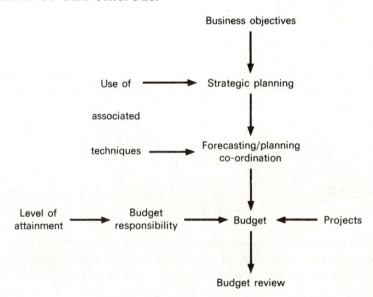

FIGURE 10.1.

The technique which embraces all activities of the business and serves to support the key aspects of the management control process is budgetary control. The importance of the technique in relation to information for management may be judged by the use of the budget to relate objectives and policies to managerial responsibility, and facilitate accountability and overall control.

The distinction between a forecast and a budget needs emphasis. A forecast is a probable event and in the planning stage it is necessary to prepare forecasts of probable courses of action for the business in the future. Arising from these forecasts, plans or budgets are prepared for the future operation of the business so that it may achieve its objectives. A budget is, therefore, a planned event usually expressed in financial and quantitative terms.

The nature of the budgetary system is governed by the size of the business. In the small organisation, one man may be able to rely upon his own observations to exercise control and the use of sophisticated techniques would be a waste of time. In a large organisation, management becomes a complex matter involving many people with varying skills and differing attitudes. Personal observation must give way to a large element of control on the basis of reported information. Budgetary control provides relevant information on what the business is trying to achieve and how it expects to transform its plans into reality.

## 10.1 REPRESENTATIONS OF THE BUDGET

A cost budget may be represented as:

1. A target of what should be spent
2. A forecast of what will be spent
3. An authority to spend
4. A limit not to be exceeded.

A target is an objective to be achieved and a forecast an estimate of performance. An authority to spend is an aspect of the control procedure where the authorisation of top management has been delegated to a lower level of management. The limit not to be exceeded is a specification extending point (3) to a control total. Points (3) and (4) may be linked in the stipulation that the manager must not exceed the spending limit without authority, recognising the view that the budget may be exceeded for good reasons.

## 10.2 THE APPROACH TO BUDGETING

The budget should be prepared by those responsible for its application and achievement in the business. Those able to take part in formulating the budgets are likely to show greater interest and motivation to achieve the plans agreed.

There are three basic approaches to the budgeting process:

1. The manufacturing facilities approach
2. The sales approach
3. The action programme approach.

The manufacturing facilities approach is given below:

£

Budgeted profit          —     Based on the desired rate of
                                return on capital employed

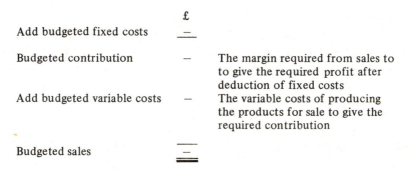

|                              | £ |                                                                                          |
|------------------------------|---|------------------------------------------------------------------------------------------|
| Add budgeted fixed costs     | — |                                                                                          |
| Budgeted contribution        | — | The margin required from sales to to give the required profit after deduction of fixed costs |
| Add budgeted variable costs  | — | The variable costs of producing the products for sale to give the required contribution  |
| Budgeted sales               | — |                                                                                          |

The sales approach works in the opposite direction:

|                                | £ |                                                    |
|--------------------------------|---|----------------------------------------------------|
| Budgeted sales                 | — | Based on an examination of the market              |
| Deduct budgeted variable costs | — | The variable costs of producing the possible sales |
| Budgeted contribution          | — |                                                    |
| Deduct budgeted fixed costs    | — |                                                    |
| Budgeted profit                | — |                                                    |

The action programme approach works as follows:

|                                                                                                                       | £ |                                     |
|-----------------------------------------------------------------------------------------------------------------------|---|-------------------------------------|
| Profit on the basis of the current year's operation                                                                   | — |                                     |
| Add/deduct the effect of action programmes originated in the current year on operations for the budget year           | — | Known as the carry-over effect      |
|                                                                                                                       | — |                                     |
| Add/deduct the effect of environment factors affecting the business in the budget year not experienced in the current year | — |                                     |
|                                                                                                                       | — |                                     |
| Add/deduct the effect of action programmes originated in the budget year                                              | — | After allowance for the carry-over effect |
| Budgeted profit                                                                                                       | — |                                     |

The deciding factor on the approach to the adopted is the key factor influencing the business in the budget period. It may be customer demand, manufacturing facilities, a shortage of materials or skilled labour and, possibly, cash. If there is a limit on, for example, manufacturing facilities this will affect the other budgets and unless output can be increased in some other way,* this will dictate the sales that can be made. Such a factor is known as the principal budget factor.

If the manufacturing facilities approach is used, it may be found that the sales level required cannot be achieved or the prices are not competitive. Action will then be required to try to reduce costs and bring the prices to a more acceptable level.

If the sales approach is used and the resulting profit is inadequate as a return on capital employed, it will be necessary to either reduce costs, increase the turnover of capital or improve sales revenue.

The action programme approach has been described by B. J. M. Edmunds as follows:

All managers with responsibility for planning and initiating action are asked to develop specific action programmes to obtain a significant improvement in profits. Each manager has, therefore, to:

(i) review the activities for which he is responsible;
(ii) decide where opportunities exist that will enable him to make a contribution to improved profits;
(iii) select from perhaps a number of opportunities those that will best repay his efforts, recognising the probable limitations in men, machines or money that exist and his own capacity for planning and implementing changes;
(iv) define the particular objectives which he has selected;
(v) review alternative methods of achieving his objectives. Select the best method and plan the detailed steps required to obtain his goal. Specify the action required, the timing and the person responsible for each critical step in the programme;
(vi) assess the impact of his plans on profits and in terms of changes in the assets to be employed;
(vii) submit his proposed plans to his superior for review.

The sum total of the action programmes determines the profit improvement that is to be made as a result of management action. This is not, however, the total profit (or loss) to be made by the firm — a certain profit level would have been reached in any case simply through the momentum that exists in the firm.†

The budget may include a statement of areas of vulnerability and alternative programmes to offset the unfavourable effects of incidents that might arise in those areas.

## 10.3  BUDGETING CO-ORDINATION

There is an interrelationship between the various types of information required for budgeting as, for example, in the matching of sales and production levels with the

*For example, components may be sub-contracted and assembly facilities extended into the manufacturing area previously used for the manufacture of the components. This action would facilitate increased output.

†B. J. M. Edmunds, 'Integrated planning and control', The Accountant, 24th October 1964, pp. 516–17.

effects of such levels on costs. The work of all members of management preparing
the budgets should be co-ordinated and the formation of a budget committee is a
useful way of integrating the efforts of functional staff.

## 10.4  ESSENTIALS OF A BUDGETARY CONTROL SYSTEM

The essential requirements for effective budgetary control are as follows:

1. The establishment of clear objectives
2. Top management support for the operation of the system
3. The use of available techniques to ensure budgets are as realistic as possible
4. The correct choice of the budget period
5. A recognition of the control period
6. The assessment of the budgeted level of attainment
7. The use of a realistic preparation timetable
8. The recognition of responsibility for control in the establishment of budget
   centres
9. Clear instructions to executives to assist them in their job of preparing the
   the budgets
10. The scrutiny and discussion of submitted budgets and, where necessary,
    explanations given to managers of changes made
11. The use of approved budgets as an essential feature of the management control
    process
12. The detailed scrutiny of actual results against the plan, and a control system
    that ensures that where action is necessary managers are advised so that action
    will be taken.

## 10.5  INSTALLATION OF A BUDGETARY SYSTEM

It takes time to install a budgetary system because:

(a) The budget as a tool of management may not be understood by managers
(b) The integrated managerial action required when budgetary control is practised
    may be a new experience for many managers
(c) Existing managerial responsibilities may not be clarified to the extent necessary
    for the budgetary system
(d) Staff may be reluctant to commit themselves to plans for the future and feel
    that it is impossible to predict the future.

For the above reasons, limited application of a budgetary system may be undertaken as, for example, the budgeting of overheads only or capital investment. This
limited application is justifiable as a stage-by-stage installation of a more complete
system, but it should be noted that the total benefits of budgetary control cannot
be obtained until comprehensive budgeting is undertaken. Many of the inadequacies

of management mentioned in this section can be resolved by experience and an educational programme to motivate staff to use the technique intelligently.

## 10.6  TOP MANAGEMENT SUPPORT FOR BUDGETING

The reluctance of managers to submit their thinking to the discipline required for budgeting may only be overcome by top management support. The discipline of recording executive commitments on paper usually makes the intentions more definite and comprehensive in their coverage.

## 10.7  THE USE OF ASSOCIATED TECHNIQUES IN BUDGETING

One of the most difficult figures to budget is the sales figure and there may be the problem of persuading the sales organisation that it is possible to forecast sales with reasonable accuracy. Budgets must be as realistic as possible and any associated techniques that may be used for this purpose, such as market research, should be adopted. Other techniques useful in the budgeting process are industrial engineering, operational research, statistics and network analysis. Management literature abounds with examples of the way in which these techniques may be used,* particularly in long-range planning, but there is considerable evidence that many of these techniques are either ignored or inadequately applied.† Prejudice, scepticism and established beliefs may all work against the application of management techniques.

## 10.8  THE BUDGET PERIOD

Companies normally develop their short-term plans in relation to long-term fore-casts. The long-term forecast may be for a period of three to five years, not in great detail because of the uncertainties involved, but in sufficient detail to serve as a sound guide for short-period budgeting. The short-term plan is usually for one year corresponding to the financial year of the business. Deciding factors are the seasonal nature of the business, the manufacturing cycle, the effort necessary to prepare the budget and the reliability of the estimates made. The type of budget might also affect the budget period chosen. For example, capital expenditure needs to be planned on a long-term basis whereas other budgets are more realistically con-sidered in the short term. A cash budget is a good example of the latter category.

For control, management require information on a more frequent basis than

*A useful glossary is John Argenti's *Management Techniques – a Practical Guide* (Allen & Unwin, 1969). The author gives in the glossary: (a) some idea of what each technique is; (b) what each technique is for; (c) who can use each technique; (d) the practical results one can expect from using each technique.

† See, for example, the reported results of a survey by H. C. Hunt printed in the *Manager* (July 1965) under the title, 'The real truth about forecasting'. Mr Hunt found that most of the forward planning was little more than intelligent guesswork.

the budget period. The control periods that may be used were described in Chapter 1. To enable comparative information to be extracted from the budget for period control, the budget is analysed by control periods.

## 10.9 THE BUDGETED LEVEL OF ATTAINMENT

The level of attainment usually incorporated in the budget is a realistic figure for the budget period: one that is reasonably attainable in the conditions that are expected to exist in the budget period although there should be an element of incentive to be a challenge to management.

Two levels of attainment may be fixed. Using sales as an example, one sales figure may represent the minimum level beyond which the sales are not likely to fall; the other, fixed at a higher level which the company hopes to achieve. The idea behind this double budget is to fix a level which can be used for judgements of risk and cash flow with a certainty not matched by the higher level used for operating control. At the operating stage differences in level of attainment can arise. If standard costing is used in association with budgeting, the standards fixed in the two techniques may be different. The desired performance standard used in standard costing may include an incentive element above the challenge element considered acceptable for budgeting. If the standard costing target is high enough, unfavourable variances are inevitable. In this situation, the budget should allow for excess incentive elements as follows:

|  | £ | Incentive level |
|---|---|---|
| 1. Budgeted profit based on standard costing standards | 10,000 | High |
| 2. Less planned budget variance (difference between items 1 and 3) | 2,000 | |
| 3. Budgeted profit based on 'expected actual' | 8,000 | Moderate |
| 4. Less operating budget variance (difference between items 3 and 5) | 1,000 | |
| 5. Actual profit | 7,000 | |

## 10.10 THE BUDGET TIMETABLE

To ensure that plans receive adequate consideration in the preparatory stages and that budgets are available in time for the commencement of the budget period, a timetable should be agreed for budget preparation. The length of time taken to prepare the budget varies according to the size of the business, the detail required, and the necessity to co-ordinate with other plans. For example, the long-term planning may advance the starting-point of the process to as much as six months for a three-year plan and two months for a one-year plan, from the start of the budget year.

Budget preparation is usually left as late as possible to get accurate information. If current information is used as a basis for fixing future budgets, and it takes three months to prepare the budget for the following year, 'actual' information for the current year will not be available. An attempt to improve the quality of the current information as a basis for budgeting is to provide an extra column to reports as follows:

| Actual to date | Budget to date | Variation to date | Revised budget to the end of the current year |
|:---:|:---:|:---:|:---:|
| £ | £ | £ | £ |
| | | | (the extra column) |

In effect, the extra column gives 'actual' to date plus the budget for the remainder of the current year on the basis of the best information available at that time.

## 10.11  BUDGET RESPONSIBILITY

To establish a budgetary control system, it is often necessary to prepare an organisation chart for the business and sort out overlapping operations and over-lapping responsibilities. Budget responsibility is bound up with the organisation structure of the business, the management control process and cost responsibility. The budgets should be prepared by the officials responsible for incurring the expenditure or controlling the sales activity. Too much stress cannot be placed upon the importance of having senior executives contribute to the preparation of the budget. Work should not be left to clerical staff who can only assemble figures from past records and make guesses about the future, since they do not know what the real plans of the executives are.

The preparation of the budget is not the job of the accountant apart from the figures particular to his own department. The accountant's role in budgeting is that of an adviser to other departments and in this sphere he can perform a valuable service to management.

## 10.12  THE BENEFITS AND LIMITATIONS OF BUDGETARY CONTROL

Benefits that may be obtained by the business that adopts budgetary control are as follows:

1. The technique relates the overall objectives to specific managers and identifies the part each executive must play in converting the intentions of top management into reality.

2. All managers are involved in the management control process in significant areas where views of lower management are not always obtained, e.g., the fixing of objectives.

3. Policies may be examined in relation to their detailed effect on company performance and a basis is provided for their review and modification as necessary.

4. Management is in the position of anticipating business problems and provided with a tool to judge their detailed effects on the organisation. Valuable information is available to deal with a problem in advance rather than the company being faced with a crisis situation demanding drastic action.

5. In the control situation, management is provided with information as a routine which would be difficult to obtain promptly without the budgetary technique in operation.

6. The decision-making discipline of identifying problems and possible solutions, ascertaining the consequences of alternative solutions and evaluating them as a basis for decision, is supported by the budgetary control process.

7. Decisions reached on problems affecting the business are likely to be more accurate because the machinery is available for all interested parties to be consulted and their combined views given appropriate attention.

8. Co-ordinated managerial activity is facilitated.

9. Accountability for results is secured in financial terms on an organised basis through the medium of plans which have been expressed in terms of their profit impact on the company.

10. The technique assists the management in using the resources of the business in the most economical way possible.

Factors preventing the most effective use of the budgetary control technique are as follows:

(a) Staff regard the technique as a pressure instrument rather than a procedure to assist the executive to do a better job.

(b) Because the technique is so closely identified with the management control process, executives imagine that the technique can replace management. There is no substitute for good management.

(c) The motivation may be misplaced. For example, managers may be satisfied with budget performance when better performance is possible and could reasonably be attained if a low level of attainment had not been agreed in the budget.

(d) The checking of estimates may be difficult and it is sometimes forgotten that budgets are estimates given in the context of defined anticipated conditions that can change.

(e) The required degree of management co-operation may not be obtained and top management support may be inadequate.

(f) Where managers know that the figures they submit for budgeting purposes will subsequently be used as a measure of their efficiency, there is built in the system an incentive to submit estimates that are not too demanding on their performance.

(g) The supporting accounting system may not be sufficiently effective.

(h) There may be deficiencies in the organisational structure of the business.

(i) Forecasting may be practised too far into the future before appropriate techniques have been developed.

(j) Not enough time may be allowed for the system to be developed and managers gain the necessary experience to use the technique to maximum advantage.


## 10.13  SUMMARY

Budgetary control can be a powerful technique in supporting the executives of a business in achieving objectives, but this is dependent upon the quality of management and the attention given to motivating staff to react favourably to the descipline the technique imposes. This discipline involves making plans in financial terms within the framework of an organisation where authority and responsibility are clearly defined and accountability is secured by using the plans as a measure of performance. The development of these plans by type and the associated budgetary reporting considerations are the subject of the next chapter.


## FOR FURTHER STUDY

QUESTIONS

1. *The purpose and nature of budgetary control*
   Your organisation has recently appointed a chairman who has little knowledge of commercial or management accounting matters. He is not able to appreciate the purpose and nature of your system of budgetary control. He also lacks knowledge of the underlying factors in the related sphere of business forecasting.
   *Required:*
   He has asked you to write a brief for him in non-technical terms, stating the overall purpose and nature of budgetary control and factors to be considered in relation to business forecasting. You are not required to discuss details of particular budgets but you must bring out important principles.

   (ACA — part)

2. *The implications of changes in budgets*
   'These budgets never work out as planned. Conditions always change. Why bother to make them?'
   *Required:*
   Discuss the implications of the argument expressed in the above quotation and state the points you would make to a manager expressing this view.    (ICMA)

3. *The introduction of budgets*
   'The introduction of forecasts or budgets is, probably, the most difficult task
   to get over to management, particularly in small businesses; and it must be
   accepted that initial attempts to produce such forward figures may not be very
   successful.'
   (N. R. Bellwood, 'Improving accounting for management in a small business',
   *Accountancy*, May 1962, p. 396)
   *Required:*
   Identify and comment on the possible difficulties inferred in this statement.

4. *The sales approach to budgeting*
   Budgeting usually begins with the sales budget. What are the implications of
   this approach?

5. *The action programme approach to budgeting*
   Describe the action programme approach to budgeting.

6. *The principal budget factor*
   What do you understand by the principal budget factor and what is the effect
   of this factor on the budgeting process?

7. *The budgeted level of attainment*
   The budgeted level of attainment adopted affects the size and type of variances
   disclosed in the budgetary system.'
   *Required:*
   Comment on this statement.

8. *The budget/control period*
   What do you understand by the budget period and what is the relationship of
   this period to the accounting control period?

9. *The budget timetable*
   'To ensure that plans receive adequate consideration in the preparatory stages
   and that budgets are available in time for the commencement of the budget
   period, a timetable should be agreed for budget preparation.'
   *Required:*
   Comment on this statement.

10. *The disadvantages of budgetary control*
    The advantages of a budgetary control system are often stressed and it would
    be wrong to assume that these advantages always accrue to an organisation
    which introduces such a system.
    *Required:*
    Discuss the reasons why these advantages need not necessarily be achieved.
                                                                          (ACA)

11. *Personality considerations in budgeting*
    The factory of the Excelsior Manufacturing Co. Ltd was situated in
    Manchester and the headquarters in London. The managing director and his

senior functional executives, apart from the factory manager, were included in the head office organisation. The factory manager was located at the Manchester factory with a small office staff for routine clerical work including basic accounting routines such as wages and stores accounts.

The background of the managing director was in marketing and he was primarily interested in sales although he maintained a close interest in production through key figures supplied by the accountant who was responsible for office administration.

The senior executives usually worked together as a team and there were few disagreements but the proposal to introduce budgetary control was met with mixed feelings. The managing director was enthusiastic, supported by the accountant, but the factory manager and sales manager had serious reservations about the proposed system.

The accountant proposed the appointment of a budget accountant responsible to himself, to administer the system. The factory manager thought that such a person would have a closer involvement with functional staff than the average accountant and he should, therefore, be responsible to general management.

The sales manager tended to be a dominant personality. He maintained that the central issue was sales and he thought the scheme impractical because it was virtually impossible to assess sales in this company.

The factory manager was worried about the paperwork involved. He maintained that it was a major job at present to deal with the administrative work required without adding to the burden. He wanted to know what support the accountant was prepared to give to functional executives involved in budgeting.

The accountant responded by saying that he was prepared to centralise accounting work. This proposal met with opposition from the factory manager who still wanted control over what he regarded as factory operations.

*Required:*

(*a*) To what extend should the managing director acknowledge the personality considerations of his executives in installing a budgetary system?

(*b*) The wishes of all the executives in this case cannot be met. What action should be taken if an executive does not co-operate?

12. *Budget construction*

The Murphy Manufacturing Co. Ltd had its headquarters in Manchester and prepared a budget at the beginning of each year for the ten operating companies it controlled. Budgeting in this company commenced with an estimated sales figure for the group based on past experience and modified as expected for the budget year. Once this figure was agreed, each operating company was allotted its share of the sales. The gross profit for each company was then calculated by an estimate of closing stock values related to cost of goods manufactured. Opening stock values were obtained from the last trading statement. The remaining costs to fix a net profit for each company were also calculated by head office.

Apparently this type of budget had been used for a number of years. Operating company management were not satisfied with the system and head office now had their doubts as to its effectiveness. The master budget at head office was analysed in detail by types of expense but no details of this kind were passed to operating companies. Subsidiary company detail was limited to main group totals such as administration, selling and distribution expenses.

One suggestion put forward to improve the budgetary procedure was to analyse the expense totals for each operating company so that some items considerably above budget in individual companies would not be hidden by items below budget. Headquarters objected to the increased work, making the point that the total figures were fixed on the lowest possible figure for the volume expected which did not allow much room for offsetting item expenses.

*Required:*

(*a*) Do you think that operating company expense budgets should by analysed in detail?

(*b*) What criticisms would you make of the way in which the budget was prepared in this company?

FURTHER READING

Bishop, S. V. *Business Planning and Control.* General Educational Trust of the Institute of Chartered Accountants in England and Wales, 1966. Chapters 1 to 3.
Chamberlain, Neil W. *The Firm: Micro-Economic Planning and Action.* McGraw Hill, New York, 1962. Chapter 18.
Welsch, Glenn A. *Budgeting: Profit Planning and Control.* Prentice-Hall, Englewood Cliffs, New Jersey, 1964. Chapters 1, 2 and 17.

# 11 Budgetary Control (2)—Budget Type Aspects

OBJECTIVE OF THE CHAPTER

To develop the budgetary programme to cater for functional requirements, including budgetary reporting considerations.

OUTLINE OF THE CHAPTER

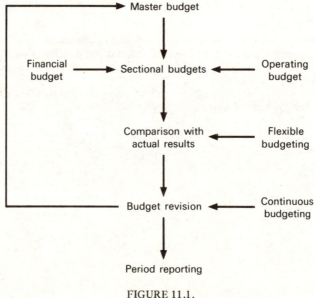

FIGURE 11.1.

When a budgetary control system is first introduced it is necessary to budget in very general terms, increasing the detail required as the installation of the system progresses. The amount of information required by officials preparing the budget will be considerable when the system is first installed. Heavy demands will be made on the accountant and he should prepare himself with the following:

1. Details of the actual results of previous years

2.  Details concerning the preparation of each budget with particular reference to items where special considerations apply.

In an established budgetary control system, internal information will still be required for budget preparation, but records will have been modified with a view to furnishing information which the budget from time to time shows to be necessary.

## 11.1  BUDGET REVISIONS

An approved budget should not be changed without good reason. Changes in circumstances since the budget was prepared will take place continually, but a distinction should be made between actual and budget variations which arise in the normal course of business but do not affect the budget; and changes in the basic conditions upon which the budget was based.

In the first case, the variances would be revealed by the periodical returns for management and it would be necessary to analyse the causes of such variances so that immediate action might be taken to remedy any wrong tendencies. In the second case, the budget as a measure of current efficiency would be of restricted value if it was not altered.

If budget amendments are considered essential, it is desirable to ensure that the system does not develop into a means of covering up inefficiency on the part of managers. This is usually accomplished by the manager completing a budget amendment form where a revision is necessary, giving the extent and reasons for amendment of the original budget. This form would pass through the normal stages of scrutiny and approval.

Continuous and flexible budgeting help to reduce the need for budget amendments. In continuous budgeting, as each control period is completed that period is dropped from the budget and another control period is added. The short control periods covered by each successive stage of the budgeting process helps to keep the budget at a realistic level of performance.

## 11.2  FLEXIBLE BUDGETING

An unchanged budget for comparison with actual results is known as a fixed budget. Where a budget is changed for different levels of activity the plan is known as a flexible budget. In Chapter 2, expense classifications were described showing the cost behaviour of particular expenses when activity changed. Recognising the relationship of each expense to the variability characteristic, it is possible to produce a budget in the form shown in Figure 11.2.

Fixed costs, by definition, will remain the same for each activity level column. directly variable costs will change in proportion to the change in the activity level; and the semi-variable costs will vary according to their particular behaviour pattern for each activity level shown.

| Flexible expense budget | | | | |
|---|---|---|---|---|
| Department _____ Year ended _____ | | | | |

| Type of expense | Activity level – Machine hours | | | | |
|---|---|---|---|---|---|
| | 10,000 | 15,000 | 20,000 | 25,000 | 30,000 |
| | £ | £ | £ | £ | £ |
| Fixed costs | | | | | |
| Variable costs | | | | | |
| Semi-variable costs | | | | | |
| Total budgeted cost | | | | | |

FIGURE 11.2. A flexible expense budget

The aim of the flexible budget is not to vary the budget objective but to provide a better control figure. For example, if the company aims to operate at 20,000 hours machine activity, whatever the actual activity, the objective is unchanged. It may be realised, however, that if actual activity is only 15,000 hours, the use of budget figures for 20,000 hours (the fixed budget) for control purposes could be misleading to management. The following figures illustrate this point:

*Data for an accounting period: machine department*

Budget:
    Production: an activity level of 20,000 machine hours
    Overhead

| | £ | *Per machine hour* £ |
|---|---|---|
| Fixed cost | 2,000 | 0·10 |
| Variable cost | 4,000 | 0·20 |
| | 6,000 | |

Actual results:
    Production: an activity level of 15,000 machine hours
    Overhead £5,000

Comparison of actual cost with the budget (fixed budget basis):

| | £ |
|---|---|
| Budgeted cost | 6,000 |
| Actual cost | 5,000 |
| A saving of expense to the extent of | 1,000 |

If the budgeted figure is adjusted to the amount associated with the level of activity achieved (use of the flexible budget) the comparison is as follows:

|                                                              | £     | £     |
|--------------------------------------------------------------|-------|-------|
| Budgeted cost                                                |       |       |
| Fixed cost                                                   | 2,000 |       |
| Variable cost: 15,000 machine hours at £0·20 per machine hour | 3,000 | 5,000 |
| Actual cost                                                  |       | 5,000 |
|                                                              |       | Nil   |

In the first example, the information submitted to management would indicate a saving in expense when, in fact, no saving had been made. The information calculated on the basis of the original budget (the fixed budget) is of limited value or even misleading for managerial control. To make the information meaningful for management the budget should be 'flexed' according to the actual level of activity. This is the flexible budget figure shown above of £5,000 and termed the budgeted expense allowance to distinguish it from the planned expense figure which remains at £6,000.

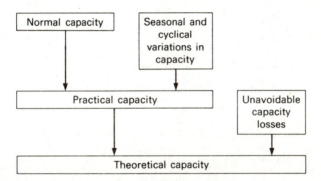

FIGURE 11.3. Capacity levels

In a flexible budgetary control system, the budget column on departmental expense statements for management, to which actual costs are compared, is completed with budgeted expense allowances for the level of activity achieved in the accounting period.

In the example above, machine hours have been used as a measure of activity. The operating level factor should be chosen with care to measure the incidence of the expense item and another measure in frequent use is direct labour hours. Both these factors are production levels of activity; for sales expenses, sales volume would be more appropriate.

The activity level is related to the capacity committed by the management for use in the budget period and this capacity may be given different interpretations as illustrated in Figure 11.3.

The rated output for the machinery in a department, assuming ideal operating

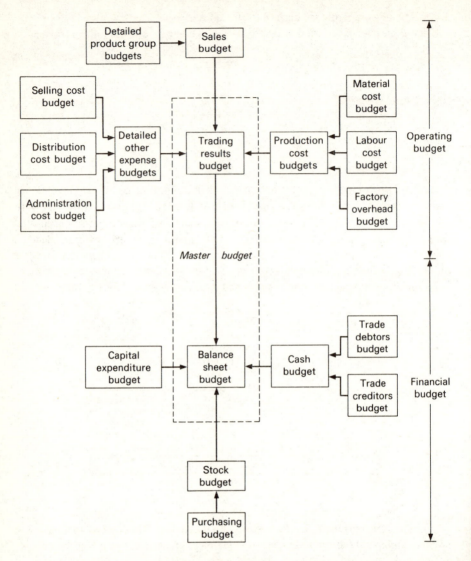

FIGURE 11.4. Relationship of sectional budgets to the master budget

conditions, is known as the theoretical capacity. When allowance is made for un-
avoidable capacity losses such as normal maintenance and holiday interruptions, the
resulting calculation is practical capacity. In an attempt to allow for the company's
long-term ability to produce and sell its products, practical capacity is usually
adjusted for seasonal and cyclical variations to give what is known as normal capacity.
It is the normal capacity figure which is usually used in budgeting to calculate the
fixed and variable overhead rates illustrated in the figures given in the example above.

## 11.3  SECTIONAL BUDGETS

The overall control budget, or master budget, is the end product of detailed functional or sectional budgets and their relationship is illustrated in Figure 11.4.

To show the interrelationship of the figures in a budgetary procedure a simple illustration is given. Quantity information is not given and analysis that would be provided in practice, such as accounting period detail, has been eliminated to show the essentials of the budgetary system.

*Data for the budget period:*

*Balance Sheet as at 1st January 19. .*

| | £ | £ | | Cost | Depn. to date | Book value |
|---|---|---|---|---|---|---|
| Share capital | | 50,000 | | £ | £ | £ |
| Revenue reserves | | | | | | |
| | | | Fixed assets | | | |
| | | | Land and buildings | 20,000 | – | 20,000 |
| Profit and | | | Plant and equipment | 45,250 | 15,000 | 30,250 |
| loss balance | | 23,000 | Vehicles | 10,000 | 5,000 | 5,000 |
| | | | | 75,250 | 20,000 | 55,250 |
| Current | | | | | | |
| liabilities | | | Current assets | | | |
| Trade | | | Stock | | 20,750 | |
| creditors | 3,000 | | Trade debtors | | 30,000 | 50,750 |
| Bank | 30,000 | 33,000 | | | | |
| | | 106,000 | | | | 106,000 |

| | Product A | Product B | Product C |
|---|---|---|---|
| Sales in units | 20,000 | 10,000 | 30,000 |
| Selling price per unit | £4 | £6 | £3 |
| Costs per unit | | | |
| Direct material: | | | |
| X (at £0·05 per material unit) | 10 material units | 20 material units | – |
| Y (at £0·025 per material unit) | 10 material units | – | 20 material units |
| Direct labour: | | | |
| Department 1 (at £0.5 per hour) | $\frac{1}{2}$ hour | $\frac{1}{2}$ hour | 1 hour |
| Department 2 (at £1 per hour) | $\frac{1}{2}$ hour | 1 hour | $\frac{1}{2}$ hour |
| Variable overhead | £0·50 | £0·75 | £0·50 |

The above figures give the following information per product unit:

| | Product A | | Product B | | Product C | |
|---|---|---|---|---|---|---|
| | £ | £ | £ | £ | £ | £ |
| Direct material | | | | | | |
| X | 0·50 | | 1·00 | | – | |
| Y | 0·25 | 0·75 | – | 1·00 | 0·50 | 0·50 |
| Direct labour | | | | | | |
| Department 1 | 0·25 | | 0·25 | | 0·50 | |
| Department 2 | 0·50 | 0·75 | 1·00 | 1·25 | 0·50 | 1·00 |
| Variable overhead | | 0·50 | | 0·75 | | 0·50 |
| Marginal cost | | 2·00 | | 3·00 | | 2·00 |
| Selling price | | 4·00 | | 6·00 | | 3·00 |
| Contribution | | 2·00 | | 3·00 | | 1·00 |

The sales budget may now be given as follows:

*Sales Budget – Year ended 31st December 19. .*

| Product group | Sales | Marginal cost of sales | Contribution | Profit/volume ratio |
|---|---|---|---|---|
| | £ | £ | £ | % |
| A | 80,000 | 40,000 | 40,000 | 50 |
| B | 60,000 | 30,000 | 30,000 | 50 |
| C | 90,000 | 60,000 | 30,000 | $33\frac{1}{3}$ |
| Totals | 230,000 | 130,000 | 100,000 | |

The column details are calculated by multiplying the unit prices and costs by the sales in units for each product.

*Given:*

*Unit Stock Movements*

| | Product A | Product B | Product C |
|---|---|---|---|
| Work-in-progress (complete as to materials only) | £ | £ | £ |
| Opening stock | 2,000 | 2,000 | 2,000 |
| Add materials issued | 20,000 | 8,000 | 28,000 |
| | 22,000 | 10,000 | 30,000 |
| Deduct production | 21,000 | 9,000 | 29,000 |
| Closing stock | 1,000 | 1,000 | 1,000 |
| Finished goods | | | |
| Opening stock | 1,000 | 2,000 | 3,000 |
| Add production | 21,000 | 9,000 | 29,000 |
| | 22,000 | 11,000 | 32,000 |
| Deduct sales | 20,000 | 10,000 | 30,000 |
| Closing stock | 2,000 | 1,000 | 2,000 |

The following budgets may now be given:
  The production cost budget
  The materials cost budget
  The labour cost budget.

*Production Cost Budget – Year ended 31st December 19. .*

|  | Product A | Product B | Product C | Total |
|---|---|---|---|---|
|  | £ | £ | £ | £ |
| Direct material cost | 15,000 | 8,000 | 14,000 | 37,000 |
| Direct labour cost | 15,750 | 11,250 | 29,000 | 56,000 |
| Variable overhead | 10,500 | 6,750 | 14,500 | 31,750 |
| Marginal product cost | 41,250 | 26,000 | 57,500 | 124,750 |
| Add opening work-in-progress | 1,500 | 2,000 | 1,000 | 4,500 |
|  | 42,750 | 28,000 | 58,500 | 129,250 |
| Deduct closing work-in-progress | 750 | 1,000 | 500 | 2,250 |
| Marginal cost of finished production | 42,000 | 27,000 | 58,000 | 127,000 |

The multiplication of the closing stock of finished goods in units by the marginal cost per unit gives the marginal cost of finished production. The use of the stock movement figures and the relevant unit costs provides the input data shown in this budget.

The figures below show the reconciliation between the budgeted sales at marginal cost and the marginal cost of finished production.

|  | Product A | Product B | Product C | Total |
|---|---|---|---|---|
|  | £ | £ | £ | £ |
| Sales at marginal cost | 40,000 | 30,000 | 60,000 | 130,000 |
| Add closing stock-finished goods | 4,000 | 3,000 | 4,000 | 11,000 |
|  | 44,000 | 33,000 | 64,000 | 141,000 |
| Deduct opening stock-finished goods | 2,000 | 6,000 | 6,000 | 14,000 |
| Marginal cost of finished production | 42,000 | 27,000 | 58,000 | 127,000 |

*Materials Cost Budget – Year ended 31st December 19. .*

| Material Type | Product A | Product B | Product C | Total |
|---|---|---|---|---|
|  | £ | £ | £ | £ |
| X | 10,000 | 8,000 | – | 18,000 |
| Y | 5,000 | – | 14,000 | 19,000 |
| Totals | 15,000 | 8,000 | 14,000 | 37,000 |

*Labour Cost Budget – Year ended 31st December 19. .*

| Department | Product A | Product B | Product C | Total |
|---|---|---|---|---|
| | £ | £ | £ | £ |
| 1 | 5,250 | 2,250 | 14,500 | 22,000 |
| 2 | 10,500 | 9,000 | 14,500 | 34,000 |
| Totals | 15,750 | 11,250 | 29,000 | 56,000 |

The above budgets are subsidiary to the production cost budget, explaining in greater detail the summary information for direct material and direct labour costs. *Given:*

*Raw Material Stock Movements*

| | Material X (units) | Material Y (units) |
|---|---|---|
| | £ | £ |
| Opening stock | 20,000 | 50,000 |
| Add purchases | 370,000 | 770,000 |
| | 390,000 | 820,000 |
| Deduct closing stock | 30,000 | 60,000 |
| Raw materials issued | 360,000 | 760,000 |

The following budgets may now be given:
    The purchasing budget
    The stock budget.

*Purchasing Budget – Year ended 31st December 19. .*

| | Material X | Material Y | Total |
|---|---|---|---|
| | £ | £ | £ |
| Materials consumed | 18,000 | 19,000 | 37,000 |
| Add closing stock | 1,500 | 1,500 | 3,000 |
| | 19,500 | 20,500 | 40,000 |
| Deduct opening stock | 1,000 | 1,250 | 2,250 |
| Purchases | 18,500 | 19,250 | 37,750 |

*Stock Budget – Year ended 31st December 19. .*

| | Material X | | Material Y | | Total | |
|---|---|---|---|---|---|---|
| | Opening stock | Closing stock | Opening stock | Closing stock | Opening stock | Closing stock |
| | £ | £ | £ | £ | £ | £ |
| Raw material | 1,000 | 1,500 | 1,250 | 1,500 | 2,250 | 3,000 |

|  |  |  |  |  |  | £ | £ |
|---|---|---|---|---|---|---|---|
|  |  |  | Brought forward |  |  | 2,250 | 3,000 |

|  | Product A | | Product B | | Product C | |  |  |
|---|---|---|---|---|---|---|---|---|
|  | Opening stock | Closing stock | Opening stock | Closing stock | Opening stock | Closing stock |  |  |
|  | £ | £ | £ | £ | £ | £ |  |  |
| Work-in progress | 1,500 | 750 | 2,000 | 1,000 | 1,000 | 500 | 4,500 | 2,250 |
| Finished goods | 2,000 | 4,000 | 6,000 | 3,000 | 6,000 | 4,000 | 14,000 | 11,000 |
|  |  |  |  |  |  |  | 20,750 | 16,250 |

The unit cost information for raw materials, work-in-progress and finished goods, enables the management to value the units of stock, and a comprehensive picture of investment in this important asset is indicated.

*Given:*

|  | £ |
|---|---|
| Fixed expenses |  |
| Factory | 30,000 |
| Selling | 20,000 |
| Distribution | 7,000 |
| Administration | 20,000 |
|  | 77,000 |

The trading results budget may now be given.

*Trading Results Budget – Year ended 31st December 19. .*

|  |  | Product A | Product B | Product C | Total |
|---|---|---|---|---|---|
|  |  | £ | £ | £ | £ |
| Sales | (A) | 80,000 | 60,000 | 90,000 | 230,000 |
| Direct material cost |  | 15,000 | 10,000 | 15,000 | 40,000 |
| Direct labour cost |  | 15,000 | 12,500 | 30,000 | 57,500 |
| Variable overhead |  | 10,000 | 7,500 | 15,000 | 32,500 |
| Marginal cost of sales (B) |  | 40,000 | 30,000 | 60,000 | 130,000 |
| Contribution (A − B) |  | 40,000 | 30,000 | 30,000 | 100,000 |
| Profit/volume ratio |  | 50% | 50% | $33\frac{1}{3}\%$ |  |

|  | £ |
|---|---|
| Deduct fixed expenses |  |
| Factory | 30,000 |
| Selling | 20,000 |
| Distribution | 7,000 |
| Administration | 20,000 |
|  | 77,000 |
| Net profit | 23,000 |

In this budget the fixed expenses are deducted from the contribution, as shown in the sales budget, to give the final net profit.

Two capital expenditure projects have been approved for the budget year as illustrated below:

### Capital Expenditure Budget – Year ended 31st December 19. .

| Project number | Details of project | £ |
|---|---|---|
| 1 | Accounting machine | 2,000 |
| 2 | Conveyor | 7,000 |
| | | 9,000 |

Customers are allowed an average of $1\frac{1}{2}$ month's credit and one month's credit is normally taken from suppliers. For this illustration it is assumed that all other outlays are for cash. The following budgets may now be given:

The trade debtors budget
The trade creditors budget.

### Trade Debtors Budget – Year ended 31st December 19. .

| | £ |
|---|---|
| Opening balance of debtors | 30,000 |
| Add sales on credit | 230,000 |
| | 260,000 |
| Deduct cash received from customers | 231,250 |
| Closing balance of debtors | 28,750 |

The opening balance of debtors is taken from the opening balance sheet and the sales on credit from the sales budget. The closing balance of debtors, allowing $1\frac{1}{2}$ month's credit, is one-eighth of £230,000. In this simple example and the trade creditors budget below, seasonal factors have been ignored.

### Trade Creditors Budget – Year ended 31st December 19. .

| | £ |
|---|---|
| Opening balance of creditors | 3,000 |
| Add purchases on credit | 37,750 |
| | 40,750 |
| Deduct cash paid to suppliers | 37,600 |
| Closing balance of creditors | 3,150 |

The opening balance of creditors is taken from the opening balance sheet and the purchases on credit from the purchasing budget. The closing balance of creditors, taking one month's credit, is one-twelfth of £37,750 (rounded to the nearest £10). Included in the fixed expenses is £7,000 for depreciation:

| | £ |
|---|---|
| Plant and equipment | 6,000 |
| Vehicles | 1,000 |
| | 7,000 |

The cash budget follows:

*Cash Budget – Year ended 31st December 19. .*

|  | £ | £ | £ |
|---|---|---|---|
| Opening bank overdraft | | | 30,000 |
| Budgeted receipts from customers | | 231,250 | |
| Deduct budgeted payments | | | |
|    Payments to suppliers | 37,600 | | |
|    Capital expenditure | 9,000 | | |
|    Wages and salaries and other payments | 157,750 | 204,350 | 26,900 |
| Closing bank overdraft | | | 3,100 |

The total of cash payments from the earlier budgets and the figure for cash received from customers from the trade debtors budget explains the change in the bank overdraft in the cash budget.

The budgeted fixed assets analysis is illustrated below followed by the balance sheet budget.

*Budgeted Fixed Assets Analysis – Year ended 31st December 19. .*

|  | Cost (A) | Capital expenditure (B) | Total cost (A + B = C) | Depn. brought forward (D) | Depn.-budget year (E) | Total depn. (D + E = F) | Book value (C – F) |
|---|---|---|---|---|---|---|---|
|  | £ | £ | £ | £ | £ | £ | £ |
| Land and buildings | 20,000 | | 20,000 | | | | 20,000 |
| Plant and equipment | 45,250 | 9,000 | 54,250 | 15,000 | 6,000 | 21,000 | 33,250 |
| Vehicles | 10,000 | | 10,000 | 5,000 | 1,000 | 6,000 | 4,000 |
| Totals | 75,250 | 9,000 | 84,250 | 20,000 | 7,000 | 27,000 | 57,250 |

*Balance Sheet Budget as at 31st December 19. .*

|  |  | £ |
|---|---|---|
| Fixed assets | | |
|   Land and buildings at cost | | 20,000 |
|   Plant and equipment at cost less depreciation | | 33,250 |
|   Vehicles at cost less depreciation | | 4,000 |
|   Total fixed assets | (A) | 57,250 |
| Current assets | | |
|   Stock-in-trade | | 16,250 |
|   Trade debtors | | 28,750 |
| | (B) | 45,000 |
| Current liabilities | | |
|   Trade creditors | | 3,150 |
|   Bank overdraft | | 3,100 |
| | (C) | 6,250 |
| Working capital | (B – C = D) | 38,750 |
| Net Assets | (A + D) | 96,000 |

Represented by

| | |
|---|---|
| Ordinary share capital | 50,000 |
| Profit and loss account balance | 46,000 |
| Capital and reserves | 96,000 |

The changes in the financial status of the business are clearly presented in the balance sheet budget. The net asset figures are taken from the budgets named by each item and the budgeted fixed assets analysis above. The ordinary share capital figure is taken from the opening balance sheet and the profit and loss account balance is calculated as follows:

| | £ |
|---|---|
| Opening balance per the opening balance sheet | 23,000 |
| Add net profit ignoring taxation per the trading results budget | 23,000 |
| | 46,000 |

## 11.4  PREPARATION OF SECTIONAL BUDGETS

In the preparation of budgets, quantities for particular qualities or grades of cost and revenue factors are multiplied by prices or rates to give costs and revenue. Past data may be used as a guide in fixing budgets but the plans must reflect expectations for the future.

For some factors that cross sectional boundaries separate data may be prepared. A good example is labour where personnel requirements for the budget period may be compiled in a document known as a manpower estimate.

### 11.41  THE SALES BUDGET

To prepare the sales budget it is necessary to assess:

1. The potential demand for company products
2. The proportion of the total demand that the company may be able to obtain.

In addition to the use of past statistics to establish sales trends, sales staff and market research can guide the sales manager in fixing the budget. Pricing and advertising policy relative to potential sales and the assessment of the relative profitability of products may alter the mix of sales. The ability of the factory to produce the products required may affect quantities used in the sales budget. Inflation, government price control and the overall economic climate are also factors that must be considered.

### 11.42  THE PRODUCTION COST BUDGET

The basis of the production cost budget is the assessment of production in the budget period, often termed the production budget. Stocks are assessed to adjust the sales budget to the production required. The production plan provides the basis for the direct material cost, direct labour cost and production overhead budgets.

Closely allied with the production budget is the purchasing budget and the plant utilisation budget. The latter budget is prepared from machine loading data.

## 11.43 OTHER EXPENSE BUDGETS

This section covers the marketing and administration functions. A review of procedures in relation to each sectional cost will indicate acceptable expense levels. The amount of detail given is governed by the significance of each cost item and, therefore, the degree of control necessary. If, for example, advertising is a major expense item for the company a publicity budget may include publicity media costs.

## 11.44 RESEARCH AND DEVELOPMENT AND CAPITAL EXPENDITURE BUDGETS

The basis of these budgets are the research and development and capital expenditure projects approved by management. The long-term effect of such projects is recognised in the budget for the period calculated as follows:

| Project | Project started in the current year £ | Budget year £ | Future period(s) £ | Example |
|---|---|---|---|---|
| 1 | 5,000 | 4,000 | | A project already a commitment for the business and to be completed in the budget year |
| 2 | | 3,000 | 2,000 | An approved project to be started in the budget year and completed in a later period |
| 3 | | 2,000 | | An approved project to be started and completed in the budget period |
| 4 | 1,000 | 4,000 | 2,000 | A project already a commitment for the business and to be completed in a period after the budget year |
| Miscellaneous costs | | 500 | | Small items of expense not significant enough for the detailed project review procedure |
| | | 13,500 | | |
| | | (the budget figure required) | | |

## 11.45 THE CASH BUDGET

The cash budget may be prepared in any of the forms described in the chapter on funds analysis (Chapter 7), although for short-term control the receipts and payments basis is usually preferred.

The other budgets may appear reasonable until this budget is prepared which may indicate cash problems in the form of a cash shortage or excess for the business. Additional capital or bank facilities or a reduction in expenditure may be needed. If the cash shortage is temporary, an alteration in the timing of expenditure may solve the problem.

A contingencies allowance should be provided in the cash budget because uncontrollable factors can significantly affect cash receipts and payments.

## 11.5  PERIOD REPORTING

After the budget is approved and becomes a commitment for the organisation in the budget period, the reporting of actual results against the budget figures and an indication of the differences (variances) becomes part of the reporting system. Budgetary information used as the comparable data in Figure 1.10 provides a typical outline budget report.

In these reports the word 'actual' should not be interpreted literally. Estimates of actual cost, sufficiently accurate for management purposes, prepared from the best information available may be shown under the heading 'actual'. There is nothing wrong in this providing it is understood by management and that the possible error in the figures is not liable to lead to erroneous conclusions.

The differences between the actual and the budget figures may be analysed by causes to assist managers in improving their performance. This aspect of the subject is developed in the standard costing chapters.

## 11.6  THE BUDGET COMMITTEE

In the previous chapter, under the heading of budgeting co-ordination, reference was made to the possible use of a budget committee as an advisory and co-ordinating body for the administration of the budgetary system. A budget committee can be useful in the following budgetary activities:

1.  To offer advice to managers responsible for preparing budgets
2.  To co-ordinate budget activity with special responsibility for reconciling the views of executives where their plans overlap and agreement is necessary to govern the preparation of other associated details, e.g., the agreement of sales levels in relation to production activity
3.  To receive sectional budgets and scrutinise the plans as a basis for any revisions that may be necessary
4.  To make recommendations to the board of the company regarding the consideration and approval of the master budget
5.  To review routine budgetary reports on actual performance as a basis for recommendations for managerial action that is considered necessary.

If the accountant is given specific responsibilities for the administration of the budgetary system he may carry the title: 'budget officer' and be appointed secretary to the budget committee. His main duties in this position would include:

(a) The calling of committee meetings and the issue of the agenda with supporting papers needed by committee members

(b) The taking of minutes and the issue of advice regarding the conduct of the meetings

(c) The selection of committee members for specific budgets and possibly additional members where specialist advice is necessary

(d) The provision of general advice to all members of the committee on technical factors affecting budget preparation

(e) The fixing of preparatory procedures.


## 11.7 THE BUDGET MANUAL

It is common practice for the budget officer to prepare a budget manual to serve as a reference document for all staff connected with the budgetary control system. A typical contents list for such a manual may include the following:

| *Budget manual heading* | *Description* |
| --- | --- |
| 1. System objectives | The objectives of the system and the way the system will operate |
| 2. Business objectives | The objectives to be achieved by the business in the budget period in relation to its long-term plans |
| 3. Company policies | The policies adopted by the business to operate in the budget period |
| 4. Organisation structure and responsibilities | The organisational structure and responsibilities of specific personnel for aspects of the budgetary procedure |
| 5. Budget timetable | Details of when sections of the budgetary procedure are to be completed |
| 6. Sectional budget preparation | Specific instructions on the preparation of each sectional budget |
| 7. Master budget procedure | The procedure for preparing the master budget |
| 8. Budget review | The procedure for the review of submitted plans |
| 9. Budgetary reports | The statements to be produced for management |
| 10. Accounting procedure | The related accounting routines to be observed |
| 11. Report review | The procedure for the review of budgetary reports. |


## 11.8 SUMMARY

The responsibility for the design and development of a budgetary control system usually belongs to the accountant with the support of top management, and in the contents of the budget manual described above there is an indication of the potential impact of this system on the affairs of the business.

The master budget summarises sectional budgets that may be classified into two types: (*a*) the operating budget; and (*b*) the financial budget. The former is associated with the trading and profit and loss statement; the latter, the balance sheet. This simplified classification requires subsidiary analysis in most companies and the analysis should follow management control requirements. Specific areas may assume greater significance in some businesses than in others but limited development of sectional budgeting may be practised. Where there is limited development of the system, the overall advantages of budgetary control are unlikely to be secured.


## FOR FURTHER STUDY

### QUESTIONS

1. *Budget revision*

   Should budgets be amended when circumstances change that affect the budget? If budget amendments are required, what amendment detail will be required by a budget committee? Design a budget amendment form incorporating your requirements.

2. *Flexible budgeting*

   Using the following operating statement, prepare a report which will indicate the advantages which flexible budgeting has over fixed budgeting. Your report should show the operating statement as it would appear if flexible budgeting were in operation.

*Operating Statement for Period*

|  | Budget | | Actual | | Variance | |
|---|---|---|---|---|---|---|
|  | £ | £ | £ | £ | £ | £ |
| Sales |  | 392,000 |  | 450,500 |  | 58,500 |
| Less cost of sales |  |  |  |  |  |  |
| Factory: |  |  |  |  |  |  |
| Material | 115,000 |  | 134,650 |  | 19,650 |  |
| Labour | 80,000 |  | 88,000 |  | 8,000 |  |
| Expenses | 60,000 | 255,000 | 71,000 | 293,650 | 11,000 | 38,650 |
|  |  | 137,000 |  | 156,850 |  | 19,850 |
| Less sales expenses | 50,000 |  | 62,550 |  | 12,550 |  |
| administration expenses | 45,000 | 95,000 | 42,500 | 105,050 | (2,500) | 10,050 |
| Profit |  | 42,000 |  | 51,800 |  | 9,800 |
| Output (Production/Sales) Units 400,000 |  |  |  | 460,000 |  | 60,000 |

Notes re budget:
1. Material and labour costs vary in direct proportion to the number of units produced
2. Factory expenses are 20% fixed, 80% variable
3. Sales expenses are 20% fixed and the remainder vary directly with the level of unit sales

4. Administration expenses are fixed up to an output level of 500,000 units
5. Sales turnover figures are based on selling prices of £1 per unit subject to the following rebates:

| Quantity (units) | Average rebate |
|---|---|
| 0–300,000 | Nil |
| 0–350,000 | $1\frac{1}{2}\%$ |
| 0–400,000 | 2% } on total sales revenue |
| 0–450,000 | $2\frac{1}{2}\%$ |
| 0–500,000 | 3% |

In calculating budget figures for intermediate sales figures, rebates are taken to the nearest 50,000 units. (ACA)

**3.** *Sales analysis for effective planning and control*
'For effective planning and control, a marketing manager needs his company's sales analysed in a number of different ways.'
*Required:*
Comment upon this quotation and illustrate your answer with a description of the usual forms of sales analysis, stating briefly the purpose of each. (ACA)

**4.** *Appraisal of the sales budget*
The preliminary sales budget figures for Metal Products Ltd for next year have been submitted to the budget committee for consideration. These are given in Table 1. The company manufactures and sells only the three products mentioned, each of which requires highly skilled labour which cannot easily be replaced. In addition to the budget figures, the actual results for this year are given in Table 2.

TABLE 1. Sales budget provisional figures for next year
(This year's budget shown for comparison purposes)
Units (000)

| Quarter | Product A (units) this year | next year | Product B (units) this year | next year | Product C (units) this year | next year | Total (units) this year | next year |
|---|---|---|---|---|---|---|---|---|
| 1 | 4 | 3 | 5 | 6 | 9 | 10 | 18 | 19 |
| 2 | 4 | 3 | 5 | 6 | 9 | 10 | 18 | 19 |
| 3 | 4 | 3 | 5 | 6 | 9 | 10 | 18 | 19 |
| 4 | 4 | 3 | 5 | 6 | 9 | 10 | 18 | 19 |
| Total | 16 | 12 | 20 | 24 | 36 | 40 | 72 | 76 |
| Selling price (per unit) | £1·00 | £1·00 | £1·40 | £1·25 | £0·50 | £0·50 | – | – |
| Turnover (£000) | 16 | 12 | 28 | 30 | 18 | 20 | 62 | 62 |

TABLE 2. Actual trading results for this year
*Sales units (000)*

| Quarter | Product A | Product B | Product C | Total |
|---|---|---|---|---|
| 1 | 4 | 5 | 9 | 18 |
| 2 | 3 | 4 | 9 | 16 |
| 3 | 3 | 4 | 13 | 20 |
| 4 | 3 | 3 | 9 | 15 |
| Total | 13 | 16 | 40 | 69 |

*£000*

| | Product A | Product B | Product C | Total |
|---|---|---|---|---|
| Turnover | 13 | 20 | 15 | 48 |
| Costs | | | | |
| Material | 8 | 10 | 9 | 27 |
| Labour | 3 | 4 | 2 | 9 |
| Direct expense | 1 | 2 | 2 | 4 |
| Fixed expense | 2 | 3 | 2 | 7 |
| | 14 | 19 | 14 | 47 |
| Profit/(Loss) | (1) | 1 | 1 | 1 |

*Required:*

(*a*) What principles should be inherent in a sales budget before it can be accepted as an integral part of overall company policy?

(*b*) Applying the principles given in your answer to (*a*) what comments would you make on the sales estimates for next year? On the assumption that these figures are the best possible in the circumstances, what action would you recommend to the budget committee?                    (ACA Modified)

5. *Purchasing and production budgets (material)*

XYZ Ltd manufacture three products, P1, P2 and P3. These are made in three production departments from four materials, M1, M2, M3 and M4. The following information is supplied:

Predetermined product cost detail:

| | | Cost per | Product | | |
|---|---|---|---|---|---|
| Material | Used in department | material unit (£) | P1 | P2 | P3 |
| | | | (units per product) | | |
| M1 | D1 | 0·50 | – | 1 | 2 |
| M2 | D2 | 0·20 | 1 | – | 2 |
| M3 | D2 | 0·25 | 2 | 1 | – |
| M4 | D3 | 0·15 | 2 | 2 | 1 |
| Rejection on final inspection at end of process considered normal | | | 5% | 10% | 10% |

Budget details:

| | £ | £ | £ |
|---|---|---|---|
| Sales for the year in £000 | 260 | 580 | 450 |
| Sales price each | 5 | 10 | 6 |

*In thousands of products*

| Stocks | | | |
|---|---|---|---|
| At beginning of year – 1st Jan. | 5 | 10 | 15 |
| At close of year – 31st Dec. | 10 | 15 | 30 |

*In thousands of material units*

| | M1 | M2 | M3 | M4 |
|---|---|---|---|---|
| Raw material stocks | | | | |
| At beginning of year – 1st Jan. | 30 | 40 | 10 | 60 |
| At close of year – 31st Dec. | 40 | 30 | 20 | 50 |

*Required:*
Prepare: (a) pre-determined material costs per product for P1, P2 and P3; (b) for the year: (i) the production budget; (ii) the production cost budget for direct material for departments D1, D2 and D3; and (iii) the purchasing budget.

(ICMA)

6. *Preparation of a cash forecast*

You are asked to assist in the preparation of a cash forecast for Brown & Co. Ltd, a wholesaler. The company ends its financial year on 31st December and the following information is available regarding the company's operations:

(a) Management believes the previous year's sales pattern is a reasonable estimate of the current year's sales. Sales in the previous year were as follows:

| | £000 |
|---|---|
| January | 360 |
| February | 420 |
| March | 600 |
| April | 540 |
| May | 480 |
| June | 400 |
| July | 350 |
| August | 550 |
| September | 500 |
| October | 400 |
| November | 600 |
| December | 800 |
| Total | 6,000 |

(b) The debtors at 31st December total £380,000. Collections are generally made as follows:

| | |
|---|---|
| During month of sale | 60% |
| In first subsequent month | 30% |
| In second subsequent month | 9% |
| Uncollectable | 1% |
| | 100% |

(c) The purchase cost of goods averages 60% of selling price. The cost of the stock at 31st December is £840,000 of which £30,000 is obsolete. Arrangements have been made to sell the obsolete stock in January at half the normal selling price on a COD basis. The company wishes to maintain the stock as of the 1st of each month at a level of three months sales as determined by the sales forecast for the next three months. All purchases are paid for on the 10th of the following month. Trade creditors for purchases at 31st December total £370,000.

(d) Recurring fixed expenses amount to £120,000 per month including depreciation of £20,000. For accounting purposes the company apportions the recurring fixed expenses to the various months in the same proportion as that month's estimated sales bears to the estimated total annual sales. Variable expenses amount to 10% of sales. Payment for expenses are made as follows:

| | During month incurred | Following month |
|---|---|---|
| Fixed expenses | 55% | 45% |
| Variables expenses | 70% | 30% |

(e) Annual rates amount to £50,000 and are paid in equal instalments on 31st December and 31st March. The rates are in addition to the expenses in (d) above.

(f) During the winter unusual advertising costs will be incurred which will require cash payments of £10,000 in February and £15,000 in March. The advertising costs are in addition to the expenses in item (d) above.

(g) Equipment replacements are made at the rate of £3,000 per month. The equipment has an average estimated life of six years.

(h) Tax will be paid in January: £40,000.

(i) At 31st December the company had a bank loan with an unpaid balance of £280,000. The loan requires a principal payment of £20,000 on the last day of each month plus interest at $\frac{1}{2}$% per month on the unpaid balance at the first of the month. The entire balance is due on 31st March of the current year.

(j) The cash balance at 31st December: £100,000.

*Required:*

Prepare a cash forecast by months for the first three months of the current year for Brown & Co Ltd. The statement should show the amount of cash in hand (or deficiency of cash) at the end of each month.

**7.** *Preparation of the master budget and cash budget (A)*

The directors of a wholesaling business have approved the following budget programme for the six months to 30th June:

(*a*)  Sales:

|  | Per month £ |
|---|---|
| January | 10,000 |
| February | 15,000 |
| March to June | 25,000 |

(*b*)  Expenses:

|  | Salaries £ | Other expenses excluding rent £ |
|---|---|---|
| January to March | 2,000 | 800 |
| April to June | 3,000 | 1,500 |

One-eighth of each month's salaries and one quarter of the other expenses would be outstanding at the end of each month.

(*c*)  Rent at the rate of £2,000 per annum is payable quarterly in arrear at 31st March, 30th June, etc.

(*d*)  Stock at the end of the month:

|  | £ |
|---|---|
| January | 10,000 |
| February | 11,000 |
| March to June | 18,000 |

(*e*)  New fixed assets which have been purchased for £20,000 are to be paid for 31st March. These assets are to be brought into operation on 31st March.

(*f*)  Bank overdraft facilities have been arranged up to a limit of £5,000. The chairman has agreed to subscribe in cash on 31st March for such additional share capital as may be required to keep the overdraft within the limit during the six months.

(*g*)  It has to be assumed that the existing terms of credit will continue and be complied with.

(*h*)  The gross profit has to be taken at the constant rate of 20% on sales.

(*i*)  The balance sheet as at 31st December of the previous year is as follows:

| | £ | | £ |
|---|---|---|---|
| Issued share capital | 30,000 | Fixed assets (Cost – £25,000) | 19,000 |
| Profit and loss account | 11,550 | Stock | 9,000 |
| Trade creditor | 8,000 | Debtors | 20,000 |
| Charges accrued £ | | Cash in bank | 2,000 |
|   Salaries 250 | | | |
|   General | | | |
|   expenses 200 | 450 | | |
| | 50,000 | | 50,000 |

The trade creditors represent the purchases for December of the previous year, and the debtors the sales for November and December of the previous year, at £10,000 per month.

(*j*) Depreciation on the fixed assets at 10% on cost has to be provided.

(*k*) Ignore interest on the bank overdraft.

*Required:*

(i) Prepare a cash budget month by month for the six months to 30th June of the budget year, showing what share capital will be issued on 31st March.

(ii) Prepare a budgeted trading and profit and loss account for the six months and a budgeted balance sheet as at 30th June for the budget year as would appear if the estimates were realised. (ICMA)

8. *Preparation of the master budget and cash budget (B)*

The balance sheet of A. B. Rubber Co Ltd, as at 30th November this year is as follows:

|  | £ | £ |  | Cost £ | Depn. £ | £ |
|---|---|---|---|---|---|---|
| Share capital |  | 25,000 | Fixed assets |  |  |  |
| Reserves |  |  | Land and |  |  |  |
| General |  |  | buildings | 10,000 | – | 10,000 |
| reserve | 10,000 |  | Equipment | 15,500 | 5,500 | 10,000 |
| Profit and |  |  |  |  |  | 20,000 |
| loss account | 2,737 | 12,737 | Current assets |  |  |  |
|  |  | 37,737 | Stock |  | 16,773·5 |  |
| Current |  |  | Debtors |  | 15,500 | 32,273·5 |
| liabilities |  |  |  |  |  |  |
| Bank |  |  |  |  |  |  |
| overdraft | 8,000·5 |  |  |  |  |  |
| Trade |  |  |  |  |  |  |
| creditors | 6,536 | 14,536·5 |  |  |  |  |
|  |  | 52,273·5 |  |  |  | 52,273·5 |

At the balance sheet date stock consisted of:

Raw materials
E156  20,000 units
E157  18,000 units
E158  22,000 units

Finished goods
Grade 1:  200 blocks of 100 units
Grade 2:  150 blocks of 100 units
Grade 3:  200 blocks of 100 units

The company manufactures three grades of rubber compound which it sells to rubber component manufacturers. The Standard Cost Master Card for the three grades shows:

*Direct standard cost per 100 unit block*

|  | Price | Grade 1 | Grade 2 | Grade 3 |
|---|---|---|---|---|
|  |  | | Quantity | |
| Direct materials |  |  |  |  |
| E156 | £0·12 per unit | 50 units | 50 units | – |
| E157 | £0·13 per unit | 60 units | 63 units | 60 units |
| E158 | £0·15 per unit | – | – | 55 units |
| Direct labour |  |  |  |  |
| Dept. 1 | £0·40 per hour | 2 hours | $2\frac{1}{2}$ hours | $2\frac{1}{2}$ hours |
| Dept. 2 | £0·60 per hour | 20 minutes | 30 minutes | 20 minutes |

The company uses the direct cost method, i.e., overheads not allocated to products. Stock and finished goods are valued at direct cost. Overheads are controlled by comparison with a budget which shows for the following year:

|  | Grade 1 | Grade 2 | Grade 3 |
|---|---|---|---|
| Budget sales |  |  |  |
| Blocks of 100 units | 2,500 | 2,000 | 2,000 |
| Selling price per block | £20 | £21 | £20 |

|  | Depreciation | Others | Total |
|---|---|---|---|
|  | £ | £ | £ |
| Budget overheads |  |  |  |
| Manufacturing | 1,500 | 5,000 | 6,500 |
| Selling | 100 | 3,500 | 3,600 |
| Administration | 100 | 2,000 | 2,100 |

Budget stock at 30th November:
    Raw materials
        E156  23,000 units
        E157  20,000 units
        E158  19,500 units
    Finished goods
        Grade 1  210 blocks
        Grade 2  150 blocks
        Grade 3  150 blocks
    Capital budget:

(a) Capital expenditure: £2,500.
(b) Note that installation of new equipment to be commenced following the end of the budget year. Total estimated cost: £10,000; £3,000 to be paid during the month following the end of the budget year.
    All outlays apart from depreciation are for cash. There will be no opening or closing work-in-progress, and taxation can be ignored. The company allows its

customers $1\frac{1}{2}$ months credit and it takes one month's credit from suppliers.
*Required:*
(a) Prepare a statement showing the budgeted profit for the budget year, twelve months ended 30th November. The statement should bring out the contribution which each product makes per block and per annum.
(b) Prepare a statement which will disclose whether or not there will be sufficient cash in hand at the end of the budget year to meet the first instalment on the new equipment which will be due almost immediately after that period.
(c) Prepare the budgeted balance sheet position at 30th November.     (ACA)

9. *The use of a budget committee and the budget manual*
You have been appointed to a new post of budget officer and will be responsible for designing and instituting a profit planning and control programme. You will also act as secretary to a top-level budget committee responsible for the executive action necessary to implement the programme.
*Required:*
Prepare a concise statement of:

(a) The chief work of the budget committee
(b) The main duties you would expect to undertake
(c) The proposed headings and basic content for each chapter of a budget manual.     (ICMA)

10. *Survey of a budgetary control system*
Write a critical survey of a budgetary control system with particular reference to:

(a) The various types of budgets
(b) Changing production and sales levels.     (ACA)

11. *Interpretative comment on budgets*
Electronic Components Ltd, a large company, realised that the evaluation of the current year's performance and its effect on the budget year would provide major assumptions for management preparing their plans. As the current year's performance for the first nine months of the year had already been reported and reviewed through the medium of the control reports, the following detail was provided for planning guidance:

(a) An analysis of cash generation and borrowing requirements. A comparison of the current year budget with the estimated results for the current year for the following:

   (i) Long-term funds available
   (ii) Long-term funds required
   (iii) Available working capital
   (iv) Required working capital
   (v) Short-term borrowing
   (vi) Total borrowing facilities

(b) Capital authorisations and expenditure. The estimated current year end position. For each project:

    (i) Project number and description of project
    (ii) Estimated total current year expenditure
    (iii) Estimated expenditure in the budget and future years
    (iv) Estimated total cost

(c) A review of significant changes in external environment which have taken place during the current year analysed as follows:

    (i) Economic changes
    (ii) Political action changes
    (iii) Competitive action changes
    (iv) Changes due to labour disputes and union relations.

The future programme for the budget year included the following:

(a) New product introductions classified as follows:

    (i) By time of release
    (ii) By budget year profit impact

(b) The impact of budgeted price factors by major product classification:

    (i) Competitive changes
    (ii) Product changes
    (iii) Cost changes
    (iv) Other factors

(c) Sales classified by:

    (i) Product
    (ii) Order types (stock orders and others)
    (iii) Sales outlets
    (iv) Market area

(d) Supply requirements by major product classification:

    (i) Planned cost of goods sold
    (ii) Increase/decrease in finished goods stock
    (iii) Total production requirements
    (iv) Planned source of production (locally produced and imported)

(e) Utilisation of production capacity — available and to be used
(f) The effect of changes in the level of production on manufacturing costs
(g) Manpower — by type of labour and function.

The above details were supported with interpretative comment as a basis for assessment.

*Required:*

(a) For the detail provided for planning guidance, suggest the interpretative comment that should be submitted to the budget committee.

(b) For the detail included in the future programme for the budget year suggest the interpretative comment that should be submitted to the budget committee.

## 12. *Installation of a budgetary control system*

Oldroyd & Sons Ltd is an old-established business manufacturing sauces, pickles and similar products, and trading mainly in the north of England and central Scotland. The company has been successful for many years and a sound position has been built up enabling good dividends to be paid to shareholders who are mainly descendants of the original founder. A minority of the shares are held by old customers and senior employees of the company.

The present managing director is 38 years of age and succeeded to the position 12 months ago on the death of his father who had held the position for over 30 years. He was formerly sales director and believes there is good scope for expansion. The board of directors have accepted his proposal to double the sales volume in four years, mainly by opening new accounts in the Midlands and south of England.

Hitherto, the only financial information available to management has been a half-yearly profit and loss account and balance sheet prepared by the company's auditors on traditional lines. In addition, each year's sales are analysed by products and by representatives' territories, of which there are five. Cost records are elementary and are not reconciled with the financial books.

On the 1st January, you were appointed chief accountant to meet the managing director's wish for 'better and more frequent financial figures'. You propose, and he accepts, that budgetary control will help to provide the necessary answer.

*Required:*

(a) With the above information in mind, indicate the steps you would take in establishing budgetary control; and the difficulties you might encounter in doing so and how you would overcome them.

(b) Draft the designs for the statements which you would recommend in order to give the managing director and other levels of management the 'better and more frequent financial figures desired.                                        (ICMA)

## FURTHER READING

Bishop, S. V. *Business Planning and Control*. General Educational Trust of the Institute of Chartered Accountants in England and Wales, 1966. Chapters 4—8.

Chamberlain, Neil W. *The Firm: Micro Economic Planning and Action*. McGraw-Hill, New York, 1962. Chapters 7—11.

Welsch, Glenn A. *Budgeting: Profit Planning and Control*. Prentice-Hall, Englewood Cliffs, New Jersey, 1964. Chapters 3—11.

# ACCOUNTING AND BUSINESS CONTROL

# 12 The Acquisition of Long-term Resources

## OBJECTIVE OF THE CHAPTER

To emphasise the importance of capital expenditure and project control with particular reference to the financial procedures that may be adopted to ensure proper project authorisation and evaluation; measure progress at all significant stages of completion; and report to management information on projects as an aid to their successful completion or modification.

## OUTLINE OF THE CHAPTER

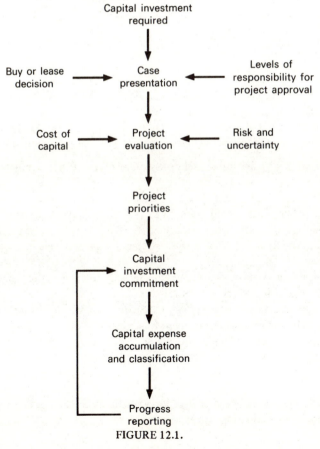

FIGURE 12.1.

215

A business requires fixed and working capital resources and before operations can commence long-term investment must be made in fixed assets. Control over this capital expenditure is important for the following reasons:

1. Most capital projects involve the company in a significant outlay of cash which has a marked effect on the use of funds in the business
2. Capital expenditure usually means a definite commitment decision which cannot normally be reversed without a significant loss
3. Current expenditure is incurred in the short term where a manager's judgements about the future are fairly reliable. Capital expenditure decisions are made relative to a longer time-scale and the longer the period, the less reliable the forecasts made. This point is developed in chapter 8
4. Management ability is stretched to the limit with some projects demanding an awareness of all relevant factors and their measurement and evaluation, where appropriate
5. Management talent and funds are often limited and the use of these resources should reflect an awareness of the priorities appropriate to the business. Information on priorities relative to proposed capital expenditure proposals is necessary
6. The completion of a project may take some time and, without adequate control information, costs may be exceeded by a significant amount or the planning project specifications not achieved.

## 12.1  ESSENTIALS OF A CAPITAL EXPENDITURE CONTROL SYSTEM

Control over capital expenditure involves a system with the following key features:

1. An understanding by key personnel of the importance of the six points noted above
2. A recognised level of responsibility for project approval
3. The ability of those submitting projects to state their case adequately
4. A knowledge on the part of the management accountant on how to evaluate a project from the financial point of view so that adequate advice can be given to management
5. An understanding by those responsible for decision-making of the techniques involved in point (4) and their significance
6. A good communication system for capital expenditure decisions and their implications at all levels of management to be understood
7. A good accounting control and reporting procedure as a check on approved projects.

The use of capital expenditure project forms of the type described in Chapter 3 support the control system as illustrated in Figure 12.2.

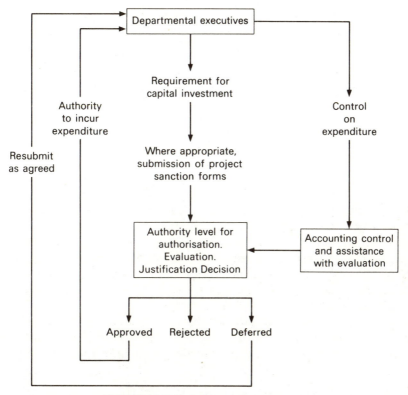

FIGURE 12.2. Capital expenditure control

## 12.2 THE COST OF CAPITAL

To acquire the resources required for business, the funds may be budgeted and obtained in accepted forms: short-, medium- and long-term capital. Good finance control will dictate that long-term assets are backed by long-term finance, but the total capital requirement in most businesses is from many sources and the cost of capital can vary significantly. The cost of capital, therefore, is not the interest rate on a specific form of capital, even though it may be planned to obtain this capital to finance the capital expenditure project for review. The cost of capital is a weighted average of debt and equity at current market rates, the weighting depending on the balanced fund structure that the company expects to maintain in the future. For example:

| Kind of capital | Capital £ | Cost of capital* £ |
|---|---|---|
| Debt | 40,000 | 3,200 |
| Equity | 60,000 | 6,000 |
| | 100,000 | 9,200 |

*The calculation of the cost of capital is a difficult matter and the subject a topic in finance that may be pursued by reference to a good text in this area. Recommended, is Chapter 11, 'Cost of capital', in *Managerial Finance* by J. F. Weston and Eugene F. Brigham (Holt, Rinehart & Winston, 1972).

Weighted average cost of capital: $\dfrac{£9,200}{£100,000} \times 100 = 9\cdot2\%$

Because of the difficulty of calculating the weighted average cost of capital, it is not uncommon for a company to fix the cut-off rate for judging capital expenditure projects by experience of what has been found to be an acceptable rate of return.

## 12.3  CAPITAL INVESTMENT COMMITMENT

The investment commitment to be considered is the incremental position, whether the costs are capitalised or treated as revenue expenditure in the books of the business. Incremental costs are the cash outflows that will be made if the project is carried out and avoided if it is not carried out. This assessment involves associated cash movements as, for example, the cash that may be received on the disposal of an existing asset at the time of replacement. When machinery and equipment is purchased, the additional investment may include current assets such as stock and trade debtors. This additional investment may be recovered (a cash inflow) at the end of the life of the project as well as the net salvage value of the machinery and equipment, where applicable.

Committed items, such as design costs, which may have been incurred preparatory to the project being seriously considered for further investment, are irrelevant in the assessment of cash flows for evaluation since they are not incremental.

## 12.4  RISK AND UNCERTAINTY IN CAPITAL EXPENDITURE FORECASTING

The possible loss of money invested in a business project is a financial risk and many uncertainties contribute to this risk. Economic uncertainties, for example, make investment forecasting difficult. As mentioned earlier in this chapter, amounts estimated are long term and the longer the term the greater the potential error in the forecasts made. Sensitivity analysis can make a valuable contribution in this area. If this technique is adopted, key figures may be changed and the effect on forecasts measured. The identification of highly sensitive areas to key figure changes gives management valuable information on the significance of forecasting errors.

Executives may be asked to supply three forecasts regarding a project:

1. The optimistic estimate of cash flows
2. The most likely estimate of cash flows
3. The pessimistic estimate of cash flows.

Forecasts (1) and (3) are not extreme estimates because these would be useless for project evaluation. Given reasonable estimates, the range of possible results are an improvement on a single forecast.

Probability distribution may improve the objectivity of the forecasts. This procedure involves weighting each forecast according to its probability and using the weighted result as the project review figure. In the example that follows, the three forecasts mentioned above have been given probability weights of ·25, ·45 and ·3 respectively (the total is 1):

| Forecast | Cash inflow of £ | Probability | Weighted result £ |
|---|---|---|---|
| 1 | 4,000 | ·25 | 1,000 |
| 2 | 3,000 | ·45 | 1,350 |
| 3 | 2,000 | ·3 | 600 |
| | | | 2,950 |

(The project review figure)

## 12.5 PRIORITIES AND THE EVALUATION OF CAPITAL EXPENDITURE PROJECTS

Investment opportunities can vary significantly in profitability to the business and the evaluation procedure should assist in establishing a scale of priorities. It is realistic to recognise that not all profitable projects can be undertaken because of lack of finance and other key factors such as management, which may be stretched near the limit by existing responsibilities.

The priority aspect is not limited to varying project opportunities; it may be applicable to a single project. For example, there may be a choice of machines that can be purchased for a specific project, involving an appraisal of their relative merits.

## 12.6 COST ESCALATION INCLUDING THE EFFECTS OF INFLATION

The costs over the life of a project may be greater than the estimated level owing to:

1. Inefficient management
2. Poor estimating
3. Changing economic conditions
4. Unexpected developments.

Only the rigorous control of costs can help the company to realise the potential envisaged from its investment opportunities.

Inflation should be recognised in project evaluation by allowing for this factor in the estimated cash flows.

## 12.7  LEVELS OF RESPONSIBILITY FOR PROJECT APPROVAL

In a small company, all capital projects may require board approval but in a large company responsibility may be delegated to various levels of management as follows:

| Type of management | Estimated project expenditure |
|---|---|
| Area manager | Up to £5,000 |
| Divisional manager | £5,000 to £20,000 |
| HQ management | Over £20,000 |

There may be a variation on this arrangement for different types of investment; essential projects being allowed on the authority of a lower level of management for amounts beyond the general scale of estimated project expenditure.

## 12.8  CASE PRESENTATION

Standardised procedures are useful in ensuring that the information required for investment appraisal is supplied as necessary. The danger is that one executive may not obtain project approval because his case has not been presented adequately while another executive, more skilful in case presentation, may obtain approval for a project of less value to the business. Executives should be educated in case presentation and the evaluation process carried out with great care. Case presentation to secure approval of a project should emphasise:

1. The relationship of the project to long-term objectives
2. The required rate of return
3. The risk and uncertainties regarding the future of the project at an acceptable level
4. The preferences relating the proposed investment to alternative opportunities
5. The weighting of the arguments put forward in favour of or against a proposal so that the relative value of these arguments may be determined
6. The assumptions on which the projections have been based
7. The relevant non-quantifiable factors and the weighting given to these factors.

The management accountant can render a useful service to management in screening submitted proposals and giving financial advice where appropriate. It is usually the management accountant who provides a predetermined and approved required rate of return on capital projects.

## 12.9  TYPES OF ASSET ACQUISITION

Capital expenditure proposals may be identified by the following categories:

1. New product
2. Cost saving

3. Replacement
4. Expansion.

This classification may be supplemented by an urgency rating such as:

(a)  Urgent – the project necessary to maintain current operations
(b)  Necessary for the future – the project is required but it is not of such immediate concern as in (a).

The emphasis in this chapter has been on projects meeting the criterion of the required rate of return. There may be essential projects with no return, such as a pollution control proposal, and a separate classification may be reserved for such projects.


## 12.10  THE BUY OR LEASE DECISION

It should not be assumed that all assets are purchased. An asset may be leased, i.e., a third party finances the purchase and the asset is rented by the third party to the user company in return for rental instalments. With outright purchase by the company the full purchase price is usually paid at the time of purchase, whereas with a leasing arrangement rental payments are made usually on a monthly or quarterly basis. Normally, the rental payments are not equal over the life of the asset. After a period, say five years, the rent may be less than the rate in the early years of the leasing agreement.

There may be an intermediate situation where the asset is obtained by hire purchase. In this case, an immediate payment of deposit may be necessary with hire-purchase repayments following in subsequent years as the relevant cash flows.

The significant difference in these arrangements from the project evaluation point of view is the timing of the cash flows. This factor is developed in the evaluation methods described below.


## 12.11  PROJECT EVALUATION METHODS

The usual methods of evaluating capital expenditure proposals include:

1. The pay-back method
2. The return on investment (ROI) method
3. The discounted cash flow (DCF) net present value (NPV) method
4. The discounted cash flow (DCF) internal rate of return (IRR) method.

To illustrate these methods, the following cash inflows are given for three projects to be evaluated where the outlay at the beginning of the project is £1,000 in each case (usually referred to as year 0):

| Year | Project A £ | Project B £ | Project C £ |
|------|-------------|-------------|-------------|
| 1 | 600 | 300 | 100 |
| 2 | 500 | 700 | 100 |
| 3 | 50 | 480 | 800 |
| 4 | 50 | 10 | 400 |
| 5 | 300 | 10 | 100 |
|   | 1,500 | 1,500 | 1,500 |

It is assumed that the cash is received at the end of each year and there is no recovery value on the £1,000 at the end of year 5.

### 12.111 THE PAY-BACK METHOD

The payback period is the time taken to recover in cash inflows the cash outflow for the investment. Using the example above, the payback periods for the three projects are:

Project A:   $1\frac{4}{5}$ years
Project B:   2 years
Project C:   3 years.

### 12.112 THE RETURN ON INVESTMENT METHOD

The average profit for the period is expressed as a percentage of the cash outflow for the investment. For each project in the example the average profit is:

|                     | £     |
|---------------------|-------|
| Cash inflow         | 1,500 |
| Less depreciation   | 1,000 |
| Profit for 5 years  | 500   |
| Annual profit       | 100   |

The return on the original investment as a percentage for each project is, therefore, 10%.

The view may be taken that an average investment should be used since there is a reduction in the value of the asset over its life. A typical formula is to divide the asset value by two which gives a return for each of the above projects of 20%. An alternative average calculation assuming depreciation at equal amounts of £200 per annum (£1,000 divided by five years) is as follows:

| Investment employed in year | £ | |
|---|---|---|
| 1 | 1,000 | |
| 2 | 800 | (£1,000 − £200) |
| 3 | 600 | (£800 − £200) |
| 4 | 400 | (£600 − £200) |
| 5 | 200 | (£400 − £200) |
| Total | 3,000 | |
| Average investment | 600 | (£3,000 ÷ 5) |

Using this average figure, the return on the projects in each case would be 16·7% $\left(\dfrac{100}{600} \times 100\%\right)$.

## 12.113 THE DCF/NPV METHOD

In this method, allowance is made for the time value of money, i.e., the recognition that money received in the future is worth less than money received today. In the above examples, this factor has been ignored. In the discounted cash flow method the view is taken that the cash inflows and cash outflows should be of the same money value for comparison — today's value (known as present value). To obtain this present value, future cash flows are discounted at a chosen discounting compound interest rate. This process is the reversal of finding a future value of an investment at compound interest and may be calculated by formula or the use of compound interest tables — in this case, Table 1 in Appendix B (Present value of £1). The explanation of the formula and how the tables are used is given in Appendix A. The factors taken from Table 1 (Appendix B) are known as discount factors.

The chosen discounting compound interest rate may be the cost of capital but whatever figure is used it is usually regarded as the cut-off rate for judging the acceptability of projects. Assuming a cut-off rate of 10%, the net present values of the three projects may be calculated as follows:

| | | Project A | | | | Project B | | | | Project C | |
|---|---|---|---|---|---|---|---|---|---|---|---|
| | £ | 10% Discount factor | Present value £ | £ | 10% Discount factor | Present value £ | £ | 10% Discount factor | Present value £ | | |
| Cash inflows: | | | | | | | | | | | |
| Year 1 | 600 | ·909 | 545 | 300 | ·909 | 273 | 100 | ·909 | 91 | | |
| Year 2 | 500 | ·826 | 413 | 700 | ·826 | 578 | 100 | ·826 | 83 | | |
| Year 3 | 50 | ·751 | 38 | 480 | ·751 | 360 | 800 | ·751 | 601 | | |
| Year 4 | 50 | ·683 | 34 | 10 | ·683 | 7 | 400 | ·683 | 273 | | |
| Year 5 | 300 | ·621 | 186 | 10 | ·621 | 6 | 100 | ·621 | 62 | | |
| | 1,500 | | 1,216 | 1,500 | | 1,224 | 1,500 | | 1,110 | | |
| Cash outflow | | | 1,000 | | | 1,000 | | | 1,000 | | |
| Net present value | | | 216 | | | 224 | | | 110 | | |

Because the net present value is positive, the actual rate of return of all three projects must be greater than 10%. If the net present value had been negative, the project return would have been less than 10% and, therefore, the projects would not have been acceptable on the basis of the cut-off rate criterion.

## 12.114 THE DCF/IRR METHOD

In the previous method, it was noted that the rates of return on each project must be greater than 10%. From the last paragraph of the previous section it may be realised that the actual DCF return would be given when discount factors are used which provide the discounted cash inflows and outflows at the same present values – in this case, £1,000. For the three projects, the nearest percentages are shown below giving projects A and B a return of 21%; and project C, a return of 14%:

| | | Project A | | | Project B | | | Project C | |
|---|---|---|---|---|---|---|---|---|---|
| | £ | 21% Discount factor | Present value £ | £ | 21% Discount factor | Present value £ | £ | 14% Discount factor | Present value £ |
| Cash inflows: | | | | | | | | | |
| Year 1 | 600 | ·826 | 496 | 300 | ·826 | 248 | 100 | ·877 | 88 |
| Year 2 | 500 | ·683 | 341 | 700 | ·683 | 478 | 800 | ·769 | 77 |
| Year 3 | 50 | ·565 | 28 | 480 | ·565 | 271 | 800 | ·675 | 540 |
| Year 4 | 50 | ·467 | 23 | 10 | ·467 | 5 | 400 | ·592 | 237 |
| Year 5 | 300 | ·386 | 115 | 10 | ·386 | 4 | 100 | ·519 | 52 |
| | 1,500 | | 1,003 | 1,500 | | 1,006 | 1,500 | | 994 |
| Cash outflows | | | 1,000 | | | 1,000 | | | 1,000 |
| Net present value | | | 3 | | | 6 | | | –6 |

Discounted cash flow methods assume that the rate of return calculated represents the reinvestment of the cash inflows at the same rate, i.e., in the above example, projects A and B: 21%; and project C: 14%.

## 12.12  OTHER FACTORS AFFECTING PROJECT EVALUATION

This section covers the following topics affecting project evaluation:

1. Taxation
2. Relationship between evaluation methods
3. Projects to be compared with differing investment amounts
4. Projects to be compared with differing investment lives
5. Variation in the assumptions used to apply evaluation methods
6. Non-quantifiable factors in project appraisal
7. Identifying the rate of return
8. Depreciation
9. Projects with constant annual cash flows.

## 12.121 TAXATION AND CAPITAL EXPENDITURE EVALUATION

Taxation is such a significant factor in cash flow that the relative profitability of investments cannot be satisfactorily considered by ignoring taxation (which includes development area allowances). The taxation factors vary from time to time and those in force at the time of writing are shown in Appendix C. Because of this government tendency to change taxation allowances, some companies prefer to ignore tax on the grounds that taxation is an appropriation of profits and it is, therefore, safer to consider the profitability of projects before tax. It is difficult to understand the reason for isolating this particular uncertainty from the other uncertainties that surround investment projects.

The delayed taxation effects should be recognised in DCF methods when the present value of cash flows is calculated.

## 12.122 RELATIONSHIP BETWEEN EVALUATION METHODS

Where the life of a project is more than double the payback period of the project and cash inflows per year are approximately equal, the reciprocal of the payback period in years as a percentage is very close to the DCF return.

## 12.123 PROJECTS WITH DIFFERING INVESTMENT AMOUNTS

When comparing the net present values of investment projects with differing investment amounts this factor should be incorporated in the ranking procedure. Providing projects have equal lives, the method adopted is to calculate the profitability index by the use of the following formula:

$$\text{Profitability index} = \frac{\text{Present value of the cash inflows}}{\text{Present value of the cash outflow}}$$

The preferred project in the ranking order is the project with the highest profitability index.

## 12.124 PROJECTS WITH DIFFERING INVESTMENT LIVES

When comparing the net present values of investment projects with differing lives, the comparison of the shorter-lived project should be made with the longer-lived project by assumed repetitive investment of the former project.

Where the assumed repetitive investment is not equal to the longer-lived project, the repetition is assumed for the length of time necessary and an estimate of the disposal value of the shorter-lived project at the end of the longer-lived project is introduced into the present value calculation.

## 12.125 VARYING THE ASSUMPTIONS IN THE EVALUATION METHODS

Two assumptions were made in the above examples. One was the cash inflow receipts assumed to be at the end of each year. This assumption may be unrealistic and the error introduced into the discounted cash flow calculations may be reduced by six-monthly period calculations, rather than the use of annual discount factors. It is a matter of judgement whether the error is sufficiently significant to justify such a procedure.

No recovery value was assumed for the projects described above. Where disposal values are expected and working capital can be recovered at the end of the project, these amounts are considered as cash inflows at the end of the project life.

### 12.126  NON-QUANTIFIABLE FACTORS IN PROJECT APPRAISAL

This chapter has concentrated on the quantifiable factors affecting project approval. Non-quantifiable factors must also be considered and accounting can make no contribution in this area. The issue is a matter of judgement and the quality of management in making the correct investment decision is crucial.

### 12.127  IDENTIFYING THE RATE OF RETURN

The internal rates of return identified for the three projects above were obtained by trial and error and when rates are close, interpolation may be used to calculate the rate of return. If, for example, project C present values for 13% and 15% are £1,020 and £968 respectively, the rate of return may be calculated as follows:

| Rate of return % | Present values £ | Net present value £ |
|---|---|---|
| 13 | 1,020 | 20 |
| 15 | 968 | −32 |
| 2 | 52 | |

$$\frac{£20}{£52} \times 2 = \cdot 77$$

Rate of return $= 13\% + \cdot 77\% = 13 \cdot 77\%$

A graph may be used for the same purpose, where the profitability index at different interest rates may be plotted on a chart using the $X$ axis for the profitability index and the $Y$ axis for the interest rate. The rate of interest required may be obtained by inspection, reading off the graph the point where the profitability index of 1 (where the net present values of cash inflows and outflows are the same) cuts the plotted curve.

### 12.128  DEPRECIATION AND CAPITAL EXPENDITURE EVALUATION

It may be noted that there was no mention in the DCF examples of depreciation. Depreciation was not ignored because the calculations in the technique provide for the recovery of the investment amount.

### 12.129  PROJECTS WITH CONSTANT ANNUAL CASH FLOWS

The cash inflows of the three projects used in the example above varied each year. Where they are constant, the present value calculations may be shortened by the use of Table 2 in Appendix B (present value of £1 per period). In this case, advantage is being taken of the annuity situation represented by the periodic inflows of equal amount for each equal period. An example follows:

| Year | Cash inflows £ | 10% Discount factors Table 1 Appendix B | Present value £ |
|---|---|---|---|
| 1 | 1,000 | ·909 | 909 |
| 2 | 1,000 | ·826 | 826 |
| 3 | 1,000 | ·751 | 751 |
| 4 | 1,000 | ·683 | 683 |
| 5 | 1,000 | ·621 | 621 |
| | 5,000 | | 3,790 |

Reference to Table 2, Appendix B, where $i = 10\%$ and $n = 5$ years gives the discount factor 3·791:

$$£1,000 \times 3·791 = \text{present value of } £3,791$$

It may be noted that the total of Table 1 factors given above give the Table 2 factor: 3,790 — the slight difference is due to approximation.

## 12.13 COMPARISON OF THE EVALUATION METHODS

| | Payback method | Return on investment method | DCF NPV method | DCF IRR method |
|---|---|---|---|---|
| 1. Recognition of the time value of money | No | No | Yes | Yes |
| 2. An indication of the speed of cash return | Yes | No | No | No |
| 3. Includes all cash flows | No | Yes | Yes | Yes |
| 4. Dependent on the reinvestment rate of return | No | No | Yes | Yes |

From the above table, it would appear that the DCF techniques are to be preferred and conceptually this is so. Considerable research indicates that many companies ignore DCF and favour the payback period because of its simplicity and emphasis on liquidity. The big disadvantage is that in the priority ranking of projects misleading data can be given because cash inflow beyond the payback period is ignored. From the earlier example a different rating may be indicated than by DCF which recognises the time value of money. These different priority ratings are shown below:

| | Project A | Project B | Project C |
|---|---|---|---|
| Payback method | 1 | 2 | 3 |
| Return on investment method | 1 | 1 | 1 |
| DCF/NPV method | 2 | 1 | 3 |
| DCF/IRR method | 2 | 1 | 3 |

There are differences of opinion regarding the DCF method preference, but the widely-held view is that the NPV method reinvestment assumption at the cut-off rate is more realistic than the higher IRR method return percentages.

## 12.14  CAPITAL EXPENSE ACCUMULATION AND CLASSIFICATION

Work on a capital project may be undertaken by company staff and company facilities may be used. Cost ascertainment procedures should recognise this possibility and a typical system may include the following features:

1. The identification of each capital expenditure project by a number
2. A capital expenditure cost sheet established for each capital job
3. The identification of costs directly incurred on the capital work on basic documents and records
4. The recording of the costs ascertained in (3) above on the cost sheet mentioned in (2) above
5. A decision made on the treatment of overheads and the amount, if any, to be added to the direct costs for the project.

The segregation of capital cost is a matter of judgement. Capital expenditure is generally regarded as the amount incurred on new assets, extensions and improvements to existing assets, such expenditure being incurred as a basis of earning revenue. Installation cost is part of the capital cost.

## 12.15  PROGRESS REPORTING

Chapter 3 referred to the financial control necessary following project approval and such a system should include the following features:

1. The use of project sanction procedure which would provide the following cost control data:

   (a)  Estimated costs for each element of cost
   (b)  Planned completion times and costs for each stage of the work to be checked

2. The provision of the costs incurred on the job as each stage is completed with certification that the job has been completed to the required standard for each stage
3. The comparison of the results ascertained in (2) with the planned costs given in (1)
4. The period reporting of the results with an indication to management of unsatisfactory performance
5. Where applicable, the revision of the control data in (1) as a result of management decision and the future use of this data for subsequent stage cost control.

It may be decided to abandon a project which is not matching the approval criteria and careful judgement is necessary to minimise project loss.

## 12.16 SUMMARY

The successful company is the one capable of making good investments and this implies an ability to identify worth-while investment opportunities; assess their relative value to the company; carry through a project to a successful conclusion; and in this process recognise cash requirements and cash availability.

## FOR FURTHER STUDY

QUESTIONS

1. *Need for and objectives of a capital expenditure control system*
   Comment on the need for capital expenditure control in a business and the objectives that should be met by such a system.

2. *Features of a capital expenditure control system*
   What are the essential features of a capital expenditure control system?

3. *Criteria for capital investment*
   Most businesses are today faced with alternative uses for available funds. What criteria would you, as an accountant, recommend should be used to decide on alternative investment opportunities? What problems would the application of your criteria bring? Give a formula for the evaluation of a capital expenditure project by the discounted cash flow method explaining clearly how each term in the formula is obtained. (ACA)

4. *Proposal sanction form interpretation*
   Consumer goods is a division of Merchandise Supplies Ltd. Divisional management require the authority of the board of directors for all capital expenditure over £20,000. The request on p. 230 (figure 12.3) for capital expenditure has been submitted to the board of directors:

   *Required:*
   Comment on this submission. (ACA)

5. *Methods of investment evaluation*
   Your company is considering investing in a project for which the investment data is as follows:

   Capital outlay: £200,000
   Depreciation: Fixed instalment method
              Project life: 5 years with no residual value
   Forecasted annual income — before charging depreciation but after all other charges:

| Year | £ |
|---|---|
| 1 | 100,000 |
| 2 | 100,000 |
| 3 | 80,000 |
| 4 | 80,000 |
| 5 | 40,000 |
| | 400,000 |

| Capital expenditure proposal | Ref. no. 5389 |
|---|---|

Location:　　Consumer goods division

Project description:　*To replace an existing machine tool with a more automatic model which has just come on to the market.*

| Evaluation: | | £ |
|---|---|---|
| **1. Capital costs:** | | |
| *New machine – purchase price* | | *33,500* |
| *Less salvage value in 8 years* | | *1,500* |
| *Net capital employed* | | *32,000* |
| | | |
| *Old machine – original cost* | | *24,000* |
| *Accumulated depreciation* | | *12,000* |
| *Net book value* | | *12,000* |
| *Current salvage value* | | *1,000* |
| *Loss if replaced* | | *11,000* |

| | | £ | £ |
|---|---|---|---|
| **2. Annual operating costs:** | | | |
| *Labour hours saved: 6,000* | | | |
| *Average wage cost per hour £0.5* | | | |
| *Saving in labour cost* | | | *3,000* |
| *Overhead rate: 125% on labour cost* | | | *3,750* |
| *Gross savings* | | | *6,750* |
| *Less: loss on old machine* | | *11,000* | |
| *Installation cost of new machine* | | *1,000* | |
| | | *12,000* | |
| *Annual cost* $\dfrac{£12,000}{8}$ | | | *1,500* |
| *Net saving* | | | *5,250* |

**3. Return on investment:**

$$\frac{\text{Net saving}}{\text{Half capital employed}} = \frac{£5,250}{£16,000} \times 100 = 32.8\%$$

*Cost of capital: 15%*

**4. Comments:**

*In view of the profitability of this proposal, sanction to go ahead is requested immediately.*

*S.Smith*　Divisional manager　　*3ʳᵈ October 19*　Date

FIGURE 12.3.

In connexion with the above, you are asked to employ methods of measuring the return on the capital employed with a view to ascertaining the value to the company of the proposed investment.

*Required:*

On the basis of the figures given above and assuming a cost of capital rate of 10%, set out calculations illustrating and comparing the following methods of evaluating return on capital employed:

(a) Payback period
(b) Rate of return on original investment
(c) Rate of return on average investment
(d) Discounted cash flow.

Taxation to be ignored.                                    (ACA – Modified)

6. *DCF calculations on a proposed machine purchase*
A machine with a purchase price of £14,000 is estimated to eliminate manual
operations costing £4,000 per year. The machine will last 5 years and have no
residual value at the end of its life.
*Required:*
Calculate:

(a) The discounted cash flow rate of return
(b) The level of annual saving necessary to achieve a 12% DCF return
(c) The net present value if the capital cost is 10%.

Ignore taxation.                                           (ICMA)

7. *Distinction between the DCF/IRR and /NPV methods*
The DCF method may be applied in two ways: one by calculating the net
present value; and the other by calculating the internal rate of return of the
investment proposals under review.
*Required:*
Comment on the distinction between these two applications of the DCF method.

8. *Different methods of proposal appraisal*
Appliances Ltd are considering the purchase of a machine and two types are
available, both costing £10,000 and both adequate for the purpose intended.
The cash inflows are as follows:

| Year | Machine A £ | Machine B £ |
|---|---|---|
| 1 | 2,000 | 4,000 |
| 2 | 2,000 | 4,000 |
| 3 | 6,000 | 1,000 |
| 4 | 3,000 | 4,000 |
|  | 13,000 | 13,000 |

The accountant, using the cut-off rate for projects in the company of 10%,
has produced the following evaluation:

|  | Machine A | Machine B | Preference |
|---|---|---|---|
| Return on investment method | 7·5% | 7·5% | None |
| DCF/NPV method: net present value | £25 | £423 | Machine B |

When asked why he ignored tax, the accountant made the point that the uncertainty surrounding the tax position of the company in the years to come prompted his belief that it was better ignored, particularly seeing that the company normally aimed for a good profits before tax figure and from this amount tax would be paid.

The factory manager said that he had mentioned non-measurable factors on his capital expenditure proposal form that justified investment in Machine A, whatever the accountant's figures may show.

The managing director also supported the investment in Machine A but for an additional reason to that given by the factory manager. He pointed out that the company would get its money back from Machine A in 3 years whereas it would take $3\frac{1}{4}$ years with Machine B.

The chief engineer said that he was rather confused by the figures presented and the statements made because the overall criterion of success for the company had been agreed as profit before tax as a percentage of capital employed. On the accountant's figures, it did not seem to matter which machine was purchased.

*Required:*

(*a*) Comment on the different methods of appraisal mentioned in the case.

(*b*) Do you agree with the accountant on the subject of taxation?

(*c*) What advice would you give to management in this case?

9. *Factors in connexion with the purchase of new machinery*

A company manufacturing metal products intends to install new capacity. The choice has been narrowed to two machines, A and B. The initial cost of A would be £10,100 and of B, £20,200. Both have an estimated life of 10 years with no scrap value at the end of their lives. A could produce 1·25 pieces per hour while running at full capacity and it is estimated that the average loss of potential full capacity running time in changing over from one product design to another would be 10%. The corresponding data for B is 3·2 pieces per hour with a changeover loss of 40%. Both machines would also lose 10% of potential full capacity running time from other causes. Running costs of both machines are otherwise the same.

At full capacity, 48 hours of running time per week would be available for 50 weeks in the year.

The management at present require a rate of return of 7% per annum to be shown before investment is undertaken.

The average income value of the output per piece before charging depreciation but after all other charges is £1.

*Required:*

(*a*) Provide a calculation for the management showing which machine should be bought if the above factors only are taken into account.

(*b*) State any other economic considerations which you think might also influence the decision.

10. *Interpretation of capital expenditure progress chart*

The chart given relates to a major development project on one of your company's products.

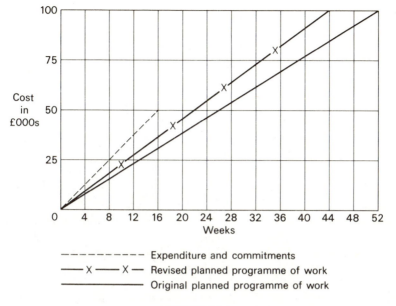

FIGURE 12.4.

*Required:*

(*a*) Interpret the significance of the information conveyed by the chart.

As financial controller, safeguarding the finances and profitability of the company, state:

(*b*) What further information you would require
(*c*) What action you would take?                                              (ICMA)

11. *The evaluation of a project with revised estimates*
Your company's required rate of return on investment projects is 20% before tax calculated on a discounted cash flow basis.

The following project for the design, development and exploitation of a new product is submitted and accepted on the grounds that it satisfies the above criterion:

| Year | 1<br>£ | 2<br>£ | 3<br>£ | 4<br>£ |
|---|---|---|---|---|
| Design | 5,000 | 500 | | |
| Drawing | 700 | 2,500 | | |
| Prototypes | | 300 | 8,500 | |
| Production drawings | | | 500 | 1,000 |
| Manufacturing costs | | | | 45,000 |
| Sales income | | | | 50,000 |
| Net cash flow | (5,700) | (3,300) | (9,000) | 4,000 |

| Year | 5 £ | 6 £ | 7 £ | 8 £ |
|---|---|---|---|---|
| Manufacturing costs | 67,500 | 67,500 | 65,000 | 65,000 |
| Sales income | 75,000 | 75,000 | 75,000 | 75,000 |
| Net cash flow | 7,500 | 7,500 | 10,000 | 10,000 |

By the end of the first year, £5,000 had been expended on design work. At this stage the project controller reports that he has made new estimates and that the probable course of the project will now be as follows:

| Year | 1 £ | 2 £ | 3 £ | 4 £ | 5 £ |
|---|---|---|---|---|---|
| Design | 5,000 | 1,000 | 500 | | |
| Drawing | | 250 | 750 | 2,300 | |
| Prototypes | | | | 700 | 9,000 |
| Production drawings | | | | | 500 |
| Net cash flow | (5,000) | (1,250) | (1,250) | (3,000) | (9,500) |

| Year | 6 £ | 7 £ | 8 £ | 9 £ | 10 £ |
|---|---|---|---|---|---|
| Production drawings | 1,000 | | | | |
| Manufacturing costs | 36,000 | 58,000 | 80,000 | 71,000 | 63,000 |
| Sales income | 40,000 | 65,000 | 90,000 | 80,000 | 75,000 |
| Net cash flow | 3,000 | 7,000 | 10,000 | 9,000 | 12,000 |

These new estimates are probably reliable within plus or minus 20%.
*Required:*
Evaluate the revised project and advise the board with full reasons what action you now recommend.                                    (ICMA)

12. *Control of internal capital expenditure work*
   It is the practice of a large manufacturing organisation to put all its capital expenditure work, with the exception of general-purpose machine tool purchase, through its civil and plant engineering sections. These sections also undertake the maintenance and repairs of the company's assets.
   *Required:*
   Describe the system you would use to ensure accurate cost ascertainment and adequate cost control of capital expenditure in this circumstance.        (ICMA)

FURTHER READING

Carsberg, Bryan. *Analysis for Investment Decisions.* Haymarket, 1974. Chapters 1, and 5–10.
Merrett, A. J. and Sykes, Allen. *The Finance and Analysis of Capital Projects.* Longmans, 1963. Chapters 1–7.
Porterfield, James T. S. *Investment Decisions and Capital Costs.* Prentice-Hall, Englewood Cliffs, New Jersey, 1965. Chapters 3 and 4.

# 13 Use of Resources (1)—Material Control

## OBJECTIVE OF THE CHAPTER

To identify stock movements in relation to the control process applicable to material, emphasising the financial aspects of these factors appropriate to production requirements and stock levels.

## OUTLINE OF THE CHAPTER

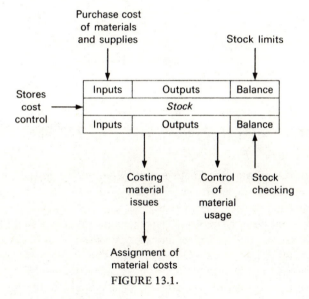

FIGURE 13.1.

In the manufacturing process, materials are required for conversion to the finished product and these resources are usually identified as raw materials. Other materials incidentally used in the manufacture of the product are frequently termed supplies. The former, including components, directly identified with the manufacture of the product are termed direct materials; the latter, usually indirectly identified with the manufacture of the product are termed indirect materials. Examples of indirect materials are maintenance supplies, and this category includes consumable stores that are a minor cost to the product, e.g., screws and glue.

235

Material control is concerned with raw materials and supplies, and while the emphasis of this chapter is on the use of these resources, the complete material control cycle cannot be ignored. This is illustrated in Figure 13.2.

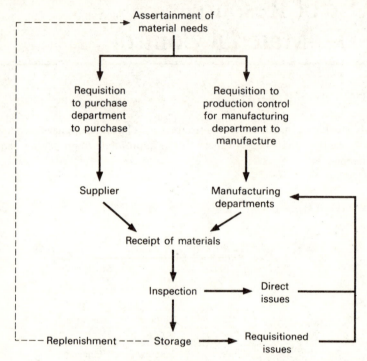

FIGURE 13.2. Basis of material control procedure

The close relationship that should exist between the purchasing, producing, servicing and accounting departments is evident from the above illustration and an integrated material control policy can best be obtained through the application of a budgetary control system. Given adequate planning, the importance of material as an expensive asset can be recognised and adequate steps taken to ensure that there are minimum losses through obsolescence, waste, deterioration and pilferage; there is no unauthorised purchase or use of materials; and costs are kept to the minimum consistent with the quality of product required and service to the customer.

## 13.1  MATERIAL CONTROL REQUIREMENTS

The procedure necessary to achieve the objectives so far described includes:

1. The clear identification of responsibilities for the various departmental material control activities and interrelationships between them
2. Where possible, the standardisation of materials to reduce costs

3. The use of a sound classification and coding scheme to assist in the efficient operation of the stores system
4. The planned programming of materials required, preferably included in budgets and production control procedures
5. An effective stores control procedure covering all aspects of storekeeping and clerical routine
6. Information for management indicating the financial effects of the material control procedure to the extent that action is required to ensure the system operates efficiently and economically.

This text is not concerned with the description of storekeeping* and production control procedures except to the extent that their administration has a financial impact and serves the requirements of a management accounting system. The aspects of primary concern for this chapter are:

(*a*) Purchase cost of materials
(*b*) Costing material issues
(*c*) Store account adjustments
(*d*) The use of material
(*e*) Stock limits
(*f*) Stores cost control.

## 13.2  STORES ACCOUNTING PROCEDURE

The basic accounting entries may be illustrated in relation to the appropriate control accounts and documents as shown in Figure 13.3.†

## 13.3  PURCHASE COST OF MATERIALS AND SUPPLIES

The debit to stores accounts (sometimes called inventory accounts) for purchases made will be reflected in stock values (inventory values), to the extent that usage has not taken place in the accounting period. If certain costs are not considered as purchase cost, and treated as a period expense to be written off in the period in which they are incurred, the calculated profit for the period will reflect this alternative treatment (purchase cost in stock values will be carried forward to a subsequent accounting period).

The choice of inputs to be considered as purchase cost is a matter of judgement. The minimum cost is usually the charge recorded on the purchase invoice which

---

*If the reader requires further information in this area a good descriptive text is: A. Morrison, *Storage and Control of Stock for Industry and Public Undertakings* (Pitman, 1967).
†The documentation is described in greater detail in Chapter 22 — Source documentation and data processing.

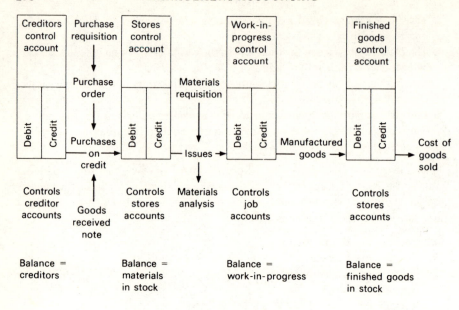

FIGURE 13.3. Stores accounting procedure

takes account of trade and quantity discounts. Subsequent costs such as receipt, inspection and storage are theoretically part of input cost but usually treated as a period expense as a matter of convenience and conservative accounting.

Cash discounts received are usually regarded as 'other income' but some companies consider that additional control information is provided if cash discounts receivable are deducted from other inputs making up purchase cost. The example to follow indicates the additional control information provided.

*Data*

Materials purchased at a value of £100
Cash discount obtainable if the purchase invoice is paid within the agreed payment term: £5
Accounting entries
    Stores account debited with £95
    Trade creditors account credited with £95
    If the creditor is paid promptly:
        trade creditors account debited with £95
        cash credited with £95 (payment to the supplier)
    If the creditor is paid outside the discount period:
        cash credited with £100 (payment to the supplier)
        trade creditors account debited with £95
        cash discounts not obtained debited with £5 (the control information).

## 13.4  COSTING MATERIAL ISSUES

Material when received may be issued direct to the production process to save the costs associated with intermediate storage. When this is possible, the purchase cost is immediately identified with production and charged to work-in-progress. Such a cost transfer is known as a specific cost and this method may also be used for stock items where the specific identification can be maintained.

If a large number of stock items are involved with rapid turnover, averaging may take place. Alternatively, cost sequence may be retained although specific identification of materials and supplies may be ignored. This variation in procedure identifies the following cost methods for pricing material requisitions recording issues to production:

1. Weighted average cost
2. First-in, first-out cost (FIFO)
3. Last-in, first-out cost (LIFO).

Other methods that may be used are:

4. Standard cost
5. Replacement cost
6. Inflated cost.

The data given below is used to illustrate these methods:

*Data for the month*

    Purchases: 2nd January    2 units at £2 each
               10th January   2 units at £4 each
    Issues: 15th January    1 unit
            20th January    2 units.


### 13.41  WEIGHTED AVERAGE COST

In this method, each purchase influences the issue cost for all items in stock at the date of receipt. There is no specific cost flow assumed. Using the given data the issues would be costed as follows:

*Materials Account*

| Date | Reference | Note | Receipts units | £ | Issues units | £ | Balance units | £ |
|------|-----------|------|-------|---|-------|---|-------|---|
| 2nd Jan. | Purchase | (i) | 2 | 4 | | | 2 | 4 |
| 10th Jan. | Purchase | (ii) | 2 | 8 | | | 4 | 12 |
| 15th Jan. | Issue | | | | 1 | 3 | 3 | 9 |
| 20th Jan. | Issues | | | | 2 | 6 | 1 | 3 |

*Notes:*
  (i) Weighted average cost at this stage: £2
  (ii) Weighted average cost at this stage: £3 (£12 ÷ 4).

The weighted average cost method averages charges to production where purchase cost inputs have varied significantly as in the above example.

## 13.42  FIRST-IN, FIRST-OUT COST

In this method, the purchase costs for the first materials received are used for the first issues made and, where a series of purchases have been made, the purchase cost inputs are used for issue costs in the same order as follows:

### Materials Account

| Date | Reference | Receipts units | £ | Issues units | £ | Balance units | £ |
|------|-----------|---------------|---|-------------|---|--------------|---|
| 2nd Jan. | Purchase | 2 | 4 | | | 2 | 4 |
| 10th Jan. | Purchase | 2 | 8 | | | 4 | 12 |
| 15th Jan. | Issue | | | 1 | 2 | 3 | 10 |
| 20th Jan. | Issues (see note) | | | 2 | 6 | 1 | 4 |

*Note:* Issue cost = 1 unit at £2 and 1 unit at £4.

The FIFO method assumes a cost flow in accordance with good storekeeping, i.e., old stock used first; but there is no specific identification of cost with the materials issued.

## 13.43  LAST-IN, FIRST-OUT COST

In this method, the purchase costs for the last materials received are used for the first issues made and, where a series of purchases have taken place, the purchase cost inputs are used for issue costs in reverse order as follows:

### Materials Account

| Date | Reference | Receipts units | £ | Issues units | £ | Balance units | £ |
|------|-----------|---------------|---|-------------|---|--------------|---|
| 2nd Jan. | Purchase | 2 | 4 | | | 2 | 4 |
| 10th Jan. | Purchase | 2 | 8 | | | 4 | 12 |
| 15th Jan. | Issue | | | 1 | 4 | 3 | 8 |
| 20th Jan. | Issues | | | 2 | 6 | 1 | 2 |

The LIFO method does not assume a cost flow identified with the materials issued. By this method the issue costs are the most recent costs and products are costed at current price levels if purchases have been recently made, or if the stock has been held for some time and material prices are not rising rapidly.

## 13.44  STANDARD COST

In this method, a predetermined cost (the standard cost) may be used as the issue cost. This involves isolating at the time of material receipt the difference between the actual and standard price as a material price variance. This difference is used as a control figure to check that the buyer is purchasing stock in accordance with an assessment of what the purchase costs should be. The materials account is maintained at standard cost as follows (assuming the standard cost at £4 per unit):

*Materials Account*

| Date | Reference | Receipts units | £ | Issues units | £ | Balance units | £ |
|---|---|---|---|---|---|---|---|
| 2nd Jan. | Purchase | 2 | 8 | | | 2 | 8 |
| 10th Jan. | Purchase | 2 | 8 | | | 4 | 16 |
| 15th Jan. | Issue | | | 1 | 4 | 3 | 12 |
| 20th Jan. | Issues | | | 2 | 8 | 1 | 4 |

The method described is part of the technique known as standard costing but the principles can be applied independently of the application of the full standard costing procedure.

## 13.45 REPLACEMENT COST

In this method issues are costed at the replacement cost of materials at the time of issue. There is no link with purchase cost unless the replacement cost, by coincidence, is the same as a previous purchase at the same price. The objective of using this method is to cost products at current price levels.

## 13.46 INFLATED COST

In this method the issue cost calculated by any of the methods described above may be increased to cover normal wastage experienced by the type of stock carried. If, for example, material deteriorates in value with storage on average by 10% of the normal cost of issues made, the cost of these issues may be calculated as follows:

|  | £ |
|---|---|
| Issue cost without wastage addition | 3·0 |
| Add 10% wastage | 0·3 |
| Inflated cost | 3·3 |

## 13.47 MATERIAL ISSUE COST METHODS COMPARED

The effects of using the various issue cost methods are as follows:

1. *Issue costs*
   Similar products manufactured in the same accounting period may be charged different material issue costs. Only the standard cost method standardises the issue cost. The weighted average cost method achieves some measure of standard-isation but a purchase in the accounting period can alter the issue cost in that same period.
2. *Stock values*
   The stock valuations at this stage of the valuation process are residual figures after correction for discrepancies between book stock and actual stock amounts. As shown in the examples, different stock valuations may be calculated.
3. *Current price levels*
   Only the replacement cost method ensures costs are at these levels, although the

LIFO method may be near to current price levels if purchases are currently being made.

4. *Complexity*

Some methods are easier to use than others. The standard cost method can give issue cost easily with a knowledge of the number of units issued. With FIFO, for example, the possibility of changing unit costs can make the calculation more complex and time-consuming where stock turnover is frequent.

The most popular methods in use are the FIFO, weighted average and standard cost methods. The choice of issue cost method is a matter of judgement as to the extent objectives will be achieved by the use of specific procedures.

Where it is necessary to maintain a minimum quantity of material in stock as a requirement to keep the factory in operation, e.g., raw sugar as the only component input to the continuous process of sugar refining (without it the refinery would close), the stock is in effect a fixed asset. If this view is adopted, this basic stock is valued at a fixed price which normally remains unchanged. Stock above the minimum is usually maintained on one of the bases described in the previous section, e.g., FIFO. The procedure is known as the base stock method.

## 13.5  ISSUE COST AS A RESIDUAL CALCULATION

A stores procedure involving extensive documentation and, in particular, the use of stores requisitions to give an issue cost is not necessarily a justifiable expense in cases where stock values can be ascertained easily and job identification is not required. In this situation the issue cost for the period may be a residual calculation modifying the basic stock control formula for materials as follows:

Basic stock control formula:

$$\text{Opening stock value} + \text{Purchases cost} = \text{Issues cost} + \text{Closing stock value}$$

Modified formula:

$$\text{Opening stock value} + \text{Purchases cost} - \text{Closing stock value} = \text{Issues cost}$$

The formula may also be used for quantities only. It may be noted that the residual figure disclosed includes possible discrepancies which are not identified as a control figure.

## 13.6  THE USE OF MATERIAL

The assignment of material costs to cost units and cost centres is through the medium of a material issues analysis illustrated in Figure 13.4.

The documents identifying the amounts required for costing purposes, which

| Document reference | Totals | Cost units | | | | | | | | Cost centres | | | | | | | | |
|---|---|---|---|---|---|---|---|---|---|---|---|---|---|---|---|---|---|---|
| *Material issues analysis — Period ended _____* | | E.g., job codes | | | | | | | | E.g., departmental codes | | | | | | | | |
| | £ | £ | £ | £ | £ | £ | £ | £ | £ | £ | £ | £ | £ | £ | £ | £ | £ | £ |
| | | | | | | | | | | | | | | | | | | |
| | | | | | | | | | | | | | | | | | | |

FIGURE 13.4. Material issues analysis

should be properly authorised by staff responsible for the costs involved, cover:

1. Material issues — stores requisitions
2. Material returned to stock — stores credit notes
3. Material transfer between jobs — material transfer notes.

Control over the use of material depends on the comparison of actual usage with the planned usage in terms of quantities and quality of materials. Control over quantities includes a check on production inefficiency which may cause excessive wastage and usage, and material mix changes which may increase costs for standard qualities of output. Control over quality includes a check on the standard of material issued to production.

## 13.7  STOCK CHECKING

The basic stock control formula, mentioned in an earlier section, provides a basis for stock checking. Where the opening stock, receipts and issues have been identified by the stores procedure, the stock position is theoretically indicated. If a stock check indicates a difference between the book stock and the physical stock, an inquiry should be carried out as necessary and authority given to write off the difference in the stores accounts, usually through an authorising document. If the stores accounts are maintained in continuous sequence for all aspects of material movement, the records are known as a perpetual inventory and continuous checking may be used to ensure the figures recorded are accurate. The expression 'continuous checking' in this context means a frequency of individual checks governed by the type of material and supplies, their value and control requirements.

The store accounts are usually maintained in quantity and value for the receipt, issues and balance data. Quantity only records may be kept as, for example, the recording of stores items of small value. In addition to the stores accounts. companies may record the quantity data on bin cards kept in the stores bin or container. The tendency is to eliminate this record, where possible, to reduce store costs.

If a stock check indicates a difference between the quantity in the stores container and that recorded on the stores ledger account, a bin card, if one is available, may be useful in finding out how the discrepancy has arisen.

The authorising document for a write-off will secure agreement between the physical stock in the store container and the recorded quantity balance on the stores ledger account. This same document, when valued, will be used to ensure that the stores control account is agreed in total value with the stores ledger accounts it represents. A check should be made periodically to ensure that this is so. Any differences should be investigated and the accounts adjusted where necessary.

Where the accuracy of stores accounts cannot be maintained by continuous checking, periodic stocktaking may be carried out at intervals dictated by accounting needs and managerial requirements.

When stock is checked, this is an opportunity for an investigation to be made of slow moving stock to prevent further investment in these items and reduce stock write-offs owing to obsolescence.

## 13.8 STOCK LIMITS

The satisfaction of production requirements for materials and supplies, with the minimum investment of funds in stock, is a difficult objective to achieve. Stock

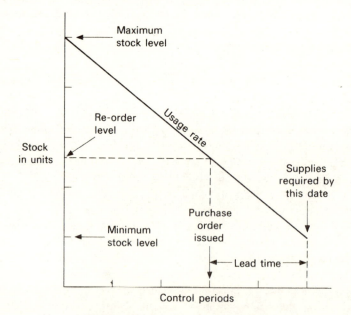

FIGURE 13.5. Stock level control factors

limits may be related to usage, lead time between orders placed and supplies received, and economic order quantities.

Usage may be identified as a range such as that fixed by maximum and minimum stock levels. If these figures are to be of any value, they should be reviewed in relation to changing production requirements. If this action is not taken, the levels designed to control stock investment may be the means of keeping and ordering materials that are not required. The relationship of the factors described in this section is illustrated in Figure 13.5. The calculation of economic ordering quantities is covered in the business decision-making section (Chapter 21).

## 13.9  STORES COST CONTROL

The costs of running a stores can be considerable and include:
  Rent and rates of stores buildings
  Depreciation of stores equipment
  Running costs of stores equipment
  Wages and salaries and labour related costs of stores staff
  Stock-checking expenses
  Discrepancy and deterioration write-offs
  Stationery.
These costs are regarded as works overhead although abnormal wastage or write-offs should not be charged to production but written off to profit and loss account.

In an attempt to reduce store costs, store items of small value may be written off to works overheads and by this procedure the documentation and clerical procedures developed for a full control system can be avoided. Where to limit the application of the procedure yet maintain adequate control is a matter of cost effectiveness. A useful guide is to list item values and their stock values in ascending order as follows:

| Category | | Stock value £ | Number of items |
|---|---|---|---|
| 1 | Stock items of low unit cost | 10,000 | 7,000 |
| 2 | Stock items of medium unit cost | 20,000 | 2,000 |
| 3 | Stock items of high unit cost | 70,000 | 1,000 |
| | | 100,000 | 10,000 |

In the illustration, only 10% of the items in stock account for 70% of the stock value, and the detailed costly procedures could be relaxed on 70% of the stock items without a marked loss of control.

## 13.10  SUMMARY

Material requirements need to be planned in accordance with production needs regarding timing of supply, quality and quantity. In addition to meeting these needs a further aim is to minimise the investment of funds in stock.

Many important factors have been identified in this chapter as matters of judgement, and the accountant should choose the financial procedure that meets the objectives agreed for the system. In particular, relevant information should be reported to management to secure effective control of this important resource — material.

## FOR FURTHER STUDY

QUESTIONS

1. *Need for stock control*

Mr Check, as the accountant of Chemical Products Ltd, had produced monthly trading statements since he joined the company at the beginning of the financial year. He had not introduced the system but had been informed that the accuracy of the periodical statements was doubted and he must do something about it as soon as possible. Early inquiries seemed to suggest that stock consumed figures were inaccurate but Mr Check was unable to secure any definite action to improve the position. The buyer and stock controller, Mr Leak, was an old servant of the company and any suggestion that his department was not running efficiently was impertinent to say the least — as Mr Leak remarked to the works manager: 'Mr Check cannot tell me my job. When he has been with the company for thirty years he may know something about the company and be in a position to advise others to the benefit of all concerned.'

Peace reigned in the accounting and stock departments until the final accounts of the company were produced and showed a profit £10,000 less than the figure indicated by the periodical statements after allowance had been made for non-comparable factors. Mr Check was on the 'mat'. It was pointed out that figures were useless unless reasonably accurate and the management had been living in a fool's paradise. A thorough investigation was required immediately. Mr Check carried out the investigation and apart from miscellaneous errors, due to faulty estimating, discovered that the stock consumption figures supplied by Mr Leak were approximately £8,000 less than the figure disclosed by the final accounts of the company.

Mr Leak's department was then subjected to a detailed investigation and it was quickly established that little control existed. The following faults were revealed:

(*a*) Materials could be obtained from store without requisitions because the storekeeper did not insist on the documentation being followed. In any case, for certain periods of the day the store was left unattended.

(*b*) Bin cards were used but in 75% of the bins checked quantities were different from those shown as book stock. No regular check appeared to be carried out.

(*c*) Many items in the store were obviously of little value and certainly of no importance to production since the required quality had not been maintained (*d*) Certain materials of good quality had not been used for eighteen months

(*e*) For certain store items, on the basis of current consumption levels, stocks were sufficient to supply the factory for the next 25 years

(*f*) During the investigation it was extremely difficult to ascertain total stocks of some store items since stock was found in different locations and in the most unlikely places

(*g*) Paperwork was in arrear and for the purpose of the monthly consumption figures any missing information, e.g., prices, were estimated. No attempt was made to check estimations and adjust if necessary in subsequent periods.

(*h*) Actual prices were supposed to be used for pricing requisitions but it was impossible to check some of the figures used to price issues.

Faced with these deficiences in the stores 'system' Mr Leak said in his defence that the purchasing side alone was a full-time job and obviously miracles were expected from him. He pointed out that while he did not wish to appear to be passing the blame on to others did Mr Check think that old man Hezekiah, aged 72, was a suitable person to hold the position of storekeeper in his department.

*Required:*

(*a*) What were the principal faults in the organisation of the stock control department? Was Mr Leak wholly responsible?

(*b*) Apart from providing accurate stock consumption figures, what other advantages would accrue from the installation of a good stock control system?

(*c*) How would you introduce a new system of stock control? Include the consideration of any organisational changes necessary.

2. *Control of inventories as a contribution to the efficiency of a business*
It is often suggested that the proper control of inventories can make a substantial contribution to the efficiency of a business.

*Required:*
Discuss this, and suggest control measures which might be applied.        (ICMA)

3. *Material cost control*
In manufacturing organisations it is frequently contended that rising prices preclude control of material costs.

*Required:*
Analyse the field of material cost control into those areas in which control is possible and indicate briefly the type of control required.        (ICMA)

4. *Sequence of movements of raw material*
A company buys raw material from which it manufactures components, which are then assembled into a final product.

*Required:*
Tabulate the sequence of movements and the operations undergone by an item

of raw material from the supplier's warehouse until the final product is des-
patched to the customer, and state by whom the different movements and
operations are controlled. (ICMA)

5. *Treatment of cash discounts receivable and stores wastage*
   (a) Describe alternative procedures for dealing with cash discounts receivable
       in the accounts of a company.
   (b) Indicate the costing treatment of wastage which occurs prior to materials
       being issued to production. (ACA – part)

6. *Different methods of pricing stores issues*
   Set out the different methods of pricing stores issues giving, briefly, the
   advantages and disadvantages of each. (ACA)

7. *Inflated cost charges for wastage*
   The A.B.Co. Ltd buys two raw materials, A and B. The stores ledger cards for
   December may be summarised as follows:

| Receipts | Material A Units | £ | Material B Units | £ | Issues | Material A Units | £ | Material B Units | £ |
|---|---|---|---|---|---|---|---|---|---|
| 1st Dec. Balance b/f | 100 | 50 | 200 | 200 | 6th Dec. Issues | 120 | | | |
| 4th Dec. Purchases | 100 | 60 | | | 12th Dec. Issues | | | 100 | |
| 13th Dec. Returns | | | 10 | | 26th Dec. Issues | 25 | | | |
| 24th Dec. Purchases | | | 200 | 240 | 28th Dec. Issues | | | 140 | |
| | | | | | 31st Dec. Balance c/f | 55 | | 150 | |
| | | | | | Wastage | | | | |

Issues are charged on the FIFO system. Stock at the end of the month is
checked by physical stocktaking. In the case of material B some wastage is
normal and, therefore, 5% is added to the cost of all issues, any excess wastage
being treated as works overhead.
*Required:*
Fill in the blanks in the above accounts and draft the stores control account for
materials A and B.

8. *Use of LIFO for pricing material issues*
   'The use of the LIFO method of pricing materials issued ensures that production
   costs are related as closely as possible to current price levels.'
   *Required:*
   (a) Describe the operation of the LIFO method; explain how it brings about
       the effect stated in the quotation and comment upon the effect of the use
       of the method on stock valuations.
   (b) Record the following transactions which relate to Component No. B1716,

using the LIFO method to price the issues and show the value of the closing stock:

19. .

| | |
|---|---|
| 1 Nov. Stock of component B1716 | 100, value £30 |
| 5 Nov. Requisition No. 8131 | 30 |
| 7 Nov. Requisition No. 8379 | 50 |
| 11 Nov. Goods received note No. 319 | 50, cost £16 |
| 18 Nov. Requistion No. 8479 | 40 |
| 21 Nov. Requisition No. 8516 | 20 |
| 25 Nov. Goods received note No. 817 | 80, cost £28 |
| 28 Nov. Requisition No. 8694 | 60 |

(ACA)

9. *Annual stocktaking and perpetual inventory*
   (a) Outline the considerations you would have in mind in preparing for the annual stocktaking in a medium-sized engineering concern.
   (b) Briefly set out the advantages which might accrue to the company if a system of perpetual inventory and continuous stocktaking were to be installed.                                                                  (ACA)

10. *Stock differences*
    The physical stock of material D7 is different from the quantity shown as stock on the bin card and also that shown as stock in the stock ledger account.
    *Required:*
    (a) Give possible reasons as to how the differences may have been caused.
    (b) Describe how you would deal with such differences in the stock ledger accounts and how you would correct the bin card.                        (ICMA)

11. *Reports on the subject of stocks*
    What reports would you submit to top management on the subject of stock?
    (ICMA)

12. *Important aspects of stores accounting to be introduced in a company*
    The Delta Manufacturing Co. Ltd produces a wide range of consumer goods; in all, twenty main products are produced, but within each main product there are different grades and qualities ranging from two grades for Product 1 to give grades for Product 20. Materials are by far the most important element of cost, accounting for approximately 55% of total cost.
    Most of the processing is done with raw materials but for some of the products, finished parts are brought in, and assembled into the finished products. Prices for most of the raw materials are subject to many and wide variations but the finished parts can be contracted for at a fixed price for the year, which has been done in the past, although prices have always gone up from contract to contract.
    Although the company was only formed eight years ago, its size, in every aspect, has trebled since then due mainly to the fact that the company were manufacturing for a sellers' market. Because of this the company has paid little

attention to cost control; as the managing director has said, 'We could sell all that we could produce at a price, easy to fix, which covered our costs and gave a desired return on capital'. However, circumstances have changed in that many other firms have entered into this field with competing products and this has made severe inroads into the company's profit position. To reduce selling prices in an attempt to counteract this competition would only lead to similar action on the part of the company's competitors and, therefore, the situation has arisen where the only control which the company can exercise on profit is through cost.

A preliminary investigation in this area has shown that the planning and control of material usage is not sound. A simple comparison of input with output has revealed that a very high wastage of materials is taking place but, because the company does not operate any system of stores accounting, it is impossible to say whether this is due to bad buying, inefficient storage, faulty processing or what.

*Required:*

You have been asked to prepare a detailed report on the system of stores accounting you would like to see introduced. Your report should touch upon all the important aspects of stores accounting including how your system will provide the necessary information which will be required when, as is the intention, a full system of cost accounting is implemented. (ACA)


FURTHER READING

Battersby, Albert. *A Guide to Stock Control.* British Institute of Management and Pitman, 1962.

Borsay, J. 'Inventory control'. *Cost Accountant*, October, 1962, p. 364–73.

Morrison, A. *Storage and Control of Stock for Industry and Public Undertakings.* Pitman, 1967. Chapters 1–8.

# 14 Use of Resources (2)—Labour Control

## OBJECTIVE OF THE CHAPTER

To outline the administrative aspects of labour control with particular reference to their financial implications. The labour control requirements are explained in the context of sound personnel policies.

## OUTLINE OF THE CHAPTER

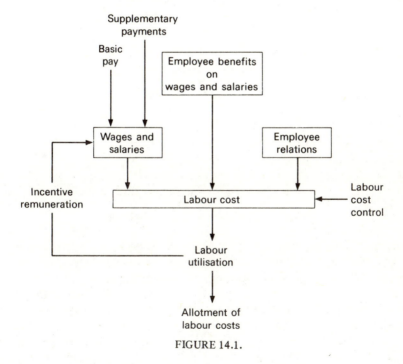

FIGURE 14.1.

Labour control follows material control in the economic sequence of converting material to the finished product but labour is not secondary. The work of the business is accomplished through individuals and although the labour control system may be described in terms similar to those used for other resources, the human element is distinctive. Each individual reacts differently to the same situation,

251

especially under varying conditions. The individual's feelings, motivation and relationships are crucial to the control process. Analysis and understanding of the individual is difficult but group behaviour is more complex and any consideration of labour control must recognise this context. Successful labour control may be thought of in terms of morale, personal satisfaction and motivation. The extent to which these factors are identified with the objectives of the organisation gives a company an asset which should be preserved and improved and not damaged by controls improperly developed or inadequately explained. The labour control cycle is illustrated in Figure 14.2.

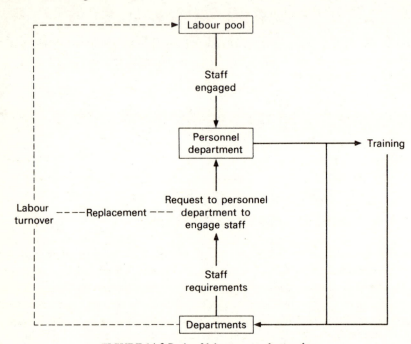

FIGURE 14.2 Basis of labour control procedure

Evident in this illustration is the central role of the personnel department. The attempt is made to provide the required number of personnel of the right type, when and where required, at the right wage or salary level.

An integrated labour control policy recognising the close relationship that should exist between the personnel department and the user departments can best be obtained through the application of a budgetary control system. Given adequate planning and control, a reasonable return on the high costs of labour is possible.

## 14.1  LABOUR CONTROL REQUIREMENTS

The procedure necessary to achieve the objectives so far described includes:

1. The establishment of a sound organisation pattern

2. The clear identification of responsibilities for the various departmental labour control activities and interrelationships between them

3. The planned personnel requirements, preferably included in budgets through manpower estimates

4. An effective authorisation procedure for incurring personnel expenditure including associated documentation

5. Information for management indicating the financial effects of the labour control procedure to the extent that action is required to operate the company effectively and economically.

This text is not concerned with the description of personnel management* and production control labour procedures except to the extent that their administration has a financial impact and serves the requirements of the management accounting system.

The aspects of primary concern for this chapter are:

(*a*) Labour recruitment, selection and training
(*b*) Wage and salary payment including incentives
(*c*) Employee expense factors
(*d*) Labour utilisation
(*e*) Labour turnover.

## 14.2 LABOUR RECRUITMENT AND SELECTION

Labour recruitment can be a significant administration cost involving staff advertising, personnel interviewing and clerical costs. On the basis of job descriptions staff may be recruited or promoted from within the organisation. The distinction should be made between replacements and the recruitment of staff for new appointments. It is possible to calculate the cost of processing job applications and a check should also be made on the cost of various sources of recruitment to ensure that the most cost effective sources are identified for future use. Interviewing cost is not restricted to the personnel department — functional managers are also involved in the selection process.

## 14.3 TRAINING

Training costs should be calculated because they can be significant in many businesses. These costs may begin with induction training and on the job instruction with costs being incurred because production is below standard. If the company maintains its own training school or pays for staff attending courses, the costs should be easy to

---

*If the reader requires further information in this area a descriptive text is *Personnel Management* by C. S. Deverell (Gee, 1968).

calculate by establishing separate accounts for the amounts paid. In other cases, an apportionment of costs, particularly wages, may be necessary.

The training costs and payment of a training levy to an Industrial Training Board may be part-recoverable by a grant from the same board, where approved costs are incurred in training employees.

## 14.4 WAGE AND SALARY PAYMENT

The basic accounting entries may be illustrated in relation to the appropriate control accounts and documents as shown in Figure 14.3.*

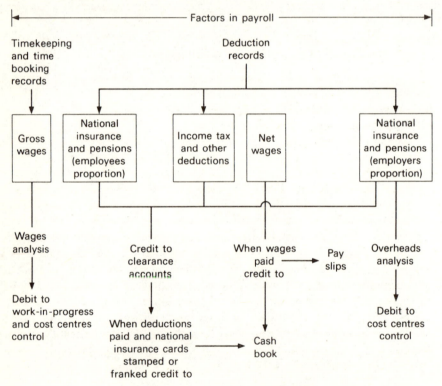

FIGURE 14.3. Wages accounting procedure

Where national insurance and pensions (employers' proportion) are allotted with the gross wages for direct workers to work-in-progress, the debit for this amount would be to work-in-progress.

It will be evident from this illustration that many types of activity are involved in wage calculation and payment and, where possible, these activities, starting with

*The documentation is described in greater detail in Chapter 22 – 'Source documentation and data processing'.

wage authorisation, should be carried out by different people. The objective of this procedure is to make fraud difficult by making such an act only possible with the collusion of two or more people.

To assist wage analysis, labour that is not directly involved with the manufacture of the product may be segregated on the payroll. Examples are factory supervision; labour employed in the factory service centres; and selling, distribution and administration staff.

In calculating the gross wages, the following items may supplement or replace basic pay:

1. Overtime and night shift payments — these amounts are at the basic pay rate plus premiums paid for work outside normal day duty times
2. Sick payments — these amounts are usually after the deduction of sick pay received from the Department of Health and Social Security
3. Holiday pay entitlement
4. Bonuses.

## 14.5  FINANCIAL INCENTIVES AND PRODUCTIVITY

To increase the productivity of labour, that is effectiveness of the use of the labour, financial incentives may be given. Some businesses prefer the payment of a higher standard of basic wages or salary with a lower proportion of financial incentives; whereas other companies prefer a comparatively lower level of basic pay associated with a higher proportion of financial incentives. With an increased standard of living, financial incentives lose some of their power to increase productivity. Money is not the only factor to ensure labour effectiveness, but the way in which remuneration is calculated is an important factor in industrial relations.

## 14.6  WORK STUDY

Incentive schemes are usually based on work study to measure the work unit values of the elements of the job to be carried out. To these work unit values allowances that are considered justifiable are added to give target times for an agreed method of working. Method study should precede work measurement with the aim of improving methods of production. If this approach is followed, incentive scheme times can be based on the best methods of doing the job.

Labour times can be affected by the workers' increasing familiarity with the job, these times reducing as familiarity increases. In these situations, labour costs are controlled by estimating changes in the labour times and a 'learning curve' may be used for this purpose. A learning curve is a graph showing the estimated labour times for increasing quantities of work produced.

Work study techniques were initially applied to direct labour but the need to tighten control over indirect labour has prompted efforts in this area of the business.

Some aspects of indirect work, such as mechanised routines in the office, could use established work study procedures (and this has been done) but other techniques have been developed such as Variable Factor Programming (VFP). In this technique, the control process features used are forward plans; work assignment in control batches according to labour time availability; recording of actual results; and action where plans are not being achieved. The forward plans are identified in the form of work targets, not developed as a basis for incentive schemes but for labour control only.

## 14.7 FINANCIAL INCENTIVE SCHEMES

There are many financial incentive schemes used in industry and there is considerable evidence* that the complications arising from their use have caused some managements seriously to question their value. It is true, however, that financial incentive schemes are being successfully used in industry and their success can be traced to the specific identification of company needs and a realistic assessment of objectives; the choice of a scheme relevant to those needs; the thorough preparation and proper introduction of the scheme; and supporting management providing the quality of working environment necessary to apply the procedure with confidence. Poor working relationships and bad management will not be improved by the introduction of a financial incentive scheme.

Financial incentive schemes have been classified in various ways and the groups adopted for this chapter† are as follows:

1. Weekly wage incentive systems (individual and group);
   Workers' earnings and direct labour costs vary

   (*a*) in the same proportion as output;
   (*b*) proportionately less than output;
   (*c*) proportionately more than output; and
   (*d*) in proportions which differ at different levels of output.

2. Longer term individual systems

3. Long-term collective systems:

   (*a*) Those based on standard production or added value
   (*b*) Those based on profits

4. Systems not directly dependent on production:

   (*a*) Those based on personal assessment
   (*b*) Those supplementary to production.

---

*See, for example, the case study by Wilfred Brown, *Piecework Abandoned* (Heinemann Educational Books, 1962).
† This classification is a slightly modified version of the one given in *Incentive Payment Systems* by R. Marriott (Staples Press, 1971), p. 45.

*Schemes where the incentives are in the same proportion as output*
A simple direct incentive of this type is the straight piece-rate where there is a constant rate of payment per unit produced.

*Schemes where the incentives are proportionately less than output*
Examples of such schemes* are:

(*a*) Barth system — in this system, as production increases the incentive payment is at a decreasing rate. Earnings are calculated on the basis of the following formula:

$$\sqrt{\text{Actual hours x Standard hours}} \times \text{Rate per hour.}$$

(*b*) Bedaux system — each work unit has a number of points (the Bedaux point or allowed minute) and each worker receives the day rate plus a bonus calculated on the points saved on work produced. The original scheme proposed a proportion of 75% of the points saved and with this percentage the formula for calculating the earnings is as follows:

$$\left(\begin{array}{c}\text{Number of}\\\text{hours worked}\end{array}\right) \times \left(\begin{array}{c}\text{Rate of pay}\\\text{per hour}\end{array}\right) + \left(75\% \times \begin{array}{c}\text{Number of}\\\text{points saved}\end{array} \times \dfrac{\text{Rate of pay}}{\text{per hour}}\Big/ 60\right)$$

The number of points saved is the time taken in minutes deducted from the number of points allowed for the work produced.

(*c*) Halsey system — where work units are completed in less than the standard time allowed for the work produced, a bonus is paid to the worker on a percentage basis of the time saved. Assuming 50% sharing of the time saved, the formula for calculating the earnings is as follows:

$$\begin{array}{c}\text{Rate of pay}\\\text{per hour}\end{array} \times \left(\text{Time taken } + \text{ 50\% of the time saved}\right)$$

(*d*) Rowan system — as in the Halsey scheme a bonus is paid on the time saved but in this system the percentage of the time rate is equal to the proportion of the time saved to standard time. The formula for calculating the earnings is as follows:

$$\left(\begin{array}{c}\text{Time} \quad \text{Rate of pay}\\\text{taken} \overset{\times}{} \text{ per hour}\\\text{i.e., time wages}\end{array}\right) + \left(\begin{array}{c}\text{Percentage of}\\\text{time saved to } \times \begin{array}{c}\text{Time}\\\text{wages}\end{array}\\\text{time allowed}\end{array}\right)$$

*Schemes where the incentives are proportionately more than output*
A scheme of this type is where a higher piece-rate is paid as increased work units are produced.

---

*Standard hours in incentive schemes are the number of hours that should have been taken to complete the work produced.

*Schemes where the incentives are in proportions which differ at different levels of output*

Examples of such schemes are:

(*a*) Accelerating Premium System – the bonus accelerates as the work produced increases.

(*b*) Gantt system – when the worker reaches standard performance a bonus, usually 20%, is paid on the time wages. Work achieved above standard performance is paid at high piece-rates.

(*c*) Emerson system – from a point below standard performance an increasing bonus is paid until 20% is reached at standard performance. Above standard performance, for every 1% increase in work units produced a 1% increase in bonus is paid.

(*d*) Merrick system – this is a differential piece-rate system where three rates are applied as follows:

Up to 83% of standard performance – basic piece-rate payment per unit produced.

At 83% to standard performance – basic piece-rate payment plus 10% per unit produced

At standard performance and above – basic piece-rate payment plus 20% per unit produced.

(*e*) Taylor system – as described for the Merrick system with only two steps:

Up to standard performance – basic piece-rate payment per unit produced

At standard performance and above – basic piece-rate payment plus 50% per unit produced.

*Longer term individual system incentives*

A good example of this type of incentive is measured day work where hourly rates are established for differing levels of performance. The worker is paid on an agreed level of performance for a three- or six-month period and a check maintained on performance achieved in that period. The hourly rates for the next three- or six-month period are then adjusted on the basis of that performance but a rate reduction may be delayed where it is expected that earlier performance standards will be regained.

*Longer term collective system incentives*

(*a*) Priestman system – where the monthly production standard for the whole works is exceeded, all workers receive a bonus in the following month equal to the percentage increase in production over standard performance.

(*b*) Scanlon system – all workers receive a bonus from a surplus calculated by deducting salaries and wages paid from a fixed percentage of added value.

(*c*) Profit sharing – all workers receive a bonus as an addition to wages and salaries based on a fixed percentage of profits achieved.

(*d*) Co-ownership – all workers receive a bonus in the form of shares in the capital of the business.

*Personal assessment incentive schemes*

Examples of such schemes are:

(*a*) Merit rating – job evaluation is used to fix a points rating regarding the extent to which identified job characteristics are applicable to the work undertaken. Examples are skills, responsibility and effort. Given this job evaluation, merit rating assesses the extent to which the individual matches the points rating. The differences in individual qualities so assessed are made the subject of a merit payment.
(*b*) High day rates – fixed hourly rates that may be established by job evaluation and above the normal rates paid in the industry for equivalent jobs
(*c*) Attendance bonuses – additional payments may be made for good attendance and time-keeping
(*d*) Length of service awards whether in the form of an additional payment, personal gifts or better conditions of employment.

*Other supplementary bonuses to assist the production process*

These bonuses include the following:

(*a*) Quality bonuses – used as an encouragement to maintain a high quality standard
(*b*) Waste bonuses – used as an attempt to minimise waste.

*The Financial Incentive Schemes Compared*

Figure 14.4 on p. 260 compares the features of the various incentive schemes and shows the rating scales which have been used.

## 14.8 EMPLOYEE EXPENSE FACTORS

Labour related expense factors, other than educational expenses already considered, include the following:

1. Employee benefits on wages and salaries – the employer's proportion of national insurance and pension fund contributions
2. Employee relations:
    (*a*) Removal and displacement expenses
    (*b*) Ex gratia pensions
    (*c*) Contributions to canteen expenses
    (*d*) Contributions to employees' entertainment, leisure and travel.

## 14.9 LABOUR UTILISATION

The assignment of labour costs to cost units and cost centres is through the medium of a labour analysis illustrated in Figure 14.5.

| Rating scale | A | B | C | D |
|---|---|---|---|---|
| 1 | Low | Easy | Yes | Good |
| 2 | Moderate | Reasonable | Partly | Average |
| 3 | High | Difficult | No | Poor |

| Effect of using the various incentive schemes | Rating scale used | Straight piece rate | Barth system | Bedaux system | Halsey system | Rowan system | Accelerating premium system | Gantt system | Emerson system | Merrick system | Taylor system | Measured day work | Priestman system | Scanlon system | Profit sharing | Co-ownership | Merit rating | High day rates | Attendance bonuses | Length of service awards | Quality and waste bonuses |
|---|---|---|---|---|---|---|---|---|---|---|---|---|---|---|---|---|---|---|---|---|---|
| 1. The level of administration costs | A | 1 | 3 | 3 | 2 | 2 | 2 | 2 | 2 | 2 | 2 | 2 | 1 | 3 | 2 | 2 | 1 | 1 | 1 | 1 | 1 |
| 2. Ease of understanding by workers | B | 1 | 3 | 2 | 1 | 2 | 3 | 1 | 1 | 1 | 1 | 1 | 1 | 2 | 2 | 2 | 1 | 1 | 1 | 1 | 1 |
| 3. Generally applicable to the company | C | 3 | 3 | 3 | 3 | 3 | 3 | 3 | 3 | 3 | 3 | 1 | 1 | 1 | 1 | 1 | 1 | 1 | 1 | 1 | 3 |
| 4. Flexibility of worker transfer | B | 2 | 3 | 2 | 2 | 2 | 2 | 2 | 2 | 2 | 2 | 2 | 1 | 1 | 1 | 1 | 1 | 1 | 1 | 1 | 1 |
| 5. Flexibility of revising working methods | B | 2 | 2 | 2 | 2 | 2 | 2 | 2 | 2 | 2 | 2 | 1 | 1 | 1 | 1 | 1 | 1 | 1 | 1 | 1 | 1 |
| 6. Standard of incentive | D | 1 | 2 | 1 | 2 | 2 | 1 | 1 | 2 | 1 | 1 | 1 | 1 | 2 | 3 | 3 | 2 | 3 | 2 | 3 | 2 |
| 7. Incentive directly related to the individual worker | C | 1 | 1 | 1 | 1 | 1 | 1 | 1 | 1 | 1 | 1 | 1 | 3 | 3 | 3 | 3 | 1 | 2 | 1 | 1 | 1 |
| 8. Management control over earnings | D | 1 | 2 | 1 | 2 | 2 | 2 | 1 | 1 | 2 | 2 | 1 | 1 | 1 | 1 | 1 | 1 | 1 | 1 | 1 | 1 |
| 9. Extent of subjective judgment | A | 1 | 1 | 1 | 1 | 1 | 1 | 1 | 1 | 1 | 1 | 1 | 1 | 2 | 2 | 2 | 3 | 2 | 1 | 1 | 1 |
| 10. Encouragement to employees to take an interest in the company's prosperity | C | 3 | 3 | 3 | 3 | 3 | 3 | 3 | 3 | 3 | 3 | 3 | 3 | 2 | 1 | 1 | 3 | 3 | 3 | 3 | 3 |
| 11. Will increase output | C | 1 | 1 | 1 | 1 | 1 | 1 | 1 | 1 | 1 | 1 | 1 | 1 | 2 | 3 | 3 | 3 | 3 | 3 | 3 | 2 |
| 12. Will assist the efficient use of machinery or materials | C | 3 | 3 | 3 | 3 | 3 | 3 | 3 | 3 | 3 | 3 | 3 | 3 | 2 | 3 | 3 | 3 | 3 | 3 | 3 | 1 |

FIGURE 14.4.

| Document reference | Labour analysis<br>Period ended _____ | | | | | | | | | | | | | | | | Totals |
| | Cost units<br>E.g., job codes | | | | | | | | Cost centres<br>E.g., departmental codes | | | | | | | | |
| | £ | £ | £ | £ | £ | £ | £ | £ | £ | £ | £ | £ | £ | £ | £ | £ | £ |
| | | | | | | | | | | | | | | | | | |

FIGURE 14.5. Labour analysis

The documents, which should be properly authorised by staff responsible for the costs involved, identifying the amounts required for costing purposes cover:

1. Timekeeping and attendance recording — registers and clock cards
2. Time booking — time sheets, job cards, operation cards, timework and waiting time tickets.

Control over the use of labour depends on the comparison of actual use with the planned use in terms of time and quality of labour. Analysis of this comparison may disclose inefficiency owing to the use of poor quality labour, but detailed investigation can show the effect on costs of associated factors such as production problems: faulty equipment, low quality material, etc.

Idle-time cost, holiday pay, overtime and night-shift premiums are usually charged to factory overhead. The overtime premium may be charged direct to a job if that work has been completed in overtime on the basis of specific customer instructions. If overtime is worked to enable the company to complete its production programme, there is no justification for charging the overtime premium to the specific job just because, in the order of the work performed, that job is completed in overtime.

The cost-centres section of the labour analysis includes wages and salaries not directly identifiable with specific units of output such as the labour costs concerned with:

1. Factory management
2. Factory service personnel, e.g., staff employed in production control, stores control, work study, maintenance and inspection departments
3. Marketing personnel, e.g., sales management, salesmen and van drivers
4. Administration personnel, e.g., general management and clerks.

Labour costs (1) and (2) are included in factory overhead; items (3) and (4) in marketing and administration overhead respectively.

To improve labour utilisation, a productivity agreement may be agreed between a company and its employees. Such an agreement gives the employee better terms and conditions of employment in return for a major change in traditional working arrangements. As a basis for such an agreement, which is aimed at a long-term solution to productivity and industrial relations problems, the following features must be evident:

(a) A conviction on the part of management and staff that a significant impact on productivity and industrial relations is possible
(b) A consultative procedure which can make possible the achievement of the desired objective
(c) An ability to recognise opportunities for significant improvements in performance that are practical and acceptable
(d) A sound management accounting system that can assist in the management process, and the provision of relevant cost information as a basis for decisions as the agreement is negotiated.

## 14.10  LABOUR TURNOVER

A significant labour cost in most organisations is labour turnover. Labour turnover can be expressed by the following formula:

$$\text{Labour turnover percentage for the control period} = \frac{\text{The number of leavers during the control period}}{\text{The average number employed during the control period}} \times 100\%$$

The numbers recorded in the formula may be modified to provide more meaningful information as follows:

1. Part-time workers — included as equivalent units, e.g., two workers employed for half each normal working day treated as one employee
2. Temporary workers — excluded
3. Special staff movements, e.g., where redundancy is created — excluded
4. Segment variation, e.g., male and female staff or skilled and unskilled workers — separate labour turnover calculations should be made for these classifications.

In an effort to reduce a high labour turnover the reasons for employees leaving the organisation should be examined. They may be classified as:

(a) Employee dissatisfaction, e.g., inadequate terms and conditions of employment including lack of promotion
(b) Employer dissatisfaction, e.g., unsatisfactory employee performance
(c) Employee circumstances, e.g., domestic and family responsibilities.

The company can do little about the influence of personal circumstances on employees leaving the organisation but attempts should be made to reduce labour turnover owing to the remaining causes.

The full cost of labour turnover is difficult to calculate because it is impossible to measure factors such as the loss of good employees who might not apply for employment with the company owing to the bad record of the organisation in keeping its staff. Some costs can be measured and these include:

(*a*) Recruitment, selection and training costs
(*b*) Production efficiency losses.

A calculation of these costs should encourage management to attempt to reduce labour turnover.


## 14.11 SUMMARY

Labour control is exercised in the company environment created by established personnel policies. If the company has a reputation for fair treatment of employees which includes adequate terms and conditions of employment and a commitment to foster good morale and industrial relations, there is a greater possibility of effective labour utilisation. The quality of management is crucial in the labour control sector.


## FOR FURTHER STUDY

QUESTIONS

1. *Gross pay calculation*

   X, Y and Z are three craftsmen employed by Decorative Gardens Ltd to work on the production of two models of decorative garden gates known as 'Tudor' and 'Regency'.

   Each craftsman completes eight Tudor gates and ten Regency gates per week. Production is then inspected for defective work.

   The company's remuneration scheme provides for employees to work a 40-hour week for which X is paid 48p per hour; Y, 54p per hour; and Z, 60p per hour. Time worked in excess of the 40 hours in any week is paid for as follows:

   The first four hours — time-and-a-third
   Additional hours — time-and-a-half.

   In addition, a bonus of 75% of time saved is paid on work completed during the week. The bonus hourly rate for all employees is 50p. No bonus payment is made on defective work.

The time allowances in hours per completed model passing inspection are as follows:

|  | Craftsmen | | |
|---|---|---|---|
|  | X | Y | Z |
| Tudor model | 5 | 4 | 3 |
| Regency model | 3 | 5 | 2 |

The following facts relate to week number 34:

(a) Hours worked: X, 44; Y, 46; Z, 40
(b) Hours worked during week number 33 on uncompleted gates brought forward to week number 34: X, 8; Y, 7; Z, 5
(c) Hours worked on uncompleted gates carried forward to week number 35: X, 7; Y, 8; Z, 3
(d) Defective work:

|  | X | Y | Z |
|---|---|---|---|
| Tudor gates | 1 | 2 | – |
| Regency gates | – | 1 | 1 |

*Required:*
Calculate the gross pay earned by each of the craftsmen for week number 34, showing basic wages (inclusive of overtime premium) separately from bonus.

(ACA)

## 2. *Labour efficiency*

The directors of the XY Engineering Co. Ltd are concerned about the ever-increasing labour costs at their Alpha factory. It is also felt that labour efficiency is very low, although this is difficult to establish because production at the Alpha factory is quite dissimilar from any of the other production units in the company and, accordingly, comparisons are not made.
*Required:*
Prepare a memorandum for the directors outlining a system of accounting for labour costs which will both control the level of expenditure and give some indication of labour efficiency. (ACA)

## 3. *Production and productivity*

Explain the difference between 'production' and 'productivity'. Give two bases for measuring the productivity of direct labour.

Using the following figures as a basis, illustrate the differing effects of a 10% increase in (a) production, and (b) the productivity of direct labour. In your calculations assume that labour is remunerated on a straight piece-work basis, and that variable overheads are absorbed to production on a direct labour-hour basis.

| | |
|---|---|
| Production (units | 10,000 |
| Labour hours | 5,000 |
| | £ |
| Production costs | |
| Direct materials | 8,000 |
| Direct labour | 2,000 |
| Factory overheads (variable) | 3,000 |
| Factory overheads (fixed) | 4,000 |

(ICMA)

**4.** *Classification of remuneration and incentive systems*
Outline the main classes into which remuneration and incentive systems can be divided. Illustrate your answer with examples.                    (ICMA)

**5.** *Profit sharing incentive scheme*
The board of a manufacturing company is considering the institution of a profit sharing scheme for all its employees.
*Required:*
Prepare a discussion paper which clearly sets out what in your opinion should be the main criteria for such a scheme to be successfully implemented. (ICMA)

**6.** *Job evaluation and merit rating*
Define and distinguish between job evaluation and merit rating. List and briefly describe the steps to be taken and the factors to be considered in job evaluation.
(ICMA)

**7.** *Possible introduction of a group wage incentive scheme*
An established company, Spare Parts Ltd, had a good record in terms of profit-ability and the quality of its management. Equipment was modern and costs had been kept low in relation to levels experienced by similar companies. Many of their competitors had introduced wage incentive schemes and from time to time the point had been raised and the decision made to leave the wage payment system (day rates) as established. The main reason for this decision was the small proportion of total cost accounted for by direct labour. Formerly, this proportion was in the region of 25% but mechanisation had reduced the figure to 8%.

A profit improvement programme introduced by the company had re-opened the possibility of introducing a wage incentive scheme, the main point in its favour being the suggestion that there was a close link between labour and the efficient use of the expensive facilities of the company and an incentive scheme should improve productivity.

A working party was established to: (*a*) ascertain whether an incentive scheme was desirable; and (*b*) if so, recommend an appropriate scheme.

The working party found agreement difficult on point (*a*) but they were unanimous that if an incentive scheme was introduced, it would be necessary to adopt a group scheme giving an incentive payment based on group output as a bonus above the base rate.

Members of the working party, supporting the introduction of a wage incentive scheme, pointed out the likely improvement in group co-ordination and efficiency where the workers' collective bonus was affected by unco-ordinated action. In addition, greater control would be possible through the medium of better information on labour use and productivity. It was also pointed out that increased production should be possible with the benefit being shared by workers and management through increased pay and reduced product unit costs.

Against this view, some members of the working party were concerned about possible labour disputes in the future as compared with the excellent labour relations at present enjoyed by the company. Standards established would need frequent alteration because of changing conditions and the flexibility of management might be seriously affected. There was some doubt about good quality standards being maintained. It was also felt that early possible benefits from increased production would be rapidly lost as the scheme became a routine for the factory.

*Required:*
Comment on the case with particular reference to the view taken regarding the desirability of introducing a wage incentive scheme.

8. *Purpose of incentive schemes and a selling application*

   (*a*) Define generally the purpose of financial incentive schemes.
   (*b*) The local managers of a company with numerous selling and service branches are paid a basic salary with a bonus on turnover. Large and small orders, wholesale and retail, carrying varying rates of profit are handled for a wide range of equipment. Bonus payments vary widely from branch to branch, and complaints from the public of poor service tend to increase.

   *Required:*
   Enumerate the points which seem to you likely to be applicable to the situation described, and outline your proposals for improvement.   (ICMA)

9. *Revision of a wages structure*
   Analysis has shown that your business is losing a large number of trained staff to other firms in the locality. The reason given at leaving interviews is 'higher wages'.
   *Required:*
   What factors need to be examined if you wish to overcome this difficulty by a revision of the wages structure?                    (ICMA)

10. *Labour analysis and the treatment of overtime*
    The AB Co. Ltd specialises in precision engineering work which is always done to order. Employees are paid weekly on a time basis.

*Required:*

(a)  Prepare in outline form a weekly statement suitable for recording the time spent by employees on each job and state how you would reconcile the hours worked as shown on the statement with the actual hours paid for and how any difference would be treated.

(b)  What principle would determine whether or not you would charge to a specific job the premium payable to employees who work on that job and how would you suggest such a premium is treated in the cost accounts?

(ACA)

11. *Reports on the subject of labour*

What information would you provide to management to keep it fully informed about the labour factor in the business?                    (ICMA)

12. *Labour turnover*

The office manager of Repair Services Ltd has had considerable difficulty in keeping staff, and the high labour turnover rate prompted an investigation into the reasons for this situation. An analysis of those leaving the office during the past twelve months showed the following:

| *Reason for leaving* | % |
|---|---|
| Personal improvement | 8 |
| Domestic responsibilities | 15 |
| Dissatisfied with salary | 45 |
| Leaving the district | 3 |
| Not satisfied with the job | 16 |
| Pregnancy | 3 |
| Other reasons | 10 |
| | 100 |

The figure that caused the greatest concern was the 45% — those that left because they were dissatisfied with their salary.

The office manager outlined his problem as follows:

(a)  He could raise the rate of pay and possibly reduce the percentage but the work in general was of a routine type. He was not certain that the work warranted staff paid at a grade higher than the one at present fixed for general clerical work in the office.

(b)  The reduction in the percentage suggested above assumed that the higher calibre staff attracted by the higher pay would stay. He thought it likely that such staff would quickly become bored with the job and leave. In other words, he thought the work low grade and only suited to low calibre staff.

(c)  He had considered trying to alter the work content of the job to create more high-grade jobs for higher calibre clerks, and in the process possibly cut down staff. He might then justify higher salary payment and reduce labour turnover. His difficulty then would be the creation of routine jobs that would be more uninteresting than they are now and that would increase the percentage leaving through being dissatisfied with the job — an already high percentage at 16%.

*Required:*

(*a*)  The routine character of the work of the office appears to be a problem. Do you think this is the central issue and, if so, could this difficulty be eased in any way?

(*b*)  How would you assess the cost of labour turnover?

FURTHER READING

*Employee Remuneration and Incentives.* The Institute of Cost and Works Accountants, 1954.

Garbutt, Douglas. *Training Costs.* Gee, 1969. Chapters 2, 4, 5 and 7.

McBeath, G. and Rands, D. N. *Salary Administration.* Business Books, 1969. Chapters 1—5.

# 15 Use of Resources (3)—Expense Control and Depreciation Methods

## OBJECTIVE OF THE CHAPTER

In the context of the expense control cycle, to consider aspects of expense control other than indirect material and indirect labour cost.

## OUTLINE OF THE CHAPTER

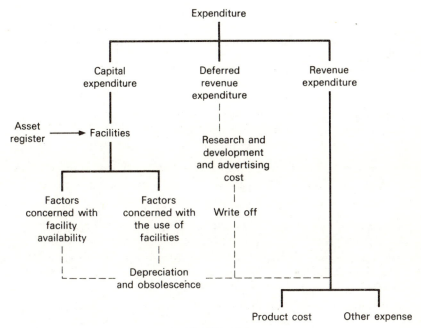

FIGURE 15.1.

General expenses tend to increase and there is a need for companies to extend the control procedures concerned with material and labour to other types of expense. There should be sound planning and authorisation procedures for incurring any expense and the provision of relevant information to ensure expenditure is incurred at levels that are in accordance with the achievement of the objectives of the business.

Chapter 12 referred to capital expenditure that may be incurred by the business and in this chapter other long-term expenditure will be considered, such as research and development and advertising cost. If these costs are not written off in the period in which they are incurred, the amount carried forward to subsequent trading periods is known as deferred revenue expenditure. The write-off in the subsequent periods is according to the expected benefit likely to be derived in those periods from the amount incurred. Such write-offs and the amortisation or depreciation of fixed assets supplement other revenue expenditure to provide product cost and period expense. Product cost is charged in the period when products are sold. Product cost for work-in-progress and products completed but not sold is carried forward to subsequent periods in stock valuations. These valuations are the subject of the next chapter. In this chapter, factors affecting services regarded as the overheads of the business are considered.

## 15.1 FACTORS CONCERNED WITH FACILITY AVAILABILITY AND USE

Records concerning specific assets may be in the form of an assets register where the following details may be recorded:

1. The asset description and identification reference
2. The asset location and location reference
3. Details regarding the cost of the asset
4. Asset changes, e.g., location, additions and sale information
5. Data regarding the asset to:

   (a) Support accounting routines, e.g., depreciation and book value calculations
   (b) Assist in the review of machine efficiency, e.g., repair and maintenance costs
   (c) Support other procedures, e.g., insurance arrangements.

To keep assets operating at an acceptable standard, maintenance should be carried out on a planned basis. It is uneconomic for all maintenance to be preventive in type and corrective maintenance is inevitable. To decide on the economic level of maintenance, the record of maintenance costs in the asset register will be invaluable.

An attempt to recognise the importance of the effective maintenance of an asset in a broader management context has resulted in the development of terotechnology. The Department of Industry's Committee for Terotechnology defines the concept as 'a combination of management, financial, engineering and other practices applied to physical assets in pursuit of economic life-cycle costs'. The application of this concept is concerned with the specification and design for reliability and maintainability of physical assets. It includes costs associated with resource management from initial installation to final asset disposal. The optimisation of life-cycle costs involves the co-operation of managers in a number of disciplines concerned with the acquisition, use, care and disposal of an asset. The comprehensiveness of the concept from the management accounting aspect is evidenced by the long-term nature of the costs relevant to an asset and the accountant should assist management concerned with terotechnology by providing life-cycle costs. The life-cycle cost is the cost of the ownership of an asset for its full anticipated life. The objective of terotechnology is to reduce life-cycle costs.

Factors concerned with the use of facilities include the following:

1. Property rent
2. Production control
3. Office management
4. Depreciation and obsolescence.

## 15.11 PROPERTY RENT

Where property in the company is owned and rented, the ascertained costs for operating units may need some adjustment so that comparability is possible. The unit where property is rented will have a rental charge included in its costs. The unit where property is owned can be made comparable by including in its costs an estimated rent for the facilities. This estimated figure is sometimes described as notional rent.

Where a company is not large enough to have several comparable units under its control, a notional rent may still be included in costs to enable the business to take advantage of interfirm comparison arrangements, either through a trade association or the Centre for Interfirm Comparison.

## 15.12 PRODUCTION CONTROL

Production control involves on the product manufacturing side of the business:

1. Quantity control
2. Quality control
3. Delivery control.

All these features have an impact on production costs and the factory manager may use the techniques of group technology and network analysis to assist in expense control. Where possible, long production runs will be attempted to reduce costs but the effect of this action on stock levels should not be overlooked. Idle time analysis, mentioned in connexion with labour control, can be applied with advantage to other facilities and a check should be made on defective production, scrap and waste.

### 15.121 *Group Technology*

In group technology, the functional layout of specialised machinery is altered by grouping work into similar types and grouping the machines to manufacture these similar work types on a flow-line basis. This procedure assists in controlling costs by reducing setting times throughput times and work-in-progress.

Management accounting is affected by group technology in the make-up of responsibility centres. In the traditional functional layout the cost centre may be a group of similar machines, such as lathes. In group technology, the cost centre may be the group which could include, in addition to a lathe, drilling and milling machines.

### 15.122 *Network analysis*

The technique of network analysis* identifies the critical path which is the most time-consuming sequence of consecutive events in producing the product. To provide this information, a flow chart is drawn on the basis of activities and events (the beginning or end of each activity) recognising the time to be taken for each activity.

The importance of this technique in the context of expense control is that resources use can be optimised by planned attempts to reduce the critical path. In addition, if costs are incorporated in the network analysis the resulting critical path is the minimum time to complete the job at the acceptable cost level.

| | | Idle machine time report | | | | | | | | | | |
|---|---|---|---|---|---|---|---|---|---|---|---|---|
| | Department | | | Week ended | | | | | | | | |
| | | Running hours | | | Idle hours | | | | | | | |
| Machine number | Standard hours | Ordinary time | Overtime | Total running hours | No work | Under repair | No operator | No material | Awaiting instructions | Awaiting set-up | Other reasons | Total idle hours |
| | | | | | | | | | | | | |
| | Totals | | | | | | | | | | | |

FIGURE 15.2. Idle machine time report

### 15.123 *Idle time analysis*

Where fixed costs are ascertained for the use of a machine, or a group of machines,

*Also known as Critical Path Analysis and the Project Evaluation Review Technique (PERT).

a rate per hour of planned use may be calculated. This rate multiplied by the idle hours identified on a return of the type illustrated in Figure 15.2 can provide management with idle machine time costs.

### 15.124 *Defective production, scrap and waste*

Scrap and waste may arise as a result of the manufacturing process and where scrap is separately identified from waste the distinguishing feature is recovery value. If the disposable material has recovery value the term 'scrap' may be used. If the disposable material has no recovery value the term 'waste' may be adopted. Defective production is output from the manufacturing process that does not meet quality standards.

A scrap cost report of the type illustrated in Figure 15.3 may be issued to management.

| Scrap report Month ended _____ | | | | | | | |
|---|---|---|---|---|---|---|---|
| Department | Scrap cost – this period | Scrap cost – this year to date | Analysis of scrap cost – this period | | | | |
| | | | Operator fault | Material fault | | Faulty tools | Other causes |
| | | | | Defective – outside guarantee period or supplier unknown | Defective – material content recoverable | | |
| | | | | | | | |
| Totals | | | | | | | |
| Details of major items scrapped during the period | | | | | | | |

FIGURE 15.3. Scrap report

Normal losses are usually considered part of the cost of good units produced and the income received from the sale of scrap, after deduction of disposal costs, credited to job costs. Where the disposal value is not significant it is usually credited to works overhead or treated as other income. This subject is also considered in Chapter 23.

Where defective production is rectified, rectification costs should be ascertained and charged to factory overhead. This amount may be a balancing figure made up as follows:

|  | £ |  |
|---|---|---|
| Cost prior to rectification | — | (May be credited to work-in-progress to recognise that the work has been taken out of production) |
| Add additional costs concerned concerned with rectification | — |  |
| Less normal cost transferred to work-in-progress or finished goods | — | (According to the condition of the work rectified) |
| Amount transferred to factory overhead for the department responsible for the rectification costs | — |  |

## 15.13 OFFICE MANAGEMENT

The quality of the organisation and control of the office in a business will have an important bearing on the use of its staff, space and equipment. In modern offices, expensive facilities are provided and to be effectively used they must be managed to the high standard required in other functions of the business.

## 15.14 DEPRECIATION AND OBSOLESCENCE

A typical definition of depreciation is 'the measure of the wearing out, consumption or other loss of value of a fixed asset, whether arising from use, effluxion of time or obsolescence through technology and market changes.'*

From the management accounting point of view, depreciation is a cost allocation process and the attempt is made to allocate the capitalised cost of the asset in a systematic manner. This process involves an assessment of:

1. The life of the asset
2. The residual value of the asset less disposal costs at the estimated time of its disposal
3. The most equitable method of spreading the asset cost over its useful life.

A leasehold life is predetermined by the lease† but most asset lives are difficult to assess. In addition to the factors affecting the life of the asset, mentioned in the above definition, maintenance may be significant in lengthening the lives of some assets well beyond the normal period for their use.

The method of providing for depreciation attempts to balance the time, use,

---

*Accounting for Depreciation* — ED15, Proposed statement of standard accounting practice (Accounting Standards Committee, 1975).
† The write-off of a lease is usually termed 'amortisation'.

obsolescence and maintenance factors affecting the rate of depreciation, and the relative importance of each factor is a matter for decision. It is common practice to apply a given method over a classified group of assets and the individual assessment of each asset, for the method of depreciation to be applied, does not take place beyond the classification group decision.

The depreciation process and its definition has tended to convey a confused understanding of the subject. The process does not:

1. Provide funds for the replacement of the asset.

   It is true that a provision for depreciation does retain funds in the business that may have been distributed as dividends but the replacement decision, if indeed an asset is replaced, is a matter unrelated to the depreciation provision. The financial transaction concerned with asset purchase may be at a price level unrelated to original cost and a different asset may be acquired.

2. Measure the loss in value of the asset.

   Some factors affecting depreciation may result in a loss of value of an asset, e.g., wear and tear and obsolescence* but the depreciation charge is a cost allocation, not a measure of value. In inflationary times, the value of assets may increase and the book value of assets (original cost less depreciation to date) is not likely to agree with the current value of assets.

3. Measure the service value of an asset.

   Unless depreciation is charged to revenue by recognising the changing value of money, the cost allocations are likely to be different from service values. In a period of inflation depreciation based on the original cost of assets will be understated.

The methods of providing for depreciation may be classified as follows:

(a)  Fixed allocations per period:†
 (i)  The straight line method
 (ii)  Endowment insurance policy method
(iii)  Sinking fund method
(iv)  Annuity method
(b)  Reducing allocations per period:
 (i)  Reducing balance method
 (ii)  Sum of years' digits method
(c)  Variable allocations per period:
 (i)  Production method
 (ii)  Revaluation method.

---

* Another example of a reduction in value is the extraction of minerals from the ground. The charge against current revenue for this process is known as depletion.

† The sinking fund and annuity methods may be classified as increasing allocations per period if the interest factor is included to give a net charge against revenue. These methods are not considered this way above because for costing purposes interest would not be netted against the constant depreciation figure.

To illustrate these methods, the following common data is provided:

Cost of asset: £5,000
Residual value: nil
Expected life of the asset: 5 years
Interest rate (where applicable): 10%

## The straight line method

In this method, the annual provision for depreciation is calculated as follows:

$$\frac{\text{Cost of asset} - \text{Residual value}}{\text{Expected life of asset}} = \frac{£5,000}{5} = £1,000 \text{ per year}$$

At the end of the five years the book value of the asset will be nil (£5,000 original cost less £5,000 accumulated depreciation).

## The endowment insurance policy method

To secure £5,000 at the end of five years in this method, an insurance company is approached to issue an endowment policy maturing in five years time at a value of £5,000. The annual premium is the annual provision for depreciation.

## The sinking fund method

In this method, if the depreciation charge is invested at 10% and subsequent depreciation provisions plus interest received are invested at 10%, the investment value at the end of the life of the asset is expected to be the original cost of the asset.* The annual provision for depreciation is calculated as follows:

$$\frac{\text{Cost of asset}}{\substack{\text{Reference to Table 3, Appendix} \\ \text{B, where } n = 5 \text{ and } i = 10\%}} = \frac{£5,000}{6\cdot105} = £819 \text{ per year}$$

The £5,000 at the end of five years is calculated as follows:

| Year | Annual provision for depreciation | Interest received at 10% of the previous end of year balance | | | | Total investment |
|---|---|---|---|---|---|---|
| | | Year 2 | Year 3 | Year 4 | Year 5 | |
| | £ | £ | £ | £ | £ | £ |
| 1 | 819 | — | — | — | — | 819 |
| 2 | 819 | 82 | — | — | — | 901 |
| 3 | 819 | 82 | 90 | — | — | 991 |
| 4 | 819 | 82 | 90 | 99 | — | 1,090 |
| 5 | 819 | 82 | 90 | 99 | 109 | 1,199 |
| | | | | | | 5,000 |

* For this illustration, taxation and investment charges and market price fluctuations have been ignored.

*The annuity method*

The funds invested in the asset in alternative use are assumed to earn interest. The asset book value at the beginning of each year is increased by this interest and the annual provision for depreciation is calculated as a constant figure to reduce the £5,000 plus interest to nil in five years. This calculation is as follows:

$$\text{Cost of asset} \times \frac{\text{Reference to Table 4, Appendix}}{\text{B where } n = 5 \text{ and } i = 10\%} = \frac{£5,000}{x \cdot 2638} = £1,319 \text{ per year}$$

The reconciliation of these amounts is as follows:

| Year | Asset book value at beginning of year | Interest at 10% | Book value of asset plus interest | Annual provision for depreciation | Asset book value at end of year |
|------|------|------|------|------|------|
| | £ | £ | £ | £ | £ |
| 1 | 5,000 | 500 | 5,500 | 1,319 | 4,181 |
| 2 | 4,181 | 418 | 4,599 | 1,319 | 3,280 |
| 3 | 3,280 | 328 | 3,608 | 1,319 | 2,289 |
| 4 | 2,289 | 229 | 2,518 | 1,319 | 1,199 |
| 5 | 1,199 | 120 | 1,319 | 1,319 | Nil |

*The reducing balance method*

In this method, a fixed percentage is written off the reducing book value of the asset each year. The formula for the calculation of this percentage is:

$$i = 100 - 100 \sqrt[n]{\frac{\text{Residual value}}{\text{Cost of asset}}}$$

For this illustration only, assuming a residual value of £840 at the end of year 5, the percentage is:

$$i = 100 - 100 \sqrt[5]{\frac{£840}{£5,000}}$$

$$i = 100 - 100 \sqrt[5]{0 \cdot 168}$$

$$i = 100 - 100 \, (0 \cdot 7)$$

$$i = 30\%$$

The provision for depreciation for each year is calculated as follows:

| Year | Asset book value at beginning of year | Provision for depreciation | Asset book value at end of year |
|------|------|------|------|
| | £ | £ | £ |
| 1 | 5,000 | 1,500 (30% of £5,000) | 3,500 |
| 2 | 3,500 | 1,050 (30% of £3,500) | 2,450 |
| 3 | 2,450 | 735 (30% of £2,450) | 1,715 |
| 4 | 1,715 | 515 (30% of £1,715) | 1,200 |
| 5 | 1,200 | 360 (30% of £1,200) | 840 |

*The sum of years' digits method*

In this method, the digits for the five years are added to give the figure: 15 (1 + 2 + 3 + 4 + 5). The provision for depreciation is then calculated by using a fraction where the denominator is 15 and the numerator the years' digit in reverse order as follows:

| Year | Asset book value at beginning of year £ | Provision for depreciation £ | Asset book value at end of year £ |
|---|---|---|---|
| 1 | 5,000 | 1,667 ($\frac{5}{15}$ of £5,000) | 3,333 |
| 2 | 3,333 | 1,333 ($\frac{4}{15}$ of £5,000) | 2,000 |
| 3 | 2,000 | 1,000 ($\frac{3}{15}$ of £5,000) | 1,000 |
| 4 | 1,000 | 667 ($\frac{2}{15}$ of £5,000) | 333 |
| 5 | 333 | 333 ($\frac{1}{15}$ of £5,000) | Nil |

*The production method*

The provision for depreciation is calculated by applying the following formula:

$$\frac{\text{Cost of asset} - \text{Residual value}}{\begin{array}{c}\text{Estimated number of production units to be}\\ \text{completed in the life of the asset}\end{array}} \times \begin{array}{l}\text{Actual number of}\\ \text{production units}\\ \text{completed in the}\\ \text{period}\end{array}$$

Assuming for this illustration, 100,000 production units are estimated to be completed in the period covered by the life of the asset and 18,000 units completed this year, the depreciation provision for this year would be:

$$\frac{£5,000}{100,000} \times 18,000 = £900$$

The production factor chosen should reasonably reflect the incidence of the use of the resources and time, a rate per hour, for example, may be considered a better measure for calculating the provision for depreciation for the period.

*The revaluation method*

In this method, the annual provision for depreciation is calculated as follows:

$$\begin{array}{c}\text{Valuation of the asset at}\\ \text{the beginning of the period}\end{array} - \begin{array}{c}\text{Valuation of the asset}\\ \text{at the end of the period}\end{array}$$

If the asset was valued at the end of year 1 at £4,150, the provision for depreciation for year 1 would be:

$$£5,000 - £4,150 = £850$$

*The methods of providing for depreciation compared*

The most widely used methods of providing for depreciation are the straight line method and the reducing balance method, but the factors that affect the choice of method are as follows:

1. The passage of time – predominently recognised by the straight line method.
2. The use of the asset – predominently recognised by the production method.
3. The rapid deterioration of assets as, for example, loose tools where the revaluation method may be used.
4. The effect of associated procedures such as costing methods which can aid the calculation of depreciation by, for example, the production method.
5. The possible onset of obsolescence and, therefore, the early write-off of the major portion of cost by using, for example, the reducing balance method.
6. Company connexion influence. The sum of years' digits method is rarely used in Great Britain but widely used in America. A subsidiary in this country may be required to follow the American practice.
7. The effect of maintenance expenditure. To equalise product costs an attempt may be made to match low maintenance costs with high depreciation or vice versa in any one accounting period. An example of this is the use of the reducing balance method but the point tends to be theoretical since the balancing of such charges would be extremely difficult in practice.
8. The intention to provide funds for the business at the end of the anticipated asset life as a result of setting aside the depreciation provision, e.g., the use of the sinking fund or endowment policy method.
9. The need to recognise that the funds invested in the asset should be providing a return, e.g., use of the annuity method.
10. The effect of taxation. To prevent the need for tax computation reconciliation, the rates used for tax purposes may be adopted by the company.

It is important to choose a method which results in a fair allocation to the accounting period and to product costs. It is possible, for example, to have misleading product cost data if two identical products are produced on two different machines and one machine is fully depreciated and the other machine is not. In this situation, a different depreciation allocation may be made in the costing records from the one adopted for the financial accounts. Alternatively, the depreciation may be treated as a fixed cost and excluded from product cost, e.g., where marginal costing is used (see Chapter 19).

*Depreciation and changing money values*

For management accounting purposes, an increasing number of companies are recognising that in a period of inflation depreciation based on cost is understated and a more realistic figure would be calculated on replacement cost. This subject is considered in greater detail in Chapter 24.

*Accounting entries for depreciation*

The original costs of assets are identified in accounts representing the principal classifications for report presentation, e.g., plant and machinery, office furniture and equipment, motor vehicles, etc. The period provisions for depreciation charged against revenue in the manufacturing and profit and loss statements for those periods are accumulated in depreciation provision accounts for each principal classification noted above. The book value of each type of asset may be easily calculated, e.g., plant and machinery asset book values can be ascertained by associating the two classified accounts as follows:

|  | £ |
|---|---|
| Plant and machinery at cost | — |
| Less provision for depreciation on plant and machinery to date | — |
| Book value of plant and machinery at the end of the current period | — |

Adjustments may be required to the accounts noted above for the following reasons:

1. An assumed life of an asset being less than previously anticipated. This may be the result of obsolescence whether of a technical nature or owing to product replacement. In these circumstances, the accumulated depreciation account should be credited with the excess depreciation to be written off to reduce the book value of the asset to the estimated recoverable amount for its remaining life. The debit for the write-off is the depreciation account for the asset account concerned.
2. An asset disposal. A credit to the asset account for the asset cost and a debit to the accumulated depreciation account for its depreciation charged to the date of disposal eliminates the asset from the accounts. The resulting book value is matched against the disposal proceeds and where there is a difference, the surplus or deficiency should be identified as a profit/loss on the disposal of fixed assets.
3. If assets are revalued, the adjustment made in the asset account to give effect to the revaluation should be the basis of revised depreciation charges in the accumulated depreciation account.

Other factors may affect the treatment of depreciation in the management accounts of the business:

(a) An assumed life of an asset revised to a period greater than the life previously anticipated. The book value of the asset less estimated residual value should be written off over the revised remaining useful life. Strictly, the annual charge for product costing should be the depreciation calculated on the basis of the total amount to be written off over the total life of that asset (usually, the original cost) divided by that useful life now estimated — a figure in excess of the balancing write-off described above. This difference in the provision for depreciation may be so small as to render the distinction unnecessary.
(b) An asset written down to its residual value or nil yet retained in use. For product costing purposes, depreciation should continue to be charged in the

costing records although the amount should reflect the revised asset life, i.e., recognise that earlier charges were higher than they should have been because the asset life was underestimated.

(c) Changes in the use of assets significantly affecting the wear and tear factor in depreciation charge assessment. An example of this is a change from single to double shift working: asset lives should be reassessed to recognise the change in asset use.

## 15.2 RESEARCH AND DEVELOPMENT

A common classification for research and development is as follows:

1. Pure (or basic) research: original investigation undertaken in order to gain new scientific or technical knowledge and understanding. Basic research is not primarily directed towards any specific practical aim or application.
2. Applied research: original investigation undertaken in order to gain new scientific or technical knowledge and directed towards a specific practical aim or objective.
3. Development: the use of scientific or technical knowledge in order to produce new or substantially improved materials, devices, products, processes, systems or services.*

The cost of routine research and development activities are included in the main expenditure classifications, for example:

Routine improvements in manufacturing methods — factory overhead
Organisation and methods — administration overhead
Market research — selling and distribution overhead.

Other significant research and development costs are either:

(a) Written off in the period in which they are incurred and often treated as a separate item in the profit and loss statement
(b) Charged to product costs where such research and development is specifically undertaken for a particular customer
(c) Carried forward to subsequent periods on the grounds that this expenditure is expected to produce income during these future periods.

In a sense, most development expenditure will benefit future trading periods but course (c) should only be followed where there is a high level of certainty regarding the benefits to be received. In most companies the view is taken that research and development expenditure is of a continuous nature subject to the appropriation of funds particular to a control period and, therefore, resonably written off in that period.

*Taken from ED14 — *Accounting for Research and Development*, proposed statement of standard accounting practice (Accounting Standards Committee, 1975).

The control of significant research projects may be assisted by the project procedure mentioned in Chapter 3. Appropriate estimated costs of the research would be included on a project sanction form and after consideration of the objective of the research work, the timing of research, limits set for particular project research costs, and the probability factor as to the success of the project, a decision would be made. Subsequent control would be ensured by the capital expenditure control procedure explained in Chapter 12, actual costs being compared with estimates at each significant stage of research, according to the agreed research programme.

## 15.3  ADVERTISING

Advertising is a significant cost in many businesses and its control presents a problem because it is difficult to relate advertising costs incurred to sales achieved. It may be possible to relate classified advertising to specific sales by using a customer response code quoted in the advertisement. An incremental approach may be tried by attempting to relate changes in advertising costs to changes in sales achieved but so many factors, difficult of assessment, enter into sales results that the problem remains.

Control of advertising cost usually concentrates on the budgetary appropriation of funds and the skilled allocation of these funds to deal with specific problems in the period. For example, advertising cost may be increased in areas where sales are decreasing because the advertising manager considers that sales potential makes such increased expenditure worth while.

## 15.4  OTHER EXPENSES

Other services affecting the company performance, recognised in the overheads of the business, are often classified as follows:

1. Utilities, e.g., electricity, water, gas and fuel oil expenses
2. Outside services, e.g., postages and telephones, cleaning, security, legal, accountancy and auditing charges
3. Financial expenses, e.g., bank charges.

### 15.41  BAD DEBTS

Bad debts may be included in selling expenses, and a check on bad debts experience may prompt more effective measures of credit control. The accountant can help by:

(a) Providing a prompt invoicing and sales accounting routine
(b) Regularly inspecting ledger balances and taking action to recover debts promptly

(c) Keeping in close touch with sales staff regarding credit limits and specific customer difficulties

(d) Taking an active part in fixing selling policies that may affect debt collection.

## 15.42  SIGNIFICANT SERVICES

Where services are significant segments of the business, control may be improved by reporting to management detailed costs, and where appropriate, revenue of these responsibility centres. Examples are transport and canteen facilities illustrated in Figures 15.4 and 15.5 respectively.

| Transport cost statement<br>Period ended _____ | | | | | | | | | |
|---|---|---|---|---|---|---|---|---|---|
| Vehicle reg. number | Vehicle based at | Total running expenses | Overhead | Total vehicle cost | Mileage | | | Miles per gallon | Running costs per mile |
| | | | | | Loaded | Empty | Total | | |
| Analysis by make and type of vehicle | | £ | £ | £ | | | | | |
| | Sub total | | | | | | | | |
| | | | | | | | | | |
| | Sub total | | | | | | | | |
| | | | | | | | | | |
| | Sub total | | | | | | | | |
| | Totals | | | | | | | | |

FIGURE 15.4. Transport cost statement

Total running expenses often include the following:

Drivers and mates wages
Fuel and lubricants
Repairs
Direct expenses
Licence
Insurance
Depreciation.

Overheads are concerned with garage administration. An alternative classification for total vehicle costs is as follows:

Running expenses
  Drivers and mates wages
  Fuel and lubricants
  Repairs
  Direct expenses
Fixed expenses
  Licence
  Insurance
  Depreciation
  Garage expenses.

| | Canteen operating statement Period ended _____ | | | | | |
| --- | --- | --- | --- | --- | --- | --- |
| | This period | | | To date | | |
| | Budget | Actual | Variance | Budget | Actual | Variance |
| | £ | £ | £ | £ | £ | £ |
| Free meals value Sales | | | | | | |
| Total sales Deduct food and supplies | | | | | | |
| Contribution | | | | | | |
| Wages and salaries National insurance Holiday pay Gas Water Electricity Crockery Maintenance Rent and rates Sundries | | | | | | |
| Total expenses | | | | | | |
| Operating profit/(loss) | | | | | | |

FIGURE 15.5. Canteen operating statement

## 15.43 INSURANCE

Insurance, the provision against a contingent liability resulting in a loss, is usually regarded as a secretarial function but the accountant can be involved in the submission of data to insurance companies and the insurance cost includes the following types of insurance cover:

1. Fire insurance — building and contents

2. Consequential loss insurance — cover against losses resulting from the interruption of trade owing to fire and other disasters such as floods and storms
3. Engineering insurance — boilers, machinery breakdown and lifting gear
4. Motor vehicle insurance
5. Employers liability insurance
6. Goods-in-transit insurance and marine insurance
7. Credit insurance
8. Cash in safe and transit insurance
9. Public liability insurance
10. Fidelity guarantee insurance
11. Products insurance — loss to persons arising from goods sold or supplied
12. Pensions schemes and life assurance.

## 15.5 RECONCILIATION OF PROFIT PER THE MANAGEMENT AND FINANCIAL ACCOUNTS

References in this chapter to amounts appearing in one set of records (e.g., notional rent) or in the management and financial accounts at different amounts (e.g., depreciation) indicate that a profit reconciliation is desirable. This is illustrated in Chapter 22.

## 15.6 A CONCLUDING COMMENT

This chapter explains the financial aspects of facilities control including the consideration of depreciation, research and development and advertising. The opportunity has been taken in this chapter to refer to aspects of other expenses which are not covered elsewhere.

## FOR FURTHER STUDY

QUESTIONS

1. *Better utilisation of plant, labour and materials*
   'It is ironic that, at a time when great emphasis is being laid on the need for better utilisation of plant, labour and materials, accountants are paying more attention to investment decision-making techniques, such as DCF, than to providing the accounting and statistical information required for optimising the use of the currently available resources.'
   M. H. Chappel, 'Information for operations planning', Management Accounting (April 1967), p. 138.

   *Required:*
   Explain and comment on this statement.

2. *Use of asset registers*

Cogs and Gears Ltd is a group with a number of subsidiary companies and for some time it has been dissatisfied with its control over assets. A student was assigned a project to examine the control system with the specific task of recommending as asset register system to be introduced into the group. Summarising sections of the report produced by the student, the following recommendations were included:

(a) The provision of an asset register for each subsidiary company to record existing assets
(b) The centralisation of asset registers and their supporting records and clerical up-dating at head office
(c) The introduction of documentation to cover the advice of:

   (i) Asset acquisitions
   (ii) Asset transfers between subsidiary companies
   (iii) Asset location changes in the subsidiary company
   (iv) Maintenance
   (v) Depreciation charges
   (vi) Insurance details
   (vii) Asset disposals

(d) The use of a coding system appropriate to the asset classification to identify separately each asset by code number.

*Required:*
(a) What information may be recorded in an asset register?
(b) Comment on the recommendations made by the student.

3. *Cost of using owner occupied premises*

Company A has two comparable operating units; one unit in owner occupied premises and the other unit in rented accommodation. When the results of the two units are compared, the manager of the rented accommodation says that he is at a disadvantage because an equivalent cost for rent is not included in the accounts of the unit in owner occupied premises.
*Required:*
Discuss the implications of the view expressed above and the action that may be taken.

4. *Value of production control*

'Effective production control can make a valuable contribution to the financial control of the business.'
*Required:*
What do you understand by 'production control' and in what ways can effective production control assist the management in the financial control of the business?

5. *Defective work rectification*
A system of job costing is operated at a small engineering works where part of the production is defective but capable of rectification.
*Required:*
Design a sheet to record an item of defective production, and the necessary variable cost additions for rectification. Show how the figures obtainable from the record would be treated in the management accounts.                (ICMA)

6. *Confusion about the nature of depreciation*
Do you agree with the following statements regarding depreciation:

(*a*) The accumulated depreciation provision shown in the accounts of the company as at the end of this year is £80,000 and this amount is available for the replacement of the assets that have formed the basis of these provisions.
(*b*) The book value of plant and machinery at the beginning of this year at £20,000 has been reduced by this year's depreciation to £16,000. This reduction represents the decrease in value of this plant and machinery.

Explain your answer.

7. *The meaning of depreciation and obsolescence and methods of providing for depreciation*
State what you understand by (*a*) depreciation; and (*b*) obsolescence.
   Outline four methods used for calculating depreciation including two methods where funds are provided at the end of the anticipated life of the asset by the setting aside of the provisions for depreciation.                (ACA)

8. *Adjustments to accounting entries for depreciation*
The accounting entries for depreciation may require adjustment for the following reasons:

(*a*) An assumed life of an asset being less than previously anticipated
(*b*) An asset disposal.

*Required:*
Describe the adjustments required, given the following information:

(*a*) Plant and machinery was purchased five years ago for £15,000 and had an estimated life of 15 years with no residual value. At the beginning of year 6, the estimated life of this plant and machinery has been reassessed as 10 years (5 years remaining life).
(*b*) Office equipment with a book value of £100 (original cost £500, less depreciation to date £400) has reached the end of its useful life and been sold for £50.

9. *Depreciation policies and depreciation rates*
Mercury Products Ltd have built a new factory to manufacture and market a new range of products demanding the latest technical equipment.

The company uses the straight line method of providing for depreciation and adopts the following rates for its assets:

Leasehold land and buildings — life of lease
Plant and machinery — 10 years
Furniture and fittings — 20 years
Motor vehicles — 5 years

Its depreciation policies include the following instructions to subsidiary company accountants:

(a) When an asset is sold in advance of its estimated life.
The difference between the book value of the asset and its disposal value is to be written off to 'Profit/Loss on the Sale of Fixed Assets' and this account closed off to 'Other Income and Expense', i.e., not considered as an expense of the period.

(b) When an asset life is found to be less than previously estimated.
The difference between the book value of the asset and the estimated recoverable amount for the remainder of its estimated life is to be written off to the 'Accumulated Depreciation Account', the charge being recorded in the depreciation account for the asset concerned.

(c) When an asset is written down to its residual value or nil yet retained in use.
No further depreciation to be charged.

(d) When it is planned that an asset will not be in use for a long period.
No depreciation to be charged until the asset is returned to normal use.

The question arose as to whether the asset lives used by the remainder of the group should be used for this subsidiary company. Detailed investigations were made by the company engineers and they examined types of asset in relation to wear and tear, asset maintenance policies, and likely obsolescence. They found that the rates calculated were similar to their normal rates but when compared with Trade Association rates for their particular industry, their anticipated asset lives were much longer, particularly for plant and machinery.
*Required:*

(a) Do you agree with the depreciation policies included in subsidiary company accounting instructions?

(b) What action would you take regarding the depreciation rate problem?

10. *The meaning of research and development cost*
What do you understand by the term 'research and development cost'? Give examples of various types of research and development.

11. *Cost control and cost ascertainment aspects of research and development*
P. Products Ltd maintains a research department which until now has been relatively small, operating on a cost budget of approximately £20,000 per annum. This represents one per cent of total cost. There is to be a considerable

extension of research activities during the budget year commencing on 1 January 19.., and research projects already under consideration are of the following types:

(*a*) Two projects for the development of new products
(*b*) One project for the improvement of a product already being manufactured, where the emphasis is on both functional aspects and cost reduction
(*c*) Three projects for the improvement of manufacturing methods.

The industrial engineer of the company, who is responsible for the research department along with all other engineering activities, expects to increase annual spending on research up to a total of £100,000. He is asking you, as the management accountant, to present your ideas on the cost ascertainment and cost control arrangements which should be applied to this function.
*Required:*
Set out your ideas in the form of a report to the industrial engineer.     (ICMA)

12. *Accounting aspects of credit control*
The company is seeking to provide a more effective credit control service.
*Required:*
You are the accountant to this company. What help can you give to the company managers to enable them to achieve their objective?

FURTHER READING

Bullock, J. and Paula, F. Clive de. *Research and Development – the Key to Future Profitability.* General Educational Trust of the Institute of Chartered Accountants in England and Wales, 1966.
Moore, Franklin G. *Manufacturing Management.* Richard D. Irwin, Homewood, Illinois, 1969. Chapters 6, 13–15, 30 and 35–7.
Paula, F. Clive de. *Management Accounting in Practice.* Pitman, 1959. Chapters 7, 8 and 10.

# 16 Investment Results

## OBJECTIVE OF THE CHAPTER

To show that the summary financial information produced to illustrate the results of investment may be used to indicate possible improvements in business efficiency and how profit improvement may be secured in significant areas of the business.

## OUTLINE OF THE CHAPTER

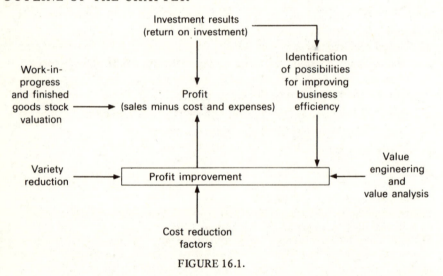

FIGURE 16.1.

In the investment results classification of financial information for management the costs of the period are matched against the revenue (sales) of the same period, the balance being profit or loss. To calculate the cost of sales, the expenses considered in the three previous chapters need to be adjusted by work-in-progress and finished goods stock values.

## 16.1 WORK-IN-PROGRESS AND FINISHED GOODS STOCK VALUATION

Reported profits can be significantly affected by the values placed on stocks and they may be valued at:

1. Prime cost — direct material, direct labour and direct expense
2. Factory marginal cost — prime cost plus variable factory overhead

3. Total factory cost — prime cost plus fixed and variable factory overhead.

Prime cost is the most conservative valuation and in a period when stock levels are increasing, profits will be understated to the extent that other costs normally carried forward to a subsequent trading period will be written off in the current period. When stock levels are reducing, profits will be overstated to the extent that only prime costs will be charged against sales, a cost figure below what may be regarded as the cost of the product being sold in the period.

Factory marginal cost is supported by marginal costing enthusiasts — a technique described in greater detail in Chapter 19. For this chapter, it may be noted that fixed expenses are considered as predominently related to the period in which they are incurred. On the basis of this argument, there is little justification for carrying these costs into a subsequent trading period, that is by including them in the work-in-progress valuation.

When total factory cost is adopted, the view is taken that the partial costs of the prime and marginal cost methods do not measure the expenditure that has been incurred in bringing the product to its present location and condition. The Statement of Standard Accounting Practice* suggests that this expenditure should include, in addition to the cost of purchase, such costs of conversion (including related over-heads) as are appropriate to that location and condition. Costs of conversion for this purpose are defined as:

(a) Costs which are specifically attributable to units of production, i.e., direct labour, direct expenses and sub-contracted work

(b) Production overheads based on the normal level of activity, taking one year with another

(c) Other overheads attributable in the particular circumstances of the business to bringing the product or service to its present location and condition, e.g., design and selling costs relating to products manufactured to a customer's specification.

Standard costs may be used in place of actual costs to value stocks. If the standard cost method is used, advantage is taken of predetermined costs mentioned in greater detail in the next chapter. Standard costs are what the costs should be, rather than what the 'actual' costs are. Stocks at standard cost may be converted to 'actual' by the use of variances (the differences between actual and standard costs calculated in the standard costing system). The view may be expressed that, providing the standard costs are realistic, the stock values should not be adjusted because the variances represent inefficiencies or improvements which should be written off in the period in which they are incurred or gained. The value at which stocks and work-in-progress are stated in the accounts can vary according to the following formula:

(a) The total of the lower of cost and net realisable value of the separate items of stock or of groups of similar items

(b) In the case of long-term contract work-in-progress, cost plus attributable profit less any foreseeable losses and progress payments received and receivable.

* *Stocks and Work-in-Progress,* Statement of Standard Accounting Practice No. 9 (Accounting Standards Committee, 1975).

The terms mentioned above may be defined as follows:

1. Net realisable value — the amount at which it is expected that items of stocks and work-in-progress can be disposed of without creating either profit or loss in the year of sale, i.e., the estimated proceeds of sale less all further costs to completion and less all costs to be incurred in distribution, marketing and selling
2. Attributable profit — that fraction of the total profit currently estimated to arise over the duration of the contract which fairly reflects the proportion appropriate to the work completed at the accounting date.

The exposure draft, ED18, suggests that stock and work-in-progress should be shown in the balance sheet at its value to the business at the balance sheet date. The value to the business is the lower of current replacement cost and net realisable value.*

## 16.2 THE STOCK VALUATIONS COMPARED

*Data*

Per unit: Prime cost: £20

Factory variable overhead: £20

Selling price: £70

Fixed costs per month: £1,500

Unit movements in the quarter:

|  | January | February | March |
|---|---|---|---|
| Opening stock | 100 | 50 | 150 |
| Add production | 50 | 200 | 50 |
|  | 150 | 250 | 200 |
| Less sales | 100 | 100 | 100 |
| Closing stock | 50 | 150 | 100 |

Period management accounts prepared on the basis of stock valued at prime cost (£20 per unit) would appear as follows:

*Method 1*

|  | January £ | February £ | March £ |  |
|---|---|---|---|---|
| Sales | 7,000 | 7,000 | 7,000 | (A) |
| Production cost |  |  |  |  |
| Prime cost | 1,000 | 4,000 | 1,000 |  |
| Variable overhead | 1,000 | 4,000 | 1,000 |  |
| Fixed cost | 1,500 | 1,500 | 1,500 |  |
|  | 3,500 | 9,500 | 3,500 |  |
| Add opening stock | 2,000 | 1,000 | 3,000 |  |
|  | 5,500 | 10,500 | 6,500 |  |
| Less closing stock | 1,000 | 3,000 | 2,000 |  |
| Cost of sales | 4,500 | 7,500 | 4,500 | (B) |
| Profit/(loss) | 2,500 | (500) | 2,500 | (A − B) |

*The Accounting Standards Committee's exposure draft on Current Cost Accounting (ED18) involves a suggested major change in accounting practice in the U.K. See Chapter 24.

Period management accounts prepared on the basis of stock valued at marginal cost (£40 per unit) would appear as follows:

*Method 2*

| | January £ | February £ | March £ | |
|---|---|---|---|---|
| Sales | 7,000 | 7,000 | 7,000 | (A) |
| Production cost | | | | |
| Prime cost | 1,000 | 4,000 | 1,000 | |
| Variable overhead | 1,000 | 4,000 | 1,000 | |
| Fixed cost | 1,500 | 1,500 | 1,500 | |
| | 3,500 | 9,500 | 3,500 | |
| Add opening stock | 4,000 | 2,000 | 6,000 | |
| | 7,500 | 11,500 | 9,500 | |
| Less closing stock | 2,000 | 6,000 | 4,000 | |
| Cost of sales | 5,500 | 5,500 | 5,500 | (B) |
| Profit | 1,500 | 1,500 | 1,500 | (A − B) |

Period management accounts prepared on the basis of total factory cost (£55 per unit)* would appear as follows:

*Method 3*

| | January £ | February £ | March £ | |
|---|---|---|---|---|
| Sales | 7,000 | 7,000 | 7,000 | (A) |
| Production cost | | | | |
| Prime cost | 1,000 | 4,000 | 1,000 | |
| Variable overhead | 1,000 | 4,000 | 1,000 | |
| Fixed cost | 1,500 | 1,500 | 1,500 | |
| | 3,500 | 9,500 | 3,500 | |
| Add opening stock | 5,500 | 2,750 | 8,250 | |
| | 9,000 | 12,250 | 11,750 | |
| Less closing stock | 2,750 | 8,250 | 5,500 | |
| Cost of sales | 6,250 | 4,000 | 6,250 | (B) |
| Profit | 750 | 3,000 | 750 | (A − B) |

The example illustrates the point made in the previous section that reported profits can be significantly affected by the values placed on stocks. February results have changed from a loss of £500 to a profit of £3,000, with a profit figure of

* Prime cost: £20 per unit plus variable overhead: £20 per unit plus fixed overhead: £15 per unit (production averaged out at 100 units per month divided into fixed cost: £1,500).

£1,500 for the second method. All three methods show different reported profits for January and March (£2,500, £1,500 and £750) although the same within each method (as might be expected with equivalent production and sales figures). It is significant to note that the marginal cost method gives a constant profit figure for constant sales and costs as one would expect. As opening and closing stocks are the same, total profit for the quarter is £4,500 for each method.

From this example, the justification is provided for the stock method chosen to be consistently applied from period to period, recognising that it is a matter for judgement which method is adopted. The supporter of marginal costing would point out that period results are easily explained if Method 2 is adopted and it is true that if accounts are to be of value to management, they must be understood. If Method 1 or 3 is adopted, the stock change effect on profits should be explained to management. In the example given, Method 1 results may be related to Method 2 profits as follows:

|  | January £ | February £ | March £ |
|---|---|---|---|
| Method 1: |  |  |  |
| Profit/(loss) | 2,500 | (500) | 2,500 |
| Period stock change x cost difference (£40 − £20) | (1,000) (50 x £20) | 2,000 (100 x £20) | (1,000) (50 x £20) |
| Method 2 profit | 1,500 | 1,500 | 1,500 |

Method 3 profits may be related to Method 2 profits as follows:

|  | January £ | February £ | March £ |
|---|---|---|---|
| Method 3 profit | 750 | 3,000 | 750 |
| Period stock change x cost difference (£55 − £40) | 750 (50 x £15) | (1,500) (100 x £15) | 750 (50 x £15) |
| Method 2 profit | 1,500 | 1,500 | 1,500 |

The conservative approach to stock valuation in the financial accounts may not be repeated in the stock valuations used for management accounts. A reconciliation of profits according to each set of accounts should, therefore, include the difference between the stock valuations adopted.

## 16.3  POSSIBILITIES FOR IMPROVING BUSINESS EFFICIENCY

The calculated profit related to capital employed gives the return on investment and a review of the investment results may indicate that business performance can be improved. Business performance may be improved by an increase in the profit margin and an increase in the turnover of capital. To secure this improvement, the identification of possibilities for improvement precedes the submission of proposals to

(a) Reduce costs
(b) Increase the volume of sales
(c) Reduce capital employed.

Ratio analysis is a valuable technique for identifying areas for further investigation and Figure 5.4 illustrates the possibilities of this approach for profit improvement, with or without interfirm comparison. Where ratios indicate poor performance, the appropriate control activity should be examined. For example, the calculation of a poor credit period of debtors result should be followed by an examination of the credit control procedure.

Trend information can be used to isolate the major factors causing the trends so that their implications can be judged to enable the business to change strategy to maintain long-term growth objectives.

All managers have a responsibility for detecting improvement possibilities and possible methods of increasing volume and reducing capital employed are illustrated in Figures 16.2 and 16.3.

The diagrams illustrate the important point that profit improvement involves the use of many techniques that have been proved in industry as being capable of improving performance. In most companies there is considerable scope for the successful application of modern management techniques.*

## 16.4 PROFIT IMPROVEMENT EMPHASIS

Where to place the profit improvement emphasis in the cost sector is a question answered by cost analysis in terms of total cost, high cost, functional cost, controllable cost and product pricing. These points are examined in greater detail in the sections to follow.

### 16.41 TOTAL COST ANALYSIS

The minimum breakdown of cost should follow the conventional pattern of:

Cost of raw materials and components
Direct labour cost
Factory overhead cost
Administration overhead cost
Selling and distribution overhead cost.

Further subjective analysis may be necessary and the overheads divided into the fixed, variable and semi-variable cost categories.

*See, for example, the book recommended in Chapter 10: John Argenti, *Management Techniques – A Practical Guide* (Allen & Unwin, 1969).

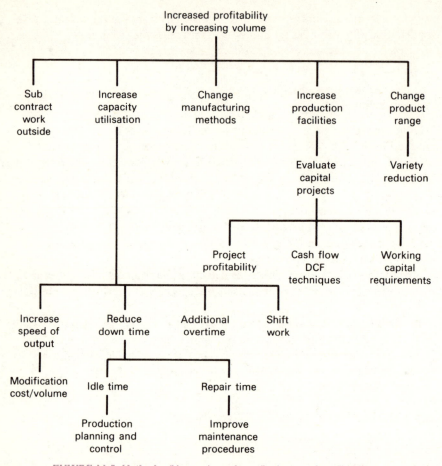

FIGURE 16.2. Methods of increasing volume for increased profitability

Apart from the need to relate cost initiation with product cost for the development of the cost reduction programme, cost ascertainment is an essential tool for the evaluation of cost reduction proposals.

In costing systems, abnormal costs are not included in product costs but from the cost reduction point of view they should not be ignored.

## 16.42 THE SOURCES OF HIGH COSTS

To recognise items that account for the highest cost is an important phase in cost reduction analysis. The reason for this is that it is normally easier to obtain a significant cost saving from such items than obtain an equivalent cost reduction from a low product cost element. This concentration on high costs should not obscure the fact that a few savings of small amount may make a significant cost reduction in total.

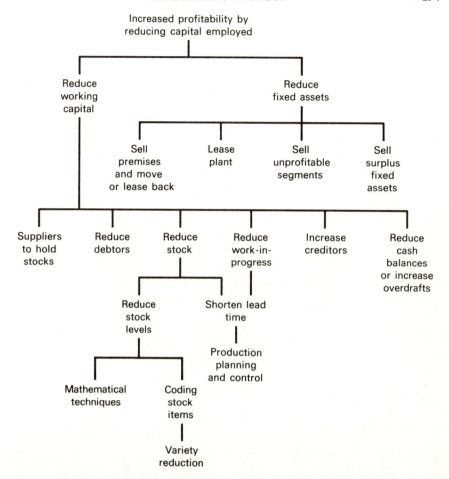

FIGURE 16.3. Methods of reducing capital employed for increased profitability

## 16.43 FUNCTIONAL COST ANALYSIS

In Chapter 8, it was mentioned that cost control is facilitated by the establishment of responsibility centres where responsibility is clearly defined. Cost reduction possibilities are best associated with these responsibility centres, rather than areas of cost for which no single manager is responsible.

## 16.44 CONTROLLABLE COST ANALYSIS

Cost and expenses analysis is the preliminary step to the analysis of functional costs between controllable and uncontrollable classifications. Cost reduction emphasis should be placed on the controllable costs for a particular level of responsibility.

## 16.45  PRODUCT PRICING

To attempt to increase profits, prices should not only stimulate demand but maintain reasonable profit margins. Prices at too high a level may result in lost sales and
under-utilisation of resources. Low prices may keep plant fully occupied but give a
poor return on investment.

   If pricing is governed by the market situation fixed by competitors, then cost
information will be required as a basis for accepting or rejecting business at the price
levels ruling in the market. Where a short-term price is required as, for example, in a
recession, the price may be fixed on the basis of marginal cost information, since
any excess of selling price over marginal cost will make some contribution to the
fixed costs which must be met although all the facilities are not being used. This
point is developed in Chapter 19.

## 16.5  COST REDUCTION FACTORS

The competitive situation forces attention on costs, and management accounting
techniques effectively applied will normally secure a measure of cost reduction. A
more dynamic approach to cost reduction involves a recognition of the following
factors:

1.  Unnecessary costs exist even in the most efficient businesses
2.  Inefficient management may generate additional costs
3.  Cost reduction generally requires change; staff usually dislike change
4.  Perfection is expensive
5.  Coverage of system exceptions is a costly matter
6.  Creative thinking may make a significant contribution to cost reduction
7.  Costs should be attacked at their source
8.  Short-term action should be related to long-term objectives
9.  Cost reduction should be maintained
10. Communication of company policy and objectives in the context of cost
    reduction.

### 16.51  UNNECESSARY COSTS

Unnecessary costs are costs that can be eliminated without reducing the quality of
the product or service provided. Little value can be gained for the business if costs
are reduced but the quality that made the product attractive to the customer is
impaired. This is not to say that existing quality standards must be assumed to be
necessary. It may be found that the needs of a customer may be met by lowering a
standard and obtaining a cost reduction as a result of this action.

   It is not unusual for temporary arrangements to become fixed because management decisions often have to be made quickly and a second examination of the
problem is not possible because time is not available. If the time is available to
consider action to secure improved cost effectiveness, something may not be done

owing to the mistaken belief that it is impossible. It is easy to find excuses for not taking action that could eliminate unnecessary costs.

## 16.52 INEFFICIENT MANAGEMENT

When a business is facing difficult times, the incentive to keep costs low is evident. In a period of prosperity this incentive is, to some extent, removed and management becomes complacent. This is when control procedures may become lax. Top management support for cost reduction should be constantly in evidence.

## 16.53 THE RELUCTANCE TO CHANGE

The resistance to change must be overcome if any real progress is to be made, but change for change's sake will not bring any real benefits to the business. The systematic approach is to study present methods and seriously question the belief that because something has been done for ten or twenty years it must be right. Not only may the work be done by a method which could be improved, but the task itself may prove to be unnecessary.

## 16.54 SYSTEM PERFECTION

The attempt to devise detailed systems of control that will operate with maximum efficiency is a laudable objective but it can be overdone. In question 4 at the end of this chapter, M. J. Glenn of Marks & Spencer, describes part of their simplification programme, and it may be noted that unnecessary refinements in systems were eliminated.

## 16.55 SYSTEM EXCEPTIONS

Procedures for the simplest of business operations can become very complex and costly to operate, if an attempt is made to cover every possibility and not rely on the common sense of individuals operating the system. It is true that management has a responsibility to make fraud difficult but systems of internal check may become too elaborate and costs can escalate alarmingly. If losses from not operating a control system are unlikely to exceed £200 per annum, it is absurd to put in a system of control costing £6,000 per annum to operate.

## 16.56 CREATIVE THINKING

The development of alternative ways of doing a job depends upon ideas and suggestions emanating from those responsible for cost reduction. One way of developing creative thinking of this type is to subject a cost reduction team to a series of questions designed to originate new ideas. Typical questions are considered in the later section in this chapter on value analysis.

    If a company has a suggestion scheme in operation this may be used as a source of ideas for cost reduction. The 'man on the job' can often see what needs to be done when this eludes others in the organisation. Suggestion schemes sometimes lapse because enthusiasm quickly wanes. A steady campaign and incentive payments are necessary to keep the programme alive and this point is relevant for all areas of activity designed to improve business efficiency.

## 16.57  COST REDUCTION SOURCES

As might be expected, the cost reduction sources follow the functions of the business which, in a manufacturing business, are principally manufacturing, marketing and financial.

Opportunities in the manufacturing area begin with the design of the product and affect every element of cost:

Material: e.g., the use of material at lower cost
Labour: e.g., the use of acceptable tolerances that reduce labour time on the job
Overhead: e.g., the design of the product to use cheaper equipment.

Preventative and routine maintenance carried out when it is convenient to the works may prevent or reduce costly breakdowns. Material, labour and facilities control in the factory can minimise costs. Techniques, such as work study, have been used for some time on the shop floor and they have not outlived their usefulness.

Opportunities in the marketing area affect selling and distribution costs. Normal cost control of area sales offices can be useful but the real savings may be secured by special cost studies on such topics as the likely profit impact of a proposed sales promotion idea or pricing policy.

In the financial area, the periodical examination of how funds are used can contribute to improved profitability. The comparatively recent use of work study in the office is testimony to the opportunities that exist for the reduction of general administration costs. Increasing office mechanisation has served to give an impetus to systems analysis. Many of the studies made necessary by the proposed introduction of office machinery could bring big reductions in office costs without the introduction of the machinery.

Attempts at cost reduction through areas of control is a reasonable practice but the best overall results can only be obtained by integrated action. For example, the sales manager's predominent interest, although not his only aim, is to secure a high volume of sales. To do this, he likes to meet the customer's specific requirements which may include speedy delivery from stock, choice from a wide product range, and special machining to the required product. The works manager's prime aim is to secure smooth production flow with long runs to produce the quality product at low cost. This requirement may include the build-up of work-in-progress stocks, good buffer stocks to prevent a sudden shortage of raw material, and the reduction in varieties of product and special machining. The accountant must look at company liquidity and may view with alarm the additional build-up in stocks. Each functional executive is acting in the interests of the business in his own function but this functional action can generate effort in opposing directions. The best overall result is only possible by integrating these conflicting efforts in a comprehensive plan. Budgetary control is a useful technique in this context to secure maximum economy in the use of resources.

## 16.58 COST REDUCTION STABILITY

It may be fairly simple to identify a cost that should be reduced. By taking the appropriate action the desired effect may be secured but the cost reduction may not be maintained. Take, for example, the case of a telephone charge that is identified as being at a level higher than necessary. An instruction is given that the cost must be reduced and a check on long-distance calls is made at the switchboard. Personnel soon hear of this check being made and restrict their long-distance calls with the result that the telephone charges are reduced to the level required. The check at the switchboard is removed, this becomes known, and the telephone charge returns to its former level. In fact, the former level of cost may be exceeded. This is not effective cost reduction. From this example the principle emerges that a simple system of continuous control should be established to ensure that cost reductions are maintained. Again, the technique of budgetary control can be useful with the problem of cost reduction stability.

## 16.6 THE COST REDUCTION APPROACH

The approach to cost reduction is important and it is not uncommon for the following wrong approaches to be made:

1. The issue of a cost reduction circular by top management as a routine instruction. Lack of top management enthusiasm is soon noticed.
2. The instruction issued that all costs must be cut by a fixed percentage. Sometimes, it is necessary to increase costs in one sector to secure large economies in other parts of the organisation.
3. The request for economies when it is evident that in some sectors of the business there is no effort to reduce costs. In fact, there may be evidence of extravagance. Team effort is required for cost reduction.

Motivation is important. In this connexion, the words 'cost reduction' may be considered a disadvantage. A cost reduction campaign can represent the negative approach. A better emphasis is the positive implication of the terms used earlier in this chapter: 'profit improvement'.

Good communications are important. Rumour quickly places emphasis on the worse aspects of cost reduction from the employee's point of view. An employee cannot be expected to give wholehearted support to a scheme which he is convinced will secure his own unemployment. The positive approach should include provision for staff changes with an equitable personnel policy communicated to all concerned at the earliest possible moment.

## 16.7  VALUE ENGINEERING AND VALUE ANALYSIS

Cost reduction at the design stages of a product is sometimes referred to as value engineering, this term embraces techniques to identify costs unnecessary according to the value of the product to the user. The procedure concerned with identifying unnecessary costs and indicating ways of eliminating them is value analysis. Value analysis, therefore, can assist the cost reduction process when applied to existing products.

The value analysis procedure is concerned with product cost, function and esteem value to the customer. When these values are assessed, the specifications of the product may be redefined to produce the product to the desired standards at reduced cost.

The assessment procedure is carried out by a team representing the various phases of the design and production process, plus an accountant. In session, their job is to co-ordinate their attitude to the product and to produce ideas that will secure the desired result of cost reduction. Ideas are usually encouraged by detailed questioning and recognising that unnecessary costs can be incorporated in any product unless a conscious attempt is made to eliminate them. Value analysis is the conscious attempt. The questions usually asked regarding the product include:*

*Function*
Are all the functions essential?
Can they be achieved more easily?
Can any be incorporated in another component?

*Material*
Can the specification be revised or another material used?
Can dimensions be reduced or increased with a less costly material?
Will design modification, changing the method of manufacture or blanking nearer to the finished size, cut wastage?

*Limits*
Can they be relaxed to ease manufacture or permit an alternative method?

*Processes*
Can the basic material, or the finished component, be made by a quicker, better method?

*Surface finish*
Are the requirements essential?

*Standardisation*
Is the component replaceable by a standard part or can the raw material be standardised?

*Taken from *Sixteen Case Studies in Value Analysis* (British Productivity Council, n.d.), p. 3.

*Direct labour costs*
Would a minor change in design or methods, or improved plant, reduce or
eliminate any labour operation?
Can assembly be improved?

Advantage may be taken of outside assistance in assessing the product. The
supplier of components used in the manufacture of a product is usually a source of
valuable advice.

## 16.8 VARIETY REDUCTION

Profits may be improved by an examination of the product range, when it may be
found that this range is too extensive and some of the products uneconomic. These
products may be uneconomic because they are produced in small quantities and the
extra costs are hidden in inadequate costing procedures. The accountant's contribution to this review of product range should be the provision of a valid manufacturing
cost for each product. There may be justifiable reasons sometimes for deliberately
selling some products at a loss but, unless there are overriding reasons, an acceptable
margin of profit should be determined before production.

A contributory factor to uneconomic variety in the product range is the pricing
policy adopted by a business. The price differentials between regular lines and fringe
products are often inadequate and this may be due to inaccurate cost information. A
revised pricing policy may include a price incentive to customers to buy regular lines
which are more profitable to the business.

## 16.9 SUMMARY

A progressive management committed to profitable operation of a business, ready
to identify good business opportunities, and motivated to realise their potential, is
in a good position to secure a good return on its investment. This discipline must
recognise the value of business acumen but, without the determination to operate
efficiently and effectively at minimum cost, the profitable growth of a company is
unlikely to be assured.

## FOR FURTHER STUDY

QUESTIONS

1. *Cost reduction programme types*
   'It is inevitable that the degree of cost reduction possible in any business over a
   period of time must, at the outset, be a matter for some speculation. Under
   conditions which constitute an ominous threat to the economic stability of an

organisation the minimum level of achievement necessary for its continued well-being will be unmistakably clear.'

(*Cost Reduction*, Institute of Cost and Works Accountants, 1959, p. 11)

*Required:*

Give features of a cost reduction programme that may be necessary when drastic action is required as envisaged in the above quotation. Compare these features with the type of cost reduction programme that may be initiated when a business is in a more prosperous position.

## 2. *The accountant's contribution to cost reduction*

The management of a well-established business finds that profits over the last few years have fallen, and are continuing to fall. It is decided to embark upon a programme of cost reduction.

*Required:*

Explain how, as management accountant, you would assist in this work.

(ICMA)

## 3. *Profit improvement emphasis*

An effective procedure for cost reduction begins with the ascertainment of costs and cost analysis is useful in indicating to management where to place profit improvement emphasis.

*Required:*

Outline the types of cost analysis that may be used in this context and explain how they contribute to determining cost reduction priorities.

## 4. *The Marks and Spencer approach to profit improvement*

'In the last few years there has been a growing awareness of the evils of excessive paperwork' and as long ago as 1957 in Marks and Spencer Ltd, 'it was realised that wasteful practices and useless statistics can accumulate automatically in every organisation unless there is a conscious recognition of the danger, and a positive determination to combat it. The Board of Marks and Spencer Ltd, issued a firm directive that everybody from the top executive to the most junior supervisor should take vigorous action to get rid of wasteful practices, and standards were not to be lowered. Emphasis was placed by the Board on the need for closer personal contact between all sections of the business. Elaborate systems were swept away, and the paperwork thrown out by the company amounted to 22 million pieces per year.' By the non-replacement of staff as they left the company, they were able to permit the staff to continue to run down for a year or two, with the result that in 1960 they were achieving a larger volume of turnover with some 20% less staff than they had in 1957. Such savings in operating costs made it possible to benefit the public by lowering prices, to help finance further development and to increase the wages of the present staff.

(M. J. Glenn, 'Simplification for efficiency', *Secretaries Chronicle,* February, 1960, pp. 46–7)

*Required:*

(*a*) Comment on this approach to securing profit improvement.

(*b*) Could this approach be used to achieve similar results in other companies? Explain your answer.

5. *Cost reduction at the product design stage*

Possibly the greatest scope for cost reduction throughout industry lies in the field of product design.

*Required:*

Outline your ideas for cost reduction in the area of product design, with particular reference to:

(*a*) Improvement of existing designs

(*b*) Cost of variety

(*c*) Use of the technique of value analysis.                              (ICMA)

6. *Cost reduction aspects relative to distribution costs*

The managing director of your company is concerned that the costs of distributing the company's products are increasing disproportionately to the costs of production. He has asked you, as management accountant, to undertake a review of the distribution costs as an initial stage in a formal cost reduction programme.

*Required:*

(*a*) Give your suggestions of how the initial review should be undertaken, together with the major aspects to receive attention.

(*b*) Within these aspects, state the main items you would investigate.   (ICMA)

7. *Problems concerned with cost reduction by standardisation*

XY Ltd, manufactured a large number of products in many sizes and in recent years had attempted to reduce costs by standardising the product range. They had achieved some success but the need remained to supply parts for their discontinued lines and this meant inflated stocks and short manufacturing runs. This necessity limited their attempts to reduce costs on the manufacture of current models because of the dislocation to production caused by the short runs for spare parts.

*Required:*

What approach could be adopted to this problem and what advantages might be claimed for your possible solution to the difficulty?

8. *The generation of ideas for profit improvement*

Ideas for profit improvement are needed as a basis for company cost reduction proposals.

*Required:*

How may new ideas be generated and encouraged?

9. *Unnecessary costs*

'Unnecessary costs exist even in the most efficient businesses.'

*Required:*

How may unnecessary costs arise? Elaborate on the point that such costs are not confined to inefficient businesses.

10. *Value analysis*

What do you understand by the term 'value analysis'? How is value analysis different from work study?

11. *Variety reduction*

'Variety reduction is a convenient label which, by its brevity, may give the mistaken impression that it concerns only the narrow field of contraction of product range.'

> (*Variety Reduction,* British Productivity Council, 1961,
> p. 1. Extract from *Target*)

*Required:*

What do you understand by 'variety reduction'? Your answer should emphasise other aspects than the 'contraction of product range'?

12. *Use of cost control manager to obtain cost control*

The Excelsior Manufacturing Co. Ltd, had always paid close attention to its costs. When a small company, the direct control was easily maintained and as the size of the company had increased the managing director wondered how to emphasise cost consciousness throughout the business. His answer was to appoint a cost control manager directly responsible to himself, whose function was to check all additional expenditure. Without the cost control manager's approval, no additional expenditure could be incurred. His authority also included the examination of current costs with the aim of securing cost improvements.

This approach to cost reduction was remarkably successful but the situation was under review because the cost control manager was overworked and there were doubts about the delegation of his power to other cost control officials. The cost control manager's success was attributed to two principal factors:

(*a*) The final authority and support of the managing director

(*b*) The knowledge and tact of the cost control manager in carrying out his job.

*Required:*

What is your view of the approach used in this company to achieve adequate cost control? What action would you take to resolve the problem now facing the company?

## FURTHER READING

*Cost Reduction.* Institute of Cost and Works Accountants, 1959.
Gage, W. L. *Value Analysis.* McGraw-Hill, 1967.
*Stocks and Work-in-Progress.* Statement of Standard Accounting Practice No. 9. Accounting Standards Committee, 1975.

# 17 Standard Costing (1)—Basic Procedure and Primary Variance Analysis

## OBJECTIVE OF THE CHAPTER

To show the value of standard costing as a management accounting technique and explain how standard costs are ascertained. This chapter also describes the basic principles of standard costing variance analysis.

## OUTLINE OF THE CHAPTER

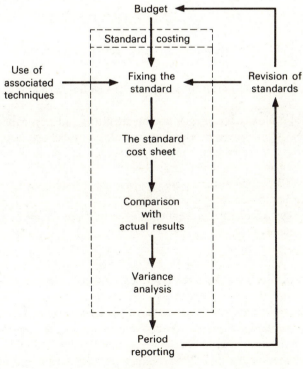

FIGURE 17.1.

A standard cost is a predetermined figure of what the cost should be in a period. The procedure that uses this data as a basis for assisting the management in controlling the business is known as standard costing.

Standard costing operates within the same managerial control cycle as budgetary control, and if the techniques of budgetary control and standard costing are compared it may be noted that each technique is based on:

1. A predetermined standard of performance – in budgetary control it is called the budget; in standard costing, the standard
2. A comparison of actual performance with the standard of performance
3. An analysis of variances by cause to point the way to action that may be taken by managers to improve performance.

The two techniques are interrelated but not interdependent. Standard costing operates in the business context of standardised operations, being concerned with detail, particularly on the production side of the organisation. By comparison, budgetary control is concerned with overall operation of the undertaking and may be applied to any type of business organisation. The overall information that forms the basis of a standard costing system is best provided by budgetary control because greater reliance can be placed on the relative accuracy of this information.

## 17.1 THE ADVANTAGES OF STANDARD COSTING

The most important advantages of using the standard costing technique are as follows:

1. The principle of 'management by exception' can be followed in the reporting system
2. The fixing of standards forces attention on quantities and rates applicable to the elements of cost and improvements in procedure can usually be secured
3. The standard costs are valuable for policy formation and profit planning – this point is particularly relevant to pricing policies
4. The standards are a practical measure of efficiency: one of the essential elements of the control process of the business
5. Economy in cost accounting procedures may result from the use of a standard costing system.

## 17.2 LIMITATIONS OF STANDARD COSTING

The use of a production standard presupposes a repetitive process, and standard costing is therefore used in mass-production factories where quantities of standard and uniform products are produced. In jobbing industries, the variety of products and non-standard products render the technique too cumbersome and costly to apply, except for components which may be uniform in special assemblies.

Companies tend to retain standards for long periods. Manufacturing conditions are constantly changing which gives the standards a rigidity and inflexibility which may work against their effective use as a measure of efficient performance.

Standards are very often regarded by management as incentives to employees and it is sometimes claimed that worker resistance to the standards is generated. This is particularly the situation where standards are used as a basis for remuneration. The efficiency a company hopes to achieve may be seriously impaired by this practice.

## 17.3  THE ESSENTIALS OF A STANDARD COSTING SYSTEM

If the advantages are to be realised and the limitations minimised, certain essentials should be evident in the standard costing system:

1. The realistic assessment of overall measures of performance within which the standard costing system can be developed
2. The use of available techniques to ensure standard costs are reliable measures of performance
3. A consideration of the length of time the standards will be in use
4. A decision on the most desirable standard of attainment
5. The choice of the appropriate level of activity
6. The preparation of standard cost sheets
7. Documentary assistance in operating the system
8. Integration into the accounting system for the business
9. Integration into the reporting system of the business
10. Variance analysis for managerial control.

The first point has been mentioned at the beginning of this chapter and the remaining points are considered in the sections to follow.

## 17.4  THE STANDARD HOUR

Fundamental to the assessment of the production operations of the business is the decision on how to express the production achieved. In this decision the basic consideration is to find a common measurement in which the output of differently measured articles can be expressed.

In some companies no one statistic is the answer. The most common unit of measurement is time, based on the 'standard hour' which is a measure of the work content of a clock hour. The measurement of work produced in terms of standard hours is, therefore, a calculation irrespective of the time actually taken to produce the work in the factory.

The assessment of the production rate is a job for the specialist and by the application of the work study technique reliable standards may be compiled. As in the case of budgetary control, so with standard costing; associated techniques such as work study can be invaluable in fixing a sound basis for the development of the control system.

## 17.5  THE REVISION OF STANDARDS

The fixing of standards is a time-consuming task and once fixed they should be capable of use for a reasonable period without alteration. For control to be effective, the standards should be currently applicable to the business, otherwise variances between the actual and standard figures will have little significance.

Research indicates that most companies revise their standards on an annual basis. The reason for this period is the reluctance of officials to increase significantly clerical costs by more frequent calculations, and the need to fit the job into the accounting timetable of work to be done at different times of the year. It has always been the case that although standards might be revised annually, significant changes would be incorporated as necessary; for example, material price changes and wage awards. With inflationary conditions, significant price movements have become more frequent and this has increased the problem of maintaining reliable standards. The type of business is a relevant factor. In food processing, for example, it is common practice to revise material prices weekly because of rapid price fluctuations.

## 17.6  THE STANDARD OF ATTAINMENT

The standard of efficiency represented by the standard costs may be set at a high or low level. There is no point in setting a standard at such a point that the level of performance is never likely to be achieved. Such a level is sometimes described as the *ideal* standard. This standard could only be attained in the most favourable conditions possible and since business conditions do not attain that level of efficiency, the ideal standard is seldom used.

If trend information is wanted, a base year standard may be fixed, against which future movements in actual costs are compared. To obtain the trend information, the *basic* standard is not changed for a long period.

A standard that may be kept longer than the budget period may be known as a *normal* standard. The word 'normal' in this sense is interpreted as an average performance expected to be attainable over the trade-cycle of the business. While such a standard might be aimed at eliminating the cost variations due to the trade-cycle, it is not very practicable since it is difficult to identify such a period in a business.

Since the objective in setting the standards is cost control, the *currently expected* standard is the level of attainment normally adopted.

## 17.7  THE LEVEL OF ACTIVITY

Standard costing procedures are usually established on the basis of a normal capacity for the financial year, i.e., an average for the year. There are two approaches to the calculation of normal capacity:

1. The average capacity to produce
2. The average capacity to produce and sell.

The calculation of average or normal capacity was mentioned in Chapter 11, and it is the average capacity to produce and sell which is usually used for fixing the standard cost. This level of activity is realistic since it recognises plant availability and marketing experience and forecasts.

## 17.8  THE STANDARD COST SHEET

The basis of the standard cost sheet detail is the technical specification for the product. This specification provides full information on quantities and times and qualities and grades of the elements of cost. Standard cost prices and rates developed from the budget complete the factory cost of the products to be produced.

The standard product cost sheet, illustrated in Figure 17.2, is used to supply the information against which actual costs are compared so variance analysis can provide

| Standard cost sheet<br>Product _____ | | | | | | |
|---|---|---|---|---|---|---|
| | Unit cost | | Revised unit cost | | Revised unit cost | |
| | £ | £ | £ | £ | £ | £ |
| Material<br><br>Quantity,<br>quality and<br>price<br>information | | | | | | |
| Labour<br><br>Time, grade<br>and rate<br>information | | | | | | |
| Factory overhead<br><br>Time, rate<br>and cost<br>centre<br>information | | | | | | |
| Factory cost | | | | | | |
| Date prepared | | | | | | |
| Prepared by | | | | | | |
| Approved by | | | | | | |

FIGURE 17.2. A standard cost sheet

the control detail for management. This sheet can be extended to record a standard selling price against which standard costs are compared to show a standard profit per unit of product.


## 17.9  CONTROL AT SOURCE

One of the byproducts of a standard costing system is the ability to design the source documentation to identify the variances as they occur, rather than wait for their calculation and submission, after the event, on statements for management.

As standard costing is applicable to repetitive processes, pre-printed job instructions can be prepared with the standard information which reduces clerical costs. The exception principle can be applied to isolate departures from the standard. For example, excess material may be supplied by the use of excess material requisitions, which require the signature of the official responsible for the variation from standard before the excess material is issued. In this way, the reason for an unfavourable variance would be known at source and immediate action could be taken to remedy unsatisfactory performance. The excess material requisitions can provide documentary proof for an unfavourable material usage variance, subsequently shown on the control reports for management.


## 17.10  ACCOUNTING SYSTEM INTEGRATION

In the case of a budgetary control procedure, the accounting system adjustments are limited to providing the additional information that may be required. The budget details are not included in the double entry accounts of the business, but retained in working papers and budget statements.

In the case of a standard costing procedure, the standard costs are part of the double entry recorded information in the books of account. The accounting system should be designed so that the results of the procedure affect interpretation as intended. In meeting this requirement, the recording system is affected by the decision as to when the variances are to be extracted. Variances may be extracted at the input or output stage. For example, in the case of raw material stock, if the material price variance is extracted at the input stage the stock will be maintained at standard cost; if this variance is extracted at the output stage, the stock will be maintained at actual cost. The result of this distinction is that variance amounts recorded on statements for management, and in the cost accounts, may be different for a particular accounting period. This is illustrated in the following example:

*Data for an accounting period*

Purchased material
at actual cost: £1,000 (1,000 units at £1 each)
at standard cost: £1,050 (1,000 units at £1·05 each)

Issued material
    at actual cost: £900 (900 units at £1 each)
    at standard cost: £945 (900 units at £1·05 each)

Variance calculations:
Method 1
    Material price variance on the basis of input to the raw materials stock account
    valued at standard cost: £50 favourable (£1,050 − £1,000)
Method 2
    Material price variance on the basis of output from the raw materials stock
    account valued at actual cost: £45 favourable (£945 − £900).

The difference is accounted for by the 100 units still in stock, valued under
Method 2 at actual cost as compared with the valuation under Method 1 at standard
cost: $100 \times (£1·05 − £1) = £5$.

## 17.11  STANDARD COSTING AND THE REPORTING SYSTEM

In the application of the standard costing technique, the ability to draw the attention of management to the causes of not achieving an anticipated profit level has its
effect on the form in which information is presented to management. Without
standard costing, the trading statement begins with the sales figure and profit is
calculated as a result of deducting the cost of sales from sales revenue. With standard
costing, the trading statement begins with the standard profit on actual sales and the
actual profit is calculated by adjusting this figure by the variances. Where a company
can take advantage of the standard costing technique in this way, the reporting
system is more effective. As an illustration, Figure 17.3 shows the two formats of
the trading statement and the figures shown are calculated in the remaining sections
of this chapter.

## 17.12  VARIANCE ANALYSIS

The calculations recorded in the section 'Accounting System Integration' (17.10)
illustrate an aspect of the important part of standard costing procedure known as
variance analysis. It is important because it is the means of interpreting operating
results and indicating situations calling for management action. Given the standard
and actual cost data, variance analysis is a mathematical exercise used to isolate
causes of variances.

### 17.121  THE BASIC PROCEDURE OF ANALYSIS

The basic procedure of variance analysis is illustrated in Figure 17.4.
    By convention, the mixed variance area (price/quantity) is regarded as part of the

## FORMAT WITHOUT STANDARD COSTING
*Trading Statement*
*Period ended*

|                              | £      | £      |
|------------------------------|--------|--------|
| Sales                        |        | 17,100 |
| Deduct factory cost of sales |        |        |
|    Direct material         | 3,780  |        |
|    Direct labour           | 3,800  |        |
|    Variable factory overhead | 2,500 |        |
|    Fixed factory overhead  | 1,200  | 11,280 |
| Profit                       |        | 5,820  |

## FORMAT WITH STANDARD COSTING
*Trading Statement*
*Period ended*

|                                | £     |
|--------------------------------|-------|
| Standard profit on actual sales | 7,200 |
| Add sales price variance        | 900   |
|                                | 8,100 |

Add/deduct cost variances:

|                          | Favourable £ | Unfavourable £ |       |
|--------------------------|--------------|----------------|-------|
| Material                 |              |                |       |
|   Price        |              | 630            |       |
|   Usage        |              | 450            |       |
| Labour                   |              |                |       |
|   Rate         | 200          |                |       |
|   Efficiency   |              | 400            |       |
| Factory fixed overhead   |              |                |       |
|   Expenditure  |              | 100            |       |
|   Capacity     |              | 100            |       |
|   Efficiency   |              | 100            |       |
| Factory variable overhead |             |                |       |
|   Expenditure  |              | 500            |       |
|   Efficiency   |              | 200            |       |
|                          | 200          | 2,480          | 2,280 |
|                          |              |                | 5,820 |

FIGURE 17.3. Trading statement formats without and with standard costing

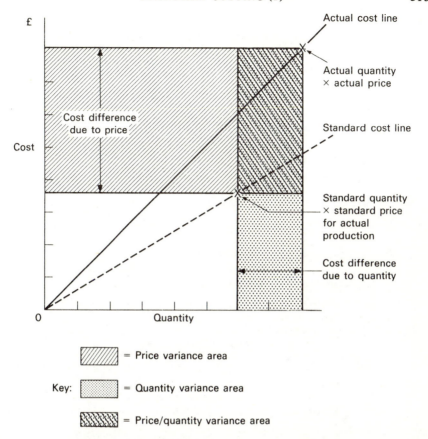

Key:  = Price variance area

= Quantity variance area

= Price/quantity variance area

FIGURE 17.4. The actual/standard cost comparison graph
(This graph is drawn on the assumption that the actual cost
is greater than the standard cost for actual production and
all variances are unfavourable.)

price variance and the analysis of the total cost variance for a particular element of
cost per the graph (Figure 17.4) may, therefore, be calculated as follows:

Price variance = the difference in price × actual quantity

$$\left(\begin{array}{c}\text{actual} \\ \text{price}\end{array} - \begin{array}{c}\text{standard} \\ \text{price}\end{array}\right)$$

+

Quantity variance = the difference in quantity × standard price

$$\left(\begin{array}{c}\text{actual} \\ \text{quantity}\end{array} - \begin{array}{c}\text{standard quantity} \\ \text{for actual} \\ \text{production}\end{array}\right)$$

$$\|$$

Total cost variance for a
particular element of cost = actual cost − standard cost for actual production

Variances should be identified as favourable or unfavourable according to the
effect of the variance on profit. If inputs or costs are being measured, a favourable

variance requires that the actual figure shall be less than the standard. If outputs or capacity are being measured, a favourable variance requires that the actual figure shall be greater than the standard. Other means may be used for indicating a favourable/unfavourable variance. They include:

1. The use of the terms 'loss' and 'gain' (the word loss being used for an unfavourable variance)
2. The use of + and − signs (the minus sign would indicate an unfavourable variance)
3. The use of the colours: black and red (a variance recorded in red would be an unfavourable variance)
4. The use of brackets (a variance in brackets could be the unfavourable variance).

To illustrate the variances described in the sections to follow, the following data will be used:

*Data for an accounting period*

| Standard profit per unit of product: | £ | £ | £ |
|---|---|---|---|
| Selling price | | | 18 |
| Less factory costs | | | |
| Direct material: | | | |
| 12 units of material at £0·25 per unit | | 3 | |
| Direct labour: | | | |
| 4 hours at £1 per hour | | 4 | |
| Factory overhead: | | | |
| Variable: 4 hours at £0·50 per hour | 2 | | |
| Fixed: 4 hours at £0·25 per hour | 1 | 3 | 10 |
| Profit | | | 8 |

Budget: Sales and production: 1,100 units
Actual : Sales and production: 900 units
        Selling price per unit: £19
        Direct material: 12,600 units of material at £0·30 per unit
        Direct labour: 4,000 hours at £0·95 per hour
        Variable factory overhead: £2,500
        Fixed factory overhead: £1,200

## 17.122 DIRECT MATERIALS VARIANCES

Following the basic procedure of variance analysis, the total variance for direct material cost may be classified into two variances:

1. The direct material price variance
2. The direct material quantity variance (also known as the usage variance — to be used in this chapter).

The formulae given applied to material cost and the illustrative data produces the following variances:

1. $\left(\begin{array}{c}\text{Actual} \\ \text{price}\end{array} - \begin{array}{c}\text{Standard} \\ \text{price}\end{array}\right) \times \begin{array}{c}\text{Actual} \\ \text{quantity}\end{array} = \begin{array}{c}\text{Direct material} \\ \text{price variance}\end{array}$

   £0·30 − £0·25)   x  12,600  = £630 (unfavourable)

2. $\left(\begin{array}{c}\text{Actual} \\ \text{quantity}\end{array} - \begin{array}{c}\text{Standard quantity} \\ \text{for actual production}\end{array}\right) \times \begin{array}{c}\text{Standard} \\ \text{price}\end{array} = \begin{array}{c}\text{Direct material} \\ \text{usage variance}\end{array}$

   (12,600 −        10,800)        x  £0·25   = £450 (unfavourable)

   (900 product units
   x 12 material units)

3. Proof of the calculations given:

   $\text{Actual cost} - \begin{array}{c}\text{Standard cost for} \\ \text{actual production}\end{array} = \text{Direct material cost variance}$

   (£3,780  −     £2,700)     = £1,080 (unfavourable)

   (12,600     (900 units x £3)     (£630 + £450)
   units
   x £0·30)

The following points should be noted:

1. The word 'direct' is usually ignored, it being understood that the above variances are concerned with prime cost
2. Where more than one material is used, separate calculations are required for each material, the results being arithmetically totalled
3. To ensure like is compared with like, actual and standard quantities are taken on the basis of units of product produced.

## 17.123 DIRECT LABOUR VARIANCES

The basic procedure of variance analysis can also be followed for the total variance for direct labour cost to give the two variance classifications as follows:

1. The direct labour price variance (also known as the labour rate variance − to be used in this chapter)
2. The direct labour quantity variance (also known as the labour efficiency, labour time or labour usage variance − labour efficiency variance to be used in this chapter).

The formulae given applied to labour cost and the illustrative data produces the following variances:

1. $\left(\begin{array}{c}\text{Actual} \\ \text{rate}\end{array} - \begin{array}{c}\text{Standard} \\ \text{rate}\end{array}\right) \times \begin{array}{c}\text{Actual} \\ \text{quantity} \\ \text{(hours)}\end{array}$ = Direct labour rate variance

   (£0·95 −     £1)     x    4,000    = £200 (favourable)

2. $\left(\begin{array}{c}\text{Actual} \\ \text{hours}\end{array} - \begin{array}{c}\text{Standard hours for} \\ \text{actual production}\end{array}\right) \times \begin{array}{c}\text{Standard} \\ \text{rate}\end{array} = \begin{array}{c}\text{Direct labour} \\ \text{efficiency variance}\end{array}$

   (4,000 −         3,600)         x      £1     = £400 (unfavourable)

   (900 product units
   x 4 hours per unit)

3. Proof of the calculations given:

   $\begin{array}{c}\text{Actual} \\ \text{cost}\end{array} - \begin{array}{c}\text{Standard cost for} \\ \text{actual production}\end{array}$ = Direct labour cost variance

   (£3,800 −         £3,600)         = £200 (unfavourable)

   (4,000
   units
   x £0·95)   (900 units x £4)    (£400 − £200)

The following points should be noted:

1. The word 'direct' is usually ignored, it being understood that the above variances are concerned with prime cost
2. The word 'wages' may replace the word 'labour'
3. Where more than one class of labour is used, separate calculations are required for each class of labour, the results being arithmetically totalled
4. To ensure like is compared with like, actual and standard hours are taken on the basis of units of product produced.

## 17.124 FACTORY OVERHEAD VARIANCES

In the case of factory overhead, the graphical representation of variable and fixed overhead is illustrated in Figures 17.5 and 17.6.

In Figure 17.6, the budgeted factory fixed cost line originates at the point of origin on the graph although the fixed cost is constant for all levels of activity. The reason for this presentation is that when the budgeted factory fixed costs are divided by anticipated capacity use for production, a rate per hour is produced. Using the illustrative data, this rate per hour is £0·25:

$$\frac{\text{Budgeted factory fixed overhead: £1,100}}{\text{Budgeted capacity: 4,400 hours (1,100 units x 4 hours)}} = £0·25 \text{ per hour}$$

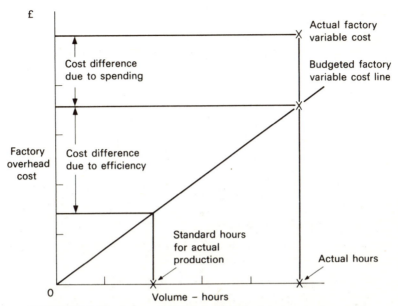

FIGURE 17.5. The factory variable actual/standard cost comparison graph
(This graph is drawn on the assumption that the actual cost
is greater than the standard cost for actual production and
all variances are unfavourable.)

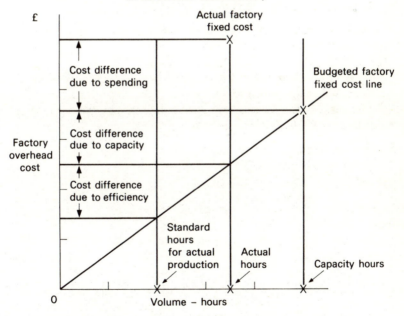

FIGURE 17.6. The factory fixed actual/standard cost comparison graph
(This graph is drawn on the assumption that the actual cost
is greater than the standard cost for actual production and
all variances are unfavourable.)

The analysis of the total variance for factory overhead cost per the graphs (Figures 17.5 and 17.6) is as follows:*

|  | Variable factory overhead cost | Fixed factory overhead cost |
|---|---|---|
| 1. Spending variance (also known as the budget or expenditure variance — overhead expenditure variance to be used in this chapter) | ✓ | ✓ |
| 2. Capacity variance[†] |  | ✓ |
| 3. Efficiency variance (also known as the productivity variance — efficiency variance used in this chapter) | ✓ | ✓ |

Using the illustrative data, the variances for factory overhead may be calculated as follows:

*Variable factory overhead*

1. Actual cost − Budgeted cost allowance[‡] = Expenditure variance
   £2,500   −   £2,000 (4,000 x £0·50)  = £500 (unfavourable)

2. $\begin{matrix}\text{Actual} \\ \text{hours}\end{matrix} - \begin{matrix}\text{Standard hours for} \\ \text{actual production}\end{matrix} \times \begin{matrix}\text{Variable} \\ \text{factory} \\ \text{overhead} \\ \text{standard} \\ \text{rate per} \\ \text{hour}\end{matrix} = \begin{matrix}\text{Efficiency} \\ \text{variance}\end{matrix}$

   (4,000 −     3,600)     x   £0·50  = £200 (unfavourable)

   (900 product units x 4 hours per unit)

*Fixed factory overhead*

1. Actual cost − Budgeted cost = Expenditure variance

   £1,200 −    £1,100    = £100 (unfavourable)

   (1,100 units x 4 hours x £0·25 per hour)

* This is not the only analysis possible and this point is developed in the next chapter. It should be noted that the illustration is on the basis of a flexible budget in use.

† Also may be known as the volume variance but the use of the term at this stage is likely to be confusing. With so many possible overhead calculations, terms may be repeated and represent different amounts. The term 'volume' is a good example. The discussion is deferred until the next chapter.

‡ The term explained in Chapter 11 (flexible budget)

2. $\left(\begin{array}{c}\text{Capacity} \\ \text{hours}\end{array} - \begin{array}{c}\text{Actual} \\ \text{hours}\end{array}\right)$ x $\begin{array}{c}\text{Fixed factory} \\ \text{overhead standard} \\ \text{rate per hour}\end{array}$ = $\begin{array}{c}\text{Capacity} \\ \text{variance}\end{array}$

(4,400 − 4,000)      x      £0·25      = £100 (unfavourable)

3. $\left(\begin{array}{c}\text{Actual} \\ \text{hours}\end{array} - \begin{array}{c}\text{Standard hours for} \\ \text{actual production}\end{array}\right)$ x $\begin{array}{c}\text{Fixed} \\ \text{factory} \\ \text{overhead} \\ \text{standard} \\ \text{rate per} \\ \text{hour}\end{array}$ = $\begin{array}{c}\text{Efficiency} \\ \text{variance}\end{array}$

(4,000 −         3,600)      x £0·25      = £100 (unfavourable)

(900 product units
x 4 hours per unit)

Proof of the calculations given:

$\begin{array}{c}\text{Actual} \\ \text{cost}\end{array}$ − $\begin{array}{c}\text{Standard cost for} \\ \text{actual production}\end{array}$ = $\begin{array}{c}\text{Factory overhead cost} \\ \text{variance}\end{array}$

£3,700      −      £2,700      = £1,000 (unfavourable)

(£2,500 + £1,200)    (900 units x £3)    (£500 + £200 + £100
                                              + £100 + £100)

If a flexible budget is not used the difference in the variances calculated is as mentioned in Chapter 11.

## 17.125  SALES VARIANCES

Following the basic procedure of variance analysis, the total variance for sales may be classified into two variances:

1. The sales price variance
2. The sales quantity variance (also known as the sales volume variance).

The standard price in this case is the standard selling price and when applied to the quantity variance it may be noted that the result would not be in terms of profit. All other variances are indicating a profit impact as a result of cost being greater or less than standard. To show the same effect for sales information, the sales quantity variance should be valued at standard profit. This assumes that costs are at standard, a basis adopted because, if there are differences between actual and standard cost, they will be identified by the cost variances. When the sales variances are calculated in this way they are sometimes termed sales margin variances.*

* The profit taken is a matter for decision and if, for example, marginal costing were applicable, marginal contribution would be used for variance calculation. The subject of marginal costing is explained in Chapter 19. In this example the profit figure quoted in the illustrative data has been adopted.

Using the illustrative data, the variances for sales may be calculated as follows:

1.
$$\left( \text{Actual selling price} - \frac{\text{Standard selling}}{\text{price}} \right) \times \frac{\text{Actual}}{\text{quantity}} = \frac{\text{Sales}}{\text{price}}_{\text{variance}}$$

$$(£19 \quad - \quad £18) \quad \times \quad 900 \quad = \quad £900$$
$$\text{(favourable)}$$

2.
$$\left( \frac{\text{Actual}}{\text{quantity}}_{\text{sold}} - \frac{\text{Standard quantity}}{\text{planned to be sold}} \right) \times \frac{\text{Standard}}{\text{profit}} = \frac{\text{Sales quantity}}{\text{variance}}$$

$$(900 \quad - \quad 1100) \quad \times \quad £8 \quad = \quad £1,600$$
$$\text{(unfavourable)}$$

3. Proof of the calculations given:

Actual profit − Standard profit = Sales total variance

$$\left( \begin{array}{l} \text{Actual} \quad\quad £ \\ \text{sales:} \\ 900 \times £19 \quad = 17,100 \\ \text{Standard cost} \\ \text{of actual sales:} \\ 900 \times £10 \quad = \quad 9,000 \\ \hline \quad\quad\quad\quad\quad 8,100 \end{array} \right) - \left( \begin{array}{l} 1,100 \times £8 \\ = £8,800 \end{array} \right) = £700 \text{ (unfavourable)}$$
$$(£1,600 - £900)$$

Where more than one product is sold, separate calculations are required for each product, the results being arithmetically totalled.

### 17.126 OTHER OVERHEAD VARIANCES

As already mentioned, standard costing is most often applied in the production departments of an organisation; but the standard cost of selling a product, delivering a package or typing an invoice can be calculated by following the principles for calculating manufacturing standard costs.

The variances are calculated by comparing the actual and standard costs for the functions of administration, selling and distribution. These total variances may be analysed by responsibility centres and products according to the classifications adopted for cost control.

### 17.13 SUMMARY

Standard costing is a powerful technique supporting the managerial control process and providing for management useful information as to the reasons why planned performance has not been achieved. The detailed standards, preferably based on budgetary information, enable the accountant to calculate variances that can render profit statements more informative and assist interpretation of such statements as a basis for executive action.


## FOR FURTHER STUDY

QUESTIONS

1. *Installation of a standard costing system and its benefits*
   Domestic Electrics Ltd, is a company engaged in the manufacture of a variety of domestic electrical products, some of the components of which are bought in and some manufactured. The labour processes are mainly machining of various kinds and assembling. Production is by batch, all products being in production most of the time; productive capacity is virtually fully employed.
   The company has a number of competitors and there is resistance in the trade to rising prices; at the same time costs are increasing.
   The newly appointed managing director is of the opinion that the company's profitability could be increased if more stringent control measures were applied.
   *Required:*
   Write a report, as a consultant, setting out and commenting upon the steps involved in the installation of a standard costing system and conclude your report with a summary of the benefits you would expect to accrue.      (ACA)

2. *Standard costing/budgetary control standards and clerical work costs*
   Hook, Line and Sinker Ltd, had been considering the possible installation of a standard costing system and the accountant, Mr Shakespeare, had passed to the managers concerned an article on the subject that had recently appeared in a professional journal. Mr Shakespeare considered that the article presented a fair summary of the advantages, limitations and essentials of a standard costing system and he awaited with interest the response from his colleagues. One day, his managing director, Mr Wordsworth, raised the topic and the following is an extract from their conversation:
   *Wordsworth:* I found your article very interesting, Bill, and I am sure the standard costing technique has a lot to offer us but I am rather confused regarding the distinction between budgetary control and standard costing.
   *Shakespeare:* Some people do write as though they were describing the same thing but . . .
   *Wordsworth:* Before you go into a long description, Bill, I'd like Walter Scott from the works to join us because the reference in the article to standards is something that is of considerable interest to him. He was mentioning to me the other day how many different standards there are and it may interest you to know his views.
   *(Mr Wordsworth telephones Walter and asks him to call in at the office.)*
   When Walter joins us you might also explain the point in the article about the expected reduction in clerical work. I find that point hard to believe.
   *(Mr Scott enters the office.)*

*Required:*

(*a*) Answer the point raised by the managing director regarding the difference between budgetary control and standard costing.

(*b*) What forms of standard are applicable to the business situation? Give examples.

(*c*) How may clerical work be reduced when a standard costing system is introduced into a company? Any qualifications you care to make?

**3.** *Preparation of product standard costs*

You are preparing standard product costs for a department manufacturing approximately 300 standard products. There are twelve production cost centres in the department which is served by ancillary services. The organisation as a whole is administered by the usual general administrative departments and executives.

*Required:*

Detail the steps which would be necessary to establish the standard overhead costs for each product, and schedule the information which would be required.

(ICMA)

**4.** *Point at which material price variances are extracted in the system*

The raw material price variance may be reflected at either of two stages in standard cost accounting procedure.

*Required:*

Describe each method separately where raw material at an actual cost of £1,020 is bought and consumed in one month, the standard cost being £1,000.

(ICMA – part)

**5.** *Causes of variances*

Indicate the causes underlying the following variances:

(*a*) Material price variance

(*b*) Material usage variance

(*c*) Labour rate variance

(*d*) Labour efficiency variance

(*e*) Overhead expenditure variance

(*f*) Overhead capacity variance

(*g*) Overhead efficiency variance.

**6.** *Labour and material cost variances*

The following standards were compiled for the manufacture of Product X150 for the material and labour elements of cost:

Material

    2 grams of P at £1 per gram

    4 grams of Q at £2 per gram

Labour

    5 hours of skilled labour at £1·50 per hour

    10 hours of unskilled labour at £0·80 per hour

Actual production in week 10 was 40 units and the remaining actual results were as follows:

Material
    75 grams of P at £1·40 per gram
    170 grams of Q at £1·80 per gram
Labour
    Skilled: 190 hours at £1·60 per hour
    Unskilled: 450 hours at £0·90 per hour.

*Required:*
Calculate the following for Product X150:
(*a*)  Material price variance
(*b*)  Material usage variance
(*c*)  Material total cost variance
(*d*)  Labour rate variance
(*e*)  Labour efficiency variance
(*f*)  Labour total cost variance.

7. *Overhead variance calculation on a fixed and flexible budget basis*

    (*a*)  How are the (i) capacity variances, and (ii) expenditure variance, as measures of the degree of efficiency of a manufacturing business, affected when budgeted and actual levels of activity do not coincide?

    (*b*)  Illustrate your answer to (*a*) by calculating the total overhead cost variance, and the individual overhead variances for expenditure, capacity and efficiency in respect of a production department to which the figures given below apply, assuming the budget is (i) fixed; (ii) flexible.

| Potential hours: | 5,000 | 5,500 | 6,000 |
|---|---|---|---|
| Budgeted cost: | £21,000 | £22,000 | £23,000 |

The product takes five hours to produce and normal capacity is 5,500 standard hours. The actual results for the period were:

        Overhead: £23,000
        Output: 1,000 units of product
        Hours: 5,200.            (ICMA)

8. *Overhead variance factors on a flexible budget basis*
    (*a*)  For a department, the standard overhead rate is £2·50 per hour and the overhead allowances are as follows:

| Activity level hours | Budget overhead allowance £ |
|---|---|
| 3,000 | 10,000 |
| 7,000 | 18,000 |
| 11,000 | 26,000 |

*Required:*

Calculate: (i) the fixed cost; and (ii) the standard activity level on which the standard overhead rate has been fixed.

(*b*)  In a period, the activity level of the same department was 10,000 hours and the actual overhead incurred was £22,000.

*Required:*

Calculate on a flexible budget basis: (i) the capacity variance; and (ii) the expenditure variance.                                                      (ICMA – part)

9. *Graph preparation for overheads and its interpretation*

The following figures for one month apply to a manufacturing company:

|  | £ |
|---|---|
| Fixed cost | 15,000 |
| Variable cost for 100 units of output | 20,000 |
| Total | 35,000  (i.e., £350 per unit) |

These figures were adopted as a basis for budgeting and standard costing. In the first month of the budget period (March), 140 units were produced at an actual total cost of £46,000. In April, 80 units were produced at an actual total cost of £29,000. The fixed expense was valid for this output range.

*Required:*

On a 'break-even' type of graph, plot the total cost line (0 to £35,000 for 100 units), and a further line representing the budget standard, for March output. Plot also the points representing: (*a*)  total actual cost for March; and (*b*) total actual cost for April.

Ascertain monthly capacity variances from the graph. What other variances, and in what amounts, are ascertainable from the graph?                  (ICMA)

10. *Preparation of a standard cost statement*

A manufacturer establishes the following standard cost per unit for his production, based on a normal volume of production of 1,000 product units per week:

|  | Per product unit £ |
|---|---|
| Standard cost of: |  |
| Labour: 10 hours at £0·50 per hour | 5·0 |
| Material: 10 grams at £1 per gram | 10·0 |
| Factory overheads |  |
|     Variable: 5 machine hours at £0·50 per hour | 2·5 |
|     Fixed: based on standard volume | 1·0 |
|       Total, per product unit | 18·5 |

His actual production for the week was 900 product units and the following were the actual costs incurred:

> Labour (8,400 hours at £0·52): £4,368
> Material (9,040 grams at £1·20): £10,848
> Variable overheads (4,000 machine hours): £2,025
> Fixed overheads: £1,010.

*Required:*

Prepare a cost statement for the week to show a comparison of the actual costs for the week with standard cost and make such analysis of the variances as is possible from the information given.

11. *Variance analysis for each element of cost and type of product*

The standard costs of the three products manufactured by your company are as follows:

|  | | | *Per unit* | | | |
|---|---|---|---|---|---|---|
|  | *Product 1* | | *Product 2* | | *Product 3* | |
|  | *Qty.* grams | *Cost* £ | *Qty.* grams | *Cost* £ | *Qty.* grams | *Cost* £ |
| Materials: A | 15 | 1·50 | – | – | 22 | 2·20 |
| B | 50 | 1·25 | 64 | 1·60 | 12 | 0·30 |
| C | 20 | 0·75 | 24 | 0·90 | – | – |
|  | hours | | hours | | hours | |
| Direct labour | 2½ | 1·25 | 2 | 1·00 | 3 | 1·50 |
| Factory overhead: Variable | | 0·50 | | 0·40 | | 0·60 |
| Fixed | | 0·25 | | 0·20 | | 0·30 |
| Standard cost | | 5·50 | | 4·10 | | 4·90 |

Transactions for the past month were:

|  | *Quantity* grams | *Cost* £ |
|---|---|---|
| Materials purchased: A | 100,000 | 10,719 |
| B | 300,000 | 7,971 |
| C | 100,000 | 3,560 |
| Material issued: A | 75,000 | |
| B | 267,560 | |
| C | 98,960 | |

Direct labour costs amounted to £7,345 and the wage analysis for the month provided the following information:

| *Product* | *Direct labour hours* | *No. of products manufactured* |
|---|---|---|
| 1 | 6,200 | 2,500 |
| 2 | 3,900 | 2,000 |
| 3 | 4,550 | 1,500 |

Actual overhead: Fixed: £1,550
Variable: £2,925

Normal manufacturing capacity for the month is fixed at:

| Product | Units |
|---------|-------|
| 1 | 2,600 |
| 2 | 2,050 |
| 3 | 1,800 |

There was no work-in-progress at the beginning or end of the month. Materials were held in stock at standard prices.

*Required:*

From the information given above, prepare a report on variances. In this report, variances should be analysed not only into elements of cost and causes but also, where applicable, into types of product. (ICMA)

## 12. *Practical use of the standard costing technique*

The managing director of a manufacturing company stated the following as the company concept for cost control:

> We fix a selling price on an estimated cost of production and when we get the order we must know promptly when our current costs are exceeding that estimate, where they are exceeding it and why, who is taking or has to take action to eliminate the excess, and if he does it quickly and effectively.

The company had a standard costing system in operation which provided variance information and when the trends were abnormal the variances were subjected to detailed investigation. It was felt that this system was not meeting the basic concept of cost control in the company as well as intended.

The company had also tended to summarise variances into net gains and losses and many of the gains reflected cautious estimating. Standards tended to represent the average of what was being achieved.

The company products had a wide product range; some simple products and others major pieces of equipment containing many thousands of parts using a wide variety of production methods.

Estimates were prepared according to the type of product by using up to twenty different forms, the basis of the information being the method planning sheet used throughout the organisation to convey manufacturing instructions to the production departments.

*Required:*

(a) Why do you think the system was not meeting the basic concept of cost control intended in the company?

(b) What should the standards represent and what action would you recommend in this case?

(c) What difficulties would you expect in applying your recommendations?

(d) How would you overcome the difficulties anticipated and what benefits would you expect?

(Based on the article: J. Hilton, 'Cost control in practice',
*Cost Accountant,* April, 1962)

FURTHER READING

Batty, J. *Standard Costing.* Macdonald & Evans, 1960. Chapters 2—6.
Chamberlain, Neil W. *The Firm: Micro-Economic Planning and Action.* McGraw-Hill, New York, 1962. Chapter 16.
Ellmer, R. E. *Marginal Costs and Variance Analysis in Management Accounting.* Macmillan, 1969. Chapters 2 and 3.

# 18 Standard Costing (2)—Further Variance Analysis

## OBJECTIVE OF THE CHAPTER

To develop the variance analysis introduced in the previous chapter. To explain the significant points emerging from the increased analysis possible when detailed actual and standard costs are compared and interpreted.

## OUTLINE OF THE CHAPTER

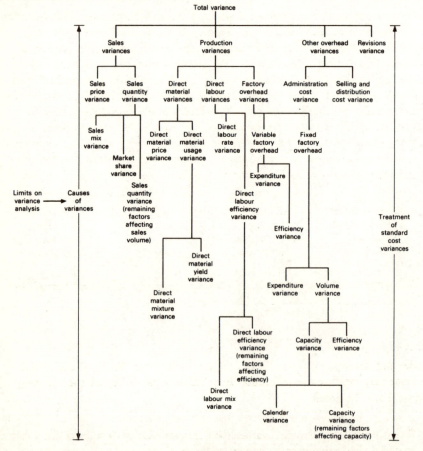

FIGURE 18.1.

A number of reasons have been given in the previous chapter why differences may exist between standard and actual costs. To the extent that standard profit on actual sales was compared with actual profit for the period, the total difference was explained in Figure 17.3. This is not the extent of a possible explanation because it is necessary to ascertain why, for example, an excess price has been paid for a particular material. This point is developed later in this chapter. Closely allied with this additional interpretation is the calculation of other variances if the subsidiary elements are recognised in terms of basic data. Any factor can be isolated by identifying the quantity data relevant to that factor and valuing the variance in relation to its principal element in the analytical process. Typical factors are described in the sections to follow.

## 18.1  DIRECT MATERIALS — ADDITIONAL VARIANCES

*Material mix*

In the previous chapter, reference was made to the analysis of material variances by type of material and this sub-analysis of a cost difference can be valuable information to management possibly serving as a basis for the purchase of substitute materials. Where more than one material is used in the manufacture of a product, the mixture of the inputs to the process may be different from the standard mix, and to the extent that the materials in the mix are priced differently, a variance may be calculated — the direct material mixture variance. It is useful to identify the main cause of the factor being measured and in this case the direct material mixture difference is clearly a quantity variance. It follows that a direct material mixture variance must be part of the direct material usage variance. The formula for calculating this variance is as follows:

$$\left(\begin{array}{c} \text{Actual quantities} \\ \text{of material inputs} \\ \text{in standard} \\ \text{proportions} \end{array} - \begin{array}{c} \text{Actual quantities} \\ \text{of material} \\ \text{inputs in actual} \\ \text{proportions} \end{array}\right) \times \begin{array}{c} \text{Standard} \\ \text{price per} \\ \text{unit of} \\ \text{material} \end{array} = \begin{array}{c} \text{Direct} \\ \text{material} \\ \text{mixture} \\ \text{variance} \end{array}$$

The quantity data due to the mix factor is priced at standard price because any difference in price will be identified by the price variance.

*Material yield*

In the manufacturing process, the output may be less than the input and a yield variance may measure this difference. In calculating the difference the following points should be noted:

1. The main cause of the yield variance is a quantity factor. It follows that a direct material yield variance must be part of the direct material usage variance.

2. Having isolated the difference due to mix, the yield comparison is in standard proportions
3. As a quantity variance the yield difference is priced at standard price
4. A standard wastage may be included in the fixing of the standard cost and if this is the case, the actual output must be adjusted for the standard loss.

The formula for calculating the direct material yield variance is as follows:

$$\left( \begin{array}{c} \text{Actual quantities} \\ \text{of material} \\ \text{inputs in standard} \\ \text{proportions} \end{array} - \begin{array}{c} \text{Actual materials} \\ \text{outputs grossed} \\ \text{up to allow for} \\ \text{standard} \\ \text{wastage in} \\ \text{standard} \\ \text{proportions} \end{array} \right) \times \begin{array}{c} \text{Standard} \\ \text{price per} \\ \text{unit of} \\ \text{material} \end{array} = \begin{array}{c} \text{Direct} \\ \text{material} \\ \text{yield} \\ \text{variance} \end{array}$$

The use of the above formulae may be illustrated as follows:

*Data for an accounting period*

| Material | Standard price per unit | Actual material inputs | Standard proportions of materials |
|---|---|---|---|
|  | £ | units | % |
| A | 10 | 100 | 80 |
| B | 20 | 20 | 20 |

Actual products produced: 95 units of Product X99
Standard wastage: 5%

*Material mix*

$$\left( \begin{array}{c} \text{Actual quantities} \\ \text{of material} \\ \text{inputs in} \\ \text{standard} \\ \text{proportions} \end{array} - \begin{array}{c} \text{Actual quantities} \\ \text{of material} \\ \text{inputs in} \\ \text{actual} \\ \text{proportions} \end{array} \right) \times \begin{array}{c} \text{Standard} \\ \text{price per} \\ \text{unit} \end{array} = \begin{array}{c} \text{Direct} \\ \text{material} \\ \text{mixture} \\ \text{variance} \end{array}$$

| Material | units | units | £ | £ |  |
|---|---|---|---|---|---|
| A | 96 (80%) − | 100 | × | 10 = 40 | (unfavourable) |
| B | 24 (20%) − | 20 | × | 20 = 80 | (favourable) |
|  | 120 | 120 |  | 40 | (favourable) |

*Material yield*

$$\left( \begin{array}{c} \text{Actual quantities} \\ \text{of material} \\ \text{inputs in} \\ \text{standard} \\ \text{proportions} \end{array} - \begin{array}{c} \text{Actual material} \\ \text{outputs grossed} \\ \text{up to allow} \\ \text{for standard} \\ \text{wastage in} \\ \text{standard} \\ \text{proportions} \end{array} \right) \times \begin{array}{c} \text{Standard} \\ \text{price per} \\ \text{unit} \end{array} = \begin{array}{c} \text{Direct} \\ \text{material} \\ \text{yield} \\ \text{variance} \end{array}$$

| Material | units | units | £ | £ |
|---|---|---|---|---|
| A | 96 (80%) − | 80 (80%) × | 10 = | 160 (unfavourable) |
| B | 24 (20%) − | 20 (20%) × | 20 = | 80 (unfavourable) |
|  | 120 | 100 |  | 240 (unfavourable) |

$$95 + (\tfrac{5}{95} \times 95) = 100 \text{ units}$$

Proof of the above calculations given:

$$\left( \begin{array}{c} \text{Actual} \\ \text{quantity} \end{array} - \begin{array}{c} \text{Standard} \\ \text{quantity for} \\ \text{actual} \\ \text{production} \end{array} \right) \times \begin{array}{c} \text{Standard} \\ \text{price} \end{array} = \begin{array}{c} \text{Direct} \\ \text{material} \\ \text{usage} \\ \text{variance} \end{array}$$

| Material | units | units | £ | £ |
|---|---|---|---|---|
| A | 100 − | 80 × | 10 = | 200 (unfavourable) |
| B | 20 − | 20 × | 20 = | − |
|  | 120 | 100 |  | 200 (unfavourable) |

(£40 favourable +
£240 unfavourable)

Alternative calculations:

| Material | Units | £ | £ | Units | £ | £ |
|---|---|---|---|---|---|---|
| A | 100 | × 10 = | 1,000 | 80 | × 10 = | 800 |
| B | 20 | × 20 = | 400 | 20 | × 20 = | 400 |
|  | 120 |  | 1,400 | 100 |  | 1,200 |

$£1,400 - (\tfrac{120}{100} \times £1,200) = £40$ (favourable): The mixture variance

$\dfrac{£1,200}{95} \times \left( 25 - \dfrac{5 \times 120}{100} \right) = £240$ (unfavourable) The yield variance

*Note:* (*a*)  Actual material inputs (120) − Actual output (95) = 25 units.
(*b*)  Actual output grossed up for wastage (100) − actual output (95) = 5 units.

## 18.2  DIRECT LABOUR − ADDITIONAL VARIANCES

### LABOUR MIX

A mixture of labour grades employed in the manufacture of the product can be
different from the standard mix of labour and this difference may be calculated in a

similar manner to the direct material mixture variance. The formula may be stated as follows:

$$\left(\begin{array}{l}\text{Actual hours of} \\ \text{labour employed} \\ \text{at standard mix}\end{array} - \begin{array}{l}\text{Actual hours} \\ \text{of labour} \\ \text{employed at} \\ \text{actual mix}\end{array}\right) \times \begin{array}{c}\text{Standard} \\ \text{labour} \\ \text{rate}\end{array} = \begin{array}{c}\text{Direct} \\ \text{labour mix} \\ \text{variance}\end{array}$$

This calculation may be illustrated as follows:

*Data for an accounting period*

| Type of labour | Standard rate per hour £ | Actual hours of labour employed | Standard mix % |
|---|---|---|---|
| Skilled | 1·00 | 100 | 80 |
| Semi-skilled | 0·70 | 20 | 20 |

$$\left(\begin{array}{l}\text{Actual hours} \\ \text{of labour} \\ \text{employed at} \\ \text{standard mix}\end{array} - \begin{array}{l}\text{Actual hours} \\ \text{of labour} \\ \text{employed at} \\ \text{actual mix}\end{array}\right) \times \begin{array}{c}\text{Standard} \\ \text{labour} \\ \text{rate}\end{array} = \begin{array}{c}\text{Direct labour} \\ \text{mix} \\ \text{variance}\end{array}$$

| Labour | | £ | £ | |
|---|---|---|---|---|
| Skilled | 96 (80%) − 100 × 1·00 = | | 4·00 | (unfavourable) |
| Semi-skilled | 24 (20%) − 20 × 0·70 = | | 2·80 | (favourable) |
| | 120   120 | | 1·20 | (unfavourable) |

The following points should be noted:

1. The quantity data due to the mix factor is priced at the standard rate because any difference in labour rate will be identified by the direct labour rate variance
2. The main cause of the mix variance is a quantity factor. It follows that a direct labour mix variance is part of the direct labour efficiency variance.
3. If no other factor affecting labour efficiency is isolated and valued, the remainder of the direct labour efficiency variance (the direct labour efficiency variance minus the direct labour mix variance) is the difference covering all remaining factors affecting the efficiency of labour. This residual effect is common in variance analysis because when subsidiary factors are identified and valued it does not follow that all aspects of the main variance will be calculated. As a total variance must be reported in full on a statement for management, this point is important. The following illustration should make this clear:

*Given variances for an accounting period*

|  | £ |
|---|---|
| Direct labour rate variance | 20 (unfavourable) |
| Direct labour efficiency variance | 80 (unfavourable) |
| Direct labour cost variance | 100 (unfavourable) |
| Direct labour mix variance | 40 (unfavourable) |
| Direct labour efficiency variance due to other factors affecting labour efficiency (the residual amount) | 40 (unfavourable) |
| Total direct labour efficiency variance (as above) | 80 (unfavourable) |

On the statement for management, the total difference could be identified as follows:

|  | *Unfavourable* £ |
|---|---|
| Direct labour rate variance | 20 |
| Direct labour efficiency variance | 80 |
|  | 100 |

If the labour mix variance is to be reported, the total difference would be identified as follows:

|  | *Unfavourable* £ |
|---|---|
| Direct labour rate variance | 20 |
| Direct labour mix variance | 40 |
| Direct labour efficiency variance | 40 |
|  | 100 |

The direct labour efficiency variance of £40 (unfavourable) in the second illustration should not be confused with the variance shown in the first illustration as £80 (unfavourable).

Other specific labour efficiency variances may be calculated to identify the amounts of idle time due to various causes, such as no materials, machine breakdown and management faults.

## 18.3 FACTORY OVERHEAD — ADDITIONAL VARIANCES

The level of activity used for overhead calculation is usually expressed in labour hours or machine hours according to the manufacturing process. This statistic may be applied in three ways:

|   |   | *Example from the previous chapter* hours |
|---|---|---|
| (i) | As an actual level of activity | 4,000 |
| (ii) | As a standard level of activity for the actual units produced (described in the previous chapter as the standard hours for actual production) | 3,600 |
| (iii) | As a standard level of activity per the original budget, i.e., the fixed budget. (The original budget planned production expressed in standard hours) | 4,400 |

The use of these different levels of activity can produce different factory over-head variances and to illustrate this point the respective costs taken from the example in the previous chapter, and reproduced below, are as follows:

Standard profit per unit of product heading:

Variable factory overhead: 4 hours at £0·50 per hour
Fixed factory overhead: 4 hours at £0·25 per hour
Actual variable factory overhead: £2,500
Actual fixed factory overhead: £1,200

Actual variable cost per hour: $\dfrac{£2,500}{4,000 \text{ hours}} = £0.625$

Actual fixed cost per hour: $\dfrac{£1,200}{4,000 \text{ hours}} = £0.30$

|   | Hours | Variable rate £ | Variable cost £ | Fixed rate £ | Fixed cost £ |   |
|---|---|---|---|---|---|---|
| 1. Actual level of activity at actual cost per hour | 4,000 | 0·625 | 2,500 | 0·30 | 1,200 | Actual factory overhead |
| 2. Actual level of activity at standard cost per hour | | | | | | |
| (a) | 4,000 | 0·50 | 2,000 | — | — | Budgeted cost allowance |
| (b) | 4,000 | 0·50 | 2,000 | 0·25 | 1,000 | Absorbed factory overhead (actual basis) |

| | Hours | Variable rate £ | Variable cost £ | Fixed price £ | Fixed cost £ |
|---|---|---|---|---|---|
| 3. Standard level of activity for actual units produced at standard cost per hour | 3,600 | 0·50 | 1,800 | 0·25 | 900 Absorbed factory overhead (standard basis) |
| 4. Standard level of activity per the original budget | 4,400 | 0·50 | 2,200 | 0·25 | 1,100 Budgeted cost |

Using the above figures, the principal methods of calculating the factory overhead variances may be compared: (Figure references apply to the table above and on the previous page)

### Method A
### (used in the previous chapter)

| | Variable factory overhead £ | Fixed factory overhead £ |
|---|---|---|
| Expenditure variance | 2,500 (1) 2,000 (2a) | 1,200 (1) 1,100 (4) |
| | 500 (unf.) | 100 (unf.) |
| Capacity variance | | 1,100 (4) 1,000 (2b) |
| | | 100 (unf.) |
| Efficiency variance | 2,000 (2b) 1,800 (3) | 1,000 (2b) 900 (3) |
| | 200 (unf.) | 100 (unf.) |
| Total factory overhead cost variance | 700 (unf.) | 300 (unf.) |

Assumptions:

(i) A flexible budget in operation
(ii) The difference in time taken and the time that should have been taken to do the work represents an efficiency factor concerned with manufacturing facilities that should be isolated

in the variance analysis.

*Method B*

|  | *Variable factory overhead* £ | *Fixed factory overhead* £ |
|---|---|---|
| Expenditure variance | 2,500 (1) | 1,200 (1) |
|  | 2,200 (4) | 1,100 (4) |
|  | 300 (unf.) | 100 (unf.) |
| Capacity variance | 2,200 (4) | 1,100 (4) |
|  | 2,000 (2b) | 1,000 (2b) |
|  | 200 (unf.) | 100 (unf.) |
| Efficiency variance (as Method A) | 200 (unf.) | 100 (unf.) |
| Total factory overhead cost variance | 700 (unf.) | 300 (unf.) |

Assumptions:

(i)  A fixed budget in operation
(ii) As Method A (ii).

*Method C*

|  | *Variable factory overhead* £ | *Fixed factory overhead* £ |
|---|---|---|
| Expenditure variance | 2,500 (1) | 1,200 (1) |
|  | 1,800 (3) | 1,100 (4) |
|  | 700 (unf.) | 100 (unf.) |
| Volume variance | 1,800 (3) | 1,100 (4) |
|  | 1,800 (3) | 900 (3) |
|  | Nil | 200 (unf.) |
| Total factory overhead cost variance | 700 (unf.) | 300 (unf.) |

Assumptions:

(i)  As Method A (i)
(ii) The efficiency factor on variable factory overhead should be recognised in the expenditure variance.

*Method D*

|  | *Variable factory overhead* £ | *Fixed factory overhead* £ |
|---|---|---|
| Expenditure variance (As Method A) | 500 (unf.) | 100 (unf.) |
| Volume variance (As Method C) |  | 200 (unf.) |
| Efficiency variance | 2,000 (2a) | 1,100 (4) |
|  | 1,800 (3) | 1,100 (4) |
|  | 200 (unf.) | Nil |
| Total factory overhead cost variance | 700 (unf.) | 300 (unf.) |

Assumptions:

(i) As Method A (i)
(ii) The difference in time taken and the time that should have been taken to do the work indicates an efficiency factor concerned with manufacturing facilities that should be represented by variable factory overhead only.

All methods represent the factory overhead cost variance affected by the two factors of spending and volume, although there are a number of interpretations of the volume variance that should not be confused:

Method A:
(i) The capacity variance is sometimes described as the volume variance, i.e., £100 (unfavourable)*
(ii) The combination of the capacity variance and the fixed amount of the efficiency variance, i.e., £200 (unfavourable) (£100 plus £100)
Method B:
The fixed and variable amounts of the capacity variance, i.e., £300 (unfavourable). (£200 plus £100)
Methods C and D:
The fixed overhead amounts only, i.e., £200 (unfavourable).

Most authorities would subscribe to the view that the volume variance is £200 (unfavourable).

Of the methods described, Method B is not recommended because the use of the fixed budget can give misleading information to management when the actual level of activity is different from that used in the original budget. To make the distinction

*It should be noted that the capacity variance is concerned with fixed factory overheads only since the operation of the flexible budget has removed any difference owing to variable factory overheads, i.e., the variable overhead section of the budget has been flexed to actual. In Method B the variable factory overhead difference arises because the fixed budget used for these calculations is at a different level of activity and, therefore, a variance is disclosed.

adopted in Method A, the analysis of the factory overhead into their fixed and variable elements is required.

Method D is a compromise solution on the difference of opinion regarding the use of Methods A and C. This solution attempts to isolate the efficiency variation from the expenditure variance, i.e., the expenditure variance in Method C of £700 (unfavourable) is analysed to an expenditure amount of £500 (unfavourable) and an efficiency amount of £200 (unfavourable). This method is not often used.

Method A has the advantage over Method C that differences between actual and budgeted expenditure may be easily explained. Itemised lists of actual expenditure can be compared with itemised lists of budgeted expenditure and differences for each item of expenditure clearly understood by management. It may also be noted that the formula for the factory overhead efficiency variance is similar to the formula for the direct labour efficiency variance. This similarity recognises the close resemblance between the use of labour time and factory facilities cost. Not all authorities would agree with the need for this efficiency calculation, maintaining that the calculation is not worth the effort.

The number of days planned in the budget for a particular accounting period may be different from the number of days available for production and where this occurs the difference is known as a calendar variance. The formula for calculating the calendar variance is as follows:

$$\left( \begin{array}{c} \text{Capacity hours} \\ \text{per the budget} \end{array} - \begin{array}{c} \text{Capacity hours} \\ \text{available} \end{array} \right) \times \begin{array}{c} \text{Fixed factory} \\ \text{overhead standard} \\ \text{rate per hour} \end{array} = \begin{array}{c} \text{Calendar} \\ \text{variance} \end{array}$$

With reference to this variance, the following points should be noted:

1. If, for example, the budget of 4,000 capacity hours were calculated on the basis of a 20-day accounting period (200 hours per day) and one day is lost, the capacity hours available are, therefore, 3,800 hours. The 200 hours is the calendar difference.
2. The main cause of a calendar variance is a capacity difference. It follows that the calendar variance is part of the factory overhead capacity variance.
3. If the overheads per the annual budget are not allotted to accounting periods (months) on a working day basis the calendar variance may arise in months of unequal duration. Where this procedure applies, the arithmetical total of these calendar variances for the year should be nil.

## 18.4  SALES – ADDITIONAL VARIANCES

The analysis of the sales variances may be by type of product and this sub-analysis of the sales price variance can be valuable information to management as a basis of pricing strategy. Where more than one product is sold, profitability may be significantly affected by the actual mix of sales being different from the standard mix of sales. Where this occurs a sales mix variance may be calculated. It is useful to identify the main cause of the factor being measured and in this case the sales mix variance is a quantity difference. It follows that the sales mix variance must be part of the sales quantity variance. The formula for calculating this variance could be similar to the formula used for the direct material mixture variance as follows:

$$\left( \begin{array}{l} \text{Actual quantities} \\ \text{of products sold} \\ \text{at standard mix} \end{array} - \begin{array}{l} \text{Actual quantities} \\ \text{of products sold} \\ \text{at actual mix} \end{array} \right) \times \begin{array}{l} \text{Standard} \\ \text{profit per} \\ \text{unit of sale} \end{array} = \begin{array}{l} \text{Sales} \\ \text{mix} \\ \text{variance} \end{array}$$

To illustrate the calculations involved, the following data for a given accounting period may be used:

| Product | Budgeted sales | Actual sales |
|---------|----------------|--------------|
| A | 800 units at £60 per unit | 1,000 units at £60 per unit |
| B | 200 units at £55 per unit | 200 units at £55 per unit |

Cost per unit, Products A and B, budgeted and actual: £50. Applying the formula:

$$\left( \begin{array}{l} \text{Actual quantities} \\ \text{of products sold} \\ \text{at standard mix} \end{array} - \begin{array}{l} \text{Actual quantities} \\ \text{of products sold} \\ \text{at actual mix} \end{array} \right) \times \begin{array}{l} \text{Standard} \\ \text{profit per} \\ \text{unit of sale} \end{array} = \begin{array}{l} \text{Sales} \\ \text{mix} \\ \text{variance} \end{array}$$

| Product | units | units | £ | £ |
|---------|-------|-------|---|---|
| A | 960 (80%) − | 1,000 × 10 | = | 400 (fav.) |
| B | 240 (20%) − | 200 × 5 | = | 200 (unf.) |
|  | 1,200 | 1,200 | | 200 (fav.) |

The above calculation is on the basis of units. An alternative is to use values as a basis giving the following formula:

$$\left( \begin{array}{l} \text{Actual sales} \\ \text{quantities} \times \\ \text{standard prices at} \\ \text{budgeted sales} \\ \text{value mix} \end{array} - \begin{array}{l} \text{Actual sales} \\ \text{quantities} \times \\ \text{standard prices} \\ \text{at actual mix} \end{array} \right) \times \begin{array}{l} \text{Standard} \\ \text{profit} \\ \text{per cent} \end{array} = \begin{array}{l} \text{Sales} \\ \text{mix} \\ \text{variance} \end{array}$$

| Product | £ | | £ | | £ |
|---------|---|---|---|---|---|
| A | 57,763 | $\dfrac{£48,000}{£59,000}$ × £71,000 | 60,000 (1,000 × £60) | .167 | 373 (fav.) |
| B | 13,237 | $\dfrac{£11,000}{£59,000}$ × £71,000 | 11,000 (200 × £55) | .091 | 203 (unf.) |
|  | 71,000 | | 71,000 | | 170 (fav.) |

*Notes:*
(i)  Budgeted sales at standard price:

£

Product A: 800 x £60 = 48,000
Product B: 200 x £55 = 11,000
                      59,000

(ii)  Standard profit percentages:

Product A $\frac{£10}{£60}$ x 100% = ·167%

Product B $\frac{£5}{£55}$ x 100% = ·091%

Proof of the above calculations:
  Profit on actual sales at standard price:

£

Actual mix basis: £71,000 − (£50,000 + £10,000) = 11,000
                         (1,000        (200
                         x £50)        x £50)

Standard mix basis: $\frac{£9,000}{£59,000}$ x £71,000        = 10,830
                                                                170
                                                          (favourable)

*Note:*
Budgeted profit

£

Product A: 800 x £10 = 8,000
Product B: 200 x £5  = 1,000
                       9,000

The calculation on the value basis is preferred because heterogeneous products require a common measure and sales values provide the relevant factor.*

*This view is supported by Professor L. R. Amey and Don. A. Egginton (*Management Accounting – a Conceptual Approach*, Longman, 1973, pp. 483–4), but not all authorities are in agreement. See, for example, Charles T. Horngren (*Cost Accounting – a Managerial Emphasis*, Prentice-Hall, Englewood Cliffs, New Jersey, 1972, pp. 871–4 and 882–7). Professor Horngren favours the units method on the grounds that a mix variance is only valid economically when complete interchangeability is possible in units. Actually, he favours a different units method which, using the figures above, would give a mix variance as follows:

|  | £ |  |
|---|---|---|
| Actual quantities of products sold at actual mix at standard profit | 11,000 | (1,000 x £10 / 200 x £5) |
| Budgeted quantities to be sold at budgeted mix at standard profit | 9,000 | (800 x £10 / 200 x £5) |
| Sales mix variance | 2,000 | (favourable) |

A market share variance may be calculated which represents the difference in profit arising from the company's actual share of the potential market as budgeted as compared with the budgeted share. The formula for this variance is as follows:

$$
\begin{array}{c}
\text{Budgeted} \\
\text{quantities planned} \\
\text{to be sold at} \\
\text{standard profit}
\end{array}
-
\left(
\begin{array}{c}
\text{Budgeted} \\
\text{quantities} \\
\text{planned to be} \\
\text{sold at} \\
\text{standard profit}
\end{array}
\times
\dfrac{
\begin{array}{c}
\text{Actual share of} \\
\text{the budgeted} \\
\text{potential market (\%)}
\end{array}
}{
\begin{array}{c}
\text{Budgeted share of} \\
\text{the budgeted} \\
\text{potential market (\%)}
\end{array}
}
\right)
=
\begin{array}{c}
\text{Market} \\
\text{share} \\
\text{variance}
\end{array}
$$

The market share variance is a subsidiary variance to the sales quantity variance. The remainder of the quantity variance represents differences due to remaining factors affecting sales volume.

## 18.5  THE REVISION VARIANCE

It was suggested in the previous chapter that changes in the standard may be delayed. To prevent these delays distorting the variances calculated for managerial attention, a revisions variance may be used to isolate the effect of such changes. The revisions variance is eliminated when the standard is adjusted.

## 18.6  THE CAUSES OF VARIANCES

The descriptions given to variances in this chapter and Chapter 17 identify reasons why standards have not been achieved: basically, pricing and quantity factors. Such information is valuable but the underlying cause may be more important, for example, the answer to the question: why a price or quantity difference? Further investigation may show a common cause for two or more variances. For example, if the input to a process is in the form of inferior materials to those stipulated in the standard, output of the required quality may only be obtainable by using additional materials. The cause is the use of inferior materials indicated in terms of variance analysis by an unfavourable material quantity and a favourable material price variance. Common causes of variances are production inefficiency, design and method changes, machine breakdowns and unavoidability of supplies.

In practice, the descriptions used for variances may be more specific than the terms used in a general text such as this book. Preference should always be given to local and technical terminology which usually conveys a more precise message to management.

## 18.7  LIMITATIONS OF VARIANCE CALCULATION

Standard cost variance analysis is a mathematical process and the calculations are precise, but this procedure may hide a lack of precision in the preparation of the standards for the following reasons:

1. Standard costs are predetermined and the future course of events may be very different from those envisaged when the standards were set
2. The basis on which the standards are calculated may vary, and generous levels of attainment may hide the inefficiencies that variance analysis is supposed to disclose to management
3. Standards are not necessarily analysed by their controllable and uncontrollable elements
4. There may be difficulties in the evaluation of performance owing to the factors for assessment of the company incorporated in the standard varying over a period of time
5. Poor performance may be outside a band of acceptable performance; not every variance from a specific standard is unsatisfactory yet a standard cost is generally established to indicate what the cost should be.

Given the basic data, detailed variance analysis can stem from the arithmetical analysis of major variances. The breakdown of an overall figure into minor elements can, however, produce insignificant figures which are of no value to management.

It is not necessary to investigate each variance, and minor variances can arise because of standard cost averaging. The total variation for a particular element of cost (actual cost compared with standard cost for actual production) may be reported by major causes and a balancing figure described as 'unexplained difference'. This is reasonable if the amount is insignificant but if the unexplained difference becomes a significant amount, further analysis is necessary. Having decided that additional analysis is not worth the cost, it may be impossible or too costly to obtain the detailed information at a later date.

Statistical techniques are useful in identifying significance, whether the considerations involve the magnitude of the amounts of the variances or their relationships and random effect.*

## 18.8 TREATMENT OF STANDARD COST VARIANCES

Two possibilities are open to the accountant in the treatment of standard cost variances:

1. Regard the variances as irrelevant to future costs and write them off against period profits
2. Regard the variances as product costs and apportion them between: (a) work-in-progress, (b) finished goods stock, and (c) cost of sales, according to the product

* A useful chapter with the title 'Assessing the significance of variances' is included in Nicholas Dopuch and Jacob. G. Birnberg, *Cost Accounting — Accounting Data for Management's Decisions* (Harcourt Brace & World, New York, 1969), pp. 376–92. The text examines significance from the following viewpoints: (a) where the variance was merely a random event within tolerable limits; (b) where the actions specified by the decision model were not accomplished within tolerable limits.

situation. That is, if the product is under manufacture, (*a*); if the product is manufactured but not yet sold, (*b*); or if the product is manufactured and sold, (*c*).

The treatment of variances will depend on their significance and cause. Minor variances can be ignored but the treatment of major variances could significantly affect the calculation of period profits. Where possible, variances are treated as period costs, but if stocks are adjusted the aim should be to isolate variances owing to inefficient operation and these should be written off in the period. Stocks represent costs carried forward to a subsequent trading period and such periods should not carry the costs of inefficiency in earlier periods.

## 18.9 THE RELATIONSHIP OF EFFICIENCY AND ACTIVITY RATIOS TO VARIANCE ANALYSIS

In Chapter 5, reference was made to the following ratios:

1. Efficiency ratio $= \dfrac{\text{Standard hours for actual output}}{\text{Actual hours worked}} \times 100\%$
   (also known as the productivity ratio).

2. Activity ratio $= \dfrac{\text{Standard hours for actual output}}{\text{Planned production in terms of standard hours}} \times 100\%$
   (also known as the production volume ratio)

3. Capacity ratio $= \dfrac{\text{Actual hours worked}}{\text{Planned production in terms of standard hours}} \times 100\%$

It may be noted that the data given in these ratios can be related to the following variances:

Ratio 1: Direct labour efficiency variance
         Factory overhead efficiency variance
Ratio 2: Factory overhead volume variance (Method C)
Ratio 3: Factory overhead capacity variance (Method A).

## 18.10 SUMMARY

Standard costing is a control technique and the value of the variance analysis depends on the extent that management is motivated to good performance and standards properly set. Revision of an original standard may be necessary. Whether to revise the standard or control performance is a question answered by variance analysis and the cause of the variance should prompt management accordingly. Favourable variances may receive less consideration than unfavourable variances but it should be remembered that they represent a departure from standard performance and merit study in order to capitalise on a favourable situation.

All variances should distinguish between long-run and short-run factors and controllable and uncontrollable differences with reference to management's responsibility for action.


## FOR FURTHER STUDY

QUESTIONS

1. *Sections of the cost variance*
   Define 'cost variance'. In practice 'total cost variance' would be divided into material cost variance, wages variance, expense variance, etc. These variances may again be divided. Into what divisions would you separate these variances?

   (ICMA)

2. *Accuracy of standard costs*
   'The arithmetical precision by which allowances are set and the use of standards suggest an accuracy and refinement which is not possible in practice. Bigger and better variance analysis seems to be the maxim of some accountants.'

   D. C. Ellis, 'Standard marginal costing in action − a case study', *Management Accounting*, February/March, 1965, p. 93)

   *Required:*
   Explain and comment on this statement.

3. *Material cost variances*
   A product manufactured is an alloy consisting of 70% Material X and 30% Material Y. In melting and pouring it is expected that a 4% loss of metal will occur. Standard prices are £200 per tonne of Material X and £100 per tonne of Material Y. For the control period, actual figures are as follows:

   Actual output: 192 tonnes
   Material issued and used by the process:
      Material X: 200 tonnes
      Material Y: 50 tonnes
   Actual material prices:
      Material X: £210 per tonne
      Material Y: £85 per tonne.

   *Required:*
   Calculate the material cost variances that can be calculated from the data.

   (ICMA)

4. *Labour cost variances*
   A gang of workers normally consists of ten skilled, five semi-skilled and five un-skilled workers, paid at standard hourly rates of £0·75, £0·50 and £0·40 respectively. In a normal working week of 40 hours, the gang is expected to produce 1,000 units of product.
   In a certain week the gang consisted of thirteen skilled, four semi-skilled and

three unskilled workers; 720 hours were worked; actual wages paid amounted to £450; 1,000 units were produced.
*Required:*
Present information in respect of the labour cost variance arising during the period. Assume each employee works the same hours.                (ICMA)

5. *Variances arising from the use of temporary staff*
The despatch department of a company pays its ordinary employees £1 per hour for a standard output of 4 work units per hour. In its budget for indirect wages, it includes 2,000 man hours of work by temporaries during its busy season, at a rate of £0·80 per hour. The temporaries are budgeted to work at the same rate as the ordinary employees.

During the current year's busy season, temporaries were employed for the 2,000 man hours, but their total output was 7,000 units and they had to be paid £1·20 per hour.
*Required:*
Calculate:

(a) The variance due to the policy of using temporaries as against using ordinary staff
(b) The variance due to the inefficiency of the temporaries
(c) The variance due to differences in wage rates actually paid to temporaries
(d) The amount to be charged in respect of work done by temporaries.
                                                             (ICMA)

6. *Different methods of calculating factory overhead variances*
Factory overhead variances are analysed below by four different methods recognised in books on management accounting:

*Method A*
(a) Actual factory overhead cost: £9,000
(b) Budgeted factory overhead cost as planned at the time the budget was prepared: £8,000
(c) Absorbed factory overhead (actual activity at standard rate basis): £7,200
(d) Absorbed factory overhead (standard activity for units produced basis): £6,500
(e) Spending variance $(a - b)$: £1,000 (unfavourable)
(f) Capacity variance $(b - c)$: £800 (unfavourable)
(g) Efficiency variance $(c - d)$: £700 (unfavourable).
*Method B*
(a) As Method A (a): £9,000
(b) Budgeted cost allowance: £7,500
(c) As Method A(c): £7,200
(d) As Method A(d): £6,500
(e) Budget variance $(a - b)$: £1,500 (unfavourable)
(f) Capacity variance $(b - c)$: £300 (unfavourable)

(g) Efficiency variance $(c - d)$: £700 (unfavourable).

*Method C*

(a) As Method A(a): £9,000
(b) Absorbed variable factory overhead (standard activity for units produced basis) plus budgeted fixed factory overhead: £7,000
(c) As Method A(d): £6,500
(d) Expenditure variance $(a - b)$: £2,000 (unfavourable)
(e) Volume variance $(b - c)$: £500 (unfavourable).

*Method D*

(a) As Method A(a): £9,000
(b) As Method B(b): £7,500
(c) As Method C(b): £7,000
(d) As Method A(d): £6,500
(e) Expenditure variance $(a - b)$: £1,500 (unfavourable)
(f) Volume variance $(c - d)$: £500 (unfavourable)
(g) Efficiency variance $(b - c)$: £500 (unfavourable).

*Required:*

Compare and comment on the above methods of calculating the factory overhead variances.


7. *Different methods of calculating sales variances*
Sales variances are analysed below by two different methods:

*Method A*

(a) Actual profit: £5,000
(b) Standard profit on actual sales at actual mix: £6,000
(c) Standard profit on actual sales at budgeted mix: £6,500
(d) Budgeted profit: £6,200
(e) Sales price variance $(a - b)$: £1,000 (unfavourable)
(f) Sales mix variance $(b - c)$: £500 (unfavourable)
(g) Sales quantity variance $(c - d)$: £300 (favourable).

*Method B*

(a) As Method A(a): £5,000
(b) As Method A(b): £6,000
(c) Standard profit on actual quantities of products sold at standard mix: £6,800
(d) As Method A(d): £6,200
(e) Sales price variance $(a - b)$: £1,000 (unfavourable)
(f) Sales mix variance $(b - c)$: £800 (unfavourable)
(g) Sales quantity variance $(c - d)$: £600 (favourable).

*Required:*

Compare and comment on the above methods of calculating the sales variances.

**8.** *Sales variances*

The A.B. Co. Ltd, budget to sell in the month of January, 2,500 grams of Product A at £3 per gram, 1,200 grams of Product B at £2 per gram and 2,000 grams of Product C at £2.50 per gram. During the month the actual sales were:

2,000 grams Product A for £5,500
1,800 grams Product B for £4,050
2,200 grams Product C for £4,950.

Budgeted costs of Product A at £2 per unit, Product B, £1·50 per unit and Product C, £2 per unit were in line with actual.

*Required:*

Calculate the effect of sales variances (price, quantity and mix) on budgeted profit and prepare a statement showing how each product has contributed to the increase or decrease in budgeted profit.                    (ACA)

**9.** *Forms of presentation of sales variances*

Speedster Car Parts Ltd, ascertain the following data for an accounting control period:

|  | Product A | Product B |
|---|---|---|
| Standard selling price per unit | £4 | £3 |
| Standard cost per unit | £2 | £2 |
| Budgeted sales in units | 100 | 50 |
| Actual sales in units | 50 | 80 |
| Actual selling price per unit | £5 | £3 |

The accountant prepares the following forms of presentation that may be used for supplying this information to management:

*Presentation 1*

|  | £ |
|---|---|
| Budgeted sales | 550 |
| Sales volume variance | 110 |
| Actual sales at standard price | 440 |
| Sales price variance | 50 |
| Actual sales at actual price | 490 |
| Standard cost of actual sales | 260 |
| Standard profit on actual sales | 230 |

*Presentation 2*

|  | £ |
|---|---|
| Budgeted sales | 550 |
| Standard cost of budgeted sales | 300 |
| Budgeted profit on sales | 250 |
| Sales volume variance | 70 |
| Standard profit on actual sales at standard price carried forward | 180 |

|                                                              | £   |
|--------------------------------------------------------------|-----|
| Standard profit on actual sales at standard price B/F        | 180 |
| Sales price variance                                         | 50  |
| Standard profit on actual sales                              | 230 |

*Presentation 3*

|                                                              |     |
|--------------------------------------------------------------|-----|
| Standard profit on actual sales at standard price           | 180 |
| Sales price variance                                         | 50  |
| Standard profit on actual sales                              | 230 |

*Required:*

Explain how the figures used in the above presentations have been calculated and comment on the forms of sales variance information suggested for possible use.

10. *Related variances*

In any business, an apparent saving in one element of cost may cause a loss in another element of cost, e.g., the use of cheaper material may result in a lower yield of finished product, or the use of lower grade labour may result in the wasteful use of material.

*Required:*

Explain how a standard costing system deals with this fact.            (ICMA)

11. *Standard profit statement preparation*

The following data relates to the manufacture of a standard product:

|                             | *Budgeted figures* | *Actual figures* |
|-----------------------------|--------------------|------------------|
| Overheads:                  |                    |                  |
|   Fixed                     | £6,000             | £6,100           |
|   Semi-variable             | £1,500             | £1,550           |
| Sales                       | 30,000 units       | 29,100 units     |
| Selling prices              | £2 per unit        | £2·25 per unit   |
| Material price per gram     | £0·075             | £0·10            |
| Usage of materials          | 300,000 grams      | 304,000 grams    |
| Wages                       | 60,000 hours       | 57,000 hours     |
| Standard hourly wage rate   | £0·25              |                  |
| Wages paid                  |                    | £14,350          |

Standard profit per unit:

|                              | £     | £    |
|------------------------------|-------|------|
| Selling price                |       | 2·00 |
| Materials: 10 grams at £0·075| 0·75  |      |
| Wages: 2 hours at £0·25      | 0·50  |      |
| Overheads:                   |       |      |
|   Fixed                      | 0·20  |      |
|   Semi-variable              | 0·05  | 1·50 |
| Standard profit              |       | ·50  |

There is no closing or opening stock of materials or work-in-progress. The normal number of working days for a four-week period is 20; in this particular period there were 19 days only.

*Required:*

Prepare a standard profit statement suitable for management control purposes.

(ACA)

12. *Standard costing and job costs*

The Heavy Engineering Co. Ltd, has a system of job costing in operation, all items of cost, where possible, being charged direct to the job. When tender prices are submitted they are based on past experience.

Although each job is costed separately, it has been found that the various jobs fall into one of three categories. Over the past few months profit, as a percentage of sales, on Category III work has been considerably less than that obtained in the other two categories and in a few cases a loss has been made. The management are, therefore, contemplating concentrating all their efforts towards getting jobs in either Category I or Category II.

Initially, this would mean that there would not be sufficient work to keep the factory working at normal capacity whereas at present a considerable amount of overtime is worked in order to meet delivery dates. No attempt is made to include in the tender price of any job a specific allowance for over-time.

Before discontinuing Category III work, the managing director asks for your advice on the matter. He illustrates his reasons for the proposed step with the final result on the most recently completed job in Category III.

*Job H24 account*

| | £ | | £ |
|---|---|---|---|
| Material | 1,060 | Job revenue | 2,850 |
| Labour | 1,200 | Loss on job | 1,060 |
| Direct expenses | 150 | | |
| Overheads | 1,500 | | |
| | 3,910 | | 3,910 |

After further investigation the following facts emerge. Overheads, not all of which are regarded as dependent on the level of output, are allocated to jobs by means of a predetermined percentage on labour cost, calculated at the beginning of each year and based on the final accounts of the previous 12 months. This percentage, 125, is applied to all jobs irrespective of the category. The original tender for job H24 was based on an estimate of £800 for materials. The whole of the material relates to the type X186 which is the basic material to all jobs, other materials being regarded as expense items and included in the direct expense estimate of £100. It is also estimated that 1,600 labour hours would be required at the average rate of £0·50 per hour.

There are various grades of labour but as the allocation of them to contracts is largely a matter of convenience, the average cost of all grades is usually a adopted when tenders are prepared. During the past period, supplies of X186 were unexpectedly exhausted by an abnormal work load passing through the factory and additional supplies had to be obtained from another source, costing £30 per unit for the 50 units purchased, which was £5 higher per unit than normal. Materials are charged out of stores on a F.I.F.O. basis and the 34 units which the job used came out of this latest purchase.

In addition, four of these units were scrapped, double the normal waste rate, because of the number of relatively unskilled workers who were employed on the job in the early stages, as a result of the demands for skilled workers on the other jobs. The job was finally completed by working overtime but a late penalty of 5% of the job price was payable. When overtime is worked the full labour cost is charged to the job and in this case 25% of the total labour cost represented overtime premiums.

*Required:*

(*a*) Reframe the existing operating statement for job H24 as if a standard costing system were in operation, taking account only of the information which is given as the basis of the standards used. This should be accompanied by a report pointing out firstly, the advantages which your method of presentation has; and secondly, the weakness of the present accounting system.

(*b*) Comment on the managing director's suggestion that the company should cease tendering for jobs in Category III, indicating the additional information you would require before a definite answer could be given.     (ACA)

FURTHER READING

Batty, J. *Standard Costing.* Macdonald & Evans, 1960. Chapters 7, 15 and 25.
Chamberlain, Neil W. *The Firm – Micro Economic Planning and Action.* McGraw-Hill, New York, 1962. Chapter 17.
Ellmer, R. E. *Marginal Cost and Variance Analysis in Management Accounting.* Macmillan, 1969. Chapters 4–7.

# ACCOUNTING AND BUSINESS DECISION-MAKING

# 19 Marginal Costing

OBJECTIVE OF THE CHAPTER

To describe the marginal costing technique and illustrate its value, particularly in decision-making. Difficulties in applying the technique are explained and also its relationship with absorption costing.

OUTLINE OF THE CHAPTER

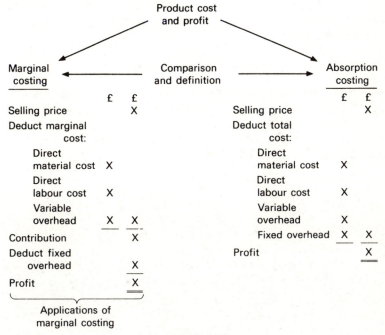

FIGURE 19.1.

Earlier chapters have introduced the techniques of cost—volume—profit analysis (Chapter 6) and flexible budgeting (Chapter 11) and the need to classify costs into their fixed and variable elements to apply these procedures. Businesses cannot afford to ignore this basic classification of costs and a serious attempt should be made to overcome the problems of identifying the behaviour of costs in context. In this area the context is a given level of output as mentioned in Chapter 2, but the behaviour of costs may be considered in other contexts such as decision-making. These cost movements, used as a basis of supplying information to management, have introduced into accounting terms such as differential costing, incremental costing and marginal costing. The similarity of these techniques has led many writers to regard them as synonymous terms. The attempt to segregate differential and incremental costing as techniques concerned with decision-making, which is correct, has not removed the confusion because marginal costing is also of particular value in decision-making.

It is not proposed to develop in detail the various interpretations of the terms used* but it is necessary to avoid confusion. For the purpose of this book, differential and incremental costs will be considered in the next chapter and marginal costing defined as the technique which uses the classification of fixed and variable costs to ascertain marginal cost as a basis for supplying information to management for profit planning and decision-making. The presentation of the marginal costs of products emphasises the effect of volume changes on the contribution of individual products to fixed costs and final profit.

The analysis described above may be incorporated in the cost accounts or confined to the working papers for specific investigations. The interpretation of the term 'marginal costing' in this country has tended to imply the latter and in the United States, the former.†

## 19.1 MARGINAL COST AND ABSORPTION COST

Marginal cost is the variable cost of one unit of a product of service. If the cost of the unit of product or service includes the allotment of fixed costs as well as variable costs this amount is known as absorbed cost.

Common data for the period reporting where the two forms of presentation are used may be as follows:

1. Absorption cost presentation

*Profit Statement*
*Period ended*

|  | £ | £ | £ |
|---|---|---|---|
| Sales |  |  | 9,000 |
| Cost of sales |  |  |  |
| Factory costs: |  |  |  |
| Direct material | 2,000 |  |  |
| Direct labour | 1,000 |  |  |
| Factory overhead | 1,000 |  |  |
|  | 4,000 |  |  |
| Less closing stock | 1,000 | 3,000 |  |
| Selling and distribution costs |  | 1,500 |  |
| Administration costs |  | 1,000 | 5,500 |
| Profit |  |  | 3,500 |

* Readers interested in these interpretations should read the article: J. Sizer, 'The terminology of marginal costing', *Management Accounting* (August 1966), pp. 308–12.
† Known in the United States as direct costing. Some authorities in this country would prefer to limit the term 'marginal costing' to the situation where the routine system incorporates the marginal principle. See, for example, *Terminology of Management and Financial Accountancy* (Institute of Cost and Management Accountants, 1974), p. 12. No such distinction is implied in this chapter.

2. Marginal cost presentation

*Profit Statement*
*Period ended*

| | £ | £ | £ |
|---|---|---|---|
| Sales | | | 9,000 |
| Marginal cost of sales | | | |
| Factory costs: | | | |
| Direct material | 2,000 | | |
| Direct labour | 1,000 | | |
| Variable factory overhead | 600 | | |
| | 3,600 | | |
| Less closing stock | 900 | 2,700 | |
| Variable selling and | | | |
| distribution costs | | 900 | 3,600 |
| Contribution | | | 5,400 |
| Fixed factory overhead | | 400 | |
| Fixed selling and distribution | | | |
| costs | | 600 | |
| Fixed administration costs | | 1,000 | 2,000 |
| Profit | | | 3,400 |

In the above examples, the following assumptions have been made:

(a) No opening stocks
(b) 1,500 units sold
(c) 2,000 units manufactured
(d) The closing stock valued at factory cost per absorption costing, i.e., 500 units: £1,000 ($\frac{1}{4}$ × £4,000)
(e) The closing stock valued at marginal cost per marginal costing, i.e., 500 units: £900 ($\frac{1}{4}$ × £3,600).

It will be noted that the difference in profit under the two methods: £100 (£3,500 − £3,400), represents the difference in the closing stock valuation (£1,000 − £900).

The term 'contribution' shown in the marginal cost presentation was introduced in Chapter 6.

When product analysis is involved, the two forms of presentation are as follows:

1. Absorption cost presentation

*Profit Statement*
*Period ended*

| | Product A | Product B | Total |
|---|---|---|---|
| | £ | £ | £ |
| Sales | – | – | – |
| Deduct cost of sales | – | – | – |
| Profit | – | – | – |

2. Marginal cost presentation:

*Profit Statement*<br>*Period ended*

|  | Product A | Product B | Total |
|---|---|---|---|
|  | £ | £ | £ |
| Sales | – | – | – |
| Deduct marginal cost of sales | – | – | – |
| Contribution | – | – | – |
|  |  | £ |  |
| Deduct fixed costs |  |  |  |
|    Factory overhead |  | – |  |
|    Selling and distribution overhead |  | – |  |
|    Administration overhead |  | – | – |
| Profit |  |  | – |

In the marginal cost form of presentation, product analysis normally ends at the contribution figure.

In absorption costing, a predetermined rate is generally used for the absorption of factory overhead to products and it is unlikely that the absorbed cost will equal the actual cost in a period. The difference, known as under- or over-absorbed cost, is incorporated in the profit statement presentation before final profit is calculated:

|  | £ |  |
|---|---|---|
| Factory cost of sales | – | (includes factory overhead absorbed) |
| Add/deduct under-/over-absorbed factory overhead | – | (e.g., under-absorption means the product has not absorbed the full factory cost, therefore, this under-absorption is added)* |
| Actual factory cost of sales | – |  |

## 19.2 MARGINAL COSTING DIFFICULTIES

The value of the marginal costing technique should be assessed with a recognition of the problems associated with its application. These may be considered as:

1. The problem of analysing costs into their fixed and variable elements. Arbitrary classifications may be used to give this analysis.
2. The tendency to concentrate on the short-term situation. In the long term, 'fixed' costs will vary.
3. Satisfactory long-range decisions can only be made given product total cost data which is not available if product analysis is restricted by marginal costing information only. In the long run fixed costs must be recovered.

* The factory overhead cost variance (actual costs – standard cost for actual production) described in Chapter 17 gives the detail of what this under-/over-absorption represents (in the standard costing system the standard cost rate is the predetermined rate).

4. Attention is focused on the contribution stage and the possible non-recognition of fixed costs by management may be dangerous.
5. In the manufacture of a product, facilities represented by fixed costs are used and the non-assignment of these costs to products is a departure from the accounting principle that attempts to match costs against revenue for profit determination.
6. In a manufacturing plant that is highly automated, the amount of variable cost may be small and this situation magnifies the problems of applying the technique.

If marginal costing is used for stock valuation, research has shown that inaccuracies arising from the difficulty of separating costs into their fixed and variable elements are not significant enough in the average business to distort the result of arbitrary classifications considered necessary. For other purposes, however, the care with which the analysis is carried out assumes a greater significance and the approach described in Chapter 6 should be adopted, particularly checking the validity of the assumptions made in the period concerned.

Information for management should be provided in relation to user requirements and if these dictate the supply of marginal cost information, management should be reminded that the information supplied for one purpose should not be used for other requirements without checking with the accounting department that the detail available is relevant to its intended use. If this rule is observed, the danger of confusing marginal cost with full cost will be lessened.

The use of the marginal costing technique should not necessarily mean that full cost data is not available. A fully developed management accounting system will have the basic data available for compilation in the manner required to satisfy the key demands of the management. Where there is the danger that fixed costs will be ignored by management if the marginal costing technique is adopted, it would appear that there are significant weaknesses in the company control system. No budgetary control system worth the name, backed by sound management would neglect this aspect of control.

The use of marginal cost as the basis of stock valuation for external reporting has not received much support and, as mentioned in Chapter 16, the Accounting Standards Committee has recommended the inclusion in stock valuation of overheads 'which relate to production notwithstanding that these may accrue wholly on partly on a time basis'.*

The fact that marginal costing has not received much support for external reporting does not invalidate its value for internal purposes — a point developed in the next section.

## 19.3 THE VALUE OF MARGINAL COSTING TO MANAGEMENT

Marginal costing is a technique of value to management for the following reasons:

1. It integrates with other aspects of management accounting, e.g., cost—volume—profit analysis, flexible budgeting and standard costing.

* *Stocks and Work-in-Progress*, Statement of Standard Accounting Practice No. 9 (Accounting Standards Committee, 1975).

2. Period reports are more easily understood. See, for example, the illustration in Chapter 16 which shows profits responding more to changing sales levels than the combination of sales and production levels. Management can more readily understand the asssignment of costs to products if these are limited to marginal cost because such costs are readily identifiable with the cost unit.
3. It emphasises the significance of key factors affecting the performance of the business in the profit-planning and decision-making areas. Chapter 6 introduced the profit/volume ratio where contribution was related to the key factor: sales. Other key factors may be applicable to the business situation such as a shortage of material; skilled labour; or machine facilities. Contribution to these factors is an important statistic for management.
4. There is a close relationship between variable costs and the controllable costs classification. This relationship assists the control function.
5. It assists in the provision of relevant costs for decision-making. Without marginal cost data, the information for management may be misleading. This is the case, for example, in decisions concerned with:

   (a) The acceptance of special orders
   (b) The possible elimination of a product
   (c) The possible outside purchase of components as compared with their internal manufacture
   (d) The selling of products in limited markets.

6. It assists short-term decision-making, particularly those decisions concerned with product short-term pricing.

## 19.4  THE ACCEPTANCE OF SPECIAL ORDERS

**Example**
A large manufacturing business offers to place a special contract with the company at a price of £20,000 for 1,000 units to be made over the next twelve months. The management of the company is doubtful about accepting the contract because estimated costs are as follows:

|  | £ |
|---|---|
| Direct material cost | 4,000 |
| Direct labour cost | 3,000 |
| Variable overhead | 5,000 |
| Fixed overhead | 8,000 |
|  | 20,000 |

**Comment**
The total cost of £20,000 is calculated on the basis of absorbed cost and the £8,000 for fixed overhead represents the allotment of the existing costs of available facilities to this proposed contract. The key question is whether these facilities could be used to better advantage if this contract was not accepted. If the answer is 'yes', the sensible course to take is to accept the more profitable business. If the answer

is 'no', the contribution towards fixed costs and profit is as follows:

|  | £ |  |
|---|---|---|
| Contract price | 20,000 |  |
| Less marginal cost | 12,000 | (£4,000 + £3,000 + £5,000) |
| Contribution | 8,000 |  |

By accepting the contract, the company has £8,000 more income towards meeting its fixed costs which it must meet whether the contract is accepted or not.

## 19.5  THE POSSIBLE ELIMINATION OF A PRODUCT

### Example

A manufacturing company makes a profit of £20,000 from the manufacture and sale of three products as follows:

| £000 | Product A | Product B | Product C | Total |
|---|---|---|---|---|
| Sales | 25 | 30 | 40 | 95 |
| Total cost | 14 | 38 | 23 | 75 |
| Profit/(loss) | 11 | (8) | 17 | 20 |

The management of the company are considering the elimination of Product B because it is making a loss. It has been ascertained that total costs may be analysed as follows:

| £000 | Product A | Product B | Product C | Total |
|---|---|---|---|---|
| Marginal cost | 8 | 20 | 13 | 41 |
| Fixed cost | 6 | 18 | 10 | 34 |
| Total cost | 14 | 38 | 23 | 75 |

### Comment

As in the previous example, the key question is whether the facilities represented by the £18,000 fixed costs allotted to Product B can be used to better advantage. The sale of a new product may not be possible but further sales effort on Products A and C may be justifiable. If better use of the facilities used on Product B is not possible and Product B is eliminated, the new profit figure is as follows:

|  | £000 |
|---|---|
| Existing profit | 20 |
| Add elimination of loss | 8 |
|  | 28 |
| Deduct cost of facilities not in alternative use | 18 |
| Revised profit | 10 |

An alternative presentation is as follows:

| £000 | Product A | Product C | Total |
|---|---|---|---|
| Sales | 25 | 40 | 65 |
| Less marginal cost | 8 | 13 | 21 |
| Contribution | 17 | 27 | 44 |
| | | Less fixed cost | 34 |
| | | Profit | 10 |

Although Product B was making a loss, its elimination has converted a £20,000 profit to the much lower figure of £10,000. The reason for this drop is that as long as the company was making and selling Product B, that product was making a contribution of £10,000 to fixed costs which had to be met whether Product B was eliminated or not. This calculation is as follows:

| | Product B £ |
|---|---|
| Sales | 30,000 |
| Less marginal cost | 20,000 |
| Contribution | 10,000 |

## 19.6 THE MAKE OR BUY DECISION

**Example**

A manufacturing company intends to sub-contract the manufacure of components which are presently costing the business £8,000 to manufacture. It has obtained a quote of only £6,000 and is satisfied as to the sub-contractor's reliability to meet its non-financial requirements. It s own cost of £8,000 is made up as follows:

| | £ |
|---|---|
| Marginal cost | 5,000 |
| Fixed cost | 3,000 |
| | 8,000 |

**Comment**

Using the criterion previously described, if the facilities costing £3,000 can be put to better use, the company intention seems reasonable. If this is not the case, the comparison is not £8,000 (make) to £6,000 (buy) but £5,000 (marginal cost to make) to £6,000 (buy). An alternative way of looking at this is that the decision to buy would involve the company in the following costs:

| | £ |
|---|---|
| Purchase price of components | 6,000 |
| Add cost of unused facilities | 3,000 |
| | 9,000 (Compare with the cost to make of £8,000) |

The non-financial factors such as the quality of the components and the reasonable certainty of meeting delivery dates can be crucial.

## 19.7 SELLING OF A PRODUCT IN A LIMITED MARKET

**Example**
A manufacturing company sells Product X in this country at a profit of £10 per unit calculated as follows:

|  | £ |
|---|---|
| Marginal cost | 8 |
| Fixed cost | 12 |
| Total cost | 20 |
| Profit | 10 |
| Selling price | 30 |

The company enjoys good profits and wishes to introduce Product X in a foreign country but finds that the maximum price per unit it could sell its product would be £18.

**Comment**
In the above assessment each unit sold would incur a loss of £2 (£20 − £18). If the company cannot extend its sales at a higher figure than £18 per unit elsewhere, foreign sales are worth consideration. As the company is profitable, its fixed overheads are covered. For every additional unit sold at £18 a contribution to fixed costs and profit is £10 (£18 minus marginal cost: £8). As fixed costs are already covered the £10 is all profit. There must be no danger to the company's existing markets by this practice.

## 19.8 SHORT-TERM PRICING

Marginal costing can be very useful in short-term pricing decisions because there may be occasions when it may be in the interests of the company to sell at under total cost for a limited period. Examples include the need to maintain production in a recession or to popularise a product. In the latter case, the company must be careful that low price selling does not lead to the loss of profitable business. In the former case, the fixed costs have still to be met and any contribution to fixed costs will be of value to the business. Using the figures in the previous example, any sale above £8 will give a unit contribution to increase profitability by offsetting fixed costs. In the recession all the fixed costs may not be covered but the loss will be minimised.

Short-term reduced pricing below total cost is a dangerous practice because of its effect on future activities of the business and profitability. Only a management knowledgeable in its use of marginal cost data in this context should apply the technique.


## 19.9  PRODUCT EMPHASIS USING THE KEY FACTOR

Where there is a key factor (sometimes called a limiting factor) affecting the company activities, the information on which product to concentrate one's attention to maximise profits may be obtained by using contribution detail for each product.

**Example**

A manufacturing company has available in the period 1,000 hours of machine capacity to product Products A and B. It is unable to increase this capacity but is able to sell whatever is produced. The contributions per unit of product are as follows:

|                | Product A | Product B |
|----------------|:---------:|:---------:|
|                | £         | £         |
| Selling price  | 20        | 10        |
| Marginal cost  | 15        | 8         |
| Contribution   | 5         | 2         |

The machine hours to produce one unit are:

> Product A: 4 hours
> Product B: 1 hour
>
> Fixed costs are £750.


**Comment**

Because Product A gives the higher contribution and to maximise profits the maximum contribution to fixed costs and profit is wanted, the company may concentrate its sales on Product A (especially considering the profit/volume ratio for Product A is 25% and Product B only 20%). If the company took this action the profit would be:

$$\text{Number of units manufactured:} \quad \frac{1,000 \text{ hours}}{4} = 250 \text{ units}$$

|               | £     |
|---------------|------:|
| Sales         | 5,000 |
| Marginal cost | 3,750 |
| Contribution  | 1,250 |
| Fixed cost    | 750   |
| Profit        | 500   |

If the company concentrated its sales on Product B the profit would be:

Number of units manufactured: 1,000 units

|  | £ |
|---|---|
| Sales | 10,000 |
| Marginal cost | 8,000 |
| Contribution | 2,000 |
| Fixed cost | 750 |
| Profit | 1,250 |

The reason for this improved result is the fact that in the example the key factor is machine capacity and for every single Product A, four units of Product B can be made and sold. The preference for Product B can be shown by calculating the contribution per unit of the key factor:

Product A: contribution per machine hour: £1·25 $\left(\frac{£5}{4}\right)$

Product B: contribution per machine hour: £2 $\left(\frac{£2}{1}\right)$

It may be unwise to eliminate Product A in favour of Product B because key factors can change and if material became the constraint, it is possible that contribution as a percentage of material cost may favour Product A to the detriment of Product B. Then it may be difficult to re-introduce Product A.

In this example, there is only one key factor but there may be more than one factor or constraint affecting company activities. The most profitable production programme to maximise profit still involves using contribution but the use of the linear programming technique is necessary — a point considered in Chapter 21.

## 19.10 STANDARD MARGINAL COSTING

The standard costing technique may be combined with marginal costing to give standard marginal costing. The combined technique is applied on the basis of product standard cost sheets prepared in marginal costing format. When standard profit statements are prepared, the standard profit on actual sales is replaced by standard contribution on actual sales. The standard contribution on actual sales is then converted to actual contribution on actual sales by the addition or deduction, as necessary, of the sales price variance and marginal cost variances, i.e., direct material, direct labour and variable overhead variances. The adjustment of the actual contribution on actual sales for fixed costs gives actual profit.

In calculating the sales quantity variance, the standard profit per unit is replaced by the standard contribution per unit to give this variance in terms of contribution.

## 19.11  SUMMARY

Marginal costing has been a controversial subject with accountants and managers for many years. Although marginal costing is not widely practised, accountants would not dispute the need to analyse costs into their fixed and variable elements. They would also recognise the value of this data for profit-planning, control and decision-making, but point to the fact that for decision-making purposes fixed costs may be incremental relative to a decision situation as well as marginal cost. In this chapter, consideration of decision-making problems has emphasized marginal costing deferring the wider issues to the next chapter.

## FOR FURTHER STUDY

### QUESTIONS

1. *The value of marginal costing*
'Marginal costing is a technique of value to management'.
*Required:*
Discuss this statement.

2. *The disadvantages of a marginal costing system*
Labour Saving Gadgets Ltd have recently engaged a new chief accountant who is a marginal costing enthusiast. The chief accountant has attempted to spread this enthusiasm to the remaining executives of the company by lecturing on the benefits of the system and emphasising that the inclusion of fixed costs in information to management makes it difficult to:

(*a*) Compare the effect of different courses of action
(*b*) Measure the true efficiency of sections and departments
(*c*) Fix selling prices so as to give the best results to the business as a whole.

The chief accountant presents a convincing case but the managing director is inclined to be cautious regarding the change which appears to be so fundamental in the accounting system. As the company uses standard costing, he feels that such a system should provide much of the information that the proposed marginal costing would provide. Without more information on marginal costing and associated accounting routines, the managing director is not very confident regarding his ability to offset the arguments put forward by the new chief accountant so that a balanced judgement on the matter may be made.
*Required:*
The managing director has asked you to

(*a*) Indicate the disadvantages of adopting marginal costing
(*b*) Advise him regarding the extent to which the disadvantages may be offset or reduced in their effect if marginal costing is adopted

(c) Explain whether an existing absorption standard costing system could provide much of the information that the proposed marginal costing would provide.

3. *Fixed/variable cost classification*

A system of marginal costing requires that the fixed and variable elements of cost in relation to output be distinguished.

*Required:*

Discuss the problems which arise in making this distinction and their implications for the provision of the marginal costing information supplied to management. (ACA)

4. *Production of profit statements on an absorption and marginal costing basis*

A. B. Co. Ltd has an opening stock of Product X of 15,000 units, and budgets to produce 150,000 units of the product in the year. The costs are budgeted as:

> Variable factory stadard cost per unit: £2
> Variable selling standard cost per unit: £0·30
> Fixed factory overhead: £75,000
> Fixed selling overhead: £30,000.

The standard selling price per unit is £4.

The actual results for the year were as follows:

> Sales: 120,000 units at £4 per unit
> Production: 130,000 units
> Unfavourable variable factory cost variance: £5,000
> Fixed overhead: factory and selling: as budgeted.

*Required:*

Prepare profit statements for the year on an absorption and marginal costing basis. Explain the reason for the difference in profits.

5. *Forecast results where an activity change is projected*

The statement of trading results for the XYZ Co. Ltd for this year is as follows:

|  | £ |
|---|---|
| Sales | 250,000 |
| Stock increase at prime cost | 22,000 |
|  | 272,000 |

| Operating costs |  £ | £ |
|---|---|---|
| Direct materials | 100,000 | |
| Direct wages | 40,000 | |
| Factory overheads | | |
| Fixed | 30,000 | |
| Variable | 70,000 | |
| Other overheads | | |
| Fixed | 20,000 | |
| Variable | 10,000 | 270,000 |
| Net profit | | 2,000 |

The board is dissatisfied with these results which are partly due to a sales activity as low as 60%. Market research indicates a possible increase of activity to 90% consequent upon selling price decreases of 5% and an additional advertising appropriation of £5,000 per annum.

*Required:*

(*a*) Prepare a statement showing the likely results of a year's trading assuming that all the changes indicated take place.

(*b*) Compare the projected results with those for this year and detail the factors which have caused the variation in net profit, calculating the amount relating to each factor.                                                  (ICMA)

6. *Possible closure of depots*

A company making a single product has a factory in the South, and distributes its production through three depots situated in the South, Midlands and North.

It is estimated that during the coming year 100,000 units will be manufactured and sold at a price of £20 per unit, the sales being spread as follows:

| South | 70,000 units |
|---|---|
| Midlands | 20,000 units |
| North | 10,000 units |

Standard costs of production are:

Direct materials: £4·80 per unit
Direct wages: £3 per unit
Factory variable overheads: 140% on direct wages
Factory fixed overheads: £400,000 per annum.

The costs of selling and distribution incurred by the depots are estimated as follows:

Fixed costs:

| South | £80,000 per annum |
|---|---|
| Midlands | £50,000 per annum |
| North | £30,000 per annum |

Variable costs:

| South | 5% of sales value |
|---|---|
| Midlands | 8% of sales value |
| North | 10% of sales value. |

From the budget for the business prepared from these figures, management is considering the desirability of closing the depots and selling organisations in the Midlands and/or North. If this is done, it is expected that all sales in these areas will be lost, but that sales in the South will remain unaffected.

*Required:*

Prepare a budget for the business from the figures provided, indicating why management is thinking of closing the depots in the Midlands and/or North.

Present additional information to help management make a decision in regard to this problem and make recommendations from your figures. (ICMA)

7. *Value of business from customer groups*

A manufacturer makes the following analysis of his customers:

| Customer group | No. in group | Yearly purchases |
|---|---|---|
| A | 40 | £800 plus |
| B | 300 | £500 to £800 |
| C | 60 | Under £500 |
| | 400 | |

Orders are obtained by representatives making a monthly call on each customer.

Analysis of his sales for the year of his three products over the above groups shows:

| | | | Products | |
|---|---|---|---|---|
| Group | X | Y | Z | Total |
| | £ | £ | £ | £ |
| A | 5,000 | 15,000 | 20,000 | 40,000 |
| B | 53,000 | 72,000 | 75,000 | 200,000 |
| C | 2,000 | 3,000 | 5,000 | 10,000 |
| | 60,000 | 90,000 | 100,000 | 250,000 |
| Gross profit margin | £18,000 | £24,300 | £25,000 | £67,300 |
| Gross profit (%) | 30 | 27 | 25 | |

| | £ | £ | |
|---|---|---|---|
| Deduct | | | |
| Advertising expenses | | 20,000 | |
| Distribution expenses | | 10,000 | |
| Salesmen | | | |
| Salaries | 6,000 | | |
| 1% commission | 2,500 | | |
| Expenses | 2,000 | 10,500 | |
| Administration and office expenses | | 9,500 | 50,000 |
| Net profit | | | 17,300 |

*Required:*

The manufacturer doubts the profitability of his business with Group C customers and asks you to comment on the position disclosed by the information given.

8. *The make or buy decision*

XY Ltd produces filing cabinets and its profits for the previous year were

as follows:

|  | £ | £ |
|---|---|---|
| Sales | | 200,000 |
| Less marginal cost of sales: | | |
| Direct material | 55,000 | |
| Direct labour | 45,000 | |
| Variable overhead | 20,000 | 120,000 |
| Contribution | | 80,000 |
| Less fixed overhead | | 40,000 |
| Profit | | 40,000 |

Company capacity is fully used at the present time. Because of the inability of the company to extend capacity for future use, the management is considering an offer from a potential supplier to supply components for £15,000 which presently cost £17,000 to manufacture:

|  | £ |
|---|---|
| Direct material | 5,000 |
| Direct labour | 4,800 |
| Variable overhad | 2,200 |
| Marginal cost | 12,000 |
| Fixed factory overhead | 5,000 |
| Factory cost of components | 17,000 |

Acceptance of this offer would release 10% of the present capacity, but further work is not yet available to absorb the capacity released if the manufacture of the components are subcontracted.

*Required:*

What additional factors should be considered before a decision is made in this case. On the information given, should the company continue to manufacture the components or accept the offer from the potential supplier?

9. *Contribution as a basis for assessing the worth of a project*

The present output details of a manufacturing department are as follows:

Average output per week: 48,000 units from 160 employees
Saleable value of output: £30,000
Contribution made by output towards fixed expenses and profit: £12,000.

The board of directors plans to introduce more mechanisation into the department at a capital cost of £8,000. The effect of this will be to reduce the number of employees to 120, but to increase the output per individual employee by 60%. To provide the necessary incentive to achieve the increased output, the board intends to offer a 1% increase on the piecework price of £0·05 per article for every 2% increase in average individual output achieved. To sell the increased output, it will be necessary to decrease the selling prices by 4%.

*Required:*

Calculate the extra weekly contribution resulting from the proposed change
and evaluate, for the board's consideration, the worth of the project.   (ICMA)

10. *Choice of contracts*

A company operates in an area where there is little prospect of increasing its
labour force. It employs 20 direct operatives, whose working week is 40 hours
each and whose average rate of pay is £1 per hour. No overtime is worked.

On 1st October, the company had to choose between two contracts with
A. B. Ltd or with C. D. Ltd, each of which would last until the end of that
year and which cannot be undertaken at the same time.

Standard prime costs for each contract and the best prices which can be
obtained are:

|  | A. B. Ltd contract | C. D. Ltd contract |
|---|---|---|
|  | £ | £ |
| Direct material cost per dozen | 5·80 | 2 |
| Direct labour cost per dozen | 2 | 4 |
| Selling price per dozen | 15 | 20 |

The company's standard overhead per week is £2,400 of which £1,600 is
variable and £800 fixed. Its overhead is absorbed by a standard rate per direct
labour hour.

*Required:*

(*a*) Calculate the total cost per dozen of each contract
(*b*) Calculate the percentage profit to sales for each contract
(*c*) State which contract you recommend the company should undertake. Give
reasons with supporting figures for your decision (assume there are no
special policy reasons which favour one contract or the other).    (ICMA)

11. *Marginal costing applicable to an agricultural problem*

On a farm of 200 acres, the farmer plans to sow 100 acres of barley, 20 acres
of kale, and to use 80 acres on which to graze milk cattle. For the barley, seed
will cost £6 per acre and fertilizers, £10 per acre. It is expected that the yield
will be 1·5 tonnes per acre, which will be sold at £60 per tonne.

The kale will cost £5 per acre for seed and £9 per acre for fertilizers. The
kale produced will be fed to the cattle.

On the 80 acres, 40 milking cows will be kept, and in addition to the kale,
other feeding stuffs will cost £2,000 in all for the year. Each cow should produce
one calf which will be sold at £40, together with an annual milk yield sold at
£300. Cows will 'depreciate' at the rate of £40 per annum per cow.

Other farm costs (which are unlikely to change, however the farm is worked)
are, per annum:

|  | £ |
|---|---|
| Farmworkers' wages | 5,000 |
| Rent, rates, etc. | 3,000 |
| General charges | 6,000 |

A suggestion is made that kale should be purchased instead of grown. If this is done it is estimated that kale will cost £30 per cow per annum.
*Required:*
Prepare figures to indicate to the farmer whether the kale should be purchased or grown. If the kale is purchased, show how the 20 acres could be used to the best advantage.                                                                 (ICMA)

12. *The possible acceptance of a special contract*
John James and his son have carried on business as haulage contractors for many years. The business specialises in the carrying of packages of all sizes, and charges are made on an area/weight basis.

A large manufacturing company has offered to place a contract with the business, the conditions of which are that in return for a truck being available each morning the manufacturing company will pay the business an annual sum of £1,000 plus £0·20 for each mile run. This charge will apply irrespective of the load and in the event of a daily load not being sufficient to fill a truck, the company will have no objection to the business using this surplus space for its own needs. It is estimated that 25,000 miles per annum will be the distance covered on the company's work.

Mr James is not certain about accepting the contract because he feels that it may not be profitable, particularly as the trade association to which he belongs issues quarterly figures of average cost per mile for businesses similar to his own, and these are always about £0·24 per mile on the basis of 25,000 miles annually.

In order to provide the service which the company desires another vehicle of the AB type will have to be purchased. This will cost £6,000 and it is the practice of the business to trade in this type of vehicle after 90,000 miles or three years whichever comes first, as by doing so an allowance of 25% on cost is obtained. On average each vehicle in Mr James' fleet covers 30,000 miles annually.

The fleet, nine AB type vehicles in all, is garaged in a large building which has an annual charge of £900 for rent and rates. There is sufficient room to garage one more vehicle. The garage staff consist of two mechanics and one labourer, whose weekly wages are £30 and £20 for a mechanic and labourer respectively. It is not anticipated that any additional help will be required here if the additional work is taken on but an allowance of 10% on the basic wages will have to be made to cover overtime. The administrative work is done by a clerk/book-keeper and an assistant whose combined wages come to £1,800 annually — these can be taken as fixed irrespective of the amount of work done.

Other expenses, such as stationery, repair material, etc., come to £2,700 per annum and over the past few years these costs have tended to move directly in relation to the number of vehicles in use. The only other assistance in the garage is provided by the two James', but as they are partners they do not take a salary but draw on their share of the profits for remuneration. If they were to employ people to do their work it is estimated that it would cost £3,600 per annum.

All other costs relate specifically to the vehicles and as far as you can ascertain they are as follows:

(a) A charge of £0·005 per mile for each tyre. All vehicles are six wheeled.

(b) Road fund licences are £150 per annum for each vehicle, and a 'blanket' insurance cover is operated which costs £180 per annum for the first vehicle and £90 for each subsequent vehicle with an upper limit of twelve vehicles.

(c) Fuel costs £0·40 per gallon but the only figures which are available on consumption are the following which have been recently collected and relate only to one vehicle. Distance will tend to vary from journey to journey depending on the number of calls which have to be made during the journey.

| Vehicle No. | Month | Miles run | Gallons used |
|---|---|---|---|
| XSG 8 | February | 2,000 | 102 |
| | March | 2,200 | 103 |
| | April | 2,300 | 110 |
| | May | 2,500 | 135 |

(d) The vehicle drivers are paid at a rate of £0·70 per hour and they work a basic week of 40 hours.

*Required:*

From the above information, prepare a statement which will indicate the profitability or otherwise of the contract and which will also give Mr James a cost figure which he can compare against the average figure issued by the trade association. This cost figure should be calculated both on the costs as they are at present and as they will be if the contract is accepted. Your statement should be accompanied by a report commenting on the results disclosed.                    (ACA)

FURTHER READING

Dixon, Stanley. *The Case for Marginal Costing.* The General Educational Trust of the Institure of Chartered Accountants in England and Wales, 1966.

Ellmer, Robert E. *Marginal Cost and Variance Analysis in Management Accounting.* Macmillan, 1969. Chapter 8.

*A Report on Marginal Costing.* Institute of Cost and Works Accountants, 1961.

# 20 Decision-making Techniques

## OBJECTIVE OF THE CHAPTER

A closer look at the decision-making context relevant costs in the decision-making situation and the techniques available to assist the decision-maker in reaching a correct decision.

## OUTLINE OF THE CHAPTER

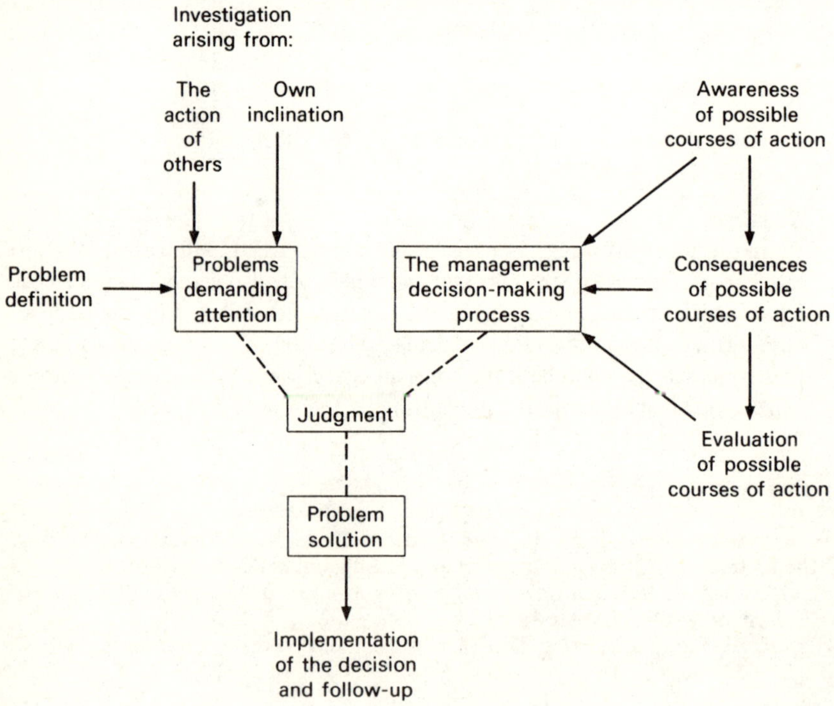

FIGURE 20.1.

Managers must make decisions and implement them in the interests of the business. The use of company resources to achieve the company objectives sets the context for decision-making, particularly when it is recognised that there are limits on the resources available to the business. These were mentioned in the previous chapter as key factors. Even in the successful business mistakes will be made arising from:

1. Inadequate information on which to make the decision
2. Misunderstanding the problem
3. Not having the time to weight up alternative opportunities
4. Inadequate resources
5. Inadequate management experience and training.

It is realistic to recognise these difficulties and try to minimise their effect on the quality of management. Some managers manage their companies by hunch, and their business instinct and experience is such that they are successful. Most managers lack this flair and need decision-making techniques to ensure their judgements have a reasonable probability of being in the interests of the business. To the extent that problems can be defined in quantitative and financial terms, the management account-ant can assist the manager with the difficult task of solving the many problems that must be resolved.

Decision-making was introduced in the previous chapter, but the wider issues were excluded for more detailed treatment in the sections to follow. These issues may be regarded as the decision-making process which involves:

1. Defining the context in which a decision must be made
2. Obtaining relevant information regarding the problem as a basis for decision-making
3. Exploring the possibilities available to the decision-maker
4. Making the decision
5. Implementing the decision
6. Follow-up action on the implemented decision.

Problems vary in their importance and it should be realised that if managerial time is expended to an unnecessary degree on minor matters, there is less time available for the resolution of significant problems. The experienced manager can assess the relative importance of problems to be resolved and allocate his time accordingly. Generally, long-term decisions require more careful consideration than short-term decisions because if mistakes are made with the latter, the consequences may not be so far-reaching for the business and the course may be changed without involving the company in significant loss.

## 20.1 DEFINING THE CONTEXT IN WHICH A DECISION MUST BE MADE

Before the decision procedure is used to attempt to find a solution to a problem, care should be taken to ensure that the problem has been correctly defined. The problem superfically indicated may be different when subjected to detailed investi-gation.

It is assumed that the problem is faced by a manager with the responsibility to take any action necessary. If the investigation of the problem reveals a greater complexity than at first anticipated, the solution to the problem may need enforcement by management at a higher level.

Of particular importance is the identification of objectives to be achieved and key factors affecting the problem. There may be practical limitations of time and cost but if a similar problem has been faced previously, advantage may be taken of that experience.

## 20.2  RELEVANT INFORMATION AS A BASIS FOR DECISION-MAKING

Of value to the decision-maker is the quantification of a problem and the statement in financial terms of relevant data to serve as the basis for decision-making. Estimated amounts and calculations should be realistic. The estimates used concern the future and the complexity of business inevitably means that precision is not attainable. To present the figures calculated as precise assessments is, therefore, misleading and managers should be informed of the approximations incorporated in the information presented to them.

Relevant information is that which bears upon, or is useful to, the action it is designed to facilitate or the result it is desired to produce. Relevance in terms of the best estimate that can be given involves the recognition of future costs and revenue for the possible alternatives, and incremental effect used as the criterion for the choice of the figures in the computation. The application of this criterion suggests that:

1. Expenditure which has taken place in the past and which will not be affected by a particular decision under consideration can be ignored. Such items are sometimes described as *sunk* costs.
2. If a cost will be incurred if a particular course of action is taken but avoided if the action is not taken, that cost is incremental. In the previous chapter, marginal cost was described in this context but the incremental cost may include fixed costs. Specific fixed costs appropriate to the decision-making situation may also be incremental if, as a result of not taking the action contemplated, they can be avoided. *Incremental* costs are sometimes described as *differential* costs.
3. If inputs in the form of resources available to the business could be put to alternative use if not used for the solution of the problem under consideration, the contribution lost to the profits of the business from not putting the resources to the alternative use is a relevant cost for the decision-making computation. Such an amount is an '*opportunity* cost' and if there are a number of alternative uses the *opportunity* cost is the value to the business of the next best use of the resources to the one being considered in the possible solution to the problem.

    The example, often quoted, to illustrate an opportunity cost is the possible use of a freehold building as offices as compared with its possible rental at, say, £5,000 per year. In the decision-making situation, where the building is being considered for use as offices, the relavant costs computation should include the £5,000 per year item which would be lost if the property is not rented.

Costs external to the accounting system, i.e., not payments and therefore not identified as outlays of the business, are sometimes referred to as *imputed* costs. An often quoted example is interest which should be considered in investment decisions where the capital outlay is different for alternative projects under consideration.

4. Common costs to alternative decisions may be ignored because they will not affect the financial result in any way.

From the above, it may be noted that all costs recorded in the accounting records are not required and even if they are relevant by type, they may need modification because: (*a*) such items are apportioned amounts only and do not reflect the incremental effect relevant to the problem for decision; or (*b*) such items are historical costs and it is the future cost level that is required. The historical costs may be a valuable guide in the estimation process when recognition is given to future changes affecting such costs.

## 20.3  EXAMPLES OF RELEVANT COSTS IN DECISION-MAKING

*Example 1*

Research cost on a new product has reached £20,000—£5,000 in excess of the original estimate. A further £10,000 is needed to complete the project and then net cash flow for the manufacture and sale of the product is expected to be £25,000. Without the £10,000 expenditure no return will be possible on the research. In deciding whether to continue the research, the relevant cost relative to net cash flow is the additional £10,000 required.

*Example 2*

A product has been discontinued and components for this product are now surplus to requirements. It is possible to sell these components for £2,000 but they cost £10,000 to make. An alternative is to modify the components at a cost of £3,000 and sell them for £6,000. The relevant costs regarding the possibility of modification are the £2,000 present sale value and the modification cost of £3,000.

*Example 3*

An asset is surplus to current requirements and the management is considering whether to sell it or use it in the manufacture of a new product in the future in place of the purchase of a new machine for that purpose. The relevant cost for its potential use for the manufacture of the new product is the difference in the disposal value now and its estimated disposal value at the end of the anticipated period of use. By using the machine rather than selling it, the present disposal value of the machine is an opportunity cost of that action.

*Example 4*

A special contract is under consideration that would use a material already in stock that cost £10,000, but if the contract is not obtained the material would have no further use and would be sold for its maximum value on disposal: £1,000. In considering whether to accept this special contract, the relevant cost of the material is £1,000.

### Example 5

The company is considering taking on additional work for a department, the work having a marginal cost of £5,000. Fixed costs are allotted to work done on the basis of direct labour hours and the allotment in this case will be £3,200. Included in the fixed costs is the foreman who will work overtime at a cost of £150 if the additional work is undertaken. The relevant costs applicable to the additional work decision are the incremental figures of £5,000 marginal cost and £150 overtime cost.

## 20.4  THE POSSIBILITIES AVAILABLE TO THE DECISION-MAKER

Initial reactions to a problem should not restrict the manager's search for other possible solutions providing the decision-maker is not confused in the process. The aim should be to identify significant possible alternatives, discarding the unlikely possibilities as soon as possible. The main alternatives can be subjected to detailed investigation in the context of the constraints imposed by the problem.

Assumptions are usually involved in these considerations, and interpretation of the possibilities available to the decision-maker will be eased if these assumptions can be expressed in quantitative and financial terms. The application of mathematical techniques to assist the manager can only be of value given valid assumptions correctly expressed.

## 20.5  MAKING THE DECISION

At the decision stage in the decision-making process all factors whether quantifiable or not must be taken into consideration. The calculations made by the management accountant are not a substitute for the judgement to be exercised by the manager who must accept the responsibility for the decision made.

Having obtained the relevant information available concerning alternative possibilities open to the decision-maker, the manager may decide:

1. To defer action. Possibly, the alternatives are so finely balanced that the manager wants further evidence to indicate the correct course of action to take, knowing that in the near future events will resolve key issues with a certainty not possible of assessment at the present time.
2. To request additional information. This action is only possible if the time is available to get this information and the cost of its provision is acceptable.
3. To make a temporary decision which can be applicable to provide more time to reach a final decision.
4. To make the final decision and take action accordingly.

The first three possibilities could be a manifestation of a manager's wish to procrastinate. They could reveal a weakness in his ability to reach a decision and act upon it without undue delay but the outcome may be sound given the circumstances of the case.

## 20.6 IMPLEMENTING THE DECISION

When a decision is made to take action all aspects of the decision must be communicated in terms which will be understood to those delegated to carry out the task.

Standards for assessment should be established, and if the decision is to be carried out in stages, the length of time each stage will take to complete and its profit impact for each stage should be indicated.

## 20.7 FOLLOW-UP ACTION ON THE IMPLEMENTED DECISION

The decision-making process operates within the managerial control cycle. This cycle is not complete until the results of the action taken are compared with the standards laid down for assessment; and, where the actual performance is below expectations, appropriate managerial action taken.

The standards laid down for assessment will invariably be derived from the factors and estimates forming the basis of the decision. The feedback of information from the implementation phase can be useful in refining the quality of the inputs to the decision-making process.

## 20.8 THE OPERATIONAL RESEARCH APPROACH TO DECISION-MAKING

The aspects of the decision-making process so far described in this chapter have tended to be combined in a scientific systematic approach known as operational research (OR). The operational researcher attempts a broad view of a problem recognising the complexity of most business situations and the need to apply scientific methods to find an optimum solution. Essential input to the model tested by the operational researcher to find the optimum solution is accounting data, but it is not the only data used. The comprehensive approach implied here requires the use of all relevant data from whatever source.

The increasing use of sophisticated electronic data-processing equipment has enabled the business to develop to an increasing extent the use of mathematical techniques to assist the decision-maker. Operational research emphasises problems involving such analysis. Statistics may come to the aid of the researcher because the volume of information to be studied may be too much to handle. Sampling may be adopted to reduce that volume.

A feature of the application of operational research is that there is rarely one correct solution. The conclusion of the study is hopefully the best answer to the problem. The investigation of a problem and its solution by the application of the operational research technique is illustrated in Figure 20.2.

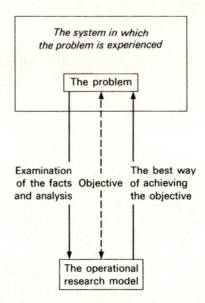

FIGURE 20.2. The operational research approach to the solution of a problem

## 20.9 THE OPERATIONAL RESEARCH MODEL

The 'model' is fundamental to operational research. A model is a representation of the problem to be solved which enables the investigator to test his theories and produce the best solution to the problem. Physical models may be used, e.g., the model of an aircraft in a wind tunnel, but financial control problems are usually in the form of a mathematical model.

The construction of the mathematical model of the actual situation must be checked for the accuracy of its representation before it may be manipulated to estimate what will happen in changed situations to derive the optimum solution to the problem. It is necessary to use a model because the use of the actual system would be costly and inconvenient. If incorrect changes were made in the actual system chaos might result.

The adequacy and reliability of the model largely determines the likelihood of the operational research approach being successful. The management accountant should be in a position to make a valuable contribution to the validity of the model where costs and profit are involved. Relevance is the key attribute of the data used, and the training of the accountant should ensure that realistic inputs are identified and applied, and outputs interpreted in the interests of the business.

## 20.10 OPERATIONAL RESEARCH TECHNIQUES

It is outside the scope of this book to describe the many techniques available in detail but it is advisable to be generally familiar with the principal methods used, and these are described below. For further information, the reader is referred to the recommended reading at the end of this chapter and selected examples in the next chapter.

Possible applications of operational research techniques include the following:

1. Marketing organisation:

   (*a*) Sales forecasting
   (*b*) Price/volume relationships
   (*c*) Distribution methods
   (*d*) Advertising evaluation
   (*e*) Product mix relationships
   (*f*) Stock levels.

2. Production organisation:

   (*a*) Production forecasting
   (*b*) Profitability of production programmes
   (*c*) Maintenance routines for machinery and plant
   (*d*) Machine loading
   (*e*) Process relationships, e.g., material mix
   (*f*) Stock levels

3. Administrative organisation:

   (*a*) Overall profitability
   (*b*) Financial forecasting
   (*c*) Accounting method, e.g., overhead apportionment.

The techniques that may be used include the following:

(*a*) *Linear programming*
   This technique is applicable where the factors in the problem are in linear relationships to each other, e.g., the allocation of productive capacity to secure maximum profit where different products may be produced. Two methods are available for linear problems: (i) the transporation method — used for routing problems; (ii) the simplex method — usually used where the problem is not of the transportation type.
(*b*) *Dynamic programming*
   This technique is applicable where the problem can be considered in stages;

the solution of one stage governing the problem at the next stage,* e.g., stock replenishment.

(c) *Simulation*

This technique is applicable where an optimum solution is required to a business problem and linear programming and dynamic programming are not used because of the large number of variables involved, e.g., the ascertainment of the profitability of a business. The simulation takes the trial and error form of considering the likely results of possible actions considered.

(d) *Queuing and congestion*

This technique is applicable to problems of congestion, e.g., how to provide a service at minimum cost where requirements are at a variable rate and the service time may also be variable. A telephone exchange illustrates this point. Queuing theory is based on the theory of probability.

## 20.11 PROBABILITY THEORY AND THE DECISION-MAKER

Probabilities are inherent in the decision-making situation since uncertainty arises whenever the attempt is made to forecast the future course of business events. The assignment of reliable probabilities to business data governs their value to the decision-maker. The assignment ranges from 1 representing certainty to 0 representing the impossibility of events. If the various possible events are listed, although none can occur at the same time, the probabilities of these events will add to one. Risk and uncertainty in capital expenditure forecasting, mentioned in Chapter 12, indicates the use of probability distribution to improve the objectivity of the forecasts.

The manager's task is to forecast the probabilities regarding the input data to the decision model. It is more reasonable for managers to be asked for this data

* Problems considered in stages where decisions are made in sequence may be presented in the form of a decision tree which diagramatically shows each decision stage as a branch leading to other consequences of the decision made:

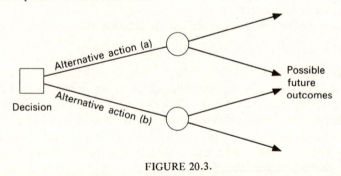

FIGURE 20.3.

Expected values of the possible outcomes, given the particular cost and probability estimates, can assist the decision-maker in choosing the best outcome.

than single figures which imply a preciseness not warranted in the decision-making situation.

## 20.12  BEHAVIOURAL FACTORS IN DECISION-MAKING

It is evident that the decision-making process is based on the assumptions, techniques and methods of accounting and economics, and the extent to which these two disciplines use mathematics and statistics. The implementation of the decision is affected by behavioural factors which may be so significant that the assumptions previously adopted in the decision model may need amendment. The problem is well reported by a committee of the American Accounting Association in the following terms:

> Implementation is frequently a behavioural problem. Economic analysis is not wrong or undesirable; it is simply incomplete. In his role as a supplier of information, the accountant must be concerned with both the economic decision models and their implementation as an entire package. The trouble at this point is that our knowledge of the behavioural effects is too fragmented. The information produced by decision models and accounting systems is supposed to exert influence or have the potential for exerting influence on the designated actions. Little systematic evidence is available concerning the complex effects of decision models and accounting information on user behaviour. Instead, the relationship is either overlooked or it is described by over-simplified assertions. Too often, the assertions or generalisations seem to be valid in one organisation but not in another, usually because they are not based on any rigorously compiled evidence that permits prediction rather than explanation.*

## 20.13  THE MANAGEMENT ACCOUNTANT'S CONTRIBUTION TO DECISION-MAKING

The management accountant provides information to guide the manager to a correct decision. His work usually confines the area in which judgement must be exercised. The position of the accountant varies considerably in each business but, however influential his position, unless he has line responsibility, he should refrain from making the decision. It is true that the information presented to the manager may clearly point the direction that should be taken by the business, and the particular decision to be made by the manager, but the key point is the responsibility of the decision-maker for actual performance in accordance with the decision made.

## 20.14  A CONCLUDING COMMENT

The processing of the facts and figures of a problem in order to be able to make deductions and inferences from them is the basic feature of the techniques

---

* 'American Accounting Association report of Committee on Managerial Decision Models', *Accounting Review Supplement*, 1969, p. 46.

described in this chapter. It is obvious that there is a very close relationship between statistics, operational research and management accounting.

It is becoming increasingly important for the management accountant to be familiar with other disciplines that have a bearing on the management of the business. In this way, if these disciplines are practised by other members of the management team, misunderstandings can be kept to the minimum and all functional executives can more effectively help each other. There is the view that accountants are losing part of their traditional role in the decision-making process because of their reluctance to take advantage of related techniques. To the extent that this is true, the management accountant can reverse the tendency by the application of the objectiveness, understanding and intimate financial knowledge of the business that he is supposed to possess.


## FOR FURTHER STUDY

QUESTIONS

1. *Poor decision-making*
   The decisions of management may not be in the interests of the business for a number of reasons.
   *Required:*
   Give these reasons and steps that may be taken to reduce the number of decision errors made.

2. *Defining the problem*
   'The most common source of mistakes in management decisions is the emphasis on finding the right answer rather than the right question'.
   *Required:*
   Comment on the above quotation.

3. *Alternative solutions available to the decision-maker*
   An essential feature of the decision-making process is awareness of the possible alternatives that should be considered before a decision is made.
   *Required:*
   How can these alternative solutions be developed and what qualifications should be made regarding their potential use?

4. *Relevance*
   'What the manager needs from the decision and control accountant is the best estimate that time and money allow him to give of the relevant figures. Where there is any conflict, it is relevance which matters and relevance today means relevance to decision and control in complex and changing organisations.'
   (D. C. Hague, 'The future of the management accountant', *Management Accounting*, August, 1966, p. 303)
   *Required:*
   What do you understand by the term 'relevance' and its significance in the context of this quotation?

5. *Relevant decision-making costs*

'Decision-making costs can be found from traditional accounting records only by re-classifications, deletions, additions, recombinations of elements and re-pricing of input factors in the process of shaping the cost conjectures to fit the concept of cost relevant for the management planning choice.'

(Joel Dean, *Managerial Economics*, Prentice-Hall, Englewood Cliffs, New Jersey, 1964, p. 17)

*Required:*

Explain and comment on this statement.

6. *Costs applicable to types of decisions*

Using whatever classifications of cost are required, state and justify the cost aggregations appropriate to the following decisions:

(*a*) Whether to make or buy in the case of an established firm

(*b*) Whether to add a new line requiring additional capital expenditure

(*c*) Whether to further process products that can be sold in their present state.

7. *Relationship of statistics to management accounting*

To what extent is the subject of statistics relevant to the study of management accounting?

8. *Trends in the type of decision-making information provided*

The type of information provided as a basis for solving the more difficult problems faced by management has changed significantly over the last twenty years.

*Required:*

Account for this trend and what effect should these developments have on accountants and the training of future accountants?

9. *Operational research*

One definition of operational research is: 'A scientific method of providing executive departments with a quantitative basis for decisions regarding the operations under their control.'

*Required:*

What does this definition mean and what reletionship does operational research have with the associated disciplines of mathematics and statistics?

10. *The place of models in decision-making*

An essential characteristic of operational research is the use of the model to find the optimum solution to a business problem.

*Required:*

What is a model in the context of the above statement? What types of models are available to the operational researcher and what contribution do they make to the successful application of operational research?

11. *TWI approach to problem solving*

The general manager's secretary was reviewing the contents of old files with a view to their disposal. She came across a card issued on a course attended by her employer when he was a supervisor with the company twenty-five years ago. The course was the Training Within Industry (TWI) Programme for Supervisors with its origin in American and adapted by the Ministry of Labour to British conditions. The secretary approached her employer, before throwing the card away, and he decided after reading the card again that he would draft some notes on applying the TWI approach to decision-making for his staff. The card is reproduced below.

---

### HOW TO HANDLE A PROBLEM
#### DETERMINE OBJECTIVE

*Step 1 – Get the facts*

Review the record
Find out what rules and customs apply
Talk with individuals concerned
Get opinions and feelings

Be sure you have the whole story and the right objective.

*Step 2 – Weigh and decide*

Fit the facts together
Consider their bearing on each other
What possible actions are there?
Check practices and policies
Consider the effect on the individual-group-production
Remember your objective

Don't jump to conclusions.

*Step 3 – Take action*

Are you going to take the action yourself?
Do you need help in taking your action?
Should you inform your supervisor of your action?
Watch the timing of your action

Don't pass the buck.

*Step 4 – Check results*

How soon will you follow up?
How often will you need to check?
Watch for changes in output, attitudes and relationships

Did your action achieve your objective?

---

*Required:*
The general manager approached you to assist him in drafting the required notes. What points would you draw to the attention of the general manager?

12. *Operational researcher's role in the business*
The new managing director, Tom Tinker of Arts and Crafts Ltd, was introduced to the company to restore the profitability of the business which had suffered in recent years. Tom Tinker's previous employer was a successful company employing the latest techniques to assist its managers, and when he arrived at

Arts and Crafts Ltd he was disturbed to find that these techniques were not used.

Discussion with other managers and the chief accountant prompted the managing director to say that he identified the weakness in the company as poor decision-making owing to the lack of appreciation of the complexity of most decisions. He also considered the need for information to be more comprehensive in its application to the business problems as an issue to be resolved.

To resolve this issue he had decided to appoint a personal assistant to himself. This assistant would have direct responsibility for the supply of relevant information for key decisions, including financial detail and the application of modern techniques as appropriate. He had in mind someone with a mathematical training and business experience in the application of mathematical models and decision theory.

The chief accountant was upset by this proposal. He put forward the argument that in the final analysis all information must be reflected in financial terms, as far as the future probability of the business was concerned, and the functional head of this service was himself. He mentioned that the proposed appointment would be a challenge to his status and authority in the company.
*Required:*
(*a*) What is your view regarding the circumstances of the case?
(*b*) As managing director, what action would you take?

FURTHER READING

Arnold, John. *Pricing and Output Decisions*. Haymarket, 1973. Chapters 1—3 and 10.
Carsberg, B. V. *Introduction to Mathematical Programming for Accountants*. Allen & Unwin, 1969. Chapters 1 and 2.
Eddison, R. T., Pennycuick, K. and Rivett, B. H. P., *Operational Research in Management*. English Universities Press, 1962.

# 21 Decision-making Problems

## OBJECTIVE OF THE CHAPTER

To apply the decision-making techniques outlined in the previous chapter and develop the solution of business problems introduced by the application of marginal costing described in Chapter 19.

## OUTLINE OF THE CHAPTER

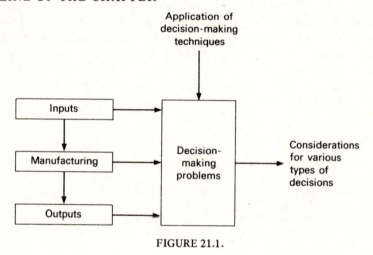

FIGURE 21.1.

For the purpose of this chapter, business decision-making problems are classified as follows:

1. Location problems, e.g., where to site the factory
2. Facilities problems, e.g., additional investment, plant replacement, purchase or lease decisions and the temporary closure of part of the business
3. Manufacturing problems, e.g., make or buy decisions (without investment), manufacturing method choice, further processing (without additional investment) and stock level decisions
4. Marketing problems, e.g., fixing selling prices and the selection of sales outlets
5. Marketing/manufacturing problems, e.g., sales and production effort preferences.

## 21.1 CONSIDERATIONS FOR VARIOUS TYPES OF DECISIONS

General considerations to be borne in mind in the decision-making process have been described in the previous chapter; in particular, the considered action should be related to company objectives, policies and long-term requirements. In this section, specific factors are noted as follows:

*Siting the factory*
1. Rent and security of tenure
2. Cost of land and buildings
3. Construction of buildings and installations, including the connexion to the necessary services
4. Location of inputs: labour and materials availability
5. Type of product and manufacturing process
6. Anticipated costs of operation and profitability
7. Distribution facilities and access to markets
8. Taxation factors.

If the possible siting of the factory is abroad, the following additional considerations are relevant:

(*a*) Local laws
(*b*) Stability of the political regime
(*c*) Restrictions on the use of parent company labour
(*d*) Currency transfer regulations
(*e*) Local taxation
(*f*) Interrelationship and trends of currencies.

*Additional investment*
1. Capital availability and its cost
2. Projected cash flows
3. Taxation
4. Time value of money
5. Return on investment
6. Risk
7. Inflation
8. Likely technological developments
9. Law and bylaws
10. Effect on existing manpower.

*Plant replacement*
1. Timing considerations regarding the asset
2. State of the asset to be replaced
3. Cost saving when production the same for the new asset
4. The ability to sell the additional output where production is greater for the new asset than the existing asset
5. Capital availability and its cost

  6. Projected cash flows
  7. Taxation
  8. Time value of money
  9. Return on investment
10. Risk
11. Inflation
12. Likely technological developments
13. Ability to dispose of the existing plant and its disposal value
14. Labour relations
15. Law and bylaws
16. Level of repair costs, increasing as the present plant life increases if plant not replaced
17. Whether to buy or lease the replacement plant
18. Manning levels and labour mobility.

*Purchase or lease of assets*
1. Capital availability and its cost
2. Projected cash flows
3. Taxation
4. Time value of money
5. Terms of the lease including references to possible restrictions of use
6. Maintenance reliability
7. Effect on profitability.

*Temporary closure of part of the business*
1. Retention of specialised labour compared with its loss
2. Labour relations
3. Cost of storage and maintenance of equipment
4. Start-up cost when the equipment is to be re-used
5. Loss in value of the plant and machinery
6. Effect on profitability
7. Cost of labour redundancies.

*Make or buy decisions (without investment)*
  1. Possible use of released capacity and facilities
  2. Whether there is an inability to expand capacity to meet other requirements
  3. Quality of goods supplied by the supplier
  4. The reasonable certainty of the supplier meeting delivery dates
  5. Whether more than one supplier is available to reduce the risk of buying
  6. Labour relations
  7. Knowledge of the processes necessary to make the product
  8. Incremental cost of making and purchasing
  9. Cost of labour redundancies
10. Availability of labour.

*Manufacturing method choice*
1. Key (or limiting) factor(s)

2. Labour relations
3. Capital availability and its cost and other investment factors, as above, where mechanisation to be compared with labour-intensive methods
4. Effect on profitability
5. Cost of labour redundancies
6. Availability of labour.

*Further processing (without additional investment)*
1. Incremental revenue
2. Incremental cost
3. Ability to sell the further processed product.

*Stock levels*
1. Capital availability and its cost
2. Storage availability
3. Stockholding cost
4. Purchase ordering cost
5. Discount availability with volume purchasing
6. Out-of-stock possibilities and minimum stock requirements.

*Fixing selling prices*
1. Future cost of products made available for sale
2. Expected demand and the elasticity of that demand
3. Capacity availability and expected volumes of production
4. Customer reactions
5. Industry practice and price controls
6. Revenue—cost—profit relationships
7. Interaction of joint products
8. Competitors' reactions.

*Selection of sales outlets*
1. Type of product
2. Type of market
3. Industry practice
4. Competitors' reactions
5. Effect on profitability
6. Cost and methods of distribution.

*Sales and production effort preferences*
1. Key (or limiting) factors
2. Possible changes in key factors
3. Customer reactions
4. Interactions of joint products
5. Other selling activity and the contribution from those products which may be affected
6. Future possibilities of work available, more desirable for the business
7. Competitors' reactions

8. Difficulty of re-entering a market in the future if a market is to be eliminated as a matter of preference
9. Effect on employees.


## 21.2  POSSIBLE SOLUTIONS TO BUSINESS PROBLEMS

In the sections to follow, problems are considered that have not been covered in earlier chapters, and the decision-making techniques already described are applied in the context of the considerations noted above.


### 21.21  PLANT REPLACEMENT

**Problem***

The central technical services department of a large organisation is responsible for the purchase of certain specialist equipment which processes work for various departments and divisions in the organisation. These departments need the services of such equipment, from time to time, but their requirement is not sufficient to warrant the purchase of a machine specifically for the use of any one department. The total demand for equipment KZ 124 is such that it is worked to full capacity (4,000 hours) and frequently work is sub-contracted out at a cost of £5 per hour.

Until now the manager of central technical services has replaced KZ 124 every three years, because after three years there is a marked increase in the likelihood that the equipment will have serious breakdowns and require major repairs. Consequently its trade-in value decreases quite substantially from the third year onwards.

A suggestion has been made that the policy of replacing this equipment every three years is not the best one to adopt. Some executives in the firm suggest a new machine each year, while others argue for a two-year replacement period. Advise management as to the optimum replacement period for KZ 124.

A new machine of type KZ 124 currently costs £16,000 and during its first year of operating will give the equivalent of 4,000 processing hours for a direct operating cost of £10,000. At the end of the first year it has a trade-in value of £14,000. During the second year of operating it will give the equivalent of 3,900 processing hours for a direct operating cost of £10,500 and at the end of this period the trade-in value will be £13,000. In the third year, the effective processing hours will be 3,600, with direct operating costs of £12,000 and a trade-in value of £12,000.

The company's cost of capital is 10%. Ignore taxation.

**Comment**

To compare the alternative policies it is convenient to take a period of six years. The figures are taken as given and operating and sub-contracting costs treated in the cash flow statements as payments made at the end of each year. The DCF

---

*A problem taken from the ACA examination in Section 5, Management Accounting (December, 1971).

calculations based on discount factors for 10% from Table 1 (Appendix B) are as follows:

*Cash Flow Statements – Years 1 to 6*

*Alternative 1 – Replacement of Machine KZ 124 every year*

| Year | Cash outflow £ | Cash inflow £ | Net cash flow £ | 10% discount factors | Net present value of net cash flow £ |
|---|---|---|---|---|---|
| 0 | 16,000 | | 16,000 | – | 16,000 |
| 1 | 26,000 | 14,000 | 12,000 | ·909 | 10,908 |
| 2 | 26,000 | 14,000 | 12,000 | ·826 | 9,912 |
| 3 | 26,000 | 14,000 | 12,000 | ·751 | 9,012 |
| 4 | 26,000 | 14,000 | 12,000 | ·683 | 8,196 |
| 5 | 26,000 | 14,000 | 12,000 | ·621 | 7,452 |
| 6 | 10,000 | 14,000 | (4,000) | ·564 | (2,256) |
| | 156,000 | 84,000 | 72,000 | | 59,224 |

*Alternative 2 – Replacement of Machine KZ 124 every two years*

| Year | Cash outflow £ | Cash inflow £ | Net cash flow £ | 10% discount factors | Net present value of net cash flow £ |
|---|---|---|---|---|---|
| 0 | 16,000 | | 16,000 | – | 16,000 |
| 1 | 10,000 | | 10,000 | ·909 | 9,090 |
| 2 | 27,000 | 13,000 | 14,000 | ·826 | 11,564 |
| 3 | 10,000 | | 10,000 | ·751 | 7,510 |
| 4 | 27,000 | 13,000 | 14,000 | ·683 | 9,562 |
| 5 | 10,000 | | 10,000 | ·621 | 6,210 |
| 6 | 11,000 | 13,000 | (2,000) | ·564 | (1,128) |
| | 111,000 | 39,000 | 72,000 | | 58,808 |

*Alternative 3 – Replacement of Machine KZ 124 every three years*

| Year | Cash outflow £ | Cash inflow £ | Net cash flow £ | 10% discount factors | Net present value of net cash flow £ |
|---|---|---|---|---|---|
| 0 | 16,000 | | 16,000 | – | 16,000 |
| 1 | 10,000 | | 10,000 | ·909 | 9,090 |
| 2 | 11,000 | | 11,000 | ·826 | 9·086 |
| 3 | 30,000 | 12,000 | 18,000 | ·751 | 13,518 |
| 4 | 10,000 | | 10,000 | ·683 | 6,830 |
| 5 | 11,000 | | 11,000 | ·621 | 6,831 |
| 6 | 14,000 | 12,000 | 2,000 | ·564 | 1,128 |
| | 102,000 | 24,000 | 78,000 | | 62,483 |

On the basis of the above figures, alternative 2 gives the lowest net present value of net cash flow but allowance should be made for inflation and taxation factors.

The cash outflow figures include, where appropriate, the capital outlay, operating costs and sub-contracting costs. The sub-contracting costs for the second year are £500 (100 hours x £5) and for the third year, £2,000 (400 hours x £5).

Machines are normally replaced when operating costs exceed the expected costs of operating a replacement machine. The saving in costs should give a satisfactory return on the increased capital investment. If the capacity of the new machine is greater than the old machine and the additional production can be sold, the sales value of this production will be considered in the replacement decision as well as cost savings. Except as a tax consideration, the written-down book value of an existing asset is not relevant to a replacement decision since the value is a sunk cost.

## 21.22 CONTRACTION OF BUSINESS

**Problem**

The accounts for the first twelve months business of a new manufacturing company showed the following profit:

*Profit Statement — Year ended 31st December 19. .*

|  |  | Product A | Product B | Total |
|---|---|---|---|---|
|  |  | £ | £ | £ |
| Sales | (A) | 15,000 | 7,500 | 22,500 |
| Direct materials |  | 2,000 | 500 | 2,500 |
| Direct labour |  | 3,000 | 800 | 3,800 |
| Works overhead |  | 4,500 | 1,200 | 5,700 |
| Administration overhead |  | 3,800 | 1,000 | 4,800 |
| Selling and distribution overhead |  | 750 | 375 | 1,125 |
| Cost of sales | (B) | 14,050 | 3,875 | 17,925 |
| Profit | (A − B) | 950 | 3,625 | 4,575 |
| Sales in units |  | 15,000 | 7,500 | 22,500 |

It is estimated that the 15,000 units of Product A to be sold next year will be at the reduced sales value of £13,500. Product costs are expected to remain the same at the above volume but the management is considering whether to abandon the sale of Product A or close the business.

If action of this type is taken, costs may be affected as follows:

*Direct materials.* Stocks on hand and ordered amount to one year's needs. Those for Product A would have no disposal value and could not be used for other purposes. Stocks for Product B could be sold without loss of value.
*Direct labour.* Each product uses the same labour and no staff would be declared redundant unless the factory was closed.

*Works overhead.* Allotted to the products in proportion to direct labour costs. If Product A is discontinued, works overhead would be reduced by £800.
*Administration overhead.* Allotted to the products in proportion to works costs. If Product A is discontinued, there will be no change in administration costs.
*Selling and distribution overhead.* 4% of sales value plus £0·01 per unit sold.

## Comment

Continuing with the present production and sales next year the revised profit would be:

|  | £ | £ |
|---|---:|---:|
| Existing profit |  | 4,575 |
| Less reduction in sales value | 15,000 |  |
|  | 13,500 | 1,500 |
|  |  | 3,075 |
| Add saving in selling and distribution costs: 4% of £1,500 |  | 60 |
| Revised profit |  | 3,135 |

Discontinuing the production and sale of Product A, the revised loss would be:

|  | £ | £ |
|---|---:|---:|
| Profit as above |  | 3,135 |
| Add avoidable costs |  |  |
| Direct materials | 2,000 |  |
| Works overhead | 800 |  |
| Selling and distribution costs: |  |  |
| 4% of £13,500 | 540 |  |
| 15,000 x £0·01 | 150 | 3,490 |
|  |  | 6,625 |
| Less reduced sales | 13,500 |  |
| stock value | 2,000 | 15,500 |
| Revised loss |  | 8,875 |

The abandonment of Product A would worsen the company position considerably. If the revised profit of £3,135 is considered a reasonable return on company investment at the present time or better prospects are anticipated in the future, the company will accept the enforced reduction in sale prices of Product A. Alternative products may take the place of Product A in the future.

The break-even point is usually higher than the point where cost factors may show that a factory closure should be considered. This is owing to the fact that costs at the break-even point will include sunk costs which are not relevant to a business decision on the possible contraction of company activities.

## 21.23 MAKE OR BUY

**Problem**

The company makes component X for Product A in a department whose costs are:

|  | £ |
|---|---|
| Direct material | 6,000 |
| Direct labour | 4,000 |
| Departmental overhead | 5,000 |
|  | 15,000 |

The managing director has been approached by a company who could supply the components for £14,000 per annum. He wishes to ascertain the financial effect of purchasing these components rather than making them in the company's own department.

The following additional information is available:

(a) The labour released by this department can be profitably employed in other sections of the business.

(b) Included in the departmental overhead of £5,000 is £1,000 for rent of buildings which can be used as an extension to the store in place of accommodation rented at the present time for £2,000.

(c) Also included in the departmental overhead is £2,500 for depreciation on a machine which cost £7,500 two years ago and a three-year life was anticipated with no disposal value. The machine will be of no value to the company if the components are purchased and it is not expected that it will have a value in the second-hand machine market.

(d) The remaining expenses of the department would be avoided if the components were purchased.

**Comment**

The relevant costs are those avoided if a particular course of action is not taken. The avoidable annual cost of purchasing if the company continues to make its components is £14,000. The avoidable annual cost of making the components, if the company decides to purchase them is as follows:

|  | £ |  |
|---|---|---|
| Direct material | 6,000 |  |
| Direct labour | 4,000 |  |
| Store rental | 2,000 |  |
| Other expenses | 1,500 | (£5,000 − £1,000 − £2,500) |
|  | 13,500 |  |

On the facts given, it would pay the company to continue manufacture of the components since there is a gain from continuing production of £500 per year. In twelve months time the situation may be different when the departmental machine needs renewal.

## 21.24 MANUFACTURING METHOD CHOICE

**Problem***

A company manufacturing a single product produces accounts for Year 1 as follows:

|                    | £       |
|--------------------|---------|
| Direct materials   | 80,000  |
| Direct wages       | 40,000  |
| Variable overheads | 30,000  |
| Fixed overheads    | 30,000  |
| Profit             | 20,000  |
| Sales              | 200,000 |

It is anticipated that sales will increase by 25% for Year 2, fixed overheads remaining unchanged.

During March, Year 2, management is considering the Year 3 programme, in which year the sales manager anticipates sales of £300,000, the selling price of the product remaining unchanged.

Present methods can be continued, though the fixed expenses would increase to £40,000, and labour may be difficult to obtain.

Alternatively, a complete revision of the method of manufacture would reduce the cost of direct wages by 25% per unit of manufacture, but would increase variable overheads to 100% of direct wages, and would increase fixed overheads to £50,000 per annum.

**Comment**

Using the figures given to assist management in making a decision on the possible revision of the method of manufacture, the following comparative statement may be produced:

*Comparative Profit Statement – Year 3 (£000)*

|                       | Present method | | Revision of method | |
|-----------------------|------:|------:|------:|------:|
|                       | £ | £ | £ | £ |
| Sales                 |   | 300 |   | 300 |
| Less marginal cost    |   |   |   |   |
| Direct materials      | 120 |   | 120 |   |
| Direct wages          | 60 |   | 45 |   |
| Variable overheads    | 45 | 225 | 45 | 210 |
| Contribution          |   | 75 |   | 90 |
| Less fixed overheads  |   | 40 |   | 50 |
| Profit                |   | 35 |   | 40 |

Under the present method, marginal costs for Year 1 are increased by 25% for Year 2 and a further 20% for Year 3. The revision of method figures are likely to be more realistic because the £60,000 for direct wages under the present method

---

*A problem taken from the ICMA examination in Part IV Advanced Cost and Management Accountancy (June, 1966).

assumes the availability of labour which is stated to be a problem. If in fact labour is difficult to obtain, a reduction of 25% on the labour required to produce units for sale to the value of £300,000 is significant. Profit is also increased and providing the return on investment is satisfactory, the adoption of the revised method of manufacture is a good proposition.

## 21.25 FURTHER PROCESSING

### Problem*

Chemical Separators Ltd produce four products: Maz, Mez, Miz and Moz, by subjecting input chemical material (known as Krudex) to an analytical process. The output proportions are Maz 40%, Mez 30%, Miz 20% and Moz 10%.

The company has capacity to process 30,000 litres of chemicals per four-week period.

An output of 20,000 litres per four-week period represents the sales demand at prevailing prices:

Maz: £3 per litre
Mez: £3·50 per litre
Miz: £4 per litre
Moz: £6 per litre

and requires an input of 20,000 litres of Krudex which costs £1·50 per litre. The labour cost of processing 20,000 litres is £10,000. The company's fixed overhead at 50% to 100% of capacity working is £10,000 per four-week period. Variable overhead has been found to be closely related to direct wages and an absorption rate of 50% thereof is applied.

The company is considering whether to subject any or all of the four products to further processing in order to produce more refined products which would be known as Supermaz, Supermez, Supermiz and Supermoz, and which would command higher prices:

Supermaz: £3·50 per litre
Supermez: £3·80 per litre
Supermiz: £6 per litre
Supermoz: £8 per litre.

Sales demands for the super products are not expected to exceed those for the products they would replace. For technical reasons it is not possible to produce both the original and the refined version of any of the four products during a four-week period, though one or more of the products can be produced in the refined version and the others in the original version.

Additional material and labour costs for the more refined process have been

*A problem taken from the ACA examination in Section IV, Advanced Costing (December, 1972).

estimated as follows:

|  | Supermaz | Supermez | Supermiz | Supermoz |
|---|---|---|---|---|
|  | £ | £ | £ | £ |
| Activating ingredients (of no significant weight or volume) | 2,000 | 3,000 | 2,000 | 1,500 |
| Direct wages | 1,000 | 3,000 | 1,000 | 1,000 |

## Comment

As a basis for the decision as to whether to undertake additional processing, the incremental revenue and incremental costs to give incremental profit or loss for the four-week period are as follows:

| | Further processing | | | | | | | |
|---|---|---|---|---|---|---|---|---|
| | Maz to produce Supermaz | | Mez to produce Supermez | | Miz to produce Supermiz | | Moz to produce Supermoz | |
| | £ | £ | £ | £ | £ | £ | £ | £ |
| Incremental revenue | | 4,000 | | 1,800 | | 8,000 | | 4,000 |
| Incremental costs: | | | | | | | | |
| Additional material cost | 2,000 | | 3,000 | | 2,000 | | 1,500 | |
| Additional labour cost | 1,000 | | 3,000 | | 1,000 | | 1,000 | |
| Additional variable overhead | 500 | 3,500 | 1,500 | 7,500 | 500 | 3,500 | 500 | 3,000 |
| Incremantal profit/(loss) | | 500 | | (5,700) | | 4,500 | | 1,000 |

The incremental revenue has been calculated as follows:

| Product | % | Output for sale litres | Increase in selling price per litre | Sales revenue |
|---|---|---|---|---|
| | | | £ | £ |
| Supermaz | 40 | 8,000 | 0·50 | 4,000 |
| Supermez | 30 | 6,000 | 0·30 | 1,800 |
| Supermiz | 20 | 4,000 | 2·00 | 8,000 |
| Supermoz | 10 | 2,000 | 2·00 | 4,000 |
| | 100 | 20,000 | | 17,800 |

Profit for the four-week period without further processing would be:

|  |  | £ |
|---|---|---|
| Sales |  |  |
| Maz (8,000 x £3) | 24,000 |  |
| Mez (6,000 x £3·50) | 21,000 |  |
| Miz (4,000 x £4) | 16,000 |  |
| Moz (2,000 x £6) | 12,000 |  |
|  | 73,000 |  |

|  | £ |  |
|---|---|---|
| Less cost of sales |  |  |
| Materials | 30,000 |  |
| Labour | 10,000 |  |
| Variable overheads | 5,000 |  |
| Fixed overheads | 10,000 | 55,000 |
| Profit |  | 18,000 |

Increased profit for the four-week period would result from further processing Maz, Miz, and Moz to give a total profit of £24,000:

|  | £ |
|---|---|
| Profit without further processing | 18,000 |
| Add incremental profit from the further processing and sale of: |  |
| Supermaz | 500 |
| Supermiz | 4,500 |
| Supermoz | 1,000 |
|  | 24,000 |

Mez would not be further processed.

## 21.26 ECONOMIC ORDER QUANTITIES

### Problem

The annual requirement for Material X is 100,000 units at a cost of £8 per unit. The material is used at a constant rate throughout the year and deliveries from the supplier are made immediately they are required. The cost of placing an order for replenishing stock is £2 per order and the cost of holding one unit of stock for one year is 20% of the cost of each unit in stock. The total ordering cost will increase as the number of orders placed are increased to obtain the 100,000 units required but the stockholding cost will reduce because less stock will be carried to meet production requirements. If less orders are placed, ordering costs will reduce but increased stocks will be maintained incurring increased stockholding costs. The order quantity where the ordering costs and stockholding costs are at the minimum is needed.

## Comment

This occurs when the ordering costs and stockholding costs are the same for a particular ordering quantity — the economic order quantity (EOQ). Taking sample order levels, costs may be incurred as follows:

| Order quantity of Material X in units | Number of orders issued | Average stock in units | Average stock value | Ordering cost | Stock-holding cost | Total cost |
|---|---|---|---|---|---|---|
| | | | £ | £ | £ | £ |
| 100 | 1,000 | 50 | 400 | 2,000 | 80 | 2,080 |
| 500 | 200 | 250 | 2,000 | 400 | 400 | 800 |
| 1,000 | 100 | 500 | 4,000 | 200 | 800 | 1,000 |

$$\left(\frac{100,000}{\text{order quantity}}\right) \left(\frac{\text{Order quantity}}{2}\right) \left(\begin{array}{c}\text{Average} \\ \text{stock} \\ \times £8\end{array}\right) \left(\begin{array}{c}\text{Number of} \\ \text{orders} \\ \text{issued} \\ \times £2\end{array}\right) \left(\begin{array}{c}20\% \text{ of} \\ \text{average} \\ \text{stock} \\ \text{value}\end{array}\right)$$

From the above table of costs the economic ordering quantity is 500 units. This figure can be calculated by the following standard formula:

$$EOQ = \sqrt{\frac{2 \times \text{Annual requirements} \times \text{Cost of issuing an order}}{\begin{array}{c}\text{Cost of holding one unit of stock} \\ \text{for one year as a percentage of} \\ \text{its value}\end{array} \times \begin{array}{c}\text{Cost per} \\ \text{unit} \\ \text{of stock}\end{array}}}$$

$$EOQ = \sqrt{\frac{2 \times 100,000 \times £2}{\cdot 2 \times £8}}$$

$$= \sqrt{250,000}$$

$$= \underline{500 \text{ units}}$$

The formula is limited to the assumptions defined in the problem but the formula can be adapted to a relaxation of the assumptions as, for example, a variation in unit prices owing to quantity discounts on purchasing larger quantities.

## 21.27 FIXING SELLING PRICES

### Problem*

A manufacturing concern has multi-purpose plant capable of operating at full capacity at 5,000 machine hours per monthly production period. It may produce three products interchangeably, for which the output and cost details are as follows:

*A problem taken from the ICMA examination in Part IV, Advanced Cost and Management Accountancy (June, 1964).

Product A
    500 units per machine hour
    Material cost, £4·25 per 1,000 units
Product B
    250 units per machine hour
    Material cost, £1·75 per 1,000 units
Product C
    1,000 units per machine hour
    Material cost, £3 per 1,000 units
Labour costs per machine hour: £1·50
Variable overhead per machine hour: £0·50
The fixed costs of the department are £10,000 per monthly production period.

The management of the company estimates from past experience that the full capacity can be used at all times if machine time can be freely moved from one product to another as dictated by demand, and is anxious to establish suitable product selling prices (per 1,000 units). The two price-fixing proposals which are being considered are:

(*a*) To fix selling prices at product costs plus 20%
(*b*) To fix prices so as to give a contribution of £3·50 per machine hour.

**Comment**
The prices fixed under proposals (*a*) and (*b*) per 1,000 units would be as follows:

*Proposal (a)*

|  | *Cost per machine hour* |
|---|---|
|  | £ |
| Product A: |  |
|     Material cost | 2·125  (£4·25 ÷ 2) |
|     Labour cost | 1·500 |
|     Variable overhead | 0·500 |
|     Marginal cost | 4·125 |
|     Fixed overhead | 2·000  (£10,000 ÷ 5,000) |
|     Total cost | 6·125 |

|  | *Per 1,000 units* |
|---|---|
|  | £ |
|     Total cost | 12·25  (2 × £6·125) |
|     Add 20% | 2·45 |
|     Selling price | 14·70 |

*Cost per machine hour*

£

Product B:
|  |  |
|---|---|
| Material cost | 0·4375 (£1·75 ÷ 4) |
| Labour cost | 1·5000 |
| Variable overhead | 0·5000 |
| Marginal cost | 2·4375 |
| Fixed overhead | 2·0000 (£10,000 ÷ 5,000) |
| Total cost | 4·4375 |

*Per 1,000 units*

£

|  |  |
|---|---|
| Total cost | 17·75 (4 × £4·4375) |
| Add 20% | 3·55 |
| Selling price | 21·30 |

*Cost per machine hour
and per 1,000 units*

£

Product C:
|  |  |
|---|---|
| Material cost | 3·00 |
| Labour cost | 1·50 |
| Variable overhead | 0·50 |
| Marginal cost | 5·00 |
| Fixed overhead | 2·00 |
| Total cost | 7·00 |
| Add 20% | 1·40 |
| Selling price | 8·40 |

*Proposal (b)*

|  | Product A | Product B | Product C |
|---|---|---|---|
|  | £ | £ | £ |
| Marginal cost per machine hour | 4·125 | 2·4375 | 5·00 |
| Add contribution | 3·500 | 3·5000 | 3·50 |
| Per machine hour | 7·625 | 5·9375 | 8·50 |
| Selling price per 1,000 units | 15·25 | 23·75 | 8·50 |
|  | (2 × £7·625) | (4 × £5·9375) | |

In Chapter 19, the use of marginal costing in short-term pricing and fixing a selling price for a product in a limited market was emphasised. At a time of recession, prices may be artificially low to get the orders for the company to remain in existence and at the other extreme cost plus prices may be possible. Companies face varied market situations which must affect pricing policy. For example, where competition is severe, prices are often governed by competitors and costs may be used as a basis for accepting or rejecting business at the price levels ruling in the market.

Prices may be fixed to give a specific return on investment for the product. In capital intensive businesses this may be considered desirable but in factories making several products the identification of fixed and working capital to specific products may be difficult. This point is examined in Chapter 5.

Where products have variable material content and value, the percentage for profit to fix the selling price may be applied to conversion cost rather than total cost to recognise a varied relationship between material cost and labour and overhead in the cost make-up of the product. This is particularly the case where some materials are purchased for assembly as compared with conversion requirements in the form of machining, finishing as well as assembly.

Standard, rather than actual, costs are used by many companies as a basis for pricing, such figures being considered an improvement on actual costs which may include the financial effects of various factors not relevant for future pricing.

Pricing policy is a complex matter and securing a balanced price structure is difficult. Pricing policy varies with the life cycle of a product and prices must be fixed on what the market will bear. Cost ascertainment provides only the basis for a pricing decision and care must be taken not to mislead management, particularly in joint product industries if costs are apportioned on arbitrary bases. Total selling values and costs are relevant because the product mix in these industries can often be varied to produce maximum profit. Sales revenue should be at a level to cover costs and provide funds for dividend distribution, the replacement of assets, and company growth and development.

In recent years, there has been a marked increase in government intervention in price-fixing in the United Kingdom. Price controls have been introduced with a severity not previously experienced by the comparatively free market economy of this country. Other countries, such as Brazil and Holland, are used to this intervention. Price controls place an added burden on the management accountant to produce relevant data to justify price increases and check that where price changes are not possible, the company can operate as profitably as possible.

## 21.28 SALES AND PRODUCTION EFFORT PREFERENCE

### Problem*

A company manufactures two models of power tool: a single-speed model and a two-speed model.

The manufacturing requirements of the two models and the available manufac-

---

*A problem taken from the ICMA examination in Part IV, Management Information and Quantitative Techniques (June, 1971).

turing capacity are:

| | Machining hours | Assembly hours | Testing hours | Warehouse space (square metres) |
|---|---|---|---|---|
| Model | | | | |
| Single-speed | 2·0 | 1·5 | 0·5 | 1·0 |
| Two-speed | 2·5 | 1·0 | 1·0 | 1·0 |
| Capacity available | 40,000 | 24,000 | 14,000 | 30,000 |

The problem is to maximise the contribution, taking into account the above production requirements and constraints, and given that the contribution per unit is £3 and £5 for the single-speed and two-speed models respectively.

**Comment**

This problem can be resolved graphically and the graph is shown in Figure 21.2. On the graph values are selected for each constraint. The machining hours constraint may be expressed as

$$2x + 2·5y \leqslant 40,000 \text{ hours}$$

which gives for $x$ (the single-speed model): 20,000 units $\left(\dfrac{40,000}{2}\right)$ and for $y$ (the two-speed model): 16,000 units $\left(\dfrac{40,000}{2·5}\right)$. Similarly, the other constraints may give the values to be plotted:

| Constraint | Expressed as | Single-speed model units | Two-speed model units |
|---|---|---|---|
| Assembly hours | $1·5x + 1y \leqslant 24,000$ hours | 16,000 | 24,000 |
| Testing hours | $0·5x + 1y \leqslant 14,000$ hours | 28,000 | 14,000 |
| Warehouse space | $1x + 1y \leqslant 30,000$ square metres | 30,000 | 30,000 |

Figure 21.2 shows that the plotting of the constraints restricts the feasibility of possible solutions and this area is known as the feasible region. The solution is to maximise the contribution from the production and sale of units of both models bearing in mind the constraints imposed. If a value of contribution is selected, say £15,000, then the equation would be

$$3x \quad + \quad 5y \quad = £15,000$$

↑         ↑

Contribution per single-speed model    Contribution per two-speed model

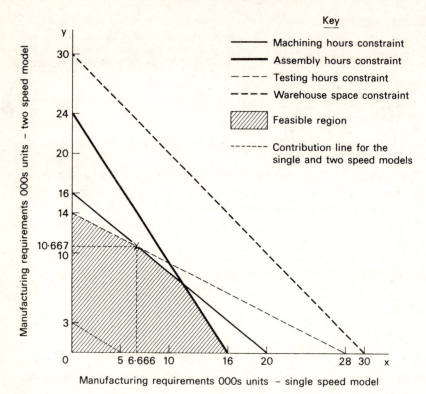

FIGURE 21.2. A linear programming solution to a sales and production effort preference problem

This detail can also be plotted on the graph as 5,000 units of $x$ $\left(\dfrac{£15,000}{£3}\right)$ and 3,000 units of $y$ $\left(\dfrac{£15,000}{£5}\right)$. Whatever the total contribution, the plotting of the equation will be a straight line with a slope parallel to the contribution line given on the graph. It follows that the solution must be where the parallel line cuts the external point of the feasible region at its furthest point from the origin and its co-ordinates must satisfy the equations:

$$2x + 2 \cdot 5y = 40,000$$
$$0 \cdot 5x + \quad y \quad = 14,000$$

These are known as the binding constraints (machining hours and testing hours).

The solution of these equations simultaneously,* or the reading from the graph,

*
|  |  |  |
|---|---|---|
|  | $2x + 2 \cdot 5y = \ 40,000$ | (i) |
|  | $0 \cdot 5x + \quad y = \ 14,000$ | (ii) |
| (ii) x 4 | $2x + \quad 4y = \ 56,000$ | (iii) |
| (i) − (iii) | $-1.5y = -16,000$ | (iv) |
| ∴ | $y = \ 10,667$ units. |  |

Substitution in equation (ii):

$$0 \cdot 5x + 10,667 = 14,000$$
$$\therefore \ x = \ 6,666 \text{ units}$$

gives the production and sale of:

|  | units |
| --- | --- |
| Single-speed model | 6,666 |
| Two-speed model | 10,667 |

The maximum contribution is, therefore:

| Model | Number of units | Contribution per unit | Total contribution |
| --- | --- | --- | --- |
|  |  | £ | £ |
| Single-speed | 6,666 | 3 | 19,998 |
| Two-speed | 10,667 | 5 | 53,335 |
|  |  |  | 73,333 |

The use of the binding constraints is as follows:

| Model | Machining hours | Testing hours |
| --- | --- | --- |
| Single-speed | 13,332 (6,666 x 2) | 3,333 (6,666 x 0·5) |
| Two-speed | 26,668 (10,667 x 2·5) | 10,667 (10,667 x 1) |
|  | 40,000 | 14,000 |

## 21.3 SUMMARY

A few of the major decisions met in business have been considered in the above sections. Taken in conjunction with the financial approach to problems described in earlier chapters, a major task of the management accountant has been described, i.e., the provision of relevant financial information to management to assist them in their decision-making task.

The earlier part of this chapter emphasises the breadth of view that must be taken by the manager and that the financial information is only part of the input to the decision-making process.

## FOR FURTHER STUDY

QUESTIONS

1. *The identification of relevant costs*

   The A.B. Co. Ltd has received a special order for Product 123. The company does not normally produce this product; however, it has decided to accept this order, provided it is profitable for two reasons:

   (*a*) To use up spare capacity and surplus materials
   (*b*) To use it as a test case to determine whether or not the company should add 123 to its product range and produce in anticipation of orders.

*Required:*

You have been asked for your opinion on the material prices which should be used for inclusion in the cost estimates for the special order and for continuous production, and you are required to give this, in non-technical language, in respect of each of the following four materials which are required for the production of 123.

(i) *Material A*

The order requires 500 grams of Material A. Material A is a byproduct of another of the company's manufacturing processes and can be sold on the open market. Production of A is very irregular and the selling price received fluctuates widely. It has been as high as £1 per gram but on occasions the price has been as low as £0·02 per gram. During the last few months the selling price has been £0·10 per gram.

(ii) *Material B*

This material was used by the company but no longer is, although there are still 2,000 grams in stock and only 1,000 grams are needed for the special order. At the end of the last financial year this was valued at £0·25 per gram and, although the current market price is £0·40 per gram, the best price that the company was recently offered was £0·30 per gram.

(iii) *Material C*

The company uses this material regularly at a rate of approximately 500 grams per week. At present there are 5,000 grams in stock at an average purchase price of £0·50 per gram. The standard price used for this in the company's standard cost calculations is £0·60 per gram and the current market price is £0·55 per gram.

(iv) *Material D*

This material is also used by the company and has a marked seasonal price variation. The average purchase price of the stock on hand at present is £0·75 per gram. If some of this is used for the special order, the company will have to go to the market sooner than expected when the price is estimated to be nearer to £0·65 per gram than the £0·55 per gram which was the anticipated next buying price. (ACA)

2. *Changing the location of a company*

The growth of the Mace Manufacturing Co. Ltd had been considerable. Its present one-acre site had been developed and no further development was possible in the area. Two small factories had been opened elsewhere but communications were difficult owing to distance, and efficiency was adversely affected by the present method of operation. Various possibilities had been considered including buying land in another part of the country for building, or purchasing an existing factory where the site would allow the necessary expansion. No existing factory meeting the requirements of the management of the Mace Manufacturing Co. Ltd could be found, and existing industrial areas were expensive.

At a meeting to consider the problem it was decided that:

(a) A move was necessary from the present site occupied by the company
(b) One of the development areas would be considered as the future site for the company.

*Required:*

(a) What preliminary action should the board of the Mace Manufacturing Co. Ltd take to implement its decision?
(b) What further action should be taken to implement the decision?
(c) What difficulties are likely to be experienced as a result of the decision to move from their present site?
(d) Assuming all details obtained, how would you attempt to overcome the difficulties mentioned in answer to question (c)?

3. *Establishing a foreign factory*
Mechanical Products Ltd was increasing its foreign trade with its main range of mechanical gadgets and this was particularly in evidence in Africa. Unfortunately, adverse factors had affected the profitability of this business and the only way of overcoming the problem, assuming the continuing trade in the area, was considered to be the opening of a factory in Nigeria to manufacture the products required in Africa.

It was realised that the following points would require investigation:
(a) where to locate the factory in Nigeria; and (b) the type of factory required in that country and its cost.

In addition, it was recognised that as the local labour was probably unaccustomed to using modern machinery it might be necessary to consider alternative methods of manufacture to those used in the UK. Labour intensive methods might be more appropriate.

Preliminary inquiries were possible at the Department of Trade and Industry and the company intended to obtain all the information possible from that source. Before sending a company representative to resolve outstanding queries at first hand at the expected location of the factory, the company intended to contact Nigeria's commercial services department for information.

Regarding the comparison of the costs of operating the factory by hand methods as compared with predominently mechanised processes, it was recognised that costs could be estimated but the extent to which Nigerians were adopting modern methods was crucial. It would be pointless to erect a factory based on labour intensive methods if modern machinery would be required in a few years time.

*Required:*
What contribution could the management accountant make to the solution of the problem outlined in this case?

4. *Replacement of plant and machinery*
In the near future, your company will be faced with the problem of deciding whether to replace certain items of plant and machinery or to carry out

extensive repairs which would increase their working lives.
*Required:*
As management accountant, advise the production director as to the main
factors which must receive consideration prior to making such a decision.

(ICMA)

5. *Company closure or product elimination*
   At the beginning of this year (1st January), Plastic Toys Ltd started a manufacturing plant. It makes three products, A, B and C, which use the same machinery
   and labour but separate raw materials. The accounts for the year are as follows:

|  | | *A* | *B* | *C* | *Total* |
|---|---|---|---|---|---|
| | | £ | £ | £ | £ |
| Sales | (A) | 17,600 | 4,200 | 3,200 | 25,000 |
| Materials | | 3,000 | 1,200 | 500 | 4,700 |
| Labour | | 5,000 | 1,000 | 1,000 | 7,000 |
| Works overhead | | | | | |
|   Foreman | | 1,500 | 300 | 300 | 2,100 |
|   Maintenance | | 1,000 | 200 | 200 | 1,400 |
|   Depreciation | | 2,000 | 400 | 400 | 2,800 |
| | (B) | 12,500 | 3,100 | 2,400 | 18,000 |
| | (A − B) | 5,100 | 1,100 | 800 | 7,000 |
| | | | | £ | |
| Less manager | | | | 4,000 | |
|   distribution | | | | 1,750 | 5,750 |
| | | | | Profit | 1,250 |

Sales in units:
    Product A: 176
    Product B:  42
    Product C:  32.

Next year, owing to competition, sales prices of Products B and C will have
to be cut; for the same volume, sales will be £3,360 and £2,240. At this volume
product costs will remain unchanged. The only volume change to be considered
is the complete abandonment of one or more products which would affect
certain cost items:

*Materials.* Cost varies directly with output. Stocks (on hand and ordered)
amount to one year's needs; those for Products A and C could be returned or
orders cancelled without loss, but those for Product B cannot be returned and
are useless for all other purposes.
*Labour;* No staff would be discharged unless the whole works closed.
*Works overhead.* This is apportioned in proportion to direct wages. Plant will

be scrapped in 10 years time (whatever the extent of use) and has at no time any resale value because it is highly specialised. Maintenance would rise by £100 per annum if either Products B or C were given up (£200 for both). *Distribution.* This consists of £500 agents' commission (2% on sales) and £1,250 railway charges (£5 per unit).

*Required:*
Draft a statement to show whether (and when) Plastic Toys Ltd should close down, or give up one or more products. Give your advice to management.

6. *The make or buy decision*
A food canning firm makes its own containers in a department whose annual costs are shown as follows:

|  | £ | £ |
|---|---|---|
| Direct material | | 8,000 |
| Direct labour | | 6,000 |
| Department overhead | | |
| Foreman | 2,500 | |
| Depreciation of machinery | 2,000 | |
| Rent | 1,000 | |
| Other expenses | 1,500 | 7,000 |
| | | 21,000 |
| General overhead at 10% | | 2,100 |
| Total cost | | 23,100 |

As an independent maker of containers is willing to supply the same quantity required for £20,000 per annum, the company asks you to report on whether this offer should be accepted and their own container department closed.

You are given the following additional information:

(*a*) All the employees, except the foreman, could be transferred without pay changes to other departments. The foreman is due to retire in four years time and is too old to learn a new job. The company would not like to dismiss him now.

(*b*) The department's buildings would be used as a warehouse in place of one at present rented at £1,500 per annum

(*c*) The depreciation of £2,000 is the charge on one large machine which originally cost £20,000. It has a 10-year life of which half has so far passed. A similar machine (new) would now cost £30,000 and last 10 years. There is no scrap value or resale value applicable to either machine.

(*d*) 'Other expenses' would be eliminated if the department was closed. General overhead would be unaffected.

*Required:*
Prepare a statement showing the financial effect of accepting the offer and closing the company's own container department now or at some time in the

future. Explain your figures and advise the company on its best course of action.

### 7. Profitability of channels of distribution

A manufacturer of kitchenware sells a range of such products through a number of channels of distribution. The products are standard and total 150 in all, while the channels of distribution cover retail outlets, wholesalers, several mail-order stores, large chain stores and overseas countries. There are 100 basic products which sell through all the channels and a further 50 specially manufactured for particular channels.

*Required:*

(a) What problems would be met in assessing both products profitability and channel profitability in this organisation and how would you deal with them?

(b) Explain what you would regard as relevant management accounting information when deciding whether or not to drop a particular product or a particular channel of distribution.                              (ICMA)

### 8. Proposal evaluation

The following information is available from the previous year's annual accounts of a passenger transport undertaking:

| | X1 | X2 | X3 | X4 | Total |
|---|---|---|---|---|---|
| | | | *Routes* | | |
| Vehicles — number used | 22 | 12 | 16 | 8 | 58 |
| Mileage | 500,000 | 300,000 | 400,000 | 200,000 | 1,400,000 |
| | £ | £ | £ | £ | £ |
| Revenue from passengers | 155,000 | 96,000 | 132,000 | 52,000 | 435,000 |
| Variable costs | 125,000 | 75,000 | 100,000 | 50,000 | 350,000 |
| Fixed costs Specific to vehicles | 8,800 | 4,800 | 6,400 | 3,200 | 23,200 |
| Garage and administration | 15,400 | 8,400 | 11,200 | 5,600 | 40,600 |
| Profit | 5,800 | 7,800 | 14,400 | | 21,200 |
| Loss | | | | 6,800 | |

*Required:*

As the accountant for this undertaking you are required to submit a report to the general manager commenting on the following problems and proposals:

(a) The rates of profitability of routes X1, X2 and X3

(b) A proposal to discontinue route X4

(c) A proposal to reduce the service on route X4 by half on the assumption that only four vehicles would be used, running a total of 100,000 miles per annum; the estimated revenue from passengers would be reduced by £20,000 per annum; and that the next year's order for replacement vehicles would be reduced by four

(d) A proposal to introduce cheap off-peak fares on route X1. The present off-peak revenue is £80,000 per annum and it is estimated that if off-peak fares were reduced by 25% there would be a 30% increase in the number of passengers using the service at off-peak periods.                   (ICMA)

9. *Further processing*

As a result of a series of processes a factory produces three joint products: A, B and C. Standard costs for the coming year are budgeted as follows:

|                    | £      |
| ------------------ | ------ |
| Direct materials   | 70,000 |
| Direct wages       | 30,000 |
| Variable overheads | 45,000 |
| Fixed overheads    | 60,000 |

Standard outputs and selling prices at this volume of production are:

| Product | Tonnes | £ per tonne |
| ------- | ------ | ----------- |
| A       | 1,000  | 150         |
| B       | 500    | 100         |
| C       | 600    | 50          |

The overhead absorption rate in respect of each process is the same and is calculated as a percentage on direct labour cost. Facilities are available to carry out further processes of a similar nature, and it is found that all three products can be further processed and sold at higher prices. Any one product, any combination of two products or all three products can be further processed, and by the addition of further materials and the application of further labour the following results can be achieved.

As a result of further processes:

|                          | Products |         |         |
| ------------------------ | -------- | ------- | ------- |
|                          | A        | B       | C       |
| Weight processed, tonnes | 1,000    | 500     | 600     |
| Cost of added material   | £10,000  | £3,000  | £7,000  |
| Cost of added direct labour | £4,000 | £2,000  | £2,000  |
| Sales value of production | £170,000 | £62,000 | £45,000 |

*Required:*

Present information to management to enable a decision to be made regarding this case, and make recommendations arising from the figures presented.

(ICMA)

10. *Optimum inventory level costs*

To determine the optimum inventory level it is necessary to compare the cost of holding the inventory with the cost of ordering and setting up production facilities.

*Required:*

Give examples of the types of costs which can fall under each category and the problems likely to arise in determining these.                    (ACA)

11. *Fixing the selling price of a new product*

The XYZ Co. Ltd are considering whether or not to market a new product NP456. A management meeting has been called to discuss possible selling prices which could be charged for this product.

*Required:*

Prepare a report outlining the factors which you think should be taken into account before a final decision is reached. Your report should indicate the cost data which you would prepare and any additional information you would require in order that this data could be assembled. Your answer should assume the following:

(a) The market for NP456 is not perfectly competitive although it is more competitive abroad than at home

(b) The capacity utilisation at the factory where NP456 will be produced has been:

| Year | % |
|------|----|
| 1 | 90 |
| 2 | 92 |
| 3 | 94 |
| 4 | 90 |
| 5 | 88 |
| 6 | 84 (to date) |

(c) NP456 requires two units of machine time on a special machine and the time available on this is likely to be restricted because of competing demands of other products. Supplies of skilled labour have also presented problems in the past although this is not likely to arise in the case of NP456.

(d) The decision to produce and sell NP456 will require an initial investment of £50,000 excluding any additional working capital requirements

(e) Although NP456 is new it is similar in many respects to other products which the company markets and falls naturally into the company's product range.                    (ACA)

**12.** *Relevant information for product pricing*

As management accountant of a large multi-product company, you are required to make a major contribution to the decision-making process by providing management with cost and revenue information which is relevant to product pricing decisions. A product management system is in operation and each product manager is responsible for developing marketing plans for his own group of products. He controls sales promotion, advertising, packing, pricing, product improvement and consequently product profit.

*Required:*

List the kind of problems facing a product manager and indicate how you, as management accountant, can assist him with product pricing decisions.

(ICMA)

## FURTHER READING

Arnold, John. *Pricing and Output Decisions.* Haymarket, 1973. Chapters 7—9.

Carsberg, B. V. *Introduction to Mathematical Programming for Accountants.* Allen & Unwin, 1969. Chapters 3—5 and 7.

Hague, D. C. *Managerial Economics.* Longman, 1969. Part 3 — Decision Techniques.

# ASSOCIATED TOPICS FOR STUDY

# 22 Source Documentation and Data Processing

## OBJECTIVE OF THE CHAPTER

To describe the flow of documentation in an accounting system and consider aspects of data processing to the extent that they are significant in the design and implementation of management information systems. Double entry book-keeping for specific accounting transactions is also considered in this chapter.

## OUTLINE OF THE CHAPTER

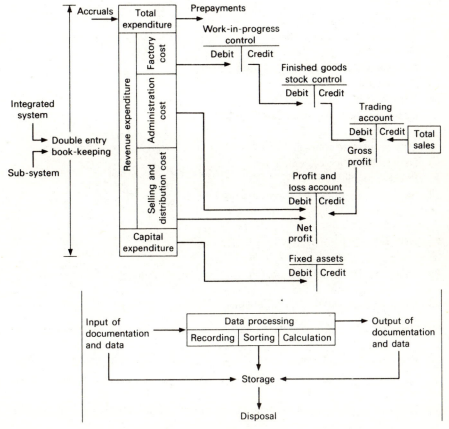

FIGURE 22.1.

419

The recording and communication of information in the business requires documents to be prepared in a predetermined way. Although information for management is not all of a routine nature, the bulk of the recording should be established as a regular routine by the use of forms.

Prior to the development of management control techniques, most recording was for the purpose of satisfying legal requirements and financial accounting. With modern control systems much of the data is now provided outside the accounting department. This necessitates close integration of effort between the accounting and other departments of the business. Monetary information may be compiled independently from other quantitative data and co-ordination is necessary to ensure that, when the two types of information are brought together in the information for management, the data is able to be reconciled.

## 22.1  ASPECTS OF SOURCE DOCUMENTATION AND DATA PROCESSING

The following aspects of source documentation and data processing are covered in this chapter:

1. Source preparation of data
2. Accuracy of documentation
3. Data sorting
4. Data summarisation and tabulation
5. Documentation costs
6. Form design
7. Document/data retention and disposal
8. Basic documentation flow
9. Data processing control
10. Double-entry book-keeping
11. Profit reconciliation
12. Impact of methods of data processing.

## 22.2  SOURCE PREPARATION OF DATA

Preferably the data should be created where action is taking place although this requirement may impede the performance of the job being recorded. This should be avoided and there may be other problems:

(*a*) Manual staff are not usually the best personnel to complete forms, and inaccurate and incomplete data is common
(*b*) The action may take place in situations where document preparation is difficult, e.g., in the open air, during dirty processes and where writing surfaces, such as desks, are not available
(*c*) The time factor relating to certain processes may rule out the preparation of the source documentation at the time production takes place.

These problems are either eliminated or minimised by the following action:

1. Clerical work for non-clerical staff kept to the minimum
2. Non-clerical staff recording being of the simplest type, e.g., it may be merely putting a stroke on a section of a pre-printed card
3. The reduction of the size of forms
4. The use of stiff paper or card in place of flimsy paper
5. The provision of writing boards
6. The make-up of forms in pads
7. The use of special pencils or other writing materials
8. Clear form design
9. Automatic recording by the machine producing the work.

## 22.3  ACCURACY OF DOCUMENTATION

Ideally the data should be prepared in the form required for further processing because the greater the transcription, the greater the probability of error and clerical costs. This might involve a journal or register entry, the punching of holes in punched cards or paper tape, recording on magnetic tape or other magnetized areas, or using some other means to assist the data processing.

The data accumulated must be reasonably accurate and in this stage of processing verification of accuracy may be attempted. Verification does not attempt to secure perfection but it includes a check that information is complete, conveys the correct meaning to a person responsible for its interpretation, and conforms to the acceptable standard of accuracy for the data under consideration. Processing difficulties may be experienced unless significantly inaccurate data is corrected early in the processing procedure.

The accuracy of the output of the accounting system in the form of information for management is only as good as the accuracy of the input fed into the system. Improved methods of data processing may only speed up the processing of inaccurate data. Many modern systems of data processing have, on installation, created real problems in establishing accuracy of input because the human capacity to correct errors at subsequent stages of the clerical process has been removed.

The usual methods of establishing a control over the accuracy of input are as follows:

1. A record of errors made to ascertain why the errors are being made and which members of staff are making them. If a staff member is persistently careless, management action will be necessary.
2. An independent check of the work done by a clerk, either in total, by spot checking, or by different methods of producing the result, e.g., alternative methods of calculation.
3. General scrutiny by an experienced official who can identify unusual features which signify processing errors.
4. The use of control totals.

5. Check digits included in codes.
6. Check programmes included in the work instructions or machine instructions.


## 22.4  DATA SORTING

To ensure the input is in a form suitable for further processing, sorting is usually necessary. It may take two forms:

(a) The arrangement of data by classifications — the types that may be used have been considered in Chapter 2
(b) The arrangement of the data in sequence — sorting input into numerical order is a good example of this.

   A particular form of sorting where data is merged in sequence is known as collation.


## 22.5  DATA SUMMARISATION AND TABULATION

The degree of emphasis required on data supplied is accomplished by condensing the input in the form of a summary or summaries. This may involve listing and tabulating to obtain the summary totals and sub-totals.
   In this operation, the relationship, order, similarity or relative value of the data may be determined to assist the interpretation of information supplied to management.


## 22.6  DOCUMENTATION COSTS

With source documentation, increased costs arise owing to:

1. A member of the business deciding he wants some information and creating a form to supply it. An existing form might be suitable.
2. Poor form design.
3. Too many copies of forms being produced. The ease with which forms can be reproduced by modern methods encourages the issue of extra copies.
4. Non-standard sizes being used.
5. The quality of the paper used of a standard higher than necessary.
6. The adoption of office equipment supplier's systems and equipment which require expensive specialised stationery.
7. Poor stationery supply control. Although economy in printing costs may be secured by the ordering of large quantities, these savings may be more than offset by the necessity to change a system and destroy the old forms.
8. The use of colour printing. A second colour necessitates an additional printing operation.

Thinking clearly of the purpose behind the documents being used and the application of form design to meet system needs can reduce documentation costs considerably.

## 22.7 FORM DESIGN

Associated aspects of form design have been introduced in the previous section but the principal features of form design are:

1. The provision of adequate space for the recording of source information. Excess space should not be provided.
2. The adoption of a simple layout. Complicated design does not assist in the completion of forms particularly where non-clerical staff are involved.
3. The use of paper or card of the type most suitable for reproduction.
4. The consideration of facilities associated with the completion of the form. This covers the following:

    (*a*) Mailing, e.g., possible use of window envelopes and standard envelope sizes
    (*b*) Filing, e.g., the provision of filing margins and the use of stiffer paper to prevent the buckling of flimsy copies
    (*c*) Office machine use, e.g., spaces fixed according to tabulation positions or printing mechanisms
    (*d*) Calculation and analysis, e.g., where pegboard summarising methods are used
    (*e*) Copying, e.g., the possible use of carbon backed forms or sensitised masters.

5. The consideration of the procedure of which the form is a part. In this respect, colour may be used to indicate the disposal of the form which should be identified with a clear title and form number. The system may require control of documents through serial numbering and the forms may be in sets for simultaneous reproduction. With sets of forms the following require consideration:

    (*a*) Information to be reproduced on the forms in the set. Certain information on the top copy may not be required on other copies. Various sizes of forms, carbons or the hatching of sections are the usual means of dealing with this problem.
    (*b*) Copying facilities, e.g., the use of one-time carbon and continuous stationery.
    (*c*) Security of the sets, e.g., binding, folding and perforating.

## 22.8 DOCUMENT/DATA RETENTION AND DISPOSAL

The large number of documents that accumulate in the average business necessitates an organised approach to document retention and disposal. One authority* suggests

---

*Office Manager's Handbook*. John Cameron Aspley (The Dartnell Corporation, 1965), p. 694.

that documents should be grouped for retention purposes into the following four classifications:

1. Vital records — records that are irreplaceable.
2. Important records — these are administrative instruments and include reports, statistical and cost studies, and the great bulk of accounting records supporting current, operating routines
3. Useful records — these are records frequently used and currently available but their loss will not seriously handicap business operations
4. Non-essential records — these records have no long-term value and are eligible for immediate destruction.

In classifying records into retention groups, consideration should be given to:

(*a*) Possible future value
(*b*) Legal value
(*c*) Possible interference with operations
(*d*) Relations with the public or customers
(*e*) Relations with government departments
(*f*) The expense of replacement in case of loss
(*g*) Availability elsewhere of identical copies
(*h*) The extent to which the same data summarises or is summarised by other records
(*i*) The degree to which the record provides essential details.

Data may be stored manually or electronically. If manually, working papers and records are used; if electronically, the usual medium is magnetic storage devices. Until the advent of the computer, accounting records formed the basis of information systems but access to such detail was slow. With electronic storage the 'bits'* of information can be identified quickly and procedures operated more efficiently. The emphasis here is on intermediate storage, i.e., where intermediate results are stored for subsequent further processing, and reading by a clerk is unnecessary. In other cases, visible records are produced.

The output of the data processing system can either be in a form suitable for subsequent processing, if this is considered necessary, or in a form for management use. In the first form the data may be similar to the input, the more common types being:

(*a*) Source documentation
(*b*) Punched cards
(*c*) Punched paper tape
(*d*) Magnetic tape.

In the second form, the output is either a copy of a document or a prepared form summarising the information required by management.

*A 'bit' is the basic unit of information recognised in a computer system and input for storage must be coded in this form so that the basic process of the computer may be carried out, e.g., in the binary digit form of 0 and 1.

In modern mechanised systems, the printed output is often designed for immediate issue to lower levels of management, but for top management transcription of the data in a more acceptable form is frequently necessary. Tabulation output from electronic installations is often cumbersome and unless staff are trained to ensure that output is clearly titled, interpretation may be difficult.

## 22.9 BASIC DOCUMENTATION FLOW

The basic documentation flow is governed by:

1. The type of information required from the system
2. The nature of the classification, accumulation, sorting, calculation, summarisation and disposal of data systems adopted
3. The volume of data to be processed
4. The speed of data processing required
5. The cost of the basic clerical operations
6. The datalinks at each stage of the data processing sequence.

It is convenient to consider the source documentation and the flow of the basic documents in respect of each element of cost as in the sections to follow.*

### 22.91 BASIC DOCUMENTATION – MATERIALS ACCOUNTING

The basic documentation in respect of materials accounting may be considered as including:

1. Purchase requisition – the request to the buyer to purchase material
2. Purchase order – the document sent to the supplier for material ordered
3. Goods received note – the document prepared when material is received from the supplier
4. Stores ledger sheet – the document showing stock movement and the book stock at a given time for a particular item of stock
5. Material requisition – the authority to issue materials from the store
6. Materials analysis – the analysis sheet that analyses the purpose for which materials have been issued and the type of material issued
7. Job card – the document that shows the cost of the job, and in the case of material accounting, direct material cost
8. Factory overhead control account – the ledger sheet that accumulates factory overhead cost pending its absorption into production, and, in the case of material accounting, indirect material cost.
9. Purchase invoice – the document from the supplier showing the charge for the material supplied

*The emphasis is on jobbing businesses. Process manufacture is considered in the next chapter.

10. Supplier's personal ledger account – the ledger sheet showing the changes in the amount owing to the supplier and the amount owed at any given time.
11. Cash voucher – the document supporting the cash payment to the supplier for material received.

The relationship of the above documents is illustrated in Figure 22.2.

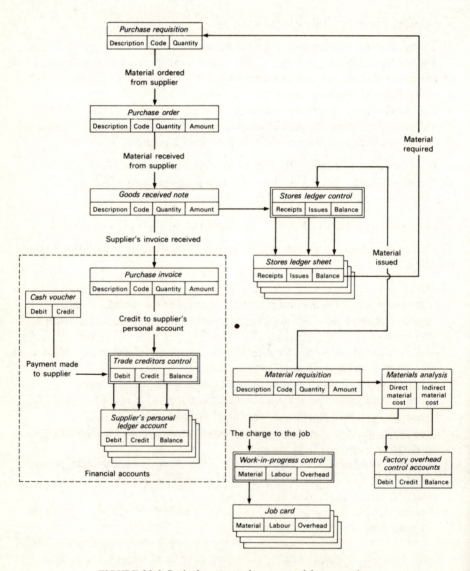

FIGURE 22.2. Basic documentation – materials accounting

## 22.92 BASIC DOCUMENTATION – LABOUR ACCOUNTING

The basic documentation in respect of labour accounting may be considered as including:

1. Time card – the record of time worked by an employee
2. Payroll – the document showing the wages payable to each employee and used as the office record
3. Payslip – the document giving the wages payable to each employee and given to the employee at the time of payment
4. Labour control account – the ledger sheet that accumulates labour cost pending its analysis for transfer to other accounts as shown by the labour analysis
5. Labour analysis – the analysis sheet that analyses the purpose for which labour cost has been incurred
6. Job card – the document that shows the cost of the job and, in the case of labour accounting, direct labour cost.
7. Factory overhead control account – the ledger sheet that accumulates factory overhead cost pending its absorption into production and, in the case of labour accounting, indirect labour cost
8. Cash voucher – the document supporting the total cash payment to employees for wages paid.

The relationship of the above documents is illustrated in Figure 22.3.

## 22.93 BASIC DOCUMENTATION – FACTORY OVERHEAD ACCOUNTING

The basic documentation in respect of factory overhead accounting may be considered as including:

1. Invoice – the document from the supplier of facilities showing the charge made
2. Materials analysis
3. Labour analysis
4. Factory overhead control account
5. Supplier's personal ledger account

    As recorded in the earlier sections

6. Absorbed overhead analysis – the document giving details of factory overhead recovery on the basis of overhead cost absorption to production
7. Job card – the document that shows the cost of the job and in the case of factory overhead accounting, the factory overhead absorbed by the product
8. Cash voucher – the document supporting the cash payment to the supplier for the facilities received.

The relationship of the above documents is illustrated in Figure 22.4.

## 22.94 BASIC DOCUMENTATION – OTHER OVERHEADS

The source documentation for administration, selling and distribution overhead is similar to the basic documentation for factory overhead except that the accumulated costs are normally regarded as period costs and do not pass through the work-in-progress control.

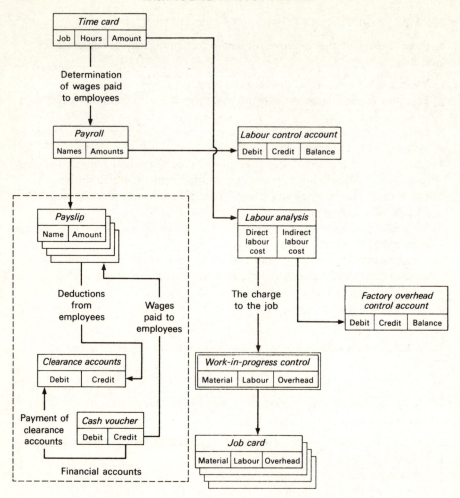

FIGURE 22.3. Basic documentation – labour accounting

## 22.95 BASIC DOCUMENTATION – SALES ACCOUNTING

The basic documentation in respect of sales accounting and its link with the factory may be considered as including:

1. Customer's order – the document received from the customer instructing the company to supply goods on the terms and conditions stated
2. Order analysis – the analysis sheet that analyses the customers' orders received to give classified order information such as product and area detail
3. Finished goods stores ledger sheet – the document showing finished goods stock movement and the book stock at a given time for a particular item of stock

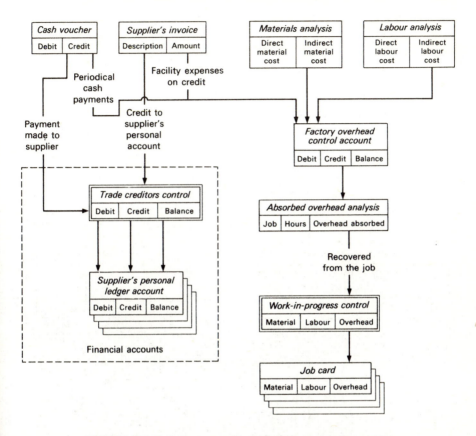

FIGURE 22.4. Basic documentation — factory overhead accounting

4. Invoice — the document issued to the customer showing the amount due for goods supplied
5. Sales analysis — the analysis sheet that analyses the invoices and cash sales to give classified sales information such as product and area detail
6. Works order — the instruction to the factory to produce the goods required
7. Job card — the document that shows the cost of the job
8. The customer's personal ledger account — the ledger sheet showing the changes in the amount owed by the customer and the amount due at any given time
9. Cash voucher — the document supporting the cash recieved from the customer for goods supplied.

The relationship of the above documents is illustrated in Figure 22.5.

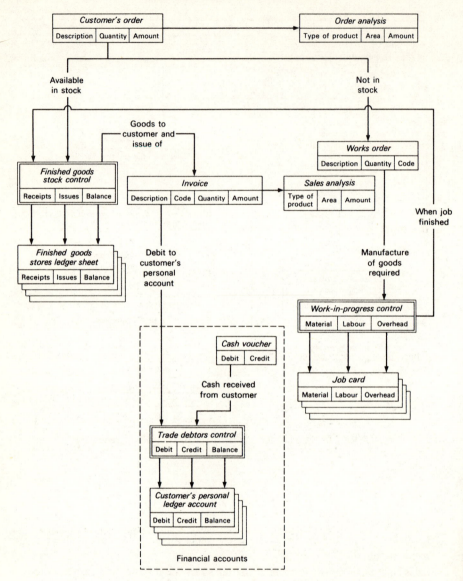

FIGURE 22.5. Basic documentation — sales accounting and the link with the factory

## 22.10 DATA PROCESSING CONTROL

In data processing the word 'control' is often used to indicate the overall check on detailed recording that may be accomplished by noting totals of this information in control accounts. The control accounts control subsidiary ledgers and the following are mentioned in the above sections:

1. Trade creditors control account
2. Stores ledger control account
3. Work-in-progress control account
4. Finished goods stock control account
5. Trade debtors control account.


Clearance accounts which hold balances pending their disposal to other accounts in the accounting system are very often called control accounts. The reason is that they control the treatment of an amount identified by the account title but they do not support subsidiary ledgers, unless cost centre records for overheads are maintained in association with such control accounts. The following accounts mentioned in the above sections are of this type:

(*a*)  Labour control account
(*b*)  Factory overhead control account
(*c*)  Administration costs control account
(*d*)  Selling and distribution costs control account.

The relationship of cost movement and these control accounts is illustrated in Figure 22.6.

The effective application of data control procedures is essential to ensure the accuracy of processed information for management. Where data processing is outside the control of the accountant he should retain the responsibility to ensure that adequate controls are built into the system. In the discharge of this function he should ensure that the controls are not excessive. This is particularly important where expensive equipment is in use that may incorporate programmed checks.


## 22.11 DOUBLE ENTRY BOOK-KEEPING

The accounting entries for specific transactions are illustrated in the following examples:


### 22.111 INTEGRATED SYSTEM – FINANCIAL AND COST ACCOUNTING ENTRIES

**Example\***
C Ltd operates an integrated accounting system and the trial balance at the 1st May 19. . was as follows:

*An example taken from the ICMA examination in Part II, Cost Accountancy (June, 1971).

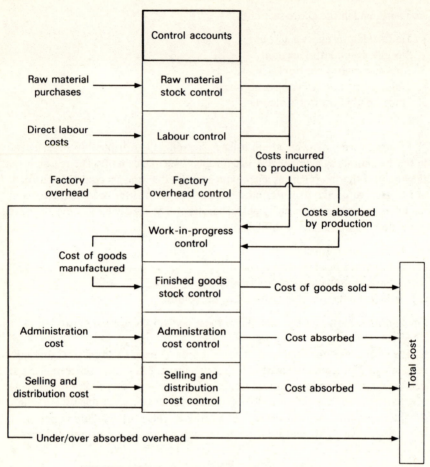

FIGURE 22.6. Cost movement and related control accounts

| *Entry reference* | | £000 Debit | £000 Credit |
|---|---|---|---|
| (a) | Raw material stock | 138 | |
| (b) | Work-in-progress | 34 | |
| (c) | Finished goods stock | 62 | |
| (d) | Debtors | 200 | |
| (e) | Creditors | | 140 |
| (f) | Expense creditors | | 58 |
| (g) | Wages accrued | | 10 |
| (h) | Bank | 40 | |
| (i) | Freehold buildings | 360 | |
| (j) | Plant and machinery at cost | 240 | |
| (k) | Provision for depreciation – plant and machinery | | 60 |
| (l) | Issued share capital | | 600 |
| (m) | General reserve | | 160 |
| (n) | Profit and loss account | | 46 |
| | | 1,074 | 1,074 |

The following information is given of the transactions that took place in May
19. .:

| Entry reference | | £000 |
|---|---|---|
| (i) | Sales on credit | 320 |
| (ii) | Purchases of raw materials on credit | 92 |
| (iii) | Raw materials returned to supplier | 4 |
| (iv) | Production overhead incurred on credit | 88 |
| (v) | Selling and distribution costs incurred on credit | 42 |
| (vi) | Administration costs incurred on credit | 37 |
| (vii) | Direct wages incurred and charged to production | 42 |
| (viii) | Raw materials issued to production | 80 |
| (ix) | Raw materials issued to production maintenance department | 10 |
| (x) | Raw materials returned to store from production | 2 |
| (xi) | Cost of finished goods sold | 210 |
| (xii) | Payments received in respect of sales | 330 |
| (xiii) | Payments made for raw materials purchased | 101 |
| (xiv) | Discounts allowed | 11 |
| (xv) | Discounts received | 3 |
| (xvi) | Payments made to expense creditors | 140 |
| (xvii) | Direct wages paid | 34 |

You are informed that:

1. Depreciation of plant and machinery is provided for at 10% per annum on cost
2. Production overhead is absorbed on the basis of 250% of direct wages incurred
3. Selling and distribution costs and administration costs incurred in May 19. . are
   charged against the profit of May 19. .
4. Work-in-progress was valued on 31st May 19. . at £39,000.

*Required:*
Open and write up the accounts for May 19. . and prepare the profit statement for
May 19. .

**Comment**
In an integrated system, the requirements for financial and cost accounting purposes
are obtained from one set of records. The accounts are maintained in what is usually
described as a general or nominal ledger. It is recognised that most of the basic data
is common to financial and cost accounting requirements which can be met by
analysis of this data as necessary.

The book-keeping procedure can be traced in the accounts shown below, using
the entry references, and the entries have been made in the following order:

1. The recording of opening entries as shown in the opening trial balance — debit
   and credit single entries as indicated

2. The recording of the transactions bearing in mind the notes given — a debit and credit for each transaction. Additional accounts are opened as necessary, e.g., the clearance accounts for factory overhead and wages.

*C. Ltd – General Ledger*
*Accounts for the month ended 31st May 19. . (£000)*

### Raw Material Stock

| | | | | | |
|---|---|---|---|---|---|
| (a) | Opening balance | 138 | (iii) | Returned to supplier | 4 |
| (ii) | Purchases | 92 | (viii) | Issued to production | 80 |
| (x) | Return from production | 2 | (ix) | Issued to production maintenance department | 10 |
| | | | | Balance carried forward | 138 |
| | | 232 | | | 232 |
| | Balance brought forward | 138 | | | |

### Work-in-Progress

| | | | | | |
|---|---|---|---|---|---|
| (b) | Opening balance | 34 | (x) | Material returned to store | 2 |
| (vii) | Direct wages | 42 | | Completed work | 220 |
| (viii) | Raw material | 80 | (4) | Balance carried forward | 39 |
| (2) | Production overhead | 105 | | | |
| | | 261 | | | 261 |
| | Balance brought forward | 39 | | | |

### Finished Goods Stock

| | | | | | |
|---|---|---|---|---|---|
| (c) | Opening balance | 62 | (xi) | Finished goods sold | 210 |
| | Completed work | 220 | | Balance carried forward | 72 |
| | | 282 | | | 282 |
| | Balance brought forward | 72 | | | |

### Debtors

| | | | | | |
|---|---|---|---|---|---|
| (d) | Opening balance | 200 | (xii) | Cash | 330 |
| (i) | Sales | 320 | (xiv) | Discounts allowed | 11 |
| | | | | Balance carried forward | 179 |
| | | 520 | | | 520 |
| | Balance brought forward | 179 | | | |

### Creditors

| | | | | | |
|---|---|---|---|---|---|
| (iii) | Material returned | 4 | (e) | Opening balance | 140 |
| (xiii) | Cash | 101 | (ii) | Raw material purchases | 92 |
| (xv) | Discounts received | 3 | | | |
| | Balance carried forward | 124 | | | |
| | | 232 | | | 232 |
| | | | | Balance brought forward | 124 |

### Expense Creditors

| | | | | | |
|---|---|---:|---|---|---:|
| (xvi) | Cash | 140 | (f) | Opening balance | 58 |
| | Balance carried forward | 85 | (iv) | Production overhead | 88 |
| | | | (v) | Selling and distribution costs | 42 |
| | | | (vi) | Administration costs | 37 |
| | | 225 | | | 225 |
| | | | | Balance brought forward | 85 |

### Wages Control

| | | | | | |
|---|---|---:|---|---|---:|
| (xvii) | Wages paid | 34 | (g) | Opening balance | 10 |
| | Balance carried forward | 18 | (vii) | Charged to work-in-progress | 42 |
| | | 52 | | | 52 |
| | | | | Balance brought forward | 18 |

### Bank

| | | | | | |
|---|---|---:|---|---|---:|
| (h) | Opening balance | 40 | (xiii) | Paid to creditors | 101 |
| (xii) | Cash from debtors | 330 | (xvi) | Paid to expense creditors | 140 |
| | | | (xvii) | Wages paid | 34 |
| | | | | Balance carried forward | 95 |
| | | 370 | | | 370 |
| | Balance brought forward | 95 | | | |

### Freehold Buildings

| | | |
|---|---|---:|
| (i) | Opening balance | 360 |

### Plant and Machinery

| | | |
|---|---|---:|
| (j) | Opening balance | 240 |

### Provision for Depreciation – Plant and Machinery

| | | |
|---|---|---:|
| (k) | Opening balance | 60 |
| (l) | Depreciation | 2 |
| | | 62 |

### Issued Share Capital

| | | |
|---|---|---:|
| (l) | Opening balance | 600 |

### General Reserve

| | | |
|---|---|---:|
| (m) | Opening balance | 160 |

### Profit and Loss Account

| | | | | | |
|---|---|---:|---|---|---:|
| (v) | Selling and distribution cost | 42 | (n) | Opening balance | 46 |
| (vi) | Administration cost | 37 | (i) | Sales | 320 |
| (xi) | Cost of goods sold | 210 | (xv) | Discounts received | 3 |
| (xiv) | Discounts allowed | 11 | | Cover-absorption of overhead | 5 |
| | Balance carried forward | 74 | | | |
| | | 374 | | | 374 |
| | | | | Balance brought forward | 74 |

*Factory Overhead Control*

| | | | | | |
|---|---|---|---|---|---|
| (iv) | Incurred | 88 | (2) | Charged to work-in-progress | 105 |
| (ix) | Materials in maintenance department | 10 | | | |
| (1) | Depreciation on plant and machinery | 2 | | | |
| | Profit and loss account | 5 | | | |
| | | 105 | | | 105 |

The following balances were transferred as follows:

(a) Cost of work completed: £220,000
    Credit: Work-in-progress
    Debit: Finished goods stock.

(b) Over-absorption of factory overhead: £5,000 (Total actual cost incurred: £100,000 less charged to work-in-progress: £105,000)
    Debit: Factory overhead control
    Credit: Profit and loss account.

The profit statement may be prepared from the profit and loss account as follows:

*Profit Statement*
*Month ended 31st May 19. .*

| | | £000 |
|---|---|---|
| Sales | | 320 |
| Less cost of goods sold | 210 | |
|    over-absorption of factory overhead | 5 | 205 |
| Gross profit | | 115 |
| Less administration cost | 37 | |
|    selling and distribution cost* | 53 | 90 |
| | | 25 |
| Add: other income: discounts received | | 3 |
| Net profit | | 28 |
| Balance brought forward | | 46 |
| Balance carried forward | | 74 |

## 22.112 SUB–SYSTEM – COST ACCOUNTING ENTRIES

**Example**[†]

L. Engineering Co. Ltd keep their financial accounts separate from their cost accounts. In the cost ledger at the beginning of the year (1st July) the balances were

---

* This item includes the discounts allowed (£11).
  † Part of an example taken from the ICMA examination in Part IV, Advanced Cost and Management Accountancy (December, 1967).

as follows:

| *Entry reference* | | £ |
|---|---|---|
| (a) | Stores ledger control | 10,000 |
| (b) | Work-in-progress control | 15,500 |
| (c) | Finished stock control | 3,500 |
| (d) | Cost ledger control | 29,000 |

Transactions for the year ended 30th June were:

| *Entry reference* | | £ | £ |
|---|---|---|---|
| 1 | Purchases of raw materials | | 55,000 |
| 2 | Wages – direct | 79,000 | |
| 3 | – indirect factory | 21,000 | 100,000 |
| 4 | Factory overhead expenses – incurred | | 36,000 |
| 5 | – absorbed | | 55,000 |
| 6 | Administration overhead expenses – incurred | | 12,500 |
| 7 | – absorbed | | 12,400 |
| 8 | Selling overhead expenses – incurred | | 7,500 |
| 9 | – absorbed | | 7,600 |
| 10 | Materials issued to production | | 57,500 |
| 11 | Sales | | 265,000 |
| 12 | Work-in-progress: value at 30th June | | 13,500 |
| 13 | Finished stock: value at 30th June | | 4,000 |

*Required:*
Show the accounts in the cost ledger for the year ended 30th June 19. .

**Comment**
To avoid the duplication of clerical effort, an integrated system is preferred but sometimes it may be necessary to keep separate records for cost accounts as, for example, when a costing system is first introduced and the accountant does not wish to dislocate an established financial accounting system. Procedures may be modified subsequently, but in the meantime, the procedure for the sub-system for the cost accounts is to establish a link with the general ledger through the medium of the cost ledger control account. This makes the cost ledger a subsidiary ledger of the general ledger as follows:

*L. Engineering Co. Ltd – Cost Ledger*
*Accounts for the year ended 30th June 19. .*

*Stores Ledger Control*

| | | £ | | | £ |
|---|---|---|---|---|---|
| (a) | Opening balance | 10,000 | (10) | Issues to production | 57,500 |
| (1) | Purchases | 55,000 | | Balance carried forward | 7,500 |
| | | 65,000 | | | 65,000 |
| | Balance brought forward | 7,500 | | | |

### Work-in-Progress Control

| | | £ | | | £ |
|---|---|---|---|---|---|
| (b) | Opening balance | 15,500 | | Cost of finished goods | 193,500 |
| (2) | Direct wages | 79,000 | (12) | Balance carried forward | 13,500 |
| (5) | Factory overhead absorbed | 55,000 | | | |
| (10) | Materials | 57,500 | | | |
| | | 207,000 | | | 207,000 |
| | Balance brought forward | 13,500 | | | |

### Finished Stock Control

| | | £ | | | £ |
|---|---|---|---|---|---|
| (c) | Opening balance | 3,500 | | Cost of goods sold | 193,000 |
| | Cost of finished goods | 193,500 | (13) | Balance carried forward | 4,000 |
| | | 197,000 | | | 197,000 |
| | Balance brought forward | 4,000 | | | |

### Cost Ledger Control

| | | £ | | | | £ |
|---|---|---|---|---|---|---|
| (11) | Sales | 265,000 | (d) | Opening balance | | 29,000 |
| | Balance carried forward | 25,000 | (1) | Raw material purchases | | 55,000 |
| | | | (2 and 3) | Wages | | 100,000 |
| | | | (4) | Factory overhead | | 36,000 |
| | | | (6) | Administration overhead | | 12,500 |
| | | | (8) | Selling overhead | | 7,500 |
| | | | | Profit and loss account | | 50,000 |
| | | 290,000 | | | | 290,000 |
| | | | | Balance brought forward | | 25,000 |

### Wages Control

| | £ | | | £ |
|---|---|---|---|---|
| (2 and 3) Cost ledger control | 100,000 | (2) | Work-in-progress | 79,000 |
| | | (3) | Factory overhead control | 21,000 |
| | 100,000 | | | 100,000 |

### Factory Overhead Control

| | | £ | | | £ |
|---|---|---|---|---|---|
| (3) | Wages control | 21,000 | (5) | Work-in-progress | 55,000 |
| (4) | Cost ledger control | 36,000 | | Under-absorption | 2,000 |
| | | 57,000 | | | 57,000 |

### Administration Overhead Control

| | | £ | | | £ |
|---|---|---|---|---|---|
| (6) | Cost ledger control | 12,500 | (7) | Profit and loss account | 12,400 |
| | | | | Under-absorption | 100 |
| | | 12,500 | | | 12,500 |

*Selling Overhead Control*

| | £ | | | £ |
|---|---|---|---|---|
| (8) Cost ledger control | 7,500 | (9) | Profit and loss account | 7,600 |
| Over-absorption | 100 | | | |
| | 7,600 | | | 7,600 |

*Profit and Loss Account*

| | £ | | | £ |
|---|---|---|---|---|
| Cost of goods sold | 193,000 | (11) | Sales | 265,000 |
| (7) Administration overhead | 12,400 | | | |
| (9) Selling overhead | 7,600 | | | |
| Balance carried forward | 52,000 | | | |
| | 265,000 | | | 265,000 |
| Under-absorption | | | Balance brought | |
| Factory overhead | 2,000 | | forward | 52,000 |
| Administration overhead | 100 | | Over-absorption | |
| Profit − cost ledger control | 50,000 | | Selling overhead | 100 |
| | 52,100 | | | 52,100 |

The book-keeping procedure follows the previous example with the opening of clearance accounts as necessary (in this case, control accounts for wages, factory overhead, administration overhead and selling overhead); but links outside the cost ledger all taken through the cost ledger control account.

The following balances were transferred as follows:

(a) Cost of finished goods: £193,500:
Credit: Work-in-progress
Debit: Finished goods stock.

(b) Cost of goods sold: £193,000:
Credit: Finished goods stock
Debit: Profit and loss account.

(c) Under-absorption of factory overhead: £2,000:
Credit: Factory overhead control
Debit: Profit and loss account

(d) Under-absorption of administration overhead: £100:
Credit: Administration overhead control
Debit: Profit and loss account.

(e) Over-absorption of selling overhead: £100:
Credit: Profit and loss account
Debit: Selling overhead control

(f) Profit: £50,000:
Credit: Cost ledger control
Debit: Profit and loss account.

## 22.113 STANDARD COSTING ENTRIES

In a standard costing system, the variances are debited or credited to their variance accounts; the double entry being completed according to their source of calculation (the control accounts). The debit variance accounts (unfavourable variances) and the credit variance accounts (favourable variances) are transferred to profit and loss account.

## 22.12 PROFIT RECONCILIATION

Where separate records are maintained for cost and financial accounts, the profits under both systems should be reconciled and the types of differences between the two sets of records that should be identified are as follows:

1. Differences in amounts where items are correctly included in both sets of accounts and correctly at different amounts, e.g., stock valuations
2. Differences in the calculated results because items have been correctly excluded from one set of accounts: either, included in the cost accounts but not in the financial accounts, e.g., notional rent; or included in the financial accounts but not in the cost accounts, e.g., interest
3. Errors in the processing of the data under both systems, e.g., items that should be included in both sets of records but excluded from one system.*

## 22.13 IMPACT OF METHODS OF DATA PROCESSING

The consideration of the nature of input to data processing systems has had the effect of dictating the form or source documentation and, with the availability of computers, their use has had a more fundamental effect. This has occurred because, as companies have increased in size, departmental specialisation has increased. To support this type of organisation, it is realised that a business should communicate information quickly between departments, establish a system of data flow between departments, and establish controls on the accuracy of this data. This may be difficult owing to:

1. The multiplicity of files maintained by many departments, ostensibly of the same data, and processed to differing standards
2. The limited use of departmental data by other departments
3. The inability to use an input transaction to update all relevant files of data
4. The relatively slow speed of processing the data.

---

*These errors may be eliminated prior to the preparation of the reconciliation statement by correcting entries as necessary.

To meet these difficulties what is sometimes referred to as the data base concept is adopted and its characteristics are as follows:

(*a*)  A single record used within the system for a single type of information
(*b*)  Any department in the organisation is provided with data as necessary irrespective of financial source
(*c*)  Data is stored and controlled according to output requirements
(*d*)  Files are automatically updated by an input transaction
(*e*)  The type of information required governs extraction arrangements
(*f*)  The centralised control of data.

## 22.14  A CONCLUDING COMMENT

The amount of paper that is created and processed through most businesses is considerable and the cost of this operation is a major item to be justified in the same way as any other cost of the business. It is important that any business examines its clerical organisation and ensures that modern methods of processing are adopted as appropriate. The size of the business is a major factor but, as the more advanced forms of equipment are used, the tendency will be to centralise data processing. This situation affects the accountant particularly as data processing is concerned with accounting transactions, establishing effective controls and the development of management information systems.

## FOR FURTHER STUDY

QUESTIONS

1. *Features of double entry cost accounting*
   What are the main features of double entry cost accounting?          (ACA)

2. *Meaning of integrated accounts*
   (*a*)  What is meant by integral accounts?
   (*b*)  To demonstrate the principles of integral accounts, give a coded list of account headings for a limited liability company.          (ICMA)

3. *Cost data flow*
   Produce a diagram showing how the elements of cost flow and accumulate to a final and total cost. Your chart should be applicable to a manufacturing organisation.          (ACA)

**4.** *Interpretation of control accounts*

The following trial balance results from entries in a cost ledger:

|  | Dr. £ | Cr. £ |
|---|---|---|
| (*a*)  Cost ledger control account |  | 11,590 |
| (*b*)  Stores ledger account | 3,790 |  |
| (*c*)  Work-in-progress account | 5,430 |  |
| (*d*)  Finished goods account | 2,350 |  |
| (*e*)  Factory overhead account | 50 |  |
| (*f*)  Administration cost account |  | 30 |
|  | 11,620 | 11,620 |

*Required:*

Explain what each balance represents and the transactions out of which it has arisen. Show a detail of the work-in-progress account.          (ICMA)

**5.** *Cost ledger accounting entries*

The following balances are extracted from a company's cost ledger as at 1st March:

|  | Dr. £ | Cr. £ |
|---|---|---|
| Raw materials — control account | 50,836 |  |
| Work-in-progress — control account | 12,745 |  |
| Finished stock — control account | 25,980 |  |
| Nominal ledger — control account |  | 89,561 |
|  | 89,561 | 89,561 |

Further transactions took place during the following quarter, as follows:

|  | £ |
|---|---|
| Factory overhead — allocated to work-inprogress | 11,786 |
| Goods finished (at cost) | 36,834 |
| Raw materials purchased | 22,422 |
| Direct wages — allocated to work-in-progress | 8,370 |
| Raw materials issued to production | 16,290 |
| Cost of goods sold | 41,389 |
| Raw materials credited by suppliers | 836 |
| Customers' returns (at cost) of good finished stock | 2,856 |
| Inventory audit — raw material losses | 1,236 |
| Work-in-progress rejected (with no scrap value) | 1,764 |

*Required:*

(*a*)  Write up the four accounts in the cost ledger
(*b*)  Schedule the remaining balances.          (ICMA)

**6.** *Cost ledger accounting entries with standard costs*

The information given below relates to a manufacturing company.

The stock balances at standard cost on 31st July 19. . were:

|  | £ |
|---|---|
| Raw materials | 150,000 |
| Work-in-progress | 90,000 |
| Finished goods | 120,000 |

The budgeted figures for the quarter ended 31st October 19. . were:

| Production in standard hours | 300,000 |
|---|---|
|  | £ |
| Production overhead |  |
| Fixed | 75,000 |
| Variable | 180,000 |

Data relating to the quarter ended 31st October 19. . were as follows:

|  | £ |
|---|---|
| Purchases of raw materials |  |
| At standard cost | 210,000 |
| At actual cost | 214,000 |
| Issues of raw materials at standard prices |  |
| For standard quantities | 206,000 |
| For actual quantities | 209,000 |
| Direct wages (296,000 actual hours) | 230,000 |
| Direct labour at standard cost | 236,800 |
| Production overhead incurred |  |
| Fixed | 74,000 |
| Variable | 185,000 |
| Administration and selling expenses incurred | 80,000 |
| Sales | 850,000 |
| Production achieved during the quarter (in standard hours) | 316,000 |

The stock balances at standard cost on 31st October 19. . included:

|  | £ |
|---|---|
| Work-in-progress | 101,600 |
| Finished goods | 150,000 |

*Required:*
From the information given above:

(a) Write up the cost ledger
(b) Prepare a costing profit and loss account showing the appropriate variances
    for the quarter ended 31st October 19. .                    (ICMA)

7. *Entries in an integrated accounting system included interim statements for
   management*
   A manufacturing company installed as from 1st August 19. . an integrated
   standard costing system.

The balance sheet of the company as at 31st July 19. . was as follows:

|  | £ | £ |
|---|---|---|
| Fixed assets at cost | 200,000 | |
| Less depreciation to date | 40,000 | 160,000 |
| Current assets | | |
| Stocks: | | |
| Finished goods | 25,000 | |
| Work-in-progress | 12,000 | |
| Raw materials | 23,000 | |
| Debtors | 33,000 | |
| Cash | 27,000 | |
| | 120,000 | |
| Current liabilities | | |
| Trade creditors | 26,000 | |
| Other creditors (including tax and dividends) | 31,000 | |
| | 57,000 | |
| Net current assets | | 63,000 |
| | | 223,000 |
| Financed by | | |
| Ordinary share capital | | 200,000 |
| Reserves and profit and loss account | | 23,000 |
| | | 223,000 |

Stocks of finished goods, work-in-progress and raw materials are shown in the above balance sheet at actual cost but before the integrated standard costing system came into operation they were revalued at standard cost.

The budget for the year commencing 1st August 19. . included the following:

| Production in standard hours | 220,000 |
|---|---|
| | £ |
| Factory overhead | 70,400 |
| Administration, selling and distribution expenses | 52,500 |
| Sales at standard selling prices | 420,000 |

The following information is given for the three months ended 31st October 19. .:

| | At standard cost 1st August 19. . £ | At standard cost 31st October 19. . £ |
|---|---|---|
| Stocks | | |
| Finished goods | 24,500 | 26,500 |
| Work-in-progress | 12,500 | 11,500 |
| Raw materials | 24,000 | 26,700 |

|                                                  | £        |
|--------------------------------------------------|----------|
| Sales, actual quantities at                      |          |
|   Actual selling prices                          | 98,000   |
|   Standard selling prices                        | 100,000  |

|                                                  | At actual cost |
|                                                  | £        |
| Payments                                         |          |
|   Received from debtors                          | 101,000  |
|   Made to trade creditors                        | 52,300   |
|   Made to other creditors                        | 13,000   |
|   Made for wages, insurance and tax              | 28,800   |
| Costs                                            |          |
|   Purchases of raw materials on credit           | 32,600   |
|   Direct wages, 54,000 actual hours              | 22,500   |
|   Indirect wages                                 | 6,300    |
|   Depreciation of fixed assets                   | 5,000    |
|   Indirect materials and expenses                | 5,700    |
|   Administration, selling and distribution expenses | 13,000 |

|                                                  | At standard prices |
|                                                  | £        |
| Purchases of materials on credit                 | 32,200   |
| Materials issued to production                   | 29,500   |

|                                                  | At standard cost |
|                                                  | £        |
| Direct wages, 52,500 standard hours              |          |
| at £0·4 per hour                                 | 21,000   |
| Materials input                                  | 29,000   |
| Factory overhead, 52,500 standard hours          | 16,800   |

For the purpose of this question, you may assume that:

(i) All wages earned for the three months, together with the insurance and tax have been paid

(ii) Indirect materials and expenses and administration, selling and distribution expenses should be regarded as credit transactions

(iii) Budgetary information for the quarter is one quarter of the budgeted yearly information.

*Required:*

(a) Record the information given above in a suitable integral form in the books of the company for the three months ended 31st October 19. .

(b) Prepare for presentation to management the interim:

   (i) Profit and loss account for the three months ended 31st October 19. ., showing clearly variances from standard

   (ii) Balance sheet as at 31st October 19. .                     (ICMA)

**8.** *Integration of the cost and financial accounts*

The A.B. Co. Ltd is a light engineering company which has doubled in size in the last five years. The company's cost accounting system has been developed independently of the financial accounting system and although a reconciliation of these two systems is attempted at the end of each year this usually requires a great deal of time and effort. It has been decided to investigate the possibility of integrating the financial and cost accounts and you have been made responsible for this investigation.

*Required:*

Prepare a report outlining:

(*a*) The types of differences between the two sets of records that may cause difficulty when reconciliation takes place at the end of the year

(*b*) What specific steps and reorganisation are required to integrate the cost and accounting records without duplication of effort and to produce relevant financial control information for management.                          (ACA)

**9.** *Reconciliation of the cost and financial accounts*

The following summary trading and profit and loss account appears in the financial accounts of the Beta Co. Ltd:

*Summary Trading and Profit and Loss Accounts*
*for the year ended 30th June 19. .*

|  | £ | £ |  | £ |
|---|---|---|---|---|
| Opening stock | 5,000 |  | Sales | 315,000 |
| Purchases | 135,000 |  |  |  |
|  | 140,000 |  |  |  |
| Less closing stock | 8,500 | 131,500 |  |  |
| Direct wages |  | 42,500 |  |  |
| Works expenses: |  |  |  |  |
| Indirect wages | 2,460 |  |  |  |
| Heat/light/power | 6,840 |  |  |  |
| Sundries | 1,200 |  |  |  |
| Depreciation | 12,200 | 22,700 |  |  |
|  |  | 196,700 |  |  |
| Gross profit carried forward |  | 118,300 |  |  |
|  |  | 315,000 |  | 315,000 |

|  | £ | £ |  | £ |
|---|---|---|---|---|
| Selling expenses |  |  | Gross profit brought |  |
| Advertising | 6,420 |  | forward | 118,300 |
| Salaries | 16,460 |  | Gain on sale of |  |
| Travelling | 3,260 |  | freehold land | 3,650 |
| Showroom | 4,830 |  | Investment income | 100 |
| Bad debts | 850 |  |  |  |
| Sundries | 2,400 | 34,220 |  |  |

Administration expenses

| | | |
|---|---|---|
| Salaries | 16,450 | |
| Printing and stationery | 2,490 | |
| Audit fee | 500 | |
| General | 2,350 | 21,790 |

Financial expenses

| | | |
|---|---|---|
| Debenture interest | 1,750 | |
| Bank interest | 3,275 | |
| Hire purchase interest | 445 | 5,470 |
| Net profit | | 60,570 |
| | | 122,050 |

122,050

*Notes:*

(a) In the cost accounts:

   (i) Works overhead, excluding depreciation, is charged at a rate of £0·05 per product produced

  (ii) Selling overhead is charged at a rate of 12% of sales turnover

 (iii) Administration expenses are charged at a fixed sum of £25,000 per annum. Included in this is an allowance of £3,000 to cover all financial income and expenditure.

(b) Depreciation in the financial accounts is calculated on a straight line basis but in the cost accounts there is a fixed annual charge equivalent to half of the straight line calculation plus a running charge of £0·025 per unit produced.

(c) The company owns the business premises but in the cost accounts, in addition to the items mentioned above, there is a notional charge of £500 per annum for rent.

(d) Items of a non-revenue nature are not included in the cost accounts.

(e) In the cost accounts, stock is valued at direct cost (material and labour) but in the financial accounts it includes an allowance for overheads.

  Opening stock consists of 5,000 units valued:

| | £ |
|---|---|
| Materials | 3,100 |
| Labour | 1,100 |
| Overheads | 800 |
| | 5,000 |

Closing stock consists of 8,000 units valued:

| | £ |
|---|---|
| Materials | 5,300 |
| Labour | 1,700 |
| Overheads | 1,500 |
| | 8,500 |

(f) Sales were 210,000 units at £1·5 per unit.

*Required:*

From the above trading and profit and loss account and the additional information given, prepare a detailed statement reconciling the profit of £60,570 as
disclosed by the financial accounts with the figure of £54,925 as disclosed in
the cost accounts.                                                         (ACA)

10. *The data base concept*

'The data base concept encompasses a central bank or file containing information about a business in a readily accessible form. Data base systems collect,
monitor, and report information to management.'

Milton J. Cooke, 'Data base revolution', *Systems and Procedures Journal*,
March/April, 1968, p. 20.

*Required:*

Explain and comment on this statement.

11. *Choice of an integrated or sub-system of cost accounting*

Mr Watkins had been appointed management accountant of Baked Biscuits Ltd
to introduce a costing system and there was disagreement as to the way in
which the double-entry book-keeping should be controlled.

Mr Elliott, the chief accountant, maintained that the only system worth
consideration was an integrated system and his reasoning was based on the
belief that any other system would be a waste of clerical effort. In any case, he
considered that any other system was old-fashioned and modern procedure was
geared to all embracing systems not independent accounting routines.

Mr Watkins was favourably inclined towards an integrated system but initial
installation of a costing sub-system was necessary for the following reasons:

(*a*) The management wanted a range of costing reports quickly and to get this
information, chaos would result if existing accounting routines were altered
on the scale required to give the classified information for costing purposes

(*b*) The financial accounting routines were operating efficiently and to maintain
this efficiency the alteration of any one routine to meet costing and financial
requirements would need detailed study and careful introduction.

Mr Elliott was influenced by these arguments to the extent that he agreed to
the sub-system introduction providing that the cost system was controlled in
relation to the financial accounts and profits be capable of reconciliation as
necessary.

*Required:*

Comment on the situation described in this case.

12. *Possible centralisation of accounting work*

Paper Products Ltd had increased in size as a result of acquiring established
companies and the accounting arrangements had continued on a decentralised
basis. Each subsidiary company had its own accounting department producing
the accounting information required by the local and parent company managements.

The new group accountant had been employed by companies operating centralised accounting systems and he felt that Paper Products Ltd should have its accounting work centralised for the following reasons:

(*a*) Greater economy of data processing
(*b*) A better information service to management
(*c*) Benefits would arise to the parent company from greater control and standardisation of accounting routines
(*d*) The corporate identity of the company could be improved by individual companies losing some of their separate identity.

As might be expected, the larger subsidiary companies objected to this point of view, mainly on the grounds of losing control of activities.

*Required:*

Comment on the case described and include the consideration of the advantages and disadvantages of the centralisation of accounting work.

FURTHER READING

Burney, A. G. B. *Illustrations of Management Accounts in Practice*. Gee, 1959. Chapter 9.
Dobson, R. Warwick. *An Introduction to Cost Accountancy*. Volume III. Gee, 1954.
McRae, T. W. *The Impact of Computers on Accounting*. John Wiley, New York, 1964. Chapters 4, 7 and 10.

# 23 Cost Accounting Methods

OBJECTIVE OF THE CHAPTER
To explain the costing sequence in the cost ascertainment procedures for jobbing and processing industries. The chapter includes the consideration of uniform costing.

OUTLINE OF THE CHAPTER

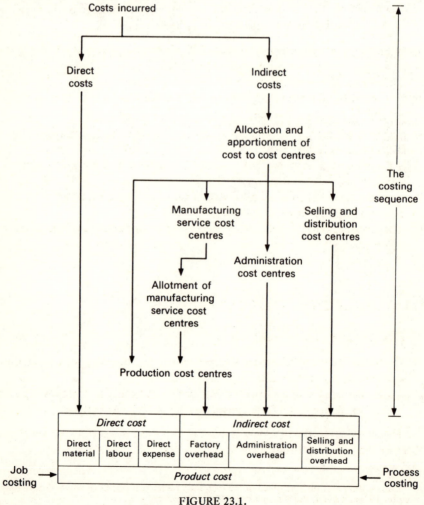

FIGURE 23.1.

450

References have been made in earlier chapters to the costing of a product by the identification of costs associated with product manufacture, administration and marketing. The costs directly identifiable with the product (direct material, direct labour and direct expense) do not present a problem, but indirect costs are more difficult to allot to a specific cost unit.* The costing sequence used involves:

1. Costing the cost centres
2. Allotting the manufacturing service cost centre costs to producing cost centres
3. Allotting the producing cost centre costs to units of production
4. Allotting the administration and marketing cost centre costs to products.

The type of manufacturing affects the costing procedure adopted and the two main methods of manufacture, jobbing and processing, use the two main types of costing: job and process costing. The principal feature of jobbing manufacture is that production orders are usually different and, therefore, costs are allotted to each job. In the early sections of this chapter jobbing manufacture will be assumed, and then processing manufacture will be considered.

Underlying the costing sequence are the following assumptions:

1. Average costs are a reasonable approximation to actual costs
2. The basis adopted for assigning costs to cost centres or cost units reasonably reflects the incidence of those costs to such cost centres or cost units
3. The period costs used have been assessed by applying acceptable accountancy conventions
4. To the extent that costs are estimated in the costing process, actual costs will not be materially different from such estimates
5. The cost accumulation reasonably reflects the economic cycle of the goods manufactured.

## 23.1  COSTING THE COST CENTRES

The costs of a cost centre are of two types:

1. Costs directly identifiable with the cost centre, e.g., the salary of a supervisor fully employed in the managing of a cost centre
2. Costs associated with a cost centre but shared with other cost centres, e.g., the rent of the factory paid for premises used by several cost centres.

The allotment of the first type of costs to cost centres is usually termed allocation because they can be attributed wholly to one cost centre.

---

* Absorption costing is assumed in the sections to follow. If marginal costing (considered in Chapter 19) is adopted, the allotment problem is largely avoided.

The problem concerns the basis adopted for the allotment of shared costs and the following are some of the bases that may be used:

(a)  Space occupied, e.g., for occupancy costs
(b)  Cost, e.g., store costs on the basis of material costs
(c)  Number of employees, e.g., labour related costs
(d)  Rating, e.g., power costs on the basis of plant horsepower
(e)  Activity, e.g., machine related costs per machine hour
(f) Capital value, e.g., for insurance.

The bases used for the apportionment of shared costs should be related as closely as possible to the type of cost and its application to cost centres. The apportionment of an expense is carried out as a result of calculating a proportion sum, e.g., if £180 is to be apportioned between three cost centres where the basic figures for calculating the apportionment are as follows:

|  Cost centre | Basis of apportionment units |
|---|---|
| A | 300 |
| B | 500 |
| C | 100 |
|  | 900 |

the calculation would be as follows:

| Cost centre | | £ |
|---|---|---|
| A | $\frac{300}{900} \times £180 =$ | 60 |
| B | $\frac{500}{900} \times £180 =$ | 100 |
| C | $\frac{100}{900} \times £180 =$ | 20 |
|  |  | 180 |

## 23.2  ASSIGNING THE MANUFACTURING SERVICE COST

It may be difficult to find an equitable basis for apportioning a single item of shared cost between cost centres. It is even more difficult to find such a basis for several costs accumulated for a manufacturing service cost centre to be apportioned between producing cost centres. It is for this reason that the apportionment is sometimes made on a two-part basis:

*Part 1.* Fixed costs of the manufacturing service cost centre apportioned to the producing cost centres for whom the service is provided on the most equitable basis available.

*Part 2.* Variable costs of the manufacturing service cost centre charged to the producing cost centres on the basis of actual use. An appropriate use rate would be calculated.

A further complication arises because service centres not only serve producing cost centres but other service centres. The apportionment may be applied repeatedly (sometimes referred to as continuing allotment) until all service department cost is allotted to producing cost centres. In practice, the procedure is often simplified by apportioning service centre costs in a set order and, once a particular cost centre costs have been eliminated, no allotment back to the cost centre is permitted. The order is often on the basis of the magnitude of cost, the aim being to minimise the inaccuracy occurring as a result of ignoring subsequent apportionments to service cost centres.

## 23.3 AN EXAMPLE OF COST ALLOTMENT TO PRODUCING COST CENTRES

**Example***
ACCA Ltd is a manufacturing company having two production departments: machining and assembly, and two service departments: maintenance and handling.

The estimated factory expenses for the quarter ending 31st March 19 . . are as follows:

|  |  | £ |
|---|---|---|
| Indirect labour | | |
| | Machining | 2,000 |
| | Assembly | 880 |
| | Maintenance | 3,970 |
| | Handling | 1,200 |
| Supervision | | 600 |
| Canteen | | 720 |
| Rent and rates | | 2,500 |
| Fuel and light | | 750 |
| Plant maintenance | | |
| | Machining | 423 |
| | Assembly | 42 |
| | Maintenance | 30 |
| | Handling | 32 |
| Plant insurance | | 188 |
| Plant depreciation | | 2,325 |

The following additional information is available and is to be used, where appro-

---

* Taken from the ACA examination Section III, Costing (December, 1971).

priate, in apportioning the expenses to departments:

|  | | Machining | Assembly | Maintenance | Handling |
|---|---|---|---|---|---|
| (a) | Floor area — square metres | 12,000 | 9,000 | 3,000 | 1,000 |
| (b) | Number of employees | 40 | 60 | 15 | 5 |
| (c) | Cost of plant | £30,000 | £10,000 | £5,000 | £2,000 |
| (d) | Plant annual depreciation rates on cost | 20% | 25% | 10% | 15% |
| (e) | Direct labour hours | 18,000 | 42,000 | | |

(f) Rent and rates and fuel and light are to be apportioned on a floor area basis; supervision and canteen according to the number of employees

(g) Of the total maintenance ocst, 10% is to be charged to handling and the remainder to the production departments on the basis of direct labour hours

(h) The cost of the handling department is to be charged to the production departments on the basis of numbers of employees.

### Calculation of the Producing Cost Centre Costs
### Factory Overhead Distribution Statement
### Quarter ended 31st March 19 . .

| Expense | £ | Allotment basis | Production cost centres | | Service cost centres | |
|---|---|---|---|---|---|---|
| | | | Machining £ | Assembly £ | Maintenance £ | Handling £ |
| Indirect labour | 8,050 | Actual | 2,000 | 880 | 3,970 | 1,200 |
| Supervision | 600 | Number of employees | 200 | 300 | 75 | 25 |
| Canteen | 720 | Number of employees | 240 | 360 | 90 | 30 |
| Rent and rates | 2,500 | Floor area | 1,200 | 900 | 300 | 100 |
| Fuel and light | 750 | Floor area | 360 | 270 | 90 | 30 |
| Plant maintenance | 527 | Actual | 423 | 42 | 30 | 32 |
| | 13,147 | Carried forward | 4,423 | 2,752 | 4,555 | 1,417 |

| | £ | Brought forward | £ | £ | £ | £ |
|---|---|---|---|---|---|---|
| | 13,147 | | 4,423 | 2,752 | 4,555 | 1,417 |
| Plant insurance | 188 | Plant cost | 120 | 40 | 20 | 8 |
| Plant depreciation | 2,325 | Actual | 1,500 | 625 | 125 | 75 |
| Cost centre total costs | 15,660 | | 6,043 | 3,417 | 4,700 | 1,500 |
| Maintenance department costs | | 10% to handling department | | | (470) | 470 |
| | | Direct labour hours | 1,269 | 2,961 | (4,230) | |
| Handling department costs | | Number of employees | 788 | 1,182 | | (1,970) |
| Producing cost centre costs | 15,660 | | 8,100 | 7,560 | Nil | Nil |

## 23.4  ASSIGNING THE PRODUCING COST CENTRE COSTS TO PRODUCTS PRODUCED

The process of assigning the producing cost centre costs to products produced is known as cost absorption and this involves the use of an overhead rate compiled from the detailed application of the general formula:

$$\text{Overhead rate} = \frac{\text{Overhead}}{\text{Absorption base considered suitable to reflect the incidence of the overhead to product units}}$$

The choice of the most appropriate base depends on a knowledge of the business. For example, if the overhead is concerned with a labour intensive manufacturing process, direct labour hours may be used to give an overhead absorption rate per direct labour hour. The factory overhead absorbed to the product might then be calculated by the application of the formula:

Direct labour time involved in the manufacture of the product  x  Factory overhead rate per direct labour hour  =  Factory overhead absorbed to the product

The absorption process may be accomplished by the use of a percentage. If, for example, direct labour cost is used for the absorption base, the factory overhead percentage may be calculated as follows:

$$\frac{\text{Factory overhead}}{\text{percentage}} = \frac{\text{Factory overhead}}{\text{Direct labour cost}} \times 100\%$$

The factory overhead absorbed to the product might then be calculated by the application of the formula:

$$
\begin{array}{c}
\text{Direct labour cost} \\
\text{incurred in the manufacture} \\
\text{of the product}
\end{array}
\times
\begin{array}{c}
\text{Factory overhead} \\
\text{percentage}
\end{array}
=
\begin{array}{c}
\text{Factory overhead} \\
\text{absorbed to the} \\
\text{product}
\end{array}
$$

If the manufacturing process is machine intensive a machine hour rate may be used and the cost centre may be the machine or group of similar machines for the manufacture of the product. Other costs may be used as the basis of absorption such as direct material cost or prime cost.

The rates or percentages of overhead absorption should be chosen with care and in general the hourly rates give a more accurate incidence of cost centre costs to cost units. The desire to achieve greater accuracy usually dictates the use of separate cost centre rates of overhead absorption where the use of the departmental resources differs in the manufacture of the products and the incidence of overhead varies between cost centres. Where the products manufactured are not dissimilar the number of units of production may be used to calculate the overhead absorption rate as a cost per unit.

## 23.5  OVER- UNDER-ABSORPTION OF OVERHEAD COST

In the previous chapter, it was noted that overhead absorbed to products may be different from actual overhead incurred. This may arise for two reasons:

1. The overhead absorbed has been calculated on a predetermined basis instead of actual as, for example, in the use of a standard overhead rate in standard costing. In this case, the actual cost may be different from the predetermined cost and the actual base used may also be different, e.g., number of machine hours actual and budgeted.
2. Seasonal costs, e.g., electricity charges are usually averaged for the year. It may be expected, therefore, that in the winter months when electricity costs are high, the cost absorbed would be less than the cost incurred. If estimating is accurate, it may be assumed that the opposite situation in the summer months will equalise such seasonal variations.

It may be expected that the difference (over- or under-absorbed overhead) at the end of the year may be of insignificant amount and the transfer of this figure to costing profit and loss account is the usual treatment, as noted in the previous chapter. If the figure is significant (costs ascertained on the predetermined basis are so inaccurate as to mislead management), the position is conceptually similar to the situation described for the treatment of standard cost variances in Chapter 18.

## 23.6  ASSIGNING OTHER COST CENTRE COSTS TO PRODUCTS

Administration and marketing costs are usually allotted to products as a percentage on factory cost, or a percentage on sales value. These methods are used because of their simplicity and the difficulty of applying more scientific methods such as separate functional rates of recovery at reasonable clerical cost. It should not be overlooked, however, that such procedures are unlikely to measure the incidence of administration and marketing costs to products with accuracy. The use of marginal costing restricting the allotment of these costs produces more meaningful information.

## 23.7 JOB COSTING

The costs accumulated as described in the above sections for each job are entered on job cost cards, the individual job being given a job number of identification. A typical job cost card is shown in Figure 23.2.

These cards for jobs-in-progress support the work-in-progress control and provide a check on estimates given, as well as serving a useful purpose in assisting estimators to bid accurately for future jobs of similar type.

The description in the previous chapter of the entries made for jobs completed follows the normal convention that profit is only taken when the work is complete and a sale is made. With long-term contracts, the period reporting of profits would be seriously distorted because such large contracts when completed would provide large profits for the period, and other years would indicate poor results when major jobs were in progress.

To overcome this problem, where large jobs are undertaken as, for example, the erection of a large building, the work-in-progress valuation is increased by a profit element and the relevant statement of standard accounting practice may be quoted as follows:

> The profit, if any, taken up needs to reflect the proportion of the work carried out at the accounting date and to take into account any known inequalities of profitability in the various stages of a contract. Many businesses, however, carry out contracts where the outcome cannot reasonably be assessed before the conclusion of the contract and in such cases it is prudent not to take up any profit. Where the business carries out contracts and it is considered that their outcome can be assessed with reasonable certainty before their conclusion, then the attributable profit should be taken up but the judgment involved should be exercised with prudence . . . The gross amount of long-term contract work-in-progress should be stated in accounts at cost plus attributable profits (if any) less foreseeable losses (if any)*

Accounting for long-term contracts is a job costing problem but the special factors introduced by the recognition of attributable profit are illustrated below and the procedure is termed contract costing.

---

* *Statement of Standard Accounting Practice* No. 9 (Accounting Standards Committee, May, 1975).

| Job cost card | | | |
|---|---|---|---|
| Customer_____         Job no._____ | | | |
| _____     Job description _____ | | | |
| Date job started _____     Date job completed _____ | | | |

| *Direct materials* | | | |
|---|---|---|---|
| Date | Voucher number | Brief details | £ |
|  |  |  |  |

| *Direct labour* | | | |
|---|---|---|---|
| Date | Voucher number | Brief details | £ |
|  |  |  |  |

| *Direct expense* | | | |
|---|---|---|---|
| Date | Voucher number | Brief details | £ |
|  |  |  |  |

| *Remarks* | *Summary* | | |
|---|---|---|---|
|  | Estimate £ |  | Actual £ |
|  |  | Direct material<br>Direct labour<br>Direct expense |  |
|  |  | Prime cost<br>Factory overhead<br>Administration cost<br>Selling and distribution cost |  |
|  |  | Total cost<br>Profit |  |
|  |  | Selling value |  |

FIGURE 23.2. Job cost card

## 23.8  AN EXAMPLE OF CONTRACT COSTING

**Example**[†]

F. Ltd is under contract to build a new factory for L.P. Ltd. The contract price has been agreed and work on the new site commenced on 1st January. Data relating to

[†] Taken from the ICMA examination in Part II, Cost Accountancy (December, 1969).

this contract is shown below:

|  | £000 |
|---|---|
| Cash received from contractee | 720 |
| Direct materials | |
|     Issued to contract | 340 |
|     Returned to central store | 8 |
|     Returned to supplier | 7 |
|     Transferred to other contracts | 15 |
|     On site at 31st December | |
| Direct wages | |
|     Paid on site | 220 |
|     Accrued on site at 31st December | 10 |
| Direct expenses | |
|     Paid | 25 |
|     Accrued at 31st December | 5 |
| Cost of work not yet certified at 31st December | 60 |
| Value of work certified at 30th November | 800 |
| Plant | |
|     Installed at cost | 100 |
|     On site, valued at 31st December | 75 |
| Overhead incurred on contract | 85 |
| Establishment charges | 60 |

## Required

Write up the contract cost account and show the valuation of work-in-progress as at 31st December.

## Comment

*Contract with L.P. Ltd., for New Factory*
*Cost Account — Year ended 31st December 19..*

|  |  |  | £000 |
|---|---|---|---|
| Direct materials | | | |
|   Issued to contract | | 340 | |
|   Returned to central store | 8 | | |
|   Returned to supplier | 7 | | |
|   Transferred to other contracts | 15 | | |
|   On site (31st December) | 20 | 50 | 290 |
| Direct wages | | | |
|   Paid on site | | 220 | |
|   Accrued on site (31st December) | | 10 | 230 |
| Direct expenses | | | |
|   Paid | | 25 | |
|   Accrued at 31st December | | 5 | 30 |
| Plant | | | |
|   Installed at cost | | 100 | |
|   On site — valued at 31st December | | 75 | 25 |
| Overhead incurred | | | 85 |
| Establishment charges | | | 60 |
| Cost of contract to date carried forward | | | 720 |

|                                                        | £000 |
|--------------------------------------------------------|------|
| Cost of the contract to date brought forward           | 720  |
| Less cost of work not yet certified (31st December)    | 60   |
| Cost of work certified (30th November)                 | 660  |
| Value of work certified at 30th November               | 800  |
| Profit                                                 | 140  |
| Allowance for contingencies                            | 56   |
| Attributable profit                                    | 84   |
| Work-in-progress valuation                             |      |
|    Cost of the contract to date         | 720  |
|    Add attributable profit              | 84   |
|                                                        | 804  |
|    Less cash received                   | 720  |
|                                                        | 84   |

The cost of the contract to date at £720,000 is a calculation of identifiable costs with the contract including £60,000 for establishment charges which is the proportion of head office costs applicable to the contract. To compare like with like, the costs must be adjusted to give the figures at 30th November when an independent valuation of the work done was carried out. The attributable profit is calculated as follows:

$$\frac{2}{3} \times \frac{£720,000}{£800,000} \times £140,000 = £84,000$$

The profit has been calculated on a figure of £800,000 but cash has only been received for £720,000. To relate the attributable profit to income, the cash proportion to the value of work done is taken. It would be unwise to make no allowance for unexpected costs and an assessment is made of this figure. One-third of the resulting profit is normally taken in accounting texts and the published accounts of large contractors show that some companies use this figure in practice.

An alternative calculation of the work-in-progress valuation is shown below:

|                                          | £        | £        |
|------------------------------------------|----------|----------|
| Cost of work not yet certified           |          | 60,000   |
| Add cash not paid for work valued        | 800,000  |          |
|                                          | 720,000  | 80,000   |
|                                          |          | 140,000  |
| Less allowance for contingencies         |          | 56,000   |
| Work-in-progress valuation (31st December) |        | 84,000   |

## 23.9 PROCESS COSTING

The distinguishing features of process costing as compared with job costing are:

1. The continuous nature of the process

2. The identification of process costs with all output from the process (i.e., the output units are not dissimilar in cost identification

3. The output of one process is either directly the input of a subsequent process or retained in a work-in-process store until required.

Processing industries such as chemicals and textile manufacture use process costing which relates costs to processes at each stage of manufacture and Figure 23.3

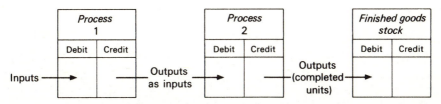

FIGURE 23.3. A simple continuous process

illustrates the simplest type of processing situation. The process may be separated as shown in Figure 23.4. In this case, the further processing in Process 2 has produced a more refined product: Product B.

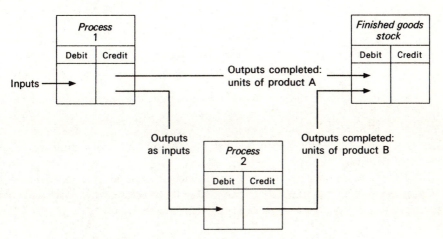

FIGURE 23.4. Further processing to produce another product

The processing situation may be more complicated and produce the output shown in Figure 23.5. In this case, incidental to Process 1 a byproduct is produced sold as Product C. The remaining output value is a joint cost of inputs A and B to Processes 2 and 3. After this processing marketable Products A and B are produced.

To calculate the costs of Products A and B, the joint costs as output from Process 1 need apportionment to give input values to Processes 2 and 3.

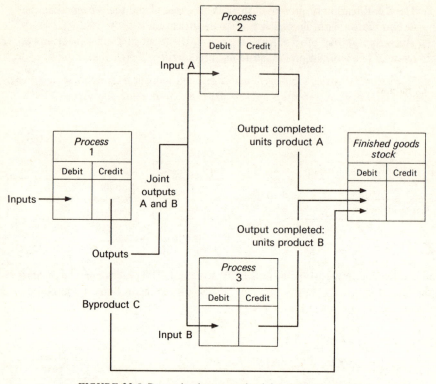

FIGURE 23.5. Processing incorporating joint and by-products

Inputs to processes in all these illustrations are the materials, labour and overheads for each process. The output of a preceding process providing the input of a suceeding process gives a material input cost to that succeeding process, i.e., the value of the input to the succeeding process is not analysed into its material, labour and overhead elements.

There may be opening and closing stocks in each process and to value these stocks an estimate is required of the stage of completion for each element of cost. The units produced and in process are reconciled and losses may be disclosed.

## 23.10 THE TREATMENT OF LOSSES AND GAINS IN PROCESS COSTING

**Example\***
Glux is produced by refining crude chemicals through a process which involves a weight loss of 15%. During Period 2, 8,000 grams of chemicals which cost £0·80 per gram were introduced into the process which yielded 6,000 grams of Glux. Wages

\* Taken from the ACA examination, Part III, Costing (December 1973).

booked to the process amounted to £1,200 and overhead apportioned thereto amounted to £1,140. The waste from the process was sold for £0·20 per gram.

*Required*

Prepare the process account to show the result of producing Glux during Period 2.

**Comment**

*Process Account for Period 2*

| | Grams | Cost per gram £ | £ | | Grams | Cost per gram £ | £ |
|---|---|---|---|---|---|---|---|
| Crude chemicals | 8,000 | 0·80 | 6,400 | Normal loss | 1,200 | 0·20 | 240 |
| Wages | | | 1,200 | Production | 6,000 | 1·25 | 7,500 |
| Overhead | | | 1,140 | Abnormal loss | 800 | 1·25 | 1,000 |
| | 8,000 | | 8,740 | | 8,000 | | 8,740 |

The cost per gram of the good units produced is calculated as follows:

$$\frac{£8,740 - £240}{6,000 + 800 \text{ units}} = £1·25 \text{ per gram}$$

The effect of this treatment is that (as mentioned in Chapter 15) normal losses are part of the cost of good units produced. The abnormal loss is taken away from the process at £1·25 per gram so that period costs are not distorted by abnormal losses. The 800 grams would be sold at £0·20 per gram and the £160 received would be offset against the £1,000 to result in a transfer of the abnormal loss to profit and loss account of £840.

In this example, the normal loss was indicated, therefore the balancing loss of 800 grams was abnormal. In examination work, where no indication is given of the nature of the loss, the balancing figure should be assumed to represent normal wastage.

Assume 7,000 grams of Glux had been produced in the above example, an abnormal gain of 200 grams would result as shown in the Process 2 account below:

*Process Account for Period 2*

| | Grams | Cost per gram £ | £ | | Grams | Cost per gram £ | £ |
|---|---|---|---|---|---|---|---|
| Crude chemicals | 8,000 | 0·80 | 6,400 | Normal loss | 1,200 | 0·20 | 240 |
| Wages | | | 1,200 | Production | 7,000 | 1·25 | 8,750 |
| Overhead | | | 1,140 | | | | |
| Abnormal gain | 200 | 1·25 | 250 | | | | |
| | 8,200 | | 8,990 | | 8,200 | | 8,990 |

Disposal of scrap would now be 1,000 grams (1,200 − 200) and the adjustment to the normal loss account to reduce the disposal value to £200 (1,000 grams at £0·20) would be made by a transfer from the abnormal gain account as follows:

### Normal Losses in Process

| | Grams | Cost per gram £ | £ | | Grams | Cost per gram £ | £ |
|---|---|---|---|---|---|---|---|
| Process account | 1,200 | 0·20 | 240 | Abnormal gain account | 200 | 0·20 | 40 |
| | | | | Cash (disposal proceeds) | 1,000 | 0·20 | 200 |
| | 1,200 | | 240 | | 1,200 | | 240 |

### Abnormal Gains from Process

| | Grams | Cost per gram £ | £ | | Grams | Cost per gram £ | £ |
|---|---|---|---|---|---|---|---|
| Normal loss account | 200 | 0·20 | 40 | Process account | 200 | 1·25 | 250 |
| Profit and loss account | | | 210 | | | | |
| | 200 | | 250 | | 200 | | 250 |

## 23.11  EQUIVALENT UNITS OF PRODUCTION

The valuation of work-in-process is accomplished by identifying the equivalent units for each element of cost. Equivalent units is the name given to the figure that represents the number of completed units in the period plus partly finished work converted into equivalent completed units. For example, if 200 units were completed in the period and 100 units only 50% complete, the equivalent (complete) units would be 250. The equivalent unit figure is required for each element of cost because the degree of completion in the use of resources may be different. For example, all the units may be completed as to material but only part completed as to labour and overhead. The product unit cost is then obtained by dividing each element of cost by its equivalent units and the result for material, labour and overhead added together. These calculations are illustrated in the two examples shown below.

*Data for both examples for Process 1 in an accounting period*

Opening work-in-process: 1,000 units complete as to material and 50% complete as to labour and overheads

|  | £ |
|---|---|
| Materials cost | 4,000 |
| Labour cost | 3,000 |
| Overhead cost | 3,000 |

Cost inputs in the period

|  | £ |
|---|---|
| Materials | 10,000 |
| Labour | 8,330 |
| Overhead | 6,270 |

Completed units: 5,000

Closing work-in-process: 600 units complete as to material and 25% complete as to labour and overheads.

There are no process losses and materials are added at the beginning of the process. Resources represented by the labour and overhead costs are used continuously throughout the processing.

*Example 1 – Weighted Average Method of Unit Pricing*

Process 1

|  | Units | £ |  | Units | £ |
|---|---|---|---|---|---|
| Opening work-in-process | 1,000 | 10,000 | Completed | | |
| Materials | | 10,000 | production | 5,000 | 32,500 |
| Labour | | 8,330 | Closing work- | | |
| Overhead | | 6,270 | in-process | 600 | 2,100 |
| | | 34,600 | | | 34,600 |

Calculation of the product unit cost:

Cost per<br>equivalent<br>unit<br>£

Material: input: cost: £4,000 + £10,000 $= \dfrac{£14,000}{5,600} =$  2·50
        output: equivalent units:
          5,000 + 600

Labour: input: cost: £3,000 + £8,330 . $= \dfrac{£11,330}{5,150} =$  2·20
        output: equivalent units:
          5,000 + 150 (25% of 600)

Overhead: input: costs: £3,000 + £6,270 $= \dfrac{£9,270}{5,150} =$  1·80
        output: equivalent units:
          5,000 + 150 (25% of 600)

6·50

    Completed production cost     5,000 units x £6·50  =  £32,500

£

Closing work-in-process

Material: 600 x £2·50  =                          1,500
Labour:   150 x £2·20  =                            330
Overhead:150 x £1·80  =                            270
                                                 ─────
                                                 2,100

*Example 2 – First-in, First-out Method of Unit Pricing*

Process 1

|  | Units | £ |  | Units | £ |
|---|---|---|---|---|---|
| Opening work-in-process | 1,000 | 10,000 | Completed |  |  |
| Materials |  | 10,000 | production | 5,000 | 32,825 |
| Labour |  | 8,330 | Closing work- |  |  |
| Overheads |  | 6,270 | in-process | 600 | 1,775 |
|  |  | 34,600 |  |  | 34,600 |

Calculation of the product unit cost:

| Units of output | Material | Labour | Overhead | |
|---|---|---|---|---|
| 1,000 |  | 500 | 500 | Opening work-in-process: half finished labour and overheads. |
| 4,000 | 4,000 | 4,000 | 4,000 | 5,000 − 1,000 units started and finished in the period. |
| 600 | 600 | 150 | 150 | Closing work-in-process complete as to material and 25% complete as to labour and |
| 5,600 | 4,600 | 4,650 | 4,650 | overheads. |

| Period costs | £10,000 | £8,330 | £6,270 |
|---|---|---|---|
| Unit cost | $\frac{£10,000}{4,600}$ | $\frac{£8,330}{4,650}$ | $\frac{£6,270}{4,650}$ |

Total

= £2·1739  = £1·7914  = £1·3484         £5·3137

Completed production cost:                        £        £

Opening balance                                10,000
Labour: 500 x £1·7914              =              896
Overhead: 500 x £1·3484           =              674
  Units fully processed during period
  4,000 x £5·3137                  =           21,255   32,825

Closing work-in-process:

Material: 600 x £2·1739            =            1,304
Labour: 150 x £1·7914             =              269
Overhead: 150 x £1·3484           =              202    1,775
                                               ─────   ──────
                                                        34,600

## 23.12 JOINT PRODUCTS AND BYPRODUCTS

In Figure 23.5 the joint costs as outputs from Process 1 require apportionment for the joint products A and B. Joint products are products produced simultaneously until the point of separation in the process and, at the point of separation, each product is of significant value to the business. Examples commonly quoted are the oil and steel industries. If a product is of small value at the point of separation and produced incidentally to the main product, the term 'byproduct' is used. Again, a joint cost requires apportionment.

Methods used for joint products to apportion joint costs at the point of separation include:

1. *The physical unit method*
   In this method, the total number of units at the point of separation are divided into the joint cost to give an average unit cost and this amount is used to value the units of each joint product. The unit used may be weight, capacity or other product characteristic recognised in the trade. The assumption is that the physical units are of equal value.
2. *The sales value of production method*
   The basis of the proportion sum for apportionment is the multiplication of the output units at the point of separation by the sales prices that will be obtained for the products when finally manufactured. There may be variations on the selling prices used such as allowance for further processing costs and selling and distribution cost, but essentially the assumption is that costs and selling prices are correlated. The effect of applying this assumption is that profits are equalised from joint products.
3. *The contribution/physical unit basis*
   In this method marginal costs at the point of separation are apportioned on the basis of physical units and fixed costs on the basis of the resulting contribution calculations when the marginal costs are deducted from the sales value of production. This method is associated with the application of the marginal costing technique.

The byproduct joint costs may be apportioned by any of the above methods but, because the byproduct is of minor value, other procedures may be adopted which do not apportion the cost but will not significantly distort the costs of the main products. These methods include:

(*a*) Treating the sales value of the byproduct as 'other income'. This method assigns the cost of the byproduct as 'nil'. Any cost incurred is, in fact, borne by the major products.
(*b*) Treating the net sales value as a credit to the main product process cost. The net sales value is the sales revenue of the byproduct less costs incurred from the point of separation, e.g., marketing costs. This method assigns the cost of the byproduct as the net sales value and, therefore, assumes no profit or loss. In fact, such profit or loss is taken by the main product.

The accounting treatment of joint products can significantly affect product costs and profits and the assumptions made should not be forgotten by management. In particular, for control and decision-making purposes the emphasis should be on total costs of manufacturing joint products and on any variations that might arise, either from inefficiency, or from taking a particular course of action as compared with not taking that action. It has been assumed above that byproducts are of relative insignificance but the choice of what is or what is not a byproduct in some industries is rather arbitrary. For control purposes, it is wiser to treat the results of arbitrary accounting procedures with caution.

## 23.13 INTER-PROCESS PROFITS

On occasions, the output of a preceding process as an input to a succeeding process is credited and charged at market prices to aid performance evaluation. The idea behind this procedure is to prevent a subsequent process manager from benefiting from efficient production in the preceding process or, alternatively, suffering from excessive transfer cost. This procedure has disadvantages. A market price may not always be available and resort to other assessments may be necessary — a problem considered in greater detail in Chapter 25. In addition, this accounting procedure of introducing inter-process profits has the effect of inflating stock values by the profit element which must be eliminated to accord with accepted conventions of stock valuation.

## 23.14 UNIFORM COSTING

Methods of cost accounting may vary between accounting units and, where a large organisation controls subsidiary units, it is common practice for the methods to be standardised so that information consolidated can be produced on a comparable basis. Such uniform methods may be extended beyond the confines of specific companies to include other businesses in the same industry of comparable type and size. These schemes of uniform costing are usually administered by a Trade Association and the procedure is similar to that outlined for interfirm ratio comparisons in Chapter 5. The amount of detail handled and the effects of adopting such a scheme are more far-reaching than ratio analysis and participating companies must be willing and flexible enough to adjust their procedures to the extent necessary. Few schemes have had long-term success* in this country because companies have not been willing to part with confidential information or adjust their costing methods as necessary. Where participation does take place, the dissemination of the best expertise for dealing with the specific problems of the industry can be valuable; but a lot of this information is freely available in the cost manuals published by Trade

* A notable exception is that administered by the British Federation of Master Printers, first introduced in 1913.

Associations.* Such a manual normally includes details of the following:

1. The uniform costing system objectives
2. The administration of the costing system
3. The chart of accounts and definition of terms
4. The treatment of specific cost items
5. The accounting methods appropriate to material, labour, overheads and revenue
6. The information that may be provided by the system and its use.

## 23.15  A CONCLUDING COMMENT

The techniques of cost ascertainment have been developed in this chapter in relation to cost elements and their relationship to the business activity being measured, whether a jobbing or processing situation. It will be noted that inaccuracies are introduced into the costing process as the sequence of cost accumulation progresses from original classification, through the procedures of cost apportionment and cost absorption. The tendency to consider the results as accurate calculations should be avoided. The only justification for such procedures is that the bases adopted reasonably reflect the incidence of costs to cost centres and cost units. Included in this justification is the belief that the degree of error introduced by these conventional procedures will not mislead management as they use the information produced to control the business.

## FOR FURTHER STUDY

QUESTIONS

1. *Calculation of machine hour rates*
It is the practice of a manufacturing business to charge overhead to jobs as a percentage of direct labour cost. The rate in use is 120%.
The overhead budget for the year is as follows:

|  | £ |
|---|---|
| Supervision | 7,525 |
| Indirect workers | 6,000 |
| Holiday pay, company's national insurance | 6,200 |
| Tooling cost | 9,400 |
| Machine maintenace labour cost | 4,500 |
| Power | 1,944 |
| Small tools and supplies | 1,171 |
| Insurance of machinery | 185 |
| Insurance of buildings | 150 |
| Rent and rates | 2,500 |
| Depreciation of machinery | 9,250 |
| | 48,825 |

*For further reading (*see* page 478) two of these uniform cost manuals are suggested because they provide excellent case studies of the practical application of costing methods in widely differing industries.

While overhead at present is absorbed into the cost of products by means of a single rate it is proposed to consider absorbing overhead by use of a separate machine hour rate for each of the four different groups of machines.

The following data is accordingly made available:

|  | Q | R | S | T | Total |
|---|---|---|---|---|---|
|  | | *Machine Groups* | | | |
| Floor space (square metres) | 1,800 | 1,500 | 800 | 900 | 5,000 |
| Kilo-watt hours (000) | 270 | 66 | 85 | 65 | 486 |
| Capital cost of machines (£000) | 30 | 20 | 8 | 16 | 74 |
| Indirect workers (persons) | 3 | 3 | 1 | 1 | 8 |
| Total workers (persons) | 19 | 24 | 12 | 7 | 62 |
| Machine maintenance hours (000) | 3 | 2 | 3 | 1 | 9 |
| Tooling costs (£) | 3,500 | 4,300 | 1,000 | 600 | 9,400 |
| Supervision costs (£) | 2,050 | 2,200 | 1,775 | 1,500 | 7,525 |
| Small tools and supplies (£) | 491 | 441 | 66 | 173 | 1,171 |
| Machine running hours (000) | 30 | 36 | 19 | 8 | 93 |

*Required:*

As adviser to the business recommending the change to the machine hour basis you are required to:

(a) State the arguments in favour of the change
(b) Calculate a machine hour rate for each of the four groups of machines
(c) Calculate the overhead to be absorbed by job A involving 4 hours in group Q, 5 hours in group R, one hour in group S and 6 hours in group T, using the machine hour rates calculated by you in answer to (b)
(d) Calculate the overhead to be absorbed by job A when the labour cost is £7 and the present method is used. (ICMA)

2. *Estimating department efficiency*

Cylinders & Tubes Ltd is an engineering company and manufactures products to customer specifications. On the basis of the specification, the company prepares cost estimates and quotes selling prices according to the formula:

Estimated materials and direct wages
Add 150% on direct wages for factory overheads
Add 15% on factory cost for all other overheads
Add 15% on total cost for profit.

The company does not keep cost accounts but the accounts for the year show the following figures:

|  | £ |
|---|---|
| Direct material | 21,000 |
| Factory overheads | 27,500 |
| Selling overheads | 3,000 |
| Sales | 75,000 |
| Direct wages | 18,500 |
| Administration overheads | 5,000 |
| Distribution overheads | 1,500 |
| Net loss | 1,500 |

In manufacturing its products, the company has two production departments and the incidence of the overhead for the two departments varies considerably.

The management of the company is very concerned at the results of the year's trading. On the basis of the formula described for the fixing of selling prices a substantial profit should have been earned rather than the loss incurred.
*Required:*
You have been asked to comment on the results disclosed:

(*a*)  Summarise your computation and observations
(*b*)  State what advice you would give to management                      (ICMA)

3.  *Under-absorption of overheads*
During the course of a year your cost accounts indicate that overheads are being under-absorbed. What are the probable reasons?

What steps would you take to deal with the under-absorption according to the cause? Give reasons.                      (ICMA)

4.  *Graphical presentation of over-/under-absorption of overhead*
The budget of a large manufacturing company shows that for the following twelve months fixed overheads are estimated at £10,000. The production budget indicates that during this period, 200,000 units will be produced for which variable overheads will be £30,000. Each unit of production requires two machine hours and these figures have been used to calculate a predetermined overhead absorption rate per machine hour which is applied to each unit of output.
*Required:*
To indicate the possible effects of any under- or over-absorption of cost, you are required to prepare a graph on which is plotted the total budget overhead cost line for output levels in machine hours from 0 to 600,000. On the same graph and for the same range of output levels, plot the line of absorbed cost based on the predetermined rate calculated from above. From the graph read off the over- or under-absorption of overheads for the following levels of output:

180,000 machine hours
500,000 machine hours                      (ACA)

5.  *Choice of activity level for overhead absorption*
The management of Perfect Products Ltd is considering the activity level to use for overhead absorption rate calculation and on the basis of estimated factory overhead have produced the following rates:

| Operating conditions | Monthly production in hours | Rate of overhead absorption per hour |
|---|---|---|
| (a) Capacity available after allowance for unavoidable capacity losses such as normal maintenance and holiday interruptions | 2,000 | £5·00 |
| (b) Average capacity use over several months in the previous year when production was at an efficient level | 1,800 | £5·56 |
| (c) Average monthly capacity use during the previous year | 1,700 | £5·88 |
| (d) Expected actual capacity use in the month | 1,600 | £6·25 |
| (e) Capacity available after allowance for unavoidable capacity losses and seasonal and cyclical variations anticipated in capacity use over the next three years | 1,500 | £6·67 |

The sales manager examining the schedule notes the emphasis on manufacturing in the operating conditions described and suggests that sales levels should be considered. The factory manager points out that operating conditions, in terms of capacity use, will be altered by such action as overtime or the sub-contracting of part of the work load and wonders whether these factors have been considered in the operating conditions described.

*Required:*

Comment on the activity levels described and discuss the points put forward by the sales and factory managers.

6. *Process accounts with normal losses and abnormal gains*

Antimuk is a cleaning material which is formed by passing chemicals A, B and C, in the proportion 3 : 2 : 1 respectively, through two successive processes, namely refining and blending. The acceptable output of the refining process is passed to the blending process into which additional chemicals D and E in the proportion 2 : 1 are introduced.

The following data apply to week ended 30th November 19 . .:

*Refining process*

Materials introduced: 4,500 grams
Cost per gram: A: £0·70, B: £0·60, C: £0·30
Labour: 200 hours at £0·60 per hour
Output: 3,500 grams

*Blending process*
Materials introduced: 2,100 grams
Cost per gram: D: £1, E: £1·20
Labour: 80 hours at £0·80 per hour
Analyst's test fee: £74
Output: 5,100 grams.

Overhead for the week of £840 is to be apportioned to the processes on a labour hour basis.

The normal output of the refining process is 80% of input and of the blending process, 90% of input. Waste material from the refining process is sold for £0·20 per gram and that from the blending process for £0·40 per gram.

It is the company's practice to complete each batch within the week and there is, therefore, no work-in-process at either the beginning or end of the week.
*Required:*
Prepare the accounts to record the production of Antimuk for the week in question.                                                                (ACA)

7. *Scrap metal pricing*
A foundry produces castings in a number of different alloys, in each of which scrap metal from previous meltings is used. It is the practice to charge this scrap metal at the average price of metal content; but as the market price of scrap metal of an identical mixture is lower, a suggestion is made that this market price should be used in the cost accounts in respect of the foundry's own scrap.
*Required:*
As cost accountant, present a report to management on the subject, illustrating your recommendations by the use of figures in respect of your most important product, the material content of which is:

> 50% material A costing £200 per tonne
> 20% material B costing £580 per tonne
> 10% material C costing £120 per tonne
> 20% scrap metal of identical mixture.

The market price of this scrap metal is £100 per tonne, and in making the alloy 5% of metal charged is lost in melting and from the production of the product in question 30% is returned to scrap metal stock to be used in future meltings.

In making the report, give consideration to the positions which arise when:

(*a*) All scrap cannot be used in future melting processes and must be sold on the market
(*b*) The scrap returned to store after pouring is (i) lower than, and (ii) equal to the input of scrap.                                                (ICMA)

8. *Process costing and the valuation of work-in-process*
A company makes a product which passes through two distinct processes, in

both of which the material brought into the process changes composition. The unit of measurement therefore also changes.

On 1st January, 19 . . the work-in-progress figures were:

|  | Units | Cost £ |
|---|---|---|
| Work-in-process, process A | 1,000 | |
| Direct material (complete) | | 5,000 |
| Direct labour (75% complete) | | 2,000 |
| Overheads (75% complete) | | 3,000 |
| Work-in-process, process B | 3,000 | |
| Direct material (complete) | | 17,000 |
| Direct labour (50% complete) | | 3,800 |
| Overheads (50% complete) | | 6,000 |

The costs of the processes for the month of January were:

|  | Process A £ | Process B £ |
|---|---|---|
| Material ex stock | 9,700 | 2,800 |
| Labour | 3,640 | 11,200 |
| Overheads | 5,400 | 21,000 |

Output details were as follows:

*Process A:* 2,000 units were completed and passed into process B. 800 units remained in progress at 31st January 19 . ., complete as to material and 50% complete as to labour and overheads.

*Process B:* 5,000 units were completed and passed to finished stock. 2,000 units remained in progress at 31st January 19 . ., again complete as to material and 50% complete as to labour and overheads.

Material passing from process A to process B is treated as direct material in process B accounts. Closing work-in-progress is always valued on the weighted average cost basis.

*Required:*

Prepare cost accounts for January from the above information, showing total and unit costs and the valuation of work-in-process. (ICMA)

9. *Preparation of a process flow chart and process cost calculation*

A continuous distillation plant processes 1,000 grams of raw material each day. The raw material cost is £1 per gram and the plant costs £1,080 per day to operate. From this there is produced the following:

| Distillate | % |
|---|---|
| A | 20 |
| B | 30 |
| C | 40 |
| Byproduct | |
| D | 10 |

Distillate A from the initial operation passes through a treating process costing £320 per day to produce product A. Distillate B has a secondary distillation costing £800 per day to produce 80% of product B and 20% of product D. Distillate C also has a second distillation costing £600 per day and produces 50% product A and 50% product C. The two streams of product A need blending before sale at a cost of £240 per day. There is no waste or loss in any process. Byproduct D is sold for £0·55 per gram. Joint costs are apportioned on a physical unit basis.

*Required:*

(a) Show in the form of a flow chart for one day the output and the build-up of operating costs for each product and the byproduct

(b) Calculate the total cost per gram for products A, B and C.          (ICMA)

10. *Process accounts kept on a FIFO basis*

The Refining Process Co. Ltd manufactures two main products MPA and MPB in three departments C, D and E. Two main raw materials M1 and M2 are used in making MPA and MPB. A byproduct BP also emerges from the production process.

The raw materials are first processed in department C. At the end of this process, BP emerges and is transferred to finished stock ready for sale. It accounts for 0·25 of the total joint weight of materials introduced into department C.

One-third of the remainder of the output of department C is transferred to department D and processed further to produce MPA. The other two-thirds of the remainder of the output of department C is transferred to department E for processing to produce product MPB. At the commencement of the process in department D water is added so that the resulting output of MPA is 25% heavier than the input received from department C. Product MPB is produced in department E with no weight gain or loss.

Details of selling prices and selling and distribution costs of the products are:

| | Selling price per gram £ | Selling and distribution cost per gram £ |
|---|---|---|
| Main products | | |
| MPA | 0·600 | 0·0800 |
| MPB | 0·300 | 0·0525 |
| Byproduct | | |
| BP | 0·025 | 0·0050 |

Department C is credited with the quantity of BP transferred to finished stock at selling price less selling and distribution costs. The remaining net costs of department C are charged to departments D and E in proportion to the net sales values of the input received by them. The respective net sales values are arrived at by reducing the ultimate sales values by the relevant costs incurred.

These are selling and distribution costs and processing costs in departments D or E after the point of separation.

The information for May 19 . . was as follows:

|  | Department C | Department D | Department E |
|---|---|---|---|
| Work-in-progress at 1st May 19 . . | | | |
| Grams | Nil | 7,200 | 11,000 |
| Cost | Nil | £2,592 | £1,705 |
| | | | |
| Input for the month | | | |
| Raw material | | | |
| Grams | 160,000 | – | – |
| Cost | £14,400 | – | – |
| Wages and overhead | £10,400 | £3,968 | £8,525 |
| Work-in-progress at 31st May 19 . . | | | |
| Grams | Nil | 8,000 | 16,000 |

Opening and closing stocks of work-in-progress in departments D and E were estimated to be 50% complete as to wages and overhead and 100% complete as to material.

|  | Byproduct BP | Main products MPA | MPB |
|---|---|---|---|
| Finished stock at 1st May, 19 . . | | | |
| Grams | Nil | 2,500 | 9,000 |
| Cost | Nil | £1,000 | £1,890 |
| Transfers from production during May | | | |
| Grams | 40,000 | 49,200 | 75,000 |
| at 31st May 19 . . | | | |
| Grams | Nil | 7,200 | 6,500 |

*Required:*
Prepare for the month of May 19 – :

(*a*) A production and cost statement for department C
(*b*) Production and cost statements for departments D and E showing in each the value of transfers to finished stock and of work-in-progress at 31st May 19 –
(*c*) Finished stock accounts for main products MPA and MPB and byproduct BP.

The accounts are kept on a FIFO basis.)                                   (ICMA)

**11.** *Joint product apportionment*

'If . . . the products are . . . truly joint products, the cost of the process can be applied to these products:

(a) On the basis of the weight, or other physical quantity of each product
(b) In respect of the marginal cost of the process on the basis of physical quantities and in respect of the fixed costs of the process on the basis of the contribution made by the various products
(c) On the basis of the selling values of the different products.'

> (*A Report on Marginal Costing*, Institute of Cost and Works Accountants, 1961, Appendix D, p. 55)

*Required:*
Discuss the above statement and the value of the methods described, using for illustration the following figures in respect of the joint production of A and B for a month:

|  | £ |
|---|---|
| Total costs | |
| Direct materials | 2,600 |
| Direct labour | 1,000 |
| Variable overheads | 800 |
| Fixed overheads | 2,200 |

Sales:

A – 100 grams at £60 per gram
B – 120 grams at £20 per gram

Production is equal to sales.                    (ICMA)

**12.** *Process costs and marginal theory*

In a factory making products from a certain grain, the following are the processes:

(a) Crushing and separating. Here the grain is crushed and the 'germ' (which contains the oil) is separated. The resultant oil goes to (b) and the other matter to (c).
(b) Oil extraction
(c) Starch grinding and drying – the final products of (b) and (c) – oil and starch – both go through
(d) Packing.

In their packed state, the oil sells at £60 a product unit and the starch at £120 per product unit. For period 6 the following details are given:

|                          | Total £ | Crushing £ | Oil extraction £ | Starch grinding, etc. £ | Packing £ |
|--------------------------|---------|------------|------------------|-------------------------|-----------|
| Grain                    | 1,200   |            |                  |                         |           |
| Labour                   |         | 160        | 120              | 340                     | 80        |
| Sundry materials         |         | 40         | 40               | 130                     | 40        |
| General works expenses   | 500     |            |                  |                         |           |
| — allocated              |         | 20%        | 34%              | 40%                     | 6%        |
| Waste sold               |         | £100       | £20              |                         |           |
| Product output           |         | 60 units   | 10 units         | 20 units                |           |

*Note:*

(i) The 'germ' is assumed to be one-twentieth of the total materials leaving (*a*)

(ii) Packing is charged in proportion to finished net units of product, all actual outlays being incurred in these proportions.

*Required:*

(*a*) Prepare a statement showing the full cost and net profit per unit of each product on the basis described above

(*b*) Comment on the usefulness of the statement prepared in (*a*) above for evaluating the profitability of the various processes. Include any alternative statement that you think would be more helpful for this purpose.

### FURTHER READING

*Cost Accountancy for Printers.* Parts 1 and 2. British Federation of Master Printers, 1971.

Most, Kenneth S. *Uniform Cost Accounting.* Gee 1961. Chapters 1, 3, 4 and 5.

*Steel Foundry Costing.* British Steel Founders' Association. Gee, 1965.

# 24 Accounting for Changing Price Levels

## OBJECTIVE OF THE CHAPTER

To show the effect of changing price levels on accounting information produced for management and consider how these changing prices may best be recognised in the accounts of the business.


## OUTLINE OF THE CHAPTER

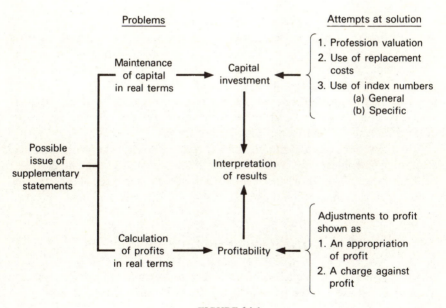

FIGURE 24.1.


Conventional accounting practice assumes that the currency unit (e.g., £ sterling) is a stable monetary unit and, in the calculation of net profit, amounts are recorded at historical cost. There has been a marked reluctance in the past to recognise that price levels have changed over the years and for a long time the general view was that if changing price levels were to be recognised, their estimated effect should be

479

treated as a matter of financial policy. A typical statement of this view is the following:

> Unless and until a practicable and generally acceptable alternative is available, the Council recommends that the accounting principles set out below should continue to be applied:

> (a) Historical cost should continue to be the basis on which annual accounts should be prepared and, in consequence, the basis on which profits shown by such accounts are computed.

> (b) Any amount set aside out of profits in recognition of the effects which changes in the purchasing power of money have had on the affairs of the business (including any amount to finance the increase in the cost of replacements, whether of fixed or current assets) should be treated as a transfer to reserve and not as a deduction in arriving at the balance for the year, that balance should be described appropriately, since it is not the whole of the profits.

> (c) In order to emphasise that as a matter of prudence the amount so set aside is, for the time being, regarded by directors as not available for distribution, it should normally be treated as a capital reserve.

> (d) For balance sheet purposes fixed assets should not be written-up, especially in the absence of monetary stability.*

The sharp decline in the general purchasing power of some currencies over recent years has prompted greater attention to the problem and the Accounting Standards Steering Committee issued in 1971 a discussion paper on 'Inflation and Accounts'. This culminated in a provisional standard for recommended application not later than the first accounting period beginning after 30th June 1974. The crux of the matter is the finding of a 'practicable and generally acceptable' procedure and the subject is controversial. In Great Britain the controversy exploded with the report of the Sandilands Committee on Inflation Accounting.†

With the volume of articles on the subject, many who chose to ignore inflation in accounting have reluctantly given it their attention but quarrel regarding the methods to be employed. Whatever the attitude adopted for external reporting the management accountant cannot ignore the issue for meaningful internal reporting.

## 24.1 THE EFFECT OF CHANGING PRICE LEVELS

As long ago as 1952, the conclusions reached by an Institute of Cost Management Accountants' study into the effect of changing price levels were as follows:

> (a) it is possible for the distribution of money profits earned by a business to involve a distribution of real capital, which results in the undermining of the real value of the interests of contributors of business capital;

> (b) the measurement in terms of money of the results of the operations of a

---

*Para. 30, Recommendation 15, The Institute of Chartered Accountants in England and Wales, 1952.
†The Sandilands Committee was appointed by the British Government in 1974 to examine inflation accounting.

business do not reflect adequately the results, in terms of real (or stable) values, of these operations.*

These points may be illustrated by the following examples:

Data:
Opening capital of £10,000 invested in an asset with a five-year life depreciated on the fixed instalment basis. The asset is rented at £3,000 per year.

*Results of operations:* Year 1 (on the historical accounting basis):

*Profit and Loss Statement – Year 1*

|  | £ |
|---|---|
| Rental revenue | 3,000 |
| Less depreciation | 2,000 |
| Profit | 1,000 |

*Balance Sheet as at the end of Year 1*

|  | £ |  | £ | £ |
|---|---|---|---|---|
| Capital | 10,000 | Asset at cost | 10,000 | |
| Profit | 1,000 | Less depreciation | 2,000 | 8,000 |
|  |  | Cash |  | 3,000 |
|  | 11,000 |  |  | 11,000 |

Data:
At the end of Year 5 the asset is scrapped with no scrap value.
*Result of 5 years' operation* assuming no withdrawal of profit (on the historical accounting basis):

*Balance Sheet as at the end of Year 5*

|  | £ |  | £ |
|---|---|---|---|
| Capital | 10,000 | Cash | 15,000 |
| Profit | 5,000 |  |  |
|  | 15,000 |  | 15,000 |

Data:
The replacement of the asset with an identical piece of equipment which costs £15,000 at the end of Year 5.
*Result of the replacement* (on the historical accounting basis):

*Balance Sheet as at the beginning of Year 6*

|  | £ |  | £ |
|---|---|---|---|
| Capital | 10,000 | Asset | 15,000 |
| Profit | 5,000 |  |  |
|  | 15,000 |  | 15,000 |

*The Accountancy of Changing Price Levels (Institute of Cost and Works Accountants, 1952), p. 45.

If a distribution of profits had been made in the five-year period the real capital of the business would have been distributed. Profits have been overstated – in fact, no profit has been made in the five-year period.

The same points are evident with stock:

Data:

Opening capital of £10,000 invested in 100 units of stock sold at £150 per unit.

*Results of operations for the year* (on the historical accounting basis):

### Profit and Loss Statement – Year 1

|                | £      |
| -------------- | ------ |
| Sales revenue  | 15,000 |
| Cost of sales  | 10,000 |
| Profit         | 5,000  |

### Balance Sheet as at the end of Year 1

|         | £      |      | £      |
| ------- | ------ | ---- | ------ |
| Capital | 10,000 | Cash | 15,000 |
| Profit  | 5,000  |      |        |
|         | 15,000 |      | 15,000 |

Data:

At the end of Year 1 the stock is replaced by identical goods costing £15,000.

*Result of this replacement* (on the historical accounting basis):

### Balance Sheet as at the beginning of Year 2

|         | £      |       | £      |
| ------- | ------ | ----- | ------ |
| Capital | 10,000 | Stock | 15,000 |
| Profit  | 5,000  |       |        |
|         | 15,000 |       | 15,000 |

The charge made against revenue has been understated by £5,000.

In addition to the points made above, changing price levels may have the following effects where conventional accounting practice is followed:

1. Financial statements are difficult to interpret, e.g., an increasing sales value may give the impression that sales revenue is increasing between periods. In fact, the increase may represent changing price levels (in a period of inflation) and the volume of sales may be static.
2. Changing price levels affect items in the accounts differently, e.g., selling prices, stock prices and wage rates do not normally move at a similar rate with each other during an accounting period.
3. Selling prices may be fixed at too low a level to maintain the real capital of the business, e.g., in the earlier illustration, if the units of stock had been sold at less than £150 per unit part of the real capital would have been eroded.

## 24.2 METHODS USED TO REFLECT CHANGING PRICE LEVELS IN THE ACCOUNTS OF THE BUSINESS

The methods that have been proposed to reflect the changing price levels in the accounts of the business, short of incorporating all adjustments for price level changes within the accounting system itself as distinct from the preparation of the financial statements, are as follows:

1. To appropriate profits for the additional depreciation on assets calculated on current price levels
2. To charge depreciation in the accounts of the business on the basis of current price levels
3. To issue supplementary statements to show the effect of current price levels leaving the conventional accounts prepared in accordance with historical cost conventions.

These methods are outlined in greater detail in the sections to follow.

## 24.3 APPROPRIATION FOR EXCESS DEPRECIATION

In this method the depreciation is divided into two parts; the first part to be based on historical cost and the second part to consist of a supplementary charge representing the difference by which the basic charge falls short of the amount which would appear as an expense if it were calculated on current price levels. The supplementary charge would be carried to a special capital reserve account from the appropriation account leaving the charge on the historical cost basis in the main profit statement as a charge against profit.

Using the data given earlier in this chapter, the profit and loss statement for the five-year period and the balance sheet at the end of Year 5 would be as follows:

*Profit and Loss Statement*
*Years 1 to 5 inclusive*

|  | £ |
|---|---|
| Rental revenue | 15,000 |
| Less depreciation | 10,000 |
| Profit | 5,000 |
| Less appropriated to capital reserve | 5,000 |
| Balance | Nil |

*Balance Sheet as at the end of Year 5*

| | £ | | £ |
|---|---|---|---|
| Capital | 10,000 | Cash | 15,000 |
| Capital reserve | 5,000 | | |
| | 15,000 | | 15,000 |

## 24.4   A CHARGE IN THE ACCOUNTS FOR EXCESS DEPRECIATION

The depreciation charged in the profit and loss statement under this method is based on current price levels. The difference between the current value and the asset cost is placed to the credit of a revaluation reserve account.

Using the data given earlier in this chapter, the profit and loss statement for the five-year period and the balance sheet at the end of Year 5 would be as follows:

*Profit and Loss Statement*
*Years 1 to 5 inclusive*

|  | £ |
|---|---|
| Rental revenue | 15,000 |
| Less depreciation | 15,000 |
| Profit | Nil |

*Balance Sheet as at the end of Year 5*

|  | £ |  | £ |
|---|---|---|---|
| Capital | 10,000 | Cash | 15,000 |
| Revaluation reserve | 5,000 |  |  |
|  | 15,000 |  | 15,000 |

## 24.5   THE ISSUE OF SUPPLEMENTARY STATEMENTS

In this case, the profit and loss statement and balance sheet are not only prepared in accordance with the historical cost convention but also on the basis of current values. This is the approach favoured by the Accounting Standards Steering Committee's provisional standard but rejected by the Sandilands Committee who specifically stated that current purchasing power supplementary statements should not be attached to current cost accounts. The current cost accounts recommended by the Sandilands Committee involve the complete integration of price level adjustments within the accounting system — a procedure adopted in Holland for many years.*

## 24.6   BASES FOR ADJUSTMENTS TO THE ACCOUNTS CAUSED BY CHANGING PRICE LEVELS

The usual bases for the adjustments to the accounts caused by changing price levels are:

1. Professional valuation
2. Use of replacement costs
3. Use of index numbers.

These bases are considered in greater detail in the sections to follow.

---

*The Sandilands Report is recommended for further reading (*see* p. 499) but a good review of the system at the Philips Electrical Industries (N. V. Philips. Gloeilampenfabrieken) that has received wide publicity is given in R. S. Gynther, *Accounting for Price-level Changes: Theory and Procedures* (Pergamon Press, 1966), Chapter 15.

## 24.7 PROFESSIONAL VALUATION OF ASSETS

A professional valuer is usually used when fixed assets are valued by expert appraisal. Subjectivity to a large degree enters into the valuation when this method is used. No two valuers are likely to agree on a valuation.

The comparison is between the book value of an asset at the date of the valuation with the current value of the asset in its existing condition.

Companies using this method usually obtain valuations periodically such as every five years. The main reason for this is the high cost of professional valuation. The effect of this is that if the price level is not stable between the valuations the revaluation is soon out-of-date.

Where the asset is not depreciated, such as land, and a professional valuation is made, a note is usually attached to the accounts of this valuation leaving the asset at historical cost. In this case, there is little possibility of confusion since the comparison is a direct one between the historical cost and the current valuation.

## 24.8 USE OF REPLACEMENT COSTS

In this case, the fixed or current assets are priced at their replacement cost, the prices being obtained from trade journals or by reference to manufacturers who supply the assets. The difficulties are:

1. The asset in use may not be currently available
2. Technological changes may mean that the existing asset may never be replaced by an asset of a similar type
3. Should the replacement cost be on a year-by-year basis or on an estimate of what the replacement cost will be at the estimated date of replacement?

The latter view is not normally taken because this would mean applying an estimate of future cost against current revenue. If replacement costs are used, current prices are obtained where possible and in other cases the technical management would be called upon to estimate notional current costs. The technological factor may also be resolved by calling on the company's technical staff to estimate what assets are likely to be needed as replacements.

The replacement costs are reduced by depreciation on the replacement cost to arrive at replacement cost written down book values. It is the difference between this replacement cost depreciation and the depreciation calculated on historical costs that forms the excess depreciation charge appropriate to the accounting period.

There is a difference of opinion regarding the back adjustment for depreciation where replacement costs indicate that the charge for earlier years should have been greater than included in the accounts. The following example illustrates this point:

Data:
An asset purchased at the beginning of Year 1 for £1,000
No residual value and an estimated life of 5 years
Depreciation on the fixed instalment method
Replacement cost at the end of Year 2: £1,500.

The charge for depreciation for Year 2 may be calculated as follows:

Method 1: $\dfrac{£1,500}{5} = £300$

|  |  | £ |
|---|---|---|
| Method 2: As above for 2 years (2 x £300) |  | 600 |
| Less already charged: Year 1 $\left(\dfrac{£1,000}{5}\right)$ |  | 200 |
| Charge for Year 2 |  | 400 |

In method 2, the depreciation for Year 2 includes the back adjustment of £100. Elsewhere in this work it has been pointed out that the provision for depreciation is not providing funds for the replacement of the asset and for this reason the usual view taken is that method 1 is appropriate.

The view may be taken that the depreciation for the year should be based on the average value to the business during the year of the fixed assets. To calculate this figure the value of the asset at the start of Year 2 is required. The fact that depreciation in earlier periods is charged on a lower valuation of assets means that depreciation will have been understated for previous years. The difference between the total depreciation amount charged for previous years and the total depreciation calculated on the revised current valuation of assets is the back-log depreciation. This back-log depreciation should not be charged against operating profit.

## 24.9 USE OF INDEX NUMBERS

Price index numbers which show the trend, rate and range of increases or decreases in prices are often advocated to adjust asset original costs to current price levels. The point arises as to whether a general or specific index should be used.

Not all prices change in the same proportions or in the same direction. A general index, such as the wholesale or retail price index attempts to indicate general inflation or deflation and the overall change in the purchasing power of money. There is no perfect general price index but as an approximate indication of current price levels they are useful. The ASC in its recommendation considered a number of indices in the United Kingdom which might be taken as indicators:

1. Gross domestic product (GDP) deflator
2. Total final expenditure (TFE) deflator
3. Consumers' expenditure deflator (CED) — formerly referred to as the consumer price index
4. Retail price index (RPI).

Because 'changes in the purchasing power of the £ are more often conceived in relation to the purchasing power of money spent by individuals on goods and services for personal use' and the RPI 'is not subject to retrospective revision and is available monthly by about the middle of the following month' the ASC recommended the use of the RPI index.

Price level changes of specific assets may be measured by special price indices prepared for them. The Sandilands Committee recommended that the government's statistical service should publish a series of price indices specific to particular industries to serve as a standard reference basis for calculating current asset values. Advocates of the use of the specific price index, such as company index calculations for each class of asset, make the point that the average change in all prices may not reflect the impact of a price level change in a particular business. An advocate of the specific price index is Professor Gynther who summarises the position as follows:

It can be said that:

1. conventional accounting maintains *money* capital only;
2. the use of one general index maintains capital in *purchasing power units*; and
3. the use of several special indices maintains capital in *physical assets*.*

Arguments can be brought forward in support of either theory particularly as the price index, general or specific, is an imperfect instrument for the adjustment of accounts. 'If it is believed that the whole or prime purpose of accounting is to assist the entity (the firm) in its daily struggles (and that only in this way will the interests of shareholders be looked after in the long term), then it is almost certain that the use of specific indexes will be favoured, i.e., so that the physical assets of the business will be maintained during the period of changing prices.†

If the application of a general index to an asset value produces a figure in excess of its future expected contribution to the business that figure should be written down to the more realistic value. This should not be made the excuse for manipulating figures.

Where the monetary amount of an asset or liability is fixed it is known as a monetary item; where the monetary amount is not fixed, it is known as a non-monetary item. Examples of the former are cash, debtors, creditors and loan capital; of the latter, tangible assets such as buildings, plant and machinery and stock.

If a general index is used, it is applied to the non-monetary items. It is not applied to monetary items. In times of inflation, monetary assets lose their value.

## 24.10 VALUE VARIATION AND INFLATION

In the above sections it may be noted that with the exception of the general index the methods adopted are measuring changing values of physical assets. Strictly these methods are not price level adjustments although they may achieve a similar result as a price level adjustment where a general price index is adopted. The reason for this is that by these methods other factors are being measured such as changing values for technical or economic reasons, and their value may change where there is

---

* 'Accounting for price level changes — one general index or several specific indexes?', *Accountancy* (July, 1962), p. 561.

† R. S. Gynther, *Accounting for Price-level Changes: Theory and Procedures* (Pergamon Press, 1966), p. 45.

no movement in the general price level. Some authorities, therefore, restrict the use of the expression 'price level adjustments' to general price index changes.

## 24.11 RECOGNISING CHANGING PRICE LEVELS IN STOCK

The changing price level problem in the case of stock is illustrated in the following example:

Data:
Opening stock: 5 units at £20 per unit
Purchases: 5 units at £30 per unit
Issues priced on the first-in, first-out basis
Sales: 5 units at £40 per unit.

The profit calculation would be as follows:

|  |  |  |
|---|---|---|
|  | £ |  |
| Opening stock | 100 | (5 units at £20 per unit) |
| Add purchases | 150 | (5 units at £30 per unit) |
|  | 250 |  |
| Less closing stock | 150 | (5 units at £30 per unit) |
| Cost of sales | 100 |  |
| Sales | 200 | (5 units at £40 per unit) |
| Profit | 100 |  |

The correct profit is £50 (£200 less £150). The other £50 has arisen owing to price movement and represents the difference in stock valuation (£150 − £100) for the same quantity of stock (5 units).

In this case, the use of the last-in, first-out method would have the desired result but it should be noted that the method is unsuitable when:

(a) Price level changes occur since the date of the last purchase of goods
(b) Sales volume is at such a level that current price levels as reflected in recent purchases are exhausted and historical prices are used at much lower levels than current costs.

To get over this difficulty, issues may be priced at replacement prices.

## 24.12 AN EXAMPLE OF ACCOUNTS CONVERSION USING A GENERAL PRICE INDEX

The two balance sheets (opening and closing) and the profit and loss account for the year are converted in terms of current purchasing power (CPP).

**Example***

The summarised balance sheets of Llewellyn Ltd as at 31st December 19.5 and 19.6 with the profit and loss account for the year ended on the latter date are given below. These were prepared using conventional historic accounting methods. The company was incorporated on 1st January 19.2 with a capital of £60,000 in £1 shares, fully paid at par on that date.

*Llewellyn Ltd*

| 31st December 19.5 | Balance Sheets as at | 31st December 19.6 |
|---|---|---|
| £ | | £ |
| | Non-monetary assets | |
| 70,000 | Fixed assets at cost | 79,000 |
| 17,500 | Less accumulated depreciation | 24,950 |
| 52,500 | | 54,050 |
| 16,000 | Stocks | 25,400 |
| | Net monetary assets | |
| 4,000 | Cash and debtors less creditors | 9,000 |
| 72,500 | | 88,450 |
| being: | | |
| 60,000 | Shareholders' capital | 60,000 |
| 12,500 | Retained profit | 28,450 |
| 72,500 | Net assets | 88,450 |

The increase in net assets, equalling the conventionally derived profit for the year, being £15,950 is as follows:

*Profit and Loss Account for the year ended 31st December 19.6*

| | £ | £ |
|---|---|---|
| Sales | | 160,000 |
| Less opening stock | 16,000 | |
| purchases | 109,400 | |
| | 125,400 | |
| Closing stock | 25,400 | |
| Cost of sales | | 100,000 |
| Gross profit | | 60,000 |
| Less depreciation of fixed assets | 7,450 | |
| other overhead expenses | 36,600 | 44,050 |
| Net profit before tax and appropriations | | 15,950 |

The following information is significant — analysis of fixed assets and depreciation as at 31st December 19.5 with conversion rates to be used, based on an index

*Taken from the ACA, Part V examination (June, 1974).

of current purchasing power:

| Year ended 31st December | Capital expenditure each year being written off over 10 years | Depreciation accumulated to 31st December 19.5 | Conversion rates |
|---|---|---|---|
| | £ | £ | |
| 19·2 | 30,000 | 10,500 | 1·154 |
| 19·3 | 20,000 | 5,000 | 1·119 |
| 19·4 | 10,000 | 1,500 | 1·087 |
| 19·5 | 10,000 | 500 | 1·056 |
| | 70,000 | 17,500 | |

Assume that the fixed assets and stocks on hand have been acquired evenly, and that cash flow is even in 19.6. Assume, also, the Consumer Price Index at

> 31st December 19.6 as 150
> 31st December 19.5 as 144
> 31st December 19.4 as 140
> 1st January 19.2    as 128.

## Comment

The first stage in the conversion process is to convert the balance sheet at the beginning of the year 19.6.

*Fixed assets and depreciation*

| Year ended 31st December | Conversion rate | Capital cost | Expenditure converted | Accumulated depreciation on cost | Accumulated depreciation converted |
|---|---|---|---|---|---|
| | | £ | £ | £ | £ |
| 19·2 | 1·154 | 30,000 | 34,620 | 10,500 | 12,117 |
| 19·3 | 1·119 | 20,000 | 22,380 | 5,000 | 5,595 |
| 19·4 | 1·087 | 10,000 | 10,870 | 1,500 | 1,631 |
| 19·5 | 1·056 | 10,000 | 10,560 | 500 | 528 |
| | | 70,000 | 78,430 | 17,500 | 19,871 |

*Stocks*

The average index for 19.5 is 142 $\left(\dfrac{140 + 144}{2}\right)$

The conversion rate is $\dfrac{150}{142} = 1 \cdot 056$

Stocks converted value = £16,000 x 1·056 = £16,896

*Net monetary assets*

It was stated earlier that if a general index is used it is not applied to monetary items.

This refers to the closing balances already in terms of current purchasing power, but the opening balances require conversion at the index for the date of the balances: 31st December 19.5, i.e., 144.

The conversion rate is $\dfrac{150}{144} = 1\cdot042$

Net monetary assets converted value = £4,000 x 1·042 = £4,168

*Shareholders' capital*

The company was incorporated on the 1st January 19.2 when the index was 128.

The conversion rate is $\dfrac{150}{129} = 1\cdot172$

Shareholders' capital converted value = £60,000 x 1·172 = £70,320.

The converted opening balance sheet in terms of current purchasing power is:

| | £ | £ |
|---|---|---|
| Non-monetary assets | | |
| Fixed assets at valuation | 78,430 | |
| Less accumulated depreciation | 19,871 | 58,559 |
| Stocks | | 16,896 |
| Net monetary assets | | |
| Cash and debtors less creditors | | 4,168 |
| | | 79,623 |
| Represented by shareholders' capital | | 70,320 |
| retained profit | | 9,303 |
| | | 79,623 |

The next stage in the conversion process is to convert the balance sheet at the end of the year 19.6:

*Fixed assets*

Additional assets in the year: £9,000 (£79,000 − £70,000)

The average index for 19.6 = 147 $\left(\dfrac{150 + 144}{2}\right)$

The conversion rate is $\dfrac{150}{147} = 1\cdot020$

| | £ |
|---|---|
| Additional fixed assets converted value = £9,000 x 1·020 = | 9,180 |
| Opening balance of fixed assets already converted | 78,430 |
| | 87,610 |

*Accumulated depreciation*

On the additional assets during the year the depreciation was charged for 6 months:

$$\frac{£9,000}{10 \text{ years} \times 2} = 450$$

$$\frac{£70,000}{10 \text{ years}} = 7,000$$

Depreciation for the year          7,450

Revised depreciation for the year:

|  | £ | £ |
|---|---|---|
| Additional assets $\frac{£9,180}{10 \text{ years} \times 2}$ = 459 | | |
| Assets at the beginning of the year $\frac{£78,430}{10 \text{ years}}$ = 7,843 | | 8,302 |
| Add opening balance of accumulated depreciation | | 19,871 |
| Converted accumulated depreciation balance | | 28,173 |

*Stocks*

The value of £25,400 in the closing balance sheet at the average conversion rate for 19.6 (1·020) gives the converted value of £25,908 (£25,400 × 1·020).

*Net monetary assets*

Already expressed in terms of current purchasing power.

The converted closing balance sheet in terms of current purchasing power is:

|  | £ | £ |
|---|---|---|
| Non-monetary assets | | |
| Fixed assets at valuation | 87,610 | |
| Less accumulated depreciation | 28,173 | 59,437 |
| Stocks | | 25,908 |
| Net monetary assets | | |
| Cash and debtors less creditors | | 9,000 |
| | | 94,345 |
| Represented by shareholders' capital | | 70,320 |
| retained profits | | 24,025 |
| | | 94,345 |

The third stage in the conversion process is to reconcile the profit figure £15,950 in the conventional profit and loss account with the profit in terms of current purchasing power of £14,722 (£24,025 − £9,303). The profit and loss account for the year 19.6 in terms of current purchasing power is as follows:

|  | £ | £ |  |
|---|---|---|---|
| Sales |  | 163,200 | (£160,000 x 1·02) |
| Less opening stock | 16,896 |  | Per opening converted balance sheet |
| purchases | 111,588 |  | (£109,400 x 1·02) |
|  | 128,484 |  |  |
| Closing stock | 25,908 |  | Per closing converted balance sheet |
| Cost of sales |  | 102,576 |  |
| Gross profit |  | 60,624 |  |
| Less depreciation |  |  |  |
| of fixed assets | 8,302 |  | Per conversion calculation |
| other overhead |  |  |  |
| expenses | 37,332 | 45,634 | (£36,600 x 1·02) |
|  |  | 14,990 |  |
| Less loss from holding net |  |  |  |
| short-term monetary assets |  | 268 |  |
| Net profit before tax and |  |  |  |
| appropriations (converted) |  | 14,722 |  |

The loss from holding net short-term monetary assets is calculated as follows:

|  |  |  | £ |
|---|---|---|---|
| Loss at the beginning of the year (£4,168 − £4,000) |  |  | 168 |
| Add loss in the year 19.6 |  | £ |  |
| Converted amount (£9,000 − £4,000) x 1·02 | = | 5,100 |  |
| Current net monetary assets difference (£9,000 − £4,000) = | 5,000 | 100 |
|  |  |  | 268 |

The reconciliation may be presented in the following form:

*Reconciliation of Profit on an Historical Basis with Profit*
*on a Current Purchasing Power Basis*
*Year ended 31st December 19. 6*

|  | £ | £ |
|---|---|---|
| Profit before taxation (historical basis) |  | 15,950 |
| Less adjustments to convert to the current purchasing power basis: |  |  |
| Stock − additional charge based on restating the cost of stock at the beginning and end of the year in pounds of current purchasing power (see note (a)) | 388 |  |
| Depreciation − additional depreciation based on cost measured in pounds of current purchasing power of fixed assets (£8,302 − £7,450) | 852 |  |
| Monetary items − net loss in purchasing power resulting from the effects of inflation on the company's net monetary items | 268 |  |
| Sales, purchases and all other costs − as increased by the change in the index at the average for the year (see note (b)) | (280) | 1,228 |
| Profit before taxation (current purchasing power basis) |  | 14,722 |

| Notes | | £ | £ | |
|---|---|---:|---:|---:|
| (a) | Opening stock | 16,896 | | |
| | | 16,000 | 896 | |
| | Closing stock | 25,908 | | |
| | | 25,400 | 508 | |
| | | | 388 | |
| | | | | £ |
| (b) | Sales | 163,200 | | |
| | | 160,000 | | 3,200 |
| | Purchases | 111,588 | | |
| | | 109,400 | 2,188 | |
| | Other overhead | 37,332 | | |
| | | 36,600 | 732 | 2,920 |
| | | | | 280 |

Using the historical accounting conventions, therefore, the profits have been overstated and the capital employed understated, giving a false picture of the profitability of the company in the period – a point developed in detail in Chapter 5.

The time-consuming process is calculating the opening position. When the details regarding fixed asset movements and accompanying depreciation have been ascertained, this information is available for future use. Plant registers properly maintained are a valuable record.

In the example, all movements have been assumed to be even. Where this is not the case, the conversion factor should be modified accordingly. Some items may already be in current value terms and, if this is the case, they should be excluded from the conversion process. An example is stock written down to net realisable value.

## 24.13 THE EFFECT OF INTRODUCING CURRENT COST ACCOUNTING

The Current Cost Accounting Exposure Draft (ED18) issued by the Accounting Standards Committee in December, 1976, contains proposals for the implementation of the main sections of the Sandilands Report on Inflation Accounting. These sections have been modified by debate to give the main provisions for Current Cost Accounting (CCA):

1. The use of current values for assets recorded in the balance sheet and current values used as a basis for depreciation calculations.
2. The charge to cost of sales for a period should normally be based on the replacement cost of the stock consumed at the date of consumption.
3. The CCA operating results should be identified in the main section of the profit and loss account. This should be followed by an appropriation section to record holding gains and losses and the amount appropriated by the directors to or from revaluation reserves.

4. The provision of a supplementary statement of change in shareholders' net equity interest after allowing for changes in the value of money.
5. The issue of a supporting note to the accounts to indicate the gain or loss to the company from holding net monetary items.

The value of the assets to the business involves the consideration of three values:

(a) Net current replacement cost (NRC) — the gross current replacement cost of assets less depreciation based on those values.
(b) Economic value (EV) — the asset's estimated future earnings potential in terms of the present value of the future cash receipts from using the asset.
(c) Net realisable value (NRV) — the asset's estimated net proceeds from its sale.

The higher of (b) and (c) should be taken and this result compared with (a). The value of the asset to the business (the deprival value) should be the lower of NRC and the higher of EV and NRV. This deprival value will normally be net current replacement cost.

Current cost accounting from the management accountant's point of view is an integrated part of the management accounting process.

## 24.14 A CONCLUDING COMMENT

With inflation at varying levels from year to year the management accountant cannot ignore its effects on the information produced for management. Economic reality dictates the recognition of specific price changes and replacement costs in conjunction with specific price indices. This action appears appropriate because it is unrealistic to assume that specific prices move in sympathy with general price changes. There are practical problems and the Accounting Standards Steering Committee felt the move to CPP adjustments was probably as much as could be expected for many companies. This was not the view of the Sandilands Committee who wanted progress to current cost accounting to be achieved at a faster rate. The Accounting Standards Committee have responded with Exposure Draft 18 and the controversy continues.

## FOR FURTHER STUDY

QUESTIONS

1. *Principles regarding the maintenance of real capital*
   In considering the accountancy of changing price levels, what are the main principles to be observed concerning the maintenance of real capital? (ICMA)

2. *Methods of providing for the excess costs of replacement of assets*
   Provision for the excess cost of replacement of some assets may be made by an appropriation of profits from the sale of goods or provision of services or by inclusion in the costs. Give the arguments supporting each possible course of action. (ICMA)

**3.** *The use of a general or specific index?*

In an attempt to prepare meaningful accounts for the business some accountants believe that index numbers should be used to adjust asset original costs to current price levels.

*Required:*

Should a general or specific index be used for this purpose?

**4.** *The calculation of depreciation on replacement cost or original cost*

What are the arguments for and against the calculation of the depreciation of fixed assets on their replacement value instead of their original cost?     (ICMA)

**5.** *The calculation of replacement cost and the appropriate depreciation*

A holding company has decided to apply return on capital employed in assessing the performance of its subsidiary companies. However, to obtain realistic figures, certain adjustments, based on price level indices to book values will have to be made.

*Required:*

From information relating to the subsidiary companies, A and B, calculate:

(i) The current replacement cost of the asset involved

(ii) The accumulated depreciation to date assuming the asset is to be reported at current value

(iii) The depreciation figure for the present year based on current values.

|  | Subsidiary Company A asset | Subsidiary Company B asset |
|---|---|---|
| Year of purchase | 1950 | 1960 |
| Purchase price | £200,000 | £550,000 |
| Life | 40 years | 40 years |
| Disposable value | Nil | Nil |
| Price level index at the date of acquisition (1st January) | 40 | 100 |
| Price level index new (31st December, 1976) | 150 | 150 |
| Depreciation method | Straight line | Straight line |

(ACA)

**6.** *The calculation of the depreciation to be charged to the current year's profit*

The following letter appeared in a professional publication:

*Calculating Depreciation on Inflated Cost*

In a publication on management accounting it is stated that the depreciation to be charged against the profits for the year is the difference between the accumulated depreciation at the beginning and end of the year. I query the method used by the ASSC to arrive at their figure of £25,000 for additional depreciation shown in Note 2 of Appendix 2 (*Provisional Statement of Standard Accounting Practice* No. 7). It seems that the figure has been calculated by reference solely to the uprated figure of fixed assets at the beginning of the year.

The following details are extracted from the publication on management accounting: The original cost of the asset was £5,000, the inflated cost at the end of Year 4: £5,500, the inflated cost at the end of Year 5: £6,300, and the depreciation charged to profit and loss account for the year (i.e., Year 5): £800.

As the asset was being written off on a straight line basis over 10 years the historic depreciation was £500, the management accounting publication showed £800 but the ASSC basis figure would be £630 (10% of £6,300). The difference of £170 represented the backlog relating to prior years and arises from the effect of continuous inflation.

Which is the figure to adopt? Can you help me?

'Puzzled'

*Required:*

Write a reply to 'Puzzled'.

7. *The replacement cost of assets with small value*

Discuss the position regarding the replacement cost of machines which have been in the factory for some years and for which the book value is small. The cost of replacing the machines will be, in some cases, four or five times the original purchase price. (ICMA)

8. *The use of the general price index for accounts conversion*

Where accounts are being converted by the use of a general price index what items would not be adjusted and why are these items left at their amounts prior to conversion?

9. *The preparation of a CPP balance sheet*

One method which it has been suggested would improve the relevance of the annual accounts is known as Current Purchasing Power Accounts.

A conventional balance sheet at 31st August 1976 in summary form is reproduced below:

| | £ | £ | | £ | £ |
|---|---|---|---|---|---|
| Share capital | | | Fixed assets | | |
| Ordinary shares | | 100,000 | Cost | 250,000 | |
| Reserves | | | Depreciation | 80,000 | 170,000 |
| Profit and loss | | | Current assets | | |
| account | | 50,000 | Stock | 60,000 | |
| 10% Debentures | | 100,000 | Debtors | 30,000 | |
| Current liabilities | | | Cash and bank | | |
| Creditors | 40,000 | | balance | 40,000 | 130,000 |
| Corporation tax | 10,000 | 50,000 | | | |
| | | 300,000 | | | 300,000 |

The share capital was issued at par on 31st August 1964. The debentures were issued at par on 31st August 1976, and they are redeemable at par on 31st August 1986. The creditors are payable on 30th September 1976; the corporation tax on 1st January 1977. Fixed assets were acquired on 1st September in the following years: 1970: £50,000; 1973: £150,000; 1975:

£50,000, and have been depreciated on a straight line basis of 10% per annum. The replacement cost of similar plant was £400,000 on 31st August 1976. Stock was acquired evenly during June, July and August, 1976 and if purchased on 31st August 1976 would have cost £70,000.

The conversion factors, based on an index of current purchasing power which it has been agreed should be used, have the following values:

*Conversion factors*

| | |
|---|---|
| 31st August 1964 | 150 |
| 31st August 1966 | 140 |
| 1st September 1970 | 125 |
| 1st September 1971 | 122 |
| 1st September 1972 | 116 |
| 1st September 1973 | 110 |
| 1st September 1974 | 107 |
| 1st September 1975 | 105 |
| Average for the year to 31st August 1976 | 104 |
| Average for the three months to 31st August 1976 | 101 |
| 31st August 1976 | 100 |

*Required:*

Prepare a balance sheet at 31st August in terms of 31st August 1976 purchasing power.                    (ACA)

10. *The form of profit reconciliation where CPP supplementary statements are produced*

'Inflation has a material effect on the published accounts of the majority of companies prepared in accordance with the normally accepted historic cost convention.'                    (ED8)

*Required:*

As an accountant in a public company, show a form of presentation to reconcile the profit on a historical basis to profit on a current purchasing power basis.

(ACA)

11. *The CPP conversion of accounts*

Balance sheets for a company on an historic accounting basis are as follows:

*31st December 1975*                                                    *31st December 1976*

| £ | £ | | £ | £ |
|---|---|---|---|---|
| 30,000 | | Fixed assets | 30,000 | |
| 10,000 | 20,000 | Less accumulated depreciation | 11,000 | 19,000 |
| 9,000 | | Stock | 18,000 | |
| 10,000 | | Debtors | 25,000 | |
| 8,000 | 27,000 | Cash | 5,000 | 48,000 |
| | 47,000 | | | 67,000 |
| | 35,000 | Shareholders' equity | | 40,000 |
| | 12,000 | Creditors | | 27,000 |
| | 47,000 | | | 67,000 |

The profit and loss statement for the year ended 31st December 1976 is as follows:

|  | £ | £ |
|---|---|---|
| Sales |  | 40,000 |
| Less cost of sales | 34,000 |  |
| depreciation | 1,000 | 35,000 |
| Profit |  | 5,000 |

*Notes on the accounts*

(*a*) Sales were made on credit
(*b*) Cash received from debtors: £20,000
(*c*) Purchases of stock on credit: £43,000
(*d*) Cash payments made to suppliers: £18,000
(*e*) The company maintains its stock account on the FIFO basis
(*f*) All transactions may be assumed to have occurred evenly throughout the year
(*g*) Fixed assets were acquired on 1st January 1960.

General price indices are as follows:

| Year | Price index |
|---|---|
| 31st December 1959 | 60 |
| 31st December 1975 | 95 |
| 31st December 1976 | 105 |

*Required:*

(*a*) Prepare the balance sheets as at 31st December 1975 and 1976 in terms of pounds of current purchasing power (31st December 1976)
(*b*) Prepare the profit and loss statement for the year ended 31st December 1976 in terms of pounds of current purchasing power (31st December 1976)
(*c*) Prove the profit in answer to part (*b*) in relation to the balances of shareholders' equity in the answer to part (*a*).

12. *The implications of changing price levels for the accounts of a business*
Brian Spender was visiting his professional friend, Roy Saver, an accountant clearly overburdened by work judging by the pile of professional magazines that had accumulated in his office but were never read. When Brian Spender entered the office, Roy Saver was glancing through the pile of magazines and an editorial in an old copy of *Accountancy Age**  had attracted his attention. Passing it to Brian he said: 'Read that, Brian':

The need for some immediate method of accounting for inflation was emphasised this week by the publication of a mechanical engineering 'little Neddy' book.
The book *Inflation and Company Accounts in Mechanical Engineering*, is

*Editorial, 26 October 1973.

the result of a study of the accounts of 126 quoted companies. It concludes that very little money was ploughed back into the industry in recent times. And it says in the worse years, if inflation is taken into account, most companies have not retained enough profits even to maintain capital.

The National Economic Development Council has given the accounting bodies a shot in the arm by using the very same basis suggested in ED8 to adjust for the plummeting value of the pound. This is despite the fact that the Government has taken it upon itself to announce an investigation into the problems of accounting for inflation.

A second event this week also points to the need to move away from historic cost accounting as the only generally used method of accounting.

The Great Universal Stores accounts published last week reveal that freehold and leasehold properties have a value of something like £110 million more than their balance sheet value.

If this were incorporated in the accounts it would increase the GUS balance sheet totals by something like a quarter.

Surely such a substantial figure should as a matter of accounting principle, be reflected somewhere other than in a note? But at present this is not necessary. GUS has done nothing wrong although it could, of course, have chosen to revalue its assets for accounting purposes.

But even the Accounting Standards Committee's ED8 would not necessarily have dealt with this situation. If property values have increased by more than the general index, they would not necessarily have been reflected by a current purchasing power statement.

Brian and Roy had a chat about the editorial and then left the office for lunch.

*Required:*

If you had been present at the conversation about the editorial what comment would you have made?

REFERENCES

*Accounting for Changes in the Purchasing Power of Money*. Provisional Statement of Standard Accounting Practice No. 7. Accounting Standards Committee, 1974.
Gynther, R. S. *Accounting for Price-Level Changes: Theory and Procedures*. Pergamon, 1966.
*Inflation Accounting*. Report of the Inflation Accounting Committee, Chairman, F. E. P. Sandilands. HMSO, 1975. Chapters 8, 9, 10, 12 and 17.

# 25 Performance Assessment

## OBJECTIVE OF THE CHAPTER

To summarise and develop features of performance assessment introduced in earlier chapters. Measures of divisional performance are considered including transfer pricing.

## OUTLINE OF THE CHAPTER

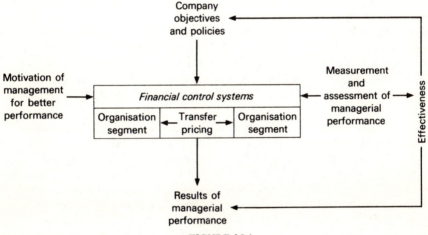

FIGURE 25.1.

The emphasis of the accounting role developed in earlier chapters is the greater involvement of the management accountant in assessing the quality of the management of the business. His unique position qualifies him to assess managerial performance objectively and a number of techniques and procedures have been shown to be of particular importance. They may be summarised as follows:

1. Planning – budgetary control
2. The use of standards – profitability, standard costing and return on capital employed
3. The use of financial responsibility centres
4. Financial control systems.

This assessment includes the consideration of the effectiveness of company objectives and policies. The use of a long-range planning group is the usual medium adopted by companies for the development of these objectives and policies in a strategy in the interests of the business.

Managerial performance may be assessed by measures other than those developed in the accounting context, e.g., productivity measurements, but management is significantly motivated by accounting controls. In decentralised organisations, for example, the method of transfer pricing adopted can influence the actions of a manager in terms of a profit level to be achieved by his own profit centre.

Efficiency audits may be conducted by specific personnel in the organisation and external management consultants. The type of work undertaken may be geared to major management problems demanding a solution or investigations of a routine character.

## 25.1  THE EFFECTIVENESS OF COMPANY OBJECTIVES AND POLICIES

Corporate planning has been shown to demand the statement of objectives to be achieved and policies to be implemented, but the development of a strategy for the business may show that policies need modification and objectives need to be defined more clearly. This development can be valuable to the business to the extent that long-run profitability may only be achieved where an organisation has clear direction and purpose. The creation of an effective corporate strategy requires a knowledge of financial analysis, business organisation and management. It also requires an ability to assess external factors likely to affect significantly the future of the business.

Company objectives and policies are applicable to the present as well as to the future but it is their relevance to the future which is likely to show their real effectiveness to the company. The future is uncertain and not all actions of management will be successful in achieving the objectives of the business. A management can act in a dynamic environment and deal with sudden reversals of fortune if they are confident that their overall strategy is soundly based and likely to be the correct course of action to follow. The periodic review of business strategy is necessary to ensure that what is planned for the business is being properly implemented. Objectives and policies may be soundly based; corporate strategy may be accurately formulated but internal factors, such as lack of management ability, or external factors, such as a rapidly changing technology, may work against the achievement of good company performance.

## 25.2  SATISFACTORY STANDARDS OF COMPARISON

There is a need for adequate standards of comparison in order to isolate the essential areas of business activity demanding managerial attention and possibly further investigation. Such analysis may be useful in indicating the appropriate action that should be taken by management.

The problems associated with finding such standards are as follows:

1. Ensuring that the standard is comparable with the information to be evaluated. This may be difficult where the standard is external, for example, another company, or internal in the form of data for a comparable period of time which might include the effects of activities not applicable to current performance.
2. Ensuring that the standard is a correct measure of performance. It is not unusual for standards to be assessments in the form of single figures of what should be attained in efficient conditions. In fact, a range of acceptable performance may be more appropriate.
3. Ensuring that the standard is realistic. While many standards are based on rigorous engineering specifications, this is not possible with all standards, and loose estimation may creep into the system to such an extent that the standards are of little value.

Of the various types of comparable data (budgets, comparable companies or departments, and historical data for comparable periods of time) budgets and standard costs are likely to be better indicators of the required performance of a business. They have their faults like all standards but they are usually prepared as a serious attempt to measure performance in circumstances expected to operate in the business. A clear definition of the terms applied and assumptions used in preparing the standards is needed.

## 25.3 FINANCIAL CONTROL SYSTEM EFFECTIVENESS

The primary requirement of a financial control system is to direct managerial attention where it is needed and the accuracy and relevancy of information output requires verification. Many companies have internal audit departments checking on the routines and procedures applicable to financial transactions. The extent of the conventional internal audit varies considerably. It may be limited to reviewing and appraising the soundness, adequacy and application of accounting routines in the usual functions such as purchasing, sales, wages and stores control. Such an audit also includes the physical verification of stock. Where such an audit is carried out to confirm the effectiveness of what are regarded as costing routines in the business, the term 'cost audit' is sometimes used.

Internal audit has sometimes been extended to an efficiency audit where the attempt is made to appraise the quality of performance in carrying out assigned responsibilities. This type of work is often limited to specific projects. A good example is the check on capital expenditure to ascertain whether the expectations which justified the investment in the project have been fulfilled.

The above reference to internal audits should be considered in perspective. There are many companies that have few systematic checks on what they are doing other than through the medium of external investigators. The statutory audit is an example, but in the sphere of management accounting the investigations carried out by cost auditors where cost-plus contracts are entered into by the company are also import-

ant. If, for example, the contract is with a government department, the actual costs
claimed by the company as a basis for fixing the price will be checked by the
government's technical cost officers.

Where a company requires an external opinion and impartial advice on the
effectiveness of its financial control system management consultants may be
employed. Consultants should be chosen with care and providing they are established
specialists in the problem area defined, valuable advice can be provided.

The effectiveness of any system is the extent to which its procedures achieve the
objectives laid down. Most control systems can be improved. Method study designed
to improve systems can make valuable recommendations to management which, if
implemented, one would hope would result in a more effective use of the resources
of the business.

Where a comprehensive check on internal control is required, the following
questions are typical of those used as a basis for specific investigation.

*General aspects of the control system*
1. Does the system of internal control appear to work effectively?
2. Are weaknesses in the business being signalled for the attention of management?
3. Are the weaknesses requiring action being brought to the attention of appropriate
   personnel?
4. Is action taken promptly regarding problems demanding attention?

*Authority and responsibility*
1. Are centres of responsibility clearly defined?
2. Have individual members of management the necessary authority to carry out
   their assigned responsibilities?
3. Are members of staff aware of assigned responsibilities and the extent of authority
   delegated?

*Work allocation*
1. Is the work fairly distributed and adequately covered by existing staff?
2. Is there a rotation of jobs to ensure adequate coverage in the case of sickness
   and holidays, and ensure the internal check is safeguarded?
3. Is the work control cycle apportioned between a number of personnel?

*Procedures*
1. Are there effective controls over documentation?
2. What is the extent of checking of accuracy incorporated in the system? Are the
   number of errors subsequently revealed reasonable and not of sufficient importance to be a serious problem?
3. What discretions are allowed in applying procedures?
4. Who initiates procedures and is there any control on changes made?
5. What are the independent checking arrangements and the extent of the authority
   of the personnel given the task, e.g., use of internal auditors?

*Relationships*
1. Is the morale of the organisation reasonably good?
2. Are working relationships between related departments satisfactory?
3. Are managers in control of their departments?

*Specific control systems*
1. Are specific control systems concerned with the acquisition of resources developed to the degree necessary, e.g., capital expenditure control?
2. Are specific control systems concerned with the use of resources developed to the degree necessary, e.g., material, labour and expense control?

## 25.4 DECENTRALISED CONTROL AND PERFORMANCE ASSESSMENT

The decentralised management structure found in large organisations necessitates the delegation of decision-making to segments of the business and the accountability of management responsible for those segments. The extent of the delegation can vary considerably and, therefore, the extent of managerial accountability will vary with each company. The management structure adopted should be chosen with care to try to ensure:

1. That management will be motivated in the overall interests of the business rather than a limited success in their own segment
2. That management will seek long-term success rather than good results limited to the short term.

To achieve these aims, the method of assessing divisional performance should also be chosen with care. The usual methods are:

(a) Conventional net profit
    If this method is adopted, the profit of the business segment will be calculated as follows:

*Division Profit Statement*
*Period ended*

|  | £ | £ |
|---|---|---|
| Sales |  | $x$ |
| Less cost of sales |  | $x$ |
| Divisional gross profit |  | $x$ |
| Less divisional overheads |  |  |
|     Administration | $x$ |  |
|     Selling and distribution | $x$ | $x$ |
| Net profit before group charges |  | $x$ |
| Less group overheads |  | $x$ |
| Net profit |  | $x$ |

The group overhead is an apportioned figure and if divisional profit statements are consolidated, the total net profit will be equal to the group net profit.

(b) Divisional net profit

If this method is adopted, the profit of the business segment is limited to the figure described above as 'net profit before group charges'. No apportionment of group overheads would be made to divisional segments.

(c) Divisional contribution

In this case the profit of the business segment will be calculated as follows:

*Division Profit Statement*
*Period ended*

|                                | £   |
| ------------------------------ | --- |
| Sales                          | x   |
| Less variable costs            | x   |
| Divisional contribution        | x   |
| Less divisional fixed costs    | x   |
| Divisional net profit          | x   |

As in the previous method, costs are limited to those incurred by the division but the marginal approach is used to give a divisional contribution.

(d) Divisional residual profit

If this method is adopted, the profit of the business segment will be calculated as follows:

*Division Profit Statement*
*Period ended*

|                                         | £   |
| --------------------------------------- | --- |
| Sales                                   | x   |
| Less variable costs                     | x   |
| Divisional contribution                 | x   |
| Less divisional fixed costs             | x   |
| Divisional net profit                   | x   |
| Less interest on divisional investment  | x   |
| Divisional residual profit              | x   |

All items in the above statement are restricted to the division but an imputed interest charge is made for assets used by the division.

(e) Net residual profit

If the residual profit concept is extended to full costs, the profit will be calculated

as follows:

|  | £ | £ |
|---|---|---|
| Sales | | $x$ |
| Less variable costs | | $x$ |
| Divisional contribution | | $x$ |
| Less divisional fixed costs | | $x$ |
| Divisional net profit | | $x$ |
| Less interest on divisional investment | | $x$ |
| Divisional residual profit | | $x$ |
| Less group overheads | $x$ | |
| Interest on non-controllable investment | $x$ | $x$ |
| Net residual profit | | $x$ |

In the divisional residual profit calculation, the imputed interest is restricted to divisional investment, i.e., investment controllable by the division. In the above calculation, imputed interest is included on non-controllable investment along with other non-controllable charges, e.g., group overheads.

The significant point emerging from the above illustrations is the extent of divisional control over specific items in the statements. Any profit figure used as a basis for judging segment performance should recognise the controllability factor.

The illustrations given are in their simplest form and Professor David Solomons has developed illustration (e) to recognise the transfer pricing situation not yet considered in detail.* For example, there may be an adjustment of the divisional net profit figure for fixed charges made to or by other divisions for transfers not priced at market value.

The profits shown are all before tax but divisional profits may be shown after tax. It is important that distortions that may be introduced by the tax calculation are avoided. A divisional segment tax calculation may be made restricting the factors to those under the direct control of the divisional management.

## 25.5 TRANSFER PRICING

Where products are transferred between segments of a group company, the pricing of the transfers can have an important bearing on the profits calculated. The usual methods adopted are as follows:

1. Cost prices
   (a) Actual absorption cost
   (b) Standard absorption cost
   (c) Actual marginal cost
   (d) Standard marginal cost.

* David Solomons, *Divisional Performance: Measurement and Control* (Richard D. Irwin, Homewood, Illinois, 1970), p. 82.

2. Cost plus prices
   (*a*) Actual absorption cost plus profit
   (*b*) Standard absorption cost plus profit
   (*c*) Actual marginal cost plus profit
   (*d*) Standard marginal cost plus profit.
3. Market prices
   (*a*) Actual market price
   (*b*) Modified market price.
4. Linear programming prices.

### 25.51 COST PRICES

Of the actual and standard cost methods, standard cost prices are preferred so that inefficiencies of the transferring segment are not passed to the receiving segment. Factory costs are usually used and if other overheads are added, there is a restriction to administration costs. Research shows that few companies use marginal cost. Its principal value to the receiving segment would be for short-term decision-making but this could be accomplished by analysing the make-up of the full-cost transfer price.

### 25.52 COST PLUS PRICES

Again, standard costs are preferred and the extent of the margin depends on the cost base. If the base is marginal cost, the margin will include the recovery of fixed costs; if the base is absorption cost, the margin will be profit. The problem with these prices is the internal friction caused by applying a standard formula. For example, the transferring segment could incur high costs and not only recover these but receive an inflated profit from the receiving segment.

### 25.53 MARKET PRICES

Wherever possible, the market price is preferred because the market price used is consistent with external pricing policy and profitability assessment. The difficulty is that a market price may not be available and in these circumstances one of the other methods may be used.

A market price may be modified by negotiation or by a fixed percentage. Unless the receiving segment is free to purchase from outside the company, negotiating a satisfactory price may be difficult because the receiving group is at a bargaining disadvantage.

### 25.54 LINEAR PROGRAMMING PRICES

Where there are supplying constraints on the part of the supplying segment and multiple receiving segments in competition for the possible supply, the optimum use of company resources may be obtained by linear programming. Optimum transfer prices may be produced but their value may be questioned when it is realised that the linear programming solution has produced the optimal allocation of resources whether the transfer prices are used or not, i.e., the objective of the exercise has already been achieved. This implies a belief in the validity of the linear programming approach which is seriously questioned by some authorities.*

## 25.6 MOTIVATION OF MANAGEMENT FOR BETTER PERFORMANCE

References to motivation that have appeared in this and earlier chapters rest on assumptions regarding human behaviour, and these assumptions may be in opposition to each other. An example is McGregor's Theory X and Theory Y.[†] The theories briefly outlined are as follows:

*Theory X*
(*a*)  The average person dislikes work and will avoid it if possible
(*b*)  Because of (*a*) autocratic management is necessary
(*c*)  The average person prefers autocratic management.
*Theory Y*
(*a*)  Work is natural if the conditions are right
(*b*)  Commitment to the organisation's aims will motivate an individual to achieve a desired result
(*c*)  The commitment in (*b*) will be secured if the social and psychological needs of the individual are relevant.

Management practices can be found to fit both sets of assumptions and, in general, where accounting techniques have been used in the context of Theory X they have not been particularly successful. For example, budgets used as a pressure instrument do not have long-term benefits for the business in terms of improved performance.

Where performance assessment shows that the desired results are not being achieved, management practice should be modified to provide better incentives to good performance. These modifications should include:

1. The designation of work that provides a challenge to the individual with a need for high performance
2. The encouragement of the individual to achieve good performance with appropriate rewards both financial and in terms of job enrichment, e.g., promotion
3. Relate company objectives to needs and aspirations of the individual
4. Improvement of communications to increase understanding and motivation of the individual.

---

* See, for example, J. Perrin, 'Aiming towards a better system of transfer pricing', *Accountancy Age,* 24 January 1975, p. 21.

[†] Douglas McGregor, *The Human Side of Enterprise* (McGraw-Hill, New York, 1960).

## 25.7 MANAGEMENT AUDIT

Many of the features of performance assessment included in this chapter have been
included by some writers in a composite term 'management audit'. There is no
generally agreed definition of what the term means but it is usually understood to
be broader in concept than the verification of the accuracy and relevancy of accounting procedures. Where such an approach takes for granted the objectives, policies
and plans of management, management audit involves the questioning of the soundness of these features of managerial control and aims to identify existing and potential organisation weaknesses.

An individual or group of individuals carrying out the type of company appraisal
considered above must operate in a senior capacity in the business. Senior executives,
including the accountant, forming a top-level management team are the most likely
individuals to reach conclusions that are not only valid but likely to be implemented.
It is preferable for an internal team to carry out such appraisals because collectively
their detailed knowledge and experience can be invaluable. Where an internal team
cannot be spared from their internal duties or an external view is required, consultants may be employed. If consultants are employed on company appraisals, precise
terms of reference should be agreed.

## 25.8 SUMMARY

Performance assessment is a difficult task mainly because so many factors affecting
good performance are interrelated and cannot be satisfactorily examined in isolation.
Control systems and the motivation of personnel are key elements in this process.
The techniques available for appraisal are imperfect but the monitoring of performance by the most effective means possible is an essential managerial task. The
experience, knowledge and status of the person(s) appointed to the task are of great
importance.

## FOR FURTHER STUDY

QUESTIONS

1. *Difficulty of making comparisons*
   'Reasonably accurate financial reports of actual performance often can be
   obtained (although the problems involved in obtaining them may be by no
   means trivial). Finding an adequate standard for comparison, however, is in
   business always a difficult matter.'
   
   (R. W. Anthony, *Management Accounting, Text and Cases,* Richard
   D. Irwin, Homewood, Illinois, 1964, p. 306)
   
   *Required:*
   Comment on the need for adequate standards of comparison for financial data,
   and on the problems associated with finding such standards.

2. *Measurement of performance for assessment*
   'Actual net profit achieved depends on three things: (*a*) profitability of products; (*b*) efficiency of cost centres; (*c*) volume.'
   *Required:*
   Give your views on this statement, explaining what is meant by profitability, efficiency and volume, and stating how each one is measured. (ICMA)

3. *The ideal standard as a measure of performance*
   What do you understand by the term "ideal standard'? Do you consider that an ideal standard is a satisfactory measure of performance? (ICMA)

4. *Presentation of efficiency measurements*
   Costs presented to management should show clearly the efficiency of departments and the profitability of products.
   *Required:*
   Write notes indicating how this is done, with special reference to standard costing, marginal costing and budgetary control. (ICMA)

5. *A check list for an internal control system*
   Internal control has been defined as comprising the form of organisation and all of the co-ordinate methods and measures adopted within a business to safeguard its assets, check the accuracy and reliability of its accounting data, promote operational efficiency, and encourage adherence to prescribed managerial policies.
   *Required:*
   As management accountant, produce a check list for the internal control system in your company. (ICMA)

6. *Management responsibility for internal control*
   Where there is a system of internal control there should also be a two-way traffic in responsibilities. The system should assist management and management should ensure that the system is capable of providing relevant information.
   *Required:*
   Discuss management's responsibilities for a system of internal control. (ACA)

7. *Cost audit*
   What do you understand by the term 'cost audit'? Your explanation should be related to a large public company which produces a variety of products which pass through many processes. In addition to the normal production which is in anticipation of sales, many 'job' orders for government departments are undertaken. These are usually contracted on a cost plus basis. (ACA)

8. *Objectives in transfer pricing*
   There arises frequently in the group company situation the problem of the pricing of intra-group company transfers, where the policy adopted can be vital to the profitability shown by the individual companies.
   *Required:*
   Suggest the objectives to be borne in mind in transfer pricing. (ICMA)

9. *Methods of transfer pricing*

Industrial Electronics Ltd has a number of subsidiary companies engaged in various sectors of the electronics industry. Most of the companies in the group, in addition to selling to the market generally, transfer components, sub-assemblies and finished products to other companies in the group.

*Required:*

Why is it important that proper consideration should be given to determining the prices at which transfers will take place between the companies? List the methods of transfer pricing which are available, commenting briefly upon the advantages and disadvantages of each. (ACA)

10. *Points to be considered in fixing a transfer price*

Evans & Jones Ltd are chemical manufacturers and two products, X and Y, are the subject of this case. Materials used for the manufacture of the two products are similar except that after testing specific lots some are used for the manufacture of product X rather than product Y.

The organisation of the business is based on the manufacturing facilities of X and Y and it can be assumed that the company is divided into two departments. Department X for the manufacture of X and Department Y for the manufacture of Y.

Material produced at the completion of product X is transferred to Department Y because it is suitable as one of the materials for the manufacture of Y but no longer of value to Department X. If Department Y purchased this material on the market it would cost, according to grade, the following:

Grade 1: £2 to £2·50 per gram
Grade 2: £1 to £1·50 per gram.

The material from Department X is considered as slightly poorer quality than Grade 2 normally available and this transferred material is charged to Department Y at £1·30 per gram.

Large quantities of the output of Departments X and Y are sold on the open market as well as to a subsidiary company that uses both products X and Y in its manufacturing operations.

The managers of Departments X and Y are in constant dispute regarding the transfer prices. The manager of Department Y considers he is overcharged for the material transferred from Department X and maintains that a more realistic price, bearing in mind that he is providing a service to Department X in moving the unwanted material, would convert his own department's trading loss into a profit. Department X also makes a trading loss and maintains that his output is used as a Grade 2 material in Department Y and a price of £1·30 per gram is not unreasonable because Department Y would have to pay up to £1·50 per gram if Grade 2 material was bought outside.

*Required:*

Comment on the transfer price problem described in the case.

11. *Management audit*

Your company has had an internal audit department for some years. This department is responsible for all internal control and, while it has been success-ful in developing a system to minimise the risk of fraud and ensure that the company's resources are preserved, the managing director has sent you a memo in which he states ' . . . the preservation of resources is no longer enough, we must develop our system for control and introduce the management audit'.

*Required:*

As management accountant, prepare a report for the managing director, indicat-ing the function of such an audit and the work which would require to be done to fulfil this function. (ACA)

12. *Company appraisal*

Packages Ltd has been a moderately successful company since its inception ten years ago and reasonably satisfied with its progress. The directors at a recent board meeting were concerned to realise that although their trade was booming, the company did not appear to have significantly benefited from such a favour-able environment. The best that could be said was that their moderate success would continue with their present profit performance and budgetary assessments for the future. Some directors felt that the real position was a deterioration with the external situation being so much in their favour.

After much discussion, the directors decided to call in consultants to assess the significant features affecting the running of the company with the object of ascertaining: (*a*) the degree of effectiveness with which the resources were being used; and (*b*) the action that should be taken to eliminate any weaknesses revealed.

The above terms of reference were given to a firm of consultants.

*Required:*

As consultant:

(*a*) What form would your preliminary investigation take?

(*b*) Outline the stages you would follow in your detailed investigation.

(*c*) What action would you take at each stage of your detailed investigation?

FURTHER READING

Anthony, Robert N., Dearden, John and Vancie, Richard F. *Management Control Systems. Cases and Readings.* Richard D. Irwin, Homewood, Illinois, 1965. Readings 6−1, 6−2 and 6−3.

Chamberlain, Neil W. *The Firm: Micro-Economic Planning and Action.* McGraw-Hill, New York, 1962. Chapter 19.

Solomons, David. *Divisional Performance: Measurement and Control.* Richard D. Irwin, Homewood, Illinois, 1965. Chapters 3 to 5.

# Conclusion

# 26 The Future of Management Accounting

## OBJECTIVE OF THE CHAPTER

To indicate the importance of future developments in management accounting and attempt to indicate the aspects of the subject that are likely to be the areas of development.

## OUTLINE OF THE CHAPTER

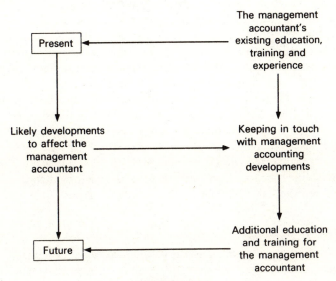

FIGURE 26.1

As businesses develop, their management needs are affected and professional staff must be alive to the changes and respond accordingly. All professions are developing and the complexity of business problems in leading to an interdisciplinary approach where individual professions are broadening the base of their qualifications. It is not suggested that each profession is professing mastery of all business disciplines but that the relevant aspects of associated disciplines are being developed as required by each profession. The effect of this trend is that if any one profession and its practitioners are reluctant or neglectful in responding to the changing business scene, other professions are available to develop further in supplying the needs of management.

The lesson for the management accountant is to assess the effect of future developments on his profession and ensure that his education and training are of the standard necessary to equip him to meet the demands expected.

## 26.1 LIKELY DEVELOPMENTS TO AFFECT THE MANAGEMENT ACCOUNTANT

The management accountant can expect to be affected by the following developments in the future:

1. *Business expansion*

   As small businesses increase in size there is a need for the introduction of management accounting techniques. When the medium-sized undertaking continues to expand, the management accounting techniques need development to cope with the marked increase in paperwork. Unless the systems are soundly based, reviewed and revised to be as effective as possible, the accounting work may be delayed, inaccurate, and in extreme cases, in a chaotic state. The accountant must recognise the early symptoms of these troubles and act in time to avoid major problems more difficult to resolve.

   The larger companies create bigger problems especially when mergers or take-overs occur. These usually involve a reorganisation of systems. Some companies resolve this problem by centralizing the work for close head-office control. Other companies decentralise their accounting work creating a uniform system. The volume of mergers and takeovers varies from time to time but it is certain that the future economic situation will encourage the formation of larger groups with the reorganisation of the accounting system and rationalisation that this entails.

2. *Economic requirements*

   In recent years a greater emphasis has been placed on national planning and there are clear indications that in an attempt to control the economy, governments are making determined efforts to influence to a greater extent the actions of companies. The trend will affect:

   (*a*) Particular trades

   Trade association activity will be intensified to protect particular trades, and the need for financial information to support their submissions to government will increase.

   (*b*) Particular businesses

   The management accountant will be involved to a greater extent in completing an increased volume of government reports and statistics.

3. *Overseas development*
   The competition from abroad will force backward businesses to revise their

   thinking regarding the use of modern management accounting techniques. Prompted by competition, the need for financial information has forced many companies to improve their systems of financial control.

   Multi-national company influence is increasing and there are other sources of finance such as capital from the Arab countries and the EEC. This development will emphasise the need to recognise nationalist and federal aspirations, and national and World Bank exchange control.

   Where companies consider opening subsidiaries overseas, the decisions are complex and the management accountant is involved in the decision-making process. There is an increasing tendency for British companies to open subsidiary units overseas.

4. *The growth in management education*
   An increasing number of managers have taken management courses and a basic topic in such courses is the appreciation of financial information for business control. The effect of this trend is that managers know what they can expect from a good management accounting system and, if they are not receiving the service they know they are entitled to expect, they will apply the necessary pressure to get what they want.

5. *Greater involvement in management decision-making*
   Management accountants are playing an increasing role as advisers to management. There is a recognition that the provision of sound advice demands a knowledge of accounting in advance of the levels of acceptable experience of ten or even five years ago. The reason for this situation is the research attack on the foundations of many accepted accounting practices of the past and the need to replace these practices with better data supply and interpretative skill.

6. *Pressure for greater cost reduction*
   The single attack on cost levels when the economic position of the business dictates that this is required is being replaced to an increasing extent by continuous cost reduction investigations. This trend will continue as a result of ever increasing costs. Interdisciplinary project teams are likely to be the most effective long-term approach to this problem.

7. *The introduction of automation and greater mechanisation*
   With increasing automation and mechanisation the proportions of cost that are fixed and variable are likely to change considerably from past relationships. This significant change will demand a reassessment of points of emphasis in information supply. Routine decisions on the basis of past cost structures will require revision.

8. *The improvement in clerical methods*
   The range of business machinery available is considerable and significant changes

have taken place in clerical methods in many companies. This is particularly evident in the use of computers and it is often possible to obtain information for management which was previously required but considered uneconomic to produce. The use of computers will increase, large companies replacing existing equipment with more sophisticated machines and smaller companies using simpler versions appropriate to their needs.

Integrated data-processing demands a unified approach to information needs and the recognition of the advantages this can bring to an organisation will increase the application of the data base concept.

9. *The development of allied techniques*

The use of quantitative methods such as mathematics and statistics in the solution of business problems has affected many accounting departments to the extent that modern developments in operational research have been incorporated in established routines. This will continue and there is considerable scope for the expansion of business modelling for corporate planning. Research shows an increasing number of companies engaged in corporate planning with the aid of the latest quantitative techniques.

Also of considerable influence in management accounting are the developments arising from behavioural studies. Attitudes to the application of budgetary control have changed as a result of these studies in regard to management participation in the fixing of budgets and the assumptions regarding management motivation. Companies that have not modified their approaches are likely to take advantage of the work of social scientists and improve their control systems.

A study of decision-making literature suggests standardised models are appropriate for managers faced with specific decision problems. Behavioural scientists have discovered that individual managers use different thought processes in dealing with problems yet this knowledge does not seem to have been applied in accounting practice. It is likely to be increasingly recognised in future.

10. *The need to improve communications*

Many companies are deficient in their communications and in the area of financial information many routine reports do not achieve the desired effect because they are too superficial. The likely development to deal with this problem is the replacement of part of the volume of routine reporting by special reports on topics investigated in greater depth.

Companies are being criticised for lack of financial information for employees and the deficiencies of conventional statements for other users. For example, increasing attention is being given to statements not recognising inflation. It is certain that an increasing output of financial statements will result from these criticisms and the likely effect will be basic statements with additional reports to meet the requirements of specific users.

11. *The growth in accounting research*

Ten years ago, the amount of research in accounting in Great Britain was minimal. In recent years there has been a growth in accounting departments in universities with a marked increase in research output. This output, and the research from overseas, is filtering through to companies, and applications are possible because universities are showing an encouraging attitude to practical considerations.

The professional accounting bodies have always attempted research but their efforts have been fragmented and little money has been allocated for the purpose. All professional accounting bodies have strengthened their technical departments and there is a growing tendency to impose their findings on industry. The ASC pronouncements and standards are an example.

12. *Consultancy assignments*

Many companies engaged consultants to investigate their financial control systems and make recommendations for improvement. In this way, management accounting techniques are developed in specific businesses. This situation will continue with investigations crossing functional boundaries to an increasing extent where the expertise of the accountant can be identified as of value to other areas of management. This demands a breadth of outlook from the modern management accountant.

## 26.2 KEEPING IN TOUCH WITH MANAGEMENT ACCOUNTING DEVELOPMENTS

Finding the time to assess the growing volume of accounting literature and extract the items worthy of more detailed study or application is a continual problem. The following approaches to keeping in touch with management accounting developments are recommended:

1. Take advantage of abstracts that convey the essence of the material available on relevant topics of interest.
2. When a good text on management accounting is identified, ensure that time is available to study its contents and understand its message.
3. Keep in touch with professional colleagues and follow up promising thoughts prompted by such conversation. Valuable ideas can be generated from discussion with colleagues in disciplines other than accounting.
4. Identify deficiencies in knowledge and experience that can be eliminated by attending a course or conference, or studying a standard text on the subject.
5. Be willing to obtain advice from service organisations organised to give technical information.
6. Establish contact with educational institutions that show they can provide relevant up-to-date information on management accounting developments.

## 26.3  MANAGEMENT ACCOUNTING DEVELOPMENTS AND THE COMMON BODY OF KNOWLEDGE

Management accounting developments are related to a common body of knowledge and studies have examined this point in depth.* The components of this common body of knowledge listed below is based on a study by the Price Waterhouse Foundation:[†]

1. Characteristics of information systems
2. The nature and function of accounting
3. Communication of accounting information
4. Economic, social, political, legal and organisational interactions with accounting
5. Mathematical and statistical interactions with accounting
6. Valuation concepts and limitations in their implementation
7. Theoretical framework for economic resource allocation
8. The conventional accounting model
9. Financial statement analysis
10. Data accumulation and transformation
11. Accounting reports
12. Decision choice, decision implementation and relevant information
13. Accounting tools as comprehensive planning devices
14. Performance evaluation and control.

To the student, such a list is a daunting prospect, but without a framework further developments cannot be considered in perspective. The ability to identify the relevant and significant aspects of apparent progress may also be seriously impaired.

## 26.4  A CONCLUDING COMMENT

Throughout this book the message has been developed that management accounting can be used as a positive force in the business, and the management accountant can significantly influence the management to achieve the objectives desired. To fulfil that responsibility, the education, training and experience of the management accountant must be of a high standard and kept up-to-date.

Whenever techniques are in the course of development, they provide a base for the publication of gimmicks and there is no shortage of exponents of high-sounding terms and phrases. A keen appreciation of what is valuable and can be realistically applied in business is a valuable attribute of the manager and management accountant.

It is the modern practice to extend the boundaries of the framework of manage-

* See, for example, David Solomons with T. M. Berridge, *Prospectus for a Profession*, The Report of the Long-range Enquiry into Education and Training for the Accountancy Profession (Advisory Board of Accountancy (UK) Education, 1974); and Robert H. Roy and James H. MacNeill, *Horizons for Profession*. A study sponsored by the Carnegie Corporation of New York and the American Institute of Certified Public Accountants, 1967.

[†] *A New Introduction to Accounting*, A Report of the Study Group sponsored by the Price Waterhouse Foundation, ed. Gerhard G. Mueller, 1971.

ment accounting to include the consideration of current moral, ethical, political, social and legal developments. The interactions of these factors with accounting cannot be ignored.

## FOR FURTHER STUDY

### QUESTIONS

1. *The balance between education and training*
   In qualifying the management accountant to follow his profession what do you understand by the terms 'education and training'? Comment on the balance between education and experience in the context of preparing the future management accountant to handle new situations that will arise in his future career.

2. *Specialisation and post-qualification education*
   Professor Solomons in *Prospectus for a Profession* suggests that specialisation is a fact of life which will be carried to greater lengths in the future.
   *Required:*
   Comment on this point in relation to post-qualification education.

3. *Taking advantage of changes affecting the profession*
   What can the management accountant do to equip himself to take advantage of changes affecting his profession?

4. *Profiting from business change*
   What can the management accountant do to help the company he serves to profit from changes affecting the organisation?

5. *Management accounting research*
   Given the facilities for research, to what aspects of management accounting would you direct your attention?

6. *Interpretation of the common body of knowledge*
   Refer to the common body of knowledge listed in the text of this chapter. What do you understand by the titles used? Quote section headings as examples of the coverage of this common body of knowledge in this book.

### FURTHER READING

Hague, D. C. 'The future of the management accountant'. *Management Accounting* (August, 1966), pp. 302–6.
Horngren, Charles T. 'The accounting discipline in 1999'. *The Accounting Review* (January, 1971), pp. 1–11.
Roy, Robert H. and MacNeile, James H. *Horizons for a Profession.* A Study sponsored by the Carnegie Corporation of New York and the American Institute of Certified Public Accountants, 1967.

# APPENDICES

# A  The Use of Compound Interest Formulae and Tables

## OBJECTIVE OF THE APPENDIX

The compound interest and annuity formulae are sometimes difficult to understand because of the various symbols used. Relationships are also sometimes difficult to comprehend. The objective of this appendix is to describe how the formulae and interest tables are derived and how they may be applied in the solution of business problems.

## FORMULAE AND DEFINITION OF TERMS

1. *Basic compound interest formula*
   Compound interest: the difference between the sum of money originally invested and the accumulated value (principal plus total interest over a total given period of time of compounding periods where the interest is calculated on principal plus interest at the end of each compounding period).
   Compounding period: the time interval between two successive calculations of interest.

   $$S_n = P(1 + i)^n$$

   Where

   $S_n$ = Accumulated value of a sum of money invested at compound interest, over a given period of time (also known as 'A' — this use avoided so that the symbol is not confused with the 'A' quoted in the basic annuity formula)
   $P$  = The sum of money originally invested (principal)
   $i$  = The interest rate for each compounding period as a percentage
   $n$  = Number of compounding periods.

2. *Present value compound interest formula*
   Evaluating the basic formula for P, the present value formula is obtained:

   $$P = \frac{S_n}{(1 + i)^n}$$

   or $P = S_n \dfrac{1}{(1 + i)^n}$

   or $P = S_n(1 + i)^{-n}$

$(1 + i)^{-n}$ is also known as $v^n$ where $v^n$ = the present value of 1 at compound interest (also known as the discount factor).

3. *Basic annuity formulae*

Annuity: a series of periodic payments of equal amount, the periods being of equal duration.

(i) $S_n = R(A)$

Where

$S_n$ = The future sum of money
$R$ = The annuity amount; the periodic payment; also known as rent
$A$ = The amount of an annuity of 1 per period; also known as $S_{\overline{n}|}i$

$$\text{or } \frac{(1 + i)^n - 1}{i}$$

and could, therefore, be written as:

$$S_n = R(S_{\overline{n}|}i)$$

$$\text{or } S_n = R\frac{(1 + i)^n - 1}{i}$$

(ii) $S = R(P)$ (The present value annuity formula)

Where:

$S$ = The present value of a series of payments; also known as $A_n$
$R$ = The annuity amount; the periodic payment
$P$ = The present value of an annuity of 1 per period; also known as $A_{\overline{n}|}i$

$$\text{or } \frac{1 - (1 + i)^{-n}}{i}$$

and could, therefore, be written

$$A_n = R(A_{\overline{n}|}i)$$

$$\text{or } A_n = R\left(\frac{1 - (1 + i)^{-n}}{i}\right)$$

4. *Periodic payment formula*

(i) Evaluating the basic formula 3(i) for $R$, the periodic payment formula is obtained:

$$R = \frac{S_n}{A}$$

$$\text{or } R = \frac{S_n}{\dfrac{(1 + i)^n - 1}{i}}$$

$$\text{or } R = \frac{S_n}{S_{\overline{n}|}i}$$

(ii) Evaluating the basic formula 3(ii) for $R$, the periodic payment formula is obtained:

$$R = \frac{A_n}{A_{\overline{n}|}i}$$

$$\text{or } R = A_n \frac{1}{A_{\overline{n}|}i}$$

$$\text{or } R = A_n (A_{\overline{n}|}i)^{-1}$$

$(A_{\overline{n}|}i)^{-1}$ is also known as the capital recovery factor.

## COMPOUND INTEREST TABLES – FORMS OF PRESENTATION

References: rate of interest: $i = 6\%$; number of years: $n = 5$.

Form (A)

6% Compound interest table

| $n$ | $(1+i)^n$ | $V^n$ | $S_{\overline{n}|}$ | $A_{\overline{n}|}$ | $(A_{\overline{n}|})^{-1}$ |
|---|---|---|---|---|---|
| 1 | | | | | |
| 2 | | (OTHER AMOUNTS NOT QUOTED) | | | |
| 3 | | | | | |
| 4 | | | | | |
| 5 | 1·33823 | ·74726 | 5·6371 | 4·2124 | ·237396 |
| etc | | | | | |
| REFERENCE FOR THE APPLICATIONS TO FOLLOW | TABLE 1 | TABLE 2 | TABLE 3 | TABLE 4 | TABLE 5 |

Form (B)

TABLE 1. Future value of £1 at compound interest
Formula: $(1 + i)^n$
(The future value of 1 at compound interest for $n$
years at the rate of interest $i$)

| $n$ | 1% | 2% | 3% | 4% | 5% | 6% | etc |
|---|---|---|---|---|---|---|---|
| 1 | | | | | | | |
| 2 | | (OTHER AMOUNTS NOT QUOTED) | | | | | |
| 3 | | | | | | | |
| 4 | | | | | | | |
| 5 | | | | | | 1·33823 | |
| etc | | | | | | | |

# MANAGEMENT ACCOUNTING

TABLE 2. Present value of £1
Formula: $v^n$ or $(1 + i)^{-n}$
(The present value of 1 in $n$ period's time at the rate of interest $i$)

| $n$ | $1\%$ | $2\%$ | $3\%$ | $4\%$ | $5\%$ | $6\%$ | etc |
|-----|-----|-----|-----|-----|-----|-----|-----|
| 1 | | | | | | | |
| 2 | (OTHER AMOUNTS NOT QUOTED) | | | | | | |
| 3 | | | | | | | |
| 4 | | | | | | | |
| 5 | | | | | | ·74726 | |
| etc | | | | | | | |

TABLE 3. Future value of £1 per period

Formula: $S_{\overline{n}|}i$ or $\dfrac{(1 + i)^n - 1}{i}$

(The amount of an annuity of 1 per period for $n$ periods
at the rate of interest $i$)

| $n$ | $1\%$ | $2\%$ | $3\%$ | $4\%$ | $5\%$ | $6\%$ | etc |
|-----|-----|-----|-----|-----|-----|-----|-----|
| 1 | | | | | | | |
| 2 | (OTHER AMOUNTS NOT QUOTED) | | | | | | |
| 3 | | | | | | | |
| 4 | | | | | | | |
| 5 | | | | | | 5·6371 | |
| etc | | | | | | | |

TABLE 4. Present value of £1 per period

Formula: $A_{\overline{n}|}i$ or $\dfrac{1 - (1 + i)^{-n}}{i}$

(The present value of an annuity of £1 per period
for $n$ periods at the rate of interest $i$)

| $n$ | $1\%$ | $2\%$ | $3\%$ | $4\%$ | $5\%$ | $6\%$ | etc |
|-----|-----|-----|-----|-----|-----|-----|-----|
| 1 | | | | | | | |
| 2 | (OTHER AMOUNTS NOT QUOTED) | | | | | | |
| 3 | | | | | | | |
| 4 | | | | | | | |
| 5 | | | | | | 4·2124 | |
| etc | | | | | | | |

TABLE 5. Periodic amount of an annuity — present value of £1
Formula: $(A_{\overline{n}|}i)^{-1}$
(The periodic amount at the rate of interest $i$ of an annuity
for $n$ periods whose present value is 1)

| $n$ | $1\%$ | $2\%$ | $3\%$ | $4\%$ | $5\%$ | $6\%$ | $etc$ |
|---|---|---|---|---|---|---|---|
| 1 | | | | | | | |
| 2 | | | | | | | |
| 3 | | | (OTHER AMOUNTS NOT QUOTED) | | | | |
| 4 | | | | | | | |
| 5 | | | | | | 0·237396 | |
| etc | | | | | | | |

## APPLICATION OF FORMULAE TO BUSINESS PROBLEMS

| *Common data* | | *Calculations showing relationship of data and the use of tables* |
|---|---|---|

Rate of interest     6%
Numbers of years     5

Cost of investment    £1,000

$\begin{cases} 237 \times 4\text{·}2124 & = £1,000\ (4\text{·}2124 \text{ from table 4}) \\ 1,338 \times 0\text{·}74726 & = £1,000\ (0\text{·}74726 \text{ from table 2}) \\ 177 \times 5\text{·}6371 & = £1,000\ (5\text{·}6371 \text{ from table 3}) \end{cases}$

Future value of
investment at     £1,338
compound
interest

$\begin{cases} 1,000 \times 1\text{·}33823 & = £1,338\ (1\text{·}33823 \text{ from table 1}) \\ 237 \times 5\text{·}6371 & = £1,338\ (5\text{·}6371 \text{ from table 3}) \end{cases}$

Periodic amount
(future value —     £237     $1,000 \times 0\text{·}237396 = £237\ (0\text{·}237396 \text{ from table 5})$
£1,338)

Periodic amount
(future value —     £177     $1,000 \div 5\text{·}6371 \quad = £177\ (5\text{·}6371 \text{ from table 3})$
£1,000)

## APPLICATION 1

£1,000 is invested at the commencement of Year 1 for 5 years at a compound
interest rate of 6%. Calculate the value of the investment at the end of Year 5.

By formula:   $S_n = P(1 + i)^n$

$$= £1,000\ (1 + \text{·}06)^5$$

$$= £1,000 \times 1\text{·}06 \times 1\text{·}06 \times 1\text{·}06 \times 1\text{·}06 \times 1\text{·}06$$

$$= £1,338$$

By tables:    $S_n = P(\text{Table 1})$

$$= £1,000\ (1\text{·}33823)$$

$$= £1,338$$

APPLICATION 2

What is the amount to be invested in a project at the start of Year 1 to yield £1,338 at the end of Year 5 at a compound interest rate of 6%?

By formula: $P = S_n \dfrac{1}{(1 + i)^n}$

$$= £1,338 \left(\frac{1}{1 + \cdot 06}\right)^5$$

$$= £1,338 \times \frac{1}{1 \cdot 06} \times \frac{1}{1 \cdot 06} \times \frac{1}{1 \cdot 06} \times \frac{1}{1 \cdot 06} \times \frac{1}{1 \cdot 06}$$

$$= £1,000$$

By tables:    $P = S_n$ (Table 2)

$$= £1,338 \,(\cdot 74726)$$

$$£1,000$$

APPLICATION 3

If £1,000 is invested in an asset now with an income flow at compound interest amounting to £1,338 at the end of 5 years, calculate the return on investment.

By formula: $\dfrac{P}{S_n}$

$$= \frac{£1,000}{£1,338}$$

$$= \cdot 74738$$

By tables:    Use Table 2 for $n = 5$. Where a figure is given as close as possible to $\cdot 74738$, the interest rate applicable for that figure is the rate of return on the investment.

$$= 6\%$$

(Note: the slight difference in this case is due to approximation)

APPLICATION 4

An income of £237 is received from a project at the start of each year for 5 years and is invested as received at 6% compound interest. Calculate the amount available at the end of the Year 5.

By formula: $S_n = R\left(\dfrac{(1+i)^n - 1}{i}\right)$

$= £237\left(\dfrac{(1 + \cdot06)^5 - 1}{\cdot06}\right)$

$= £237\left(\dfrac{(1\cdot06 \times 1\cdot06 \times 1\cdot06 \times 1\cdot06 \times 1\cdot06) - 1}{\cdot06}\right)$

$= £237\,(5\cdot6371$

$= £1,338$

By tables:   $S_n = R(\text{Table } 3)$

$= £237\,(5\cdot6371)$

$= £1,338$

## APPLICATION 5

An asset is purchased at £1,000 and is expected to have a life of 5 years with no residual value. If the funds invested in this asset could earn interest at the compound interest rate of 6%, calculate the annual cost of this investment. (This is the annuity method of providing for depreciation.)

By formula:  $R = \dfrac{A_n}{A_{\overline{n}|}i}$

$= \dfrac{A_n}{\dfrac{1 - (1+i)^{-n}}{i}}$

$= \dfrac{A_n i}{1 - \dfrac{1}{(1+i)^n}}$

$= \dfrac{£1,000 \times \cdot06}{1 - \dfrac{1}{1\cdot06 \times 1\cdot06 \times 1\cdot06 \times 1\cdot06 \times 1\cdot06}}$

$= \dfrac{£60}{1 - \dfrac{1}{1\cdot338}}$

$= \dfrac{£60}{1 - \cdot7475}$

$= \dfrac{£60}{\cdot2525}$

$= £237$

By tables:   $R = A_n\,(\text{Table } 5)$

$= £1,000\,(\cdot237396)$

$= £237$

APPLICATION 6

An asset is purchased for £1,000 and is expected to have a life of 5 years with no residual value. Future funds are to be made available by investing a constant amount plus the compound interest at 6% received from the investment in each of the five years of the life of the asset. Calculate the constant amount. (This is the sinking fund method of providing for depreciation.)

$$\text{By formula:} \quad R = \frac{S_n}{\dfrac{(1+i)^n - 1}{i}}$$

$$= \frac{£1,000}{\dfrac{(1+\cdot 06)^5 - 1}{\cdot 06}}$$

$$= \frac{£1,000}{\dfrac{(1\cdot 06 \times 1\cdot 06 \times 1\cdot 06 \times 1\cdot 06 \times 1\cdot 06) - 1}{\cdot 06}}$$

$$= \frac{£1,000}{5\cdot 6371}$$

$$= £177$$

$$\text{By tables:} \quad R = \frac{S_n}{\text{Table 3}}$$

$$= \frac{£1,000}{5\cdot 6371}$$

$$= £177$$

APPLICATION 7

If £1,000 is invested in an asset now, production costs are expected to be reduced by £237 per year for 5 years. Calculate the rate of return on the investment.

$$\text{By formula:} \quad \frac{A_n}{R}$$

$$= \frac{£1,000}{£237}$$

$$= 4\cdot 2194$$

By tables:   Use Table 4 for $n = 5$. Where a figure is given as close as possible to 4·2194 the interest rate applicable for that figure is the rate of return on the investment.

$$= 6\%$$

(Note: the slight difference in this case is due to approximation.)

APPLICATION 8

A building is leased for 5 years at an annual rental or £237 payable at the end of each year. If cash can be invested at the compound interest rate of 6% calculate the cash equivalent of the lease.

$$\text{By formula: } A_n = R\left(\frac{1 - (1 + i)^{-n}}{i}\right)$$

$$= £237\left(\frac{1 - (1 + \cdot06)^{-5}}{\cdot06}\right)$$

$$= £237\left(\frac{1 - \dfrac{1}{1\cdot06 \times 1\cdot06 \times 1\cdot06 \times 1\cdot06 \times 1\cdot06}}{\cdot06}\right)$$

$$= £237\left(\frac{1 - \dfrac{1}{1\cdot338}}{\cdot06}\right)$$

$$= £237\left(\frac{1 - \cdot7475}{\cdot06}\right)$$

$$= £237\left(\frac{\cdot2525}{\cdot06}\right)$$

$$= £237 \,(4\cdot2124)$$

$$= £1,000$$

(Note: the figure above correct to four places of decimals does not give 4·2124, but the slight difference is due to approximation.)

$$\text{By tables: } A_n = R \,(\text{Table 4})$$

$$= £237 \,(4\cdot2124)$$

$$= £1,000$$

## A CONCLUDING COMMENT

Management accounting requires an understanding of compound interest relationships if relevant data is to be submitted to management for decision-making purposes.

# B Compound Interest Tables

## TABLE 1. Present value of £1

| n | 1% | 2% | 3% | 4% | 5% | 6% | 7% | 8% |
|---|----|----|----|----|----|----|----|----|
| 1 | ·990 | ·980 | ·971 | ·962 | ·952 | ·943 | ·935 | ·926 |
| 2 | ·980 | ·961 | ·943 | ·925 | ·907 | ·890 | ·873 | ·857 |
| 3 | ·971 | ·942 | ·915 | ·889 | ·864 | ·840 | ·816 | ·794 |
| 4 | ·961 | ·924 | ·889 | ·855 | ·823 | ·792 | ·763 | ·735 |
| 5 | ·952 | ·906 | ·863 | ·822 | ·784 | ·747 | ·713 | ·681 |
| 6 | ·942 | ·888 | ·838 | ·790 | ·746 | ·705 | ·666 | ·630 |
| 7 | ·933 | ·871 | ·813 | ·760 | ·711 | ·665 | ·623 | ·584 |
| 8 | ·924 | ·854 | ·789 | ·731 | ·677 | ·627 | ·582 | ·540 |
| 9 | ·914 | ·837 | ·766 | ·703 | ·645 | ·592 | ·544 | ·500 |
| 10 | ·905 | ·820 | ·744 | ·676 | ·614 | ·558 | ·508 | ·463 |
| 11 | ·896 | ·804 | ·722 | ·650 | ·585 | ·527 | ·475 | ·429 |
| 12 | ·887 | ·789 | ·701 | ·625 | ·557 | ·497 | ·444 | ·397 |
| 13 | ·879 | ·773 | ·681 | ·601 | ·530 | ·469 | ·415 | ·368 |
| 14 | ·870 | ·758 | ·661 | ·578 | ·505 | ·442 | ·388 | ·341 |
| 15 | ·861 | ·743 | ·642 | ·555 | ·481 | ·417 | ·362 | ·315 |
| 16 | ·853 | ·728 | ·623 | ·534 | ·458 | ·394 | ·339 | ·292 |
| 17 | ·844 | ·714 | ·605 | ·513 | ·436 | ·371 | ·317 | ·270 |
| 18 | ·836 | ·700 | ·587 | ·494 | ·416 | ·350 | ·296 | ·250 |
| 19 | ·828 | ·686 | ·570 | ·475 | ·396 | ·331 | ·277 | ·232 |
| 20 | ·820 | ·673 | ·554 | ·456 | ·377 | ·312 | ·258 | ·215 |

| n | 9% | 10% | 11% | 12% | 13% | 14% | 15% | 16% |
|---|----|----|----|----|----|----|----|----|
| 1 | ·917 | ·909 | ·901 | ·893 | ·885 | ·877 | ·870 | ·862 |
| 2 | ·842 | ·826 | ·812 | ·797 | ·783 | ·770 | ·756 | ·743 |
| 3 | ·772 | ·751 | ·731 | ·712 | ·693 | ·675 | ·658 | ·641 |
| 4 | ·708 | ·683 | ·659 | ·636 | ·613 | ·592 | ·572 | ·552 |
| 5 | ·650 | ·621 | ·594 | ·567 | ·543 | ·519 | ·497 | ·476 |
| 6 | ·596 | ·565 | ·535 | ·507 | ·480 | ·456 | ·432 | ·410 |
| 7 | ·547 | ·513 | ·482 | ·452 | ·425 | ·400 | ·376 | ·354 |
| 8 | ·502 | ·467 | ·434 | ·404 | ·376 | ·351 | ·327 | ·305 |
| 9 | ·460 | ·424 | ·391 | ·361 | ·333 | ·308 | ·284 | ·263 |
| 10 | ·422 | ·386 | ·352 | ·322 | ·295 | ·270 | ·247 | ·227 |
| 11 | ·388 | ·351 | ·317 | ·288 | ·261 | ·237 | ·215 | ·195 |
| 12 | ·356 | ·319 | ·286 | ·257 | ·231 | ·208 | ·187 | ·169 |
| 13 | ·326 | ·290 | ·258 | ·229 | ·204 | ·182 | ·163 | ·145 |
| 14 | ·299 | ·263 | ·232 | ·205 | ·181 | ·160 | ·141 | ·125 |
| 15 | ·275 | ·239 | ·209 | ·183 | ·160 | ·140 | ·123 | ·108 |

### TABLE 1 (*contd.*)

| n | 9% | 10% | 11% | 12% | 13% | 14% | 15% | 16% |
|---|---|---|---|---|---|---|---|---|
| 16 | ·252 | ·218 | ·188 | ·163 | ·142 | ·123 | ·107 | ·093 |
| 17 | ·231 | ·198 | ·170 | ·146 | ·125 | ·108 | ·093 | ·080 |
| 18 | ·212 | ·180 | ·153 | ·130 | ·111 | ·095 | ·081 | ·069 |
| 19 | ·195 | ·164 | ·138 | ·116 | ·098 | ·083 | ·070 | ·060 |
| 20 | ·178 | ·149 | ·124 | ·104 | ·087 | ·073 | ·061 | ·051 |

| n | 17% | 18% | 19% | 20% | 21% | 22% | 23% | 24% | 25% |
|---|---|---|---|---|---|---|---|---|---|
| 1 | ·855 | ·848 | ·840 | ·833 | ·826 | ·820 | ·813 | ·807 | ·800 |
| 2 | ·731 | ·718 | ·706 | ·694 | ·683 | ·672 | ·661 | ·650 | ·640 |
| 3 | ·624 | ·609 | ·593 | ·579 | ·565 | ·551 | ·537 | ·525 | ·512 |
| 4 | ·534 | ·516 | ·499 | ·482 | ·467 | ·451 | ·437 | ·423 | ·410 |
| 5 | ·456 | ·437 | ·419 | ·402 | ·386 | ·370 | ·355 | ·341 | ·328 |
| 6 | ·390 | ·370 | ·352 | ·335 | ·319 | ·303 | ·289 | ·275 | ·262 |
| 7 | ·333 | ·314 | ·296 | ·279 | ·263 | ·249 | ·235 | ·222 | ·210 |
| 8 | ·285 | ·266 | ·249 | ·233 | ·218 | ·204 | ·191 | ·179 | ·168 |
| 9 | ·243 | ·226 | ·209 | ·194 | ·180 | ·167 | ·155 | ·144 | ·134 |
| 10 | ·208 | ·191 | ·176 | ·162 | ·149 | ·137 | ·126 | ·116 | ·107 |
| 11 | ·178 | ·162 | ·148 | ·135 | ·123 | ·112 | ·103 | ·094 | ·086 |
| 12 | ·152 | ·137 | ·124 | ·112 | ·102 | ·092 | ·083 | ·076 | ·069 |
| 13 | ·130 | ·116 | ·104 | ·094 | ·084 | ·075 | ·068 | ·061 | ·055 |
| 14 | ·111 | ·099 | ·088 | ·078 | ·069 | ·062 | ·055 | ·049 | ·044 |
| 15 | ·095 | ·084 | ·074 | ·065 | ·057 | ·051 | ·045 | ·040 | ·035 |
| 16 | ·081 | ·071 | ·062 | ·054 | ·047 | ·042 | ·036 | ·032 | ·028 |
| 17 | ·069 | ·060 | ·052 | ·045 | ·039 | ·034 | ·030 | ·026 | ·023 |
| 18 | ·059 | ·051 | ·044 | ·038 | ·032 | ·028 | ·024 | ·021 | ·018 |
| 19 | ·051 | ·043 | ·037 | ·031 | ·027 | ·023 | ·020 | ·017 | ·014 |
| 20 | ·043 | ·037 | ·031 | ·026 | ·022 | ·019 | ·016 | ·014 | ·012 |

### TABLE 2. Present value of £1 per period

| n | 1% | 2% | 3% | 4% | 5% | 6% | 7% | 8% |
|---|---|---|---|---|---|---|---|---|
| 1 | ·990 | ·980 | ·971 | ·962 | ·952 | ·943 | ·935 | ·926 |
| 2 | 1·970 | 1·942 | 1·914 | 1·886 | 1·859 | 1·833 | 1·808 | 1·783 |
| 3 | 2·941 | 2·884 | 2·829 | 2·775 | 2·723 | 2·673 | 2·624 | 2·577 |
| 4 | 3·902 | 3·808 | 3·717 | 3·630 | 3·546 | 3·465 | 3·387 | 3·312 |
| 5 | 4·853 | 4·714 | 4·580 | 4·452 | 4·330 | 4·212 | 4·100 | 3·993 |
| 6 | 5·796 | 5·601 | 5·417 | 5·242 | 5·076 | 4·917 | 4·767 | 4·623 |
| 7 | 6·728 | 6·472 | 6·230 | 6·002 | 5·786 | 5·582 | 5·389 | 5·206 |
| 8 | 7·652 | 7·326 | 7·020 | 6·733 | 6·463 | 6·210 | 5·971 | 5·747 |
| 9 | 8·566 | 8·162 | 7·786 | 7·435 | 7·108 | 6·802 | 6·515 | 6·247 |
| 10 | 9·471 | 8·983 | 8·530 | 8·111 | 7·722 | 7·360 | 7·024 | 6·710 |
| 11 | 10·368 | 9·787 | 9·253 | 8·761 | 8·306 | 7·887 | 7·499 | 7·139 |
| 12 | 11·255 | 10·575 | 9·954 | 9·385 | 8·863 | 8·384 | 7·943 | 7·536 |
| 13 | 12·134 | 11·348 | 10·635 | 9·986 | 9·394 | 8·853 | 8·358 | 7·904 |
| 14 | 13·004 | 12·106 | 11·296 | 10·563 | 9·899 | 9·295 | 8·746 | 8·244 |
| 15 | 13·865 | 12·849 | 11·938 | 11·118 | 10·380 | 9·712 | 9·108 | 8·560 |

## TABLE 2 (*contd.*)

| n | 1% | 2% | 3% | 4% | 5% | 6% | 7% | 8% |
|---|---|---|---|---|---|---|---|---|
| 16 | 14·718 | 13·578 | 12·561 | 11·652 | 10·838 | 10·106 | 9·447 | 8·851 |
| 17 | 15·562 | 14·292 | 13·166 | 12·166 | 11·274 | 10·477 | 9·763 | 9·122 |
| 18 | 16·398 | 14·992 | 13·754 | 12·659 | 11·690 | 10·828 | 10·059 | 9·372 |
| 19 | 17·226 | 15·679 | 14·324 | 13·134 | 12·085 | 11·158 | 10·336 | 9·604 |
| 20 | 18·046 | 16·351 | 14·878 | 13·590 | 12·462 | 11·470 | 10·594 | 9·818 |

| n | 9% | 10% | 11% | 12% | 13% | 14% | 15% | 16% |
|---|---|---|---|---|---|---|---|---|
| 1 | ·917 | ·909 | ·901 | ·893 | ·885 | ·877 | ·870 | ·862 |
| 2 | 1·759 | 1·736 | 1·713 | 1·690 | 1·668 | 1·647 | 1·626 | 1·605 |
| 3 | 2·531 | 2·487 | 2·444 | 2·402 | 2·361 | 2·322 | 2·283 | 2·246 |
| 4 | 3·240 | 3·170 | 3·102 | 3·037 | 2·975 | 2·914 | 2·855 | 2·798 |
| 5 | 3·890 | 3·791 | 3·696 | 3·605 | 3·517 | 3·433 | 3·352 | 3·274 |
| 6 | 4·486 | 4·355 | 4·231 | 4·111 | 3·998 | 3·889 | 3·785 | 3·685 |
| 7 | 5·033 | 4·868 | 4·712 | 4·564 | 4·423 | 4·288 | 4·160 | 4·039 |
| 8 | 5·535 | 5·335 | 5·146 | 4·968 | 4·799 | 4·639 | 4·487 | 4·344 |
| 9 | 5·995 | 5·759 | 5·537 | 5·328 | 5·132 | 4·946 | 4·772 | 4·607 |
| 10 | 6·418 | 6·145 | 5·889 | 5·650 | 5·426 | 5·216 | 5·019 | 4·833 |
| 11 | 6·805 | 6·495 | 6·207 | 5·938 | 5·687 | 5·453 | 5·234 | 5·029 |
| 12 | 7·161 | 6·814 | 6·492 | 6·194 | 5·918 | 5·660 | 5·421 | 5·197 |
| 13 | 7·487 | 7·103 | 6·750 | 6·424 | 6·122 | 5·842 | 5·583 | 5·342 |
| 14 | 7·786 | 7·366 | 7·982 | 6·628 | 6·303 | 6·002 | 5·752 | 5·468 |
| 15 | 8·061 | 7·606 | 7·191 | 6·811 | 6·462 | 6·142 | 5·847 | 5·576 |
| 16 | 8·313 | 7·824 | 7·379 | 6·974 | 6·604 | 6·265 | 5·954 | 5·669 |
| 17 | 8·544 | 8·022 | 7·549 | 7·120 | 6·729 | 6·373 | 6·047 | 5·749 |
| 18 | 8·756 | 8·201 | 7·702 | 7·250 | 6·840 | 6·467 | 6·128 | 5·818 |
| 19 | 8·950 | 8·365 | 7·839 | 7·366 | 6·938 | 6·550 | 6·198 | 5·878 |
| 20 | 9·129 | 8·514 | 7·963 | 7·469 | 7·025 | 6·623 | 6·259 | 5·929 |

| n | 17% | 18% | 19% | 20% | 21% | 22% | 23% | 24% | 25% |
|---|---|---|---|---|---|---|---|---|---|
| 1 | ·855 | ·848 | ·840 | ·8·33 | ·826 | ·820 | ·813 | ·807 | ·800 |
| 2 | 1·585 | 1·566 | 1·547 | 1·528 | 1·510 | 1·492 | 1·474 | 1·457 | 1·440 |
| 3 | 2·210 | 2·174 | 2·140 | 2·107 | 2·074 | 2·042 | 2·011 | 1·981 | 1·952 |
| 4 | 2·743 | 2·690 | 2·639 | 2·589 | 2·540 | 2·494 | 2·448 | 2·404 | 2·362 |
| 5 | 3·199 | 3·127 | 3·058 | 2·991 | 2·926 | 2·864 | 2·804 | 2·745 | 2·689 |
| 6 | 3·589 | 3·498 | 3·410 | 3·326 | 3·245 | 3·167 | 3·092 | 3·021 | 2·951 |
| 7 | 3·922 | 3·812 | 3·706 | 3·605 | 3·508 | 3·416 | 3·327 | 3·242 | 3·161 |
| 8 | 4·207 | 4·078 | 3·954 | 3·837 | 3·726 | 3·619 | 3·518 | 3·421 | 3·329 |
| 9 | 4·451 | 4·303 | 4·163 | 4·031 | 3·905 | 3·786 | 3·673 | 3·566 | 3·463 |
| 10 | 4·659 | 4·494 | 4·339 | 4·193 | 4·054 | 3·923 | 3·799 | 3·682 | 3·571 |
| 11 | 4·836 | 4·656 | 4·487 | 4·327 | 4·177 | 4·035 | 3·902 | 3·776 | 3·656 |
| 12 | 4·988 | 4·793 | 4·611 | 4·439 | 4·278 | 4·127 | 3·985 | 3·851 | 3·725 |
| 13 | 5·118 | 4·910 | 4·715 | 4·533 | 4·362 | 4·203 | 4·053 | 3·912 | 3·780 |
| 14 | 5·229 | 5·008 | 4·802 | 4·611 | 4·432 | 4·265 | 4·108 | 3·962 | 3·824 |
| 15 | 4·324 | 5·092 | 4·876 | 4·676 | 4·489 | 4·315 | 4·153 | 4·001 | 3·859 |
| 16 | 5·405 | 5·162 | 4·938 | 4·730 | 4·536 | 4·357 | 4·189 | 4·033 | 3·887 |
| 17 | 5·475 | 5·222 | 4·990 | 4·775 | 4·576 | 4·391 | 4·219 | 4·059 | 3·910 |

TABLE 2 (*contd.*)

| n | 17% | 18% | 19% | 20% | 21% | 22% | 23% | 24% | 25% |
|---|-----|-----|-----|-----|-----|-----|-----|-----|-----|
| 18 | 5·534 | 5·273 | 5·033 | 4·812 | 4·608 | 4·419 | 4·243 | 4·080 | 3·928 |
| 19 | 5·585 | 5·316 | 5·070 | 4·844 | 4·635 | 4·442 | 4·263 | 4·097 | 3·942 |
| 20 | 5·628 | 5·353 | 5·101 | 4·870 | 4·657 | 4·460 | 4·279 | 4·110 | 3·954 |

TABLE 3. Future value of £1 per period

| n | 1% | 2% | 3% | 4% | 5% |
|---|-----|-----|-----|-----|-----|
| 1 | 1·000 | 1·000 | 1·000 | 1·000 | 1·000 |
| 2 | 2·010 | 2·020 | 2·030 | 2·040 | 2·050 |
| 3 | 3·030 | 3·060 | 3·091 | 3·122 | 3·153 |
| 3 | 4·060 | 4·122 | 4·184 | 4·246 | 4·310 |
| 5 | 5·101 | 5·204 | 5·309 | 5·416 | 5·526 |
| 6 | 6·152 | 6·308 | 6·468 | 6·633 | 6·802 |
| 7 | 7·214 | 7·434 | 7·662 | 7·898 | 8·142 |
| 8 | 8·286 | 8·583 | 8·892 | 9·214 | 9·549 |
| 9 | 9·369 | 9·755 | 10·159 | 10·583 | 11·027 |
| 10 | 10·462 | 10·950 | 11·464 | 12·006 | 12·578 |
| 11 | 11·567 | 12·169 | 12·808 | 13·486 | 14·207 |
| 12 | 12·683 | 13·412 | 14·192 | 15·026 | 15·917 |
| 13 | 13·809 | 14·680 | 15·618 | 16·627 | 17·713 |
| 14 | 14·947 | 15·974 | 17·086 | 18·292 | 19·599 |
| 15 | 16·097 | 17·293 | 18·599 | 20·024 | 21·579 |
| 16 | 17·258 | 18·639 | 20·157 | 21·825 | 23·657 |
| 17 | 18·430 | 20·012 | 21·762 | 23·698 | 25·840 |
| 18 | 19·615 | 21·412 | 23·414 | 25·645 | 28·132 |
| 19 | 20·811 | 22·841 | 25·117 | 27·671 | 30·539 |
| 20 | 22·019 | 24·297 | 26·870 | 29·778 | 33·066 |

| n | 6% | 7% | 8% | 9% | 10% |
|---|-----|-----|-----|-----|-----|
| 1 | 1·000 | 1·000 | 1·000 | 1·000 | 1·000 |
| 2 | 2·060 | 2·070 | 2·080 | 2·090 | 2·100 |
| 3 | 3·184 | 3·215 | 3·246 | 3·278 | 3·310 |
| 4 | 4·375 | 4·440 | 4·506 | 4·573 | 4·641 |
| 5 | 5·637 | 5·751 | 5·867 | 5·985 | 6·105 |
| 6 | 6·975 | 7·153 | 7·336 | 7·523 | 7·716 |
| 7 | 8·394 | 8·654 | 8·923 | 9·200 | 9·487 |
| 8 | 9·897 | 10·260 | 10·637 | 11·028 | 11·436 |
| 9 | 11·491 | 11·978 | 12·488 | 13·021 | 13·579 |
| 10 | 13·181 | 13·816 | 14·487 | 15·193 | 15·937 |
| 11 | 14·972 | 15·784 | 16·645 | 17·560 | 18·531 |
| 12 | 16·870 | 17·888 | 18·977 | 20·141 | 21·384 |
| 13 | 18·882 | 20·141 | 21·495 | 22·953 | 24·523 |
| 14 | 21·015 | 22·550 | 24·215 | 26·019 | 27·975 |
| 15 | 23·276 | 25·129 | 27·152 | 29·361 | 31·772 |

TABLE 3 (contd.)

| n | 6% | 7% | 8% | 9% | 10% |
|---|------|------|------|------|------|
| 16 | 25·673 | 27·888 | 30·324 | 33·003 | 35·950 |
| 17 | 28·213 | 30·840 | 33·750 | 36·974 | 40·545 |
| 18 | 30·906 | 33·999 | 37·450 | 41·301 | 45·599 |
| 19 | 33·760 | 37·379 | 41·446 | 46·018 | 51·159 |
| 20 | 36·786 | 40·995 | 45·762 | 51·160 | 57·275 |

TABLE 4. Periodic amount of an annuity — present value of £1

| n | 1% | 2% | 3% | 4% | 5% |
|---|------|------|------|------|------|
| 1 | 1·010 | 1·020 | 1·030 | 1·040 | 1·050 |
| 2 | ·508 | ·516 | ·523 | ·531 | ·538 |
| 3 | ·340 | ·347 | ·353 | ·360 | ·367 |
| 4 | ·256 | ·263 | ·269 | ·276 | ·282 |
| 5 | ·206 | ·212 | ·218 | ·225 | ·231 |
| 6 | ·172 | ·179 | ·185 | ·191 | ·197 |
| 7 | ·149 | ·155 | ·161 | ·167 | ·173 |
| 8 | ·131 | ·137 | ·143 | ·149 | ·155 |
| 9 | ·117 | ·123 | ·128 | ·135 | ·141 |
| 10 | ·106 | ·111 | ·117 | ·123 | ·130 |
| 11 | ·096 | ·102 | ·108 | ·114 | ·120 |
| 12 | ·089 | ·095 | ·101 | ·107 | ·113 |
| 13 | ·082 | ·088 | ·094 | ·100 | ·107 |
| 14 | ·077 | ·083 | ·089 | ·095 | ·101 |
| 15 | ·072 | ·078 | ·084 | ·090 | ·096 |
| 16 | ·068 | ·074 | ·080 | ·086 | ·092 |
| 17 | ·064 | ·070 | ·076 | ·082 | ·089 |
| 18 | ·061 | ·067 | ·073 | ·079 | ·086 |
| 19 | ·058 | ·064 | ·070 | ·076 | ·083 |
| 20 | ·055 | ·061 | ·067 | ·074 | ·080 |

| n | 6% | 7% | 8% | 9% | 10% |
|---|------|------|------|------|------|
| 1 | 1·060 | 1·070 | 1·080 | 1·090 | 1·100 |
| 2 | ·546 | ·553 | ·561 | ·569 | ·576 |
| 3 | ·374 | ·381 | ·388 | ·395 | ·402 |
| 4 | ·289 | ·295 | ·302 | ·309 | ·316 |
| 5 | ·237 | ·244 | ·251 | ·257 | ·264 |
| 6 | ·203 | ·210 | ·216 | ·223 | ·230 |
| 7 | ·179 | ·186 | ·192 | ·199 | ·205 |
| 8 | ·161 | ·168 | ·174 | ·181 | ·187 |
| 9 | ·147 | ·154 | ·160 | ·167 | ·174 |
| 10 | ·136 | ·142 | ·149 | ·156 | ·163 |
| 11 | ·127 | ·133 | ·140 | ·147 | ·154 |
| 12 | ·119 | ·126 | ·133 | ·140 | ·147 |
| 13 | ·113 | ·120 | ·127 | ·134 | ·141 |
| 14 | ·108 | ·114 | ·121 | ·128 | ·136 |
| 15 | ·103 | ·110 | ·117 | ·124 | ·132 |

TABLE 4 (*contd.*)

| n | 6% | 7% | 8% | 9% | 10% |
|---|-----|-----|-----|-----|-----|
| 16 | ·099 | ·106 | ·113 | ·120 | ·128 |
| 17 | ·096 | ·102 | ·110 | ·117 | ·125 |
| 18 | ·092 | ·099 | ·107 | ·114 | ·122 |
| 19 | ·090 | ·097 | ·104 | ·112 | ·120 |
| 20 | ·087 | ·094 | ·102 | ·110 | ·118 |

# C Aspects of Taxation and Management Accounting

## OBJECTIVE OF THE APPENDIX

To explain aspects of taxation that have a bearing on the work of the management accountant. The appendix includes a consideration of expansion area incentives.

## THE PRINCIPAL TAXES CONCERNED

The principal taxes that are the concern of this appendix are:

1. Direct taxation

   (a) Income tax payable on the incomes of unincorporated businesses
   (b) Corporation tax payable on the incomes of companies
   (c) Income tax deducted from employees on behalf of the Inland Revenue
   (d) Income tax deducted from debenture interest payments on behalf of the Inland Revenue.

2. Indirect taxation

   (a) Value added tax
   (b) Duties on purchases, e.g., petrol
   (c) Licences, e.g., road fund licences.

   In addition to the above central government taxes, local government taxation is paid in the form of rates. Rates, duties and licences are incorporated in the business accounts as current operational expenses. Collections on behalf of the Inland Revenue are paid at prescribed intervals to the Collector of Taxes. The remaining items are described in greater detail in the sections to follow.*

## INCOME TAX ON INCOMES OF UNINCORPORATED BUSINESSES

The personal circumstances of the owners of unincorporated businesses (sole traders and partnerships) affect the tax liability which is calculated by reference to the

---

* This appendix is based on the tax position at the time of publication. Where dates are particularly relevant they are stated in the text.

following allowances and rates (1977/78):

*Allowances*

| | £ |
|---|---|
| Personal | |
| Single person | 945 |
| Married person | 1,455 |

| Children | First child £ | Other children £ |
|---|---|---|
| Not over 11 on 6th April 1977 | 196 | 170 |
| Over 11 but not over 16 on 6th April 1977 | 231 | 205 |
| Over 16 on 6th April 1977 | 261 | 235 |

| | £ |
|---|---|
| Dependent relative | 100 |
| (Single woman) | 145 |
| Housekeeper | 100 |
| Daughter's services | 55 |
| Blind person | 180 |

*Tax rates*

A basic rate of 34% is charged on the first £6,000 of income left after deducting all allowances and reliefs. The following higher rates are then applied:

| Taxable income £ | Rate £ |
|---|---|
| 6,000– 7,000 | 40 |
| 7,001– 8,000 | 45 |
| 8,001– 9,000 | 50 |
| 9,001–10,000 | 55 |
| 10,001–12,000 | 60 |
| 12,001–14,000 | 65 |
| 14,001–16,000 | 70 |
| 16,001–21,000 | 75 |
| 21,001 and above | 83 |

The investment income surcharge is an additional rate as follows:

| | Age up to 65 £ | Over 65 £ | Rate % |
|---|---|---|---|
| Investment income | up to 1,500 | up to 2,000 | Nil |
| | 1,501 to 2,000 | 2,001 to 2,500 | 10 |
| | 2,001 and above | 2,501 and above | 15 |

## CORPORATION TAX ON INCOMES OF COMPANIES

Corporation tax is payable on the profits of companies shown in the tax computation which adjusts period profits in the company accounts for the following:

1. Permanent variations in the amounts allowable for tax
2. Variations in the amounts allowable due to timing differences.

The rate of corporation tax for the year 1975/76 (1st April 1975 to 31st March 1976) is 52%. For small companies the rate is 42%. These rates applied to assessable profits provide a figure known as mainstream corporation tax (MCT). In advance of the normal payment of this tax to the Inland Revenue is a payment known as advance corporation tax (ACT). This tax for 1976/77 (1st April 1976 to 31st March 1977) is calculated as $\frac{35}{65}$ths of the dividends paid to shareholders. This is equivalent to 35% on gross payments, this being the basic rate of tax for 1976/77.* The ACT is payable to the Inland Revenue within three months of the dividend payments and the balance of MCT is due nine months after the end of the company's financial year.

Under the provisions of the Finance Act 1972, capital expenditure incurred anywhere in the country after 21st March 1972 on machinery and plant (other than private passenger cars) qualifies for a 100% first year capital allowance for the period in which the expenditure is incurred. Capital expenditure incurred after November 1974 on the construction of industrial buildings qualifies for a capital allowance for the first year of 54% followed by annual writing down allowances of 4% of cost.


## EXPANSION AREA INCENTIVES

Benefits are available to companies moving to special development, development and intermediate areas, defined by the Department of Industry to encourage businesses to locate their activities in regions of low industrial concentration. The incentives obtainable are as follows:

1. Regional development grants
    (a) New machinery, plant and mining works
        Special development areas     22%
        Development areas             20%
        Intermediate areas            Nil
    (b) Buildings and works (other than mining works)
        Special development areas              22%
        Development and intermediate areas   20%
2. Selective assistance
    (a) Loans — at concessionary rates of interest.
    (b) Interest relief grants — an alternative to loans. Grants towards the interest of finance provided from non-public sources.
    (c) Removal grants — where an undertaking is moved from any part of Great Britain outside an assisted area into one of these areas.
3. Department of Industry factories — possibly a two-year rent free period, and sale on favourable terms.

* The basic rate of tax for 1977/78 is agreed at 34% and the ACT rate will be $\frac{34}{66}$ths.

Regional development grants are not deducted from the cost of the asset in computing the tax allowances. The accounting treatment of the grants is usually to deduct them from the cost of the acquisition of the fixed asset.


## STOCK INCREASE RELIEF

Tax relief is available for increases in stock values applied to profits for the year ended 31st March 1976. The relief is calculated as follows:

|  | £ |
|---|---|
| Closing values of stock and work-in-progress for the year | – |
| Less opening values of stock and work-in-progress for the year | – |
| Increase in stock values | – |
| Less 15% of trading income for the year | |
| (trading income is the assessable profit as computed by applying | |
| Schedule D, Case 1, with the deduction of capital allowances) | |
| Stock increase relief | |

If the stock values fall during the year there is provision for the recovery of relief for previous years up to the maximum of the relief previously granted.


## VALUE ADDED TAX (VAT)

As the name suggests, this tax is charged on the value added and paid in full by the final consumer. This is shown in the following illustration where the prime producer is assumed to have made no purchases and after manufacture the goods reach the final consumer via the retailer. The current standard rate of VAT of 8% is used in this illustration.

| Stage | Value added £ | Buying price £ | Business | Selling price £ + VAT at 8% = £ | VAT paid to Customs and Excise £ (Output tax – Input tax) £ £ |
|---|---|---|---|---|---|
| 1 | 100 | Nil | Prime producer | 100 + 8 = 108 | 8(8 − Nil) |
| 2 | 50 (£150 − £100) | 108 | Manufacturer | 150 + 12 = 162 | 4(12 − 8) |
| 3 | 50 (£200 − £150) | 162 | Retailer | 200 + 16 = 216 | 4(16 − 12) |
| 4 | 50 (£250 − £200) | 216 | Consumer | 250 + 20 = 270 | 4(20 − 16) |
| | 250 | | ——8% of value added equals—→ | | 20 |

The businesses concerned are collecting VAT on behalf of the Customs and Excise Department and this collection is in stages, the amount of payment being the net amount of tax on outputs and inputs. Some businesses are zero rated* and in this case VAT is not charged to the customer and they are refunded the input tax by the Customs and Excise Department. Some businesses that do not charge the customer VAT are not refunded the input tax. These businesses are known as exempt firms[†] and, except in the case of these businesses, all others do not suffer the cost of full input VAT. Arising from this effect, turnover should exclude VAT on taxable outputs.

## SUMMARY

Taxation is a significant item and decision-making should be made after tax has been considered. Timing of allowances and payments are important including the situations where the business is merely collecting tax on behalf of the government. In the case of VAT, for example, the relationship of output and input taxes and credit terms can affect cash flow. Tax allowances for machinery, plant and buildings are the same for the country as a whole but incentives for industry in areas for expansion can be very valuable to a business.

---

* For example, businesses with an annual sales turnover not exceeding £5,000 per annum.
† For example, food, construction and pharmaceutical businesses.

# D Management Accounting in Retail Organisations

## OBJECTIVE OF THE APPENDIX

To modify the cost centre classification in the main text to reflect a retail organisation. The appendix describes the co-ordination of the selling function and the buying responsibility. This information enables the management accountant to estimate gross profit for period profit statement reporting.

## A RETAIL CLASSIFICATION

The principal divisions of a retail business are as follows:

1. General administration
2. Personnel
3. Accountancy
4. Sales promotion
5. Merchandising
6. Transport
7. Property maintenance.

In a small organisation, the cost centre classification may be limited to the principal divisions of the business shown above and the branches. It is usually found that this limited classification is inadequate for cost control purposes and additional cost centres may be formed. Additional cost centres within the framework of the principal divisions of the business may be as shown below:

| Principal division | Additional cost centres that may be formed |
| --- | --- |
| 1. General administration | Typing pool and possibly a centralised filing department |
| 2. Personnel | Canteen |
| 3. Accountancy | Internal audit |
| 4. Sales promotion | General advertising, display and exhibitions (separate cost centre for each exhibition) |
| 5. Merchandising | Buying (separate cost centre for each buyer); selling, warehousing (separate cost centre for each warehouse) |
| 6. Transport | Transport pools (separate cost centre for each transport pool); maintenance depots (separate cost centre for each depot) |

7. Property                Separate cost centre for each property main-
   maintenance             tenance depot.


## RETAIL SELLING AND BUYING CONTROL

In the retail situation it is common practice, particularly in the case of the larger
organisations, to keep stock records at selling prices, but it depends on the type of
merchandise sold. When stock records are kept on the selling price basis it is necessary
to keep a note of any reductions in the selling price. These reductions might arise
owing to allowances to customers, damage to goods in stock or ordinary seasonal
price reductions. The selling price of goods, once fixed, should not be reduced without the authority of the buyer concerned. The amount by which the goods are
reduced in price is termed the mark-down. Shrinkages are similar to mark-downs in
effect, being a percentage on sales to cover unascertainable losses due to the cutting
down of a bulked commodity for sale in smaller quantities. Such percentages are
fixed as a result of experience in the class of merchandise affected.

It is advantageous to maintain stocks at selling prices because greater control on
selling can be exercised. Once fixed, the anticipated gross margin on each article of
merchandise can only be adjusted by the mark-down system. The reasons why
anticipated prices are not realised may be found by an analysis of the mark-downs.

Where stock levels are indicated at selling price it is necessary to reduce the figures
to cost for buying control purposes. This is accomplished by the application of the
cumulative mark-up rate for the appropriate category of merchandise. The cumulative
mark-up is calculated by reference to opening stocks and purchases to date at cost
and selling price. An example is given below to make this clear:

|  | Cost £ | Selling price £ | Calculation of the cumulative mark-up |
|---|---|---|---|
| *Period 1* | | | |
| Opening stock | 1,500 | 2,000 | $\frac{£2,000 - £1,500}{£2,000} \times 100 =$ 25% on selling price |
| | | | (Cumulative mark-up at the commencement of the period) |
| Purchases | 800 | 1,000 | |
| | 2,300 | 3,000 | $\frac{£3,000 - £2,300}{£3,000} \times 100 =$ 23.33% on selling price |
| | | | (Cumulative mark-up at the close of Period 1) |

|  | Cost £ | Selling price £ |
|---|---|---|
| *Period 2* | | |
| Opening stock | 1,500 | 2,000 |
| Purchases to date (Periods 1 and 2 combined) | 1,600 | 2,000 |
| | 3,100 | 4,000 |

$$\frac{£4,000 - £3,100}{£4,000} \times 100 = \begin{array}{l} 22 \cdot 5\% \text{ on} \\ \text{selling} \\ \text{price} \end{array}$$

(Cumulative mark-up at the close of Period 2)

The original opening stock plus purchases does not go on indefinitely. Usually at the end of a six-month period, the cycle of calculations is again commenced with the opening stock at cost and selling price being the figures at the close of the previous six months.

The amount a buyer may be allowed to spend in a period can be calculated by preparing the following statement:

| | £ |
|---|---|
| Budgeted sales at selling price | — |
| Add budgeted closing stock | — |
| | — |
| Less budgeted opening stock | — |
| Purchasing allowance at selling price | — |
| Less budgeted gross profit margin | — |
| Purchasing allowance at cost | — |

The above statement is prepared from the sales and stock budgets. Control over buyers is exercised by adjusting the period figures by the following:

1. *Actual stocks different from budgeted stocks*
   This applies to opening stocks since the control statement covers the future period and, therefore, budgeted closing stocks remain as stated. Where the actual stock is greater than the budgeted stock the purchasing allowance must be reduced by this amount. Where the value of the actual stock is below that of the budgeted stock the opposite effect must be reflected in the calculation of the purchasing allowance.

2. *Commitments*
   This term not only refers to the commitments for the future period but also outstanding commitments from the preceding period. This figure is deducted from the purchasing allowance.

3. *Changes in budgeted sales*
   A decrease in the budgeted sales will necessitate a reduction in the purchasing allowance, an increase in the budgeted sales having the opposite effect.

4. *Actual sales different from the budgeted sales*
   Should actual sales show an increase over budgeted sales, the purchasing allowance will be increased by the difference. On the other hand, the opposite effect will be recorded where actual sales are below the budgeted sales.

## ESTIMATING GROSS PROFIT

A typical retail trading statement for a period may appear as follows:

|                                      | £     | £     |
|--------------------------------------|-------|-------|
| Net sales                            | 4,000 |       |
| Service charges for credit facilities | 100   | 4,100 |
| Opening stock                        | 6,000 |       |
| Add purchases                        | 1,600 |       |
|                                      | 7,600 |       |
| Less closing stock                   | 4,514 | 3,086 |
| Gross profit                         |       | 1,014 |

At selling prices the stock movements may be shown as follows:

|               | £      |
|---------------|--------|
| Opening stock | 8,000  |
| Purchases     | 2,000  |
|               | 10,000 |
| Sales         | 4,000  |
| Mark-downs    | 40     |
| Wastage       | 20     |
| Closing stock | 5,940  |
|               | 10,000 |

Mark-ups may be calculated as follows:

$$\text{Current mark-up} = \frac{£2,000 - £1,600}{£2,000} \times 100 = 20\%$$

$$\text{Cumulative mark-up} = \frac{£8,000 + £2,000) - (£6,000 + £1,600)}{£8,000 + £2,000} \times 100 = 24\%$$

The closing stock in the trading statement may be calculated as follows:

£5,940 −   (£5,940     ×     24%)        = £5,940 − £1,426

          Closing stock    Cumulative
          at selling       mark-up
          prices

                               = £4,514

The gross profit may be estimated given the following merchandise statistics:

1.  Stock movements at selling prices
2.  Other trading revenue (in the example, service charges)
3.  The cumulative mark-up

The estimate is calculated as follows:

|  | £ | £ |  |
|---|---|---|---|
| Gross profit on net sales | 960 |  | (24% of £4,000) |
| Add service charges | 100 | 1,060 |  |
| Less mark-downs at cost | 31 |  | (£40 less 24% of £40) |
| wastage at cost | 15 | 46 | (£20 less 24% of £20) |
| Gross profit |  | 1,014 |  |

The value of this statement form is that it shows the gross profit that should have been obtained and the explanation why the actual gross profit was different from that figure. In the example, the difference is explained by reductions in the prices to customers (mark-downs) and stock losses (wastage).

The closing stock in the stock movement statistics is a residual figure of book stock checked by stock checking. Where discrepancies are disclosed these are reported to management as wastage.

In the illustration, only one classification of merchandise has been shown. Where various classes of merchandise are sold at different gross margins, the merchandise statistics are classified by principal mark-up groups. The estimated gross profit is the total of separate group calculations.


## A CONCLUDING COMMENT

Many features of the techniques of management accounting applied to manufacturing companies are applicable to retail businesses. The abundance of books on the subject of management accounting for manufacturing industry, as compared with the re-markable scarcity of similar literature for the retail trade should not imply that management accounting is not applied in retailing or that its practice is not of equal value to retail organisations.

# Index

Abnormal cost 43, 67, 296
Absorbed overhead analysis 427
Absorption 455, 456
Absorption costing 66, 356
Accelerating premium system 258
Accountability 27
Accounting 4
    Cash and accrual 29—30
    Terminology 35
Accounting for changing price levels
    479—499
Accounting research 519
Accounts charts 70—71
Accounts conversion
    General price index 488—494
Activity, business 32
    Control of costs 151
Activity ratio 91, 345
Administration cost 53, 67
Administration cost ratio 87
Advertising 282
Allotment 455—457
Amortisation 274
Annuity method 277
Application of funds 127, 129
Applied research 281
Apportionment 84—85, 452—454
Asset acquisition types 220
Asset ownership costs 271
Assets register 270
Attendance bonuses 259
Attributable profit 291—292, 460
Automation 517
Availability ratio 91
Average capacity 311
Average capital employed 83—84
Avoidable cost, see incremental cost

Bad debts 282
    Provision 124

Balance sheet 69—70
Balance sheet ratios 89
Barth system 257
Base stock method 242
Basic standard 310
Bedaux system 257
Behavioural factors 151, 383
Bin card 244
Break-even analysis, see cost—volume—
    profit analysis
Break-even chart 109—112
Break-even point 107
Budget
    Amendment form 187
    Balance sheet 197
    Capital expenditure 196, 199
    Cash 197, 199
    Committee 200
    Labour cost 194
    Manual 201
    Material cost 194
    Period 178
    Production cost 193, 198
    Purchasing 194
    Representation 174
    Research and development 199
    Responsibility 180
    Revisions 187
    Sales 192, 198
    Stock 194
    Time-table 179
    Trade debtors 196
    Trade creditors 196
    Trading results 195
Budgetary control 149, 152, 173—182,
    186—202, 308
    Approach 174
    Benefits and limitations 180
    Coordination 176
    Essentials 177

Budgetary control (*contd*)
  Installation 177
  Level of attainment 179
  Sectional budget preparation 191
  Use of associated techniques 178
Business closure 390
Business contraction 394
Business control
  Accounting and 6
Business expansion 516
Business objectives 159–169, 501
  Communication 169
  Establishment 146, 163
  Nature of 162
  Principles applicable 161
Buying control 546
Buy/lease decision 221
By-products 467

Canteen cost 284
Capacity changes 42
Capacity ratio 91, 345
Capital acquisition 8, 9, 30, 42, 69
Capital employed 70
  Divisional and product assessment 84
Capital expenditure 50
  Accumulation and classification 228
  Control essentials 216
  Evaluation methods 219, 224–227
  Priorities 219
Capital increases/decreases 125
Capital investment 9, 30, 42, 70
  Commitment 218
Capital turnover ratio 87
Case presentation 220
Cash control 131
Cash cycle 52
Cash discounts 238
Cash flow 52, 126
Cash voucher 426, 427, 429
Central services 68
Centre for Inter-Firm Comparison 91,
  148, 271
Changing price levels
  Accounting 68, 479–495
Characteristics 10, 26–27
Classification 25–35
  Financial statement 5

Natural/normal 30–31
Retail 545
System effectiveness 26
Coding 71
Common body of knowledge 520
Communication 150
Compound interest
  Formulae 525–533
  Tables 534–539
Continuous budgeting 187
Continuous checking 243
Contract costing 458–460
Contribution 66, 107, 358
Control
  Period 19, 179
  System types 151
Control accounts 431
Controllability 27, 297
Conversion cost 64, 291
Coordination 152
Co-ownership 258
Corporate model 169
Corporation tax 541
Cost accounting methods 451–469
Cost control 295–297, 312
Cost element ratios 90
Cost escalation 219
Costing the cost centres 451
Cost of capital 217
Cost of sales 64, 290
Cost reduction 298–301
Cost structure 162
Cost–volume–profit analysis 101–116
  Formulae 113–116
Creative thinking 299
Creditors 52
Creditors to purchases ratio 88
Critical path 272
Current assets 50
Current cost accounting 494–495
Current liabilities 50, 125
Currently expected standard 310
Current ratio 87, 89
Customers order 428
Customers personal ledger account 429

Data
  Basic documentation flow 425–430
  Retention and disposal 423

Sorting 422
Source preparation 420
Summarisation and tabulation 422
Data division 41—53
    Characteristics 26
    Limitations 26
Data processing 419—441
    Method impact 440
Day rates 259
Debtors 52
Decentralisation 504
Decision-making
    Accounting and 6
    Internal management responsibilities 5
    Problems 388—407
    Techniques 374—383
Decision tree 382
Defective work 273
Delivery control 271
Depletion 275
Depreciation 124, 226, 274—281
    Accounting entries 279
    And changing money values 279
    Back log 486
    Methods compared 279
Deprival value 495
Design department 50
Development 281
Differential cost 376
Direct costs 63
Direct expense 63
Direct labour cost 63
Direct materials cost 62, 235
Discounted cash flow 223—224
Distribution 47
Dividend yield 90
Divisional facilities 84
Documentation 423—430
Double entry book-keeping 431—440
Drawing office 48
Dynamic programming 381

Earnings 44
Earnings per share 90
Economic cycle 7—8
Economic order quantity 245, 400
Economic value 495
Efficiency improvement 294—5

Efficiency ratio 90, 345
Emerson system 258
Employed assets 70
Employee expense factors 259
Endowment insurance policy method 276
Equivalent units 464
Estimating department 49
Excess material requisition 312
Executive action 150
Expansion area incentives 542
Expense control 269—285
Extraordinary expenses 43

Facility availability 270
Factory cost 62, 291
Factory cost of goods completed 62
Factory cost ratio 87
Factory marginal cost 290
Factory overhead 63—64
Factory overhead control account 425, 427
Field sales 46
Financial data
    Division limitations 26
Financial incentives 255, 256
    Schemes compared 259—260
Financial objectives 168
Finished goods stock 290
Finished goods stores ledger sheet 428
First-in, first-out cost 240
Fixed assets 82
Fixed budget 187
Fixed cost 32—33
Fixed investment 52
Fixed to total assets ratio 88, 89
Flexible budget 187
Forecast 173
Form design 423
Forward planning, accounting and 6
Functional cost 297
Funds 52, 125
    Analysis 123—132
    Sources 123
    Uses 123
Further processing 391, 398

Gantt system 258
Goods received note 425

Gross profit 65
  Estimation 548
Gross profit ratio 87
Group technology 271

Halsey system 257
Historical cost 83

Ideal standard 310
Idle assets 82
Idle time analysis 272
Implementing a decision 379
Imputed cost 377
Income tax 540–541
Incremental cost 376
Index numbers 486
Indirect costs 63
Indirect materials 235
Industrial relations 255
Inflated cost 241
Inflation 219, see also changing price
  levels
Information
  Chart 14
  Provision 152
Inspection department 49
Insurance 284
Intangible assets 82–3
Integrated system, double entry
  431–436
Interfirm comparison 91
Internal audit 503
Internal control 503–505
Internal rate of return 224
Interpretation
  Financial statement 5
  Of capital employed 82
  Of information 16
  Of profit 84
Inter-process profits 468
Interstatement ratios 88
Investment results 9, 31, 44, 290–303
Invoice 427, 429

Jobbing industry 308
Job card 425, 427, 429, 458
Job costing 457–458
Joint products 467

Key ratios 86–88

Labour analysis 261, 427
Labour control 251–263
  Account 427
  Cycle 252
  Recruitment and selection 253
  Requirements 252
Labour turnover 262
Labour utilisation 259
Last-in, first-out 240
Lead time 244
Learning curve 255
Leasing 390
Least squares technique 104
Length of service awards 259
Level of activity 310, 336
Levels of responsibility 220
Life-cycle costs 270
Limited market selling 363
Linear programming 381, 406, 507
Liquidity 27, 52
Liquid ratio 87, 89
Long-term contracts 291

Maintenance 270
Maintenance department 48
Make or buy decision 362, 390, 396
Managed cost 34
Management 4
  Authority 149, 153, 504
  Behavioural aspects 151
  Guidance 150
  Relationships 15
Management accountant 12
Management accounting
  Definition 4
  Framework for 7–12
  Its emphasis 11
  The future 515–520
  Topics 4–7
Management audit 510
Management by exception 149
Management by objectives 169
Management consultants 504, 510
Management control 9
  Elements of 146
  Process 145–153
Management education 517

Management techniques 295
Manager, actions 8—9
Manufacturing method choice 390, 397
Manufacturing statement 62—64
Marginal cost 107, 356
    Economist's 106
Marginal costing 66, 355—366
    Difficulties 358
    Its value 359
Margin of safety 107
Mark-downs 546, 548
Marketing information 44—47
Marketing objectives 163
Market research 45
Mark-up 548
Materials control 235—246
    Requirements 236
Materials credit note 243
Materials issue analysis 242, 425, 427
Materials issue costing 239—241
    Methods compared 241
Materials requisition 243, 425
Materials transfer note 243
Materials use 242
Mathematical techniques 379
Merit rating 259
Merrick system 258
Mixed costs 103
Model 382
Monetary assets 52
Monetary relationships 90
Motivation 152, 252, 301, 508

Net assets 70
Net current replacement cost 495
Net present value 223
Net profit 65
Net profit ratio 87
Net profit to ordinary shareholders
    equity ratio 89
Net quick assets 125
Net realisable value 292, 495
Net residual profit 507
Net sales 65
Network analysis 272
Net worth 70
Night shift premium 255
Non-monetary relationships 90
Normal losses 273

Normal plant capacity 189, 311
Normal standard 310

Obsolescence 274
Office management 274
Office mechanisation 300
Operating assets 70
Operating profit 65—66
Operational control 9
Operational research 379
    Model 380
    Techniques 381
Opportunity costs 376
Order acceptance 360
Order analysis 428
Organisation chart 12—13
Organisation structure 12—13
Output cost 66
Outside investments 84
Over-absorbed overhead 64, 456
Overseas development 517
Overtime premium 255, 261
Overtrading 51
Owners equity 81

Part-time workers 262
Payback 222
    Reciprocal 225
Payroll 427
Payslip 427
Performance appraisal 149, 501—510
Period cost 43
Perpetual inventory 243
Personnel objectives 167
Piecework rate 257
Planned range of activity 102, 105
Planning 146
    Integration 147
Planning and progress department 49
Plans: long- and short-term 147
Plant availability 311
Plant location 389
Plant replacement 389, 392
Policies 160, 502
    Formation 160
    Relationship with objectives 160
Practical plant capacity 189
Preventative maintenance 300
Price earnings ratio 90

Pricing decisions 298, 303, 363, 391, 401
Priestman system 258
Primary ratio 85
Prime cost 62, 290
Probability theory 382
Procedures 503
Process 28
Process costing 460–468
Process losses and gains 462–464
Product analysis 357
Product development 45
Product elimination 360
Product emphasis 364, 391, 404
Product pricing 298
Production control 271
Production cost 47
Production department 28, 48
Production method 278
Production objectives 164
Productivity 255
Profitability index 225
Profit and loss statement 65–69
Profit disposal 9, 31, 44
Profit graph 102
    Assumptions 102
Profit improvement emphasis 295–298, 301
Profit on disposal of fixed assets 124
Profit pattern 162
Profit reconciliation 285, 440
Profit sharing 258
Profit statement ratios 89
Profit volume ratio 113
Programmed cost 43
Progress reporting 228
Project evaluation 221
Property rent 271
Purchase cost of materials 237
Purchase invoice 425
Purchase order 425
Purchase requisition 425
Purchasing department 49
Pure research 281

Quality bonuses 259
Quality control 271
Quantity control 271

Queuing and congestion 382
Quick assets 52

Rate of return identification 226
Ratio analysis 78–93, 295
    Limitations 79
Rectification costs 274
Reducing balance method 277
Regional development grants 542
Regression line 103
Reinvestment 83
Relevant costs 377–378
Replacement cost 84, 241, 485
Report
    Narrative 18
    Review 19
    Tabular 17
Reporting 12–19
    Flexibility 17
    Integration 15–16
    Routine/Special 17–18
    Terminology 15
Research and development 42, 50, 281–282
    Objectives 166
Reserves 70
Resources acquisition 215–229
Resources available 42
Resources use 9, 31, 43
Responsibility accounting 149, 162
Responsibility centres 27, 148
Responsibility fixing 148
Retail selling 546
Return on capital employed 80, 85
Return on capital employed ratio 87
Return on investment 80–81, 222
Return on owners equity 81
Revaluation method 278
Revenue 44
Risk 149, 218
Routine maintenance 300
Rowan system 257

Salary payment 254
Sales analysis 429
Sales office service 47
Sales promotion 46
Sales service 46
Sales to current assets ratio 88

Sales to debtors ratio 88
Sales to fixed assets ratio 88
Sampling 379
Scanlon system 258
Scattergraph 103
Scrap 273
Selling and distribution costs 68
Selling and distribution costs ratio 87
Semi-variable cost 33
Service departments 28
Services, central 12
Sick payments 255
Simulation 382
Sinking fund method 276
Solvency 130
Sources of funds 127, 129
Standard cost 240, 291
Standard costing 149, 307–322,
     330–345
  Advantages 308
  Double entry 440
  Essentials 309
  Limitations 308
Standard cost rates 311
Standard cost sheet 311
Standard fixing 148, 179
  Revision 310
Standard hour 309
Standard marginal costing 365
Standard of attainment 310
Statistical techniques 149, 379
Stepped costs 103
Stock checking 243
Stock control 52
Stock increase relief 543
Stock levels 245
Stock limits 244
Stocktaking 244
Stock turnover ratio 88–89
Stock valuations 290
  Changing price levels 488
  Compared 292
Stores accounting 237
Stores cost control 245
Stores ledger 243
Stores ledger sheet 425
Straight line method 276
Strategic planning 9
Sub-process 28

Subsidiary ratio 85
Sub-systems 152
  Double-entry 436–439
Suggestion schemes 300
Sum of years' digits method 278
Sunk costs 376
Supplementary statements 484
Suppliers personal ledger account 426,
     427
Supplies 235
Surplus cash 82
System integration 312
  Double entry 431–440
System review 299
Systems analysis 300

Tangible assets 70
Taxation 84, 225, 540–544
  Deferred 125
Taylor system 258
Technical specification 311
Terminology 35
Terotechnology 270
Theoretical capacity 189
Timebooking records 261
Timecard 427
Timekeeping records 261
Tool room 48
Total assets 82
Trading statement 64
Training 253
Transfer pricing 507–509
Transport cost 283
Trend information 148, 295
Turnover of capital 80, 85

Uncertainty 218
Under-absorbed overhead 64, 456
Undertrading 52
Uniform costing 468
Unnecessary costs 298, 302
Utilisation ratio 91

Valuation of assets 83, 485
Value added 65
Value added tax 543
Value added to plant and machinery
     ratio 89
Value analysis 302

Value engineering 302
Value of output 65
Value of output to net sales ratio 89
Variability 27
Variable cost 32, 43
Variable factor programming 256
Variance analysis 149, 187, 313–322,
   331–345
  Basic procedure 313
  Limitations 343
Variances 187, 291
  Administration, selling and
    distribution cost variances 322
  And the reporting system 313
  Calendar variance 340
  Causes 343
  Direct labour cost variance 318
  Direct labour efficiency variance
    317, 335
  Direct labour mix variance 333
  Direct labour rate variance 317, 335
  Direct material cost variance 317
  Direct material mix variance 332
  Direct material price variance 316
  Direct material usage variance 316,
    333
  Direct material yield variance 332
  Factory overhead capacity variance
    321, 337–339

Factory overhead cost variance 321,
  338
Factory overhead efficiency variance
  320, 337–339
Factory overhead expenditure
  variance 320, 337–339
Factory overhead volume variance
  338–339
Market share variance 343
Revision variance 343
Sales mix variance 341
Sales price variance 321
Sales quantity variance 321
Variety reduction 303

Wage analysis 255
Wage payment 253
Warehousing 47
Waste 273
Waste bonuses 259
Weighted average cost 239
Work allocation 503
Working capital 50, 82, 125
  Requirements 130
Working capital cycle 130
Work-in-progress 62, 290
Works office 48
Works order 429
Work study 255, 300, 309

# MANAGEMENT ACCOUNTING
... a major new text for undergraduate and professional students

## Special features

- development of subject within a logical classified framework
- clear statement of objectives at the start of each chapter
- diagrammatic outlines of main topics covered
- basic principles and techniques applied to current business practice
- in-depth explanations of planning, control, and decision-making processes
- selections of discussion questions, exercises and case studies based on practical examples and examination problems
- over 110 illustrations

## Readership

- degree studies
- professional stage examinations of Institute of Cost and Management Accountants, Association of Certified Accountants, and Institutes of Chartered Accountants in England and Wales, in Scotland, and in Ireland
- HNC/D Business Studies and related courses
- qualified accountants and managers

Prospective authors are invited to write to the Technical Department, William Heinemann Ltd, 15 Queen Street, London W1X 8BE

434 91960 8

£6.50 NET

Norman Thornton received his M.A. from Nottingham University and his M.Sc. from Bradford University. He is a Fellow of the Institute of Cost and Management Accountants and an Associate Member of the British Institute of Management.

He began his teaching career in 1955 as a part-time lecturer at the Manchester College of Commerce and joined the full-time staff in 1962. His present appointment is Principal Lecturer in Accountancy at the Manchester Polytechnic in the Faculty of Management and Business, although previously he has held senior executive accounting positions in industry.

Norman Thornton has written two other books on accounting and has contributed to a third one on business organization. He is also the author of two research reports and his current research interests are concerned with financial control problems in small/medium-sized manufacturing companies.

## New and Bestselling Books from Heinemann

*Statistical Method for Accounting Students*
D. Pitt Francis
1978/434 90580 1/310 pp

*Elements of Accounting*
(incorporating Fundamentals and Preparation of Accounts)
J. Kellock
1978/434 91046 5/246 pp

*Partnership and Other Special Accounts*
J. Kellock
1972/434 91044 9/160 pp

*A Modern Approach to Company Accounts* (incorporating Company Accounts)
J. Kellock
1978/434 91047 3/320 pp

*Cost and Management Accountancy for Students*
J. Batty
1978 (Third edition)/434 90110 5/ 480 pp